TERRORISM
TODAY

CHRISTOPHER C. HARMON

FRANK CASS
LONDON • PORTLAND, OR

First published in 2000 in Great Britain by
FRANK CASS PUBLISHERS
Newbury House, 900 Eastern Avenue
London IG2 7HH

and in the United States of America by
FRANK CASS PUBLISHERS
c/o ISBS
5804 N.E. Hassalo Street
Portland, Oregon 97213-3644

Website: www.frankcass.com

Copyright © 2000 Christopher C. Harmon

British Library Cataloguing in Publication Data
Harmon, Christopher C.
Terrorism today. – (Cass series on political violence;
no. 7)
1. Terrorism
I. Title
303. 6′25

ISBN 0 7146 4998 8 (cloth)
ISBN 0 7146 8059 1 (paper)

Library of Congress Cataloging-in-Publication Data
Harmon, Christopher C.
Terrorism today / Christopher C. Harmon.
 p. cm. – (Cass series on political violence)
Includes bibliographical references and index.
ISBN 0-7146-4998-8 (cloth). – ISBN 0-7146-8059-1 (pbk)
 1. Terrorism. 2. Terrorism–Prevention. I. Title. II. Series.
HV6431.H365 2000
303.6′25–dc21

99–37193
CIP

Printed in Great Britain by
Creative Print and Design (Wales), Ebbw Vale

DEDICATION

was not invented by the US Marine Corps,
but sometimes it seems that way to me.

Contents

Foreword

PAUL WILKINSON

As we approach the twenty-first century there is no sign of any slackening of academic interest in the study of terrorism and political violence. The growing stream of books and articles published on these subjects bears witness to this continuing concern; their contents reflecting the fact that terrorism is seen as a major threat to human rights and political and economic stability in many countries, with significant implications for the well-being of the wider international community.

Inevitably in such a relatively new and fast-growing field of inter-disciplinary study, the quality of published academic work is highly variable. At one extreme are seminal works by the leaders in the field, and at the other there have been dozens of publications by authors anxious to 'band-wagon' in a newly fashionable subject but with nothing fresh or interesting to say, and little or no knowledge of the existing body of literature. It is therefore incumbent on every author and publisher working in this field to ask searching questions before bringing out a new book. Is the work adding anything of lasting value? Has it got anything original, interesting or perceptive to say about certain aspects of its subject? In short, is the reader going to learn anything worthwhile from the book? Or is it simply ideas and information that are readily available elsewhere?

In his Preface to *Terrorism Today* Christopher Harmon claims that: 'The most apparent contribution attempted by the present volume is its examination of terrorism today, years after the end of the Cold War.' It is indeed a great strength of his book that it covers new groups and trends as well as 'variations on older patterns', and that it is based on up-to-date sources. The author demonstrates an impressive grasp of a wide range of literature and data on contemporary terrorism, and this undoubtedly makes *Terrorism Today* an extremely valuable introductory survey text for university students and for the general reader, indeed for all those who, as the author puts it, are 'interested in knowing more about what contemporary terrorism is and where it is tending'.

However, in my view, Christopher Harmon is far too modest in his claims for the book. He is in reality providing much more than a well-researched and authoritative guide to contemporary terrorist groups and trends. A particularly valuable and refreshing feature of the book is that it presents and sustains a very clear, carefully thought out and consistent position that the means of terrorism can never be morally justified, whatever the professed ends of its perpetrators. A hallmark of terrorist campaigns is that they involve the deliberate killing of civilians. Hence, although Harmon does not equate terrorism with war, he does see terrorism as analogous to war crimes. At a time when there is a great revival of interest in normative theory of politics and international relations Harmon's moral argument, presented with great clarity and a quiet conviction, will undoubtedly stimulate further reflection and debate. The reader who remains unpersuaded by Harmon's moral argument can still learn a great deal from his discussion.

The author does not neglect to explore the beliefs, demands, grievances and motivation and the political, social and economic conditions which together constitute the underlying causes of terrorism. In addition to incisive summaries of the beliefs and demands of some of the major groups, the author also includes invaluable, lengthy, illustrative quotations taken from the manifestos, leaflets and other publications of terrorist groups and leaders. He constantly makes clear the distinction between political objectives or cause professed by the perpetrators of violence and the issue of the legitimacy of terrorism as a means of struggle. But Harmon argues that even a morally persuasive cause or objective cannot legitimize the use of terrorist means for its attainment. There are always alternative ways of pursuing your goals: ways that do not involve the deliberate killing of civilians.

A particularly refreshing feature of *Terrorism Today* is that it explodes the myth that terrorism is an obsession or problem unique to Western countries. He rightly emphasizes that contemporary terrorism poses the greatest danger to the fragile emerging democracies of the Third World and the CIS countries. For example, he reminds the reader that the vast majority of victims of Islamist fundamentalist terrorist groups have been members of the civilian populations in Muslim countries. And he points out that most of the terrorist violence committed today is carried out by groups or regime supporters attacking fellow members of their own native country. Harmon clearly has no sympathy with the Chomskyist conspiracy theory that holds the United States and its allies responsible for instigating and promoting most of the terrorism in the modern world.

One of the major weaknesses of much American literature on terrorism is that it is almost totally preoccupied with international terrorist activity; that is, attacks involving the citizens of more than one country. Christopher Harmon's book recognizes from the outset that 'many insurgents and guerrillas often choose to commit terrorism' and that 'some of them rely upon it'. His survey is particularly well balanced because it provides informed treatments of both new and long-established groups and both international terrorism and terrorist campaigns based mainly or entirely within the frontiers of one country. Harmon does not set out to survey the use of terror as a political weapon for internal repression and control by states, but he does include some discussion of state-sponsored terrorism and its impact on foreign countries. In assessing the strategic significance and influence of terrorism in the post-Cold War international environment the author shows a welcome realism, warning against the rather comfortable assumption, so popular in America at the end of the Reagan era, that terrorism is no longer a major problem and that we have the necessary package of 'solutions' to deal with it when it arises.

Christopher Harmon reminds his readers that although there are very few cases of terrorism alone succeeding in delivering strategic goals 'it very often succeeds at the tactical level'. But he wisely also warns us not to underestimate the strategic potential of the weapons of terrorism. For example, weak governments can be brought to the verge of collapse. Even strong governments are 'driven to distraction and international embarrassment'. He cites the example of Colombia at the end of 1998, when the incoming president made extraordinary major concessions to the guerrillas (employing terrorism as a frequent weapon) in their 'liberated zones', 'clearly compromising national sovereignty'.

Hence, although it is still true that terrorism is a faulty weapon which often misfires, in certain circumstances it can still have a major impact on politics and international relations far beyond the purely tactical level. For example, the assassination of Prime Minister Yitzhak Rabin and the Hamas suicide bus bombings in Israel undoubtedly affected the outcome of the 1996 general election in Israel, and hence the whole future of the Peace Process and the prospects for implementing the Oslo Accords.

There are many other examples to remind us that it would be dangerous to underestimate the threat terrorism can pose to peace and stability both within the borders of a specific state and internationally. For example, terrorist attacks on Israel's northern border and the attempted assassination of Ambassador Argov in London were the catalyst for the Israeli invasion of Lebanon in 1982. President Reagan was compelled to withdraw the American forces stationed in Lebanon as part of a multi-national peace-keeping force in the wake of the Islamic Jihad bombing which resulted in the deaths of 241 US marines. And in the mid-1990s mass hostage-takings by Chechen rebels ultimately forced Russia to negotiate the withdrawal of its troops from Chechnya and to grant autonomy to the Chechens.

Nor should we overlook the importance of three other recent or current developments. First, we should be aware of the danger from terrorists experimenting with new approaches to politics by combining the use of political wings or fronts to fight elections with the retention, and sometimes the use, of their terrorist cells to coerce or intimidate their opponents and to increase their grip on their own community. For example, the IRA continues to use its strategy of the Armalite and the ballot box in Northern Ireland, and by June 1999 had very nearly succeeded in gaining entry to the new Northern Ireland power-sharing executive without decommissioning a single ounce of semtex or a single rifle or machine-gun. This case and the case of Colombia show the huge dangers posed where terrorists cleverly combine politics and the threat or use of violence and where governments respond to such challenges by further concessions or appeasement. The danger in such cases is that democracy and the rule of law may be undermined by the weakness of governments.

The second worrying development is the weakness of the international community in failing to face up to the responsibility of applying the *aut dedere aut judicare* (either extradite or ...) principle in dealing with those suspected of major terrorist crimes. In 1999 we have seen the unedifying spectacle of Abdullah Ocalan, the founder and leader of the PKK, being passed from one EU country to another because none of them had the courage to bring him before a court of law to answer serious terrorist charges involving the death of large numbers of Turkish citizens, including civilians. In a 1991 television interview, quoted by Christopher Harmon, the interviewer said to Ocalan: 'The type of actions you carry out sometimes results in women and children also being killed.' Ocalan replied: 'Do you know how I cope with the results of those actions? I consider those actions as a means of spreading our cause. A small group is eliminated, but a great humanity will be created in its place' (p.194).

In view of Ocalan's record and the large amount of information in the possession of the EU states on his involvement in terrorism it is disappointing that Germany flatly refused to try Ocalan when the Italian authorities, who had him in their charge, sought to enlist the Germans' help. If major EU countries are unwilling to apply criminal justice procedures in such a case how can one expect other countries to take such obligations seriously? Even though it is true that Ocalan was eventually captured in Kenya – in circumstances which have still not been fully explained – and returned to Turkey where he stood trial, the early response of the EU states when he arrived in their jurisdiction showed up the underlying weaknesses in the structure of international judicial cooperation on terrorism.

In the case of Osama Bin Laden, wanted by the US on charges of masterminding the terrorist bombings of the American embassies in Nairobi and Dar es Salaam in which over 250 died, the Afghan authorities were unwilling to extradite the suspect to the US. The US resorted to the use of cruise missile strikes against alleged terrorist training camps in Afghanistan and against a factory in Sudan that the US claimed was linked with Bin Laden and the production of a precursor for chemical weapons. The use of military force certainly gave vent to America's desire to punish the perpetrators and it probably led the Taliban to place Bin Laden under greater constraints in Afghanistan. However, Bin Laden survived the attack, and continues to pose a threat. Hence, although I agree with Christopher Harmon that military force must be one of the options considered by democratic governments responding to terrorism, I personally believe that its utility against this type of threat is very limited and we should not exaggerate its value or depend on it as our major means of dealing with international terrorist challenges.

The third significant development we should be concerned about is the 1995 case of a religious cult in Japan using a weapon of mass destruction, Sarin nerve gas, in an attack on the Tokyo subway system. This was the first major weapon of mass destruction attack by a substate group, and it raises the question: now that the weapons of mass destruction threshold has been crossed will other groups seek to copy this method or use other types of weapons of mass destruction with the aim of causing large-scale loss of life, injury, destruction of property or disruption?

Professor Harmon is right to conclude that we should not exaggerate the threat. After all, four years have elapsed since the Tokyo attack without a repetition. Terrorists can get a major impact with conventional weapons – as in Oklahoma or at Omagh – at much less risk to themselves. Even so, even if it remains a low-probability threat, a weapon of mass destruction terrorism attack could have such devastating and lethal consequences that governments do need to enhance their intelligence, crisis management and security measures in case the worst-case scenario should come to pass.

In brief, I strongly recommend Christopher Harmon's excellent survey, *Terrorism Today*, as a wide-ranging and balanced assessment of contemporary terrorist groups and trends and the risks they pose to the international community. It will also make a useful contribution to the moral and civic education of the new generations of students.

Paul Wilkinson
University of St Andrews
June 1999

Preface

Terrorism is about power. The famous remark attributed to Vladimir Lenin, that 'the purpose of terror is to terrorize', is less direct than it sounds; terror is not an end in itself, but a means to political power and a way to hold political power. The general fear that pervades a political and social order, the psychological state of imbalance, and the particular and material damage to life and property done by terrorists are intended to advance some political purpose, be it short- or long-range, limited or unlimited. This is one of the reasons I have resisted the temptation to title this work about current events and current trends as 'The Changing Nature of Terrorism'. Terrorism has always had one nature. Capable of different expressions, such as hot rage, cold contempt, and even 'humane' indulgence of certain victims, terrorism never loses its essential nature, which is the abuse of the innocent in the service of political power.

Robespierre and his French revolutionary compatriots are said to have introduced the art of terrorism into modern politics in the West; they sought to gain power, and then use it to transform France, and then perhaps Europe. Many nineteenth- and twentieth-century communists have had similar, but global, aspirations. Such secularist revolutionaries still gain headlines on occasion, but now they have religious rivals who are equally fierce, equally 'internationalist', equally grounded in ideology, and equally determined upon new forms of political arrangements at home and abroad. Neofascists and other militant nationalists flourish today, using terrorism against the innocent to secede from decrepit states, shape new polities, or drive out ethnic and religious minorities which do not fit plans for national political 'purity'. Around the globe are innumerable other groups and minuscule clans, living more on determination than substantive popular support, fighting with arson and robbery and assassination to win adherents and alter some narrow dimension of the political or social order.

There are as well the anarchists, with their resilient dreams and arguments for wrecking a status quo. Today's anarchists are kin to those who murdered politicians in Russia, England, Spain, France, and the United States nearly a century ago. In small groups, and occasionally as loners, such as the American 'Unabomber', they strike with bombs and arson. They do not strive to change government but to make it impossible. Americans are facing another, newer class of anarchist spirit yet more limited cause. Some 'militias' oppose not all government but certain of its layers, especially the national federal. Their hope is for the end of 'overweening government'; but they say they respect local and county government, even as they avow freedom from federal taxes, refuse the draft, and defy subpoenas. A very few of this spirit have turned to terrorism, while others appear well prepared for it.

Traditional tactical patterns – some centuries old – remain in the global terrorism picture of the late 1990s. For example, there is little new in a case of a southwest Asian in a religiopolitical fury stabbing another person as would some thirteenth-century *siciari*. Today's knife-wielder may be a very modern Hindu nationalist. His victim is a symbol of some clear difference or inchoate political threat: perhaps a Muslim youth in Kashmir, or a Sikh businessman in the Punjab, a Christian from a nearby neighborhood, or an attaché from a foreign embassy. Terrorists have always attacked public conveyances and their helpless and crowded passengers. A decade and a half ago, the FMLN was systematically ruining the locomotives of El Salvador. Six and seven years ago, there were mass murders on South African trains. Today, most terrorist attacks on trains and busses occur in southern Asia. Nothing tactical has changed; the sad difference is only in the victims' names, which are invariably missing from the short foreign press articles describing what happened. To take another example, the most common of all newspaper articles about terrorism has long been that of the assassination of a well-known motorist, attacked while stuck in urban traffic. The assailants approach, and escape, on foot or motorcycle. The murder of four American businessmen in Karachi in November 1997 is one more new instance of a very old tactical pattern.

Equally familiar, a half-century after Mao's triumph in China, are the terrorist techniques of rural insurgency. In Peru today on any evening may be found a forced assembly of local people at a harangue by Shining Path insurgents. The unarmed villagers listen with varying degrees of fear and interest, feeling distinctly vulnerable. They feel almost exactly as did peasants half a world away in China in 1937, southern Vietnam in 1967, or Cambodia in 1997, for in such a jungle clearing the political authority close at hand is no listless minor official from the capital but the fearsome youth in a red kerchief. My study considers insurgents' terrorism as well as other types. The book thus contains many references to 'insurgents' (broad-based organizations seeking revolutionary power by overt and covert means) and 'guerrillas' (who attack military targets in unconventional ways). Such armed parties are by no means always reducible – logically, legally, or morally

– to 'terrorists', who murder, maim, or menace the innocent, especially unarmed civilians. Yet many insurgents and guerrillas often choose to commit terrorism; some of them rely upon it, heavily and self-consciously. Given the world-wide significance of guerrilla warfare and insurgency, and the way so many of their practitioners use terrorism, it is reasonable to include them in any thorough treatment of terrorism.

Contemporary terrorism also reveals certain new trends and dangers. Powerful, portable weapons can now bring down airliners, wreck high-speed trains, or poison thousands in a building. Two dozen civilian aircraft have been destroyed in the air by shoulder-fired missiles, which manufacturers world-wide are continuously improving. Terrorists have practised using such an obvious delivery system as the ultra-light aircraft, and doubtless they will also study remotely piloted aerial vehicles. When Chechen separatists, engaged in both guerrilla war and terrorism against Russia, took to placing nuclear material in a Moscow park, they pointed to dangers that easily exceed even those of the 1995 nerve gas attack on the Tokyo subway.

Terrorist training is acquiring new home states, so the fall of the Soviet bloc has not ended the illegal and immoral use of sovereign territory for training sympathetic foreigners in such arts as sabotage and assassination. The governments of Egypt and other states roundly condemned Sudan for becoming a terrorist training ground, and the UN censured Khartoum. Many governments recognize and condemn the transnational terrorism of Iran, which includes both patronage of foreign groups and use of its own agents to murder Iranian dissidents in Europe. Syria has moderated some behavior yet remains active and culpable. War-torn Afghanistan joined these states somewhat involuntarily as a terrorism exporter during the very epoch when Castro's Cuba and Sandinista Nicaragua were departing from the pattern.

Crime and narcotics-dealing is changing some revolutionaries. In Colombia, FARC and ELN, once impassioned and ideological groups of the hardest Marxist-Leninist credentials, have lost their old revolutionary 'purity' and turned their terrorism in a new direction – development as criminal cartels. They not merely live, but flourish, on hundreds of millions of dollars a year drawn from Colombia's population and economy by such means as extortion of cattle ranchers, theft from mines and oil companies, and 'taxation' of narcotics dealers. Personal computers manned by FARC and ELN clerks track the flow of this enormous guerrilla wealth. Insurgency and the drug business have partially merged; together they are ruining Colombia.

From Latin America to Lebanon, terrorists are trying new approaches to politics. Certain groups such as M-19 and Hezbollah have made extraordinary efforts to enter normal public life – the former group doing so wholeheartedly and irrevocably, the latter still using its numerous Shiite gunmen. M-19 and Hezbollah are now factors in the formal political process, with parties in parliament, offices open to the public, and respectable press spokesmen who talk economics, social welfare, and constitutional law. They represent contemporary possibilities in a traditional pattern of revolutionaries who use a dual 'fight and talk' strategy, working the jungle trail and then the hallway in government, or working both at the same time, seeking complementary advantages. Their expectations are doubtless maintained by awareness of such men as Yasser Arafat and Nelson Mandela, derided for decades as terrorists by most governments and now honored by state receptions in Washington and London.

The prospect that they might succeed – that terrorists can eventually destroy a government, or even take power – deserves full consideration. The present volume takes note of the many more limited ways in which terrorism works. It very often succeeds at the tactical level. It sometimes succeeds at the strategic level, as by lending life to political issues that might otherwise disappear from a nation's mind. Attacked by sustained terrorism campaigns, some weak governments can indeed fall, and they have. Or, strong governments are driven to distraction and to international embarrassment. At the end of 1998 the incoming president of Colombia made incredible overt concessions to guerrillas in their 'liberated zones', clearly compromising national sovereignty. Terrorism works. At the very least, it works well enough that, despite all its abhorrent characteristics, it continues to be pressed into service.

This book treats seriously the ideas and writings of terrorists, not only their bloody acts. The charters and communiqués that the groups write, and the interviews they eagerly arrange with friendly newspapers, are as instructive as the incendiaries they leave in department stores or under diplomats' cars. One can learn more about the Unabomber from reading his nearly endless manifesto than one can from studying the pattern of his package bombs. Politicians are wrong to use the word 'mindless' so often when denouncing terrorist bloodshed; they are not thinking when they do. Many terrorists are calculating and clever. Hundreds of them are well-educated. Most often, terrorism is not mindless; it is the calibration of violence and fear for political effect.

The most apparent contribution attempted by the present volume is its examination of terrorism today, years after the end of the Cold War. Since the late 1960s there have been hundreds of books on terrorism: some of them were very good; most of them are now badly out of date. The world is witness to new events, new groups, and emerging trends, as well as variations on older patterns. What is new deserves analysis; what seems familiar deserves a fresh look. So while I have been lecturing and writing on terrorism since 1982, the sources used for the present volume are mostly those of the 1990s.

It is hoped that this volume will be of assistance to university students, journalists, social scientists, military professionals, security analysts, and others interested in knowing more about what contemporary terrorism is and where it is tending.

Christopher C. Harmon

Acknowledgments

This project began in 1991, and advanced well during the latter half of the next year thanks to my wife, Laura, whose work in the law freed me from teaching responsibilities and allowed steady work on drafts of the initial chapters. She also handled the exacting preparation of the bibliography.

Dr Harold W. Rood, professor of government and international relations at Claremont McKenna College and Claremont Graduate School in California, has steadily and generously supplied important and sometimes unique information on global terrorism, especially from foreign newspapers and magazines. It has been over 20 years since I began my terrorism studies under Dr Rood; he remains a model teacher and a great friend.

Over recent years, chapters have been scrutinized and improved by good friends, including Paul Guppy with the US Congress, Major Kevin Smith of the Air Force, Dr David Tucker who directed policy within the Office of Special Operations and Low Intensity Conflict at the Pentagon, Mr Dennis Teti with his admirable and remarkable understanding of political affairs, and Lieutenant-Colonel Les Stein of the Marine Corps. No one has helped more, or is a better friend, than Dr James Anderson, a Research Fellow writing on national security issues for a foundation in Washington, DC.

I frequently profited from the expertise of fellow faculty and students at the Marines' Command and Staff College, including Dr Kamal Beyoghlow (on the Middle East); Major John Ross (on the American militias); Lieutenant-Colonel Carl Shelton (on both those subjects); and Lieutenant Commander Dave Lavender (on weapons of mass destruction). Of course, my writing is based *entirely* on open-source information and represents my own analysis and views. Nothing in these pages can be taken to represent the position of the US government, Department of Defense or Marine Corps.

Special thanks to Mr Frank Cass, Ms Rachel Joseph and Ms Margaret Wallis for their interest and their aid. And I am very grateful to Professor Paul Wilkinson, co-editor not only of this book series, but of *Terrorism and Political Violence*, a journal admired by all of us in this field of scholarship.

1

Politics and Policies

Introduction

Terrorism is the deliberate and systematic murder, maiming, and menacing of the innocent to inspire fear for political ends. That definition, proffered by analysts in 1979, has never been surpassed for clarity and concision.[1]

Now a well-established feature of world politics and conflict, terrorism is used by single-minded small groups, state agents, and broader insurgent movements to seek political and military results judged difficult or impossible to achieve in the usual political forums or on the battlefield against an army. Terrorism is always political, even when it also evinces other motives, such as the religious, the economic, or the social.

But while all terrorism has a political purpose, it certainly is distinguishable – technically and morally – from civil dissidence, other forms of civil violence, or revolution, which are also political phenomena. All the others are possible – some of them occur regularly – without terrorism. Consider civil dissidence. In late 1996 when the Serbian government refused to announce election results which the public presumed had favored the political opposition, street demonstrations became daily occurrences. The Serbian government denounced these as 'terrorism',[2] but no one was fooled; such demonstrations grow from Europe's long and venerable democratic tradition of nonviolent opposition to injustice. Terrorism is also sometimes used in conjunction with legitimate forms of political struggle. But alliance with legitimate methods cannot justify illegitimate ones; terrorism remains distinguishable from legitimate methods of political struggle.

Viewed from a military perspective, terrorism is a form of fighting which manifests certain characteristics of war: for example both are violent and often lethal; both are driven by political purposes, and both may sometimes use 'guerrilla' tactics. But legitimate war is not directed at the innocent. Terrorism is usually readily distinguishable from war by its ends, too. Many wars are legitimate but war crimes are never so; similarly, many forms of military violence may be justified, but not terrorism. Terrorism is a type of political depravity which unfortunately has become commonplace.

Although there have been incidents of terrorism throughout history, it was not until the late 1960s that terrorism emerged with real force and came to hold a powerful position in international politics. The year 1968 is the best marker of this modern trend. It was then that the Palestinians introduced political air piracy in Europe, in part as an alternative strategy to the conventional battle which had brought disaster to the Arab coalition that in 1967 made war on Israel. The year 1968 was independently one of violence in China and revolution in France. In Latin America, a rise in anti-US attacks occurred with slayings by the Rebel Armed Forces of Guatemala; John Gordon Mein became the first ever American ambassador to die at the hands of terrorists.[3] Events in these countries were closely watched by active and nascent terrorist groups everywhere else. In the United States, 1968 became a year of hot political turmoil and violence; events as different as the news of the Viet Cong Tet Offensive, and radicals' street fights outside the Democratic national convention in Chicago, encouraged the spirit of militancy. Among the most active and successful were the Black Panthers, whose concept of racial 'self-defense' included publishing exhortations to ambush and murder policemen.[4] Admiring the Panthers but differing from them were the largely white, university-going, internationally minded Students for a Democratic Society, from whose ranks in turn came the terroristic Weathermen. Other groups in the United States included the tiny, short-lived, multi-racial 'Symbionese Liberation Army' – a nihilistic failure at everything except crime.

The years after 1968 witnessed the regular and often devastating use of violence against the innocent to advance political ends. Groups such as the Tupamaros in Uruguay, the Red Brigades in Italy, and leftists in Puerto Rico raised indigenous challenges to political authority in their democratic host states, sometimes kidnapping or killing foreigners to underscore their wilfulness. Terrorism helped to create new governments in Cuba and Nicaragua in 1959 and 1978 respectively, and both then fostered international terrorism elsewhere.[5] The evidence is clear that terrorism wrecked established democratic governments in Uruguay and Turkey, which fell to military coups in April 1972 and September 1980. Observing these successes, and indeed sometimes involved in them, foreign powers such as the Soviet Union and its allies were encouraged to use similar means to advance their state interests and such global revolutionary causes as 'anti-capitalism', 'anti-imperialism', and 'anti-Zionism'. Debate over whether Warsaw Pact states were aiding international terrorism is no longer fruitful; the mass of evidence pouring forth from Communist Party archives in Moscow, Berlin, Budapest, and Bucharest since 1989 has settled any question.[6]

The end of the Cold War has had decidedly mixed effects. It signaled the end of a number of governments which had trained and employed terrorists, and even meant the formal sundering of entire states. It meant that others in the region enjoy a much-improved defense posture but also unprecedented new domestic tensions and political strains which are sometimes spawning terrorism. Most of the killings in post-communist Russia have been for private reasons, or linked to organized crime; but during the 1990s there has developed a pattern of execution of journalists, bankers, and even members of parliament. Several car bombings have also clearly been political. In Germany meanwhile, 1991 was the first year in which the number of indigenous rightist radicals exceeded that of the leftists. Today neofascists do almost as much damage to life and property as once did the German left.[7] Other conflicts still engender deliberate use of violence against the innocent for political purposes. Despite widespread hopes at the beginning of the 1990s that terrorism would no longer be a major threat, there have been some 300 to 440 incidents of international terrorism during most years of this decade.[8] The lethality of the average attack has risen markedly – a trend security officials expect to continue beyond the 1990s.[9]

That great continuous swath of southwest Asia and the Middle East which former US National Security Advisor Zbigniew Brzezinski called 'the arc of crisis' continues to yield international terrorists year upon year. To take just examples of anti-US attacks: in northern India in Kashmir there were two cases of the taking of American hostages in 1994 and 1995, and Donald Hutchings is still missing.[10] In Pakistan, two US embassy employees were murdered in March 1995. Afghanistan has a score of camps that train international terrorists, including some of those involved in the New York City World Trade Center bombing and tunnel plots.[11] Iraq's government dispatched agents to assassinate former President George Bush. In Israel and Palestine, Hamas attacks wounded four Americans in 1994. Another bomb, on a bus, killed 21 Israelis and two American students – an engaged couple. Operatives from northern Sudan, home to as many training camps for international terrorists as Afghanistan, were integral to the frightening and potentially devastating New York City plots. Sudan is also the best of allies to Iran, the world's most active terrorist state. Even Saudi Arabia, previously calm within this arc of crisis, faces new problems with terrorists: vehicle bombings killed Saudis and Americans in November 1995 and June 1996.

Once seemingly protected, American soil itself has been seared by spectacular bombings in New York City and Oklahoma. Less direct concerns also fester, such as worrisome dalliances by American citizens with foreign terrorism sponsors. A tour of anti-American Middle Eastern capitals by Nation of Islam chief Louis Farrakhan in early 1996 disturbed the Congress into holding a hearing. There were federal court proceedings against various Palestinian terrorists' schemes of clandestine organization and fundraising in Milwaukee, Tampa, and the northern Virginia towns of Arlington and Alexandria. Many US problems are US-made: home-grown militias and semi-autonomous political criminals have stockpiled weapons, indulged in hate speech, and even staged attacks, drawing down on them a strong federal policing effort. At Waco, Texas, and Ruby Ridge, Idaho, American officers concerned about terrorism shot other Americans. Unknown attackers who derailed a passenger train in Arizona in October 1995 left behind typed letters referring to the Waco and Ruby Ridge deaths, condemning the Bureau of Alcohol, Tobacco and Firearms for its involvement.[12] Radicalized by such incidents, and by such right-wing hate literature as *The Turner Diaries*, Timothy McVeigh placed a truck bomb at the Oklahoma City federal building in 1995, killing 168 people – more than any other domestic terror attack in US history.

If terrorism is best defined by its calculated abuse of the innocent for political purposes, there is reason to survey the political objectives which prompt such actions by militants of the modern day. The most important types are adumbrated below.

Anarchism

Anarchists perceive themselves as the 'purest' of terrorists, for their politics are the most outside all norms. They live for their overriding commitment to and exultation in the destruction of the state's authority, and for the dream of complete freedom. Terrorists of this bent say and write little about whatever political and social forms might follow; many of them expect that political forms will not survive at all. This supposition defies two ancient rules of human behavior: nature abhors a vacuum; and tyranny is the normal and almost predictable opposite of anarchy. Nihilists to some observers, incomprehensibly violent to most, the anarchists have been more than a passing phenomenon in the modern age. As long ago as 1869, Russian thinker Sergey Nechaev published in his pro-terrorist tract *Catechism of the Revolutionist* this still unrivaled description of the mind and politics of the anarchist:

> Everything in him is absorbed by a single exclusive interest, a single thought, a single passion – the revolution. In the very depths of his being, not only in words but also in deeds, he has broken every tie with the civil order and the entire cultured world, with all its laws, properties, social conventions, and its ethical rules. He is an implacable enemy of this world, and if he continues to live in it, that is only to destroy it more effectively.[13]

The era prior to the First World War was most promising for anarchists in the West. Intellects like Nachaev fostered the proper spirit. Fyodor Dostoevsky struck a contrary and satiric note in his novel *The Possessed*, where a group of anarchists were so unclear in their purposes and inchoate as a collective that they had real difficulty even organizing a meeting. But in Russia, revolutionary spirit stirred by anarchists and varieties of communists and others led to the murder of one Tsar in 1881, and the death of another toppled in 1917. As befits its philosophy, the anarchist movement was internationalist in character. As is so often true of terrorist movements, it could claim many limited successes. Activists in the United States and western Europe murdered President McKinley and five other heads of state in the two decades leading up to the First World War, and they killed or terrorized innumerable others in public places with knives, guns, and home-made bombs.[14]

Anarchism revived during the turbulent and disoriented years of the Vietnam War, and was given credence by militants, naïve persons, and imprudent university professors. It has flourished in the last 30 or so years of the twentieth century. Much of the German student movement of the early 1960s and 1970s loved what nineteenth-century anarchists and communists called 'propaganda of the deed', and they revealed certain other traits of anarchism; that doctrine became focused into a white-hot beam through a few of its members who went beyond anarchist thought and speech to terrorism. Groups such as June 2 and Baader–Meinhof were the result. One window into such souls is the 1971 memoir of Michael 'Bommi' Baumann, *Terror or Love?* It chronicles a young student's nihilism, and his early education in the writings of communists like Mao, Marx and Che, as well as celebrated anarchists like Proudhon, Bakunin, and bomb-throwers who published accounts of their own exploits. Their tales of destruction thrilled him; he went from mere counter-cultural student organizations and study groups to a 1968 arrest for slashing hundreds of automobile tires. Baumann next moved in a drug-using and drug-selling crowd of pranksters and revolutionary agitators called 'The Central Committee of the Roaming Hash Rebels', a small foretaste of today's organizational nexus between political terrorism and narcotics' trafficking. Then came his role in the terrorism and anarchism of the June 2 Movement. Baumann's rambling, shoddy volume includes a final chapter revealingly entitled 'I Don't Have a Message'. An earlier passage describes how his 'collective' went so far beyond street violence and leaflet distribution:

> Political practice doesn't have to be terrorism, it can be anything – even daycare, things like that. But we just happened to be active in that area [terrorism]. We saw it as political work inside the total framework ...We began to destroy the dilettantism. We began to get arsenals together.[15]

These young men and women expected to further a national revolution; they did at least succeed in tearing gaping holes in the social and political fabric of the self-consciously democratic post-war West German republic. Their successors, including remnants of the mostly anarchist Revolutionary Cells and the mostly communist Red Army Faction, now face a firm and thorough national domestic security system: once tested almost to the point of terminal failure, it has rebounded and fortified itself. No dimension of the German militant left, whether anarchist or communist, today appears capable of threatening the existence of the country's parliamentary order. In recent years, news is far more often of the parole of aging internees than of new bloody acts.

This German anarchism was echoed in certain strains of American thought and activity. The Vietnam era's legitimate American student movement spawned small numbers of terrorists whose violent activity aimed at social life without defined social order. The Weathermen moved into clandestine attacks against the government. For every gifted and angry German woman like Ulrike Meinhof there was in America a Bernardine Dohrn. Today, few American relics of that anarchism survive. There are small chains of leftist revolutionary bookstores. Readers of magazines may still spot advertisements for *The Anarchist Cookbook*, complete with recipes for bomb-making. Or they may download this aging volume's newer equivalents from the Internet. Among the most recent to be computer-accessible is by 'Jolly Roger', who dispenses for free hundreds of pages of detailed practical advice on making explosives, committing sabotage, exploiting the telephone system, and hacking into computers.[16]

Anarchism can be a mix of high ideals and blatant propensity to

violence. It also sometimes blends its vague political and philosophical
doctrine with other systems of ideas, such as communism or ecological
defense. There is evident anarchism in many of the writings of extreme
American 'eco-warriors' and animal rights proponents. The latter would
raise up the animal, but in doing so drag down the deepest meaning of
the human, and virtually abolish the significance of the soul and the
intellect. They believe that 'humanism' must be dramatically reduced in
importance in favor of a 'biocentrism' with equality of all living things,
from the virus to the grizzly bear. That position so deprecates reason that
it makes true discussion of government and politics rather absurd, while
inviting in wilful violence to take reason's place.

Some ecological zealots, feeling that humans are 'overrunning'
earth, look favorably upon world trends like AIDS which would cull the
human population. Others are millenarians, thinking themselves to be
'in a war with industrial civilization'. Their heroes are those willing to
be violent against designated classes of 'evil' persons or property.[17]
'Arson, property destruction, burglary and theft are "acceptable crimes"
when used for the animal cause', according to the chairman of People
for the Ethical Treatment of Animals. A political scientist writing for an
issue of *Animals' Agenda* adds an explicit defense of terrorism:
'Terrorism carries no moral or ethical connotations. It is simply the
definition of a particular type of coercion. It is up to the animal rights
spokesperson either to dismiss the terrorist label as propaganda or make
it a badge to be proud of wearing.'[18] The Internet site of the Animal
Liberation Front proudly lists hundreds of attacks on the property of
meat-packers, grocery chains, and the like.[19]

Some 'Eco-Warriors' would not go beyond occasional sabotage of
property and other propaganda of the deed. Others attack corporations,
private property, and private persons, such as industrialists, rather than
strike at government directly. As a matter of policy, they may want
limited administrative or regulatory changes, as in land use policy, but
they are readily distinguishable from pure anarchists of unbounded
demands. Animal liberationists, who have acted and sought attention in
England since 1976 and the United States since 1982, probably consider
their acts moral protests with little serious threat to the political order.[20]
No anarchist political movement has developed out of the last two
decades of attacks on the property of logging companies and
government officials responsible for forestry management, road
building, hydroelectric dams, or other life-altering modern creations.

Edward Abbey's whimsical novel *The Monkey-Wrench Gang*[21] set a
light tone for what has come to be called 'ecotage' or 'monkey-
wrenching'. Its fictional characters have a view of politics which

combines bemusement, cynicism, perhaps philosophical nihilism, and varying degrees of hatred for selected technocrats and bureaucracies. Their moralism and political indignation are layered throughout by a sense of wit and 'twisting the lion's tail', like that of their antecedents among the German student collectivists and pranksters. But the novel's characters also end up in a shooting war with law enforcement. One fan of Abbey's novel is 'Earth First!' founder David Foreman, who pleaded guilty to federal charges related to property destruction at sites in the western states.[22] Foreman's arguments for 'ecotage' are also laced with humor and the argument that such activity should be fun – 'refreshment for the urban-fatigued spirit'. Foreman writes in his *Confessions of an Eco-Warrior*[23] that sabotage of selected 'enemy' property by monkey-wrenchers is positive because it does not threaten individual human life. Instead it relies upon spectacle and cleverness to draw public attention to the damage man is doing to nature. Foreman does not see sabotage of foresters' vehicles or logging machinery as revolutionary, i.e. it need not show a desire to overthrow the democratic order.[24]

Should this illegal 'ecotage' be described as a 'terrorism'? The movement is decentralized by design, which is a hallmark of anarchistic groups but no indicator of terrorism. The practitioners have never killed, most are explicitly opposed to injuring people, and there have been no more than a few injuries inflicted during two decades of ecotage. Yet, many members believe themselves to be 'at war', one founder of the movement writes openly: 'This is *jihad*.'[25] They deliberately attack the property of fellow citizens, and such damage arguably falls within the definition given above for terrorism; the perpetrators threaten the innocent, using occasional destruction of their property as a means to their own political and social ends. Eco-warriors do not seek a climate of general fear, but they do aim their sabotage to intimidate and disrupt classes of foresters, loggers, and the like, and they aim to change forestry policy and other governmental policies, such as those on land management and sales. Their methods are illegitimate without implying a fundamental revolution of the democratic political order. The 'ecotage' activists are best understood as single-issue fanatics whose actions are brazenly illegal and sometimes very destructive. Their tactics recall those of Dutch laborers of old who protested conditions – but not necessarily the political order – by placing a well-aimed *sabot* (wooden shoe) in the finely balanced, humming machinery of the workplace, thus giving posterity the noun 'sabotage'. The movement's commitment to anarchism seems limited, and the proclivity towards terrorism very limited.

'Limited anarchism' certainly does take terrorism's recognized form

'Industrial Society and its Future'[26]

The Unabomber Manifesto:

1. The Industrial Revolution and its consequences have been a disaster for the human race. They have greatly increased the life-expectancy of those of us who live in 'advanced' countries, but they have destabilized society, have made life unfulfilling, have subjected human beings to indignities, have led to widespread psychological suffering (in the Third World to physical suffering as well) and have inflicted severe damage on the natural world. The continued development of technology will worsen the situation ...

166. Therefore two tasks confront those who hate the servitude to which the industrial system is reducing the human race. First, we must work to heighten the social stresses within the system so that a revolution against it becomes possible. Second, it is necessary to develop and propagate an ideology that opposes technology and the industrial society if and when the system becomes sufficiently weakened. And such an ideology will help to assure that, if and when industrial society breaks down, its remnants will be smashed beyond repair, so that the system cannot be reconstituted. The factories should be destroyed, technical books burned, etc ...

182/183 ... We have no illusions about the feasibility of creating a new, ideal form of society. Our goal is only to destroy the existing form of society. But an ideology, in order to gain enthusiastic support, must have a positive ideal as well as a negative one; it must be FOR something as well as AGAINST something. The positive ideal that we propose is Nature. That is, WILD nature ...

in the ecologically and scientifically obsessed 'Unabomber'. Some
interest in legitimate democratic discourse, as well as twisted hatreds of
technology dating back to sabotage by the English Luddites, are
apparent in the manifesto written by Theodore Kaczynski. There ends
the similarity with pacific lovers of nature. As spokesman of the
'Freedom Club' – a collective of exactly one – he crafted and mailed
parcel bombs that maimed, murdered, and menaced scientists, forestry
company officers, and others he thought were damaging man and the
environment. These bombs were such effective 'propaganda of the deed'
that the *New York Times* and the *Washington Post* submitted to his
demand to print his 35,000-word tract, covering eight newspaper pages.
The manuscript, 'Industrial Society and its Future', details hopes for an
intellectual and practical struggle for a more natural world. Reform will
not be enough; complete revolution is required, the manifesto states.
And yet the author does not wholly denounce the idea of government.
The tract may responsibly be labeled semi-anarchistic.

Nor are 'pure' anarchists easy to discover among state sponsors of
terrorism. Most of the organized bombers seek to destroy one political
form or another – not politics simply. Libyan dictator Mommar Qaddafi
is a revolutionary who 'exports' anarchy while fiercely holding the reins
of domestic power at home. He comes closer to anarchism in his global
activities than his philosophical convictions. Qaddafi ought not be seen
only as a lunatic, or only as a former satrap of the Soviet bloc, which he
served for two decades, sponsoring violence that created a revolutionary
atmosphere which Moscow and Tripoli alike could exploit. Qaddafi has
occasionally tried to advance his political thought, collected into *The
Green Book*.[27] But that volume gets a poor reception as a thin blend of
socialism, panArabism, and revolution abroad; readers find a paucity of
substance to his musings about 'a third way between capitalism and
communism'. Second is the image he has deserved and fostered of
supporting incongruous violence, such as the most nihilist terror groups,
the Japanese Red Army and the Abu Nidal Organization. Third and most
revealing is his patronage of both leftist and rightist organizations
engaged in terrorism. Two decades ago, Libya provided these polar
extremes in Italy with material aid, doubtless hoping chaos would result.
And one decade ago, his exclusive British agent for distribution of the
political dogmas of the *Green Book*, was the neofascist National Front.[28]
Apart from virulent antisemitism, what such extremists of left and right
most have in common is the determination to wreck the status quo. They
will argue later, atop the rubble heap, about what to do next.

Not unlike German 'autonomists' and squatters living in vacant
buildings and occasionally battling other militants or police in the

streets, the Libyan leader seems bent upon activity without certitude about what that activity should lead to. He talks of 'democratic' activism by local Libyan organizations, but is entirely attached to leadership and power. He fears and represses the new Muslim fundamentalism, which threatens his secular regime as it does that of the FLN in Algeria. Now that his Soviet allies are gone, there arguably remain only three constants in Libyan policy: the leader clinging to his own powers; the unending diplomatic gambits aimed at securing bilateral and multilateral alliances in the Mahgreb, elsewhere in Africa, and the Middle East; and the support for revolutionary groups reliant on terrorism for their impact. The latter commitment will remain iron-clad, even as he wrestles with dissidents and periodic attempts to organize a coup against him at home.

Qaddafi provides secure training quarters and steady material and diplomatic support to the gunmen of Abu Nidal, the enigmatic and obsessive Palestinian nationalist now declining badly in his third decade of warfare against Yasser Arafat. Libya is host to permanent representation from many other groups – not just such Middle Eastern entities as the Palestine Islamic Jihad,[29] but groups whose names and origins indicate the internationalism and adherence to global revolution which characterizes Qaddafi's foreign affairs. He supports the Japanese Red Army Faction, which may have been involved in a lethal bombing of Milan's US officers' club in April 1988 on the second anniversary of the US bombing of Libya. Qaddafi's money has long flowed into Muslim hands in the Philippines, where groups organize against Manila and against the regnant Catholicism of the social environment. Not long ago, analysts watched the quiet flow of Libyan support to the guerrillas and terrorists of the Moro National Liberation Front; now the news is of Libyan aid to a splinter group from that front called Abu Sayyaf. Growing since 1991, its acts include massacres of uncooperative villagers (as in Ipil, Mindanao, April 1995); bank robberies to obtain funds; and some efforts to use explosives, as against international aircraft. Some of Abu Sayyaf's 200 militants have studied or worked in the Middle East, including Libya.[30]

Such actions partly reflect Libyan Islam, and partly Qaddafi's internationalist anarchism. Both strains of thought, as well as old-fashioned realpolitik directed against Washington, explain the efforts of Libya to reach into the western hemisphere. Libya has been generous to some Latin dissidents. Its diplomats and agents were so active in Central America in the 1980s that the US State Department published a special report exposing its clandestine activities,[31] while a senior Costa Rican minister called Libya the single greatest threat to his country's internal democratic order. North American dissidents favored by Qaddafi

include the American Indian Movement. AIM's representatives attend
conferences in Tripoli and other Libyan cities, although there has been
no evidence of terrorist training. Libya made an effort to take advantage
of black criminal gangs, supplying financial aid to 'El Rukns' in
Chicago. In 1996 Libya startled American authorities again by
promising $1 billion in aid to the Nation of Islam radical Louis
Farrakhan, provoking Department of Justice lawyers to determine
whether he ought declare himself an agent of Tripoli under the US
Code's Foreign Agents Registration Act.

Such activity, and the participants' boastful communiqués that have
surrounded it, evince a vague but real strategic conception linked to
larger hopes of anarchy and global revolution. It is that Libya can unite
'oppressed people of color everywhere' – be they in Palestine, Japan, or
the United States – against world domination by Zionism, capitalism,
the US armed forces, etc. Thus, Libyan beneficiaries world-wide include
anarchists but also various nationalists, communists, and politicized
Muslims. Commitment to revolution, and the propensity of many of
them for using terrorism as a means, connect such diverse aid recipients
to each other. All are connected to Tripoli.

Communism

At war with many features of natural or conventional political life,
communism shares important characteristics with anarchism. Both are
anti-establishment, anti-bourgeois, and anti-capitalist. They are both
even opposed to reforming the system: true revolutionaries condemn
reformers, because reforms in a 'corrupt system' can lengthen its
lifespan. Terrorists kill as many reformers and liberals as they do more
obvious designated public enemies, which is why Peru's Shining Path
murders dedicated members of rural government and aid workers in
Lima's slums. Such deaths help assure that agricultural problems and
hunger persist, and that government remains inadequate and
dysfunctional; the better to prepare for the revolution led by Shining
Path. Communism and anarchism are alike in one further way: both are
millenarian, promising human happiness in a future world unrestricted
by government in any form. But here begin the differences. Anarchism
by no means shares communism's fundamental commitment to a
lengthy stage of government, a stage in which, ironically, the most harsh
and pervasive government is permissible and even expected. The
accurate Marxist description for the former Soviet Union and the current
system in Cuba and China is 'state socialism', viewed as a vital but

transitory phase in the necessary process of historical change. When socialism has triumphed world-wide, states are to give way, allowing the dawn of that idyllic condition passingly mentioned by the young Karl Marx in which every person will be utterly free, social relations will be humane and fulfilling, and no man will rule another, for there will be no government at all. Such visions 'redeem' the revolutionary violence of the current state socialist phase of history, in the eyes of communist believers.

Vladimir Lenin was less patient than Marx and more disposed to action and to the use of general fear for revolutionary purposes. Opposing the use of terrorism when it was an isolated mindless act, when his party would not control it, or when circumstances seemed unfavorable, Lenin nonetheless endorsed its use where and when it would serve to advance communist revolution. For example, in the pamphlet 'Where to Begin' (1901) he wrote that the 'individual attack, completely isolated from any army whatsoever', could be useful in militant politics when local revolutionary organizations are not strong. And in a 1905 letter from Swiss exile which he directed to comrades in a St Petersburg 'Combat Committee', he prodded revolutionaries towards robbery, arson, and other terroristic acts, insisting that they quit talking about bombs and start using them.[32] Generating fear – among even the innocent – for political purposes did not end with the attainment of power in 1917. Lenin indicated as much verbally when founding the Cheka, the first KGB. Fellow Bolshevik Leon Trotsky brazenly published the book *Terrorism and Communism* to demonstrate just how far a nascent revolutionary government could go, should go, and did go, to advance the revolutionary process. Both Lenin and Trotsky thus helped introduce the twentieth century to state-sponsored terrorism. And both then helped 'export' it abroad, along with clandestine operations, organization, intelligence, and overt political struggle. This range of foreign operations was aimed at weakening 'bourgeois' states and bringing other communist parties into political power.

Only some of the globe's Marxist-Leninist groups flourish today, after the decline of the Soviet model. A few Latin organizations fight on in Colombia,[33] Honduras, and Peru. The latter's small Castro-inspired MRTA proved capable of staging a four-month, high-profile hostage-holding in the Lima Embassy of the republic of Japan, but it was crushed in April 1997, and with it MRTA has disappeared as an effective force,[34] leaving the field to communist rival Shining Path. Such fighters as persist in the region must pretend to be indifferent to the peace settlements which have quieted their central American neighbors: El Salvador's FMLN laid down their arms and performed well in nationwide elections in March 1997; Guatemala has a peace agreement which took full and formal effect that month; Nicaragua's Daniel Ortega may be a loser in democratic politics but he continues his fight legitimately in the open political arena. In Europe, groups combining nationalism with Leninism remain powerful; these include Spain's ETA and the Kurdish Worker's Party, PKK. These groups' communiqués make them appear rather unmoved by the dismantling of the Soviet empire. The letters and manifestos they send to the press or litter at the scene of bombings may go almost entirely unreported in the American media, but they have a major impact in Europe. They sometimes give evidence of reappraisal but also of continuing faith; for them the flame of the communist dream still burns brightly, symbolized by fires burning where revolutionaries are operating.

Consider 'Revolutionary Organization 17 November' in Greece. It is continuously active, over two decades old, and has never suffered the conviction of one of its militants by the courts. Typical of the group's many strikes was a rocket attack on the offices of Procter and Gamble in Athens in June 1990 to protest corporate 'stealing from the Greek people'. The '17 November' group has also maintained its record of assassinations of Americans, begun in 1975; American military personnel were murdered in June 1988 and in March 1991. A communiqué of 1989 reveals how the group has managed to rationalize the fall of the Soviet Bloc: '[W]hat is happening in these countries consists of the ruin of Stalinism, and not socialism ... it was not the labor class that was in power in these countries but a bureaucratic, technocratic and party labor aristocracy that had imposed itself on the labor class with undemocratic, violent and bloody methods.'[35]

The globe's rural-based Maoist communist insurgencies also rely on terrorism. For them, terror is one arm of a struggle emphasizing political appeal, political activity, and mass political development. An original thinker, Mao Tse-Tung shared and expanded the Leninist concern that violence be directed by and tied closely to political work. Mao published stinging criticisms of revolutionaries who disdained grass-roots political development work or showed interest mainly in the gun. He opposed 'the small group mentality', 'the purely military viewpoint', 'warlordism', and 'roving gangs'.[36] His analysis virtually prefigured such groups of the 1990s as the urban '17 November' and others of rural Che Guevarist type; indeed, it foretells the reason for Che's failure in Latin America. A small group like Che's can always operate in Bolivia; a small group like 17 November can always assassinate someone; but this may not necessarily win political support; Mao's theory and practice shows understanding of the difference.

The Maoist variant of communism has appeared to be the strongest in the immediate post-Cold War world. Certainly it demonstrates no inhibitions in using terror to advance its ends, and it has succeeded in attracting a certain popular support. From Shining Path (Sendero Luminoso) in Peru to the New People's Army in the Philippines to the Cambodian Khmer Rouge, Maoist revolutionaries have astonished both the indigenous peoples and foreign observers with their skill in political organizing and their ruthlessness in killing the innocent. The Maoist policy is to take power in revolution and recreate the state; Maoist strategy is the patient creation of political organizations and base areas, protracted rural conflict, and eventual conquest of urban areas. This approach is alive elsewhere, as among the 'Naxalites' of West Bengal, and it often has appeal among the world's deeply poor. Because Maoism so long ago repudiated the Soviet Union, its death leaves neoMaoists unfazed.

Peru's Shining Path suffered the arrest of its principal, Abimael Guzman, in 1992, just as national power seemed within its grasp. And yet while today Sendero Luminoso is thrown back into the strategic defensive it still operates in zones around the countryside. It also draws foreign financial and political support. Backers include small Maoist parties grouped together as the Revolutionary Internationalist Movement. The understrength US chapter of this international organization is the Revolutionary Communist Party of long-time activist Bob Avakian, with small units in Los Angeles, San Francisco, New York, and he maintains an active and combative Internet site.[37] Sendero and its allies also publish propaganda in multiple languages, especially in northwestern Europe. Shining Path is clearly the most successful Maoist organization outside of Asia today.

From about 1996 to his capture in July 1999, Shining Path was moving under the direction of Oscar Ramirez Durand, 'Comrade Feliciano'.[38] Formerly a Sendero military leader, he emerged as the most capable of the opponents of any new peaceable direction for the organization. He reasserted control over its international offices, which began drifting after Guzman was jailed in 1992. More fundamentally, Durand kept the group active in the Peruvian countryside whence comes its true strength (former efforts by Guzman to penetrate urban areas were less than successful). Sendero is now emphasizing rebuilding and organizational work, such as appointing delegates, setting up 'people's committees', and propaganda work like collecting villagers to hear speeches against cooperation with the Peruvian army. But if Mao would have politics lead, he would never divorce politics from violence, and Shining Path continues ruthlessly to use the innocent to underscore its differences with democracy in Peru. In 1996 Sendero murdered a woman who was a community leader in a Lima shantytown and dynamited her body before leaving leaflets about. Another victim was a businesswoman married to a district mayor; she was ambushed driving her car. In 1996 these Maoists also invaded and sacked the little town of Marona in Leoncio Prado Province, murdered dissident members in a village to the south of Trujillo, bombed an electrical company in a district of Lima, and clashed with army troops in Tocache Province.[39]

Neofascism

The doctrine of fascism shares very few traits of anarchism: a rejection of moderation, wildness of character, and the preference for propaganda posters featuring black. Black was the traditional color of the anarchists before Hitler ever set it alongside red and white to produce his own symbols; today black remains the favorite of both anarchists and neofascists. But fascism, properly understood, has much more in common with communism. To begin with, both are of revolutionary character. Both would overturn the entire order, and then create a new order of the most far-reaching and despotic sort. This was well understood by one of the first dissidents to leave this early twentieth-century movement: a senior Nazi party official in Danzig, Herman Rauschning, who wrote the book *Revolution of Nihilism*.[40] Fascists believed they were revolutionaries, and they were; they despised the slow, quarrelsome nature of parliamentary government; they wanted to exploit the powers of the press rather than leave it free to make criticisms that divided the polity; they pioneered new ideas about economics and called themselves national *socialists* for the clear reason that the economy was to be state-directed, not free.

It is a telling fact about German politics after the First World War that while rightists and leftists fought often in the streets, they also sometimes cooperated in the Reichstag against the democratic center, and recruited heavily from each other's parties and paramilitary gangs.[41] While one must beware parallels to fully legal, overt, contemporary political parties, it is worth noting that today, former Waffen SS member Franz Schoenhuber, deputy chairman of the Brandenburg section of the new Germany's 20,000-strong right-wing 'Republikaner' party, sees promise in the old German communists. Schoenhuber has boasted that East German party and army men are a 'gigantic pool of recruits'. Another observer notes that former communists seem to flourish in the new rightist party.[42] Evidently, what the extremists hate most is parliamentary democracy, not other extremists.

One cultural/political feature of the neofascist groups of Europe is that, like their antecedents led by Hitler and Mussolini, they are dominated by males.[43] Hitler made known his view that nature ordains for women intimate association with the 'three Ks' of *Küche, Kinder, Kirche* (kitchen, children, church).[44] Today's illegal far-right European organizations feature virtually no women of the stature of Alessandra Mussolini, the dictator's granddaughter and a member of parliament, holds in Italy's legal 'National Alliance' party; indeed, she has no west European political parallel at the moment. Among the region's rightist militants and terrorists, the norm is the male. Females are usually hangers-on, or girlfriends, or supporters.[45] This contrasts sharply with the many west European and American and Latin terror groups whose women often fight and sometimes hold political or military leadership positions.

'Blood and soil' was an atavistic phrase Bismarck used to help forge nationalism and reject the moderation and accommodationism he detested in parliamentary politics. It well captures the spirit of the fascist movement which followed, and the spirit of neofascism today. To the nationalism of the nineteenth century the twentieth added ideology, and the notion of cultural war. Neofascists of today like Ewald Althans of Munich, an articulate, rising star, speak and write of a need to 'purify' their country by excluding Jews, foreigners, and blacks. Sixty years ago the demand was for a Germany that was 'free of Jews'; today it must be 'free of foreigners'.[46] 'Hitler is a hero to me', declares Althans. 'Hitler managed to open the door for supercivilization.' Flags at his rallies recall the geopolitical concept tied to Nazi cultural aspirations; some flags bear maps depicting a future Germany extended to the wider borders it had in 1937, including lands now inside Poland, Russia, and other countries.[47]

Neofascists in today's Europe hate many of the same things that quietly animate the larger, legitimate legal political parties like the German 'Republican Party'. Both overt political voices and covert terrorist groups want a stronger, better-defined, and more culturally pure nation. They dread economic recession. They are indignant about the inrush of poor foreigners from eastern Europe, southwest Asia, the Middle East and northern Africa. They retain the traditional radical right-wing obsession with the imperialist threat of great foreign powers, especially the United States. They retain the appalling fixation on indigenous Jews and certain others. People of Romanian and gypsy stock have been savagely beaten in hate crimes in as gentle and pacific a country as the Czech Republic, which is now arranging semi-isolated compounds to control and protect Romanies.[48] In Germany, depredations against Turks and other immigrants are well-known. In France the National Front, a constitutional rightist party led by Jean-Marie Le Pen, is flourishing; it may well not be militant enough to be called neofascist.[49] In Italy the far right has occasionally given expression through terrorism – suspicions of the 1980s centered upon the P-2 Lodge, for example. But the greater threat from the Italian right today is not from terrorists but from fully legal parties like the Northern League which would separate the nation by region or transform it from its current status as a liberal political culture.

Internationalism is a weak creed among Europe's neofascists. After all, for racialists of the legal or militant bents, internationalism is somewhat illogical. The Nazi party gave internationalism very limited attention in the 1930s and 1940s. They cultivated and made use of persons of Indo-European racial stock outside the Austro-German region, and they even made bizarre efforts to demonstrate racial linkages to their Axis partners, the Japanese. Similarly, today's fascist terrorists wish to have but not rely on international contacts. They maintain connections of sympathy, travel, and money to: Germans and other Caucasians in such European countries as France, Belgium, and Holland; Italians who cling to the legacy of the first fascist, Mussolini; racial German communities in Latin America, where many fled from Germany during or after the Second World War; Croatia, where a few individual Germans have fought as ideological allies in the early 1990s and returned later to rejoin neoNazi groups at home; South Africa, where Dutch and German peoples have flourished for hundreds of years; and of course the United States, former home of Gary 'Rex' Lauck, jailed in Germany for publishing the neofascist literature that often shows up in the hands of German thugs.[50]

Another American whose writing supports a revival of fascism is Milton John Kleim, Jr. His 'National Socialism Primer', posted on the Internet,[51] is a remarkable combination of Nazi ideology and information age spin. Kleim's tract accurately echoes many standard Nazi themes but updates the appeal to an audience of the 1990s. 'Blood and Soil' refers to the relationship between People and Homeland, Kleim writes, and to 'the origin and miracles of Life, the Ideal of organic lifestyle, and the importance of truly creative work'. National Socialists are not 'male Chauvinists' or 'androcentric'; that is a media myth; the correct view is one of woman's uniqueness, not subservience. Nor should National Socialists be derided as 'right-wing fascists', the tract continues, because the establishment's left–right spectrum is confused, and also there is nothing wrong with fascism properly understood. National Socialism constitutes an alternative to the failure that is democracy, 'a

Profile of William Pierce, American NeoNazi

Citizen of West Virginia: Dr William Pierce has lived in many states but currently resides in Hillsboro, WV. Middle-aged, he was a physics professor at Oregon State University in the early 1960s before becoming a white power activist.

Past Associations: Editorship of the *National Socialist World*. Membership or office-holding posts in the American Nazi Party, and its successor, the National Socialist White People's Party, as well as the Washington DC-based Liberty Lobby.

Head of the National Alliance and editor of its newspaper *The National Vanguard*.

'Churchman': Pierce's organization had tax exempt status as an 'educational' institution before losing it in a court ruling. However, part of his extensive acreage in West Virginia enjoys tax-free status as a church, the 'Cosmotheist Community'.

Radio host: Dr Pierce has a short-wave radio show called 'American Dissident Voices'. After the April 1995 Oklahoma City blast, he broadcast his prediction that Jews, homosexuals, politicians, 'female executives', and others were generating such resentment among 'normal Americans' that terrorism was forthcoming 'on a scale that the world has never seen before'.

Publisher: National Vanguard Books catalogues. These begin with a personal epistle and then offer a variety of newspaper reprints, books, and tapes which center on such themes as Celtic and Norse history and culture, contemporary race studies and relations, German history and military history, the Nazi movement of the pre-Second World War period, etc. One may order Hitler's autobiography *Mein Kampf*, or a tape with songs exalting the white race, or novels by Pierce.

Author: *The Turner Diaries*. Once an underground paperback, this novel has become a mass seller, thanks to reports that Oklahoma City terrorist Timothy McVeigh read, discussed, and even sold the book. Written by Pierce under the pseudonym Andrew Macdonald, the *Diaries* is a look at – and apparent argument for – a forthcoming race war in America. The story includes a truck bombing against a federal building and prolonged insurgency by white supremacists, who eventually win. The new regime follows up civil war with mass terror, especially against Americans of color, white women who consorted with them, and liberal journalists.

The Legacy: Timothy McVeigh, convicted for the Oklahoma City truck-bombing, is not the first admirer of *The Turner Diaries* to be jailed for terrorism. In the early 1980s Robert Matthews founded 'The Order' in the Pacific Northwest to the end of carving out a geographical 'whites only' zone. It is now known that 'The Order' functioned along lines drawn in the novel. They robbed banks and printed counterfeit money to sustain operations. They murdered a Jewish radio host, committed other crimes, and sought to spark nation-wide revolution. 'The Order' met its end in arrests and a gun-fight with police in 1984.[52]

controlled system of 'choices' that all invariably lead to the same end'. Genuine democracy, as Hitler understood, means popular support, more than it does popular choice. What of 'human rights'? They are a 'clever sham', because what matters are not the rights espoused by the Jewish-controlled media, but the truest of all human rights, the right of a nation to self-determination. Kleim's primer ends with a call to all 'brothers and sisters' and the exhortation to advance 'the Triumph of the Aryan Will'.

Organized fascist politics have little overt support in the United States. Publicists such as Lauck and Kleim are usually seen as gadflies or oddballs. By leaving the Ku Klux Klan, David Duke has done better than they at making racism seem acceptable to mainstream America, but while he ran in presidential elections in 1988 and 1992, he fared badly, and is generally regarded as a caricature, not characteristic, of American sentiments. Nation-wide, the KKK is a diminishing silhouette of its sheeted self. Every announced Klan rally invariably becomes the scene of a counter demonstration, rallying two, three, or ten times as many anti-racists as KKK marchers. American skinheads are younger, more numerous, and often violent. But some of them are actually anti-racist. Moreover, skinheads in the United States are remarkably difficult to organize; recruiters in the states encounter that problem as quickly as do neofascist recruiters when hunting for comrades amidst violent European football fan clubs. Neofascists might be thought to have better luck recruiting from American 'patriot' groups, as a number of them are white, male, gun-owning, and angry, as the stereotype suggests. Yet many militiamen detest state power, rather than exalt it as fascists do. Like the 'Freemen' besieged in their Jordan Montana compound for 81 days in 1996 by police, militiamen tend to be individualists who despise government precisely because of its alleged authoritarian tendencies. Many 'patriot' group members would never join an overtly neofascist movement. Most women in the American militia movement today feel similarly.

National separatism

Militant separatists may have fascistic dedication to their race and culture, and be willing to go to every extreme to realize these ends. Other separatists are not racist at all. The 'Republicans' of the Irish National Liberation Army (INLA) and the rival Irish Republican Army (IRA) Provisionals do not appear to manifest organizational racism, and the *Green Book* for training volunteers warns against it: 'Republicanism has an international dimension which means respecting as equals other nationalities and races. Anyone who pays lip service to international solidarity and then slips into mimicking the racist attitudes which are typical of an imperialist mentality should be immediately upbraided.'[53] In a typical Irish terror attack by Loyalists or Republicans the victim is not even English; he is an Irishman, whether policeman, militant rival, fellow-traveler of suspect loyalty, or member of the unarmed public.

National separatist terrorists need not necessarily be bent upon following the stage of destruction with their own brand of dictatorial rule, although in practice they usually are; techniques used to gain power too often are predictors of techniques used to govern once in power.[54] National separatists' conceptions of economics also may vary widely: there are fascists with their limited socialism, communists like the former Armenian Secret Army for the Liberation of Armenia, or even capitalists, such as Afrikaner groups of South Africa. Religion may be their guide, as it is for the Palestinians of Hamas, or Sikhs favoring creation of an independent 'Khalistan' by remaking part of northern India.

Unlike the 'state', which may be a composite of any number of national groups, 'nation' carries with it the full sense of lingual, cultural, and sometimes ethnic and religious cohesion. The fight for national independence against a central state government is an old tradition, especially since the partial remaking of Europe along ethnic lines after the First World War by the Versailles Conference. The dismantlement of Czechoslovakia, Yugoslavia, and the Soviet Union along ethnic or national lines, and the simultaneous unification of the German nation, are thus consistent with this older pattern. These ruptures are themselves spurring further disintegration, fostering ideas of national independence among distinctive but small populations whose struggles may succeed initially yet ultimately produce unviable states. Slovenia, the Slovak Republic, Macedonia, and the smaller fragments of Yugoslavia are among those which the future will challenge, and which any major European war may destroy. While the birth of some new mini-states has been surprisingly pacific, their future trials may be accompanied by indigenous or foreign-sponsored terrorism.

There has been no general connection between the disintegration or creation of European states and terrorism. Terrorism – domestic and international – did have a small role in the genesis of Croatia and Armenia. But most of Europe's former separatist terrorist groups have not yet enjoyed success. No one speaks any more of violent separatists in Brittany, active up until 1978, or the tiny groups in Wales that burned English holiday houses in the early 1980s. There has been no violent separatist campaign in Scotland,[55] even now when ancient Scottish heroes are bathed in the attentions of commercial movies and books; instead, a plebiscite has just enhanced the Scots' control of their internal affairs. Some very old separatist struggles within Europe do continue to percolate. ETA, or Basque Homeland and Liberty, remains strong despite rashes of important arrests in the 1990s. Europe is also ever more familiar with militants favoring an independent Kurdistan, especially the terroristic PKK, which in many countries, especially Germany, is a star of fighting quality and unashamed boldness. In Corsica, French rule is bedeviled almost daily by petty bombings.

Corsica's terror organizations wage their separatist fight against France in a classic war of the weak against the strong that commenced in 1975. France has resisted stoutly; indeed, a national high court determined in 1991 that even the phrase 'the Corsican people' is unsuitable in legislation because Corsica's place within France is unquestionable and the constitution recognizes no separations by race or origin.[56] Nevertheless, several groups, led by the National Front for the Liberation of Corsica (FLNC), carry on the low-intensity conflict. Corsican terrorists do not usually kill; there have been just 100 deaths in two decades of continuous attacks.[57] But injuries are not unusual, and the commercial damage has been immense. The tactical specialty is the string of bombs, which over one night, or even a few hours, damages numerous French or foreign-owned or managed properties. For example, on one occasion in May 1992, 30 holiday bungalows were leveled by the FLNC. All were owned by the French Ministry of Finance and Economics, which the separatists count as sufficient cause. There was also a proximate cause: the timing registered a protest against the sentencing in Paris of two Corsican militants.

All such attacks are intended to develop a sense of Corsican political and cultural identity. They further polarize opinion on the island, subtly undermining French authority. And they bleed the tourism trade of the foreign moneys it draws to the island. But these are interim, not ultimate, objectives. What do the terrorists claim as policy ends? The groups do not always confine their political propaganda to slogans daubed in paint at sites of their attacks. There are declarations, including this one from the early years, explaining attacks on the mainland: 'Our people target the privileged political, military, and economic structures of the colonialist French state and in so doing fight for their liberation.'[58] A recent declaration reflects more contemporary political angles – or perhaps the skill of the speaker from A Cuncolta Naziunalista, the FLNC's overt political front.[59] As he told the French daily Le Monde: 'Our main claims, in descending order, are recognition of the Corsican people, commitment to a process of economic development, the establishment of a specific education system and the official acceptance of the Corsican language, and the reform of the institutional framework, with the disappearance of the two departments in particular.'[60]

The Corsican terrorists' fight would break away two of the 96 departments constituting France. Their effort recalls the example of the Algerian FLN, which waged prolonged war against French authority, winning in 1962 and thus wiping out the three French departments built in north Africa. That FLN victory inspired many similar nationalist movements, especially those battling European colonial powers. Today, Corsican fighters continue testing the authority of Paris over the island, but they cannot expel the French. They lack a strong outside political ally and supplier. Their indigenous political support has dissipated by more than half, down to perhaps 10 per cent of the populace. But if the terrorists' bombs sometimes sound like mere fireworks, they do continue to sound. The Corsicans must know the story of the terrorism campaign on their Mediterranean neighbor, Cyprus: Cypriot rebels never defeated the British army, but they won independence by refusing to give up.

No less resistant, and far more powerful, is the IRA, the best-publicized separatist terrorist organization in the world. Just as the Corsicans see themselves as a final vestige of French imperial holdings, the Irish 'Provisionals' have watched the British empire erode during the twentieth century and consider themselves its last and most important colonial victim, still unliberated. They have fought 'for more than eight centuries of relentless and unremitting warfare that has lasted down to this very day', according to an in-house publication.[61] Irish nationalists have used military force, political struggle, and flagrant terrorism among the Irish and British peoples to overthrow London's authority. They have also engaged foreign allies, including American citizens with Irish roots. The fight has included sites throughout Ireland, Britain, and NATO countries like Spain and Germany and Belgium. Many IRA men have died; many others have spent decades in prison or fought long legal battles. The 1998 peace accords in one sense reflect the fact that neither side can win. The nationalists won 'Home Rule' in 1921 and 1922 but remain unable to 'liberate' the six counties of the North.[62] Nor can Britain win, a fact symbolized by the recent transfer of leadership of the anti-terrorist fight from Scotland Yard's 'Special Branch', which bore the responsibility for a century, to MI5, a national intelligence service tasked with resisting subversion and espionage.

The Provos of recent decades have blended Marxism–Leninism and nationalism; a successful government run by the IRA would presumably impose upon its countrymen both political dictatorship and the economics of state socialism. The same appears to be true of the IRA's small rival, the INLA, which splintered from the IRA in 1975. Like many contemporary terror groups, including IRA, ETA, and Hezbollah, the INLA is credited with an overt political front group – the Irish Republican Socialist Party. When a senior party official was hurt in a June 1997 car bombing, a press report stepped cautiously by describing the IRSP as 'linked' to the INLA terrorists. The INLA has no more than a hundred operatives yet is riven with internecine tensions. Notable murders and retaliatory murders underscored the divisions in 1987 and again in mid 1996.[63] Other INLA violence earlier in the 1990s struck down less guilty victims. INLA operates on both sides of the Irish border,[64] as its arms-smuggling operations indicate.

This minuscule Irish 'army' may or may not coordinate activities with the IRA Provos.[65] But it is noteworthy that it did cease violent operations during the highly publicized 18-month pause the Provos made in 1995–96, and it did then announce an end to the ceasefire when the Provos returned to the militant path. The INLA press release of 22 March 1996 declared that the renewed armed struggle would include 'retaliation'. In classic fashion, the communiqué threw the moral blame for INLA terrorism over upon the battered democratic political system: 'If this [return to armed action] appears to be a retrogressive step, then you should be asking what you did to prevent it. It has been the failure of the "political process" to deliver – not those of us who stood back despite mounting provocation.'[66] With the 'Good Friday' 1998 accord signed by the IRA, the rival INLA seems again to be restraining its own terrorists.

Of all national separatist groups, one of great consequence that is little known among Westerners is the Tamil Tigers of Sri Lanka. When the British Empire ruled Ceylon, it seemed from the outside to be a dreamy land of tea, contemplative religion, and political peace. Trincomalee possesses a natural harbor which Admiral Nelson noted as the very best in the world; it still serves as a vital naval base. But the end of foreign rule seemed threatening to Tamils, who make up only 18 per cent of the population and are Hindu rather than Buddhist like most other Sri Lankans. When the ethnic Sinhalese/Buddhist majority asserted itself in ways that were sometimes heavyhanded and discriminatory, a Tamil separatist leader arose. In 1976 Velupillai Prabhakaran founded the LTTE, or Liberation Tigers of Tamil Eelam (the last two words propose a name for the new homeland). Seeking to carve an independent Tamil state from the northeastern provinces of the teardrop-shaped island, the Tigers have fought for two and a half decades, using politics, force, and terror. Their hallmark is a capsule of

Basque separatists: ETA

'Basque Homeland and Freedom' (ETA) is an example of mixed success and failure in employing terrorism to advance the political object of national independence from Spain.

ETA is the strongest of the Basque militant groups, and dates back to 1959. The founding documents of the 'Etarras' anticipate a remade Europe in which boundaries will follow ethnic lines. There is allegedly to be no tolerance for either racism or dictatorship.

ETA draws support from Basque populations on both sides of the Spanish–French border. A well-organized political front, Herri Batasuna (HB), functions like Sinn Fein does in Ireland, providing diplomatic 'cover' and overt popular support, and possibly also illegal material assistance, to the military and clandestine political wings. But popular support via this front is waning; the Basque population is showing war fatigue.

Money comes from extortion of Basque businessmen, robbery, kidnapping, and systematic 'revolutionary taxation' of Basque persons of average means. One kidnapping yielded $3.29 million.

International connections with West European terror groups have been numerous but not always very substantive. ETA was inspired by the FLN's success in Algeria in 1962 and still sends members to Algeria for training. There are special links – prompted by culture, language, and politics – with extremists in Latin and Central America. ETA has maintained connections to Cuba, and there were varieties of traffic to and from Nicaragua up through the year of the electoral defeat of Daniel Ortega's Sandinista regime in 1991.

Fully half the attacks by ETA are directed at security forces and army personnel, rather than unarmed civilians. (For most terror groups, attacks on the unarmed dominate.) The national police force, the Guardia Civil, has borne the brunt of one quarter of all ETA attacks prior to 1981. Many others have also died in the campaign: overall, 800 have perished since 1968. ETA claimed ten new victims between January 1996 and February 1997.

The ETA of the late 1980s was second only to the IRA in strength among the European groups. But the 1990s have been hard. Arrests by French and Spanish police have decimated the ranks and captured many top leaders of the three sections: political, military, economic. Yet over the years the fight has forced Madrid to concede many aspects of political and cultural control to indigenous Basque authorities. There is a Basque parliament, and the police force in the region is all-Basque. The limited autonomy does not satisfy ETA, but it marks a true change in Spanish politics, and has satisfied many a voter in the four Basque provinces of Spain.

The 'Jarrai Movement' is the latest phase of Basque militancy. It is a sort of *intifada* of Basque youth – as many as 2,000. The political front HB and a few young Members of Parliament are reported to provide indirect leadership. An ill-defined group of ringleaders 'vet' and indoctrinate very young children, and then loose them for street actions in which police cars, public phones, and other government property is vandalized by the hooded teenagers. One campaign was against journalists. Because many of the youth are but 12 or 13 years old, when caught they invariably become an embarrassment to try in court.

cyanide, worn about the neck; scores of men and women have swallowed their dose to commit suicide when capture seemed inevitable. The typical Tiger fights with fervor, possessing both the nationalism arising from his geopolitical position and the ideological training characteristic of his Marxist–Leninist organization.

LTTE's policy end of separating the ethnic Tamil region in northern Sri Lanka is pursued by a variety of strategies. Terrorism of the Sinhalese majority is only the most apparent. Equally important, and a hallmark of the group from its first years, is the strategy of eliminating moderate Tamils or other groups which compete with LTTE, such as the former People's Liberation Organization of Tamil Eelam.[67] This is a standard approach of terror groups, though one too little noted by observers. Another Tiger strategy is to use a combination of politics and armed force to exert ever-growing power within and over the Tamil population throughout Sri Lanka. This effort, less necessary in the more Tamil-populated northwest, is now concentrated in the northwest, but it is a factor in Tamil areas everywhere on the island. A fourth strategy is to use international publicity for the plight of Tamils living in Sri Lanka, concentrating on human rights issues.[68] LTTE keeps an Internet site, rich with color, artwork, and histories of facets of the armed movement and the Tamils more generally.[69] Ethnic connections across international boundaries are nearly always exploited in revolution, and many Tamils among the 50 million living across the Palk Strait in India have felt the draw – or the pressure – of activists gathering political support and money for the Tigers' fight in Sri Lanka. Once aid flowed freely; recently, New Delhi has moved to constrict the stream. Other ethnic Tamils abroad also contribute to the cause of Tamil independence: there are Tamil populations in North America, 2,000,000 Tamils in Malaysia, and more elsewhere.[70]

War erupted in 1983 and has ground on ever since. The Tigers are waging a full-blooded insurgency against Sri Lanka's armed forces, in addition to campaigns of terrorism of civilians and government officials and innocent Tamils. There are 10,000 fighters available to the Tiger organization, which loses hundreds of them a year in pitched fights. LTTE long held Jaffna, the northern provincial capital and the largest Tamil city, retaken in an army offensive in 1995. In classic guerrilla fashion, the LTTE retreated into jungle hideouts and slowed the state's advance with tactics designed to hurt and to hinder. The LTTE also boasts a naval force – the only significant terrorist group to have one, now that the PLO's naval cells are no longer on the attack against Israel. No less than seven Sri Lankan navy combat vessels were engaged and destroyed in the year prior to April 1996. A government convoy moving troops in the region in February 1998 was attacked by two dozen craft and lost a troop ship.[71]

These engagements with government forces have a parallel in the Tamils' devastating terrorism against civilians. Explosions have become grimly familiar in the capital Colombo. When on 31 January 1996 a bomb blew the facade off the nine-storey Central Bank, killing 90 and injuring 1,400, it may not have seemed as foreign to Sri Lankans as the Oklahoma City bomb was to Americans. The economic price of years of such terrorism and insurgency is almost incalculable. Any estimate including property damage in urban and rural settings, expenditures by the government for all manner of security forces, medical costs for aiding the injured, etc. must quickly run into billions of dollars, all lost to a comparatively small economy.

Religion

The single most important fact about international terrorism since the end of the Cold War is not the renewal of nationalist separatism, but the rise of the religiously motivated gunman. Religion, ordinarily a wellspring of hope, life, and virtue, stirs such deep passions that it also sometimes leads to violent action, to war, and even to terrorism. This is especially true where the earthly and the spiritual realities are deemed inseparable – a conception foreign to many modern westerners but essential in such diverse creeds as the Cult of the Assassins in eleventh-century Iraq and Syria, the Sikh religion of the sixteenth century through the present, or the Islamic Resistance Movement (Hamas) that began in Gaza in 1987. The current trend towards religious terrorism is in contrast with the 1980s, when Westerners knew little of it, except that hostages had been taken by Shia in the Middle East. Our world since 1991 has been embroiled in regular eruptions of mass murder by 'faithful soldiers' of a half-dozen religions.

In the three years before 1997, men motivated along religious lines, whether orthodox or eccentric, have assassinated the Prime Minister of Israel; attempted to gun down Hosni Mubarak of Egypt; slaughtered dozens of Muslims worshipping in a mosque in Hebron; shattered Israeli streets and city buses and their unsuspecting passengers; tried to blow up a New York skyscraper, New York City tunnels and the UN building; hijacked an Air France passenger jet hoping to dynamite it over Paris; murdered and maimed scores of civilians in French cities based on a power struggle in Algeria; murdered tens of thousands more in the Algerian countryside; injured 5,500 Japanese by releasing nerve gas in the Tokyo subway system; and blown up 28 American servicemen stationed in Saudi Arabia to help that country thwart Iraq. The US Federal Bureau of Investigation has announced that Islamic radicals are now the single greatest terrorist threat *inside* US borders.[72]

An astute observer of contemporary insurgencies – which often rely heavily on terrorism – has noted that, in the post-Cold War era, insurgency has moved in one of two directions: either towards organized crime (e.g. in Latin America) or towards religion. As established twentieth-century ideologies like communism and fascism have lost their prestige, and with 'Western materialism' leaving so many unsatisfied, religion's attractiveness, always strong, is being further enhanced. The search for meaning, for justice, and problems of modernization will all help bring religious violence to the fore, according to this view.[73] In the northern African and Middle Eastern regions, especially, religion may motivate new insurgencies. These will usually employ terrorism as well as other methods, because the apocalyptic nature of religious extremism tends to sweep aside reservations about individual suffering; all seems forgiven by the 'greater good'.

An apt symbol of the transformation of the moment is the Palestinian revolution. Led for decades by the notably secular Yasser Arafat and diverse Palestinian leaders under the umbrella of the PLO, the insurgency against Israel and other Middle East regimes showed a mix of nationalism with varieties of Marxism. Religion was hardly a factor: the 'Christianity' of a PLO chief like George Habash of the PFLP was not taken seriously inside or outside the movement; the role of the Muslim Brotherhood, long a feature of regional politics, was both weak and quiet; the Muslim faith of many PLO leaders had no discernible effect on their politics or brutal tactics, and was indeed covered over during extensive dealings with communist patron states.

Today the PLO has achieved new status by governing a secular 'statelet' in Jerico, Gaza, and other enclaves. The Palestinian insurgency that continues, and employs terrorism in full measure, is driven by rival Palestinian forces, most of them religious. Palestinian Sunnis flock to Hamas and Palestine Islamic Jihad. Palestinian Shiites support Iranian operatives. Hezbollah is a major force in Lebanon and has attempted to gain power by force in Bahrain, where there are 600,000 Shia.[74] These activists regard the celebrated peace treaties worked out in Madrid and Oslo as a sell-out to PLO secularism and a failure to wrest all of Palestine from Israeli control. The religious groups' speakers deride and despise Arafat, his government, and his often-vicious police enforcers and jailers.[75] They go abroad to train in foreign encampments and return to wage war on Israel when Arafat has committed himself publicly to peace. They dream of the day they will impose the faith of the Koran on the region and see all Palestinians living under the true law of their God.

The 36-article Charter of Hamas is a spiritual and political declaration of war on Israel, Zionism, allies of Israel and Zionism, and others opposed to creating a religious state throughout Palestine. It displays no doubts about whether the Koran supports the use of violence to convert souls or establish political rule; saturated with Koranic language and quotations, the Charter's words dictate that the faithful take to the path of *jihad* and promise unceasing commitment until the ultimate objective is realized. Hamas members – from diplomats to would-be suicide bombers – find in the Charter the touchstones of life and death. Ideology, objectives, strategies and methods, and the Hamas position *vis-à-vis* other Islamic movements or the PLO are all addressed. Spirit and intellect are each appealed to by the vigor and argument of the tract. The Charter also sinks into the most crude stereotyping, to include favorable references to the 'Protocols of the Elders of Zion', an infamous fraud depicting Jews as driven to dominate the temporal world.[76]

Americans are increasingly aware of a pattern in their own history of sporadic outbursts of religious militancy which threatened innocent life. In the 1930s, there were adherents of Father Coughlin and his inflammatory antisemitic radio show; one group of followers stockpiled explosives and weapons and planned strikes on public buildings, a list of named Congressmen, and other targets.[77] The white supremacist, ultra-Protestant[78] Knights of the Ku Klux Klan date back to the post-Civil War years and have a subsequent legacy of violent opposition to Catholicism, Judaism, and above all the rights of black Americans. A traditional scourge in many US states and Canada, Klan members still conduct terrorism on occasion. For example, between 1977 and 1980, a single Klan (and Nazi party) member, Joseph Paul Franklin, rampaged through half a dozen states, killing persons associated with the Jewish faith or with interracial personal relationships.[79] But the once-powerful KKK is in steep decline, attacked by law-suits and increasingly at odds with public opinion in a multiracial North America. There are now no more than 3,000 Knights in the United States.[80] Former Klansman David Duke perennially engages in politics, and maintains a telephone hotline and an Internet web page, but did no better than third in primaries for open national congressional seats in 1996 and 1999, running from his home state of Louisiana.

More dangerous is Christian Identity, another terror group which gains modest legitimacy from its affiliation with religion. Their long-established doctrine holds that white Anglo-Saxons (in England and the

Excerpts from the Charter of Hamas

In the Name of Allah, the Merciful, the Compassionate

You are the best community that has been raised up for mankind. Ye enjoin right conduct and forbid indecency; and ye believe in Allah. And if the People of the Scripture had believed, it had been better for them. Some of them are believers; but most of them are evil-doers.

... the Islamic Resistance Movement erupted in order to play its role in the path of its Lord. In so doing, it joined hands with those of all Jihad fighters for the purpose of liberating Palestine ... For our struggle against the Jews is extremely wide-ranging and grave, so much so that it will need all the loyal efforts we can wield, to be followed by further steps and reinforced by successive battalions from the multifarious Arab and Islamic world, until the enemies are defeated and Allah's victory prevails.

The Islamic Resistance Movement ... is characterized by a complete comprehensiveness of all concepts of Islam in all domains of life: views and beliefs, politics and economics, education and society, jurisprudence and rule, indoctrination and teaching, the arts and publications, the hidden and the evident, and all the other domains of life.

Hamas regards Nationalism as part and parcel of the religious faith. Nothing is loftier or deeper in Nationalism than waging Jihad against the enemy and confronting him when he sets foot on the land of the Muslims. And this becomes an individual duty binding on every Muslim man and woman; a woman must go out and fight the enemy even without her husband's authorization, and a slave without his master's permission. This does not exist under any other regime, and it is a truth not to be questioned.

... the so-called peaceful solutions, and the international conferences to resolve the Palestinian problem, are all contrary to the beliefs of the Islamic Resistance Movement. For renouncing any part of Palestine means renouncing part of the religion ... There is no solution to the Palestinian problem except by Jihad ...

United States) are the true 'chosen people of God', not the Jewish people. The movement thus mixes racial hated of Jews with evocations of the Bible. It is by no means a conservative Christian 'fundamentalist' church, because it preaches race war. In the 1980s and 1990s Christian Identity has been an ideological father to groups engaged in paramilitary training, hate speech, and sometimes terrorism: the Covenant, Sword and Arm of the Lord; the Christian-Patriots Defense League; Aryan Nations, with its slogan 'One God, One Nation, One Race'; 'The Order' begun by Bob Matthews, who got many of his best recruits from Christian Identity; and Posse Comitatus, whose adherent Gordon Kahl shot down a pair of federal marshals in North Dakota and later died in a gunfight with Arkansas officers. Randy Weaver, whose son and wife were shot by federal officers in the Ruby Ridge stand-off, is also a Christian Identity follower, though not one linked to terrorism.[81]

Pro-State terrorism

This final type of terrorism can not always be reliably deemed 'right-wing'. Its purpose is to maintain the power of a state – whatever its ideology – or to preserve[82] advantages held by particular groups. Most often, pro-state terrorism involves illegal clandestine violence against revolutionaries attempting to change those power relations or undermine the state. Pro-state terrorism is as important in contemporary world politics today as are the subversive varieties. From death squads in central America seeking to suppress communist revolution, to Loyalists in Northern Ireland who would hold on to British governmental ties, these groups seek to assure the survival of the political status quo and protect their own powers within it. The 'deliberate and systematic murder, maiming, and menacing of the innocent ...' is as crudely effective and as morally troubling when the policy end is strengthening, rather than replacing, the political status quo. This is especially true when the state which is supported by illegal armed parties is unworthy of its citizens. And most despotisms are indeed utterly unworthy.

Modern political figures like Robespierre and Lenin were seminal thinkers about, and skilful practitioners of, terrorism aimed to undergird their own regimes. They have spawned many heirs. In the 1960s and 1970s, some Latin American countries unwilling or unable to institute healthy political changes illegally used state powers to frighten classes of their own citizens into submission. Usually without Leninist efficiency, these illegal partners of government combined inside political support, intelligence from police and other official sources, sometimes army modes of transportation and weaponry, and anti-communist passion – the latter being in abundance in these largely Catholic populations. The results included nocturnal house invasions, morning body counts along stream beds and rural paths, courts that reliably supported prosecutors, and vigils by relatives and defense lawyers for what became known as 'the disappeared'. In Guatemala alone, endless insurgency and pro-state terrorism combined to kill 100,000 people and make 40,000 others 'disappear'.[83] The wider political legacy has been two-fold: more states than not successfully repressed insurgency and sometimes terrorism as well; and more countries than not still shudder over the struggle, even now as, freed from dictatorship, they join the ranks of the democracies.

Spain was a healthy democracy with a mild Socialist Party government in the 1980s. But between 1983 and 1987, certain members of government undertook the killing of terrorists of ETA. Grupos Antiterrorists de Liberacion, or GAL, were formed by Spanish police, acting undercover or with aliases, and by contract thugs of various nationalities. These pro-state assassins doubtless believed they were 'retaliating' against known terrorists, especially those they could not reach who were hiding in France. But the hit squads of GAL killed 27 persons, and some of them were innocent of ETA activity. When journalists and a Madrid magistrate exposed the death squads' organization and finance by the Spanish state, the otherwise strong 1992 re-election prospects of Filipe Gonzalez were crushed. Today, Spain's 'dirty war' of the mid 1980s is a fixture of politics, and there are ongoing trials of persons involved in this attempt to turn terrorism against its ETA initiators.[84]

Far less clear are relations between the Loyalist terrorists of Northern Ireland and the British government which has been in charge there directly since the 'troubles' became urgent about three decades ago. 'Orangemen', Protestants of the six counties of Ulster, have militias among them which have been killing in earnest. After the 1985 Anglo-Irish Agreement prompted their fears the status quo would change, Loyalists ratcheted up their activity; their killings jumped to five times the earlier levels, or about 40 deaths a year.[85] In the late 1990s, Loyalists are killing as many persons a year as Nationalist groups such as the IRA.[86] A study of Loyalists who join militias finds the numbers are highest when Protestants have the most cause to fear a united Ireland, as when Sinn Fein's Gerry Adams was negotiating directly with Tory Prime Minister John Major. At present, neither side truly expects Irish unification.

That Irish and British police frequently arrest and convict Loyalist terrorists indicates two things. One is that the government does not endorse the Loyalist crimes, even if radical Irish Nationalists find such a judgment inconceivable.[87] Second, there are simple practical problems with all 'pro-state' terrorism, beginning with credibility and legitimacy. If citizens fear political revolution or change, they tend to look to their own government as their guarantor if it has legitimacy, not any paramilitary. The state, even when under attack, may not need or want the 'help' of pro-state terrorism, and any association with terrorists undermines its own political legitimacy, and thus its efforts against revolution. A related problem is manpower. In a credible state, convinced right-wingers probably support the government and may already work for it, as in the civil service or by legally bearing arms in the police or army. They may simply wish to serve the state in that capacity, rather than become involved logistically or personally with pro-state terrorists. Thus, argues one analyst of Northern Ireland's troubles, the most likely sources of Loyalist militia manpower are not government, police, or military personnel, but those who have been refused entry to such organizations, or have retired from them.[88]

In conclusion, the phenomenon of terrorism grows out of political purposes. These are usually crystallized in policy statements that can be found in the organizations' charters, formal statements, and communiqués. While the words may not always be honest, or may not be coherent, let alone persuasive, they exist, and with their accompanying acts of terrorism demand to be understood. The declared policies serve various group needs, including appeals to a wider audience, public justification of crimes against the innocent, and internal purposes such as recruitment and indoctrination. The groups' objectives vary widely, but all have a strong political component, even the contemporary religious groups. From the political foundations there arise other opportunities and problems for terror groups; subsequent chapters address the strategies with which they advance their political goals, operate, acquire funds, and the like.

Transnational terrorism sponsored by state governments is well known as a strong component of the terrorism phenomenon of today. As foregoing sections on anarchism, communism, and religion suggested, Libyans, Soviets or Algerian Muslims can have very different political motives for fostering international attacks. States like Iraq and Syria sponsor international terrorism for no ideology at all, but for immediate purposes of state, such as silencing dissidents or intimidating a neighbor. We will continue to address the purposes, strategies, and practices of state-sponsored terrorists, but without singling them out as a category distinct from all others. For while they are political, they are of innumerable political types.

The Ulster Volunteer Force

A Protestant and pro-British organization with Irish and Irish–English membership, UVF is dedicated to protecting the Protestant heritage and perpetuating British authority in the six counties of Northern Ireland.

The UVF's origins in 1912 were a reaction against a movement to give Ireland 'home rule' within the British Commonwealth – a movement that largely succeeded in 1921–22.

The UVF hunts many enemies of its political objectives, including the IRA and other Republican paramilitary and terrorist groups. But most attacks are against Catholic civilians, as in the 'tit-for-tat' retaliatory actions that follow IRA kills. And a significant minority of the UVF's victims are Protestant civilians, a fact indicative of terrorist groups' ruthless treatment of their own people.

There are frequent allegations that the UVF and other Loyalist militias receive intelligence, equipment, and even training from British intelligence. The credibility of these claims is questionable but difficult to judge.

Membership numbers about 500 active supporters, and includes many ex-servicemen and some who sought to serve in Irish or British security forces but were refused. Some criminals are present, as in virtually all terror groups. Court convictions have restricted operations and recruitment.

Funding is from domestic sources within Ulster and possibly England. It includes not just donations but contributions forcibly extracted by extortion, and by criminal racketeering and bank robbery.

Rival Loyalist groups include the larger and more politically dominant Ulster Defence Association, and the Loyalist Volunteer Force, a group of dissatisfied UVF members who took their own path in 1997, and have already killed many Catholic civilians.[89]

Notes

1. Adopted by The Jonathan Institute in Jerusalem at a 1979 conference; *Terrorism: How the West Can Win*, ed. Benjamin Netanyahu (New York: Farrar, Straus, Giroux, 1986), p. 9.
2. *New York Times* (13 January 1997).
3. David Tucker, *Skirmishes at the Edge of Empire: The United States and International Terrorism* (Westport, CN: Praeger, 1997), p. 2.
4. See for example the party newspaper the *Black Panther* in such years as 1968 through 1971. Recently (15 June 1997), Eldridge Cleaver appeared with Mike Wallace on '60 Minutes', which rebroadcast illuminating footage from an interview the two did in that earlier period.
5. Two publications replete with evidence of this are *The Challenge to Democracy in Central America* (Washington DC: Departments of State and Defense, June, 1986), and *The Sandinistas and Middle Eastern Radicals* (Washington DC: Department of State, August 1985).
6. One of a dozen good European reports on the new evidence is 'East Bloc's Terrorism Role Unveiled', *Corriere Della Sera* (Milan) (15 July 1990), trans. and repr. in Joint Publications Research Service, JPRS, *Terrorism* (7 August 1990), pp. 1–2. An example of American coverage is the front-page story in the *New York Times*, 28 June 1990. Dr Tucker, *Skirmishes at the Edge of Empire*, mentions additional sources in pp. 25–7 and his accompanying footnotes.
7. *Washington Post* (16 August 1992). German authorities were counting 39,800 'neo-Nazis and other members of the radical right' as active in 1991. They carried out almost 1,500 attacks, or four times higher than the previous year. In 1997 there were 48,000 right-wing radicals, and 790 attacks; *Washington Post* (7 May 1998).
8. The optimistic view in 1991, reflecting news of what the US State Department called a 17-year low in international terrorism, appeared in such publications as *USA Today* (11 February) and *Time*. The statistics for 1997 were consistent with events of the mid-1990s; see the State Department's *Patterns of Global Terrorism: 1997* (Washington DC: GPO, April, 1998).
9. See for example the report on a San Antonio, Texas, speech by the Pentagon's expert Peter Probst, *Quantico Sentry* (Quantico, VA), 19 September 1997.
10. Hutchings is presumed held by a Muslim separatist group called Al-Faran since July 1996. There were three European hostages in his party, but the Norwegian was beheaded by the terrorists. The two British citizens may also be dead, according to an Indian police report; *Washington Post* (7 October 1997). In 1999 Hutchings' wife continues with the search for him.
11. Of innumerable indicators that anti-American violence has come and will come from the Pakistan–Afghanistan region, one of the smallest is within a long report on international terrorism which John Thor Dahlburg filed from Kandahar. Visiting a hospital where 'Taliban' youth were readied for surgery after bloody fighting around Kabul, the American reporter was shocked to have a Taliban leader walk up to him, smile, and say 'From the Koran will come the power that destroys you'; *Los Angeles Times* (7 August 1996). For this and a hundred equally useful *Los Angeles Times* articles I have Dr Harold W. Rood to thank.
12. FBI, *Terrorism in the United States: 1995* (Washington DC: Department of Justice, 1997), p. 3. This bomb was the only incident the Bureau describes as domestic US terrorism for that year.
13. Sergey Nechaev, *Catechism of the Revolutionist* (1869), repr. in Walter Laqueur and Yonah Alexander (eds), *The Terrorism Reader: A Historical Anthology* (2nd

edn., New York: Meridian, 1987), p. 68.

14. Anarchists killed President Carnot of France in 1894, Premier Canovas of Spain in 1897, Empress Elizabeth of Austria in 1898, King Humbert of Italy in 1900, President McKinley of the United States in 1901, and Premier Canalejas of Spain in 1912. Their less successful attempts included four aimed at assassination of heads of state in Europe in 1878 alone. Barbara W. Tuchman, *The Proud Tower* (New York: Macmillan Co., 1966), p. 63. See also James Joll, *The Anarchists* (New York: The Universal Library, 1966), p. 129, etc.

15. Michael Baumann, *Terror or Love?* (1971; New York: Grove Press, 1979), p. 48. See also pp. 27, 34, 50–6, and the references to Frantz Fanon, Mao Tse-Tung, and others.

16. My copy of the 'Jolly Roger' volume was downloaded by Major John Ross, USMC, in late 1996.

17. Martha F. Lee, 'Violence and the Environment: The Case of "Earth First!"' *Terrorism and Political Violence*, 7:3 (autumn 1995), p. 119.

18. The quotations appear in a Cal Thomas column in the *Washington Times* of 22 June 1997: the first, from Alex Pacheco, had appeared in the *New York Times*; the second, by Kevin Beedy, was in the March 1990 issue of *Animals' Agenda*.

19. http://www.ANIMAL-LIBERATION.NET

20. For example, in 1992 the Animal Liberation Front so damaged the Mink Research Facility at Michigan State University that Rodney Coronado was handed a sentence of 57 months in jail, three years' further probation, and a restitution bill for $2,000,000. FBI, *Terrorism in the United States: 1995*, p. 6.

21. Edward Abbey, *The Monkey-Wrench Gang* (New York: Avon Books, 1976). Abbey penned a successor: *Hayduke Lives!* (Boston, MA: Little, Brown, 1990).

22. FBI, *Terrorism in the United States: 1991* (Washington DC: GPO, undated).

23. Dave Foreman, *Confessions of an Eco-Warrior* (New York: Harmony Books, 1991). Another book with many references to Edward Abbey is by Christopher Manes, *Green Rage: Radical Environmentalism and the Unmaking of Civilization* (Boston: Little, Brown, 1990). The latter's subtitle is suggestive of the anarchism of some 'ecoterrorists'.

24. Some members of 'Earth First!' declare themselves opposed even to ecotage. Judi Bari, for example, who helped organize opposition to logging of old-growth forests in northern California, furthered a division within 'Earth First!' by publicly opposing any kind of property sabotage. She was nearly killed by a bomb in her car in May 1990 – a bomb which supporters said must be the work of the logging industry or the government, but which law enforcement authorities think she may have knowingly been transporting. Bari moved out of the spotlight on environmental issues and died of cancer in 1997.

25. 'This is *jihad*, pal. There are no innocent bystanders, because in these desperate hours, bystanders are not innocent', writes an 'Earth First!' founder living in Missoula, Montana, in the group's journal (issue of December/January 1995; my italics). This is Mike Roselle, the same man who funded the short-lived periodical 'Live Wild or Die', which once published an ecotage 'hit list'. That list became notorious when a private investigator determined that the Unabomber had probably read it; the Unabomber's last two victims were in fact on that published list. For a distinctly noncommittal view of these linkages, see Richard Leiby's article 'Madman or Eco-Maniac' in the *Washington Post* (17 April 1996).
    The morally impaired view that 'There are no innocents' was perhaps first announced in terrorism trials in the proceedings against Emile Henry, a French anarchist whose crimes included the 1894 bombing of a café catering to the middle

and working classes of Paris; Joll, *The Anarchists*, pp. 136–7.

26. The Unabomber's manifesto, entitled 'Industrial Society and its Future', was printed in the *Washington Post* on 19 September 1995. (The full text also quickly appeared on the Internet.) The *New York Times* shared the costs of publication with the *Post* but did not print the document. Both papers acted with the support of the Attorney-General and the FBI, which hoped to flush out the bomber's identity.

   Understanding of Kaczynski has been enhanced by release of personal letters and journal material. On 29 April 1998, 100 new journal excerpts were released in federal court proceedings; some appeared in that day's *New York Times* and other papers. And in December 1998, Chris Waits and Dave Shors published a book about the case and the diaries.

27. This Libyan volume is not to be confused with the *Green Book* used to train Irish Republican Army personnel; see my Chapter 3, and here below, n. 52.

28. Patrick Harrington, a leader of Britain's neofascist National Front, has stated that 'We are ideologically sympathetic to the position of Col Gaddafi' (*Sunday Telegraph*, 10 April 1988), in JPRS, *Terrorism* (26 May 1988), p. 34.

   Better known in the UK is the pattern of Libyan aid to the IRA. Recent confirmation of such aid includes articles on Thomas 'Slab' Murphy, a liaison, in *The Times* (16 and 17 May 1998), and excerpts from Sean O'Callaghan's new book *The Informer* in the *Daily Telegraph* (19 May 1998), etc.

29. *Patterns of Global Terrorism: 1995*, p. 23.

30. The Moro National Liberation Front struck a peace accord with Manila in late 1996, but Abu Sayyaf has continued its brutal activities in Mindanao. The group's leader is a former teacher of Islam, Abdurajak Abubakar Janjalani, who has allegedly ordered his men to 'kill and behead all Christians' during engagements or terror acts. Estimates of group strength have been as high as 700 but 200 may be more realistic. Their objective is an Islamic republic, carved out of the southern Philippines. Some members may have trained in Afghanistan. Philippine press coverage of the new group's activities has included stories by such Manila-based periodicals as the *Philippine Daily*, *Manila Standard*, and *Business World*, as well as radio and television reporting; see JPRS, *Terrorism*, e.g. issues of 19 January and 19 October 1995, and 10 April and 26 April 1996. See also Peter Chalk's 'Bin Laden's Asian Network' in Jane's *Pointer* (1 December 1998).

31. Department of State, *Libyan Activities in the Western Hemisphere* (Washington DC: GPO, August 1986).

32. Scholars often disagree about Lenin's views on terrorism and on the importance of such sentences as I cite in the text. For example, Joan Witte writes a remarkably long article about Lenin and terrorism but does not cite this revealing letter from his hand. Yet she does state that in the 1905 period Lenin wanted violent action to topple the Russian regime, and that in 1906 Lenin penned this missive: 'The Resolution of the Unity Congress entitled "On Guerrilla Actions" ... is perfectly clear. "Parallel with" work among the masses it recognizes "active struggle" against the perpetrators of violence, which undoubtedly means killing them by means of "guerrilla actions".' Even so, Witte's conclusion is that Lenin opposed terrorism except the kinds wielded directly by the party and by the army after power is taken (in 1917). See 'Violence in Lenin's Thought and Practice: The Spark and the Conflagration', *Terrorism and Political Violence*, 5:3 (autumn 1993), pp. 135–203.

   A contrasting analysis of Lenin *re*. terrorism and its utility prior to the success of the 1917 revolution may be found in Roberta Goren, *The Soviet Union and Terrorism*, ed. Jillian Becker (London: Allen & Unwin, 1984), pp. 19–27. I find this the more successful presentation of Lenin's spirit and views. Naturally one does best by consulting Lenin's writings directly.

33. So well established in Colombia's rural areas that they command as much as 40 per cent of the country by one estimate, the guerrillas are now forming clandestine networks in Bogota. There may already be 300 cells in the capital, according to a leaked police report; *Daily Telegraph* (22 May 1998).

34. Although some MRTA cadres remain at large, Foreign Policy Research Institute expert Dr Michael Radu makes this comment following the deaths of all MRTA terrorists inside the Japanese Embassy: 'This group was moribund before; now it is buried'; 'The NewsHour' with Jim Lehrer (24 April 1997). Radu is coauthor with Vladimir Tismaneanu of one of the best English language books written on the latter twentieth-century's *Latin American Revolutionaries: Groups, Goals, Methods* (Washington DC: Pergamon–Brassey's, 1990).

35. Communiqué issued 12 October 1989. This, and several full communiqués of other years, appear in the valuable document collection of Yonah Alexander and Dennis Pluchinsky, *Europe's Red Terrorists: The Fighting Communist Organizations* (London: Frank Cass, 1992), p. 45, etc.

36. See, for example, the December 1929 essay 'On Correcting Mistaken Ideas in the Party', *Selected Military Writings of Mao Tse Tung*, 2nd edn (Peking: Foreign Languages Press: 1967), pp. 53–5.

37. See, for example, the Revolutionary Worker's 'Message from the Revolutionary Communist Party, USA to the Communist Party of Nepal (Maoist) on the One Year Anniversary of the People's War in Nepal', downloaded from the Internet 4 January 1999 from http://www.mcs.net/~rwor

38. Reuters' story of 21 April 1998, downloaded from the CNN Internet on 4 January 1999 at http://www3.cnn.com/WORLD/americas/9804/21/RB002252.reut.html

39. Various press sources, especially *La Republica* (Lima), *Expresso* (Lima), and Agence France Presse (Paris), as repr. in June and July 1996 in editions of FBIS, *Terrorism* and FBIS, *Latin America*.

40. Herman Rauschning, *Revolution of Nihilism* (1939; New York: Alliance Book Corporation, 1940).
    See for example p. 22: National Socialism's 'revolutionary, irrational character ... continually prompts it to any possible revolutionary destruction of existing institutions ... This irrational element in National Socialism is the actual source of its strength.'

41. On left–right ambiguities and collusion between the world wars, read Nikolai Tolstoy, *Stalin's Secret War* (New York: Holt, Rinehart & Winston, 1981), pp. 85–8. NeoNazi allegiance to Ernst Roehm is noted by the annual German 'Report on the Protection of the Federal Constitution' for 1983. A second popular 'father figure' of the neofascists is said to be Gregor Strasser, a socialist and a senior NSDAP figure. 'They also have sympathies with such organizations as the [leftist] Irish Republican Army, the Basque guerrilla group ETA and the Palestine Liberation Organization', noted the *Los Angeles Times* of 7 April 1984 in summarizing the report from Bonn. See Chapter 5.

42. The theme is captured in the article title, 'Fine Young Fellows: The Radical Right Republicans Draw Former SED Members and Former GDR Officers', *Der Spiegel* (4 May 1992), in FBIS, *Western Europe* (15 May 1992), pp. 14–15.

43. This is my conclusion. For a view that goes much further, see Michael Schmidt, *The New Reich: Violent Extremism in Unified Germany and Beyond*, trans. Daniel Horch (New York: Pantheon Books, 1993), p. 64. He writes: 'The Nazi scene is really a completely male society, with all the attendant elements of male

chauvinism, militarism, and homosexuality ... The considerable percentage of gays, especially in leadership positions, corresponds roughly to the percentage of homosexual functionaries in the Third Reich.' It may be relevant that Michael Kuhnen, a neofascist leader whom Schmidt interviewed many times, died of AIDS in 1991.

44. Seattle University Professor Emeritus of History, Charles Robert Harmon, telephone interview of November 1996.

45. This is safe as a generalization. An essay dealing with the few known female radicals in the British neofascist movement is by Martin Durham, 'Women and the National Front', in *Neo-Fascism in Europe*, ed. Luciano Cheles, Ronnie Ferguson, and Michalina Vaughan (Harlow: Longman, 1991), pp. 264–83.

46. The respective German terms are *Judenfrei* and *Auslanderfrei*.

47. Ewald Althans, interview with the *Daily Telegraph* 12 March 1992, in FBIS, *Western Europe* (3 March 1992). See also Ingo Hasselbach, with Tom Reiss, *Fuhrer-Ex: Memoirs of a Former Neo-Nazi* (New York: Random House, 1996), p. 157, etc. At his meetings of the 'National Alternative', Hasselbach displayed the flag of the German *Reich* of 1870.

48. 'Czech Towns Put Gypsies Into "Ghetto"', *The Times* (26 May 1998).

49. For example, in March 1997 2,200 delegates met in Strasbourg. 'The National Front and its president, Jean-Marie Le Pen, are notorious in much of France for their blunt statements about race and immigration. Le Pen has embraced 'inequality of the races', called for the deportation of immigrants to create jobs for 'real' French people and dismissed Nazi death camps as a historical 'detail'; *Washington Post* (30 March 1997).

50. My sources for these observations about neofascism's international connections are varied. One treatments is the aforementioned *Neo-Fascism in Europe*; see for example pp. 251–5. NeoNazi terrorist leader Michael Kuhnen told of connections to organizations in Belgium, France, and the United States, and of the financial connections of some neofascists with Latin American narcotics wholesalers; Schmidt, *The New Reich*, pp. 40, 42. See also Hasselbach, *Fuhrer-Ex*, Chs. 15 and 16. Gary Lauck served four years in jail and was then deported to the United States in March 1999.

51. Kleim is not mentioned in many reports on American extremists, but Carl Shelton, now Lieutenant-Colonel, USMC, located the second edition of the 'National Socialism Primer' on the Internet. It carried – and in January 1999 still carries – the date of 17 April 1995.

52. Diverse sources, including William Pierce's book catalogues, *The Turner Diaries*, and research by the Anti-Defamation League, *Danger: Extremism. The Major Vehicles and Voices on America's Far-Right Fringe* (New York, ADL, 1996).

The most recent murder linked to *The Turner Diaries* may be that of James Byrd Jr, a black man seized in the street in Jasper, Texas and dragged to death behind a truck. The suspects may be linked to the KKK; one told police 'We're starting *The Turner Diaries* early'; *Washington Post* (13 June 1998).

53. The IRA's *Green Book*, according to Patrick Bishop and Eamonn Mallie, was created in prison in the mid 1970s and edited by a Sinn Fein activist before distribution to volunteers; *The Provisional IRA* (London: Corgi Books, 1992), p. 346. The text of it is difficult to find. One copy – purportedly in full – appears as an annex in Martin Dillon, *25 Years of Terror: The IRA's War Against the British* (1997 edn; London: Bantam Books). See p. 380 on 'internationalism' versus racism.

This *Green Book* should not be confused with the IRA General Headquarters handbook on guerrilla war I cite frequently in Chapter 3, or the political tract by Colonel Qaddafi mentioned in this chapter.

54. When one considers the way most terrorist groups run their organizations, and control the people within their rural 'liberated zones', one sees portents of the future if these groups should take power. The Tamil Tigers and the Khmer Rouge provide two among many examples of such groups; the former ruthlessly controlling all those Sri Lankans that it can, and the other having already proven its character in the seat of national power.

55. A 'Tartan Army' of a few unemployed Scots carried out several sabotage actions in 1975 and were promptly arrested and sentenced to jail. Nothing more has been heard of this 'Army for Freeing Scotland'. Peter Janke, *Guerrilla and Terrorist Organizations: A World Directory and Bibliography* (New York: Macmillan, 1983), p. 104. The book includes capsules on small Welsh and Breton groups. On Scotland's newest political and peaceable change, see *Foreign Report* (30 July 1998).

56. Chris Ryan, *Tourism, Terrorism, and Violence*, Conflict Studies no. 244 (London: Research Institute for the Study of Conflict and Terrorism, September 1991), p. 12.

57. *New York Times* (15 January 1997); *US News and World Report* (14 December 1998).

58. Quoted by Janke, *Guerrilla and Terrorist Organizations*, p. 31, and apparently dating to 1979.

59. A Cuncolta Naziunalista is a political front for the terrorists of FLNC, as demonstrated by 1997 revelations about an extortion case which tied the overt and covert organizations together. See the *New York Times* (15 January 1997), or the similar story in the *Washington Post*. An excellent review of the long conflict appears in *L'Express* (Paris, 2 December 1998).

60. Interview with Charles Pieri, *Le Monde* (Paris, 28 May 1996), in FBIS, *Terrorism* (28 June 1996), pp. 113–14. Other useful materials on Corsican violence include: Agence France Presse (Paris), 22 May 1992, in *JPRS: Terrorism* (2 June 1992), p. 20; FBIS, *Terrorism* (5 February 1996), p. 64; and 'Corsica Pacified?', *The Economist* (24 February 1996), p. 54.

   According to *The Economist*, there have been some 3,000 bombs in the last five years alone, but 'only a small proportion are claimed by nationalists. Most of the violence comes from the feuding and commercial rivalry of the powerful clans that dominate this racket-ridden island.'

61. The IRA *Green Book*, as cited by Bishop and Mallie, *The Provos*, p. 346.

62. The IRA has won a half-loaf but no more; see for example the Anthony McIntyre admission, 'We, the IRA, Have Failed', *Guardian* (22 May 1998).

63. INLA's Belfast Brigade assassinated another INLA member, Desmond McLeery of County Armagh, in May of 1996, at a bar. The faction responsible telephoned the BBC to claim credit and blame the victim for helping kill INLA leader Geno Gallagher in west Belfast the previous January. Press Association (London: 29 May 1996), in FBIS, *Terrorism* (28 June 1996), p. 131.

64. 'Some observers reckon that the INLA in Northern Ireland has 50–70 members, with perhaps 20–30 in the Irish Republic. These members would not necessarily be active on a full-time basis'. Sean Boyne, 'INLA: The Deadly Hand of Irish Republicanism', Parts 1 and 2, *Jane's Intelligence Review* (January and February 1997). The first part of this series includes several paragraphs on 'Inter-republican feuds' of the sort described above between members of INLA.

65. Although the conventional view is that the IRA and INLA do not coordinate their activities, Tim Pat Coogan writes that they do combine for certain 'joint ventures'.

And of course, both oppose the non-violent Marxists of the left, including the IRA 'Officials'. Tim Pat Coogan, *The IRA: A History* (Niwot, CO: Roberts Rinehart Publishers, 1993), pp. 348, 407–12.

66. Communiqué issued through the 'Socialist Republican Publicity Bureau' in Belfast, and cited by the Press Association (London: 22 March 1996), in FBIS, *Terrorism* (5 June 1996), p. 128. The INLA argument resembles that of the Provos in resuming their own operations, which may be found in press reports repr. in FBIS, *Terrorism* (19 October 1995), p. 87.

67. LTTE reportedly executed the head of this group, called PLOTE, in January 1995.

68. This section on Tamil Tiger objectives is indebted to an excellent US Department of Defense publication now a decade old, *Terrorist Group Profiles* (Washington DC: GPO, 1988), p. 120. The authors included Mr Peter Probst. For budget reasons, there has not been a second edition, even after the last Chairman of the Joint Chiefs of Staff repeatedly expressed concern about 'force protection' for Americans deployed abroad.

69. http://www.eelamweb.com

70. See for example 'Malaysian Authorities Detain LTTE Activists, *Daily News* (Colombo: 28 March 1996), in JPRS, *Terrorism* (6 June 1996), p. 18, as well as *Patterns of Global Terrorism: 1995*, pp. 54–5. In early 1999 Sri Lanka dispatched an official to Australia to attempt to reduce the flow of contributions from Australians to the Tigers.

71. Paul Harris, 'Tamil Tigers Intensify War to Establish Homeland', *Jane's International Defense Review* (May 1996), pp. 56–8; *Los Angeles Times* (24 February 1998).

72. Speech by John P. O'Neill, chief of the counter-terrorism section, FBI, cited by the *Washington Times* (28 April 1996).

73. Dr Steven Metz, *The Future of Insurgency* (Carlisle, PA: Strategic Studies Institute, Army War College, 10 December 1993), pp. 1–25.

74. At Qom, the Iranian holy city, Iran's intelligence services have been training Bahraini activists since 1993. Two large groups of them were tried and convicted in Bahraini courts in the spring of 1997; see for example the *Washington Post* (27 March 1997).

75. The year 1997 witnessed a barrage of criticism of the Palestinian Authority by Palestinian activists, civil rights monitors, and press. But former terrorists cannot give up their methods quickly. The political arguments that yield terrorism also favor dictatorship and ruthless methods of governing.

76. Hamas (Islamic Resistance Movement), 'The Charter of Allah', intro. and ed. by Raphael Israeli, in *The 1988–1989 Annual of Terrorism*, ed. Yonah Alexander and H. Foxman (Netherlands: Kluwer, 1990), pp. 99–134. With kind permission of Kluwer Law International.

77. Major Brian Pulsifer of the US Air Force directed me to the article by Philip Jenkins, 'Home-Grown Terror', *American Heritage* (September 1995), pp. 38–9. Several plots of Christian zealots of the 1930s sound remarkably alike to those of the 1990s.

78. 'White supremacist ultra-Protestantism' is the phrase Warren Kinsella uses to describe the KKK and its large Canadian following; *Web of Hate* (Toronto: HarperPerennial, 1995), p. 19.
    The KKK is more racist than religious, but the latter can also be a visible characteristic. For example, if the Louisiana version of the KKK oath quoted below may be taken as representative, the primary loyalties of the inductees are to the group and to the white race, but also avowed is support for 'the free practice

of the Christian faith – in public institutions – but also in the separation – of church and state'. Next follows the line: 'I will diligently fight against Communism – and Zionism' (since both are thought to be opposed to true Christianity). This oath of 1980 is twice replicated in Jerry Thompson, *My Life in the Klan* (Nashville, TN: Rutledge Hill Press, 1988).
79. The killer also shot pornographer Larry Flynt and his lawyer in 1978 after becoming enraged by a cartoon Flynt published depicting sex between a black man and a white woman. Franklin is serving multiple life sentences for murders and faces further charges; *New York Times* (16 February 1997).
80. From years of seeing news reports of KKK rallies I have derived my own rule: Wherever ten or 20 of the robed ones venture a public display, they will be massively outnumbered by disgusted counter-protesters. See, as one example, 'Ex-Klan Leader Gets 3 Years for Conspiracy', *Star-Ledger* (Newark NJ: 29 August 1992). I take this public response to the KKK's political activity as an indicator of the essential health of American democracy.
    'Today's KKK is the weakest and most fragmented it has been since World War II', according to the Anti-Defamation League, *Danger: Extremism*, p. 239.
81. Ibid., pp. 221–3; Martin Durham, 'Preparing for Armageddon: Citizen Militias, the Patriot Movement and the Oklahoma City Bombing', *Terrorism and Political Violence*, 8:1 (spring 1996), p. 67.
    The least hateful, most idealistic component of the militant Christian right in America today is an altogether different case-study from 'Christian Identity'. It is the anti-abortion movement. Although many of its leaders have consistently condemned violence, the movement's resistance to promulgating terrorism has been partially dissolved by the momentum of efforts to protect the unborn, by zeal, and perhaps by personality disorders of a very few who turned to terrorism. There is now a lethal edge to what is generally a moral movement by the gentle and the genteel. The change in anti-abortion activities from prayer and demonstrations to occasional violence underscores the significance of the initial definition of terrorism, which includes the concept of 'menacing'. Those menaced may not seem innocent to the perpetrators, but the law does protect them, be they doctors that perform abortions, clinic workers who assist them, or political organizations lobbying for abortion rights. These circles have come to know fear because of violent acts. Early in the 1990s some of the first menacing was apparently by 'Lambs of God' who telephoned to tell doctors their own children might not remain safe unless their practices were abated. Some anti-abortionists also menaced clinic workers and clients both by sabotage of property at clinics, and even firebombings, invariably done at night when it was believed no one would be harmed. The final stage was political combustion and outright murder: shootings at clinics occurred in several states, including lethal attacks in Massachusetts and Florida. Perhaps shocked by this bloodshed, the movement quieted its public activities somewhat; incidents of violence declined after the December 1994 Massachusetts killings.
    But the 1998 murder of a Buffalo, New York, doctor shows the potential for such attacks to endure because the practice of abortion will continue. There are few more divisive American political and social questions. 'This is what you get! You should pray the rosary', shouted John Salvi III in a high-pitched voice 'like a preacher' as he fired a rifle at personnel at one Massachusetts clinic. Salvi's attorneys claimed he was insane; he may be; that is not the usual defense in the clinic incident trials, any more than it is a good explanation for terror attacks of other kinds. Perhaps more typical of the anti-abortion terrorists is James Anthony

Mitchell, a Catholic who attended several anti-abortion rallies and then, acting alone, torched a Falls Church VA clinic in February 1997. He did so because 'lives are being lost much as they were in Nazi death camps'.

82. The term 'preservationist' is that of National Defense University's Bard O'Neill, author of *Insurgency & Terrorism: Inside Modern Revolutionary Warfare* (Washington DC: Brassey's, 1990), pp. 20–1. It is a useful term. While 'preservationist' terrorism by Northern Irish militias is intended as 'pro-state' violence, Afrikaner or KKK terrorism today is intended to preserve advantages for an ethnic group but is not 'pro-state' because it contravenes the governments' interests in South Africa and the United States respectively.

83. *New York Times*, 30 December 1996. While violence in Guatemala has diminished greatly since the phased 1996–97 peace accord, terrorism remains a specter. The Roman Catholic bishop who supervised a 1,400-page study of human rights abuses during the long internal struggle was murdered two days after publishing his report. No perpetrator has been identified, but four major stories assessing the act appeared in the *Los Angeles Times* from 28 through 30 April 1998.

84. Peter Taylor, *States of Terror: Democracy and Political Violence* (London: BBC Books, 1993), pp. 98–104. See also the detailed *New York Times* articles of 12–14 February 1997.

85. Steve Bruce, 'Loyalists in Northern Ireland: Further Thoughts on Pro-State Terror', *Terrorism and Political Violence*, 5:4 (winter 1993), p. 252.

86. British statistics not contested by partisans on either side indicate that while the Nationalists (IRA, INLA, etc.) have killed more than the Loyalists, the latter have been 'making up for lost time'. In the 14 months before June 1994, police brought 138 charges against Protestant paramilitaries and 83 against Catholic organizations like the IRA; *New York Times* (22 June 1994).

87. For example, the New York weekly the *Irish People* headlines suspicions of cooperation between anyone in government or security forces, on the one hand, and 'orange' militias on the other.

88. The analysis in this paragraph is largely derived from Steve Bruce, 'The Problem of 'Pro-State' Terrorism: Loyalist Paramilitaries in Northern Ireland', *Terrorism and Political Violence*, 4:1 (spring 1992), pp. 67–88. This article engendered a response in a later issue of the journal by J. Cusack and M. Taylor; Bruce continued the exchange with a further article for the winter 1993 issue, cited above.

89. Diverse sources, including the April 1998 issue of *Patterns of Global Terrorism*, p. 20.

2

Strategies

Introduction: ends and means

Strategy is the considered application of means to advance certain ends. Terrorism can certainly be a strategy, and not merely a tactic, or incidental event. In nearly all the kinds of groups described in Chapter 1, terrorism is chosen for definite purposes; it is a chief means to advance political ends. While sometimes it is the *only* well-developed means a given group employs, successful terrorists invariably use additional means and forms of effort: political, social, military, or even humanitarian.

Because terrorism is a strategy, it may be used by different groups or governments for very different ends. It often serves multiple purposes: the same kidnapping can be intended to shock the public, to cripple a politician, and to raise operating funds, all at once. This chapter will link the concept of strategy to the unique features of terrorism, briefly examine the strategies most characteristic of the different political types of terror groups, identify the most common three strategic objectives of all terror groups, and conclude with a consideration of the question: 'Does terrorism succeed?'

Special characteristics set terrorism apart and bear upon its use as a strategy. Unlike political parties and their fights, terrorist activities are illegal, and explicitly anti-legal. Yet, unlike typical crime, or transnational organized crime, terrorism is directed at a public purpose; its money-making is incidental to that end. Unlike armies, including guerrilla forces, which employ force against other armed parties, terrorists distinguish themselves by targeting civilians, the unarmed, and the innocent. Unlike both police forces and armies, which act or claim to act with the purpose of restoring law, peace, and order, terrorists aim to shred the status quo and make a 'new order' of their own design. Most use of force in non-terroristic settings aims to destroy or reduce an identified threat; the very essence of terrorism is in the calculated use of violence to spread alarm through a wider audience; the actual target may be almost incidental to the desired effects, which expand outward like shock waves.

While every terror group has a strategy, it may be well- or ill-defined. Some groups may have only the vaguest long-range plans while focusing merely on operations. Leadership is often the key to the thoroughness or lack thereof with which terror groups plan. An informal committee of Red Brigade principals shaped and debated strategic plans with attentiveness, and then disseminated them to be studied by the urban 'columns'.[1] Abimael Guzman of Shining Path presumably developed his long-range strategic plan by himself,[2] but he then boldly published it for the faithful – and the world – to read in his underground newspaper. Other considerations impinge on planning: what is the nature of the state, or enemy, being attacked? Is there a definite timeline, like the impending world war expected by Aum Shinrikyo, or the Marxist conception of an active historical process, which must be served? Or are the terrorists relatively free from such service? At this moment, do societal and political circumstances favor more or less violence in relation to political effort? How well can a proposed plan adapt to what the enemy does? After all, a living, rational enemy often changes, or innovates. A pro-state terrorist organization succeeding in one year might find international human rights groups exposing it completely in the next year, forcing major strategic recalculations by the terrorists.

Every strategist, including terrorists, must ask 'What is the desired end state?' Here again the spectrum can be broad. States may foster international terrorists as a tool of policy; the sponsor trains, funds, and exports violent foreigners to injure or prod a rival government, and may later 'corral' that violence if it attains its purpose or ceases to be useful. Insurgent groups often use terror in their drive to take full political power. Some anti-status quo terrorists may only seek strategic concessions within their own state, such as greater autonomy for their region or ethnic group. 'Traditionalist' terrorists may want no changes to laws or the polity at all, but they propagandize and attack to perpetuate a social atmosphere in which their own rights and privileges remain paramount *vis-à-vis* other social or racial classes.[3] Individual terrorists may find the clandestine struggle so appealing that it almost becomes an end in itself, a way of life. But while such nihilism is present by degrees in anyone willing to maim and murder the innocent, it is a mistake to think that nihilism, rather than purpose, is the essence of the typical contemporary terrorist organization.

Types of terrorist groups and strategy

Anarchists are intent upon opening whole new worlds to human possibilities. Like their writings and lives, their strategies reflect that urge. Some in squatter groups and 'ANTI-FA' (anti-fascist) groups in major European urban centers see a connection between political street violence and the social stroke of founding communes which defy the paradigms of modern government, urban civilization and private property. The 'Unabomber', for his part, sees terrorism and publicization of it as his individual effort towards restoring some conception of 'wild nature', relatively free of technological and human presence. Like some other revolutionaries of the left, anarchists see a close interrelationship between economics and politics, between property and governance. They would destroy both to transform human arrangements. Destroying either property or government by degrees can produce chaos, which to anarchists is an end and a means. For such thinkers, organizing a disciplined insurgency may not be possible or appropriate, but terrorism can be. The arson fire or the bomb hurled symbolizes everything: the goal of destruction; breaking a link in the chains of authority; the desire to shock and grab attention; the general unsettling of society; the challenge to all norms. The anarchist's willingness – indeed eagerness – to be lethal demonstrates a determination to drive out compromisers, reformers, and 'liberal progressives' who fail to see that the system must be destroyed.

The weaknesses typical of today's anarchist strategies are several. Some branches of anarchism are nonviolent and can not be won over to the side of terrorists. Among those who would commit terrorism, the impetus may be psychological or personal, more than political, rendering organization difficult. Most who are inclined to be violent are urban; there is only sporadic rural activity, and overall far too small a following to support a movement of national character. As today's movements seem peculiar to a city, or a region, there is little to no international action to support the local efforts.

Communist doctrine does not just accept but enthusiastically anticipates revolutionary violence. In making strategy, communist terrorists understand the considerable powers of the state, on the one hand, and the realities of citizens' attachment to their property, on the other. But if the bourgeois state is built upon dictatorship and general economic 'theft,' so too must the solution mix politics, economics, and force. Communists of the extreme sorts make their strategy one of parallel branches: political organization, agitation and propaganda, and violence against property and life. The violence is calibrated based on circumstances and leaders' direction. The doctrinaire Leninist terrorist of today, such as a Kurd of the PKK, conceives power as centered around a professional cadre which directs all branches of revolutionary effort – even disallowing terrorism that is inopportune. The Trotskyite groups, not unknown in Latin America and Europe one and two decades ago, conceive the revolution as endless, a continuous process of recreation of human consciousness and political forms. Out of power, close to power, or in power, they would deploy terrorism and other violence in large helpings and with few reservations. The Maoists, such as a New People's Army Filipino, have no confidence in the solely clandestine approach, or the *coup d'état*. Their strategy is inherently long-term, and explicitly advances political education and organization as much as violence. Since the first decades of the century, Maoism has also symbolized the rural insurgency rather than urban, reflecting the difference between Mao and early twentieth-century Chinese Leninists about where true revolutionary opportunity and power lay. 'Focoism' of the Che Guevara sort is another communist sect, surviving in ideologically weakened form in such groups as the Colombian ELN and Peru's MRTA. It places violence on a primary plane, expecting that armed clashes and fear will draw political fealty and spark revolutionary spirit.

All these successors to Marx may differ on some strategic issues such as whether to build alliances with existing political parties, whether to create front groups, and whether to emphasize national issues or admit to an aggressively 'internationalist' posture. All are more willing than was Marx to openly use and discuss terror; they think 'history' must be spurred along by revolutionaries' attacks. For communist doctrinaires, terror is rarely without a role: in the beginning, terror transforms and polarizes the population; in the middle, it is used in tandem with political struggle to infiltrate the open minds, to bend the more opinionated, and to break the resolutely anti-communist. After victory, terror retains a primary place as a method of protecting the new government, disciplining the party, initiating mass activity, and slowing tendencies towards 'deviation'. Every communist movement to attain power has continued to use terror, through state agencies, to hold power.

Fascism had similar strategies for gaining and holding power. Politics and violence were deemed inseparable at all stages of struggle by these early twentieth-century movements. Propaganda and violence helped discredit the state while making a revolutionary consensus and even community. Political action, street-fighting, and quick *coups d'état* placed Mussolini and Hitler in power, and state power was then used to batter down domestic opposition and foreign enemies. Fascism evinced a special interest in power – and visual demonstrations thereof; thus fascism's enormity, whether in public architecture, mass political organizations, military parades, or wars of conquest. European and American neofascism is less ambitious, and far less successful. While it can count many extremists, it has undeveloped political and social roots. European neofascists of most countries are marginal figures, not the cutting edge of a coming political power. The German, Austrian, Scandinavian, and American groups virtually all lack the kind of gifted and charismatic leadership that can change this picture.

Neofascism, like its progenitor, is identifiable by what it opposes. By degrees, neofascists may be anti-rational, anti-capitalist, anti-religious, or anti-conservative. By near unanimous consent, they are anti-semitic, xenophobic, anti-pacifist, anti-individualist, and anti-democratic. Such feelings, and the doctrinal emphasis on will, supply the flagrant fighting spirit of today's neofascist terrorist groups. Their very essence is their willingness to fight. The movement is not without a conception of political action, and it works to distribute propaganda, and makes public gestures and peaceable demonstrations. But there has been little else. There is sporadic interest in exploiting the Internet, generally unsuccessful attempts to link up with the Skinhead movement's legions of followers,[4] and a low level of liaison with the nonviolent legal right wing. In the German case, no leader, from Manfred Roeder in the late 1970s to Heinz Hoffmann of the next years to Ingo Hasselbach who quit when the Berlin Wall came down, has crafted a strategy that profits fully from right-wing but nonviolent political opinion.[5] Doubtless the hatred of parliamentary spirit, and the wariness of the legal rightists, are great obstacles. But the result is that the neoNazis' public profile, apart from its political criticism and Holocaust revisionism, is in its terror attacks. These beatings and firebombings of foreign worker hostels have been expressive, heavily covered by media, and imitated by other radicals. They have changed German public opinion by drawing attention to the presence of foreign labor in a country of some unemployment, and as such these terrorist acts have contributed to raising new standards on immigration.

National separatists have no predictable ideology beyond nationalism, nor any predictable strategy. The nationalist cause has been legitimated and empowered by many trends in modern history and law, but history is no determinant for strategy. Nationalists and their leaders may chose an urban or rural focus; a preponderance of politics over violence or the reverse; direction of armed attacks at the hostile army, at police, or only against civilians, etc. Many separatist leaders opt to enhance cultural awareness, or political action, or legal efforts; this does

NeoNazis on the Internet

Racialists interested in 'white power' can find reading and reinforcement and ongoing discussion at multiple sites on the Internet. A symbol of the new information age, the world wide web is also an instantaneous communicator of violent political speech. It is practically free, and it is much more difficult to police than printed matter or political rallies. One German group comprising dozens of like-minded bulletin boards, the 'Thule Network', is even encrypted, and both a loyalty test and background check are mandated before access is permitted.

'Nordic' and 'Aryan' persons can seek out web sites for the legal rightist parties active in what might be called racially-appropriate countries. There is Alleanza Nazionale, the Italian rightist party. The British National Party is described (by a US white-power web page) as '... working for a future for the British people, and for other white Western nations beleaguered by liberalism, internationalism, and the totalitarian cult of anti-white racism'. The Norwegian 'Fatherland Party' maintains a young members organization, 'Fatherland Youth', with its own page.

Anti-semitism, revisionism on the holocaust, tirades against foreigners or immigrants, slurs on blacks and other examples may be found on the web pages. From Canada comes 'The Zundesite', home page of Ernst Zundel, popular revisionist on the Jewish pogroms – or 'holohoax', as one Skinhead web page calls it. Canada also has a white-power site called 'Scarborough Skinheads', while French participants offer the 'Charlemagne Hammer Skinheads' page. There are web sites for German language racists, and whole sections of web sites on American groups of similar type. One page is for 'White Aryan Resistance' or WAR, the organization of Tom Metzger, who was set back for years to come by a civil suit that convicted him of inciting the youths that murdered an Ethiopian man in Portland, Oregon. For those looking to pick a fight on the keyboards, 'Skinheads USA' offers links to the left – sites of foreign and domestic 'Communist Dirtbags and other Wankers'.

The American neofascist Milton John Kleim Jr, who has posted a 'National Socialism Primer' on the Internet, has also written an online essay 'On Tactics and Strategy for USENET'. He exhorts his politicized readers to exploit the opportunity to establish a web page for a few hundred dollars and thus reach tens of millions of Internet users. Kleim writes:

> USENET offers enormous opportunity for the Aryan resistance to disseminate our message to the unaware and the ignorant ... It is the only relatively uncensored [so far] mass medium which we have available ... NOW is the time to grasp the WEAPON which is the INTERNET and wield it skillfully and wisely.

Former Ku Klux Klan official Don Black of West Palm Beach, Florida, equally enthused, set up the Internet page 'Stormfront' for people 'fighting to preserve their White Western culture'. 'It's almost like having a TV network ... The benefit is that we reach tens of thousands of people, potentially millions.'[6]

not often garner them headlines. Others turn directly to terrorism as their main effort, as have two entirely different Palestinian groups: Abu Nidal and Palestine Islamic Jihad.

A road between pacific effort and pure terrorism has been chosen, and then followed with great skill for three and a half decades, by other Palestinian national separatists: the PLO. Yasser Arafat's organization has used almost every known strategic tool to shape its political environment and opportunities. They used terror to polarize opinion within Israel, pitting part of the electorate against others over the Palestinian question. Simultaneously, these terror attacks catalyzed nationalist fervor in the Palestinian diaspora. The PLO struck at Israeli soldiers to hurt them while building their own sense of martial power and justifying their use of the sobriquet 'guerrillas'. They created fronts and clandestine sub-organizations to escape the international pressures that their terrorism created. They deployed scholars and wordsmiths to court foreign public opinion and write popular histories and news to their own taste. They extracted funds systematically from Palestinians at work all over the Middle East. They murdered certain Palestinians who dared to challenge their control over refugee camps, or worse, dared to seek election for offices in the Israeli administration of the West Bank. Their gunmen were armed and trained by the hundreds by Warsaw Pact countries, while their diplomats garnered humanitarian aid by the million from innumerable other governments and agencies. And from the early stages through the political contests of tomorrow, the PLO has worked in and through the UN, winning high levels of political support.

Religious revolutionaries tend towards apocalyptic visions. When these visions assume concrete political dimensions, they can have grandiose and sometimes violent consequences. The belief system of extremist religion may energize and embolden the faithful beyond ways good for society, and may indeed justify terrorism as readily as they can an *intifada* of popular and largely nonviolent resistance. The harsh logic of a religious movement as it turns violent dismisses humanness. Children, women, and men find themselves separated into categories according to their views, or their enthusiasm for their views. Powers of discrimination that should be divine are appropriated by officious clerics who then judge what doctrines and which persons are viable. The Old Testament, Sikh scriptures, and the Koran, not to mention countless base books, such as those penned by Aum Shinrikyo master Shoko Asahara, may all be quoted or misquoted to justify violence. The rigorously controlled environment of a cult, a clandestine religious order, or a politico-religious terror organization may foster an environment where blood may be the price members pay for losing a theological or political or strategic dispute. 'Apostates' who have been taught the proper path, yet stray, like the novelist Salman Rushdie, can be sought out with more grim determination than others who never believed. As there are no higher stakes than those of religion, once violence is unleashed it can be impossible to stop even when it goes beyond the end state of the terrorists. Ambush is followed by funeral, and funeral by suicide bombing. No greater contrast can be imagined than that between the pacific democratic climate of Japan and the cult of Aum Shinrikyo, with its murders, its deployments of poison gasses, and its passion for a coming apocalyptic war. And yet the greater surprise is that today, many of those arrested are already released, and many others are returned to the fold.[7] The Japanese polity, so sensitive to civil liberties, even now declines to suppress this cult.

In 1998 Osama Bin Laden took religio-political terrorism to Africa. Only that continent's northern tier of states had been known for international religious terrorism; other Africans had escaped Islamic extremists' bombs. But Bin Laden is a new activist with a new strategy: world-wide attacks on all available Americans. He has repeatedly promised to strike at both military personnel and civilians, and he knew the latter to be particularly ill-defended in Africa. Indeed, Ambassador Prudence Bushnell told Washington repeatedly and in writing that she feared for her employees and required a new embassy;[8] she was later injured in the bombing. Bin Laden, scion of a construction fortune in Saudi Arabia, was patient enough to build his cells well in Africa, and his simultaneous bombs at US embassies in Kenya and Tanzania on 7 August 1998 announced his level of operational skill. Osama Bin Laden's peculiar views of religious struggle do not permit him public regrets over the hundreds of deaths and casualties, or the fact that 95 per cent of the dead were Africans and other non-Americans. As the terrorist declared to American correspondents visiting him in Afghanistan in the last days of 1998, 'The US knows that I have attacked it, by the grace of God, for more than 10 years now.'[9] Such views, and iron determination to carry them out, place this man in the unusual position of having injured in peacetime as many Americans as were battle casualties during the 1991 Gulf war to liberate Kuwait.[10]

Government terrorization of its own subjects has always been a reality of politics, and contemporary affairs are witness to many descendants of Robespierre and Lenin. Iraq's regime surprised many foreign analysts with its remarkable durability during the war with Iran and the subsequent Gulf War against the international coalition. It has since survived despite an American effort to help Kurds and other marginalized Iraqis, US missile strikes in 1993 and 1996,[11] a joint

British–US air raid of 70 hours' duration in late 1998, and a decade of strict UN economic sanctions. Lethal and pervasive internal security forces are the first answer to this question; Saddam Hussein's own skill and luck are another. Iraq's foreign affairs also have long evinced interest in and capacities for terrorism. The foreign terror groups which presently enjoy Baghdad's patronage are Abu Nidal, the Arab Liberation Front, aircraft bomber Abu Ibrahim, the Kurdish Worker's Party, the People's Mujahideen of Iran, and Abu Abbas's Palestine Liberation Front, which carried out the *Achille Lauro* piracy.[12]

Iraq made elaborate efforts during the Gulf War to concert terrorism against the countries which sent armies to defend Kuwait and Saudi Arabia. Part of Saddam Hussein's strategy was the use of terrorism to divide the coalition and weaken the will of its belligerents. He dispatched scores of terrorist teams, giving them access to *plastique* sent via diplomatic pouches. He also called overtly for world-wide attacks by terrorists, and many foreign groups friendly to Iraq responded – or acted on their own. There were 275 international terrorism incidents[13] during that short war in 1991 – almost as many as occurred in all of 1996. One unapologetic Iraqi ally, Yasser Arafat, directed or permitted the occurrence of Palestinian attacks on two US soldiers in Jidda, Saudi Arabia, according to one report.[14] In Yemen and in Germany there was automatic weapons fire upon US embassies; in the latter case, the Red Army Faction took credit. In Turkey, a staging area of logistics heads and air bases, and a partner in NATO, Dev Sol and other terrorists hit Western targets. A US customs agent was killed at Incirlik air base, and there were bombings of an American consulate and the Turkish–American Association in Adana. In Athens, the 17 November Organization carried out seven bombings in just four days as the war began; they were 'acting in solidarity with the people of Iraq'.[15] In Manila, an Iraqi diplomat's sons were found to possess bomb-related chemicals in their home and were detained. Another diplomat was killed while placing a bomb at the US Cultural Center in Manila. And there was at least one plan for killing President George Bush – by a pro-Iraqi individual in the United States. That he was arrested before he could carry out the attack[16] was symbolic, for the net effects of all the terrorists' world-wide efforts were dramatically limited. Counter-terrorism and cooperation among governments of unparalleled intensity thwarted Saddam Hussein's terrorism strategy.[17]

While strategy may be considered according to the ideological or political types of those who execute it, it may as usefully be studied from a second perspective. There are several very common kinds of strategy, despite the diversity of the groups, and other distinctions between terrorism by states, insurgent armies, small groups, or individuals. Three broad types of effort of national or strategic consequence are the political, the economic and the military. This order is significant: many terrorists try to avoid engagements with military personnel, but nearly all seek out economic targets for good reasons in their campaigns, and all want political gains at the expense of the existing regime.

Political strategies

Political strategies may seek to weaken or destroy a political power; some are intended to build political support; some do both. First and foremost, terrorism is intended to break or ruin the sense of social and political calm in a country. Whether the targeted country be truly peaceful, or merely quiescent under dictatorship, this strategy often works. 'Disorder' in enemy ranks, or within the enemy's home, rather than destruction of all his armed forces, is the overall strategic objective counseled by Chinese general Sun Tzu. Like the successful general in *The Art of War*, clever terrorists sometimes seek to disorient and confuse the enemy so as to break his spirit and confound his plans. Terrorism is a strategic weapon because the disorder, anarchy and paralysis it can produce affects an entire country or multiple countries.

Few tactics have so steadily proven their capacity to shock the public and make governments appear impotent as the attack on a civilian airliner. Hijackings were perhaps the archetypal terror attack of the late 1960s and early 1970s. They rattled the world order. They permitted terrorists to alert untold numbers world-wide to their political cause through free media access and by stringing out the captivity of the passengers.[18] When governments invented counter-terror forces to handle such criminal theater, terrorist strategists innovated too, by putting bombs aboard aircraft, thus producing unprecedented casualty figures while also manipulating the worst fears of hundreds of millions of people who travel by air. Among the first casualties in this new pattern was a Canadian airliner that disappeared beneath the surface of the Atlantic one night in 1985, taking 328 entirely unwitting victims, probably murdered to attract attention to the cause of Sikhs fighting in India. Pan Am 103 was blown up over Lockerbie, Scotland, in December 1988, apparently to satisfy Libya, or Libya and Iran (which had itself lost a passenger liner that held radio silence while too near a US warship in the Persian Gulf). France has suffered two devastating aircraft bombings. A UTA airliner was destroyed over Africa in September 1989, killing 171. France indicted four Libyan officials for the bombing, which seemed aimed at deterring French support for the regime in Chad, then quarreling with Libya. In 1995 suicide bombers of the Algerian and Islamic GIA nearly succeeded with a plan to load an Air France liner with fuel and detonate explosives in its cockpit as it passed over Paris. French commandos recaptured the aircraft on a ground stop, saving hundreds of lives inside and outside the plane. There could be no more shocking method for warning the people and government of France to cancel their strong support for the secular FLN regime in Algeria.

On the ground in the world of daily politics, too, terrorist actions spread anarchy for the purposes of discrediting government. Threats, attacks on property, and selective killings or hostage takings often serve multiple tactical purposes. They deter those who would serve in government. They inhibit its administrative work and may in 'liberated areas' controlled by guerrillas completely banish the government's presence. They may block the distribution of goods and services, which engenders broad dissatisfaction among even the apolitical. Each successful attack – be it the kidnapping of a politician or a road block at which armed gangs elicit 'revolutionary taxes' – is a pointed reminder that the government is unable to act, or even to defend itself, against a minority.

By its provocations and spread of a sense of anarchy, terror may bring about a 'crackdown' by the government. A state might double the police force, or impose martial law, or take other measures to suppress terrorist organizations or their allies.[19] Remarkably, even such a reaction from government is not always deemed a disadvantage by terrorists. Perhaps the single most important modern pamphlet on terrorist strategy, written in 1969 by the Brazilian terrorist and theoretician Carlos Marighella, is the *Minimanual of the Urban Guerrilla*, found in a hundred safe houses in the last three decades and translated into a dozen foreign languages. Marighella realized that terrorism does undermine public confidence in government, and does force government into a reactive posture, but as repression increases, the government angers its own populace. 'The people refuse to collaborate with the authorities, and the general sentiment is that the government is unjust, incapable of solving problems, and resorts purely and simply to the physical liquidation of its opponents.' The public's support for the terrorists increases, furthering governmental actions that undercut its own efficacy. In such ways, argues Marighella, a normal political situation is translated into a violent military one.[20]

The Marighella model has survived its author and prospered, in a variety of ways.[21] During the mid to late 1990s states engaged in rough counter-insurgency efforts – and targeted for it by influential critics and human rights monitors – were Peru, Egypt, India, Guatemala, Mexico, and Turkey, to mention but a few. Such national and international spotlights on government use of force can be of strong help to the terrorists' political campaign and security concerns. To take a second example, in the late 1980s and early 1990s, many analysts understood Italian right-wing terrorism as an attempt to use fear to create greater authoritarian controls. That is, the neofascists did not so much plan to take full political power but to force government into a more despotic position, more akin to what the right wanted and more likely to show a stern face to the left. Marighella appears again in an altogether different setting. In 1993 a Hamas leaflet listing several dozen political objectives demanded that loyalists embarrass Yasser Arafat's Palestinian Authority (PA), which was cracking down on religiously motivated Palestinian organizations like Hamas. The 'program of confrontation' is to be so effective that it forces redeployment of Israeli forces into areas handed over to Arafat! The bald exhortation of the leaflet is for: 'Escalating operations in order to force the occupation to reoccupy other areas and impose a security siege on areas under the PA's control.'[22]

All terrorists aim to discredit and destroy the government in power; most also work hard to build up their own alternative. Constructive or 'positive' political strategy, for terrorism, may include the spreading of political propaganda, creation of nascent activist groups or fronts, and even formation of political alliances with established political parties or other organized groups. In this light, the long periods of covert and overt revolutionary activity for such leaders as Yasser Arafat and Daniel Ortega appear as journeymen's years, in which they exercised authority over an ever-growing segment of the nation, gaining experience and credibility at the same time.

Propaganda is a veritable terror group standard. Lenin believed that operating a newspaper was a multifaceted way of making political and ideological inroads. 'A newspaper is not only a collective propagandist and a collective agitator, it is also a collective organizer', he noted in his own newspaper.[24] Today *Iskra* ('Spark') is forgotten; even its famous successor *Pravda* ('Truth') went broke in 1996. But Lenin's point was sound. As one infiltrator in the US terrorist group Weathermen discovered, selling their paper *Prairie Fire* on the streets was a way for a cadre to prove commitment, make contacts with prospective recruits, and also to make a little money for the Weathermen. It is for such reasons, as well as for the content of the newspaper, that dozens of terrorist groups today publish. The IRA's *An Phoblacht* ('Republican News') is available from 58 Parnell Square in Dublin; it sells throughout

A Leaflet of 'Hamas'
(Islamic Resistance Movement)

Many of the political strategies of Hamas, a Palestinian Islamic extremist group, are highlighted in a leaflet distributed on 9 October 1993 among its cadres. Reprinted in a Jordanian newspaper, and excerpted here, the leaflet opposes peace accords which helped create the 'Palestinian Authority' led by Yasser Arafat. In the eyes of Hamas, Arafat and his political organization are too secular and too willing to accept a limited geographical entity, instead of fighting for all of Palestine and then ruling it according to the Koran.

First, the most important clauses and goals of the program
1. Isolating the National Authority from the people and showing its dependency on the occupation authorities.
2. Enhancing Hamas' political and public position in preparation for leading the Palestinian street after the agreement fails...

Second, the most important clauses of the confrontation's policies and rules
1. Dealing with the self-rule authority as a dictatorial clique that does not serve the people or the Palestinian cause.
2. Gradually escalating confrontations with the Palestinian Authority as its shortcomings emerge...
4. Depicting and highlighting by every means the injustices Hamas and certain people suffer at the hands of the Authority, with an eye to winning the public over to Hamas...
6. Endeavoring to widen the rift within Fatah [Arafat's guerrilla organization] ranks...

Third, meeting the confrontation's needs
1. Establishing new Hamas institutions.
7. Cooperating with mosque preachers.
8. Issuing a daily and weekly newspaper.
13. Drawing up a plan to infiltrate self-rule institutions, the police, ministries, government bodies, and universities.
16. Establishing private colleges.
17. Setting up charity institutions that do not carry Islamic names in order to benefit from international aid.
18. Activating the security and surveillance organ and collecting information to understand how the enemy thinks, to resist him, and to torpedo his plans before they are implemented.

Fourth, highlighting the outlines of the confrontation's program
3. Continuing to issue the intifada's periodical statement...
4. Continuing the war of slogans, pamphlets, and flags adorned with the caption: 'No god except Allah' in order to belittle the Authority.
5. Escalating operations in order to force the occupation to reoccupy other areas and impose a security siege on areas under the PA's control.[23]

Europe, and can be purchased in New York. Its stories, in turn, are picked up by editors of sympathetic organs like the *Irish People*, the New York-based weekly, or more mainstream newspapers.

Where security is tight, or where the climate of opinion or laws circumscribe overt activism, terror groups may be restricted to a few copies of a press release accompanying an armed attack, or the very discrete distribution of leaflets in public places. There should be no underestimating the powers of small missives. While many persons throw leaflets away, some personalities are readily swung on the cord of a single idea,[25] as is this hard-core anti-semite, a Swede in the teaching profession:

> First I belonged to a leftist group. I have always been committed to some cause. Then one day someone gave me a leaflet. That leaflet changed my life, even if it was only three pages long. When I had read it I understood that it all was a lie, the Holocaust had never happened, it was a dizzy feeling ... At first I was ashamed, I did not dare to tell anyone that I had these thoughts, these doubts ... I had become an anti-Semite ... At my work as a teacher in a public school I had to pretend that nothing had happened, but now...when I have met others who feel like I do, I dare to come out more and more as an open anti-Semite.[26]

In 'Palestine', printed propaganda handouts helped further the *intifada* from its beginning. That movement is today sometimes represented as 'the success of the barefoot soldier' and even as a symbol of the transformation of contemporary politics.[27] The leaflet flourishes there still. In a March 1994 incident, Fatah Hawks loyal to Yasser Arafat were distributing propaganda by car in a Gaza refugee camp when they became embroiled in a fire fight with undercover Israeli troops that left six Hawks dead.[28] Others distributing leaflets in the region include Kach and Kahane Lives, the right-wing Jewish organizations founded – respectively – by an American rabbi and by his son. Kach press releases that threatened Arabs with expulsion and promoted violence appeared in the months prior to the Hebron rampage by Kach activist Baruch Goldstein, who murdered no less than 29 worshippers in a few moments with an American-manufactured MI6 assault rifle.[29] At one time the elder Kahane had run for parliament, in addition to his other political activities; now, stained by terrorism, both Kahane groups are banned in Israel.

Radio and television may be more efficient ways of transmitting news and propaganda, given their almost instantaneous impact and their ability to shape the news. One mark of terror group sophistication and

financial strength is the move into such media. Hezbollah publishes a
daily and a weekly newspaper. It runs 'Mansar TV'; late 1998
programming included film only several hours old of Hezbollah
attacking Israeli soldiers near Markaba, Lebanon, killing or wounding
seven.[30] The organization's radio, 'Voice of the Oppressed', beams out of
the Bekaa Valley. An Israeli air raid took it down for three months
during 1995.[31] But few states are as willing as Israel to take such
counter-measures against propaganda outlets. In past years, the
communist Czech government allowed Red Brigadists who had slipped
behind the Iron Curtain to make propaganda broadcasts back into Italy;
Rome mounted no violent response, and rarely even complained in
public.

The newest forms of propaganda come over the Internet. Selected
IRA/*An Phoblacht* articles can be read on the worldwide web, and
'Provisional' Sinn Fein (of Gerry Adams) and the alternative
'Republican' Sinn Fein both run web sites. Indeed, most radical groups
of international significance operate Internet sites, or have others do so
for them in the way that various 'Committees for the Support of the
Revolution in Peru' serve Sendero Luminoso by online agitation,
propaganda, and product sales. The Tamil Tigers' home page glitters
with color and art work, and includes well-written English-language
histories of the group's armed forces, the Tamil people, their
independence drive, and their fights with the Sri Lankan army. In the
United States, beginning in the early 1990s, the web joined talk radio as
a powerful tool for passing racist propaganda, as well as for advancing
the more benign right-wing opinions of many militias. The respected
Southern Poverty Law Center has an Intelligence Project monitoring
179 'active Patriot web sites',[33] though most of these are not linked to
terrorism.

A different form of political strategy, highly effective when
successful, is the use of front groups – organizations which aid terrorism
while wearing a guise of legitimacy. Some of the best models are in the
communist world, where brilliant success was achieved by 'layering' of
political organizations one inside another. In the 1960s, the North
Vietnamese communists controlled the carefully named National
Liberation Front of South Vietnam, doing so subtly enough to
continuously divide Western strategists and observers about its
authenticity as a South Vietnamese movement. Even some NLF leaders
were deceived about the degree of their own autonomy, according to the
memoir of one secret NLF leader, Truong Nhu Tang.[34]

In more contemporary guerrilla and terrorist politics fronts are rather
common. It has long been apparent that Sinn Fein ('Ourselves Alone')

The 'Unabomber' as press agent

This passage of the Unabomber's manifesto[32] explains the nexus between his environmental ideals, his politics, and his intent to use violence to capture a lethargic public's attention and advance his cause.

... freedom of the press is of very little use to the average citizen as an individual. The mass media are mostly under the control of large organizations that are integrated into the system. Anyone who has a little money can have something printed, or can distribute it on the Internet or in some such way, but what he has to say will be swamped by the vast volume of material put out by the media, hence it will have no practical effect. To make an impression on society with words is therefore almost impossible for most individuals and small groups. Take us (FC) for example. If we had never done anything violent and had submitted the present writings to a publisher, they probably would not have been accepted. If they had been accepted and published, they probably would not have attracted many readers, because it's more fun to watch the entertainment put out by the media than to read a sober essay. Even if these writings had had many readers, most of these readers would soon have forgotten what they had read as their minds were flooded by the mass of material to which the media expose them. In order to get our message before the public with some chance of making a lasting impression, we've had to kill people.

is a front for the IRA. For example, in the autumn of 1981, spokesmen for the 'provisional' branches of both IRA and Sinn Fein made it publicly apparent that they were coordinating strategy in seeking elected posts in government, something both had disdained. Sinn Fein went on to take 10 per cent of the vote in the next year's election, and its quarterly publication *Iris* described the effect in Britain as 'the ballot bomb'.[35] The intertwining of the political front and the gunmen was revealed anew by the many 1997 media interviews with defector Sean O'Callaghan, who had served in Sinn Fein and IRA hierarchies simultaneously. The 'Republicans' have a powerful strategy of combining the Armalite rifle and the ballot box.[36] The front, Sinn Fein, effectively communicates the IRA's views and negotiating positions, and puts the face of political legitimacy on them. It publicly solicits financial aid in Ireland and America and it wields limited powers of local government. Any attempt to suppress Sinn Fein's voice would doubtless be met with greater violence from the IRA.[37]

The Spanish Basque political party Herri Batasuna (HB) fronts for ETA.[38] It has been a persistent, though not very powerful, helpmate to the terrorists. Among its more frustrating years was 1992, when important arrests badly injured the ETA organization on both sides of the border with France; while the armed underground most needed support, their political front was itself in disarray. HB chief Inaki Ensaolo had been questioning the 'effectiveness of the armed struggle in light of the steady weakening of ETA's military potential and lack of social support'. Polls of Basques have increasingly shown they think ETA terrorism is failing. A majority of Basque political parties signed an extraordinary document which said as much: the Anjuria Enea Pact condemned the strategy of terrorism as a means of achieving Basque autonomy. But HB could not condemn its own.[39] One creative move it did take was to open contacts with another important regional player, the Basque Nationalist Party. No breakthrough was produced, however, for when the post-conference communiqué appeared it read: 'while HB considers ETA to be the violent expression of a conflict which has not been resolved satisfactorily, the Basque Nationalist Party believes that the ETA only represents itself'.[40]

HB's troubles of 1991–92 were followed by further evidence of discontent in July 1997. They indicate just how difficult it is to make calibrated violence against the innocent an effective tool of politics in an open democratic society.[41] In a despotism, or under totalitarian rule, men may look to anyone strong enough to fight back and may disregard the ugliness of methods used. But within a society of citizens, as against subjects, the public may well look askance at violence, especially when it is targeted at the innocent. The challenge, for the political fronts in such societies is to be radical but not so much that the populace rebels against the terrorists instead of the government.

In its political strategy, Peru's Shining Path has mastered propaganda, and it has organized indigenous front groups. What is more surprising about this group, known for a Peruvian focus and primitive localist economic ideas and overt contempt for foreign communist regimes, is its effective international political effort. So wide-ranging and visible are organized supporters in northwestern Europe that in 1992 an irritated President Fujimori gave the press a lengthy list of notable *émigrés* and other militant opponents of his government. It detailed Shining Path organizations that included the Committee for the Defense of Human Rights in Peru, the Belgian outlet where journalist Luis Arce Borja publishes the different lingual versions of Shining Path's newspaper *El Diario Internacional* and has also marketed an edition of leader Abimael Guzman's writings. In Spain, Sendero can count on the Committee for the Support of the Peruvian Revolution, the Union of the Marxist–Leninist Struggle, and various cultural fronts. Britain features a Peru Support Group in London, the Sol Peru Committee, etc. Sweden's activists are reported to include Carlos La Torre Cardenas, who is father-in-law to the Shining Path founder. There are Swiss chapters of supporters headquartered in Geneva, as well as Danish and German groups. French supporters included Duran Araujo, a nuclear engineer, allegedly a Shining Path leader slated to be foreign minister in the organization's government-in-exile. Other French helpers are to be found in music and theater groups that help disseminate Sendero views, and 'Jose Carlos Mariategui Study Clubs' promoting that intellectual father of the Communist Party of Peru.[42]

Another network supports Peru's communist revolution from Europe but is third-world in its orientation: the Revolutionary Internationalist Movement (RIM). An alliance of pro-Maoist parties concerned with reconstituting the international communist movement in the wake of the collapse of the Soviet Union, the RIM took its small place on the world stage at a press conference in London in 1984. Readily admitting to 'profound crisis in the ranks of Marxist–Leninists', the declaration in 20 languages declared that 'the advance of the People's War in Peru inspires and strengthens the Marxist–Leninist forces the world over...' RIM's publication *A World To Win* appears from presses in Nottingham, England, in Farsi, Spanish, English, and Turkish. The Turkish publication is of special interest, because Kurds loyal to the PKK, and other leftist Turkish militants, are strongly interested in, and supportive of, Peru's Shining Path.[43] Internet sites friendly to RIM occasionally post bulletins from its 'Information Bureau' or advertise subscriptions to *A World To Win.*[44]

Such internationalism is visible in the majority of terror groups' political strategies, to include even neofascists some would presume might avoid foreign contacts. Most well-organized revolutionaries eventually seek explicit endorsement by recognized political and cultural institutions, such as the United Nations, which can offer political support, access to international media, and economic support. Examples of insurgencies which achieved success within the UN at the same time as they conducted terrorism and other low-intensity conflict are the Algerian FLN, who turned from rebels to rulers in 1962, and Arafat's Palestinians, who used the UN to nail down repeated endorsements of the PLO as the 'sole legitimate representative of the Palestinian people', an important prelude to the PLO's recent acquisition of recognized governmental powers.

The United States is almost as popular a forum. While it often lacks what the UN can offer as a neutral forum, the United States nonetheless is one key to Security Council decisions. America has a wide-open media market. Many of its citizens donate money to causes they admire. The United States is home to thousands of universities and political action organizations which might be coaxed to take an interest in a foreign people's troubles. Congress is a hub of power to which foreign organizations invariably would connect themselves. Organizations with records as fearsome terrorists which nonetheless successfully cultivate some American Congressmen include the Irish Republican Army and its front Sinn Fein,[45] as well as the Iranian dissident group 'People's Holy Warriors', Mujahedeen Khalq. Possessing armor and other trappings of conventional war, this considerable insurgent organization is based in Iraq and enjoys its patronage because it attacks Iran. But guerrilla war against the Iranian armed forces is the smaller part of its strategy; public bombings and other terror acts are the Mujahedeen Khalq's specialty. Despite the innocent blood on its hands, the Khalq carefully worked the halls of Congress – where playing on anti-Iranian sentiment is not difficult – and elicited words and letters of approval for its work for 'freedom and human rights' by such powerful congressmen of 1993 and 1994 as Senator Howell Heflin of Alabama and Robert Torricelli of New Jersey who chaired the House Foreign Affairs Committee.[46]

The most surprising form of political action for a terrorist group is to fold directly into the established political process. Purist revolutionaries and certain other terrorists might damn this notion. But those with more limited political hopes, or those who regard themselves as defeated, do indeed consider a negotiated solution of sorts. While required to renounce violence in many cases, they may nonetheless enjoy the advantages of respected national forums of debate, access to local elections, or participation in a national coalition government. The IRA's political wing Sinn Fein and Lebanon's Hizballah have often won seats in the national parliaments, as well as lesser electoral bodies. Colombia's April 19 movement and El Salvador's left-wing guerrillas, once Cuban and Soviet defeat in the Cold War became evident, went much further, subsuming themselves wholly and pacifically in the democratic political process.

Terrorists are thus fully aware of major choices open to them. There is the ballot, which most long since rejected. There is the bullet. There is the dual strategy of bullets and ballots – 'fight and talk' Part of strategy is the art of adjusting long-term goals to realities and circumstances. When circumstances change, some groups do reassess, and redirect their efforts. That is the explanation for the amazing 1998 success of Gerry Adams and Sinn Fein over the other more violence-oriented partisans among the IRA.

Economic strategy

The second strategy much used by terrorists is economic. Political and social effects of dislocation are dramatically enhanced by such economic terrorism as taking over public highways to 'tax' drivers; arson campaigns against large corporations; sabotage of oil pipelines; bombings and extortion which increase insurance prices and operating costs; protracted efforts to disrupt the export of manufactured goods or agricultural crops; bank robberies; etc. Frequently under-reported are terrorism's campaigns against tourism and tourist facilities. They garner much of some nations' foreign incomes, and terrorism against them is intended both to directly harm the property owners and to harm the government. The state experiences losses in tax revenues, additional expenses for everything from fire trucks to police, and decline in foreign investment. In a typical warning, a Kurdish PKK European front, the National Liberation Front of Kurdistan, announced in June 1997 that all tourism regions in Turkey were now designated 'danger zones', to be targeted because tourism 'finances the Turkish State's war'.[47]

In Peru, Sendero Luminoso's Abimael Guzman once boasted of fighting 'the most economic war on earth'.[48] Government studies tally damage in the last decade and a half at well over $20 billion, a staggering figure in a country whose entire annual federal budget is only about $2 billion. Shining Path ideology favors a return to pre-capitalistic farming practices which feature near-total self-reliance and little to no trade with surrounding communities. This means that such Sendero attacks as dynamiting the national power grids not only waste infrastructure and underscore propaganda, but also represent a small direct step in the affected area towards Sendero's economic program: the autarky of its 'liberated zones'. The economic damage and destruction to the country helped provoke the *autogolpe* by which Alberto Fujimori greatly increased his own presidential powers. But there was a real short-term cost: Peru lost dearly in foreign confidence and foreign investment. Only later, after the repression seemed to work to the marked disadvantage of terrorism, did investment return to former levels.

Since communist ideology closely links totalitarian economics and politics and aims of social progress, communist activists have long understood how a noncommunist political order can be shaken – even shaken into ruins and dust – by repeated, prolonged attacks upon the economy. The most notable example of a prolonged attempt to win with this strategy was in the 1980s in El Salvador. An alliance of five guerrilla parties, the FMLN, made economic war their premier strategy. The guerrillas' Radio Venceremos made this clear, as in 1985 when announcing yet another ban on use of the national roadways and rails: 'This national traffic paralyzation … is part of our sabotage of the dictatorship's war economy.' Over many years, the insurgents employed most imaginable tactics, from machine-gunning crop-dusting planes, to dynamiting bridges, to burning cash crops, to systematically destroying nearly all the country's locomotives, to cutting roads and thus isolating rich crop-exporting regions. In the words of one American reporter, the FMLN alliance rendered 'massive physical damage and reduced export earnings (and) turned El Salvador into an economic basket case dependent on the American dole'.[49] But continued US aid, intense effort by millions of noncommunist Salvadorans, and indigenous leaders like President Napoleon Duarte helped the country and its democracy triumph.

Bank thefts are another tactic in terrorism's economic strategy. Systematized ideologically by Carlos Marighella, bank robberies symbolically hurt international capitalism, while also garnering funds for underground operations. International narcotics exports by political groups undermine the health and productivity of capitalist countries where the drugs feed destructive personal habits. Such sales are also more lucrative than virtually any other known manner of feeding terrorists' coffers; one cannot understand the PLO of the 1980s or Colombia's FARC in the 1990s without understanding the economic benefits of narcoterrorism.[50]

In Colombia, where 'liberated zones' are now accepted even by the previously sovereign government, one may observe the full range of terrorism's economic efforts. There are regular bank heists – 'expropriations' in the parlance of the perpetrators, who deem capitalism illegitimate and think it their right or duty to 'steal from the thieves'. There are regular interruptions of highway traffic; commercial truck drivers lose cargoes, or vehicles, and private automobiles are emptied of passengers and all are robbed in actions called 'revolutionary taxation'. Oil pipelines are bombed scores of times in a single year; ELN has declared them all 'military targets'.[51] The overall national effect of the two main terrorist groups' economic strategy, apart from its furtherance of a general sense of insecurity and dislocation, is to reduce commercial intercourse, escalate law enforcement costs, and bring down tax receipts by governments. Industries such as mines and private interests as small as cattle ranches or agricultural centers are bilked on a recognized schedule by agents of guerrilla organizations; the victims face arson or murder if the fruit of their labor is not shared on demand. The peculiar local phrase for the extortion of cattle ranchers is 'vaccination' – a wry suggestion that regular payments are the rancher's inoculation against death.

So large are the Colombian guerrillas' economic operations that they have turned from bookkeepers to computer operators to track their illicit wealth. Diskettes recovered from an ELN safe house in February 1992 depict the amazing riches of this organization in precise terms. The balance sheets showed annual income of 14.5 billion pesos derived from kidnapping, and another 19 billion pesos in extorted receipts from coal- and gold-mining operations. Threats to construction and public works projects and other sorts of persuasion enforced a flat 15 per cent 'tax' by ELN on the overall value of these building contracts, yielding another seven billion pesos a year. The result is that an organization of only about 2,000 men and women has the economic power of the country's 45th largest corporation. And yet all this somehow fails to match the economic impact of still another guerrilla, terrorist, and organized crime group, which was once Colombia's premier communist organization: FARC. It is Colombia's 23rd largest commercial entity.[52] All these terrorist takings are a direct loss to the national economy. To them are added the costs of extra security, as well as millions in extorted payments to the well-organized revolutionaries. Colombia's national stresses include narcotics, political corruption, violent attacks on the judiciary, and the counter-insurgency war;[53] all these have connections to the terrorism problem; terrorism and its economic strategies and effects are thus as insidious as any other Colombian problem.[54]

Northwestern Europe lacks the Latin states' developed insurgencies; its economic damage from terrorism there comes in different kinds and from fewer hands. The major categories affecting the northwest European states at present are attacks that undermine tourism, direct physical damage to property from bombings, and the overall net domestic economic drain from underwriting insurance and providing security. Tourism can be lost to even one well-publicized terror attack. Recovery always take longer. After the TWA 847 hijacking by Shiites who boarded the plane in Athens, disturbing publicity spread world-wide. The US State Department placed a travel advisory on Greece due in part to its reputation for laxity. Pan American World Airways temporarily ceased flying into Athens. Greece and other Mediterranean countries were also affected by the *Achille Lauro* hijacking, and there were other terror attacks in Europe. A million Americans canceled vacation plans or chose to holiday within the United States, where terrorism had nearly disappeared. The Greek government undertook a prestige offensive.[55] So sensitive have the Greeks remained that when TWA 800 went down off the New York coast in August 1996, the first trace of commentary noting the flight's origination in Athens was swiftly met by an indignant guest editorial in the powerful *New York Times*.

Many terror groups in western Europe have demonstrated their understanding of the economic impact they may have in a targeted country by combining fear, international publicity, and property damage at tourist installations. In Corsica, which shares with the Greek islands the appeals of sun, sea, sand, and separation from urban congestion, terror groups have targeted hotels, beach houses, and offices for airlines and tourism. Attacks on these facilities leave damage and serve notice of a political aspiration. When the owners are Italian, Spanish, or French, the same attacks carry an anti-imperialist message about not 'exploiting' local people and sending money off the island. The Mediterranean coastline most closed by violence in the 1990s has been that of Dalmatia, Croatia, on the Adriatic. Conventional and unconventional warfare over recent years ruined the tourism trade there;[56] it had long served as one of the few sources of Yugoslavia's foreign income. Only by the autumn of 1997 were there slight signs of recovery – and this modest revival is always at risk from further fighting.

Direct property damage done by terror attacks can also be economically disastrous. The IRA has battered Britain with TNT, Czech-made 'Semtex' *plastique*, rocket bombs, and ready-to-hand fertilizer mixes. There is a remarkably favorable ratio of expenses required to create a large bomb *vis-à-vis* the economic damage it renders. Vehicle bomb damage to London's Docklands on 9 February

1996 was about 75 million pounds sterling, and the explosion in Manchester on 15 June of that year cost Britain as much as 300 million pounds sterling.[57] The New York-based *Irish People*, reported these bombings by emphasizing their economic costs.[58] The IRA's terrorism is indeed calculated to translate into an economic drain on England. In the careful words of an official briefing often given at the British Army Staff College, the IRA 'terrorists have maintained a steady level of violence using a variety of methods (in part to) persuade public opinion in the rest of the UK that Northern Ireland was costing too much in financial and human terms and that we should withdraw'.[59]

The less dramatic but pressing costs include insurance – often underwritten by the government – to protect industries and businesses in Britain and Northern Ireland; pay and training bills for thousands of security forces; and the human costs of death in and outside Northern Ireland. MI5 devoted 44 per cent of its annual budget to 'Irish and other domestic' subversion in 1993.[60] Each year 3.5 billion pounds sterling is expended to protect the citizens of Ulster, preserve the economy, and keep alive administration, public construction, and social and welfare programs. Northern Ireland receives a third more economic aid per person than many sectors of Britain;[61] London pays these bills because it must, and because of its economic counter-insurgency strategy, matching terrorist damage with public investment and aid.

France, not forgetting the crisis caused by the 1986 bombing campaign in Paris by Middle Eastern terrorists, responded thoroughly a decade later when a new series of bombs began. The violence is perpretated by Algerians indignant at France's 1.2 billion-dollar aid program to the FLN-controlled government, which religious militants see as secular and repressive. But police work is expensive and it looks oppressive. By autumn 1995, tourism was declining, merchants were complaining, the number of police on security duties had risen to 20,000, and the secretary-general of the Paris police union believed the crisis was distorting the nature of police work and could presage the imposition of emergency powers. Army personnel were already helping with security.[62] Poland is among the other European countries making oversized security outlays in the hope of preventing the sort of problems experienced by Paris and London. The Poles devoted one trillion zloties (about $74 million) to bomb squads and counter-terrorism police during 1991. Only 23 bombs were detonated or found that year, yet those and other alerts required attention by many of the 132,000 employees of various government services[63] at a time when Poland had pressing burdens in making its transition to democracy.

Countries bidding for such international extravaganzas as the World

Trade Fair or the Olympic Games must consider the massive and rising costs of paying for counter-terrorism. The 1984 Los Angeles Games cost $100 million for security – an astonishing figure at the time. One will never be sure how many plots – by such groups as white racists of 'The Order' and the nationalists of the Armenian Secret Army for the Liberation of Armenia (ASALA) – were evaded,[64] but the games proceeded flawlessly. In 1988, South Korea met the expensive and dangerous challenge of sponsoring the Games in a country often showing political stress fractures and threatened continuously and overtly by a hostile and jealous northern neighbor. There were no terrorist acts. The 1992 Olympics took place in Spain surrounded by worries that included explicit ETA threats. Madrid and Barcelona oversaw security efforts that cost some $350 million. Hoping to match the peacefulness of all these host cities, Atlanta marshaled up 16,000 police who worked 12-hour shifts six days a week, supplemented by a large FBI force and over 1,000 personnel from the Marines, Army, Air Force, and National Guard. New technologies for crowd observation and control were deployed. The final bill came to at least $300 million. And yet someone still marred the peace by a pipe bomb attack in Olympic Park.

Few question such security measures; long-planned public gatherings are too obvious an attraction for terrorists. But no economist can doubt that the huge sums measured out in dollars and man-hours could not be more productively spent on other human services, on tax relief or on debt-reduction – a point which is not lost on terrorists.

One final view of terrorism as an economic strategy may be considered. Self-consciously 'humane' terrorists may see property damage – which frightens but does not kill – as a 'moral' alternative to actions which render human damage. A range of militants have touted their own attacks in this way, including 1970s groups such as the right-wing Warriors of Christ the King in Franco's Spain, and the left-wing Revolutionary Brigades of Portugal, the Corsican National Liberation Front, and the Breton Liberation Front in France.[66] Some religious terrorists in the United States today may aim strictly at property damage when they attack abortion clinics but do so only at night, with fire or foul-smelling chemicals.[67] America's odd new brand of dissenters, the 'sovereignty' advocates, may also threaten ownership and property. Montana's 'Freemen' and members of the self-declared 'Republic of Texas' did not just refuse to pay legitimate taxes; they were printing bogus bank checks or 'warrants' and engaging in massive commercial fraud.[68] Printing false currency has been a favored activity of American right-wing terrorists; counterfeiting yields cash for them as surely as it packs a political punch against the federal government.

Terrorism's economic costs:
The Barcelona Olympics of 1992

Like Korea, sponsor of the 1988 Olympic Games, and the United States, sponsor of those of 1996, Spain spent prodigiously to protect its sports spectacular.

Security work began far in advance of summer 1992, with contingency plans drawn up and detailed development of the human and technical systems for protecting athletes and for crowd observation and control. The many foreign specialists involved included Israelis and Americans; the FBI's lead man arrived fully three years before the games commenced. Spanish–French cooperation was particularly significant, given their shared Basque ETA problem; liaison became especially intensive once the distractions of protecting the Albertville Winter Games passed away in early 1992.

For the Barcelona games, Spain drew heavily upon police forces from all over the country, and upon the Guardia Civil.

The price of all the security was the highest in the history of the Olympics, including the elaborate efforts in Atlanta four years later. As much as $350 million was spent to protect the games in Barcelona.

Spain's games went unmarred by terrorism.[65]

Military strategy

The third strategy employed by many contemporary terrorists is the military option. Despite speaking of themselves as 'guerrillas' and calling their several hundreds of militants 'armies', many terrorist strategists deliberately avoid confrontation with the state army. For most others, doing military damage has only tertiary interest. Terrorists prefer to attack nonmilitary targets – for the shock and psychological reasons, and because those targets are undefended and 'safe' to hit. ASALA, the Armenian Secret Army for the Liberation of Armenia, conducted dozens of attacks during the late 1970s and the 1980s, but virtually none was against the Turkish military personnel whom ASALA reviled as 'fascist' in press releases. On one occasion, when striking an airport with two functioning areas, one serving civilian aircraft and the other military, ASALA attacked the civilian facility only.

Yet many groups practising terrorism also make guerrilla attacks on military forces or installations. And all political terrorism does have at least limited military effects, in the following respects. By its nature and intention, a terror campaign affects the entire country, and thus its security forces. Any important attack by a revolutionary group is a direct challenge to the state; to the degree it succeeds, it weakens the prestige of the government's arms. Citizens demand to know why they are not being protected, and such sentiment undermines the government further. Pressures mount for augmentation of police forces, for militarization of police forces, or for the creation of special military units to use overseas against the international terrorists or their sponsors. There may also be pressures for direct intervention in internal politics by the state's armed forces – 'transforming a political situation into a military one', as Carlos Marighella might have said.

In El Salvador, during the 1970s and 1980s, leftist guerrillas killed army and police personnel as freely as they attacked civilians. In only six months of 1981, 2,000 security force members died in encounters with them,[69] a traumatic experience for any nation, but especially for one so small, where such casualty figures touch every province and town. In Spain, uniformed personnel suffer high casualties from Basque terrorists. ETA attacks the army, especially with bombs aimed at vehicles carrying troops. But ETA's specialty is killing members of that democratic country's national police force, the Guardia Civil.[70] United States military installations at home have not been successfully attacked by terrorism since the decline of the domestic left wing a generation ago. Several plots by local militias obsessed with a 'New World Order' dominated by the UN were foiled in Michigan and Texas.[71] It is abroad that US personnel and bases are commonly attacked by terrorists. Peacetime bombings at NATO bases, service clubs, and barracks have killed or wounded hundreds of American service personnel in the last decade and a half. While there were arguments over whether the Marines on peacekeeping duty in Beirut in 1983 were a legitimate military target, the statistic was cold and clear: 240 dead. In June 1996 another vehicle bombing – of the Khobar Towers residence at an air force base in Saudi Arabia – killed 19 and wounded some 500. All these represent important damage to military forces in peacetime; all were successful 'indirect attacks' by weaker and smaller armed parties.

Armed conflicts between groups using terrorism and guerrilla attacks on a nation's police and military forces serve the useful purpose of dispersing and tying down the state's armed personnel. Traditional guerrilla strategy is to 'appear everywhere and be nowhere', so that the smaller armed force can attack at moments of numerical advantage. In both the guerrilla war and terrorist environments, the effect of this strategy on the state is to require it to deploy forces widely and visibly to reassure the populace, and to keep them in a high state of readiness. The overall effect may be studied in such cases as Germany in the late 1970s and Northern Ireland today. Not only do the deployments tire the state, the overall effect is to make a liberal democracy appear to be its precise opposite: an armed camp. Terror group propagandists then use that public sense to effect, as when German radicals occasionally exulted in the 'police state' effect because it successfully 'exposed the latent fascism' of the Federal Republic.[72] In such ways does this third form of strategy support the first: terrorism's political effort against government.

Defense budgets can be drained by requirements for continuous surveillance, patrolling, and training for counter-terrorism action. Government spends less on more desirable social programs, costing it political appeal. Foreign borders may be less well protected. Ultimately, a national armed force intended to resist foreign neighbors may be entirely distorted in its purpose and preparation, twisting inward upon the nation as an agent of repression. Every battalion which Pakistan deploys against its own dissidents[73] or Indian-sponsored terrorists today is distracted from service on the Indian border, or from training for full-scale war. India has similar problems. Sikh militias and terrorists in northwestern India may or may not wish to serve the interests of Pakistan, but they do so by distracting and tying down innumerable Indian national police and military personnel, who are bled with classic 'bite and flee'[74] guerrilla tactics. This combination has made a continuous battleground of parts of a giant world state: India. In

Colombia, internal security has so deteriorated because of FARC and ELN insurgents that British Petroleum Exploration contracts with the Colombian Ministry of Defense to underwrite an army battalion of 650 men to assure its oil operations minimal protection.[75] FARC and ELN make enough guerrilla attacks on the Colombian armed forces to require a continuous national effort on the part of the army to keep order.

An altogether different effect of military damage by terrorists is to weaken a state in order to prepare it for assault by an outside power. This might occur by chance, or it can be part of a foreign design, a 'softening attack'. The prospect that indigenous Euroterrorists might act in conjunction with the Warsaw Pact must have been pondered by NATO defense planners in the mid 1980s. After all, fuel pipelines were attacked in Belgium and Germany; military bases and trains were bombed; and there were incidents of known and suspected Warsaw Pact reconnaissance of critical bridges, theater nuclear missiles, etc. In 1986 German and Italian communist terrorists opened new and lethal campaigns against the American-sponsored Strategic Defense Initiative. European laboratories, researchers, and officials associated with SDI were bombed, shot, or burned out. Any doubts about the terrorists' strategic purposes were voided by the leaflets they published to mark the murders. Any doubts about Soviet approbation of these events should be weighed alongside the ongoing Soviet propaganda offensive against SDI at that time.[76]

As with their political and economic methods, the military strategies of terrorists do not merely destroy; they have positive advantages. Battles provide experience, or 'blooding', draw recruits, capture weaponry, and may lead to foreign support. Operations develop logistical infrastructure and means of finance. Depending upon dogma and doctrine, today's terrorist leaders may anticipate that terrorism can be combined with clandestine organization and guerrilla combat experience to develop from a marginal underground into a truly national military capability. That is in fact the Maoist model of the development of protracted guerrilla war – from low-level violence and propaganda, to a second phase of mixed or 'mobile' warfare featuring formal military units, and ultimately to a third rather conventional phase of operations by regular armies. This was, in sketch form, the history of the Vietnamese communists. Today it serves contemporary groups including Shining Path and the Tamil Tigers. Both have advanced through formative stages of violence, from terrorism and tactically impressive guerrilla attacks to a next phase of conducting occasional conventional military operations.[77] Since 1992 Shining Path has fallen back considerably, into the Maoist 'first phase' of warfare. But for their part the Tamil Tigers remain in this middle stage, very strong, if also short of full military capability to destroy the armed forces of Sri Lanka.

Conclusion

The making of strategy includes questions of limits on both ends and means. If terrorism groups were examined from the perspective of a conventional military thinker, their notable weakness might dictate a cautious strategy, with marked limits on both ends and means. But terrorists may or may not consider strategy that prudently. Others begin with expansive ends and deliberately repudiate virtually all limits on means; harm to the unarmed and innocent is the least of their concerns.

Typically, terror groups envision themselves as locked in an unlimited effort towards an extraordinary end, such as total anarchy, or the revolutionary seizure of full political power, or the creation of a holy and perfect religious kingdom on earth. A minority are more modest or more practical: they declare a struggle towards greater autonomy within a state, perhaps, or better protection of their own lives and political positions. The usual extremism of the ends bears directly upon choice of means. 'By any means necessary' is a phrase made famous by Malcolm X, leader of the black American 'Nation of Islam'. Actually, there were many means that man disdained to use. And, before he was murdered, he journeyed to Mecca and came back speaking as a minister, denouncing violence, and thus rejecting his own claim to any and all means. But for terrorists, strategy embraces 'any means necessary' as surely as it rejects virtually all limits. Terrorism's normal tactics include earning operating funds from cocaine sales, extortion, mass murder, tearing apart families to deter candidates from competing for office, and fashioning bombs of nails and compressed gas for use on crowds at metro stations. These are means of terrorism, chosen by strategists of terror groups. They view related strategic questions – such as whether to halt attacks, or mix in legitimate politics, or ally with organizations in nonviolent struggles – as prudential issues. They do them all if they calculate that they will be useful, just as they carry on the 'deliberate, systematic murder, maiming, and menacing of the innocent to inspire fear and gain a political end'.[78]

For group members, the decision to adopt terror stamps the group, often indelibly, with a definite spirit and character. It shapes the group's image, in country and abroad. It thus affects what foreign help it will receive, and how it will be treated in the international press. The decision is a catalyst that escalates and advances the fight. It dramatically furthers social polarization, and it has an effect on recruitment. In theory, there can later be a strategic retreat from the position of terrorism. By increments, some groups do lessen the proportions and types of force they employ, often in the service of a calibrated 'fight and talk' strategy. Terrorism can even be laid aside altogether, as several groups have done in Central and Latin America. But more commonly, groups embarked upon conflicts of unlimited ends and means do not come to terms easily. Three and a half decades after their dramatic terrorist campaigns opened on the Malay Peninsula, the communist party of Malay was still fighting, still losing, and still mustering some 2,500 militants.[79] Their leader Chin Peng guided them from 1948 until his surrender in 1989, directing strategy from the jungles, from Thai border refuges, and apparently from China. It took nearly half a century to break the man's will.

The terrorist's dream is not always so drawn-out, or so empty. Twentieth-century revolutionaries using terror, as well as sophisticated other means – political, economic, or military – have risen to grasp and hold power: Bolsheviks, Chinese Maoists, the nationalist Algerian FLN, 'focoists' lead by Castro and Che, and the Sandinistas. Daniel Ortega only lost Nicaragua for his party when the Soviet bloc collapsed and he felt driven to face elections. But Fidel Castro welcomed in the year 1999, and another anniversary in power, with a scorching anti-capitalist speech from the same city hall balcony in Santiago de Cuba where he first declared victory exactly 40 years before. For the baldest possible exhortations to the utility of terrorism, few can rival Abu Daoud, a surviving gunman from the 1972 Munich Olympics massacre of Israeli athletes. Recently celebrating the 25th anniversary of that affair, he told the press: 'Munich put the Palestinian cause inside every house.'[80] This is true. Ultimately Yasser Arafat would denounce such terrorism, but only when it had ceased to serve him well, and today there is a 'statelet' for the Palestinians under his authority, expanding by increment into a grudgingly acquiescent Israel.

Such illustrations of strategic successes by terrorism are outnumbered by the flagrant failures.[81] But they are beacons, enough to hold the eyes of the aspiring gunman, the intense ideologist, and the small, unknown group active underground. Consider a second perspective: Revolutionaries using terror have a high capacity for achieving their broadest and most typical initial strategic objective, the wrecking of normality and political order. Terrorists of recent memory have successfully smashed governments in Uruguay in 1973 and Turkey in 1978 and again in 1980. These partial strategic successes which lead to military interventions are important for terrorism, whether or not the militants proved strong enough to take power. A third perspective is the tactical, valuable because many militants are more interested in actions and short-term gains than strategic issues. There will always be knots of malcontents like the 'Symbionese Liberation Army' of California who can rob banks, and kidnap a society woman like Patty Hearst; they do not always see beyond, to the day when their only 'base' – a single house – is incinerated in a battle with police;[82] or if they do, they may not be entirely averse to such 'martyrdom'. Terrorism's list of tactically successful actions has been bottomless. In open democratic societies, it remains regrettably easy, especially in the years before the group carries a strong police profile, to win tactical victories. The average attack readily produces two kinds of important results: death or wounding of a victim, and headlines. Both magnify the reputation of the claimants. These limited gains alone, as much as ideological faith and practical long-term plans, can continue to spur terrorists to action.

Notes

1. *Court Depositions of Three Red Brigadists*, ed. Sue Ellen Moran (Santa Monica, CA: RAND, February 1986).
2. A good review of the strategic plans of the Shining Path founder is in Simon Strong, *Shining Path: The World's Deadliest Revolutionary Force* (London: HarperCollins, 1992), pp. 101–7. Like lesser researchers, Strong must rely heavily on Guzman's rare interviews with the Sendero newspaper *El Diario*. But understanding Guzman as a loyal Maoist is of great use in understanding his strategy.
3. Yemeni tribes have been taking foreigners hostage for many years as a means of bargaining with their own government for civic improvements, etc. There were a hundred such kidnappings during the 1990s, notes the *Washington Post* (30 December 1998). A world away is another example, the American Ku Klux Klan, whose members joined in part out of hopes to preserve their racial and religious privileges; Kathleen M. Blee, *Women of the Klan: Racism and Gender in the 1920s* (Berkeley, CA: University of California Press, 1991), p. 1.
4. For example, American Gary 'Rex' Lauck, calls his group the NSDAP Overseas Organization, and its foreign appeals have included calls to Skinheads to join in with 'members of the great world-historical Aryan racial movement'. Quoted by the Anti-Defamation League in its report on the United States in 'The Skinhead International: A Worldwide Survey of Neo-Nazi Skinheads', from the Internet, 21 March 1996. But what is worthy of note is the weakness of far-right internationalism. One of many indicators is that in some 300 pages of excellent material on 'Terror From the Extreme Right' in the spring 1995 issue of *Terrorism and Political Violence*, there is little or no material on neofascist internationalism.
5. This is my conclusion. For another perspective, see Michael Minkenberg, '*The New Right in France and Germany:* Nouvelle Droite, Neue Rechte, *and the New Right Radical Parties*, in *The Revival of Right-Wing Extremism in the Nineties*, ed. Peter Merkl and Leonard Weinberg (London: Frank Cass, 1997), pp. 79–85.

6. Don Black's web site 'Stormfront' was begun in March 1995 and remains active in January 1999 at: http://stormfront.org and Black's personal information is attached thereto at: http://www.stormfront.org/dblack/

   Most information for this inset was gathered from the Internet in 1996 by colleague Carl Shelton. Especially useful were (1) the 'Stormfront White Nationalist Resource Page', with a lengthy list of foreign neofascist sites; it recorded a third of a million 'hits' by net-users in the 20 months before December, 1996. (2) 'Skinheads USA Link Page.' (3) 'Cyberhate', a collection of news stories from mainstream publications about white supremacists on the net. (4) 'The Skinhead International: A Worldwide Survey of Neo-Nazi Skinheads,' with its report on US groups by Ken McVay, drawing on work by the Anti-Defamation League. On Lauck, see the Anti-Defamation League, *Danger: Extremism: The Major Vehicles and Voices on America's Far-Right Fringe*, ed. Alan M. Schwartz, (New York: Anti-Defamation League, 1996), pp. 68–70.

7. Kevin Sullivan of the *Washington Post* reported the seemingly impossible story of Aum's recovery in the *International Herald Tribune* on 30 September 1997. Subsequent stories appeared in the New York Times News Service (e.g. *Daily Bulletin* (Pomona, CA: 11 October 1998) and *L'Express* (Paris), 29 October 1998. That French journal reports 5,500 faithful, 500 living in the communes, and some 30 installations owned by the group.

8. *USA Today* printed a report on the story on 12 August 1998: http://11167.8.29.16/news/world/bomb043.htm and later the *New York Times* followed with a lengthy report on 9 January 1999 at: http://www.nytimes.com/library/world/africa/010999africa-bomb.html. The latter reported that interviews with officials show that Bushnell's 'concerns were more intense, more well-founded, more specific, and more forcefully expressed than has previously been known'.

9. Rahimullah Yusufzai, 'Conversation with Terror', *Time* (11 January 1999), from the Internet.

10. My estimate depends upon the still unproven link to the Khobar Towers' bomb of 1996, which killed 19 American servicemen and wounded 500. During 1996, although after that bombing, Osama Bin Laden twice threatened to attack US personnel in Saudi Arabia; US Department of State, *Patterns of Global Terrorism: 1996* (Washington, DC: GPO, April 1997), p. 3. The death tally for the two 7 August 1998 bombs in east Africa was 224, 12 of them Americans.

   Recent investigative journalism reporting on Bin Laden is voluminous. A good beginning is always the reliable *Foreign Report* by Jane's publications, e.g. 13 and 27 August, and 24 December 1998. On 23 December 1998 Bin Laden renewed his call for deaths of Americans and Jews, and refused to decline weapons of mass destruction if they should become available; ABC Evening News, 24 December, and the following day's *Washington Post*.

11. Force was used against Iraq in 1993, including use of missiles in June against an intelligence center in Baghdad, retaliation for the Iraqi attempt to murder President George Bush. In September 1996 military force was used because of Iraqi moves against Kurds in country.

12. See any 1990s issue of the US Department of State annual *Patterns of Global Terrorism*.

13. US Department of State, *Patterns of Global Terrorism: 1991* (Washington, DC: GPO, 1992), p. 1.

14. William Safire, *New York Times* (27 May 1991).

15. Paraphrase by a Greek official, in the *New York Times* (30 January 1991).
16. In New Jersey, Jamal Mohammed Warrayat believed he was negotiating with an Iraqi diplomat in a plot to kill President Bush; he was in fact dealing with the FBI and was arrested. A US official reported that there were more than five potential schemes, all involving 'lone zealots', which were uncovered or prevented in the period after Iraq invaded Kuwait. Reports on these matters appeared in such newspapers as the *Providence Sunday Journal* (RI) (20 January 1991).
    For further remarks on how coalition forces contained the Iraqi attempt to use terrorism as an adjunct to war, see Chapter 6 below.
17. These notes on Iraqi teams, plastic explosive sent via diplomatic pouch, and the successful international counter-terrorism effort are from *USA Today* (23 September 1998). But as my research in this Chapter 2 paragraph shows, the *USA Today* statement that 'Not a single American was injured' pertains only to activities by Iraqi nationals; allies of Iraq did launch successful terror attacks.
18. This combination of shock and propaganda is what terrorist theoretician Carlos Marighella calls 'the war of nerves'; *Minimanual of the Urban Guerrilla* (1969; repr. in Adelphi Papers no. 79, London: International Institute for Strategic Studies, August 1971), p. 36.
19. When the Tupamaros assaulted Uruguay in the late 1960s, they transformed a country with a small police force and an army the size of the capital's fire department. Soon the army was large and preparing for a coup, and one in 20 economically active persons worked for security services. Unpublished lecture by Ellen Jacoby (Seattle University faculty, and subsequently headmistress of British schools, Montevideo), at Seattle University (January 1983), p. 10.
20. Marighella, *Minimanual of the Urban Guerrilla*, p. 40. An older formulation of the idea was in anarchist Peter Kropotkin's 1880 essay 'The Spirit of the Revolt': 'The government resists; it is savage in its repressions. But, though formerly persecution killed the energy of the oppressed, now, in periods of excitement, it produces the opposite result. It provokes new acts of revolt, individual and collective; it drives the rebels to heroism; and in rapid succession these acts spread, become general, develop.' Excerpted in *The Terrorism Reader: A Historical Anthology*, revised edn, Walter Laqueur and Yonah Alexander (eds) (New York: Meridian, 1987), p. 95.
21. In addition to the examples in this paragraph, another appeared recently in Israel's 'Security Zone' in southern Lebanon. The township of Hasbaya was Druze and pro-Israel. But Hamas deployed one of the roadside bombs that are now such common weapons there, killing several Israeli soldiers. The Lebanese and Israeli authorities' response to this provocation transformed the social and political spirit in the area. For example, Moslem clerics were taken into custody for not condemning the attack. Now, 'Israel has lost Hasbaya ...' according to *Foreign Report* (3 December 1998).
22. 'Hamas 1993 Plan to Torpedo Gaza–Jerico Accord', *Al-Aqsa* (Jerico) (1 January 1995), in JPRS, *Terrorism* (19 January 1995), pp. 20–1. See the excerpts in the inset in this chapter.
23. Ibid.
24. Part of his the essay 'Where to Begin', in the May 1901 issue of *Iskra*, these words reappeared in Lenin's book *What Is To Be Done* (1902; Peking, Foreign Languages Press, 1975), p. 202.
25. Paraphrase of an expression of T. E. Lawrence.
26. Interview with an activist (13 April 1991), by Helene Loow, 'Racist Violence and Criminal Behavior in Sweden: Myths and Reality', *Terrorism and Political*

Violence, 7:1 (spring 1995), p. 127.
27. The lectures and writings of Dr Martin van Creveld, especially, argue that war and politics have been transformed in recent years, making low-intensity conflict the most useful strategy and rendering traditional conventional war capabilities useless in the face of 'barefoot armies' moved by nationalism or some other source of will.
28. The printed appeal was characteristic of leaflets: its availability was a limited show of political presence, and its text made specific arguments, such as calling on local residents 'to respect orders issued by the Hawks', and warning Palestinians that 'some renegade gangs were using the name of the Hawks to commit robberies'. Paraphrase by the *Washington Post* (29 March 1994).

Leaflet distribution is apparently the main function of Hizballah activists operating in the United States, according to former CIA counter-terrorism director Vincent Cannistraro, quoted by Paul Wilkinson, 'Hezbollah: A Critical Appraisal', *Jane's Intelligence Review* (August 1993), p. 370.
29. *Washington Post* (1 March 1994).
30. *Foreign Report* (3 December, 1998).
31. *Foreign Report* (17 September 1992; 1 August 1996).
32. This passage is a transcript of most of paragraph 96 of the Unabomber manifesto 'Industrial Society and its Future', *Washington Post* (19 September 1995).
33. 'The Patriot Movement: Fewer, but Harder, Patriot Groups in 1997', Intelligence Report, Spring, 1998, downloaded 19 January 1999 from http://www.splcenter. org/intelligenceproject/ip-4fl.html

For other Internet sites, including some mentioned in the text paragraph above, see Bibliography. For a very simple guide to 'The Internet: A Terrorist Medium for the 21st Century', see Kelly R. Damphousse and Brent L. Smith in *The Future of Terrorism: Violence in the New Millennium*, ed. Harvey W. Kushner (Thousand Oaks, California: Sage Publications, 1998), pp. 208–24.
34. Truong Nhu Tang, with David Chanoff and Doan Van Toai, *A Vietcong Memoir* (New York: Vintage Books, 1986), p. 92, etc. His clandestine role as an NLF leader came to nothing when, in 1975, the North overran not just the South Vietnamese Army but many of the communists there working for Hanoi. His complicated work for the NLF included a further layer of deception, a 'Movement for Self-Defense' which he helped form from noncommunists – people in Saigon 'who had prestige and broad associations themselves among the city's groups and factions'. In short, North Vietnam set up the NLF as an attractive front in the South, and the NLF followed with its own fronts, further 'de-communizing' its image.
35. Cited by Adrian Guelke and Jim Smyth, 'The Ballot Bomb: Terrorism and the Electoral Process in Northern Ireland', in *Political Parties and Terrorist Groups*, ed. Leonard Weinberg (London: Frank Cass, 1992), pp. 112–13.
36. Danny Morrison said in a speech of November 1981: 'Who here really believes that we can win the war through the ballot box? But will anyone here object if, with a ballot paper in this hand, and an Armalite in this hand, we take power in Ireland?'; *Sunday Tribune* (Dublin: 8 November 1981), quoted ibid., p. 112.
37. The last point, about the implied threat of IRA retaliations should measures be taken to shut up Sinn Fein, is owed to Guelke and Smyth, ibid., p. 122. This book may be the first to so directly analyze the relations of various organized political parties and fronts with terror groups.
38. HB and ETA both closely watch Irish affairs. When the gunmen and political men in that country made a unilateral ceasefire and then the 'Good Friday' accord of

spring 1998, their Spanish counterparts took note and, in October, made a similar political gambit. They declared a ceasefire and at the time of writing the Basque militants are wrangling for political advantage and (temporarily) withholding most terrorism. See Richard Boudreaux's excellent article in the *Los Angeles Times* (23 October, 1998).

39. HB had similarly refused to share in the general Basque criticism of three ETA bombings in Madrid on 17 November 1991, instead blaming the government for the cycle of violence in terrorism's classic maneuver of transference of moral blame (see Chapter 5). This information on ETA and HB is from Spanish-language materials translated by JPRS, including the interview with Esnaolo by a Madrid news agency on 19 August 1991 as repr. 19 September 1991; see also JPRS, *Terrorism* for 6 December 1991, 30 January 1992, and 7 August 1992.

40. RNE-1 Radio Network (Madrid), 30 July 1992, in JPRS, *Terrorism* (7 August 1992), p. 29.

41. HB was faring no better in July 1997. After ETA kidnapped and killed a local Basque politician, Spain erupted in protests, including protests by Basques. An HB party office was attacked by a mob, and there was other evidence of public repudiation of ETA's terrorism.

42. 'Shining Path Supporters in Europe Named', *El Comercio* (Lima), 16 September 1992, in JPRS, *Terrorism* (8 October 1992), pp. 6–8. Mariategui is a hero to Guzman.

43. Simon Strong, pp. 244–52. Strong also documents a network of support groups called Peru People's Movement, with chapters in Italy, Spain, Germany, France, Greece, and Switzerland.

   The Internet carries pages for many SL support groups, including the 'El Diario Internacional' site designed by Detroit supporters.

44. A 1998 May Day call to international revolution (in Peru and elsewhere) was carried by the *Revolutionary Worker* (US) on 3 May. A Maoist site carries a 26 June 1995 editorial by Luis Arce Borja himself against frauds and other 'Bastard Children of the RIM' who criticize or exploit the revolution in Peru. The 'Revolutionary Worker Online' publishes both for charge, and information for free on the Internet, from its address in Chicago, Illinois. And there is a loud new voice on the Internet calling out to the English-speaking 'anti-imperialists' in the western hemisphere: the 'Maoist Internationalist Movement', which prints 'MIM Notes' on its web site periodically; their language is scorching. All documents were downloaded 4 January 1999.

45. IRA supporters like Sinn Fein and its North American counterpart NORAID (Irish Northern Aid Committee) have enjoyed success cultivating American politicians. America's ethnic Irish population, a powerful historical relationship, and the warmth for Ireland of American statesmen as different as Ronald Reagan and 'Tip' O'Neill over decades have helped build American affection for the Irish. But illegal financial and arms assistance from the eastern shores of the United States to anti-British militants in Ireland dates at least from the 1920s and has been an established pattern since. In 1995 and 1996, President Clinton overturned all past policy and twice granted visas and diplomatic courtesies to Sinn Fein chief Gerry Adams. A new wave of private money – this time overt – has now passed eastward. NORAID fund-raisers and political events in the northeastern United States successfully draw Congressmen such as Peter King, Charles Rangel, Joe Moakley, and Joseph Kennedy. They all have legitimate interests in Irish affairs and Irish–American affairs. However, NORAID is registered with the Justice Department as a foreign agent (of Sinn Fein). And whatever the Congressmens'

intentions, media organs of pro-'republican' Irish activism report their presence at NORAID and related events as an argument against British authority in Northern Ireland, an argument against extradition to Britain of US-held Irish terrorists or terrorist suspects, etc. See for example the *Irish People* (13 July and 10 August 1996).

46. Ohio Rep. James Traficant also reportedly supported the Mujahedeen Khalq. Many in both houses of Congress have wittingly or otherwise signed letters supportive of the organization because it opposes the Iranian regime. All this occurs despite the State Department's steady warnings that the Khalq is a terrorist organization responsible for thousands of deaths, according to Peter Waldman, *Wall Street Journal* (5 October 1994).

47. MED TV in Turkish (London: 12 June 1997), in FBIS, *Terrorism* (14 June 1997).

48. Abimael Guzman, interviewed by *El Diario* (date unknown); quoted by Strong, *Shining Path*, p. 126.

49. The best single article on the guerrillas' economic strategy is that of William Montalbano (whose reports of the time did not favor US policy or US persistence in aiding the Salvadorans in their war effort); see 'Strategy of Destruction by Rebels in El Salvador Risky', *Los Angeles Times* (29 May 1983). The Radio Venceremos broadcast quoted above was on 19 February 1985, cited in FBIS, *Central America* that day, p. 8. Another broadcast that August included announcement of a reopening of commercial traffic and boasted that, in the guerrilla ban now ending, 'The FMLN has dealt one of its hardest blows on the country's shaky war economy', Radio Venceremos, cited in the *Washington Times* (26 August 1985). Reports reprinted in FBIS, the *New York Times,* and other sources of that period sometimes referenced explicit statements about the tactics of economic war made by guerrilla leaders such as Joaquin Villalobos.

50. US governmental reports on terrorism and on narcotics are useful, but see especially Dr Rachel Ehrenfeld, *Narco-Terrorism: How Governments around the World Have Used the Drug Trade to Finance and Further Terrorist Activities* (New York: Basic Books, 1990).

51. *Washington Times* (19 March 1998). The Cano Limon oil pipeline, for example, has been attacked more than 500 times in a decade. This is a campaign against the country's leading economic export.

52. *Semana* (Bogota), in JPRS, *Terrorism* (13 August 1992), pp. 6–10.

53. This pessimistic view of Colombia's future is attributable in part to regional expert Richard Millett of Southern Illinois University. Interview of 4 September 1997, Quantico, VA.

54. June 1998 brought election to the presidency of an anti-corruption campaigner, Mr Pastrana; time will tell whether he can halt Colombia's dangerous slide. Current Colombian government estimates show guerrilla group revenues of $800 million annually, more than half of it from protecting narcotics trafficking. *Washington Post,* 13 July and 27 December, 1998.

55. Chris Ryan, *Tourism, Terrorism, and Violence*, Conflict Studies #244 (London: Research Institute for the Study of Conflict and Terrorism, September 1991), pp. 1–2. *Wall Street Journal* (26 June 1985); *USA Today* (12 February 1986); and *Washington Times* (7 April 1986).

56. 'La Croatie en mal de touristes', *L'Express* (Paris) (22 August 1996), p. 61.

57. *Washington Post* (11 February 1996); *Irish People* (29 June 1996). Another bomb hit downtown London in April, 1992, causing 400 million pounds worth of damages, according to the sources of Peter Taylor, *States of Terror: Democracy and Political Violence* (London: BBC, 1993), p. 114.

58. The *Irish People* is a newspaper which successfully walks the accepted American line of giving limited support for violence cast as 'just struggle for freedom'. It does so in such ways as advertising upcoming fund-raisers for Irish welfare causes closely tied to political groups like Sinn Fein, awarding elaborate coverage to allegations of torture and abuse by security forces, reporting on many IRA attacks without condemning the human damage they do, labeling terrorist attacks 'military' actions (or quoting partisans who do so) even when the acts were public bombings, etc. Coverage is also given to noncontroversial matters. The paper makes appeals to the American character of its readers, even printing the lengthy text of George Washington's 'Farewell Address' when its 200th anniversary occurred in 1996.

59. A British Army Staff College briefing, 'Northern Ireland: A Campaign Profile'. Unpublished; revised September 1992, pp. A–20.

60. MI5 has for the first time gone public, releasing a detailed self-profile and permitting a photograph of the new director; *Daily Telegraph*, 17 July 1993.

61. Britain's subsidy figure to each citizen of northern Ireland averages 2,370 pounds sterling a year, according to British government and private sources used by *The Economist* (6 November 1993).

62. *International Herald Tribune* (21 June 1995); Associated Press and *London Observer* articles in the *Washington Times* (28 August 1995); *Washington Post* (28 October 1995).

63. Polish Press Agency (Warsaw), 11 August 1992, in JPRS, *Terrorism* (13 August 1992), p. 2.

64. According to a principal figure in The Order, Mr Denver Parmenter, the group had vague plans to bomb the 1984 Olympic Games in Los Angeles and/or to poison its water supply. Interview by 'Turning Point', ABC Television, a 1995 segment rebroadcast on 10 July 1997. ASALA, with a strong presence in the Los Angeles area, opposed any participation in the games by Turkish athletes, and sent written threats to this effect; *Armenian Allegations: Myth and Reality: A Handbook of Facts and Documents* (Washington DC: Assembly of Turkish American Associations, 1986), p. 69.

65. The author is appreciative of a most helpful telephone interview in 1997 with Mr Dave Maples, who served on the US task force in Spain and later served in the Atlanta office of the FBI.

66. Information from Peter Janke, *Guerrilla and Terrorist Organizations: A World Directory and Bibliography* (New York: Macmillan, 1983).

A recent case of damaging property without loss of life, to affect government, was the mafia bombing of art galleries and similar public buildings in Italian cities such as Florence to protest against the crackdown on organized crime. Convictions for the 1995 bombings came in mid 1998.

67. Several anti-abortion militants have killed, of course; recently a sniper murdered Buffalo, New York, abortionist Dr Barnett Slepian. An Internet site, 'The Nuremberg Files', allegedly promotes violence against abortionists, reports the *Washington Post* (15 January 1999); it has since been banned.

68. The leader of the so-called 'Republic of Texas' was convicted 14 April 1998. Charges included passing off $3.4 million in fake financial documents.

The 'Freemen' leadership were similarly convicted, in July 1998. One of them, together with ranch partners, had once received $676,000 in governmental aid for farming; *New York Times* (30 April 1996).

69. An estimate by the Salvadoran rebels themselves which others deem reliable, according to the *Los Angeles Times* (1 January 1982). Using terrorism and guerrilla

war, they fought their way almost to strategic parity with the government in the early 1980s, drawing on aid from Cuba, the Warsaw Pact, and even captured American rifles sent from Vietnam. The FMLN fully expected a massive upset of the military and political status quo. Their 'Radio Venceremos' did a revealing series on Vietnam in May 1985, praising that country's protracted struggle against 'the same North American imperialist enemy' the Salvadoran Communists were facing, and promising that 'We, too, can defeat imperialism if we follow the Vietnamese road.' Cited in the *New York Times* (19 May 1985).

70. ETA also hits the usual terrorist targets: judges, prison officials, local politicians. See the Department of State, *Patterns of Global Terrorism: 1997* (Washington DC: GPO, 1998), p. 17.

71. The Michigan Militia plotted against the National Guard base at Camp Grayling in mid 1995, and two right-wingers planned an attack on Fort Howard Texas for Freedom Day festivities, 4 July 1997; Major Jon L. Ross, USMC, 'Arming For War: The Military Threat to the US Military', unpublished master's paper (Command and Staff College, Quantico, VA, 8 April 1998).

72. In Italy, like Germany, the presence of heavily armed national and local police transformed the appearance of the country during the 'years of lead'. I saw another illustration of the psychology this evokes while observing a public rally of leftists against NATO in Padua one day in 1982. On sale was a cheaply produced, thick photocopied dossier which ostensibly detailed all the foreign military installations on the peninsula. They included a map, so heavily inked that many NATO areas nearly merged on the page. Propaganda thus sought to foster the idea that Italy was both militarized and occupied.

73. Internal troubles include MQM, the Muttahida Qaumi Movement, an Urdu-speaking sect of Muslims deemed responsible for nearly 1,000 deaths in 1998 and also believed responsible for the huge bomb near Lahore which was meant to kill Prime Minister Nawaz Sharif; *Washington Times* (5 January 1999).

74. 'Bite and flee' was the slogan of the Italian Red Brigades as well as other terrorist groups. An earlier use of interest is in Mao Tse-Tung, *Guerrilla Warfare*: Guerrillas 'may be compared to innumerable gnats, which, by biting a giant both in front and in rear, ultimately exhaust him'. Fleet Marine Force Reference Publication 12-18, *Mao Tse-Tung on Guerrilla Warfare* (Washington DC: Headquarters, US Marine Corps, Department of the Navy, April 1989), p. 54.

75. *New York Times* (22 August 1996).

76. German laser research and other labs and industries were attacked, and then followed the murders of Karl-Heinz Beckurts, Director of Research at Siemens Company, an SDI contractor, and Gerold von Braunmuhl of the Foreign Ministry, a principal advisor on talks with the United States on strategic defense. Communiqués in both murder cases by the Red Army Faction identified the motive: 'great responsibility' for SDI-related 'secret negotiations' and research. Then in Italy, the Air Force general and Defense Ministry officer most closely associated with Italian support for 'Star Wars' development, Licio Giorgieri, was murdered by the Red Brigades, who left a 14-page leaflet entitled: 'No to Italian adhesion to star wars – Italy out of NATO'. It may also be relevant that at this time England underwent a wave of nine deaths of talented scientists, some of them doing defense work. See James A. Courter of the US House Armed Services Committee, 'Warfare in Peacetime', an address to the International Churchill Society, Dallas, Texas, 31 October 1987, *Proceedings of the International Churchill Society: 1987* (Hopkinton, NH: ICS, 1989), p. 56.

77. Mao Tse-Tung, *Selected Military Writings of Mao Tse-Tung*, 2nd edn (Peking:

Foreign Languages Press, 1963), pp. 181–2, 244–8, 279–80. Mao does not discuss terrorism, but the aforementioned pages well express his thesis that a small revolutionary group can develop into one that challenges, and eventually overcomes, a state army and political apparatus. Shining Path, the New People's Army, the Khmer Rouge, and other terrorist groups of today were founded by adherents of Mao.

78. Please see the definition at the opening of Chapter 1.

79. Janke, *Guerrilla and Terrorist Organizations*, p. 355.

80. Associated Press report in the *News-Leader* (5 September 1997). This deserved broad coverage but did not get it; as in many other cases, I am indebted to Dr Harold W. Rood for my copy.

81. Any encyclopedia of terrorist groups is full of examples of failures. Walter Laqueur of Georgetown University has long argued that terrorism fails; see his articles in *The New Republic* and the latest 'Post Modern Terrorism' in *Foreign Affairs*, 75:5 (September/October 1996), pp. 24–36.

82. Patty Hearst, daughter of a newspaper magnate, described the SLA, her own kidnapping, and the bloody end to six members of the group in a Los Angeles house in 1974 in her book *Every Secret Thing*, with Alvin Moscow (New York: Doubleday, 1982). The SLA leader, a convict named Donald De Freeze, was meticulous at planning small actions, but rather dimwitted about larger or longer-range plans.

3

Terror Group Operations

Introduction

Sun Tzu in the fourth century BC laid down epigrammatic sentences and brief chapters on *The Art of War* to capture the multiple dimensions of military and psychological war. These also seem to describe many features of guerrilla war and terrorism in the latter half of the twentieth century. For example, Sun Tzu argues that the purpose of operations is to create disorder, more than destruction. Speed and deception are the essence of war. Intelligence is key to everything. Sun Tzu also devoted a chapter to fire, which at the end of the 1990s reminds readers that arson is one of the most common terrorist weapons.

Today's insurgent movement and terror leaders virtually never mention Sun Tzu, however; they are more likely to train recruits on twentieth-century derivatives. Mao Tse Tung's writings, indebted to Sun Tzu while also very creative, have been favored by many contemporary guerrilla groups and terrorists. The practices of the Viet Cong have also been a modern inspiration. Well reflecting the continued 'serviceability' of such older ideas is the *Handbook for Volunteers of the Irish Republican Army*, created by the IRA's General Headquarters in 1956.[1] The IRA's doctrine is familiar to those who know Sun Tzu, or Mao, or the norms of guerrilla or terrorist fighting: strike hard but then disengage; concentrate for attacks but disperse quickly; move fast; be adaptable; change methods constantly; surprise is key; master intelligence. Above all, create disorder in the enemy camp.

At the higher, strategic level of war, the IRA General Headquarters argues something that has been true ever since the Second World War. Awesome conventional and nuclear power cannot necessarily overwhelm the power of guerrilla warfare; indeed, reasonable fear of overusing the former may well make the latter the most practical of all approaches. How useful has been the heavily-gunned warship, or nuclear weapon, to Britain in its fight in Northern Ireland? 'In the age of the H-bomb, strangely enough, the tactics of guerrillas are being widely copied', declares the IRA's *Handbook*; they are 'the blueprint of warfare in the atomic age'. Such tactics remain powerful today in our own age of partial atomic disarmament. Via them, and Sinn Fein's powerful politicking, the IRA of today has made itself the globe's most challenging and innovative terrorist organization. That potency bore heavily upon the willingness of others to come to the negotiating table and create the Easter Accords of 1998 which presently constrain the IRA from using its capabilities.

The IRA sniper rifle may strike from a perch in an abandoned building, hitting an Irish constable once at 500 yards, and then it vanishes, perhaps not to be used again for weeks. The modest commercial truck, its inner walls lined with disguised explosives, may accompany hundreds of other vehicles along roadways well watched by a large security establishment, and then pause near a bank building just long enough for the driver to disappear and detonate his cargo from a safe distance with an electronic beeper. Barrels full of simple farm fertilizers may be buried beneath a roadway and set off as an army convoy passes, detonated by a small charge of 'Semtex', one of the world's most lethal and pliable chemical compounds.[2]

Innovation

Faced with such IRA tactics, Britain has proven a calculating and clever enemy, inventing elaborate technical and other counter-measures. And to meet them, in turn, the IRA has continued to be masterful at innovation. Sometimes the group has evolved technological fixes for problems; sometimes it has relied more upon the human factor. For example, British helicopters are capable of considerable range, high speed, and night operations, and they have often cornered 'Provos'. But the IRA has responded, with heavy machine guns and even mortars, downing several helicopters and threatening all others. In one striking case, the IRA bombed an army convoy – but only after correctly predicting that when it did so British reinforcements would arrive by helicopter and land at an obvious and appropriate spot. All went as the IRA expected, so its second bomb at the landing site inflicted even more casualties than the earlier explosion.[3] Such double-bombings are now being used by other terrorists outside Ireland.

IRA vehicle bombs have led British and Irish security forces to enhance perimeter defenses, as with police cordons near public buildings believed to be targeted. Faced with this good ground defense, the IRA has sometimes relied upon stealth, penetrating the perimeter to leave a bomb, and boast of it. But the group has also made use of the mortar, reaching out from a distance to inflict great damage. Military outposts or bases have often been struck with mortars, and even 10 Downing Street was damaged during a February 1991 Cabinet meeting by mortar fire from a truck stopped nearby. Alert police in plentiful numbers have recently faced another, more devilish challenge. To get close to stationary targets like police headquarters and army posts, the IRA has several times seized members of a family – usually one hostile to the IRA – and threatened all with death unless one willingly becomes a human suicide. That person is forced, under the closest supervision, to drive a truck bomb to the target personally, detonating it before security forces can turn it away.[4]

Internationalism

IRA operations have had a wide range – at least as wide as the Atlantic Ocean. The group's declared policy of 'creating a Socialist Republic'[5] and its Marxist–Leninist sentiments give it an inherent internationalism, as do other practical imperatives of the fight. The IRA has linked up with foreign terror groups like the Marxist–Leninist ones on the Continent, kept company with foreign helpmates like the PLO and Libya, carried out operations abroad (especially in Europe), attended international terrorist 'summits', sent recruits to training sites in distant states, and raised revenues in lands where British police power can not reach.[6]

There have been four main theaters of IRA operations, three of which include scenes of the group's terror attacks. The foremost is in Northern Ireland, where the battle lines are drawn the deepest and the fighting has been the heaviest. The second theater is in Britain itself, 'the belly of the beast' deemed responsible for the strife. The third is on the Continent, where British troops with NATO offer occasional targets and where sympathizers of many nationalities live. Attacks there are never numerous but neither do they ever cease completely. The fourth theater is America, home to millions of ethnic Irish and millions more of partial Irish blood. The United States resembles the southern 26 Irish counties in so far as it is a source of political and financial and intelligence support but not of 'combat' operations. There are no 'targets' important enough to justify fouling the pool of public support in which guerrillas and supporters may swim. It makes sense for the IRA to kill in Gibraltar or in Belgium or in London, as they have; it would be self-defeating to spill blood too close to American sympathizers, which is why the IRA does not murder anyone in the United States. This fact points to the overwhelming difference between terrorist operations and normal military methods: terrorism is more political than military, more designed to change opinion than to destroy combat capabilities. IRA visitors and Sinn Fein spokesmen do go to the United States ... to make telephone calls. And senior American politicians take many of those calls.

Geographical bridges

Contemporary terror groups are more ideologically nationalist than were the communist actors of only a decade and a half ago, but their operational range is still international. Support, money, training facilities, and targets draw terrorists abroad. For example, there are consistent paths etched through Cyprus, Greece, Bulgaria, and Yugoslavia. These states are convenient bridges between the Middle East, where much terrorism originates and other terrorism may draw sustenance of logistical kinds, and Europe, where ethnic support groups are many, targets abound, and publicity for each strike is guaranteed. They are easy to enter and leave because they see millions of foreigners a year and cannot possibly control their borders perfectly. Their governments have political reasons to be indulgent, or are lax towards given groups. Greece, when governed by the Pan Hellenic Socialist movement, PASOK, has been almost kindly to Palestinian militants[7] and the Kurdish Worker's Party, PKK. Bulgaria, once a favored crossing-point for organized crime and terrorists of both right and left,[8] has probably changed little; the communist regime that had superb border controls but secretly indulged leftist terrorists and their criminal associates has been replaced by a democratic weakling that has trouble resisting passage of any terrorists, with or without their criminal associates. The same was true of Yugoslavia, which during the 1970s and 1980s was possibly the most culpable state in the region for permitting access and egress to wanted terrorists. The pattern was already firmly established by 1985 when, following the *Achille Lauro* hijacking, the murder of American Leon Klinghoffer, and all the surrounding scandal, the tactical leader of the mission, Abu Abbas, fled back to the Middle East by way of Belgrade.[9]

Yemen is another sort of transit point, useful for its obscurity as Cyprus is for its centrality. Yemen was a popular training spot in the

Terrorist transit points: Cyprus

Cyprus has long been a haven for advocates, activists, and operatives for terror groups. Strategically located in the eastern Mediterranean, badly divided between Greek and Turkish populations and governments, open to travelers, businessmen, and others so representing themselves, home to innumerable diplomats with privileged baggage, magnet for shipping and vacationers and air travel, Cyprus is, perhaps unwittingly, the Mediterranean world's most convenient starting point for places terrorists want to go to.

Terrorism has all but institutionalized itself on the island. A document released after the Cold War shows that Cypriot terrorists were among the many foreigners brought for special training to KGB intelligence schools.[10] Weapons intended for terrorists and guerrilla groups have passed through the island or been moved to or from there by Cypriot-registered ships; one involved a major shipment to the IRA.[11] Long before renouncing terrorism, the PLO kept open offices, overt commercial interests, and other agents operating without persecution on the Greek side. In times past, this has been a meeting place for IRA personnel come to see the PLO.[12] Among Palestinians on Cyprus there have been factional struggles, some of them including quiet assassinations or other blood-letting.[13] Most diplomats and tourists are safe on the island, but beneath the surface much clandestine life goes on.

Terrorists have often come from or passed through Cyprus to strike elsewhere, especially in Europe or the Middle East. A quarter-century ago, a campaign on US soil against Israeli targets was linked to a Cypriot resident, Khaled Mohammed el Jassem, an ethnic Palestinian presumed to be with Black September; his fingerprints tied him to bombings of Israeli commercial targets in New York City in 1973. Finally arrested in Rome in 1991, Jassem has now been convicted in a New York trial.[14] Another Cypriot caught security officials' eyes in the 1970s. Panaviotis Paschalis was a roving correspondent for the Cypriot Communist Party's newspaper *Harachi*, as well as for East German television, a job that reportedly permitted him to serve as an intermediary between several international terrorist groups and their sponsors in East German intelligence.[15] In October 1980, when France suffered the infamous bombing of the Rue Copernic synagogue, the crime was initially blamed on indigenous French neo-fascists, but later evidence pointed to men who arrived from Cyprus and left Paris immediately after the attack.[16]

A series of professionally made letter bombs aimed at Israel was mailed from Cyprus in December 1989 and January 1990.[17] Today's Palestinian terrorists, many of whom are anti-Arafat Moslems, also know the value of Cyprus: Hamas is using the island as a base. Some Hamas operatives have successfully returned to Cyprus after being declared *personae non gratae* elsewhere, doing so by legally changing their names in foreign countries and acquiring new visas.[18]

Government establishments on Cyprus are also part of the operational support structure of international terrorism. These include foreign state embassies and missions where terrorist contacts can safely be made, where checks may be cut, where communications channels are available, and where safe houses can be arranged before or after difficult operations. Radical Arab governments have large missions in Cyprus. Cyprus itself apparently permits terrorist training. Palestinians train there in non-military arts such as intelligence, disguise, operations management, and propaganda. Despite official denials from Athens, the Kurdish PKK has had training camps in Greece and on the Greek side of Cyprus too.[19] Cyprus presumably serves the PKK in lesser ways too, as it has many other groups: operatives may pass through, going from Syria into Turkey, for example, knowing that they are less suspicious arriving from an intermediate country. [20]

Drug-trafficking, money-laundering, and Russian mafia figures all seem to have blossomed in Cyprus.[21] In the midst of a 1995/96 global scandal over counterfeit US currency, much of it circulating in the Middle East, Cypriots and other nationals were arrested in a fake currency operation based in Larnaca and in Lebanon and involving Hezbollah and its patrons. Cyprus then appeared on a short list of countries in which the US Secret Service wanted to open a new office.[22]

1970s; Socotra and other sites welcomed many foreign terrorists.[23] Yemen has since turned noncommunist, and fought a civil war. Remarkably, the country has now re-emerged as a terrorist training ground all over again – this time for Muslim extremists, especially Islamic Jihad personnel and followers of Osama Bin Laden.[24] Terrorists see the same advantages there that ship captains have always recognized: a distant and ignored – but geographically accessible – location. Internal weakness is another advantage terrorists seek in states like Yemen. Some regions of today include ungoverned 'gray areas'.[25] Weak internal controls combine with weak border controls, yielding countries like Lebanon and Afghanistan which, all but lacking sovereignty, are ripe for abuse by internal groups, outside powers, and foreign terrorist organizations.

'Terror triangles'

Other countries possess other advantages to international terrorist operatives. Some countries feature multiple borders with adjacent countries of value to the terrorists. What might be called 'terror triangles' have already appeared on two different continents. One such entity lies in and around the odd, notable, southward extension of Holland called the Maastricht Appendix. Bordered by Luxembourg, Germany, and Holland, and close to France as well, this multistate and multinational intersection is marked with prominent cities and rivers and has become a new gathering place and transit area for terrorists operating in northwestern Europe. Arabs and Kurds and many other foreign and indigenous groups exploit the freedom there; one may move between several countries in a single day, or change money with ease in one of four different states. Cologne, just east of Maastricht, is home to a remarkable concentration of Arabs, including some militants, such as FIS 'executive authority' spokesman Rabah Kebir. He calls for the overthrow of the Algerian government and reportedly took part in a deadly car bombing at Algiers Airport before escaping to German exile in 1992. Another prominent Algerian activist in the area is a self-described religious teacher, Cemaleddin Khan, called the 'Khomeini of Cologne'. German sources say fund-raising for Hamas and many other terrorist activities go on in the area of Aachen/Aix-la-Chapelle. Once famous as the capital of Charlemagne, today it is most known for its role in European commerce, and its utility to terrorists who can operate in a range of important countries all from the same small multinational center point.[26]

A similar locus for terrorism interests is the region called Iguazu, where Paraguay, Argentina, and Brazil all touch, near the Parana River. A Lebanese exile community has been settling in during the recent years of civil war in Lebanon. Criminal trade of older types is now overlaid with political organization and logistic effort favoring Hezbollah, the Lebanese Shiite organization. There has been strong suspicion that the bombers of the Argentine–Jewish Mutual Association in 1994, and possibly the 1992 bombing of the Israeli Embassy in Buenos Aires, are Hezbollah members or agents coming from or through the Iguazu region. The two attacks killed some 125 people and injured hundreds more.[27] Iguazu possesses natural and exploitable racial and political links to Lebanon, with all its fermenting discontents, and probably to Iran as well.

Cultural linkages

Other aspects of geography which are exploitable by terrorists are determined by commonalities of culture. Spain, for example, is a natural bridge to Latin America. Spain's special lingual, religious, and cultural affinities to the Latin nations in the western hemisphere helped make it a source of support to terror groups there in the critical 1970s and 1980s when Uruguay, Nicaragua, and El Salvador were under leftist siege. ETA Basques and other violent foreigners sheltered in Castro's Cuba and reportedly still do; they were also welcome in Sandinista Nicaragua.[28] Spain and other western European states are attractive for their private wealth, as well; the narcotics trade, aided by such wealth and European demand, links Latin America to Spain. Other moneys flow westward for reasons of sympathy or ideology: wealthy individuals as well as church groups in Spain and western Europe have given large and small sums to such Latin groups as the Shining Path of Peru. Sendero, for its part, has moved personnel to western Europe to profit from the openness of democratic societies and the open purses of sympathetic Catholics, Spanish people, and others with an interest in Peru's poor, Peruvian revolutionaries, or both.

Spain is also a bridge to Africa, as it has been for millennia. Spanish culture reflects its central position between western Europe and the peoples of northern Africa. Algerian FLN operatives and their enemies in the right-wing French death squads both used Spain as a base and safe-haven during the Algerian civil war of the 1950s and early 1960s. Once in power, the FLN government supported many revolutionaries from western Europe, Central America, and even the United States, including Black Panthers and hijackers. The Basques of ETA have almost always been a presence in FLN-ruled Algeria.[29] And some of today's ETA members involved in killings of Spanish in Madrid or in the Basque lands have trained in Algeria. This Algerian assistance to terrorists from Spain is doubtless 'unofficial'. But the irony is that today the FLN is the archetypal 'status quo' government, assaulted by Muslim extremists and criticized by democratic parties who want to remake Algeria. Spain, for its part, wrestles not only with such North African support for its secular Basque nationalists but with Algerian Islamic extremists who despise the governments in Algiers and Madrid alike. Activists of the GIA, or Armed Islamic Group, had constructed a network in Catalonia and other eastern coastal areas of Spain when Spanish police interrupted their efforts in March 1996. In the town of Puigcerda, with a large Arab population, safe houses yielded documents linking the suspects to terrorist operations in Europe, including GIA bombings in Paris. This network in Spain also sheltered terrorists fleeing Algeria or heading further north and east into continental Europe.[30]

Training

The types of training required for terrorist operatives vary widely, as indicated by the diverse published accounts by trainees and by observers. Carlos Marighella, the Brazilian author of the *Minimanual of Urban Guerrilla Warfare* who died battling security forces, taught that an almost impossibly wide range of technical skills are necessary or useful. These range through document forgery to fundamental medicine to small arms handling to flying a plane. As physical training is vital, he encouraged hiking, camping, swimming, and training as a frogman, in addition to the more predictable hand-to-hand skills of self-defense and combat.[31] Personal accounts by other terrorists underscore the need for exercise to build strength and release tension. This is evident in the memoirs of such American militant groups of the early 1970s as the Weather Underground (infiltrated for the Federal Bureau of Investigation by Larry Grathwohl) and the Symbionese Liberation Army (whose swift life and death has been chronicled by hostage Patty Hearst). Some of today's American radical rightist militias put themselves through equally demanding physical and 'combat' training.

While only a few of the new American 'Patriots' have demonstrated an inclination to terrorism, the movement has proven capable of, and interested in, small arms training. It has been less impressive for, its handling of explosives, document forgery, and other techniques detailed by Marighella and others of the far left in decades passed. Militiamen are taking advantage of large private farms and remote rural sites which may be found in most states in America to drill and practice shooting. A widely publicized report identifies training locations in 23 states (half of which prohibit private militias). Named groups include the 'Washington State Militia' in Snohomish County, the 'Army of Israel' near Zion National Park in Utah, several chapters of the 'Ohio Patriots', the 'United States Militia' in Key Largo, Florida, and many others throughout the United States.[32] The 'Arizona Viper Militia', broken in summer 1996, was found to have trained for two years in remote forest areas and at an abandoned mine. They owned more than 100 rifles and hundreds of pounds of ammonium nitrate. This explosives find was important for two reasons: the same chemical was the main ingredient for the Oklahoma City bomb of one year previously, and no one has ever been arrested for the explosion that derailed an Amtrak train in Arizona in 1995.[33]

The American northwest has seemed particularly hospitable to right-wing militias and terror groups for a number of reasons, including expanses of unsettled territory where training may occur and new communities may be founded; a regional culture that is not averse to guns; a legacy of personal independence; and, for some, demographic distance from black, brown, and other non-white Americans. The mostly white northwest is seen by some as 'a last preserve' of that race; such was the thinking of 'The Order' which operated and committed terrorist acts in Washington State in the 1980s, and today's Hayden Lake Idaho-based 'Christian Identity', a blend of religion and politics dominated by anti-Jewish and anti-black themes.[34] Although many racists are not involved in terrorism, some associated with Christian Identity's ideas and the Hayden Lake scene have been, leading to the deaths of two dozen people in the past decade and a half.[35] In one recent case, a technically sophisticated, self-trained handful of men calling themselves the Aryan Republican Army stole an estimated quarter-million dollars from banks in four midwestern states in 1994–95. They reportedly funneled some of the cash to other extremists just as had the first famed right-wing group, The Order.[36]

There are apparent advantages to taking one's training outside the home country, and contemporary terror groups have done so, when possible. Since the collapse of Soviet bloc support, international terrorism is training in some new regions and several old standbys. One of the latter is the Bekaa Valley. Syria controls that Lebanese valley and thus its encampments of Hezbollah, the Kurds of PKK, and probably other groups such as remnants of the Japanese Red Army (four of whom were finally arrested only in 1997 after they ceased to have any utility for their sponsor). Syria itself may still use its intelligence services directly to sponsor terror acts; it certainly did a decade ago, and it remains on the State Department's list of state-sponsors of terrorism because Syrian territory is still used for terrorist training. Prime beneficiaries of President Assad's policy have been PKK[37] and other Turkish groups of the far left. This newest indulgence of anti-Turkish radicals and Kurds is but one more page in a thick ledger; both the left and the right from the Turkish underground have often trained in Syria. Mehmet Ali Agca claimed he received training in Syria before shooting the Pope in St Peter's Square in 1981, and US satellite photography demonstrated the existence of a Dev Sol camp near the Syrian–Lebanese border in 1990. In the following year, during the Gulf War, Dev Sol killed several Americans stationed in Turkey.[38] Despite years of denials, prevarication, and promises to cease aiding the PKK, Damascus permitted and helped pay for that Kurdish organization's training and operations, at least until the October 1998 bilateral accord with Ankara.[39]

Afghanistan and the Sudan, two countries dominated by extremist Muslims, are probably the largest trainers of international terrorists at present.[40] Taliban's assumption of internal powers and better border controls will probably not change that Afghan picture. While a reduction of brigandage can be expected, the same is not true of the present and future flow of foreign and Afghan Muslims, trained in violent arts and loosed upon the secular world. Presently, at as many as two dozen sites in Afghanistan, Muslim foreigners are working to master intelligence operations, assassination, explosives handling, small arms, and hand-to-hand combat, and other dimensions of low-intensity conflict useful to waging *jihad* in western and other countries. The Hezb-e Islami organization of famed Sunni *mujahideen*, Gulbuddin Hekmatyar, is among the most effective at training foreigners; many hundreds are present in his network of camps at Shahar Siyab, Kanjak, Jubi, and Baktia.[41] Egypt's lethal 'Islamic Group' has a base in Afghanistan as well. The enormous extent of the problem has been confirmed by Arab intelligence, western governments, and independent journalists, to say nothing of a spreading record of court documents of terrorists convicted at points world-wide. The chief plotter of the New York City harbor tunnel bombing, Ramzi Yousef, and others convicted (as he was) for the New York Trade Center Tower's bomb, are among the many who underwent training in Afghanistan.[42]

Sudan has captured African attentions by flagrant cultivation of guerrilla and terrorist trainees from virtually all countries surrounding her. The evidence against Sudan emerged in the open press in 1991 and

1992, only a few years after an Islamic-dominated government took power. By 1994 the regime admitted to making use of some 2,000 Iranian military experts to train its army;[43] the presence of training camps for foreigners was widely known; and Iran's influence in the country had become remarkably strong. By 1995 there were obvious training links to Algerians wrecking their own country in civil war. Two Sudanese diplomats and other Sudanese gunmen were involved in the murder attempt against Egypt's Hosni Mubarak, then visiting Addis Ababa. Other Sudanese were shown to be linked to terror plots in New York City. By 1996 the UN had slapped sanctions on the Sudan and warned it against further terrorism.[44]

Pakistan and India are also training terrorists, especially each other's ethnic militants. This practice has bloodied civilians in both countries and obsessed the two governments for years, though coverage of it rarely holds Western attention. Now the reality of the systematic border violations and malicious intent involved in each country's exploitation of the other's religious and ethnic divisions has become too pronounced to be ignored by the world.[45] The centerpiece of tension is the revolt in Kashmir, jointly administered, disputed since 1947, and especially contentious since the end of the Afghan war against the Soviets. It has cost at least 20,000 lives since 1989.[46] The Pakistani government has previously admitted to giving moral, diplomatic, and political support to those fighting for independence, while denying material support. But Pakistan has trained and sheltered terrorists who have struck in India, including the group Harakat ul-Ansar, which took Western hostages in July 1995 and then murdered at least one of them.[47] The immediate aim was one of the most common in terror operations: winning release of jailed comrades-in-arms. The case is but one more in a lengthening low-intensity war between two powerful neighbors.

Many Palestinians have had training with the Abu Nidal Organization, which in the mid and late 1980s had camps in Iraq, Syria, and Libya. Abu Nidal's recruits undergo a six-month course with emphasis on martial discipline, physical training, political indoctrination against the 'Zionist enemy and Arab reactionary regimes', skill with small arms including the ANO's trademark Polish WZ63 submachine pistol, and elementary intelligence techniques. In more advanced courses, notes a defector, 'we learned how to kill people with a variety of methods, how to enter buildings quietly, stalk people through the streets, and then escape'. Emphasis was placed upon secrecy: personnel were repeatedly advised that secrecy was their best friend. Counter-intelligence policy dictated use of code names even within cells in the camp, which severely limited one's knowledge of other recruits; some

Training of international terrorists in Pakistan

India and Pakistan have trained separatists, religious fundamentalists, and other militants in their low-intensity conflict. Trainees of only one of the Pakistani groups, Harakat ul-Ansar, have later been engaged not only in Kashmir but also Burma, Tajikistan, and Bosnia-Herzegovina.

Evidence for the Pakistani training activities has been growing. One Indian press source speculates that the conclusion of the anti-communist *jihad* in Afghanistan has allowed Pakistan to turn its attention to the next 'target' – Kashmir, the disputed territory lying between India and Pakistan.

Outside Sopore, Pakistan, near the border, a Hezb-ul Mujahideen (Party of Holy Warriors) commander named Mohammad Abu Nasar proudly introduced some of his combatants to a foreign reporter in late 1992. He claimed that in all more than 4,000 Kashmiris had received training in Afghanistan; evidently many were prepared to fight for a Muslim state in Kashmir. A Sudanese from Khartoum said he had arrived under the sponsorship of the Muslim Brotherhood in the Sudan; Yasin Salin Masood come to the camp 'to share in the *jihad*'. 'There are 300 to 400 Arabs here, from Libya, Algeria, Bahrain and other places', he related.

Sikh separatists including members of the Khalistan Liberation Force also train in Pakistan for operations across the border into India. Occasionally, terrorists captured in Europe give evidence of having begun in – or transited through – Pakistani camps. *Jane's Intelligence Review* goes so far as to state that 'Pakistan is currently the world's leader in hosting international terrorist organizations.'[48]

trainers even wore masks. Later, once the recruit was trained and trusted, sophisticated individual instruction helped the would-be terrorist to operate in target areas by arranging plausible cover stories, handling money and weapons, avoiding police surveillance, and maintaining contacts with superiors.[49] Today, Abu Nidal recruits probably still train in Iraq and Syria, where they enjoy a presence; they are definitely training in other long-friendly countries such as Lebanon, Libya, and Sudan.[50]

Much is known about the training of recruits in the mainstream PLO, if only because tens of thousands of boys, girls, men and women have been involved. Most recruits went through months of physical, technical, and political training; many had more advanced instruction. One former PLO camp contained a full-size mockup of a passenger liner for the training of recruits for hijackings. Some PLO cadres made themselves experts on particular European airports, especially Athens and Rome. Others learned to be pilots, and for a time one Red Sea island served as a PLO air base. For more typical guerrilla operations, the network of PLO camps and facilities included a huge sports stadium in Beirut and offered extensive and impressive curricula, taught by Arab specialists as well as instructors from throughout the Soviet bloc. As proven by document caches – like those discovered by Israel when invading Lebanon in 1982, and those scanned into the personal computer of Vladimir Bukovsky when he worked through Communist Party archives in the mid 1990s – many PLO recruits went directly to Warsaw Pact military schools or terrorist training camps to enhance skills in conventional and unconventional warfare.[51]

By the early 1990s, the postcommunist age, it was Japan's cult 'Supreme Truth' that was dispatching members to Russia. Aum Shinrikyo had many contacts and associates in Russia and claimed 30,000 recruits there. This compared with a claimed 10,000 adherents in Japan itself, and small offices in New York. The spectacular excesses of Aum violence were made possible not only by leadership and ruthlessness but by attention to the logistical bases of terrorism. In their rise and fall, they demonstrated the continuing relevance of the Carlos Marighella manual which exhorts recruits to master complicated subjects that are the necessary underpinning of successful operations.

Organization

Recruits, once given initial training, are subsumed into the organization. Perhaps the least dramatic and most direct responsibility of terror group

AUM SHINRIKYO'S TECHNICAL TEAMS

At its height in Japan, Aum provided technical training for personnel that was partly legal and partly clandestine.

There was overt, successful recruiting of talented young students of Japanese technical schools and universities. These graduates brought with them such useful degrees as physics, chemical engineering, and computer science. One recruit was a salesman for a chemical company; his dealer's license could be exploited by Aum. Hard-working and talented, these personnel help explain not only the cult's capacity for construction, demonstrated by its many installations, but for its killing capabilities.

Specialists worked on laser weapons, chemical weapons, and many simpler weapons. Lab workers manufactured in house the poison gasses used to kill Japanese on several occasions and the technical apparatus for their dispersal. There were several effective types of dispersers; fortunately a primitive and clumsy 'delivery method' was used in the 1995 sarin attack on the subway, rendering that attempt less murderous than it could have been. Many other types of talent were sought out. Aum had lawyers in a 'Justice Ministry' to deal with the cult's property holdings and fended off government inquiries over unexplained deaths. Aum, like many insurgencies, even had its own hospitals. One of these hospitals treated a member of an Aum assassination team poisoned in a botched sarin attack on a powerful Buddhist leader.[52]

Aum sought out members of the Self-Defense Forces of Japan to exploit their military skills. For weapons, and for training, some members went to Russia. Leader Shoko Asahara himself met with Russian military officials and visited the Kantemirovsky military base outside Moscow. The second in command of 'Supreme Truth', Kiyohide Hayakawa, visited Russia some 20 times and was in charge of military relationships. At least two groups of senior Aum members, including veterans of the Japanese Defense Forces, were in Russia in 1994 for training in small arms from Spetznaz men – GRU special forces skilled in assassination, intelligence-gathering, and sabotage. It was Russian plans that Aum Shinrikyo used to make both sarin gas and AK-47 rifles in Japan. The group also bought a Russian military helicopter and showed serious interest in buying tanks and possibly nuclear weapons.[53]

This last dimension of Aum activity illustrates an earlier theme: many terror groups are ambitious to grow into far larger and nationally powerful movements – taking part in the status quo while transforming it, as do Peru's Shining Path, Lebanon's Hezbollah, and the like. As the terror groups grow, they increasingly come to need the conventional weapons, the equipment, and many of the methods of full insurgencies.

leaders is to create and manage the clandestine organization required for operations. The latter are as diverse as armed action, administering training of many types, money-raising, the gathering of intelligence, counter-intelligence against penetration of the group by other terrorists and by security forces, etc. Whether a group's objective is to survive as a persistent thorn in the government's paw, which may be all that the Greek group November 17 expects, or whether it is to develop into a full-blown insurgency that rivals the government in power, which has always been the intention of the New People's Army in the Philippines, eye-catching actions can only succeed when supported by a quiet, systematic, effective infrastructure.

Clandestine cells make up the heart of this structure; they are its essence, whether or not the group also has overt political fronts. Clandestine cell structures were vital to such early twentieth-century movements as the Bolsheviks and the IRA. Others evolved readily out of Second World War resistance movements in Soviet Russia, France, and Scandinavia, and were promptly copied after 1945 by insurgents eager to take advantage of global changes and opportunities opened up by the war. The Vietnamese, Malaysian, and Philippine movements all included methods and personnel from the anti-Japanese war. To these were added entirely new movements, especially the FLN insurgency in Algeria. While French forces managed to destroy the cell structure in the Algerian capital, they could not do so in the countryside, nor could they deal effectively with army units across the borders in safe havens in Tunisia and Morocco.

The cell has many variants, but the essential principle is simple and effective. Each is part of a hierarchy and is responsible to a single point of contact above. Within each cell, which is typically three to ten persons, a member may not even know all his or her compatriots. When an action is in preparation and execution, a person or a cell or a group of cells may act in ignorance of the strategic purpose of the action, or even about the full dimensions of the operations; one knows only what one must.[54] The result is an organization which can act decisively and quickly. Also, such an organization cannot easily be 'rolled up' by security forces who capture some personnel and use them to identify the others. Only a senior leader can give away that kind of intelligence to security forces, and he or she rarely does. Infiltrators are always possible, but they may be members of an organization for months and still know few of its personnel.

The Basque 'Etarras' (ETA) are typical of contemporary terrorist organizations. Aiming at Basque autonomy, they have carried on covert organization and armed struggle since 1959, developing new members from nationalist circles, student groups, and workers' unions. Three- to five-person cells have always been the norm, and each is usually based on very familiar home ground where members are known to townspeople and familiar with the geography. A major study estimated that there were 100–200 such cells operating in northern Spain 15 years ago.[55] These numbers are much lower today, as the 1990s have been harsh for ETA. Unprecedented French assistance removed their transborder sanctuaries and combined with Spanish efforts to round up top terrorist leaders.

Some cells are 'illegals' – 'wanted' men and women known to the police, living on ETA salary, and conducting the majority of the armed actions. Others are 'legal', that is, members unrecognized by the police and able to move about openly, while serving the ETA as organizers, intelligence specialists, couriers, and links to the outside world.[56] Still others operate as supporters, supplying food, shelter, false documents and the like, but never fully subordinating themselves to the group with formal membership.[57] All three categories of ETA members take part in the effort at recruitment and political organization. Leaders watch both overt and covert Basque organizations for promising individuals, with an eye to recruitment or promotion of them. For example, a survey of ETA leaders among Basques on the French side of the border has shown that they began their involvement in worker movements or youth groups of the 1970s and were then recruited into the ETA by its historical leaders.[58] A sound mix of talented overt and covert activists yields a range of membership that can manage all kinds of activities: nonviolent nationalism; clandestine liaison work with overt fronts and external support groups; and 'direct actions' such as killings.

ETA organization can be considered from a third perspective, beyond those of cell structure and a division into illegals, legals, and supporters. As documents seized from an ETA organizer named 'Santi Potros' reveal, there is a committee structure based upon the political, economic, and military rubrics. An executive committee of eight, to which a considerable staff reports, controls all three divisions of work. Political branch activities are broken out regionally and also functionally: Connections and Propaganda, International Connections, and Regional Connections to both French centers of support like Biarritz and Bayonne, and the 'inside' of Spain.[59] Overt public support groups have become a common political strategy for terrorist groups, and ETA's political wing coordinates activity with 'Herri Batasuna'. HB organizes nonviolent activists and amenable nationalist groups, and helps to depict Spain's democratic government as disguised Francoism, enmeshed in a state of perpetual war of subjugation with Euskadi, the Basque homeland.[60] Street marches and other campaigns focus on nationalist causes, incidents of government repression, and above all, ETA actions and ETA prisoners.

Abu Nidal created and still rules his small group 'Fatah' – The Revolutionary Council, sometimes referred to as ANO, the Abu Nidal Organization. He is a fierce, dedicated, and self-educated individual from a family that lost its property when the state of Israel was formed. Nidal was in the PLO, but broke away in 1974 and began hunting and killing Palestinians loyal to Arafat. ANO was most active in the 1980s; in 1985 alone it perpetrated the airport massacres at El Al airline's desks in Vienna and Rome, and hijacked the jetliner that was shot up and burned in Malta. More recently it has been less active, and 1988 brought a report that Nidal was ill and hospitalized. Unlike ETA, the Nidal group has never known collective leadership; the personality of its chief is reported to be all-controlling and paranoiac; he and a very few lieutenants micro-manage everything, and even those senior lieutenants are slavishly subordinate. Members accept strict orders on every aspect of personal life or risk death. Indeed, many have already died in internal purges after arousing the slightest suspicion. Therefore if Nidal is ill, his singular importance is now a grave disadvantage to the group.

ANO is secular and nationalist but its structure is familiar to students of communist movements. Abu Nidal is General Secretary and sits among the membership of the powerful 'Politburo', which itself is the key to the larger 'Central Committee'. Below that committee there are some 40 persons of the 'Revolutionary Council' from which the group's formal name derives. Beneath these superstructures, all dominated personally by Nidal, are 'committees' and 'directorates' – no discernible qualities differentiate the two rubrics. These is an Intelligence Directorate, an Organization Directorate, a Membership Committee, the Political Directorate, a Finance Directorate, the Committee for Revolutionary Justice, the Technology and Science Committee, and the People's Army.

Because ANO has been ejected in years past from host countries (Iraq, Syria, Poland), it has adapted to the problem of its fundamental undesirability and ugly profile. It keeps a foot in each of two countries: Nidal rules from Lebanon, but the offices of the chief of staff of the General Secretariat, Dr Ghassan al-Ali, are in Libya. There are ANO archives, staff, 'politicos', and fighters in both countries. These personnel are tracked by the Organization Directorate and the Membership Committee, with computers to help account for their whereabouts and records. Manpower levels have fluctuated widely.[61]

The Political Directorate – not to be confused with the ruling Politburo – is responsible for public affairs and publications. Such things may seem to be beyond the interest of a murderer like Abu Nidal. In fact, Nidal himself has served as editor-in-chief of the principal ANO journal, a weekly with a circulation of 12,000 called *Palestine the Revolution*. He also writes for other in-house publications, and keeps abreast of political and foreign affairs by reading and by including intellectuals among his top leadership.

The ANO Financial Directorate naturally lacks the PLO's hundreds of millions, but it does own foreign bank accounts in Switzerland, Austria, Spain, and other countries, with investment companies in Europe, and holdings world-wide. Some accounts are in Nidal's true name, Sabri al-Banna; others are under pseudonyms. Some are joint accounts with another ANO principal, but the leader periodically reshuffles these, often to remove the other ANO officer's name. Recent years have witnessed both losses and gains in the ANO's financial accounts. With the fall of communism in Poland, they lost the trading company SAS, based in Warsaw and dealing in goods and arms.[62] A collapse of no less importance was that of the Bank of Credit and Commerce International, based in London and holding millions of Nidal's funds. On the other hand, an inflow from Arab governments continues, and when Yasser Arafat sided with Iraq in the Gulf War, and Arab governments slashed contributions to the PLO, it seems that ANO's accounts enjoyed an increase. One estimate of ANO wealth at that time ran as high as $400 million.[63]

Nidal's other directorates include the Technical, charged with producing fake passports and such, the Scientific, which specializes in implements of killing, and the Committee for Revolutionary Justice, which oversees ANO prisons, interrogations, and probably burials.[64] The People's Army is a militia, not just a cadre of terrorists; it is centered in Lebanon and has wide experience in the refugee camp wars. The military commander ranks as a Politburo member. Like many groups, ANO keeps the structure and titles which could permit expansion. Under different circumstances or strategic choices, ANO could have developed into a true guerrilla army. By contrast Fatah, Arafat's main guerrilla wing, can now call upon some 6,000 fighters in Lebanon, and almost as many more elsewhere, while Nidal's 'People's Army' is less important than the ANO Intelligence Directorate which handles his terrorist operations.

Intelligence

Intelligence has a pronounced operational role in terror groups and terror operations. The use which ANO makes of its intelligence directorate to carry out terror attacks is not unique; Syria and other sovereign governments have used their intelligence networks for identical purposes, as in 1986 when Syrian air force intelligence attempted to destroy an El Al flight from London by bringing a bomb aboard via an unsuspecting pregnant Irish woman.[65] Syria's army intelligence organization, for its part, today virtually owns the Palestinian group led by Abu Mussa called 'Fatah Uprising', which has camps in the Syrian-controlled Bekaa Valley.[66]

Intelligence must precede operations but it has still higher functions, including an essential role in the making of military and diplomatic strategies. Sun Tzu and modern masters of war recognize how intelligence can offset enemy advantages in men, money, and *matériel*. Thus the IRA's 1956 *Handbook* states, 'Information gathering is a continuous operation', including collection, analysis, and distribution. Among the many obvious 'targets' of intelligence work are persons deemed appropriate for assassination, routes of escape, location of safe houses, etc. At the higher, operational and strategic levels, the groups investigate such problems as the methods of operations of security forces state-wide, the availability of contacts and conduits offered by foreign powers in embassies nearby, prospects for use of adjoining countries' territory, political and military trends in the targeted country, and so forth.

Intelligence is a key to other requirements for success, such as surprise. As the IRA manual notes, 'The guerrilla's great weapon is surprise. To achieve this surprise, intelligence must be first-class. The guerrilla must know everything about the enemy and his battle order, his strength and his weakness – even his plans for anti-guerrilla activities.'[67] Knowledge offers not only tactical opportunity but engenders an overall sense of confidence, as Mao well understood and as the IRA *Handbook* once again captures: 'Good intelligence breeds good morale. And for the guerrilla, morale is everything. It is this morale that gives the guerrilla his determination and his daring.'[68]

The need of the professional to 'know everything' about his enemy explains the almost obsessive reconnaissance and record-keeping which precedes most terror attacks. While some see in terrorism only passion and blind fury, successful attacks are often months in planning. The seizure of Colombia's Palace of Justice, and the typical Palestinian attack on Israeli beaches with high-speed boats, are examples of operations to which much time and training are devoted. Safe houses and training camps often contain small mock-ups of targets, and newspaper files on targeted persons, as well as personal disguises, false documents used in reconnaissance, and similar evidence of preparation.[69]

Some terrorist intelligence efforts may be sophisticated enough to be of use to the powers that patronize them. West European terrorists 'at rest' behind the Iron Curtain sometimes wrote political reports for their Warsaw Pact handlers or gave them long debriefings. And Stasi files show that the PLO was sometimes asked by its handlers to make reports on West German intelligence operations in Beirut.[70] That would be logical, given that PLO terrorists were often the beneficiaries of Eastern Bloc intelligence on various targets, including industrial sites in West Germany.[71] At the very least such attacks of the 1980s as those on NATO fuel pipelines executed by the Belgian communist combatant cells are the sort of venture that could be of strong interest to Warsaw Pact war planners. Thus, terror groups' relations to outside powers may be significant even in peacetime.

For revolutionary terrorists, more than for pro-government killers, there is also a requirement for strategic intelligence, the kind which is the most difficult to acquire. At the strategic level, uncertainty is the greatest. But, within their obvious limits, violent activists nonetheless learn what they can. Terror groups show a strong appetite for studies of the government's political caste, information about individual foreign leaders who are visiting, the plans and activities of hostile governments, and relevant events and trends in international politics. Their diverse files captured in safe houses are one testament to this. Another is the very visible way in which the end of the Cold War found insurgent and terror organizations grappling with new problems of philosophy and strategic intelligence. Groups as disparate as Central American guerrillas, PLO factions, the South African ANC, and the German Red Army Faction (RAF) were visibly destabilized by the consequences of the Soviet collapse. In two agonized treatises released to the public, the RAF discoursed upon internationalism, the Soviets' role in it, the new environment in European politics, the need for national political change, and the overall failure of the RAF to advance such change.[72] By April 1998 these conversations were apparently over; the group formally announced its complete disbandment.

Some rightist paramilitaries and terrorists aiming to enforce the status quo, rather than overturn it, have successfully established intelligence liaisons with security forces. Armed with information systematically gathered by the entire police force and military net for legitimate purposes, 'death squads' have been able to select victims from 'known leftist' or communist parties, trade unions critical of the government, and dissident social organizations. The squads are able to act with some certainty about their victim and with some surety that their own terrorism is unlikely to go punished.

A document of strategic intelligence

Excerpts from Germany's Red Army Faction's
reassessment of 1992

In 1989, we, the RAF, began to apply more thought and discussion to the understanding that, for us and for all of those who have a record of resistance in the FRG, things cannot go on as they have done. We have come to the conclusion that we must seek new guidelines for a policy that is truly able to bring about changes for human life. This makes it necessary for us to reassess our own history and the joint history of all those who have been active in the resistance, and to think about what we did wrong and about the important experience that we or others gained, and what significance our experiences can have for the future.

Our starting point was (1) The fact that we were all facing a completely changed situation regarding the international balance of power – the dissolution of the socialist state system, the end of the cold war. We were faced with the fact that we had failed to accomplish our objective: to achieve a breakthrough in the joint international struggle for liberation. The liberation struggles were generally too weak to hold their own against the imperialist war, which was extended to all levels.

The collapse of the socialist states, which was essentially caused by unsolved internal consistencies, has had a disastrous effect on millions of people throughout the world ... [New] struggles for liberation can develop only from each people's sense of awareness of its own specific and individual history, authentic conditions and objectives. Only from this can new international power develop. Many of our comrades from the Tricont [the Third World] have repeatedly said as much in our discussions, and in their individual countries they found and implemented the beginnings of a completely new policy – and we will do so here, as well. This shared objective makes us feel close to them.

(2) We ourselves were confronted with the fact that the policy we pursued in the years before 1989 had not strengthened us politically, but weakened us ... [W]e no longer managed to attract people ... [A] situation in which we, the guerrillas, make all the decisions ourselves, while the others have to follow us, cannot go on. Although we might often put it differently, this was the reality ...

We very much reduced our policy to attacks against imperialist strategies, failing to look for immediate positive objectives and to show how an alternative was able to exist here and today ...

For everything that is now beginning and for all those who are looking for new directions, attacks by us against top officials of the state and the economy with intent to kill cannot advance the process that is now necessary ...

By preventing the conflict from escalating, we have now taken a step on our own initiative to open this political space. It now remains to be seen how the state will react ... [If the state continues] to bank on war ... then we consider the phase of halting the escalation over – we will not stand idly by and do nothing ... [T]he answer to war can only be another war.

Red Army Faction
10 April 1992[73]

An important 1989 investigation in Northern Ireland disclosed that British security forces were passing intelligence along to Protestant militias like the now-banned Ulster Defense Association. More than 90 people were arrested, and one former army officer pleaded guilty to 20 charges of terrorism, including plotting to kill a member of Sinn Fein and four others. Irish activists claim security file leads often have led to deaths or injuries of IRA activists and sympathizers.[74] In 1996, in the new republic of Slovakia, there was evidence – enough to provoke strong public words from the US Ambassador and from an Austrian judge – that the security services of Prime Minister Vladimir Meciar dealt with political rival Michal Kovoc by kidnapping and drugging his son. Police investigators on the case were dismissed; a key witness has died in a car explosion.[75] By May 1997 some observers were speculating that such indicators of strife within Slovakia might doom its narrow chance for early entry into NATO; the small new republic was subsequently dropped from 'first round' selection for both NATO and the European Union.

Whether pro-state or anti-state, violent parties must assemble, process, and store the tactical and operational kinds of intelligence which they need. Terrorists have traditionally been keepers of files. The communist Khmer Rouge insurgents were as organized and as totalitarian as the Nazis, patiently assembling photo-files of tens of thousands of their innocent victims of the mid 1970s, as at Tuol Sleng prison. Today the Khmer Rouge terrorists would probably record such a holocaust on CD-ROM.[76] Modern technical equipment has come into increasing global use, steadily replacing the pens and paper files of old. Videotape is used for reconaissance and making training films.[77] Video, computers, and other such technologies are common in terrorists' offices and safehouses; files are increasingly kept on computers. Typical recent finds by police include personnel records, finances, and intelligence files on targets, including personal data on public figures such as bankers, politicians, army generals, prominent Jews, etc. During 1992 alone, police raids on hideaways yielded computer diskettes on Colombia's ELN, Peru's Shining Path, and German and Austrian neoNazis.[78] Subsequently there have been more recoveries of diskettes.

In January 1995 in Manila, smoke from a bomb-making effort attracted Filipino police to an apartment. They recovered a Toshiba laptop personal computer with files on the terrorism operations of Ramzi Ahmed Yousef. Yousef was a principal in the New York Trade Towers explosion, has been linked to an attempt to blow up the Israeli Embassy in Bangkok, and has been convicted of a 1994 airline bombing that killed a Japanese citizen. The talented graduate in electrical engineering had little trouble making bombs or handling computers. He had also undergone armed training inside Afghanistan before becoming a leader of world-wide Islamic terrorism. His plans in the Philippines were for a dozen bombings of American airliners in Asia. Detailed on the computer were money transfers, airline schedules, and a threatening letter. An identification card photograph for one of Yousef's accomplices had been scanned in; this man later confessed to providing false documents to the bombers. Some of this evidence had been deleted from the computer but, recovered from the hard-drive by a technical expert, it became the prosecution's best ally in the New York court, where Yousef and two accomplices were convicted in September 1996.[79]

The American Unabomber was different, and truly old-fashioned. He hated computers, and targeted computer scientists with old-fashioned bombs, sometimes delivered in hand-crafted wooden boxes. Ted Kaczynski was thus the exception who proves the contemporary rule.[80]

Counter-intelligence

According to the closing passage in the IRA's 1956 *Handbook* for volunteers, 'Counter-intelligence … means guarding our own security, denying information to the enemy and tracking down enemy agents.'[81] A newer IRA manual shows the battle scars of years of successful British intelligence efforts and penetrations of the IRA: the *Green Book*, written in prison in the mid 1970s and then edited by a Sinn Fein activist before publication and distribution to volunteers, offers more than a few sentences on counter-intelligence. The *Green Book* sketches the many dangers facing a clandestine organization and orders recruits to avoid loose talk in public places, which may be overheard; drinking, which has often led to boasting or to chatter in pubs about members or their activities; and pro-'republican' public events, an obvious magnet for security forces. The *Green Book* also covers techniques for resisting interrogations: members are advised to expect three kinds of abuse: physical, to include possible torture, psychological torture, and humiliation. Counter-measures include sound education in the ideals of the IRA movement and psychological tricks for dealing with isolation and physical pain. Political discussion is to be avoided at all costs, as police often attempt it to loosen up a suspect who has resisted more direct forms of interrogation. Other tricks are to be expected, such as display of an IRA accomplice's faked confession.[82]

Nearly all terrorist groups are paranoid as regards police agents, and obsessive about their secrecy and their cell structure. In the Irish case, as in the Palestinian, rival nationalist groups are as eager to penetrate them as are government security forces. Terror groups protect themselves with training and indoctrination, with internal security measures, with Maoist-style 'self-criticism' sessions designed to extirpate personal traits which could prove dangerous to the group and, in many cases, with horrendous punishments. All these weed out the weak and strengthen the others against penetration. Close family relations and cell structures also may forestall government infiltration; a primary reason for Western governments' failures against Hezbollah terrorists is the integrity of the Lebanese group's family-based structure.[83]

Irish terrorism was plagued by police penetration in the nineteenth century. When the IRA 'Provos' experienced similar problems in the early 1970s, they cut down their traditionally large 'columns' and became more decentralized, organizing more around the cell of only three to five persons.[84] Yet in Northern Ireland in the years leading up to the recent 'Good Friday' accord, some Catholics were turning against the IRA by informing on the gunmen among them. The IRA admitted this trend in Belfast in early 1997, and British authorities confirm it based upon secretive contacts with citizens. The 'Republicans' countered with public warnings against any of their own who so inform.[85]

The most public contemporary counter-intelligence problem for the IRA today is an insider who turned willingly to the police. Sean O'Callaghan was an IRA commander by the age of twenty-five and then one of the most senior IRA leaders of the 1970s, responsible for more than three score attacks and robberies. But, struck by conscience, and the callousness of a senior IRA member who spoke cynically after the killing of a police department female, O'Callaghan turned. He became an informer for the Irish national police, the Garda Siochana, despite also being IRA chief of the important 'Southern Command', which manages operations in Britain. O'Callaghan was able to abort one well-developed bomb plot against Prince Charles and Princes Diana, in 1983, and in the next year betrayed his organization's incoming arms shipment from Boston, $2 million worth of cargo aboard the ship *Valhalla*. O'Callaghan, released from jail, doubtless lives in great danger, especially if he continues with lecture tours in England and America and his writing. He is on record about the IRA's ties to the political front Sinn Fein; O'Callaghan was a ranking member of that, too.[86]

Successful compromise of terrorist groups may be the best single weapon of security forces. In Italy, the once-impenetrable Red Brigades were broken open not just by good detective work but by 'turning' hardened members into repentants – *pentiti* – and using them in court against their associates; eventually, hundreds were locked up. The

Irish Republicanism's fear of police infiltrators

In the low intensity conflict in Northern Ireland, security forces cultivate informers within the terror groups and their political organizations so as to be warned of pending attacks, and for evidence in trials. Terror groups aggressively promote counter-intelligence efforts to dilute this threat to their structures and operations. And politicians and media organs favoring the cause of total independence from England trumpet the government's intelligence operations as unfair and grotesque, if not criminal. Following are some opening paragraphs of a typical story in the 'Voice of Irish Republicanism in America', the weekly New York City newspaper the *Irish People* (4 October 1997).

Eight weeks into a ceasefire, the RUC [Royal Ulster Constabulary] admitted that it is still deeply involved in a strategy of infiltrating and compromising the nationalist community by using informers. This unprecedented admission followed a Sinn Fein press conference on Thursday, when Councilor Cathal Crumley introduced three recent targets of the RUC's recruitment attempts.

Crumley blasted the RUC's 'ongoing trawl for informers', and he challenged those who were saying that the RUC were acceptable in relation to drugs and traffic matters. Crumley pointed out that all three victims, young men in their early 20s, had been approached while in contact with the RUC for so-called 'community matters'.

All three were visibly shaking at the press conference. One man, too frightened to be identified, revealed how he came into contact with the RUC as a result of drunken driving. He had no license but was told there would be no charges if he supplied the RUC with information about certain republicans – members of Sinn Fein. When the youth refused to cooperate, he was followed and approached again by plainclothes RUC two weeks ago.

Brigades are now gone; there were 1992 reports of a modest renaissance, but even this came to nothing. It is believed by some European officials that terrorists have transitioned into 'part-time' terrorism work and otherwise 'bourgeois' lives to make their affairs more impenetrable. The West German Red Army Faction's consistent problem has been its minuscule size; it has paid little attention to political organization and has thus never been able to add to its hard core of several dozen gunmen. But neither have arrests and shoot-outs snuffed it out entirely, and no additional RAF members have been captured for many years.

When foreign intelligence agents and adverse political pressures build, some groups may even try to solve their counter-intelligence problems temporarily by changing the name of their organization or assuming new names for certain operations.[87] The PLO seems to have often switched names for its most active operational units over the years whenever adverse publicity or outside penetration risks became too high. The PLO's Black September unit, though disavowed by Yasser Arafat, included his own brother-in-law, Hasan Salamah, and other loyalists when it murdered Israeli athletes and German security personnel at the Munich Olympics in 1972. In the 1980s, 'Force 17' emerged as an internal security unit of the PLO but expanded into terrorism and long-range operations, such as murdering three Israeli tourists in Cyprus in 1985. Then, while that organization allegedly became quiescent,[88] another emerged, also controlled by Arafat and thought to derive directly from 'Force 17' personnel: the 'Hawari Group', named after the colonel who led it. He carried out attacks in Europe in 1985 and then bombed TWA 840 over Greece in April 1986;[89] incredibly, the plane did not crash, although four American passengers died. Arafat later brought forth the 'Fatah Hawks', hooded young men who acted as the PLO's bullies and enforcers of his government in the occupied territories. Arafat has thus come full-circle, from the archetypal terrorist of the 1960s to the sponsor of pro-state terror against Palestinians as this century ends.

Counter-intelligence needs have driven the IRA to selectively execute some of its own members – for suspicion about informing, or crimes such as theft. Never has the IRA conducted anything like the bloody self-purges which have wracked a number of terror groups. Abu Nidal may have killed hundreds of his own men in 1987 and 1988, burying some victims in the floor of one of his own compounds.[90] In the years immediately prior to those, the Colombian FARC and the Philippine NPA – separately – became caught up in fears about treason and penetration and left scores of suspected followers in mass graves. The most publicized purge of recent decades was the work of the Japanese Red Army Faction. Isolated for weeks in a safe house, the JRA turned as brutally ugly towards its own as they had been toward unarmed civilians. Self-criticism sessions escalated into screaming and vicious recriminations, until one member after another was tortured and murdered.[91]

No US terror group is known to have committed such a sweeping purge.[92] Among the current 'patriot militias' something like the opposite tendency is evident. The 'weakness' of the American militias – a JRA spokesman would be swift to say – is in fact their belief in individuality. The militia are more a movement than a hard class of tight groups, and they probably ignore many methods of counter-intelligence so self-evident to hard terrorists. In today's US militias, defectors are permitted to drift away. Partners to illegal actions have often turned state's evidence without later being murdered, as they would be so readily in Ireland or Mexico or Peru. A veritable parade of American militiamen and women have testified before courts (whose legitimacy they reject) since the Oklahoma City bombing. Groups everywhere face incredibly close scrutiny by diverse local, country, state, and federal police agencies. The Arizona Viper Militia recognized the counter-intelligence problem clearly: recruits had to swear not only to 'enter into moral combat against enemies of the US Constitution' but additionally to kill anyone trying to infiltrate their group. One counter-intelligence measure used was clandestine review of members' long-distance telephone records to see if there were suspicious calls to such Washington DC entities as the FBI, the Bureau of Alcohol, Tobacco, and Firearms, or other law-enforcement offices. An Arizona policeman nonetheless penetrated the group, taped its proceedings, and landed many members in court on weapons charges.[93]

One American white supremacist has now written a concept paper on 'Leaderless Resistance' as an innovative way around the counter-intelligence problems of hierarchies. Published about 1992, it circulated quietly in the racist underground and now appears on an Internet page. Authored by Louis Ray Beam, military veteran and former Grand Dragon of the Texas Knights of the Ku Klux Klan, the short essay argues for moving beyond traditional 'pyramid'-style power structures, and the cell structure of clandestine movements as well. The cell system's faults are said to be their derivation from communists and the inherent requirements for top–down authority, a large bureaucracy, and plentiful money. While the cell system is better than overt pyramid structures for counter-intelligence, Beam says, they still get penetrated by 'ZOG or ADL intelligence agents' – that is, federal authorities of the US–Zionist–Occupied government and spies from the New York-based Anti-Defamation League.

L. R. Beam's answer is the leaderless resistance of the 'Phantom Cell'. 'All individuals and groups operate independently of each other, and never report to a central headquarters or single leader for direction or instruction ...' Having the same outlook, being independent and responsible, and keeping aware by using computer mail, leaflets, newspapers, and other normal means, the cells and individuals act spontaneously. Beam states that his model is indeed practical, and is based upon the American Revolution's effective 'Committees of Correspondence'. According to the essayist, the ruination of the Koresh compound at Waco, Texas, came when the Federals could focus all their efforts and resources on a single point; 'conversely, the LAST thing federal snoops want ... is a thousand different small phantom cells opposing them'.[94] The concept of leaderless resistance, somewhat new to militias, has already been the practice of some ecoterrorist movements in America.

Weaponry

In its pages on 'Arms' the IRA General Headquarters pamphlet describes a number of techniques which still remain in use in the 1990s by the Provos, including preparation and use of a variety of explosives, special culvert bombs for burial beneath roadways, and deployment of snipers. It is emphasized that 'Almost any small arms weapon can be a guerrilla weapon', including submachine guns, grenades, pistols, automatic rifles, rifles, mortars, and rocket launchers. All these have been deployed in past strikes by the IRA, and all remain in regular service today. In that respect the IRA is very typical of contemporary terrorism.

Dynamite exhilarated one of Europe's first terrorists, German anarchist Joachim Most, who thought its possibilities endless; today a supply of dynamite stolen from a mine or a construction project is not an unusual part of an IRA weapons cache.[95] A stick of the material is a commonplace weapon of a guerrilla column of Shining Path in Peru, where good weapons are less available than they are in Ireland; a larger cache of dynamite is not an unusual find for European police investigating terrorists. Dynamite is also readily available in the United States, and has often been used in bombings. The apparent serial bomber sought by authorities in Atlanta, Georgia, in 1997 has used high-quality dynamite to destroy an abortion clinic and at a bar attracting homosexuals. That bomber has also used the devilish IRA tactic of double-effect bombings, deploying a second device that hurts people rushing to the scene of the first.

Plastic explosive is only passingly mentioned in the *Handbook* as a malleable substance useful for 'cutting' – that is, directing limited explosions, to open a masonry wall, for example. The modern IRA has used it independently and liberally for bombs, such as those carried in a briefcase, or as a detonator for larger fertilizer bombs, just as non-Irish groups often do. Stocks of Czech 'Semtex' *plastique* were once plentiful, and when they became depleted the Libyans replenished them generously, leaving large supplies still in IRA hands despite regular expenditure of the material over the past decade. In a typical IRA attack of 1992, for example, 'volunteers' placed a Semtex bomb within a police perimeter in London, and boasted as follows in a statement:

> Yesterday, and for the second time within four weeks, an active service unit of the IRA succeeded in breaching very heavy security around the seat of British government administration in Whitehall to plant a 5lb Semtex device ... [T]he heart of British administration was paralyzed, and the attendant disruption will serve to focus attention on their Irish war ... [96]

The grenade was an obvious and a potent terror weapon from the beginning: 'Carlos' sprung on the European scene with grenades in attacks such as that against 'Le Drugstore' in Paris in 1974, and other terrorists have continually renewed the implement's infamy, as did Abu Nidal in a series of European attacks on crowds in the 1980s. In March 1997, grenades thrown into a political rally for the Khmer National Party, the main democratic opposition, wounded leader San Rainsy and 112 others and killed 11 people, including American political advisor Ron Abney of Georgia.[97] There is speculation that the grenade attack was a prelude of things to come, arranged by pro-Vietnamese communist Hun Sen, who seized power in a subsequent coup of July 1997. While the IRA makes less use of the grenade than some groups, weapons shipments intended for the IRA but seized by police have often included quantities of grenades.

The IRA's most common weapon in small, short-range, high explosives is something else: the mortar. Acquired on the black market or by theft, or more often rigged in home-made forms in basement workshops, mortars are used from both rural and urban hides, and against both military and civilian targets. Some are armed with explosives that are part Semtex. Many mortar attacks miscarry: 71 such attacks during the mid-1970s produced no injuries. But the IRA became more proficient with time. For instance, a rack of tubes was successfully used against a Royal Ulster Constabulary barracks at Newry in 1985, killing nine people and wounding 32. IRA mortars had a devastating impact during March and July 1994 in well-timed strikes at security force helicopter landing areas.[98] One of the most creative and ingenious use of mortars was popularized by the IRA and by Japanese terrorists of the 'Middle Core Faction' during the 1970s and 1980s. The groups place mortars in the back of an altered vehicle, creating a truly 'mobile launcher' for urban terrorism. The method was used in 1991 in a bold attack on 10 Downing Street. It proved to be a psychological victory that could have had even greater impact had one of the shells not struck a tree in the Prime Minister's garden rather than the residence itself. The IRA carried out another truck-based mortar attack on Britain's Quebec Barracks in Germany in June 1996, but missed the targeted fuel dump. The pattern of IRA use of home-made mortars was underscored twice more in 1996 when police raided a farm south of Dublin and found 44 tubes, shells filled with Semtex, and additional supplies of Semtex. Several months later a bunker near Hackballscross, along the North–South border, was found to hold 21 tubes with frames for mounting.[99]

The sniper rifle is commonly used in many low-intensity conflicts. The IRA have long favored the American Armalite, the principal cause of death for more British soldiers than any other IRA weapon. Another staple of urban terrorism is the readily hidden small submachine gun, sometimes with folding stock, long relied upon by Middle Easterners and Latin Americans. In the 1970s the Czechs ceased production of the famous Skorpion VZ61, and eventually its use became eclipsed by a black-market Israeli Uzis and by the Polish WZ63. Other political killers employ the first-rate German Heckler and Koch MP5, just as do some government special forces. A best-known staple of recognized state armies for 50 years, and more recently a favorite of terrorist bands, is the 30-round capacity Kalashnikov. Its popularity is a reflection of its compact size, high rate of fire, simplicity, superb reliability, and low price.[100] Merely modest rates of accuracy are not a problem for Kalashnikov users; most terrorist acts take place at exceedingly short range.

Apart from bombings, a majority of terror tactics involve using one or two weapons at very close range. Side arms are standard-carry weapons for terrorists. Easily handled by man or woman, the pistol is readily disguised on the person and useful for attack. In 1996 there was a typical instance in America. Two militiamen of the 'Phineas Priesthood', an eastern Washington State group motivated by white racism and the 'Christian Identity' politicized religion, were found to be transporting a number of weapons, including a .357 magnum pistol; each also wore a .22 derringer.[101] Pistols and rifles can be acquired over the counter in a typical American sports shop, a large hardware store, or any of the 168,000 federally licensed arms dealers in the United States. That reality may be what most scares many of the critics of the new American militias: most 'Patriots' have no criminal records, and thus can legally purchase small arms.

Terrorists today acquire weapons by simple legal purchase in some cases, but there are more common sources. One is the black market. Its independent dealers may be readily found in Russia, Eastern Europe, the United States, and innumerable other countries. In the 1970s Switzerland was a geographically convenient locale where terrorists bought weapons for European operations. There are also government suppliers ready to sell quietly, such as the state-run Omnipol, now of the Czech Republic and formerly a chief seller for the Warsaw Pact. The democratic Prime Minister Vaclav Havel came to office determined to end what he thought a dirty business, the export of arms, but economic concerns compelled a change of mind. China is perhaps the world's largest small arms exporter. Recently seized caches have included hundreds of assault rifles on their way into the United States, for which several Chinese officials were later convicted. The case showed that it is dangerous to imagine that 'entrepreneurs' sell Chinese-made weapons without government authorization. But in less authoritarian countries, state-arranged or state-permitted deals with indigenous legitimate producers bring important dollar amounts into the producing country's export accounts. This explains how some weapons reach world markets from the United States, Russia, Brazil, etc. Once abroad, the weapons can be sold to second and third parties, including terror groups.

Theft is also a common source of terrorists' weapons. Many a revolution or insurrection has begun with crude assaults on police stations, armories, or government warehouses in the expectation of getting better arms. Swiss court documents of 1977 reveal that in the first half of the decade of the 1970s, European anarchists stole tons of weapons, including mines, from lightly guarded Swiss armories. They resold the *matériel* from a centrale in Zurich; customers included Carlos and other terrorists from the Basques, the French left, and the IRA. Arsenal thefts have also been a profound problem in America. A US army report of the early 1970s concluded that enough weapons had been stolen by groups such as the IRA from American depots to arm eight battalions (about 8,000 men).[102] American military bases like Camp Lejeune, North Carolina, Devens, Massachusetts, and Fort McCoy in Wisconsin, have experienced more recent thefts or black-market sales by persons with inside connections.[103]

Many American weapons from the black market are illegally sold over the southern border, to Mexico and Central America. Latin American leftist groups of the 1970s and 1980s enjoyed more direct outside suppliers, at times: archives opened in Sofia in 1993 revealed that communist Bulgaria gave tens of millions of dollars-worth of weapons to such Central American parties as the Nicaraguan Sandinistas, the Honduran Communist Party, and Salvadoran insurgent chief Jorge Shafik Handal.[104] Terror groups do not get everything from abroad, however. Mao's Chinese revolutionaries in the 1940s enjoyed use of considerable Soviet *matériel* but also acquired tons of weapons within China. The Filipino NPA fought a protracted insurgency using weapons stolen from the armed forces of the Philippines. And revolutionaries of the 1970s and 1980s in Latin and Central America acquired many weapons by buying, stealing, or capturing them directly from the army's arsenals, from police and soldiers they killed, and from defectors from security forces.

A final source of weapons is manufacture in the underground. The burgeoning literature on the new American 'Patriot' movement indicates that, despite their residency in a country where nearly all own or can obtain personal weapons, the militias also manufacture some of their own.[105] Skilled craftsmen may modify weapons to make them fully automatic, or fashion silencers, or merely 'saw off' shotguns to make them easier to conceal and draw. Bombs are most often fashioned one at a time and for a particular target, ordinarily from materials stolen or purchased separately from different sellers. The 1995 and 1996 militia cases broken by American police nearly always included making or stockpiling illegal explosives, or both. In Georgia, a militia experimented with explosives over a number of weeks, and a police recording indicates they may have contemplated bombing federal targets.[106] In West Virginia, a militia spent $50,000 for floor plans of a FBI building nearby, while also making and stockpiling pipe bombs.[107] In Nevada, two men with tax liens against them prepared a hundred pounds of explosive and wheeled them to an IRS office in Reno, only to have the blasting cap fail.[108] This incident is the latest in a decade-old pattern of actions against federal tax authorities in Western states, especially Arizona, California, and Nevada.[109]

Experimentation with explosives throughout the United States has redoubled recently. The state of Maryland sees pipe bombs used or discovered every month, for example. Two explanations are probable. First there are the examples of two successful truck bombs built of readily available commercial chemicals, one by Islamic radicals in New York City in 1993, and the other, made of fuel oil and ammonium nitrate by army veteran Timothy McVeigh, in Oklahoma City in 1995. Second is the proliferation of information on how such bombs, and smaller pipe bombs, can be made with remarkably little difficulty. Detailed manuals, with names like *The Terrorism Handbook* and *The Anarchist Cookbook* are available through the mail or the Internet. Following Oklahoma City, there are wider sales of such pro-terrorist literature as *The Turner Diaries*, which describes a hypothetical truck bombing of a federal building. The net result is a dramatic escalation of home-made bombs, by tinkerers, by individuals with a personal vendetta, and by political groups. Some of these bombs have killed, like that at the Atlanta Olympics; most are eventually discovered by police because of accidents or the amateurishness of the experimenters.[110]

The home-manufacture of terrorist weaponry is complicated work and not easy to disguise from the curious or prying eyes of neighbors, police, and the retailers upon whom weapons makers may rely. And the work is dangerous – as evidenced by the injuries of terrorists every year. In the United States, there have been such cases at least since the May 1970 day when 'Weathermen' in a New York townhouse blew themselves up while making timer-activated black powder pipe bombs. In East Jerusalem, on 12 April 1996, a hotel room was blown to bits by its occupant; the Hezbollah agent, an accountant and Lebanese Shiite, mishandled the bomb he was carrying; the American C-4 military explosive blinded him and mangled three of his four limbs beyond repair.[111] In Northern Ireland, explosions that hurt terrorists instead of intended victims are common enough so that the expression 'own goals' has been adopted from football to describe the irony and the failure. Sean O'Callaghan, the celebrated IRA defector, writes of his days as a bomb-school instructor, and one occasion when he barely survived an accidental explosion in the course of preparing materials for a training session.[112]

Despite such risks, terror and insurgent forces usually have shops which can make weapons and bombs, modify commercial weapons for special purposes, equip guns with silencers, etc. Two operations for acquiring surface-to-air missiles for the IRA took place in the United States in 1991 and 1992 and involved surface-to-air missiles;[113] one plot involved making components in an engineer's basement, while the other aimed at acquiring missiles in an illegal sale. Peculiarly unable to buy shoulder-launched missiles despite their prevalence on the world market, the IRA has continued to seek other sources for them because of the immense problem of protecting IRA gunmen from British helicopters. Always a staple of British counter-insurgent activity in northern Ireland, the helicopters are useful firing platforms and, as the *Handbook* notes, are also for troop movement and reconnaissance.

General Headquarters chose to print nothing more about them in its 1956 book, not possessing proven tactics for counteracting them. But subsequent efforts have brought down several helicopters.[114]

Case-study of operations: Iran

Today, Iran is an archetype in the studied employment of terrorism for state purposes. It makes an ideal case study of how terrorism operates, for Iranian terrorist activities are broad, diverse, and successful.

Ever since attaining power in 1979, the Muslim extremists of Shia faith have determined upon expansion of their realm, both religious and political. Those two are not readily separable. Nor are Iranians from non-Iranians, in some sense. Lebanese of Hezbollah see themselves, the future of Islam, and the authority of Tehran's government as all linked. The clerics of Hezbollah regard their own state, Lebanon, as artificial and far too secular. What is real to them is the authority of the clerics who rule the esteemed state of Iran. That foreign state is effectively the center of their political universe, as proclaimed in Hezbollah's founding document, issued in Beirut, the 'Open Letter to the Disinherited in Lebanon and the World'.[115] Tehran is thus the capital of a boundaryless movement. Its many strategies for this expansion of influence include normal religious leadership, diplomacy, and a massive expansion of conventional military power. But, in addition, there is a full-dress effort using militants – both Iranian and foreign – to intimidate opponents and attack the power of those resistant to the regime's policies. The operations Tehran conducts in this direction could fill a textbook.

To begin with, Tehran is cautious about how often it lays claim to its terrorism. It loudly flaunts the religious edict promising money for killing novelist Salman Rushdie. But usually, Iranian terrorism is given a dignified veil. Tehran often acts through clandestine agents who issue no proclamations, or it acts through 'cut-outs' – well-known groups like Hamas and Hezbollah – which are Palestinian and Lebanese rather than Persian, and which may also not claim credit in their own name.[116] Violence is required; bloody results are requisite, and even apparent; but the actual directors and perpetrators of violence are hidden to discourage great power retaliation and to protect the state's shaky and limited respectability. Iran wants and indeed has legitimacy; it also wants the world to know it has a capacity to shock the public, as by assassinations of dissidents in foreign capitals.[117]

From Tehran, an operational hub of world-wide militancy, spokes reach outward to the world, helping to transmit and widen Tehran's power, and helping to mobilize the distant foreign Muslim groups. Consider the Iranian embassies and consulates in most of the world's countries. Terror operations can hardly have better helpmates than the diplomatic structure, with its protected buildings, protected diplomatic pouches, and protected cross-border communications. A German secret service study and a German prosecutor's indictment of an Iranian terrorist are among the many European sources documenting heavy employment of the Iranian embassy in Bonn and the consulate in Berlin for conducting intelligence and money-raising for terrorism, for organizational activities related to terrorism, and for other acts of political violence and retaliation in Europe.[118] The German people have in recent years become even more aware of such Iranian activities than are Americans, but commercial interest in bilateral trade has muted their outrage.[119]

Another vital spoke in the Iranian organization is its 'Revolutionary Guards', or Pasdaran. Thousands of these paramilitaries are deployed abroad, especially in the Bekaa Valley and Sudan, where some of them staff guerrilla and terrorist camps in which scores of foreigners are trained. There are an estimated 2,000 Revolutionary Guards in the Sudan today, and these camps, protected by the powerful fundamentalist man behind the Sudanese throne, Hassan al-Turabi, have proved to be sources for many terror acts abroad. At home in Iran, other Pasdaran guards help train indigenous Iranians as well as avid foreigners in a dozen camps within Iran, camps containing as many as 5,000 men and women. The largest of these include the Imam Ali camp in east Tehran where Saudi dissidents train, and the Nahavand camp to the southwest of Tehran, where Lebanese of Hezbollah train.[120] The Revolutionary Guards (essential to Iranian promulgation of Iranian terrorism abroad) once controlled the Office for Islamic Liberation Movements, which in turn handled many formal Iranian relations with Hezbollah and other foreign Shiite terrorists. But in 1983 that office was brought under the Ministry of Foreign Affairs of the government of Iran. This may imply closer control by Tehran; certainly it means more official relations. Hezbollah, which has always taken in tens of millions of dollars annually in Iranian subsidies, is probably now even more officially the pupil and proxy of Tehran.[121]

Thirdly, there is the Iranian Ministry of Intelligence and Internal Security, known by the initials MOIS. Intelligence Minister Ali Fallahian is not embarrassed to boast of how his 'security department' terrorizes counter-revolutionaries at home and abroad. Some agents are entirely secretive; others work as properly accredited Iranian diplomats. For example, a press attaché at the Iranian consulate-general in Istanbul,

Moshen Kargar Azad, is believed to be among those involved in the assassination of Iranian dissidents, some 50 of whom have died in Turkey in recent years. Similarly, in Germany, it was apparently the consulate-general in Berlin, Amani Farani, who was the 'handler' of the hit team of Iranian and Lebanese Hezbollah men who murdered four Kurdish leaders in the Mykonos restaurant in Berlin. Intelligence Minister Fallahian then took credit for his office and regime when speaking on television on 30 August 1992:

> [The counter-revolutionaries] have been forced to flee abroad. We have continued our operations. We are now pursuing them and observing them constantly. We have managed to inflict setbacks on these units outside Iran or on the borders. As you know, one of these units is the Kurdish Democratic Party. Last year, we were able to deal decisive blows to its members.[122]

A fourth, virtually unknown, Iranian mechanism assisting with global terrorism is the 'Organization for the Liberation of Revolutionary Fighters'. This is a classic front group, a legal organization of specialists in international law, economics, finance, and foreign affairs whose narrow mission for the government is freeing Iranians or pro-Iranians in official trouble in foreign states. OLRF is said to employ both overt and covert pressures, but its activities are mostly legal. It moved swiftly in mid 1995 when Argentina was holding seven Lebanese suspected of bombing the Jewish–Argentine friendship center in Buenos Aires. The men were not held or interrogated as long as Argentine law permits, and then they were all declared innocent and released. In that same year, the Organization was reported to be at work to free Kazem Darabi, on trial in Germany for the aforementioned murder of the Kurdish leaders in Berlin. In France, meanwhile, freedom was somehow arranged for Iranian intelligence officers arrested at Swiss request following the 1990 murder of an Iranian opposition leader, Kazem Rajani. Just before they were to be extradited from France, the duo was released and allowed to fly from Paris to Tehran.[123]

Innocent-looking, and not less effective, perhaps, are Iranian state and state-dominated organizations which aid schools and mosques abroad in ways that enhance Islam's political power, cover unusual financial transactions, and create social opportunities to recruit potential fighters and terrorists. Iran (like Saudi Arabia and other countries) uses such foundations, funds, and charities to supply aid to many institutions in Afghanistan (with its Islamic schools of terrorism and guerrilla warfare) and many other countries in the promising southern reaches of Eurasia. It is an Iranian charity backed by the government, the 15th

Khordad Foundation, that brazenly offers the $2 million bounty for the death of Salman Rushdie, the novelist accused of blasphemy.[124] The politically pregnant programs of aid and of religious charity managed by such entities – whose names include the Martyrs' Foundation, the Foundation of the Oppressed, etc. – make gifts to families of those deceased in conflict, donate large sums to Islamic centers of religious study abroad and foreign mosques, and tender humanitarian aid to communities made desperate by natural or man-made violence. Such programs are both the model for, and the mirror of, smaller, localized efforts by Hezbollah, the Iranian-supported Lebanese organization which feeds the hungry, helps hospitals, and performs other humanitarian services, even as it dispatches one terrorist cell after another to die blowing up targets in Israel or the occupied territories. Indeed, the parallel between Iranian humanitarian operations and those of Hezbollah is an excellent one, since it is Iranian money that pays for much of Hezbollah's charity.[125]

A sixth spoke, and easily the most unofficial, is Tehran's relationship to actual or apparent 'freelancers' of international terrorism. These are the least affiliated and thus the hardest of all to trace; their inspiration may or may not be Iranian; their operational ties to Tehran may be loose or nonexistent. Yet they can be an ally to Iranian revolutionary policy in a rich way no state official can match, while never embarrassing Tehran. By some new evidence, this may apply to Osama Bin Laden. Well known for patronage of anti-Soviet *mujahideen* in the Afghan war, this Saudi found disfavor in his home country, relocated to the Sudan, and became a suspect in international terrorism of pro-Muslim varieties. His Sunni – not Shiite – faith places one more increment of distance between himself and the revolutionary Iranian clerics and civil rulers. Someone like Bin Laden needs no direct guidance, and his importance may be enhanced, not mitigated, by the absence of hard links to a sovereign government. He can patronize terrorism and offer Tehran deniability while carefully avoiding strikes on any person or institution favored by the distant patron regime.[126]

As a final method of exporting Iranian influence, Tehran cultivates alliances with sovereign states that share its ambitions. The closeness of bilateral relations with the Sudan is now well known. Less noticed are Tehran's relations with Damascus. There are operational, continuous, and highly useful connections from Iran to Syria. On the surface Iran's relationship with Syria is awkward: the former is religious, Shiite, revolutionary and fiercely anti-Western; the latter is secular, Alawite-ruled, concerned about stability and a post-Assad transition (he is elderly and sick) and determined at present to keep communications to Europe and America open. The Iranian dream is for a region dominated by Shia Islam; the Syrian interest is pan-Arab and not religious. But the two states share a long background of radicalism, use terror for state purposes such as the taking of Western hostages, and oppose certain regional powers like Iraq. They therefore cooperate.

Iran thus illustrates the strong roles which terrorism may play in statecraft. Since 1979, by itself through two subsequent decades, and often in league with other groups, and states like Sudan and Syria, Tehran has enhanced its power in and outside the region. It drove American and French military forces from Lebanon in 1983; the West 'hurriedly ran away from three Muslims who loved martyrdom', boasted Hezbollah cleric Sadiq al-Musawi.[127] It has itself amassed remarkable – though not complete – influence of political, economic, and clandestine varieties in Lebanon, while maintaining strong relations with rival Syria and winning new plaudits from Turkey, a NATO linchpin. Iran has not merely matched Syria's program of violence but exceeded it, in its number of actions, in their effects; and in the brazenness of the actions. A string of dead abroad grows longer monthly. Slapped with sanctions, Iran continues to draw large European contracts, to amass conventional Russian arms, to further invest in chemical, biological, and nuclear programs. It has worked a deal with its famous enemy Iraq whereby both help the latter smuggle oil beneath UN barriers. Iran's revolutionary zeal has remained strong – despite an ever-youthful population. The regime holds up the bright flame, and many Muslims world-wide look to it. Hezbollah cleric Ibrahim al-Amin has proclaimed, 'Islam rules through the regime in Iran, and it will eventually rule the entire earth.'[128] That is of course but a dream. But it is one which Iranian operations strive to bring to fruition.

Conclusion

The contemporary terrorist who is successful is a calculating, responsive, innovative being. He is first of all mentally prepared. There are old manuals by leftists and nationalists, like Marighella and Mao. The new *Turner Diaries* and various Internet essays serve white racists. There is a long array of published works on technical aspects of the necessary crafts. Doubtless there are new books of inspiration and instruction which are presently known only in the clandestine world. The terrorist studies intelligence, and he is drilled in counter-intelligence. He or she seeks to know all one can about the enemy, from the national level strategic targets to the operational and tactical level

Syrian–Iranian cooperation: An aspect of international terrorist operations

Syria under the governance of Hafez al Assad has long been a prime sponsor of Palestinian, Kurdish, Turkish, international communist, and other terrorists who require operational assistance, such as safe haven, weapons, money, intelligence support, and training. It still is. When Lebanon surprised the world in February 1997 by arresting several members of the Japanese Red Army, long resident in the Bekaa, no one mentioned that the JRA chief, a woman named Fusako Shigenobu, maintains her residence in Damascus and goes untouched. When the Popular Front for the Liberation of Palestine murdered two Israeli hikers in mid-1995, a boast of the action was published by George Habash's PFLP office in Damascus.[129] When Turkey carried its war against Kurdish insurgency over the border into the PKK headquarters in northern Iraq, leader Abdullah Ocalan relocated his base to the Syrian side of the Turkish border. During the mid-1990s he thus moved more often within Syria and the Syrian-controlled Bekaa Valley than in Iraq.[130]

Iran shares Syrian contempt for all these targeted regimes, especially Israel and Turkey. And Iran has ties to Syria, well described by a recipient of the patronage of both states: the spiritual head of Hezbollah, Ayatollah Sayyid Muhammad Husayn Fadlallah. 'Syria and Iran have a joint strategy based on the struggle against Israel and imperialism. We would like to reiterate that our relationship with Damascus is a strategic one based on Syria's stands, which are hostile to Zionism and US colonialism … We take a strategic view of relations with Syria. If problems occur from time to time, we do not believe they are serious enough to affect this strategic integration.'[131]

Syrian embassies in the Middle East are closely involved in cash and intelligence assistance to terror groups, just as are Iranian diplomatic entities. Damascus puts its official structures in the service of Tehran where it deems it appropriate, as when sponsoring high-level meetings to coordinate terrorist organizational activity – literally, terror 'summits'.

Weapons shipments from Iran to Hezbollah recipients in Lebanon go via Syria, and must go with Syrian permission, since many Hezbollah camps are in Syrian-controlled parts of Lebanon, including Janta near the border.[132] Iran's embassy in Damascus is well known as a prime facilitator of terrorist liaisons.

Hamas, well known as a recipient of Iranian cash aid, has received some of that via the Iranian embassy in Damascus. One conduit has been Imad al-Alami, an engineer who travels regularly between the two capitals and is thought to reside in Damascus. Reportedly he serves there as the contact point for Hamas.[133] Syrian state interest in maintaining relations with Iran and with Iranian-dominated terror groups like Hamas is reflected in financial transactions in Damascus and in other kinds of quiet operations requiring, at minimum, 'benign neglect' by Syrian officials. These include permitting free transit to terrorists, as when in early 1994 four Hamas members going to Iran for terrorist training used Damascus as their travel route.[134]

persons, places and things that allow actions taken to make the appropriate impact. The most sophisticated of today's terrorists use computers to store data on membership, targets, and finances, and work with scanners and keyboards and electronic mail to send illegal propaganda and communications across international lines.

For more physical and tactile training, there are still schools of violent arts for foreign students in such Cold War locations as the former Yugoslavia, Yemen, Lebanon, and Afghanistan. There are also new schools managed by new personalities and groups – in some of those same locations, and in new areas of southwest Asia, northern Africa, and the United States. Some states pay for or protect these schools; in other cases the 'faculty' do not have or want such contact. From the tent flaps and doors of such places there emerge women and men who are better skilled at fighting, killing, use of small arms, bombs, document forgery, and the like. The graduates have dispersed world-wide, and live in innumerable countries, as do the famous 'Afghani'. Indeed, today's terrorists have as many foreign connections as did the international left of 1970 or 1980. This is true even of what might be taken for inwardly focused groups. The religious zealots of Lebanon's Hezbollah have cells in Asia and Latin America; Aum Shinrikyo had a larger membership in Russia than in Japan; Canadian neoNazis look to German and American comrades for inspiration, and to the latter, especially, for an occasional training opportunity or a friendly foreign speaker. Foreign connections include not only sympathetic persons or allied outposts, but also convenient way-stations, nodes in the international highway system which are inadequately policed but frequented by foreigners whose contact terrorists seek.

Financial aid and arms may flow in from abroad too, as from private donors, web site solicitations, foreign states, and internationally-minded private groups, be they legal or not. International organized crime remains as central as always to distributing and moving arms. But while some terrorists get along with remarkably few weapons – the same Colt .45 is used year after year to kill the men November 17th targets in Greece – insurgents must broaden and deepen their networks, or they die.

Technical and organizational structures vary widely at the end of the 1990s. As Chapter 4 will indicate, groups from Hamas to Sendero Luminoso to the Algerian GIA have killed as frequently with the knife as with any more elaborate apparatus. The psychological and political impact remains more important than the device used. But mature groups do invariably move beyond, towards more complicated weapons and new modes of fighting and winning attention, to include even weapons of mass destruction. Organizationally, the classic cell structure and hierarchy still predominate, but so too flourish their opposites, found in the American militias, ecoterrorists, or autonomous Islamic extremist groups where decentralization may be the prized key. Meanwhile, some older guerrilla groups have been devoting less time to insurgency and more to evolving into stable, businesslike managers of complex systems. FARC runs its own government within Colombia, while the PLO continues to adjust itself to ruling its own new territories.

It is apparent that while terrorists most love action, their success depends on intelligence, organization, training, etc. Individuals may well join the underground for its action, but they learn that to survive there they must spend more time debating, planning, rehearsing, and waiting than in using weapons. Second, the hallmark of the terrorists who gain their objectives is innovation. From tactical twists, to new weapons, to strategic shifts into peace talks, the most accomplished groups are showing flexibility and imagination, not just individual technical skills.

Notes

1. IRA General Headquarters, *Handbook for Volunteers of the Irish Republican Army: Notes on Guerrilla Warfare* (publisher unknown; 1956), p. 5. This is not to be confused with a newer IRA manual, called the *Green Book*, which will be discussed shortly, and which explicitly quotes from Mao (the 'Three General Rules of Discipline and the Eight Reminders').
2. The diversity and sources of IRA explosives and weapons are described by many of the specialized sources noted in this chapter. including Tim Pat Coogan, *The IRA: A History* (Niwot, CO: Roberts Rinehart, 1993). Also see such brief reviews as the US State Department, *Patterns of Global Terrorism: 1990* (Washington DC: GPO, April, 1991), p. 17.
3. Coogan, *The IRA*, p. 356. Vietnamese communists used similar tactics against South Vietnamese and American helicopters during their war.
4. Dr Daniel Fitz-Simons, 'A Snapshot of the IRA Today'. Lecture at Command and Staff College, Marine Corps University (12 February 1997). IRA attacks of the mid 1990s also reveal this pattern.
5. Coogan, *The IRA*, p. 414, citing the IRA *Green Book*.
6. A dozen prominent books of the last two decades have detailed the IRA's connections with foreign terrorist groups, including Coogan's *The IRA* (see Ch. 23 discussing arms traffic and other contacts), and John Laffin's *The PLO Connections* (London: Corgi, 1982), pp. 102–3; 122–3, emphasizing training and high-level meetings between the PLO and the IRA.
7. Over the years, the UK-based intelligence journal *Foreign Report* has detailed comings and goings through Greece of Palestinian terrorists, noting even that Fatah owned a 'safe house' outside the Athens airport which was protected on the perimeter by Greek policemen. Like all European countries, Greece has also been the scene of attacks by Palestinians.
8. Investigations after the shooting of Pope John Paul II revealed Bulgarian state

complicity in many aspects of terrorism and organized crime, such as arms trafficking. The Pope's would-be assassin, Mehmet Ali Agca, stayed in Sofia for 55 days before going to Rome for the attack, as *Foreign Report* noted (4 July 1991) in its last comment on the old case. Two full-length accounts of the assassination and Bulgaria's role were written by Paul Henze of RAND and Claire Sterling, then an Italy-based journalist.

9. Abu Abbas was a member of the PLO executive council and chief of the Palestine Liberation Front; he was greeted at Belgrade airport and escorted away by officials from the PLO, which had an embassy there. Other incidents of similar indulgence of terrorists include a 1978 denial of extradition when West Germany sought four Red Army Faction members in Zagreb, and protection from foreign police of the celebrated 'Carlos the Jackal' in 1976 when he arrived in Belgrade on an airplane from Algiers. See 'Why Abbas Chose Yugoslavia', *Wall Street Journal* (23 October 1985), and 'A Look at the Yugoslav–Libya Link', in the European edition (6 June 1986), both by Rep. Jim Courter of New Jersey.

10. Documents covering the years 1979–81 discussed KGB intelligence service school training of terrorists from Cyprus, Lebanon, and Chile. 'There were a particularly large number of them at the time', noted a news report on a Russian government commission's continuing work in Communist Party of the Soviet Union archives; Moscow Russian Television Network (13 August 1992); repr. 23 September 1992 by Joint Publications Research Service: JPRS, *Terrorism*, p. 23.

11. An IRA-related example occurred in 1973. A Cypriot-registered ship of nearly 300 tons, *Claudia*, tried to move 250 rifles, 240 small arms, anti-tank mines, and explosives to the IRA; Coogan, *The IRA*, p. 328. In the mid 1980s there was a report of a major weapons movement from eastern Europe to Africa, and it had a Cypriot connection. More recent terrorism cases are noted above in Chapter 3.

12. Laffin, *The PLO Connections*, p. 103.

13. For example, the Greek news source *Alithia* (Nicosia) reported on 26 August 1992 that Abu Nidal might target one or more PLO cadres who were on Cyprus; in JPRS, *Terrorism* (28 August 1992), p. 22. Other indicators of PLO presence on the island have been in *Foreign Report*.

14. *New York Times* (9 March 1993). Cyprus is a scene of continuous struggle between Palestinian terrorists and Israeli intelligence and police services. There have been deaths on the island for this reason. See for example the repeated references to Cyprus on the terrorist incident list in Patrick Seale, *Abu Nidal: A Gun For Hire* (New York: Random House, 1992), pp. 47–9.

15. *Foreign Report* (21 May 1980).

16. The short-lived French group FANE was suspected, and while there was good cause for doubting that, FANE remained the 'favorite' suspect of most commentators, and is occasionally so mentioned even today. Ten years after the bombing, *Manchester Guardian Weekly*'s Peter Lenon writing from Paris stated that the infamous Rue Copernic bombing of 1980 'turned out to be the work of the Palestinians'; 'Le Pen and the Kristallnacht of Carpentras' (27 May 1990). Regarding such ambiguities of left and right in Europe, see Chapter 5.

17. The ten letter bombs postmarked in Cyprus were recalled in a news story on a later series of letter bombs sent to the United States from Egypt, and intercepted by US police in Washington DC and Leavenworth KA; *Washington Post* (4 January 1997).

18. The source on Hamas operations on Cyprus is the Israeli Ambassador. 'Israeli Government Asks Cyprus to Cooperate Against Hamas', *Alithia* (Nicosia; 10 March 1996), in FBIS, *Terrorism* (16 May 1996), p. 4.

After other Islamic terrorists struck the Egyptian embassy in Islamabad in 1995, Cyprus was one place that felt ground tremors. One of the groups that claimed that explosion in Pakistan, the Islamic Movement of Victory or of Martyrs, apparently circulated a leaflet in Cyprus warning that it could be the next target area. Threatening especially Israeli targets on the island, the leaflet read, in part:

> In the name of God. This is why we are giving sincere and honest advice to all young people on the island of Cyprus, to this friendly country and its people, to keep away from every Israeli organization, embassy, and association in Cyprus and all countries so that they may not become a target of injuries and so that there may not be innocent victims in our battles with the Zionist enemy. We will strike with force, violence, and without mercy. In the name of God. If you worship God he will bless you and steady your steps.

Quoted in *Alithia Tis Dhevteras* (Nicosia), 4 December 1995, in FBIS, *Terrorism* (1 February 1996), p. 2.

19. Turkish sources have often pointed to PKK personnel and safe havens on Cyprus. The issue of PKK bases on Greece proper is more notable. Bill Gertz reports that CIA sources tell of official Greek support to the Kurdish PKK. During the 1990s the Greek government's National Intelligence Service helped supply a training ground on the island of Euboea, where weapons and explosives were used, as well as a safe house near Athens used by PKK operatives working in Europe. However, when control of the PASOK party passed from Andreas Papandreaou to Costas Simitis in January 1996, the Greek government moved to reduce the relationship, writes Gertz; *Washington Times* (10 September 1996).

20. There is a new antiterrorism pact between Cyprus and Israel, signed in early 1995; 'Minister to Sign Antiterrorism Accord with Israel', Nicosia Cyprus Broadcasting Corporation Radio Network, 9 January 1995, in JPRS, *Terrorism* (19 January 1995), p. 50. The growth of Israeli operations on the island is enumerated by *Foreign Report* (26 November 1998).

21. *L'Expansion* (Paris; 6 March 1996), *FBIS-TDD* (14 May 1996), p. 81. The US media has shown no awareness of the clandestine life of Cyprus, but a happy exception is William Safire, 'Primakov in Cyprus', *New York Times* (2 July 1998).

22. See 'Special Report: Iran, Syria Still Flood Mideast with Forgeries', COMPASS Newswire (18 October 1995). *Foreign Report* on 22 June 1995 noted that Hezbollah agent Abu Hadi Hamadi of Lebanon had just been in Cyprus to reorganize party offices already there; 'Hezbollah plans to use Cyprus as a transit base for agents traveling to Europe'. See also the Government Accounting Office report, *Counterfeit US Currency Abroad: Issues and US Deterrence Efforts* (Washington DC: GPO, February 1996), p. 48.

23. Laffin, *The PLO Connections*, p. 102, etc.

24. For example, Adil Abd al-Quddus, an Islamic Jihad leader with a background in the war in Afghanistan, resided in Yemen and engaged in terrorist work with Yemenis. Yemen would not extradite him to Egypt, despite Cairo's request. The man later moved to the Sudan, and then to Austria. More troubling are Yemen's government-subsidized Koranic schools called 'scientific institutes' which Egypt describes as training camps for Islamic Jihad. *Foreign Report* (28 March 1996). March 1998 brought a new report in a related publication, Jane's *Pointer*, of a Yemeni terrorism leader named Abd-al-Majid al-Zandani attending a terrorists' summit in the Sudan the previous October (p. 11). The US State Department identifies Hamas and Palestine Islamic Jihad in Yemen; *Patterns of Global Terrorism: 1997* (Washington, DC: GPO, April 1998), p. 28.

Osama Bin Laden's organization has attacked Americans in Yemen, according to the 27 August 1998 *Foreign Report* excerpt of an alleged CIA paper; see also Yossi Melman's essay in the *Los Angeles Times* (23 August 1998). He reports an abortive 1992 attempt by Bin Laden to bomb the US embassy in Yemen. For news on attacks in 1998 in Yemen and the Bin Laden connection, see the Telegraph Group Limited's wire and Internet report of 3 January 1999, *Washington Post* of 30 December 1998, and the *Christian Science Monitor* newswire for 4 January 1999.

25. Dr Roy Godson's National Strategy Information Center in Washington DC and Mr Peter Lupsha are among the first in American policy studies to do useful work on the post-Cold War problem of 'gray areas' and 'gray-area phenomena'.

26. Relying upon the Cologne office of the Federal Office for the Protection of the Constitution and other sources, *Stern* (Hamburg) published a remarkable and detailed account 'Germany Could be a Scene of Terrorist Attacks' on 5 January 1995, pp. 90–2. *Focus* (Munich) reported on Hamas activities in Aachen and Berlin (15 March 1996), pp. 57–62, with quotations of rally speakers shouting for the blood of the king of Jordan, Israeli Jews, etc. Meanwhile, the Belgian press is watching Antwerp and nearby cities. Its reports cover Arab and North African activity that includes arms shipments intended for Algerian terrorists fighting back home. Antwerp is also the port at which authorities intercepted an incoming ship with a peculiar cargo – a massive mortar, believed intended for a terror attack somewhere on the continent. Iranian aid was apparently involved. On the small arms traffic going the other direction (to Algeria, etc.), see *Le Vif-L'Express* (Brussels: 8–14 March, 1996), p. 20, and other reports translated by and appearing in issues of JPRS, *Terrorism*.

27. The most detailed published report on Iguazu may be that of *Ma'Ariv/Shabat* (Tel Aviv: 7 October 1994), in JPRS, *Terrorism* (1 November 1994), pp. 6–ll. Less convincing is 'Trafficker Claims Knowledge of Embassy Attack', in *Buenos Aires* (Buenos Aires) (26 November 1992), in JPRS, *Terrorism* (2 December 1992), p. 2. Hezbollah/'Islamic Jihad' claimed credit for the attack on Israel's embassy in Buenos Aires, and provided a videotape of the group's reconnaissance of the target to support the statement. As foreign attentions focused on the problems at Cuidad del Este, the 5 March 1998 issue of a Brazilian daily *Folhas de Sao Paulo* reported fundamentalists leaving their hiding places to relocate elsewhere in Latin America.

28. ETA members remained in Nicaragua even after 1990 elections in which Daniel Ortega gave power over to democracy and Violeta Chamorro, according to *Patterns of Global Terrorism: 1990*, p. 23. The annual report for 1993 and the world press covered the discovery of an arms cache in Managua connected to ETA. Basque ETA terrorist fugitives still live in Cuba; eight were named by *ABC*, a Spanish newspaper, cited in *Foreign Report* (4 December 1997).

29. Algeria opened itself up to sympathetic foreigners for training about 1968. Palestinians were in evidence there continuously thereafter; for example, a Fatah camp trained Swedes in 1969. Others arriving for training in the early 1970s included Italian and German leftists and members of Marxist nationalist organizations like the Breton and Corsican separatists, the IRA, and ETA. The ETA came in considerable numbers, especially after 1975, and Algeria was probably their most favored foreign locale after southern France. One source is Robert Clark, *The Basque Insurgents: ETA, 1952–1980* (Madison, WI: University of Wisconsin Press, 1984), pp. 233–5.

Algeria was also a long-favored place for hijackers seeking safe haven. The PFLP's first hijacking was of an El Al plane; they took it to Algeria, and 32 Jewish hostages spent five weeks there. In later years, American hijackers occasionally

        chose Algeria as a place to flee.
30. *ABC* (Madrid: 29 March 1996), in FBIS, *Terrorism* (5 June 1996), p. 122.
    Hezbollah is also of concern to Spanish authorities, having been identified on at
    least one occasion for smuggling explosives for attacks in Europe, according to
    Paul Wilkinson, 'Hezbollah – A Critical Appraisal', *Jane's Intelligence Review*
    (August 1993), p. 370.
31. Marighella, *Urban Guerrilla Minimanual*, p. 22.
32. Southern Poverty Law Center, *False Patriots: The Threat of Antigovernment
    Extremists* (Montgomery, AL: Southern Poverty Law Center, 1996), pp. 20–1.
    Morris Dees, who heads the center, and his team have been bold in its publishing
    and in its legal pursuit of right-wing extremists, especially the KKK. The many
    other reports of right-wing training areas include books about The Order, such as
    Stephen Singular, *Talked to Death: The Life and Murder of Alan Berg* (New York,
    Beech Tree Books, 1987).
33. See the 3 July 1996 stories on the Arizona Viper Militia in the *Providence Journal
    Bulletin*, the *New York Times*, etc.
34. Dale Jacobi, reportedly in charge of religious instruction, and Rodney Skurdal, the
    security head, arrived together at the compound in September 1995. They were
    adherents of Christian Identity and gave seminars in which they spoke out against
    Jews and Blacks; *New York Times* (28 April 1996).
35. Morris Dees makes and supports this argument in *Gathering Storm: America's
    Militia Threat* (New York: HarperCollins, 1996); see pp. 10–12, 22–4, etc. Brent
    L. Smith found that of 173 persons indicted by the FBI for terrorism between 1980
    and 1989, '103 were members of or associated with a loose coalition of right-wing
    groups frequently referred to as being part of the Christian Identity Movement.'
    Quoted by Mark S. Hamm, 'Terrorism, Hate Crime, and Anti-government
    Violence: A Review of the Research', in *The Future of Terrorism: Violence in the
    New Millennium*, ed. Harvey W. Kushner (Thousand Oaks CA: Sage Publications,
    1998), p. 77.
36. Peter Kevin Langan ('Commander Pedro'), Scott Anthony Stedeford, Kevin
    William McCarthy, Mark Thomas, and Michael William Brescia have been
    indicted for bank robbery and use of the proceeds to buy weapons and fund
    recruiting. Guthrie had attended Hayden Lake gatherings of Aryan Nations and
    espoused Christian Identity ideas, and one of the group's safe houses was in
    Elohim City, 'a heavily armed Christian Identity community in Oklahoma near the
    Arkansas border'. Langan is a self-proclaimed ordained minister in a church
    believed affiliated with the KKK. He and the others also favored *The Turner
    Diaries*, which was the model for the original rightist terror group The Order, and
    like that organization ARA donated some bank raid proceeds to other extremist
    groups. There is a sensationalistic profile of the Aryan Republican Army in the
    Washington Post (13 February 1997).
37. The normally reserved *New York Times* reports that foreign support *is* the PKK's
    main strength, 'especially from Syria', proffers evidence, and judges that Syria
    uses PKK as an instrument to press Turkey 'to accept certain political demands,
    especially in a quarrel over water, and regarding Turkey's new military
    cooperation with Israel' (3 July 1996).
38. The State Department's Bureau of Intelligence and Research documented the Dev
    Sol presence in a Lebanese border region under Syrian control in the autumn and
    winter of 1990–91; see the INR letter of 11 December 1991 repr. as Appendix IV
    to Daniel Pipes' monograph *Syria Beyond the Peace Process* (Washington DC:
    Washington Institute for Near East Policy, 1996).

39. Evidence has been assembled by Daniel Pipes, ibid., pp. 59–64.

40. One Jane's freelancer argues that Pakistan is the country that trains the most international terrorists; I agree only that it has a place somewhere in the top ten. Thomas Hunter, 'Bomb School: International Terrorist Training Camps', *Jane's Intelligence Review* (March 1997), p. 136.

41. *Al-Watan Al-'Arabi* (Paris) (6 January 1995), in JPRS, *Terrorism* (19 January 1995); Anthony Davis, 'Foreign Combatants in Afghanistan', *Jane's Intelligence Review*, (July 1993), pp. 327–31; Tim Weiner, 'Blowback from the Afghan Battlefield', *New York Times Sunday Magazine* (13 March 1994).

42. Weiner, ibid., p. 53.

43. The Sudanese admission was noted by the Heritage Foundation's admirable Middle East analyst Jim Phillips; *Washington Times* (27 April 1994). Coverage of the Sudanese training camps has appeared since 1992 in the *New York Times*; see for example Chris Hedges' article in the 24 December 1994 issue, which ends with these notes: 'The decision to increase the Sudan's role in regional conflicts has been accompanied by a new stridency against the West. The state-controlled television spends hours each day broadcasting messages calling for a 'holy war' against 'infidels', playing martial music as armed militias march across the screen and flashing pictures of the latest martyrs.'

44. An excellent unofficial source on Sudanese terrorism and the international response is the 'Military Issues Paper' written in 1996–97 by Mr Art J. Schoenwetter at Command and Staff College, Marine Corps University, Quantico, VA, titled 'Should the US Attack Sudan?'

45. 'Hundreds of battle-hardened Afghan rebels have slipped into the northern Indian state of Jammu and Kashmir and are fighting alongside local Muslim separatists and raising the level of the insurgency against Indian troops, intelligence officials said today'; *New York Times* (24 August 1993). Examples of Indian reports of Pakistani involvement include 'Pakistan, Terrorism and Kashmir', from the Global Hindu Electronic Network, via Internet (8 February 1996), and 'Top Pakistan-Trained Militants Killed in Kashmir', Doordarshan Television Network (Delhi), 15 November 1992, in JPRS, *Terrorism* (2 December 1992), p. 19.

46. The estimate of the Indian Home Minister was 18,000 (*Washington Post*, 7 June 1998), but by mid 1998 the *Washington Post* and the *New York Times* were indicating 20,000 dead as the minimum, while some Muslim groups place the figure at over twice that high. Most who die are civilians.

47. See for one recent report the *Washington Post* (7 June 1998). The State Department's annual report on terrorism has long used such euphemisms as 'There were credible reports … ' of Pakistani help to militants in Kashmir. Now it uses stronger language and offers concrete cases, such as that of Harakat ul-Ansar (HUA); see recent issues of State's *Patterns of Global Terrorism*. After a US ban the group has renamed itself ul-Mujahideen.

48. Hunter, 'Bomb School'; multiple reports repr. in JPRS, *Terrorism* (28 August and 11 September 1992); and Richard Ehrlich, 'Outsiders Join 'jihad' in Kashmir', *Washington Times*, 2 November 1992.
   Pakistan has also been helpful to the United States on many issues. For example, the government is credited with aiding US authorities in apprehending and extraditing murderer Mir Aimal Kasi.

49. Yossi Melman, *The Master Terrorist: The True Story Behind Abu Nidal* (New York: Adama Books, 1986), pp. 22–3, and Seale, *Abu Nidal*, pp. 11–24.

50. Hunter, 'Bomb School'; and *Patterns of Global Terrorism: 1995*.

51. See veteran Middle East correspondent John Laffin's Ch. 9, 'Schools for Terror',

in *The PLO Connections*. British authorities such as Laffin and Robert Moss, the long-time editor of *Foreign Report*, covered such training camps in their writing at a time when most mainstream American journalists and scholars still resisted evidence on the subject. The Israeli haul of PLO documents from Lebanon has been sifted by Ray S. Cline and Yonah Alexander, *Terrorism: The Soviet Connection* (New York: Crane Russak, and the Center for Strategic and International Studies, 1984). Former Soviet dissident Vladimir Bukovsky reports on Soviet training of foreign radicals, insurgents, and terrorists in 'Secrets of the Central Committee', *Commentary* (October, 1996), see pp. 38–40. His book based on 3,000 pages of documents, *Judgment in Moscow*, has been published in French and German.

The eventual foundation of a Palestinian government in small parts of Palestine has been rich in ironies, one of which is that today there are many middle-level and senior PLO men and women, in the police departments and other governmental structures, with terrorist training in their backgrounds, while their work day-to-day is to contain the new terrorists of Hamas and Hezbollah in the name of stability.

52. Special Report, 'Terror in the Heart of Japan: The Aum Shinrikyo Doomsday Cult', in the English-language *Japan Times* (Tokyo: July 1995), pp. 5–39.
53. *The Straits Times* (Singapore: 1 May 1995); *The Daily Yomiuri* (26 April 1995); Kyodo News Service, in English (19 May 1995); Reuters (2 June 1995), in JPRS, *Terrorism*. Another good source on Russian links to Aum, on such subjects as AK-47s and laser technology, is D. W. Brackett, *Holy Terror: Armageddon in Tokyo* (New York: Weatherhill, 1996; uncorrected proof).
54. See for example the aforementioned *Minimanual of Urban Warfare* by Marighella, p. 39.
55. Clark, *ETA*, pp. 209–10. The book by Clark, now teaching at George Mason University in Virginia, has not been superseded by a better one in English, and remains a prime source, as for the three authors of a newer (1993) article on ETA in *Terrorism and Political Violence*.
56. A good illustration of this intelligence work occurred in December 1995, when ETA car bombed a Madrid target and killed six civilians working for the Defense Ministry. Police determined that the well-planned operation had important surveillance help from anonymous ETA 'legals'. *El Mundo* (Madrid: 12 December 1995), in FBIS, *Terrorism* (1 February 1996), p. 104.
57. Clark, *ETA*, pp. 210–11.
58. 'Biodata, Comments on ETA Leadership Residing in France', *Tiempo* (Madrid: 14 December 1987), repr. in JPRS, *Terrorism* (3 March 1988) pp. 48–50.
59. Francisco S. Llera, Jose M. Mata, and Cynthia L. Irwin, 'ETA: From Secret Army to Social Movement – The Post-Franco Schism of the Basque Nationalist Movement', *Terrorism and Political Violence*, 5:3 (autumn 1993), p. 123. The document seizure occurred in 1987.
60. Ibid., p. 121. Herri Batasuna could produce as many as a quarter-million votes in 1987; it has since lost some of its support. Polls show a public weariness with Basque terrorism and in January 1988 all other Basque parties signed an agreement opposing ETA's terrorism. Nonetheless, ETA is 'increasingly committed to a dual strategy of electoral and armed struggle', according to Llera *et al.*
61. ANO manpower was estimated at 500 in 1988 by the Pentagon's *Terrorist Group Profiles* (Washington, DC: GPO, November 1988), p. 5. The figure rose into the low thousands in the latter 1980s, only to sink again with purges and deaths of some 600 cadres in 1987–88. Current strength is difficult to judge, but must be no

more than several hundred, according to US government reports and Israel's Dr Ariel Merari, of the Jaffee Center for Strategic Studies at Tel Aviv University, lecturing at The Heritage Foundation, Washington DC, 2 October 1996.

62. Displeased by the presence of Abu Nidal's organization in Poland, the US State Department prepared a damning White Paper on the problem, and then used it as a lever to get Warsaw to expel Nidal. Enough was apparently done to satisfy the State Department and pre-empt publication of the 29-page report, but its existence was noted in the open press.

63. Seale, *Abu Nidal*, and James Adams' article on financing of terrorism in *The Sunday Times* (3 November 1991), repr. in *Current News: Terrorism* (Washington DC: Department of Defense: December 1991).

64. Patrick Seale, the British scholar, covers such harsh facts as those on the Nidal prisons in his book. Another important book on the Nidal group, which tends to confirm Seale's dark view, is written by an Israeli, Yossi Melman, *The Master Terrorist*.

65. Samuel M. Katz, *Israel versus Jibril: The Thirty-Year War Against a Master Terrorist* (New York: Paragon House, 1993), pp. 124–9.

66. *Foreign Report* (13 July 1995).

67. IRA, *Handbook for Volunteers*, p. 7.

68. Ibid., p. 7.

69. In a typical case, dated 1990, British police broke up an IRA cell operating in mainland Britain, seizing 50 kilos of 'Semtex', diverse firearms, car bombs, disguises, combat clothing, and a target list that included politicians, businessmen, members of the armed services, and a 'well-thumbed copy of *Who's Who*'. Press Association (London: 22 January 1992), in FBIS–*Western Europe* (23 January 1992), p. 6.

70. When ten Red Army Faction terrorists left West Germany for the East, the GDR, 'gave them refuge – in exchange for long debriefings with the insatiably curious Stasi,' according to a retrospective article about hijacker Monica Haas by the *Los Angeles Times* (27 February 1996). Stasi files demonstrate that there was an accord between its chief and the PLO security boss Abu Iyad (Salah Khalaf, since killed). 'Comrade Minister Erich Mielke' offered weapons, while the PLO's duty would be to provide East Germany information on West German intelligence activities in Beirut. Jonas Bernstein, 'When in Need, Terrorist Groups Turned Eastward', *Insight* (21 January 1991).

71. Cline and Alexander, *The Soviet Connection*, pp. 44–5.

72. The two RAF documents may be found in Dennis A. Pluchinsky, 'Germany's Red Army Faction: An Obituary,' *Studies in Conflict and Terrorism*, 16:2 (April–June 1993), pp. 135–57. The second of these RAF proclamations, which I excerpt in this chapter, is dated 10 April 1992 and has appeared in FBIS, *Western Europe* and in Yonah Alexander and Dennis Pluchinsky, *Europe's Red Terrorists: The Fighting Communist Organizations* (London: Frank Cass, 1992).

73. From Alexander and Pluchinsky, 'Germany's Red Army Faction'.

74. In a 1992 case, court evidence that the Royal Ulster Constabulary had leaked evidence about a wanted man named Sean Mackin appears to have been one reason American legal and political figures supported Mackin. That man also asked to remain in New York and not be extradited, and he was in fact given political asylum; *Irish People* (19 January 1992).

75. Brief electronic mail interview with US Ambassador Ralph Johnson, while he was in Bratislava (March 1997). The Ambassador confirmed the suspicions he noted publicly in late 1996, and added that the case of the prime minster and the abuse

of a political opponent's son suggested a pattern of such behavior by security forces.

76. This is a computer feature meaning 'Compact Disk; Read Only Memory'.

77. Examples are Colombian FARC and the multinational team that attempted to assassinate Georgian leader Eduard Shevardnadze in February 1998.

78. On Austria, see articles in FBIS–*Western Europe* (17 January 1992), or the account of police searches of Gottfried Kussel's apartment by Ingo Hasselbach, with Tom Reiss, *Fuhrer-Ex: Memoirs of a Former Neo-Nazi* (New York: Random House, 1996), pp. 271–2.

79. See Christopher Wren's columns on the trail for the *New York Times*, including those of 10 July, 14 and 29 August, and 6 September. The final story concerns the convictions; the penultimate article includes the defense allegation that computer files had been tampered with after confiscation.

80. Indications of Unabomber's anger over computers includes a letter to Yale University computer scientist David Gelernter, sent in April 1995, two years after Gelernter had been injured by a package bomb. The letter ties computers to invasions of privacy, genetic engineering, excessive economic growth and environmental degradation. It attacks the professor's book, *Mirror Worlds* for trying to justify computer research. Text quoted by the *Washington Post* (27 April 1995). At least five of the Unabomber's victims were directly related to computer sales or research.

81. IRA, *Handbook for Volunteers*, p. 38.

82. Patrick Bishop and Eamonn Mallie, *The Provisional IRA* (London: Corgi Books, 1992), p. 346, give the background to the *Green Book*. Tim Pat Coogan's Ch. 34 concerns 'Anti-Interrogation' in the IRA's *Green Book*. This alleged IRA text itself is appended to Martin Dillon, *25 Years of Terror: The IRA's War Against the British* (Toronto: Bantam Books edn, 1997), pp. 353–84.

83. 'I worked 10 years against these people, 10 years, and I was unable to corrupt them', says a Lebanese official who monitored Hezbollah clans; *Washington Post* (1 December 1996).

84. Walter Laqueur, *The Age of Terrorism*, rev. edn (Boston: Little, Brown, 1987).

85. *New York Times* (14 January 1997).

86. Released in December 1996, Sean O'Callaghan served eight years of a 539-year sentence. He has given many interviews, including one to the *Los Angeles Times*, 28 February 1997. See also his article 'The Lying,' for the *National Review* (27 January 1997), pp. 31–5. His book *The Informer* was published in May 1998 in Britain by Bantam. For criticism of O'Callaghan see the unsigned feature 'O'Callaghan – the Truth', in the *Irish People* (15 March 1997), pp. 8–9.

87. Abu Nidal called his group 'Black June' when he first organized independently; subsequent assumed names have been Al-Asifa (The Storm), Arab Revolutionary Brigades, Black September (not the sponsor of the Munich massacre, a Fatah operation), and Revolutionary Organization of Socialist Muslims. This list, while long, is current only through 1987.

88. Force 17 is not reputed to have further engaged in international terrorism. It did make the press in mid 1997 when a squad of its police killed a Palestinian man, apparently for personal reasons of one Force 17 member.

89. Attribution of the TWA 840 bombing to the Hawari Group, and the statement that it is 'part of Yasser Arafat's Fatah apparatus', may be found in *Patterns of Global Terrorism: 1989* (Washington DC: GPO, 1990), p. 56.

90. See Patrick Seale, *Abu Nidal*.

91. On the JRA, see Chapter 5.

92. Certainly there have been executions. For example, for counter-intelligence reasons, 'The Order' killed an 'ideological relative' from the Aryan Nations Church, Walter West; Singleton, *Talked to Death*, pp. 212–13.

93. *New York Times* (3 July 1996).

94. The Internet site for the 'Independent White Racialists' – festooned with the words 'hate' and 'Nazi' – urged readers interested in 'White survival' to study the concept of Leaderless Resistance. It offered the L. R. Beam essay by that name and suggested that it had originally appeared in *The Seditionist*, downloaded 21 March 1996. On Beam as a KKK author of the 1983 *Essays of a Klansman*, see Dees' *Gathering Storm* and Warren Kinsella, *Web of Hate: Inside Canada's Far Right Network* (Toronto: HarperPerennial, 1995), p. 11.

95. 'The principal destructive agent used in the North has been gelignite ... obtained ... from quarries all over Ireland and England and from America where in New York it took five years and a suspiciously large amount of explosives to blast out the New York City Water tunnel.' Coogan, *The IRA*, p. 285n. Varieties of IRA bombs are described by Christopher Dobson and Ronald Payne, *The Terrorists: Their Weapons, Leaders and Tactics* (New York: Facts on File, 1979), Ch. 7.

96. IRA statement, published in slightly longer form in the *Irish People* (22 February 1992), under the paper's heading 'War News: Whitehall Brought to Standstill'.

97. *Washington Post* (31 March 1997), and subsequent press articles.

98. The *Irish People* (23 July 1994). Both incidents were in County Armagh; the first was against an RUC helicopter and the second against a British 'Puma'; security forces were injured in each attack.

99. A description of the mortar attack on Downing Street, and a photograph of the frame of tubes used against the Newry Barracks, may be found in Coogan's book. The June and October 1996 discoveries of more mortars appeared in Pinkerton serials: *Pinkerton Risk Assessment Services* (Arlington, VA), 13:36, 40, (September and 4 October 1996, respectively).

The *Irish People* regularly reports both successes and failures with mortar attacks, as on 11 July 1992. The many other sources include the periodical *Pointer* (London: Jane's: September 1996), pp. 1–2.

100. The IRA has never favored the Kalashnikov but was reported in the 1970s to possess a small number. *Claudia*, seized in 1973, had among its weapons intended for the IRA 250 Kalashnikovs. Dobson and Payne, *The Terrorists*, p. 102.

101. The source of the weaponry is unclear. An arrest in 1995 of the same men led to nothing because the guns in their possession were not illegal.

According to the *Seattle Post-Intelligencer* of 11 October 1996, Charles Barbee and Robert Berry belonged to 'America's Promised Ministries', a section of the Christian Identity movement, which is based in Idaho and has spawned racist activism. Other Identity suspects have adopted the name. 'Phineas Priesthood' draws its name from Phineas, whom the Bible's Book of Numbers describes as a priest who used a lance to kill an Israelite man and a prostitute from another ethnic group. The killings stopped a plague that had been inflicted against Moses and his people, according to Numbers. The paper cited a source with Seattle's 'Northwest Coalition Against Malicious Harassment' who said the biblical passage could be alleged to justify violence against race mixing, for example.

For a different account of the arrests, and Phineas Priesthood bank robberies, see FBI, *Terrorism in the United States: 1996* (Washington DC: GPO, undated; June 1998).

102. Coogan, *The IRA*, p. 330, quoting then-Congressman Les Aspin's words of

2 September 1975 concerning a US Army report.

103. *Washington Post* (3 October 1996).

104. See Raymond Bonner in the *New York Times* (27 January 1994). The archive reveals much other aid from Sofia to non-state actors, including military training for Chilean and Salvadoran leftists, cash for Bangladeshi communists, scholarships for Turkish communists, and military aid for the PLO. The Central Committee once sent 3,000 Kalashnikovs as well as machine guns and ammunition to Libya, which forwarded them to Libyan favorites in the ongoing civil war in Chad.

105. According to one report, 'The underground militia movement relies heavily on the illegal arms trade in the United States and abroad. Automatic rifles are obtained routinely through this weapons network, and semi-automatic rifles are purchased and easily converted to machine guns'. Southern Poverty Law Center, *False Patriots* (Montgomery, AL: 1996), p. 25.

106. *Washington Post* (3 November 1996).

107. *Seattle Post-Intelligencer* (12 October 1996); *Washington Post* (3 November 1996).

108. *Washington Post* (4 August 1996). The FBI's annual report on terrorism describes incidents by persons or groups, such as 'Up the IRS'.

109. The anti-IRS movement eventually stirred in Congress as well, prompting dramatic hearings in October 1997 about abuse of average citizens – an echo of militia complaints going back many years.

110. The proliferation of bombings in the United States, many non-terrorist, is a story that has been tracked by the *New York Times* and the *Washington Post*, for example. A more authoritative source is the FBI's *Bomb Summary* utilizing information gathered by the Bureau's Bomb Data Center.

111. Douglas Frantz and Catherine Collins, 'The Accountant is a Terrorist', *New York Times Magazine* (10 November 1996), pp. 45–9. '[S]uicide bombs are usually crude affairs, made from TNT extracted from old land mines and concealed beneath bulky clothing. [Hussein Mohammed Hussein] Mikdad's radio, packed with C-4, was a sophisticated instrument that offered the chance of escape.'

112. O'Callaghan's *National Review* account was written in Maghaberry prison in Northern Ireland, from which he was released in early 1997.

113. FBI, *Terrorism in the United States: 1982–1992* (Washington DC: GPO, undated), p. 5. Four men were arrested in New York and Connecticut, and two others were convicted in a Florida case.

114. On IRA weapons, and the long history of their shipment from the United States since at least 1867, the best catalogue of evidence may be by Jack Holland, *The American Connection: US Guns, Money, and Influence in Northern Ireland,* (New York: Viking, 1987). Specialized journals fill in the picture for the last decade. One may also see for example the *Irish People* for stories on alleged IRA attempts to buy or make shoulder-fired missiles in the United States, or *USA Today* on 24 September 1996.

115. One of many indicators of the self-conscious link between religious and state power is in Article 10 of the Iranian constitution: 'All Muslims form a single nation, and the government of the Islamic Republic of Iran has the duty of formulating its general policies with a view to the merging and union of all Muslim peoples ...' Quoted by Dr Richard Shultz, Jr, 'Iranian Covert Aggression', *Terrorism and Political Violence*, 6:3 (autumn 1994), p. 284.

For relevant passages of Hezbollah's 'Open Letter' (Beirut, 16 February 1985), and statements of Hezbollah clerics as to their allegiance to Iran, see Ch. 2 of

Martin Kramer, *Hezbollah's Vision of the West*, Policy Paper no. 16 (Washington DC: The Washington Institute for Near East Policy, 1989).

116. 'Islamic Jihad, Islamic Jihad for the Liberation of Palestine, the Revolutionary Justice Organization and the Oppressed of the Earth are names which are used exclusively to claim credit for violent acts such as bombings and kidnappings, directed mostly against Western targets. Hezbollah's does not want to be held directly accountable for such acts, even when they serve the aims of the larger movement'. Kramer, *Hezbollah's Vision of the West*, p. 19.

117. For an instance of Iran's public discussions of terrorism, see Iranian radio and press articles reprinted in FBIS, *Terrorism* (26 April 1996).

118. *Foreign Report* and European press stories in JPRS, *Terrorism* have frequently detailed Iranian activities in Germany since the end of the Cold War. Clearly such activities have official Iranian support.

119. *Foreign Report* (6 February 1997), alleges a direct link between Germany's status at the top of the list *re.* Iranian commercial offerings, on the one hand, and German willingness not to point the finger at Iran on terrorism, on the other.

120. This evidence was apparently disclosed by intelligence sources in the wake of two bombings of American military interests in Saudi Arabia in 1995 and 1996 and is reported by *USA Today* (2 August 1996), and subsequently echoed by Thomas Hunter, *Bomb School*. The initial *USA Today* story included yet another denial by the Iranian regime, but one which can as easily be read as an admission: the Ayatollah Ali Khameni was reported to have warned in a radio address that Iran would continue to retaliate for US support for Israel: 'When we said that the fire will spread to you too, you did not believe us. All those countries that supported terrorism, especially the United States, will be hurt by terrorism.'

121. Magnus Ranstorp, 'Hezbollah's Command Leadership', *Terrorism and Political Violence*, 6:3 (autumn 1994), pp. 319, 323. This remarkable piece of scholarship details the development of the Hezbollah operational structure and its many diverse relations with Iran. It also corroborates much of what *Foreign Report* has published on Hezbollah in recent years.

122. James Bruce, 'Iran's Covert Acts Proving Intolerable', *Jane's Intelligence Review* (August 1996), from the Internet.

123. This paragraph is closely based upon an issue of *Foreign Report* (2 November 1995).

124. To commemorate the 1997 anniversary of the Iranian revolution of 20 years before, the 15th Khordad Foundation temporarily elevated the bounty on Salman Rushdie's head by a half million dollars – to a total of $2.5 million. *Washington Post* (15 February 1997).

125. Ranstorp, *Hizbollah's Command Leadership*, pp. 320–1; and Kramer, *Hezbollah's Vision of the West*, especially Ch. 2.

126. Italian Red Brigadists attacked a thousand targets but never Soviet interests, a fact more important than Westerners' speculations about the exact degree of influence Moscow and Prague had over Red Brigade operations. Osama Bin Laden's Muslim operatives never kidnap Iranian diplomats or carry out car bombings in Tehran or Qom, but invariably they do direct their violence at enemies of Iran, leaving speculation about their apparent autonomy to others. Such a combination of loosely unattached terrorists and others directly run by the state served Moscow well for decades. The USSR was never bombed by American air forces, and neither has Iran been attacked by the United States despite 20 years of consistent exportation of political violence.
Among the many who see ties between Bin Laden and Iran are Senate Judiciary

Committee chairman Orrin G. Hatch, who also links him to Syria and Sudan; *New York Times* (14 August 1996).

Bin Laden's activities appear to include arranging a shipment of 20 tons of C-4 (high explosive) from Poland to Qatar; two tons of it went on to Saudi Arabia before the Khobar Towers bombing, say US officials; *Washington Times* (24 October 1996).

127. Kramer, *Hezbollah's Vision of the West*, p. 38.
128. Speech by Ibrahim al-Amin, *al-Ahd* (12 February 1988), cited by Kramer, ibid., p. 28.
129. 'PFLP Admits Killing, Vows to Keep On', Paris AF (20 July 1995), in FBIS, *Terrorism* (31 August 1995), p. 31.
130. *Foreign Report* (16 November 1995), p. 4.
131. Interview with Ayatollah Fadlallah by *al-Hawadith* (London: 10 July 1987), cited in Kramer, *Hezbollah's Vision of the West*, p. 34.
132. *Washington Post* (1 December 1996).
133. 'UK Intelligence Sources Uncover Hamas Terrorist Funding Operation', *The Times* (16 April 1996), in FBIS, *Terrorism* (18 June 1996), p. 3.
134. After the 25 June 1996 bombing in Dahrahn, Iranian and Syrian links were suspected. The Saudis named a man with important contacts with the Iranian embassy in Damascus, and asked formally to see his body. Syria declared the man had already been buried. Thomas Freedman, *New York Times* (6 November 1996).

4

Current Trends and Future Threats

Major political forces and problems

The 1990s have offered hopeful signs about our future security. Democracy possesses the global prestige it has always deserved, and in Latin America and parts of central Europe democracy has never been stronger than it is today. The collapse of the Soviet bloc has discredited Marxism–Leninism, probably the most destructive ideology of modern times, and one which ruled much of the globe in the twentieth century. Virulent political forces have erupted to threaten sovereign states and regional stability; but these are under watch by the global community, which has intervened – if only sometimes, and sometimes too slowly – with military force to limit the worst excesses, as in Bosnia, Somalia, and Rwanda. The Republic of South Africa is making a transition to a more democratic state; we have seen the end of decades of cross-border terrorism of the African National Congress, as well as its counterpart, South African commando activities in Angola, Namibia, and Mozambique. Finally, peace accords, partially brokered or indebted to the international community's diplomats or military forces, have brought a tenuous cessation, or at least a reduction, of political killing in Somalia, Northern Ireland, Guatemala, El Salvador, and areas controlled by Israel and the Palestinian Authority. Such accords, together with wide democratic progress in Latin and Central America, and the Soviet withdrawal from Afghanistan improved international terrorism statistics. The year 1992 was the lowest out of 17 on the US State Department's charts of terrorist activity. There followed other relatively 'safe' years: 1996 and 1997 each brought about 300 international incidents[1] – an abhorrent number but one dramatically lower than the terrorism tallies of the early and mid 1980s.

Unfortunately, terrorism is here to stay. No sooner had the optimistic news about 1992 appeared than a Pakistani shot up a line of cars waiting to turn into the Langley Virginia base of the CIA. Mir Aimal Kasi killed two people and maimed three more.[2] It took over three years to find and apprehend the gunman on the Afghan border, and he was promptly celebrated in his Pakistani hometown with parades and speeches on his heroism. Upon his November 1997 conviction in a Virginia court for murder, terrorists in Pakistan instantly retaliated by killing four more Americans.[3] This case, boiling over with anger between two otherwise friendly states, is but one reminder that terrorism will remain with us.

There are many other such cases. The Yugoslav communist state permitted transit and even provided training to terrorists, and had liaisons with Libya, but independent Bosnia has been rent by more lethal evils. A post-Cold War creation, the Palestinian Authority, is a 'statelet' composed of a half-dozen separated small regions, joined administratively and legally to the capital Jericho. A boon for many Palestinian moderates, it has done equal harm to the preconceptions of the most radical. There is now a new place on the global terrorism stage for Hamas and Palestine Islamic Jihad, which regard Yasser Arafat as a traitor for creating a state in only part of Palestine, and for creating a state that is secular and not religious.[4] A ceasefire in Northern Ireland lasted 17 months, only to explode in early 1996. Now there is another, and all hopes are upon making it work. In Colombia, while M-19 terrorists have completely merged with the democratic political process, their rivals in FARC and ELN have remained alienated, leaving the nation bleeding internally.[5] War is returning to Angola. In Nicaragua, a few 'Re-Contras' emerged as a low-level threat to the uneasy peace between the communists and other leftists of the Sandinista front and the more democratic-minded majority of the electorate. These right-wing gun carriers in the mountains have been but a small problem, and a purely Nicaraguan concern. So are the arms caches within Nicaragua dating to recent years of Sandinista–Central American guerrilla cooperation; a dozen discoveries occurred after the peace.[6]

The useful and commonplace role terrorism has within insurgency[7] is another reason for expecting no diminution of terrorism in the near future. In the post-Cold War world, insurgency is flourishing, and most insurgent groups are killing civilians more often than military men. The doctrine of most insurgencies supports this practice; terrorism is usually deemed acceptable on strictly pragmatic grounds; leaders advise using it if and when it helps the movement. This is the case, for example, with Marxism–Leninism, and if that doctrine is less popular today than before, it does remain attractive to revolutionaries in some parts of Europe and in Asian countries, both east and southwest. The Maoist variant is upheld today by large insurgent groups in Peru, Cambodia, and the Philippines.[8] Doctrines mixing communist-style ideology with nationalist extremism, like that of JVP (Janatha Vimukthi Peramuna) which tore at Sri Lanka during the 1980s, can be found in new outcroppings in central Europe and Asia. A religious model of insurgency,[9] newly powerful, is burning across the Maghreb and all the way to Iran. A moderate Arab country like Egypt faces the influx from several directions, especially Sudan. All the aforementioned types of insurgents may employ terrorism in their war for the population. Most use terror within their countries, and some have used it internationally, either quietly or with dramatic effect.

Insurgency has also adapted to the post-Cold War environment by wedding itself increasingly to organized crime.[10] There is a marked trend of combining two familiar forms, political terrorism and private intimidation, in an overlapping of policy and greed. This has developed particularly in Latin America, where purist rhetoric about the higher human things – once the staple of revolutionary leaders – has given way to systematic practices of selling contraband, dealing directly with drug cartels, and hostage-taking for reasons that are monetary more than revolutionary. Colombia's powerful Marxist–Leninist insurgents FARC and ELN have devolved into professional extortionists and calculating businessmen, with computerized accounting systems, sophisticated money-laundering, first-rate communications, and corporate resources.[11] FARC alone earns half a billion dollars a year just from protecting the drug trade.[12]

Thus the 1990s have demonstrated that terrorism has heartily survived the atrophication of communism and the end of the Cold War. Terrorism flourishes as a small-group activity, as a component of insurgency and revolutionary warfare, and as an adjunct of the new organized crime. The present chapter highlights some important sources of current terrorist threats, and then turns to the tactics and techniques of future terrorism.

Nationalism

A major reason why terrorism will maintain a place in the forseeable future is the prevalence of nationalism. Violent nationalist movements sometimes enjoy a deep and wide ethnic base which may be ceaselessly drawn upon for passion and personnel. And by its nature it may grow even in the absence of coherent political ideology. Already, nationalism has had a role in the partition of two multinational states, the post-First World War creations Yugoslavia and Czechoslovakia. It has shorn Russia of many holdings, and spurred separatist Chechens to savage

Death tallies of 'low-intensity conflicts' around the world

The figures below reflect *selected* conflicts and approximate totals for all deaths from all political causes (not only terrorism) for a given recent period, with a comment on status in April 1999.[13]

Afghanistan	unknown	since 1989	continuous fighting, with new prospects for an end
Algeria	80,000	since 1992	worsening in latter 1990s
Cambodia	unknown	since 1979	sporadic terrorism, declining
Chechnya	40–80,000	1992–96	accord stopped war August 1996
Colombia	40,000	for decades	deteriorating, and out of government's control
Corsica	100	since 1975	averaging a bomb per day
Cuba	very low, but unknown	since 1962	occasional foreign attacks, in Cuba and in the United States
Egypt	1,200+	1993–97	ongoing
Guatemala	100,000+	1961–96	accord signed December 1996
Kashmir	20,000	since 1989 in this phase	ongoing
Kurdish insurgency	37,000+	since 1984	serious, and internationalized; guerrilla war and terrorism
Northern Ireland	3,350	since 1969	peace accord of April 1998, but occasional terrorism
Palestine	800+	tally of September 1993–97	tension and violence
Peru	30,000	since 1980	quieter since setbacks to terrorism of 1992, 1997 and 1999
Philippines (separatist, South)	15,000	continuous	mixed status; recurrent Middle Eastern involvement
Philippines (NPA insurgency)	11,250	1988–97 figures only	steady decline; now quiet
Spain (Basque)	800	since 1968	September 1998, suspension of ETA attacks
Sri Lanka (Tamil insurgency)	tens of thousands	since 1975	guerrilla war and terrorism
Yugoslavia (Bosnia)	over 250,000	1991–95	now quiet in most areas
Yugoslavia (Kosovo)	unknown	1998–99	strong beginnings in 1998; guerrilla war, terrorism, massacres

guerrilla fighting and such terrorism methods as mass hostage-taking and a nuclear threat by the rebels. Excepting former Yugoslavia most of the remainder of central Europe has resolved border issues and made other transitions with gratifying moderation. Nationalism has also shown a harsh visage in the east and south, around the centers of population of the Kurds and the Palestinians, respectively.

The Kurds are one underappreciated nationalist problem of the present and future – a fact well disguised until the late 1998 Italian arrest of Kurdish Worker's Party (PKK) chief Abdullah Ocalan.[14] Militant activists are working virtually wherever there are Kurds, whose 20 million include large communities in western Europe. The radicals want political power, and a Kurdish state amidst Turkey, Iraq, Syria, and Iran for the Kurdish diaspora. PKK militants dominate the movement in western Europe and have colored it red with Marxist–Leninist ideology, extortion against Kurdish emigrants, and bombs against legitimate governments of Europe too. Not only Syria has patronized PKK. Russian mafia figures supply many of its guns, via Turkish towns such as Sarp and Kapikule.[15] And Iran has been a regular arms supplier. Turkey, a NATO stalwart, feels these Kurdish pressures acutely. Ankara's low-intensity conflict with the Kurds is a massive economic drain, and it often boils up into fully-fledged war, repeated incursions into Iraq, and surprising military cooperation between nations as different as Turkey and Israel.

The issue of independence for Kashmir, bordering Pakistan and India and home to both Muslims and Hindus, has been a leading, unceasing source of bloodshed. Yet it is unclear that independence would mean peace, any more than division of Pakistan and India in 1948 could forestall a series of conventional wars between those sovereign states. To the southwest, New Delhi has wrestled successfully with Tamil militants in India's populous province of Tamil Nadu. But across the narrow Palk Strait, in Sri Lanka, radicals of a much smaller Tamil population demand their total independence from the rest of the country, once a pearl of Indian Ocean beauty. The Tamil insurgents who mix Marxism–Leninism with national separatism have been a devastating human problem for the region for a quarter of a century. Religious and ethnic and political differences are traditional, and have in recent years become so violently pronounced that there may be no solution save a new spirit of multinational unity on the island-state. The steep decline of recent years in terrorism by right-wing Sinhalese might seem like an opening for reciprocal moderation by Tamils. Instead, the 'Tigers' and other Tamil militants remain a spear – not merely a thorn – in the side of their Sri Lankan countrymen.

When dividing a state, rather than building one that had not existed, nationalists – both terrorist and non-terrorist – face the theoretical and practical problem of where the process of political division should stop. One of American President Abraham Lincoln's arguments against secession of the American South was that once the process began, there was no longer a barrier – in practice or principle – to a train of further secessionist movements. He was proved right by the Confederacy's internal divisions, and the secession of West Virginia from Virginia. Today countries such as Russia face this problem; having just given up vast territories garnered in hundreds of years of war and diplomacy, Russia may also lose Chechnya. Georgia, itself so newly released from Moscow's grip, now fights to keep minuscule Ossetia and Abkhazia within Georgia. Central Europe knows this problem well: Czechoslovakia was a conception that seemed to make sense when it was created out of the larger multinational Habsburg Empire. But it was swallowed up twice by aggressors within only a decade of the mid twentieth century. That state, barely defensible when whole, has wilfully divided itself into two smaller nation-states, raising the question of whether the Czech Republic and that of Slovakia verge upon the untenable in terms of their economic strengths and capacity for self-defense. Similarly, it is unclear who besides Moldavians and Macedonians honestly judge those two new countries with tiny populations as capable of preserving their national lives in a future European war. Such small entities have neither the determined and overwhelmingly powerful ally that Cuba once had in the Warsaw Pact, nor the supreme geographical advantages of a Switzerland. All they have is is *de jure* independence for this moment in history.

It is a sign of the times that Italians, who once angered the Florentine Machiavelli by their rampant internal divisions, and found no real unity until the late nineteenth century, should again contemplate division of their peninsula. The change could only leave it weaker. Yet the Northern League has drawn many to the cause of national dismemberment. A minor terrorism campaign by separatists on the Austrian border festers, and Seborga, a tiny town of 300 voters on Italy's northern Mediterranean coast, declared itself sovereign in 1995, and took to printing money and stamps as the Principato de Seborga.[16] Rome's problem with such divisiveness reflects similar tendencies in some other parts of Europe.

Such instability, and tensions within nations, may lead to future terrorism in Europe. So too might tensions between existing or new states: Moldova *vs* Trans-Dniester; Macedonia *vs* Greece; Albania *vs* Serbia because of the guerrilla war in Kosovo, etc.

Clash of civilizations

As the tensions between secular and religious factions of Palestinians suggest, many post-Cold War security problems do not fit the mold of an ethnically cohesive nation seeking self-determination against an overbearing foreign state. Instead, some of the globe's hottest struggles are intranational. Certain contemporary scholars seek to explain modern-day violence as a 'clash of civilizations' rather than conflicts between states.[17] That view appears to account for some struggles in Africa and Asia, as well as the former Yugoslavia. And in the Middle East, most fighting today is among various peoples within single states. Such violence can spawn terrorism; it is a consolation of sorts that it does not usually or necessarily spawn *international* terrorism too.

The central Asian republics, newly emergent from Soviet and communist shadows, are a complicated mix of Muslims and Orthodox Christians, as well as differing ethnic groups. The divides between their civilizations have thus far produced skirmishes, riots, and tension, but a minimum of international terrorism. A subtle battle of wits, money, preachers, and agents of political influence is helping to shape the future of the region. Turkey had evidently aspired to lead the Muslims of Central Asia, and spent heavily on mosques and educational materials; so does Saudi Arabia. But neither state is extremist; the now-infamous Saudi terrorist Osama Bin Laden was driven out of his country.[18] It is Iran which works hardest for, and now holds, influence among some of the politically militant who dwell in this region of Islamic civilization.[19]

Sunni Muslims have not been a check on the militant Shi'ites. Indeed, Sunnis are producing enough of their own extremists to count as a leading threat for the international community in the future. Some Sunni extremists are willing to use terrorism for their own politico-religious aspirations, and some appear to operate in league with Shia Iran. Already, the Palestinians of Hamas and Palestine Islamic Jihad have committed scores of terrorist acts and killed many foreigners. Sudan's ruling cleric, Hasan al-Turabi, is a Sunni. Algeria's extraordinarily violent GIA (Armed Islamic Group) is also Sunni. Lebanon has a small new Sunni fundamentalist group called the Partisans' League which in July 1995 murdered a sheik who headed an association of Islamic philanthropists in Beirut, perhaps because the man was too close to Syrian influence.[20] Thousands of internationalist-minded Muslims with war experience or training in Afghanistan – called 'Afghani' or 'Afghansi' – and now living in southwest Asia and the Middle East, are also Sunnis. Many are linked to terrorism, as is one of their Sunni financial patrons, ex-Saudi and construction-heir Osama Bin Laden.

It is symbolic of such contemporary supranationalist currents that an east European nation like Bosnia could find itself in 1992 hosting as many as 2,000[21] internationally minded *mujahideen*, some with training in Afghanistan, some trained in Bosnia by experts from Lebanon's Hezbollah or the Sunni militia Tawheed, and most of them presumably organized and paid for their Bosnian service by Tehran. A minority of Bosnian Croats who share the Muslim faith have also been trained by Hezbollah specialists. And both national groupings have enjoyed assistance from Iranian arms shippers, whose airlink to Zagreb airport is complemented by overland smuggling. Tehran and its 'Afghani' have taken part in what is in many respects a traditional Balkan war pitting Croat against Serb against Muslim. These internationalists for Islam have reportedly taken part in terrorism, not just war: bombing of a bread-line in May 1992; killing of ABC television producer David Kaplan in August 1992; assassination of a British peacekeeper in 1994; and murder of the deputy chief of the Bosnian intelligence agency in September 1996.[22] Such actions, and the identifiable training camps facilitating them, ultimately attracted the attentions of the United Nations; most foreign Muslims have now left the country; some may have folded into the Bosnian Muslim population.

Environmentalism

Some 'nonpolitical' issues have legal and political consequences. They have already incited profound anger and cross-border communication. These are environmental issues, including protection of forests, animal rights, water shortages, and overpopulation. While all have become political issues, thus far none seems to have developed a strong international organization engaging in terrorist violence. There appear to be three reasons. First, mutual awareness and communication have not yet become collaboration; real organization by the militants is limited and in some cases missing. Second, some extreme activists deliberately operate in a decentralized manner to prevent police penetration; Internet documents and home pages give counsel on this strategy.[23] Third, there is good reason to believe that the motivations of the people now involved are not sufficiently political and rarely militant; the average ecological activist favors a nonviolent approach. But these issues have the capacity – in moral, sentimental, and political terms – to become militant movements. Like the abortion issue of today, or the Vietnam War protests of two decades ago, they may prove capable of turning idealism and healthy activism onto a path of political criminality.

Over a decade ago, when Puerto Rican Macheteros published a

communiqué justifying their ongoing attacks on US military targets as 'a war of national liberation', they included their opposition to the US National Park Service's plan to permit commercial logging in the island's national rain forest at El Yunque.[24] This was unusual. It will not be so in the future. There is now sabotage and 'ecoterrorism' in the UK and the United States, despite the pacific intentions of most environmentalists. 'Preserving lynx habitat' was the announced motive of the Earth Liberation Front's arson against a ski resort in Vail, Colorado, in October 1998, which cost damages of $12 million.[25] Animal rights activists have apparently directed their bombings, arson, and sabotage at harming property rather than human life. But their willingness to use violence could become a model for other ecological groups. There has been no reported political violence against the innocent based upon the selective destruction of British cattle herds because of concern about 'mad cow disease'. But has deforestation in the northern and southern hemispheres emboldened political enemies? If acid rain can singe Canadian–American relations, can it produce violence on either side, especially if coincident with unemployment in the logging industry? As battles over water rights and access to rivers strain relations between cities and farming interests of the American southwest, between Turkey and Syria, and between Israel and Lebanon, will terrorism be one product of strained relations?[26]

It no longer seems incongruous that pro-environmental groups would consider violence to prevent or cause certain public actions. In this age, even sovereign states' national security documents devote attention to environment issues. In 1985 few would have imagined that pollution would appear as an issue in a seminal government report on national security; by 1995, countries as different as the United States and the Republic of Lithuania devoted defense departments' explicit attention to just that problem.[27]

Instability

Global instability has increased since 1990, and that may increase terrorism. But on balance, it has not. Refugees from totalitarian countries – who seek escape, not creation of fear or propagation of a political program – have occasionally hijacked aircraft as a way to the outer world; they did so to escape the Soviet Union and they can and still do so to leave China and Cuba. Other refugees may use the same method to flee poverty or an overwhelming personal problem. When an Ethiopian passenger jet crashed in the Comoros Islands in late 1996 there was speculation that the three perpetrators harbored only private grudges against their government. They wanted to leave.[28] Millions do, and their methods will sometimes resemble the methods of terror, though their purposes can not be more different. Refugees and exiles do not usually become practitioners of terrorism against the regime they have fled; they usually have other concerns, like re-establishing themselves in a new world.

But sometimes that reassuring pattern does not hold. Even though Cuban Americans inhabit the southern and eastern shores of the United States by the hundreds of thousands, living peaceable lives, their sentimental attachments, and sometimes offerings of largesse, have been a temptation and supplement to the tiny minority which believes in violence. The latter have included the Party of National Democratic Unity, which sent Miami-based 'commandos' into an armed engagement in Cuba in October 1994.[29] Better known right-wing groups include Alpha 66 and Omega 7, which have often operated within America against official Cuban visitors or Castro sympathizers. Such incidents, and Florida-based speedboats heading south across the straits to fire rifles at beach targets, attack shipping piers, or make other acts of sabotage against Cuba, violate international and US neutrality laws. The attacks in Cuba endanger civilians who may hate the Castro regime as much as do some ethnic Cubans in Florida.

Instability caused by poverty will foster new and unpleasant political problems, possibly including terrorism. Especially vulnerable are the vast slum belts which surround many Latin, Asian, and Middle Eastern cities. Capitals like Mexico City, Sao Paulo, Manila, Tehran, and Cairo are living with explosive population growth. This places in the hands of government agencies, or conversely in the hands of revolutionary organizations dedicated to destroying governments, legions of young women and men with few good prospects – the veritable working capital of violence. Lima, Peru, is rimmed with millions of human beings, most of them relocated or driven from the countryside, and few possessing means of earning a decent living. Thus far, the Maoists of Shining Path and the Castroites of Tupac Amaru (MRTA) have been intriguingly unable to exploit these human resources. The insurgents have attempted political organization and terror but have made few inroads;[30] others may do better in the future, or do better in other countries where discontent is as evident. Poverty, when it ignites a proper moral indignation, may become twisted into a motive for terrorism.[31]

Even a stable country is affected by world instabilities. Venezuela resents incursions of Shining Path organizers and logisticians from Colombia's insurgents; but it will not close its borders because of this incremental damage to internal stability. The Nordic countries and

France, long reputed for tolerant spirits and tolerant laws, have attracted so many foreign residents and would-be citizens, including innumerable Middle Easterners, that popular attitudes have chilled against immigration, especially since a few immigrants actively support terrorism. The United States, with its remarkably porous borders and indulgent domestic laws, cannot possibly consistently prevent violations of its sovereignty. The size, wealth, and attractiveness of the United States supplement the liberality of its social order to make it a magnet for travelers, émigrés, and legal or illegal immigrants. There are several millions of illegal aliens living in the United States and the number leaving and entering each year is also great.[32] In the south, US defenses have been saturated by the influx; there are 200,000 Nicaraguans – many of them illegal – in Miami alone. In the north, along Canadian borders, there are virtually no defenses against malevolent political intruders, and some have quietly entered the United States in this way. Legal travel and illegal cross-border movements are thus two different forms of 'instability', each of which may permit transfer of terrorists' intelligence, money, and equipment, and of course personnel. A number of foreign terror groups operate within the United States today, especially extremist Muslims of Hamas, Islamic Jihad, and even Hezbollah.[33]

Peace-keeping forces and humanitarians

Strict definitions of terrorism may distinguish between such targets as soldiers and humanitarian assistance personnel. Guerrillas and terrorists are also highly conscious of the differences, though they may not honor them. What seems apparent about the future is that both military and civilians overseas will be targeted for purposes indigenous to violent groups. Indian troops sent into Sri Lanka to make peace in the Tamil war in 1987 may have been told they were 'peace-keepers', but during a humiliating 32 months there they suffered 4,200 casualties.

Forces deployed abroad impermanently as NATO or UN makers of peace or keepers of peace[34] are aware that they are exposed to terrorism risks even though their mission, in doctrinal terms, is one of 'operations other than war'. To avoid the anger of indigenous belligerents, analysts and political leaders have made it a dogma of intervention that the outsider must be neutral, and remain neutral, between the competing parties. But this offers only limited protection. The harsh reality of most UN Charter interventions is that there will be aggrieved parties, however small or unrepresentative, who naturally view US, European, or other international military personnel as intruders. They *are* intruders. Almost by definition, in a violent situation into which the UN introduces forces, some indigenous party or another will feel that the international action is blocking its path to power, or its opportunity to destroy its enemy.[35] A UN-managed cooling off period may work in some cases; this has been the persistent hope for Bosnia as several expected withdrawal dates have come and gone.[36] In other cases it will fail, for hatreds run too deep and belligerents' war aims are unlimited. This has been true in Cyprus, still tight as a trigger finger despite a consistent UN peace presence since 1964. Most intervening forces can be waited out by eager belligerents, which is sadly what should be expected in Bosnia once NATO leaves.

Peace-keepers subject to calculated and calibrated attacks have included the UN blue helmets in Cambodia. The very reasons the world appreciated the outside intervention in Cambodia – creating a sense of calm, less fighting, and an opportunity for free elections – were the same reasons the Khmer Rouge hated those bringing about such conditions. As a feared and unpopular party, the Khmer Rouge could be damaged by several rounds of free national elections. As revolutionaries, they would be stopped cold by something as friendly-sounding as 'peaceable enforcement of the status quo'. Therefore their terrorism against the blue helmets was utterly logical. And now that the UN forces are gone, and the pro-Vietnamese Cambodians of Hun Sen have snatched power – in part by their own terrorism – remnants of the Khmer Rouge may turn again to insurgency, to terrorism, or both to reassert themselves or rebuild their shrunken 'liberated zones'.[37]

Peace-keepers will face attacks because terrorism works. Militants well know the story of the remarkable strategic effect of one bomb upon the world's greatest military power. In 1983, despite all their idealism about helping war-ravaged Lebanon, President Reagan and Secretary of State Shultz withdrew American peace-keeping forces from Beirut. A single truck bomb killed a building full of Marines in an attack that was never punished. The fate of this mission – one of peace-keeping that had gradually assumed more forcible character – is another part of the pattern of indicators: even if indigenous belligerents appreciate the intervention, neighboring powers may not. While Lebanon was a deeply troubled country, it was never in Syria's interests to have the US Marines help. The Assad regime viewed Lebanon as a weak territory and an opportunity for Syrian hegemony. Syria (like Iran) thus aided terror groups in Lebanon and possibly the very truck bombers who attacked US and French targets in Beirut in 1983;[38] once the United States withdrew, Syria secured hegemony over much of Lebanese territory. Appropriately, those Syrian-held lands include the Bekaa Valley, notorious then, as now, for terrorist training.

In Bosnia, the flagrant injustices done to Muslims by other ethnic groups, Belgrade's policies, and an international arms embargo sponsored by the US all helped produce yet another opening for Iran and another problem for international peace-keepers. The introduction of Iranian Revolutionary Guards and terrorist agents was the first such semi-overt deployment into the northern Mediterranean world. For that region, Tehran had hitherto relied only upon its embassies and the limited cover they provide. It now was able to give military and unconventional training directly to an entirely new group of Muslim warriors, and doubtless to recruit for is own purposes. Bosnia ultimately points back to Beirut: even where peace-keeping proceeds well, and is desired by many indigenous parties, international peace-keepers may face attack sponsored from outside powers which do not wish for such success and such results.

Attacks on humanitarian missions and peace-keepers will include sniping, hostage-taking, efforts at compromising soldiers on an individual basis, intimidation of military units by bomb threats, and outright attacks on sleeping quarters and other installations with grenades, small arms, or logistical sabotage such as poisoning water supplies[39] or foodstuffs. Neither a gentle nor a fierce posture can guarantee the safety of Americans. Two operations in October 1993 illustrate this. Haiti faced hunger, misery, and right-wing terrorism. Yet US Navy vessels bearing medical personnel and food were prevented from landing by a combination of several patrol craft, sniping from the shore with small arms, and a mob mobilized on the docks of Port o' Prince. Having been promised a 'benign environment', the US commander wisely refused to put his unarmed relief personnel in harm's way.[40] That same month the complicated Somalia relief operation became more complicated with the deaths of many American Rangers hunting a clan leader who was bullying other Somalis. US withdrawal from 'Operation Continue Hope' followed early in the next year.[41] These two cases a half-world apart demonstrated that relief efforts in a place of non-vital interest to the United States can be destroyed by political violence. The lesson has not escaped Washington, nor the enemies of Washington. Nor has it escaped the UN, whose experts at relief occasionally show signs of 'peace-keeping overstretch'.[42]

To terrorists, it will mean nothing that governments regard their citizens who work for the Red Cross, or the Peace Corps, or Doctors Without Borders, as unarmed and utterly without a political agenda. What will matter most is the cold calculation by terrorists and insurgents as to whether the aid workers are more useful as aid-givers, as hostages, or as dead foreign bodies. If any terrorist, guerrilla, or militia leader calculates that the foreign aid workers are ameliorating crisis conditions while they, the gunmen, seek to foment crisis for political reasons, the aid workers may become victims. If the international assistance rendered appears to improve the American image, Americans at hand may be dealt with as undesirables. If tormented minds perceive humanitarian aid workers as spies – a common accusation against the Peace Corps – they may be abused, expelled, or seized. Aid workers are both 'available' and utterly defenseless against hostage-takers. That combination made medical and education work in Beirut a dangerous occupation in the early 1980s. Today it is causing shudders among Red Cross professionals world-wide. Six were murdered in their beds in Chechnya in December 1996, bringing the tally of that organization's workers killed on foreign duty since 1990 to 18 – a higher number than were killed during the entire Cold War.[43] In Somalia, kidnappings of relief workers have become so commonplace that in April 1998 the Red Cross simply withdrew.[44]

Anger at Jews and Israelis

The anti-semitic and anti-Zionist causes of much global terrorism are well recognized today. American soil has been one locus of many acts of such violence. At least two Palestinians have committed terrorism in the United States: Sirhan Sirhan assassinated Robert Kennedy in 1968, and Ali Hassan Abu Kamal shot up a half-dozen visitors on the observation deck of the Empire State Building in 1997; both men left written evidence of their motives. More broadly, there is a pattern of hate speech and violence from right-wing American militias and 'patriot' groups against Jews, Israel, and a perceived enslavement of US policy to both. Individuals and organizations are outraged over US aid to Tel Aviv, particularly in light of perceived underfunding of such US problems as the farm crisis. Many radicals go so far as to call their own federal government 'ZOG', or Zionist-Occupied Government.[45] The underground bestseller *The Turner Diaries* favored by extremists like Timothy McVeigh is full of such commentary.[46] So are radio broadcasts in 'the heartland', made by militant spokesmen with local and even national followings. Fanatics in the Christian Identity movement actually anticipate a race war in the year 2000 in America.[47] The anti-semitism and white racism of American 'Christian' groups like these have parallels with views of certain black American radicals, secular or religious, especially several outspoken current or former aides to Nation of Islam Minister Louis Farrakhan. Black American radicals have largely confined their assaults on 'Jewish interests' in America to the rhetorical, thus far. But they represent a complex American problem, especially where connected to terrorism-prone foreign governments.[48]

Posse Comitatus against American Jews

Yes, we are going to cleanse our land. We're going to do it with a sword. And we're going to do it with violence.

You're damn right I'm teaching violence. God said you're going to do it that way, and it's about time somebody is telling you to get violent, whitey ...

[S]tart making dossiers, names, addresses, phone numbers, car license numbers, on every damn Jew rabbi in this land, and every Anti-Defamation League leader or JDL leader in this land, and you better start doing it now ... You get these roadblock locations, where you can set up ambushes, and get it all working now.

Radio broadcast by William Gale,
Former spokesman for Posse Comitatus
Radio KTTL-FM, Dodge City, Kansas[49]

One of several reasons why Americans will remain frequent targets of international terrorism is the consistent and strong US support for Israel. The charters of Hamas and Hezbollah explicitly condemn the American alliance with Israel; the latter document favors confrontation with 'the imams of infidelity of America, France and Israel', and states 'We are moving in the direction of fighting the roots of vice and the first root of vice is America'.[50] Many of contemporary history's international terrorist spectaculars, like the massacres at Israel's Lod Airport, the Munich Olympics, and the 1985 Vienna and Rome airport assaults, were directed against Israelis. Subsequent years show that both US interests and Israel's are among those most targeted in transnational attacks;[51] often the reasons are similar, or linked. But if the connection between Washington and Tel Aviv is a lightening rod, every US administration in recent history has tendered powerful diplomatic, economic, military, and intelligence assistance to the Middle East's most democratic state. The Democratic Clinton administration is perhaps even warmer to Israel than was the Republican Bush administration.

The Camp David accords negotiated by President Carter and cultivated by all his successors directly engage Egypt, dooming that state to a share of the enmity of haters of Israel or Jews. Secular and religious 'rejectionists' of peace have proven themselves enduring in their capacities for anger and organization. Islamic extremists shot President Sadat and they now direct their antipathies to President Mubarak, nearly shot in Addis Ababa in 1995. Such crimes, like the manifestos or broadcasts that sometimes accompany them, reveal a pattern larger than animosity towards Israel, and animosity for US support for Israel. The enmity of anti-Jewish radicals is extended to any conservative or moderate Arab government that maintains decent relations with Israel. Governments at risk today from anti-Israeli terrorists include all those of the Gulf Cooperation Council and others in the Middle East such as Jordan, Egypt, and Tunisia.[52]

State sources of future terrorism

As actor, the state may be more predictable, and harder to hide, than small groups and insurgents using terrorism. But a state is able to call on so many resources which prove advantageous: ability to plan operations; good intelligence; expertise in weapons training; ways to move personnel about covertly; and other assistance that may be offered via embassies, consulates, foreign-deployed agents, military personnel, or state-run businesses. In the space of one generation, terrorism became a common adjunct of state power, and it remains such in the post-Cold

War era for many governments and groups. There is nothing in present threat assessments to suggest that traditional terrorism users will abandon this tool. And there is everything to suggest that if, for example, Islamic zealots take power in Algeria or Libya or Egypt, there will be both domestic and international terrorism against political opponents of the kind now faced by Iranian citizens,[53] Iranian exiles and non-Iranians such as author Salman Rushdie.[54] Conservative Arab regimes know as well as Israel the damage that can be done by foreign regimes which murder, maim, and menace the innocent to advance purposes of state.

It is noteworthy that so many of the most serious threats from the sovereign state category are in North Africa and the Middle East. The US State Department's entire list of governmental sponsors is only seven long but includes the geographic proximates Libya, Sudan, Syria, Iraq, and Iran. Many other governments – from these states' nervous neighbors to distant capitals in Western Europe – see similar threats from similar sources.

Consider Syria. While Abu Nidal and Ahmad Jibril may enjoy only limited success with terrorism, Syria, as a state sponsor of those groups, has succeeded manifestly. First the Assad regime succeeded by making such violence an arm of state power.[55] Then, more recently, it succeeded by publicly disavowing violence while ratcheting down its use as well, so as to foster other purposes of state. Syria's regular use of terrorism as a dimension of its international relations is most evident *vis-à-vis* Israel and Turkey, before all other countries. There is a long pattern of successful and sometimes spectacular operations, such as attempts at three major bombings in 1986. Two of those plots succeeded: an attack on an El Al ticket counter in Madrid, and another on Berlin's German–Arab friendship society. At the last moment, security interdicted the third attempt – coaching a love-smitten woman into unwittingly smuggling a bomb aboard an El Al jet leaving Heathrow, London. Syria is now more subtle. Assad calculates that there are advantages to be had in 'cold peace' with the Western powers, suggested by token support in the Gulf War and occasional rebuffs to known terrorists such as Abu Nidal. But Assad also retains his revolutionary credentials by encouraging Middle Eastern antipathies to Israel and by giving safe haven and training to a variety of violent international groups.

The tension between these Syrian positions is evident in a March 1996 broadcast by Damascus Radio:

> Syria condemns terror and will continue to condemn it at every opportunity, but what Israel defines as terror is national struggle

against occupation. National struggle is a legitimate right of nations, as is written in the UN charter. The Israeli occupation of the territories and collective punishment which Israel imposes on the citizenry is terror.[56]

Syria thus patronizes such Palestinian terrorists as the technically proficient Ahmad Jibril of the PFLP–GC, and the zealous, less technically advanced Hamas and Palestine Islamic Jihad.[57] Secular Syria is also generous with Shiite terrorists from Hezbollah as part of its influence campaign in Lebanon and the region. The most dangerous group in Europe (while the IRA is inactive) may well be a Syrian ally, the Kurdish PKK. For many years, its leader Abdullah Ocalan kept his residence and main offices in Damascus, and training camps in Syria as well, e.g. above Hama.[58] This convenience was interrupted suddenly in October 1998 when Turkish pressures and other factors led Syria to turn out Ocalan and many of his men.[59] It would be foolish to regard this expulsion as permanent, given Assad's record. While terrorism has been highly useful to Syria, its effects are apparently contained in the Middle East. Damascus does not seek or possess the global reach of an Iran or a Libya.

Sudan has less money to offer than Syria but more room. The military regime which follows directives of the articulate, British-educated Muslim cleric Hasan al-Turabi has welcomed foreign militants in by the hundreds.[61] Sudan is thus a newcomer to the longstanding business practised by such neighboring territories as Libya and the Bekaa Valley. Iranian Revolutionary Guards and other experts provide training at as many as 20 camps scattered throughout Sudan. This activity, and the way Cairo now feels surrounded by the Iranian–Sudanese connection, has angered the Mubarak government, among other neighbors. Once a Nile backwater, Sudan is no longer ignored by the world; with Islamic fervor, partnership with Tehran, propaganda by al-Turabi,[62] and the potent weapon of international terrorism, the country has emerged as a new focal point of revolution in North Africa, a region of mostly status-quo powers. Lacking the will and infrastructure to deal with its immense internal problems, the Sudan has turned outward to create problems for other states. It does not need weapons of mass destruction, but only trained cadres of the militant and foreign-born.

Iraq, initially a pro-Western state, moved towards the Soviet bloc in the 1970s, and then maintained fair relations with both superpowers during the 1980s while it was continuously at war with Tehran. Iraq is home to, and supportive of, Abu Abbas, whose Palestine Liberation

Ahmad Jibril: a Syrian protégé

Origins Syrian army captain and demolition expert Ahmad Jibril is the founder of the Popular Front for the Liberation of Palestine – General Command. He broke away (in October 1968) from George Habash's PFLP. Now 50 years old, Jibril still dominates the PFLP–GC's (General Command's) internal power arrangements, while Syria has been its chief patron.

Objectives 'The violent destruction of the Jewish state in battle.' Rejection of interim compromises with Israel and steady opposition to the peace process.

Strength An early estimate put manpower at 250. Strength today may be similar. Repeated Israeli raids have not succeeded in eliminating the group.

Range Successful operations, arrests, and published intelligence reports show that, apart from a group presence in the Middle East, there are PFLP–GC cells in European countries, especially Sweden and Germany. Some of the Swedish/Scandanavian network was blown in a failed operation against El Al in June 1980. Rebuilt, the network was again crippled by arrests in Stockholm, Goteborg and Uppsala in mid-May 1989.

Major Operations PFLP–GC has three characteristic types of operations. There are low-tech attacks on Israeli citizens. There are high-tech operations against targets such as airliners in western Europe; these, with their demonstrations of engineering expertise, have become Jibril's signature activities. Finally, there are occasional assaults that approximate guerrilla attacks – i.e. assaults on military targets (albeit during times of peace).

First actions included a 1970 attack on a school bus in Moshav Avivim which left dozens wounded and 11 children dead. Another bus attack in 1990 on Israeli tourists in the Suez Canal area killed nine and critically wounded twice as many.

Operations of a second type have shown similar chronological range. PFLP–GC first attacked a civilian airliner in 1970, bombing Swiss Air flight 330 over Aargau, Switzerland; 47 people died. Another incident was the attempt against a 1972 El Al flight departing Rome. There is evidence that, two decades later, Jibril remains in action as an airliner bomber. With good cause, he was the first suspect in both the 1988 bombing over Lockerbie, Scotland, that brought down Pan Am 103, and the next year's Tenere Desert, Niger, crash of UTA 772; these two crimes killed 341 innocent people. Subsequent investigations may have pointed more strongly to Libyan perpetrators.

Guerrilla-style attacks on military targets in peacetime have included sophisticated operations in Israel and Europe both. A remarkable 1987 assault on an Israeli Defense Force unit featured multiple hang-gliders and left considerable damage. In that year and the next, there were bombings of US military trains in Europe under the direction of a PFLP–GC commander named Hafiz Dalkamoni.[60]

State Patronage Syria trained Ahmad Jibril as an army officer and has since continuously supported his terrorism. PFLP–GC's headquarters is near Damascus, and the Syrians give the group training bases in Syria and the Bekaa Valley, which is controlled by Syria. The group never harms Syrian interests.

Lebanon – which does not firmly control its own territory – is home to some bases of the PFLP–GC, including even a naval facility. These PFLP–GC installations often come under Israeli attack.

Weapons caches have included sophisticated Soviet bloc arms such as wire-guided anti-tank missiles, hand-held surface to air missiles (SAMs) and infra-red or night-vision rifles. The Soviets trained many PFLP–GC cadres in the USSR. Hundreds of Soviet weapons arrived for the group via freighters berthing in Syrian or Lebanese ports.

Libya provides considerable financial support, and may even assist PFLP–GC guerrillas who fought alongside Libyans in Chad.

Iran also supports the Jibril group, despite PFLP–GC's entirely secular character. But apparently Iranian financial aid has not been generous.

Front murdered American traveler Leon Klinghoffer aboard the hijacked cruise liner *Achille Lauro*. Baghdad also was an early supporter of PLO defector Abu Nidal; Nidal's locus later shifted to, and then away from Syria; all the while Iraq has done Nidal no harm and helped his small, nihilistic Palestinian group enormously. Another Palestinian group with a record of terrorism including attacks on aircraft, the organization lead by Abu Ibrahim, has enjoyed patronage of Baghdad.[63] The failed, but extensive, attempt by Iraq successfully to exploit these and many non-Palestinian terrorist assets will be explored in Chapter 6. One of Baghdad's non-Palestinian terrorist clients is the 'National Liberation Army' of the 'National Council of Resistance', based 60 miles north of the Iraqi capital. Fiercely opposed to the clerical rule of Iran, these exiles aspire to power themselves. They maintain a large conventional army and also frequently carry out bombings within Iran. Not surprisingly, they have been counter-attacked by Iran – with car bombings, aircraft, and even Scud missiles. The force is another example of an old pattern of international relations, whereby exiles in waiting near a border are maintained by a patron, to be used or not used as appropriate by the outside power – in this case Baghdad.

Iran is the most active of the world's state sponsors.[64] Like Iraq, it murders its own *émigrés* to remind nationals at home or abroad of their vulnerability and their purported responsibility to the regime. Some of the most remarkable events in international terrorism in the 1990s have occurred in European capitals like Paris, where Iranian teams of killers have employed patience, stealth, good planning, and weapons sometimes no more considerable than knives or handguns to murder one Iranian exile after another, usually because of political activities for democracy or against the mullahs. These murders – 11 are confirmed for 1994 and 1995 alone – are now so common they may receive only a few lines in foreign newspapers.[65] US State Department statistics released in April 1998 confirmed Iran's status as the leading global state sponsor of terrorism, even though President Clinton and his Secretary of State, less than two months later, publicly sought a warming of bilateral relations.

Iran's activities include wholesale support for Hezbollah: figures for yearly financial aid range from 30 to 100 million dollars,[66] in addition to full diplomatic support. It is not insignificant that Hezbollah has probably already killed more Americans than any other international terror group.[67] Iranian money and *matériel* flow to many other effective groups, including Bin Laden's group Al Qa'ida, Hamas, and Palestine Islamic Jihad, as well as extremists in Latin America and Asia like Abu Sayyaf. Nor has Iran been content to work at the lower levels of violence. There are nuclear programs at Esfahan, Bushehr, and two sites just west of Tehran. There may also be a relevant Iranian–South A relationship: Hezbollah had been permitted terrorist camps in Natal, and now there is new evidence of cooperation on nuclear energy between Tehran and Pretoria. Iran's indigenous chemical agent production and its work on biological weapons has long been proceeding. Iran has acquired the ballistic missiles and technology necessary to get poisons and toxins to external targets; it used this capability against Iraq between 1985 and 1988.[68] Weapons platforms such as submarines and two-man minisubs could also support use of weapons of mass destruction.[69]

It is not only sovereign states that are training terrorists. 'Gray-area' states such as Lebanon do so as well – sometimes intentionally, sometimes in spite of themselves. Afghanistan remains embroiled in violent civil war. The Taliban (meaning 'student') militia, a relatively new coalition of mostly Sunni fighters, has proceeded from success to success and now controls nearly all Afghan territory. Taliban, supported by Pakistan, may itself protect as many as 400 trained terrorists, including people whose connections reach the Mubarak assassination attempt in 1995 and the devastating double-bombing of US embassies in eastern Africa in August 1998. After the 1998 attacks the United States sent missiles into camps run by Osama Bin Laden in Afghanistan.[70] Taliban's actual control over the terrorists in its midst remains an unknown; its policy on the export of violence is as unclear as the future of Afghanistan itself. Similarly, while Taliban may oppose drug use, Afghanistan is now the world's largest grower of raw opium, with all the implicit connections to international crime.

The two greatest powers of East Asia are not deeply involved in the export of terrorism. Certainly Russia and China are maintaining capabilities to make and use weapons of mass destruction and also arming a number of radical foreign regimes. Moscow has continued its drive, including some support for insurgents in Georgia and other nearby states, to reincorporate many of the old territories into itself. This newest phase of a pronounced pattern since the seventeenth century also employs covert moneys, conventional diplomacy, and occasional use of force or lesser bullying.[71] China is hardly benign, but neither is it exporting trained personnel to murder, maim, and menace the innocent abroad for the policy ends of Beijing. The strongest and longest extant Chinese commitment has been to the Khmer Rouge, but that weapons aid is now much curtailed, which may help explain the guerrillas' plummeting strength within Cambodia.[72] There were many defections from the Khmer Rouge in 1996–98, as well as the house-arrest and then death of Pol Pot himself. It was not a pro-Chinese Khmer Rouge officer but a defector from that organization, the long-time pro-Vietnamese Hun

Sen, who grabbed state power in 1997. Political terrorism, especially against Funcinpec Party politicians, plagued Cambodia during 1998,[73] but it is not apparently linked to Beijing.

Japan is no sponsor of terrorism but a state which sometimes suffers from it. The Chukaku-Ha ('Middle Core Faction') was active up through the very early 1990s, attacking police stations or targets associated with the imperial family, and sometimes foreign interests in Japan, especially airports. It has faded, but may still possess many cadres. The smaller and much more deadly Japanese Red Army attacked in Japan and then increasingly only outside the country; it is now largely inactive in both realms. The leading threat to Japan and foreigners in Japan tomorrow may be from the right. Thus far incomprehensibly quiet, Japanese militant traditionalism is likely to arise – in political or religious form – to deplore what it sees as the bourgeois corruption of parliamentary politics, the decline in traditional culture, general lack of interest in religion, or the weakness or liberality of Japan's foreign policy. In that last case, it could mean attacks on Russians, Chinese, or others deemed rivals for territories such as the Kurile Islands.[74] Either left, or right, or the two acting in unspoken accord, could forge new militant opposition to Japan's slowly expanding role in international peacekeeping. Leftist arsonists have already pointed in this direction.[75] The left may also carry out attacks against, or in protest of, Japan's formidable armed forces. American armed forces personnel will be attractive individual targets for Japanese 'anti-imperialists', xenophobes, racists, and almost anyone with resentments that can be focused on foreigners. Instances of crime and incivility by American troops in Okinawa, and the last decade of hard economic years for Japan, could favor such assaults.

North Korea has been and remains today Asia's most flagrant supporter of clandestine international violence. This is the view in the region – not a mere obsession of Washington. Pyongyang's agents blew up much of the Burmese cabinet in 1983. Five years later, they deployed the two-person team that blew a Korean Air Line jet out of the sky in a bid to discourage visitors to the upcoming Olympic Games in Seoul. North Korea still harbors Japanese hijackers and other radicals. It is brazenly involved in international crime, using embassy personnel to sell contraband, including large quantities of narcotics. Like Cuba, North Korea makes an occasional nod to public relations, as it did with a modest apology for letting a submarine full of commandos loose in South Korea in September 1996. But another submarine became stranded at the boundary with South Korea in June 1998, one more small symbol of continuity in Pyongyang's policies despite the world community's demands for change. The communist government remains as it was, and militant internationalism will keep its role, both in justifying totalitarianism at home and for foreign policy reasons. It is likely that too much attention is being paid to whether the North will invade the South.[76] Cash and food reserves are too low, and, more importantly, neither of the great powers that aided the 1950 invasion would be party to a Kim Jong-Il coalition war in the year 2000. But terrorism, on the other hand, is warfare on the cheap; terrorism can best be done without risking destruction of the North Korean state; terrorism does not require – and indeed can be done best without – prior consultation with Beijing and Moscow. North Korean terrorism is thus to be expected – almost anywhere in Asia. Outside Asia, Korea has not made armed attacks, and it long ago discontinued its practice of providing hundreds of military advisors to African armies.

In all of Latin and Central America, only one sovereign state is charged by the United States with supporting international terrorism: Cuba. Its position on the State Department's terrorism list is tenuous, because there have been no recent confirmed acts by Havana. But the regime remains suspect, for reasons that go beyond the 1996 shoot-down of two small civilian aircraft from the Cuban–American relief group 'Brothers to the Rescue' based in Florida. Cuba has an extraordinary history of exporting violence, especially to neighboring weak states, a policy discernible as soon as Che Guevara and Fidel Castro attained power. It is still an advocate of Marxism–Leninism, and Castro is personally hostile towards 'bourgeois' states and especially the neighboring United States. Cuba remains a safe-haven for terrorists of such foreign countries as Spain, the United States, and Chile.[77] There are appropriate suspicions that Cuba continues its involvement in narcotics trafficking, which not long ago was a source of scarce foreign capital; this may be continuing quietly – despite occasional publicity-grabbing acts of cooperation with US authorities.[78] However, no pattern of overt violence, such as flagrant support for renewed terrorism by Puerto Rican militants,[79] is expected in the near future, even though the latter need it to bounce back from obscurity and imprisonment. The new climate of Latin and international politics, more than Havana's infamous fiscal problems, may keep Castro on a semi-legitimate international path.

The more general problem of state sponsorship of terrorism in the Latin region is that of indigenous death squads and abusive police units. Some of these enjoy access to intelligence, weapons, and vehicles of the government security services. Mexico has proven over and over again that corruption runs to its political core, literally crippling enforcement of laws against narcotics and refugee trafficking. Colombia and Peru have shallower pockets of corruption within armed forces and police that permit advantage to traffickers and left-wing terrorists. Argentina and Guatemala are democracies but have nightmarish legacies of recent police fierceness that may dissipate only a decade or more from now. Most Latin states are by and large quiet; many are among the world's calmest states; year after year; terrorism reports count few to no international incidents linked to Bolivia, Brazil, Paraguay, Uruguay, etc. Their governments must remember that illegal and corrupt government practices by individuals and groups of the far right may engender inappropriate public and activist support for terrorists of the still-entrenched left. Both extremes can still threaten the democratic center which, throughout the 1990s, has been on the ascendant in that continent.

Technologies and tactics of terrorism in the next decade

Turning from the broad political sources of terrorism to its technical and tactical types, the most pressing current threat is that of *the individual or small group with simple automatic weapons.* There is no more likely combination, for the near future of terrorism, than this sort of attack. There are hundreds of millions of automatic weapons in human hands around the world. Each now possesses the potency, in the presence of a crowd, to do extensive human damage in a matter of seconds. And the evident trend is towards man-portable guns with large magazines but overall construction that is lighter and shorter than that of traditional rifles; being more portable they are more useful than ever to terrorists. Nothing more than such commonplace portable weapons as guns and grenades are used in some of the largest massacres, including the Egypt Air jet hijacked to Malta and destroyed there (1985), the Rome and Vienna airport attacks by Abu Nidal and Libya (1985), and the Islamic Group's assault on foreign tourists visiting ancient temples in Luxor, Egypt (1997). The same two kinds of simple weapons were the staple of infamous terrorist attacks inside religious buildings in Ankara (1986) and Jerusalem (1995). Single assassinations can be accomplished with yet less firepower; within the United States, there have been political murders with pistols or rifles. By one tally, of victims including only writers and journalists, 13 have perished in the United States in recent years,[80] many presumably due to entanglements with foreign ethnic groups.

The small bomb is a less controllable but deadly terror weapon that can be readily used by a single killer or small group. Home-fashioned pipe bombs were a plague in Puerto Rico in the 1970s and 1980s before separatists like the Armed Forces of National Liberation (FALN) and Los Macheteros were jailed. In most cases they were intended to intimidate, more than to kill. Today's bombers within the United States include anti-abortionists, anti-federal government activists, and loners like the philosophically minded ecowarrior Ted Kaczynski. Most are unwilling to become a suicide bomber to ensure maximum casualties. They nonetheless often succeed at placing small charges where they can cripple or kill an enemy or his associates. Car booby traps, made not to devastate an area but to kill an occupant, have been unusual in the US, as compared with Lebanon, Sri Lanka, or the UK and Northern Ireland. Most such US attacks are aspects of organized crime. Car bombs require sophistication; the radio-controlled bomb used to kill Chilean Ambassador Orlando Letelier and US associate Ronnie Moffitt in Washington DC in 1976 is one of the rare US cases of successful political terrorism with this weapon.[81] Other kinds of small bombings are common in America, both for personal and political motives. A bomb can send a loud political message while containing physical damage to an immediate circle.[82]

The second major level of threat – less common than the first but also markedly more dangerous – is attack by *a group with professional skills and a medium-grade conventional weapon*. There had never been a terrorist-inspired assault on the US public by a large bomb in a vehicle until 1993; since then, truck bombs at the New York World Trade Center and the federal building in downtown Oklahoma City together killed 174. The first bomb also left a thousand others injured, and the second made casualties of hundreds more. The FBI classified the Oklahoma City device as a 'Weapon of Mass Destruction' – a term hitherto reserved for chemical, biological, or nuclear weapons. There is nothing like either attack in modern American political history, not even any of the terrorist strikes during the Vietnam War. For hint of a parallel, one must go back to the bombing and rioting in Haymarket Square, Chicago, of 1886 in which seven police died and more than 70 were injured. The danger in the near future is indicated not just by the two truck bombs but by the relative simplicity of their construction. A similar plot, against the Lincoln and Holland Tunnels in New York City, involved mass amounts of hand-mixed liquid explosives. Pre-empted by arrests, it achieved no more than scaring commuters who drive that artery. But others might have noticed that a later, moderate-sized, and probably unintended fire in 1996 in the new cross-channel Franco-British tunnel caused injuries, closed the passages for weeks, and cost some $85 million to repair. Such an accident brings to mind terrorist scenarios. One also considers the damage that could be done if a normal automobile stocked with explosive were driven aboard a car ferry and detonated when the vessel moved away from shore. Cities like Seattle and New York move hundreds of people at a time on such ferries, and there are similar traffic patterns throughout Asia, back and forth across the English Channel, and in other regions.

To date, no surface-to-air missile (SAM) has dropped an American passenger jet from the skies. But this must be considered in part the result of good fortune. Few scenarios are more simple, regrettably, because civilian airliners are not fitted with the kind of flares combat planes drop to distract heat-seeking missiles. A team possessing a British 'Red Eye', a North Korean or Chinese shoulder-fired SAM, or an American 'Stinger' could position itself in a boat near Washington's National Airport or off the New York coast near Kennedy International.[83] Similar opportunities are available inland near large airports. The Chicago street gang that linked up with Libyan money may have sought to buy a missile for just this purpose in 1985.[84] Large airports serving international traffic give terrorists targets at predictable and publicly available times; the planes arrive from or leave for countries of openly known political allegiances. They may also be attacked on the ground. Vigilance, good planning by transportation authorities, and reasonable police capability are required for a free society to forestall attacks of this sort. There have been cases of pre-emption of terrorist plans against airports.

The pattern of terrorist attempts to acquire heat-seeking missiles seems to offer a new case annually in American courts alone. In 1990 Colombian nationals under investigation by the Polk County Florida Sheriff's Office sought to buy Stingers and automatic military weapons in order to kill Colombian officials and US Drug Enforcement Agency employees in Colombia, and to shoot down Colombian helicopters. The end receiver for the buy was to be the Medellin cartel, which uses terror against the government to restrict its counterdrug operations and to oppose extradition of terrorists and narcotraffickers to the United States.[85] Narcotics traffickers of today are often better equipped than the police forces arrayed against them, and air defense missiles have a natural place in the criminals' arsenals. In 1991 three Croatians were arrested by US Customs agents for trying to buy 20 Stingers, as well as guns, for use against Serbia. In 1992 an Iranian army colonel reputed to be Iran's chief trafficker in Europe and the United States, was arrested in Madrid; he had violated international COCOM (Coordinating Committee) military commerce regulations in seeking to buy the Stinger. Spain was a COCOM member, as was the United States where the Stingers are made.[86] Proponents of the IRA conspired to procure weapons that included a Stinger in 1993 in Tucson, Arizona, and were arrested in that year;[87] this foiled another IRA effort against the British helicopter in Northern Ireland. And in 1994 Cuban exiles of 'Commandos F-4' were arrested in Miami while seeking various weapons, including Stingers, for an attack on Cuba.[88]

There is a more troubling pattern: successful acquisition and use of heat-seeking missiles. Cases of such use by small groups now include the Palestinian PFLP outside Rome's airport (1973), and outside Nairobi airport (1976); in Rhodesia where an airliner crash killed 38 (1978); the destruction of a UTA flight 772, a passenger liner over Chad (1988); the shooting-down of an Italian aircraft near Sarajevo (1992); three aircraft downed over the Republic of Georgia (1993–94); loss of a World Food Program 727 over Angola (1994); LTTE destruction of two Sri Lankan air force transports, killing 94 people (1995), and PKK use of Russian shoulder-fired missiles to down two Turkish helicopters over northern Iraq.[89]

The list of successes will grow, barring counter-measures by civil air authorities. Many active groups possess man-portable missiles. Several hundred Stinger missiles provided to Afghan *mujahideen* for use against the Red Air Force are unaccounted for. There may have been as many as 30 of the missiles obtained by Iran from an Afghan convoy near their mutual border in 1987, and by one account, Iran's Revolutionary Guards own a half-dozen, at a minimum. Qatar found Stingers on the black market and refused to return them to the United States in 1988. North Korea is believed to possess Stingers. Other violent groups reported to possess man-portables include the Algerian GIA, the Tamil Tigers, Chechen rebels, and some Central Americans. Finally, there are others who have made unconfirmed claims to possess such weapons: the Islamic Renaissance Party in Tajikistan; and Abu Sayyaf, the break-away Muslim group in the Philippine island of Mindanao which has ties to Middle Eastern extremists.[90]

Heat-seeking missiles and the newer infra-red missiles are improving. The technology is becoming lighter, more lethal, and more readily available. Some experts think very well of the Russian successor to the old 'Grail' SA-7, especially the 'Gimlet' SA-16, which is credited with 'kills' of airliners over the former Soviet Union. China is exporting a highly portable 'fire-and-forget' model with considerable technical potency. Called the 'Vanguard' or QW-1, it weighs less than 17 kilos and yet can strike aircraft as high as 4,000 meters.[91] Given that China has a steady record of weapons sales to Iran, North Korea, and almost any party with cash, however radical,[92] this development is of real concern.

The old-fashioned rocket-propelled grenade (RPG), developed by armed services to stop tanks and kill bunkers full of infantry, retains its full range of terrorist potential. Simpler to use and easier to acquire than heat-seekers, the RPG line has been made for decades by many major powers and can be found in army arsenals all over the world.[93] When Washington DC, in its periodic bouts of terrorism concern, contemplates such physical defenses as a fence of wrought-iron bars around the Capitol, it must consider whether a LAW rocket-launcher or other RPG could not be simply thrust between the bars and fired with effect from that fence line. A mentally disturbed man recently stuck an automatic rifle through the White House fence, though his light bullets had little effect.

A deadly 'mid-tech' threat which goes strangely undiscussed by terrorism analysts and journalists covering hostile groups is the ultralight aircraft. Readily available from manufacturers in the United States, Germany, and other countries, requiring little operating skill and nothing more than a city street for take-off, these minuscule aircraft could be used to drop a small bomb, spread chemical or biological toxins, or transport a suicide bomber. After a decade and a half of car bombs in the globe's crowded public places, it seems almost bizarre that a small airplane or ultralight has not been used in a major urban area terror attack. Like the nerve gas attack in a city subway, this is surely something which, so readily conceivable, is likely to occur.

Attacks by a group with professional skills and a medium-grade weapon of some type are not merely possible today but almost inevitable. Most types of terror groups favor such strikes. Some analysts of the early 1980s made a little-supported argument that 'black' or fascist terrorists kill *en masse*, while the 'red' or communist terrorists 'attack more selectively'. In fact, both have killed civilians in large numbers, individually and in mass attacks. 'Red' bomb attacks include all those by George Habash's PFLP and the IRA Provisionals; the New People's Army's 'false flag' operation that left dozens dead or wounded at a Manila rally in 1972; Ahmad Jibril's plots against civilian airliners; and the Tamil LTTE Tiger car bombs that shatter buildings in Sri Lanka. On the right, Europe's neofascists have bombed and bloodied such public facilities as train stations and highway tunnels. The United States has its own brands of extremists willing to use all the powers a medium-grade weapon offers. If the perpetrators of the wreckage in Oklahoma City are the only anti-federal 'patriots' thus far to begin the mass-murders sketched out in *The Turner Diaries*, they have nonetheless made a noteworthy beginning. There are doubtless others with equal delusions of conspiracy, and they too may forge dangerous plans for themselves. Fortunately, most militias have never killed and do not wish

The ultra-light aircraft threat

Modern terrorist training sometimes includes aviation skills – not only in hijacking, but in the handling of a range of aircraft.

The PLO experimented with varieties of aircraft for years. Pilots were trained with expert foreign assistance in Yugoslavia, Libya, Syria, Lebanon, and in the Soviet bloc. A nascent PLO air detachment, 'Force 14', was established on Kamaran Island off Yemen in the Red Sea. Eventually, personnel of the PLO obtained enough expertise such that individuals served formally on flight teams of an accommodating international airline, that of Mauritania.

Iran has trained militants in the use of small aircraft at bases associated with military or terrorist activity. On the Gulf coast, Bushehr is such a base, and trainees there have been flying Pilatus Porters, maybe as a prelude to suicide missions. *Jane's Intelligence Review* is equally concerned about Iranian acquisition of Cessna Citations and Dassault Falcons, which could be used to destroy 'the homes of heads of state in the Gulf and Near East regions in suicide attacks'. There are recent reports of these terrorist training activities in northeastern sites in Iran.

Ultralight aircraft are easy to acquire and to fly. In 1990 *Jane's Defense Weekly* summarized ultralight training thus far: Palestinian factions aided by Syria, Libya, and Iran have already worked seriously with mini-aircraft and have made purchases of such craft from companies in western Europe. Ahmad Jibril, whose PFLP–GC terrorizes Europe with sophisticated airline bombs, worked through Syria to contract with a West German company as far back as 1981, and his group and others have bought a number of mini-aircraft since. By the end of the 1980s, Jibril, Abu Nidal, Abu Abbas, and various Shiite groups all possessed some very light aircraft.

Many attacks have already been attempted, though usually with little success. The Palestine Liberation Front tried to attack Israeli oil refineries with two powered hang-gliders in March of 1981. In November 1987 the PFLP–GC launched four hang-gliders from Sultan Yaakub, in Syrian-controlled Lebanon, against the Israeli army; one pilot did land and inflict 16 casualties before being shot. In 1989 there were attacks by Shia militia suicide bombers using very light aircraft.[94]

The potential uses of powered small aircraft for bomb runs, commando raids, suicide bombings, radio-controlled non-human bombs, and disbursement of chemical or biological agents, are blatant and deeply disturbing.

to do so.[95] To such political paths there are now also religious parallels; many groups around the world would not hesitate to use large-scale killing for their 'religious' purposes.

The third level of terrorist threat for the coming years is that of a *highly skilled group with a weapon of mass destruction.* Chemical, biological, and nuclear agents have the capacity to take thousands, even hundreds of thousands, of lives. Not long ago, the view prevailed among many experts that the great barrier to employment of such weapons would be the profound and widespread loathing they would engender among the 'audience' they were supposed to attract. America's best terrorism analyst, Brian Jenkins, had enunciated that view a quarter-century ago, regarding nuclear dangers.[96] He was right, regarding nuclear dangers. But did 1995 bring dusk over such hopes? With nerve gas in Tokyo, a religious cult demonstrated that in an 'unlimited war' upon the world there are no limits on weaponry. Two years earlier, a truck bomb nearly toppled a New York skyscraper. Thus the world's two greatest financial capitals have seen proof that cultists in the service of a zealous religiopolitical leader (the Aum cult's Asahara; Egypt's Sheik Rahman) were fully prepared to create mass death and mass mayhem for political–religious purposes. 'Aum' actually expected war imminently, war which would destroy most of Japan; it thus had little fear of its own fearsome weapons. Such professionalized groups, with or without state assistance, may attempt physical destruction on a scale formerly contemplated mainly by warlords or states. Terrorism, said to be the poor man's weapon, holds out chemical, biological, and even nuclear prospects for making a modest group of limited means more noteworthy – or temporarily more powerful – than some sovereign countries.

National governments, with the coldest deliberation, have already used chemical weapons. Belligerents in the First World War began it. Still horrified a quarter-century later, most belligerents in the European theater of the Second World War disdained chemical attacks for fear of retaliation. Italy did use them in Ethiopia, and Japan turned them upon the Chinese. Later wars would bring other usage: Egypt, against Yemen in the mid 1960s; Soviet-bloc armies in both Laos and Afghanistan (it appears) Iraq against Iran in the long *sitzkrieg* war of the 1980s; and then, incredibly, in March 1988, Iraq against its own rebellious (Kurdish) population in Halabjah, a city in northeastern Iraq. To these powers must be added the short list of states with proven records of terrorism sponsorship that produce or stockpile chemical weapons, including Syria, Libya, possibly still Iraq, and certainly Iran. By 1996 Tehran had already produced several hundred tons of chemical agents that kill by choking, blistering, or other means. No UN-sponsored bombing campaign has interrupted Iranian developments. A half-world away are other producers, the communist states of Vietnam and North Korea. Russia had an enormous chemical and biological production record in its late Soviet years. It is now unaggressive but profoundly troubled, and subject to frequent thefts of its national war *matériel*. Russia has publicly released a manifest of its chemical munitions inventory, and these stockpiles presumably still exist. These states might provide a weapon to an allied radical group, judging that the enormous damage resulting would not – or would not soon – be traced back to them. As a pre-war terror weapon, or against a particularly detested enemy, such use is highly probable. Or, such states or scientists trained by them might sell technical advice or weapons themselves to terrorists for cash.

Small groups with strong technical skills can also make chemical agents themselves, as did Aum, recruiting for the purpose from the 'hard sciences' departments of Japan's fine universities. Home-made cyanide and sarin were used in several Aum attacks,[97] at least one of them lethal, additional to the 20 March 1995 strike against the Tokyo subway. That better-known assault killed 11 and caused severe sickness in thousands. With proper fan or aerosol systems for correctly distributing its nerve gas, Aum might have achieved its obvious purpose – wholesale death. Subsequent seizures of Aum properties yielded not only more sarin gas components but at least one bottle of a stronger nerve agent, VX, discovered buried on the property of an Aum member.

Tactical opportunities for the use of chemicals are not difficult to imagine. 'Rejectionists' of the Palestinian–Israeli peace accords could strike a blow against the Israeli nation by placing vats of lethal chemical just downwind of a new Jewish housing settlement in Palestine. Several simultaneous attacks of that kind might throw Israel into a panic that would do almost as much physical damage to moderate Palestinians as to Jewish people. Or, German neoNazis with technical help from even one 'Nordic' scientist could hurl chemical bombs into a major political rally of Muslims in Cologne, or anarchists and squatters in Berlin. American troops in Saudi Arabia, or a US mission in Jordan or Egypt, might experience chemical attack during peace-time when some radical Middle Eastern state is angling for greater power in the region. Libya is well prepared for making just such various attacks. Its bombers and missiles could serve as conventional delivery mechanisms, but Libya would be the first to see the advantages of instead using 'cut outs' like its favored nihilistic groups, Abu Nidal and the Japanese Red Army. Libya has invested years and tens of millions of dollars into a chemical weapons industry and proved its readiness to use them at least once –

against Chadian troops in 1987. While that air-dropped agent was supplied by Iran, Libya has now manufactured at least a hundred tons of its own blister and nerve agents at Rabta and Tarhunah, underground facilities within 100 kilometers of Tripoli.[98]

Biological attacks are more frightening than chemical attacks for three good reasons. First, they are invisible, and may take longer to kill, making bio-agents harder to anticipate and evade than many chemicals. Second, instead of dispersing in the air, sometimes within minutes as will many chemicals, biological war agents may spread, linger, and even propagate. One US government test years ago dropped dummy 'anthrax'-filled light-bulbs into subway tunnels and the air moved by the trains dispersed the agent until it 'killed' thousands. Under proper weather conditions, a single warhead landing in the American capital could kill more people than did the Hiroshima bomb. Third, biological weapons are cheap relative to their immense lethality. They are hundreds of times more cost-effective per victim for the terrorist group than the atomic, chemical, or conventional bomb.[99]

The only known uses of biological warfare before the twentieth century were in the sporadic cases in which besiegers catapulted plague-infested bodies over defensive walls in a bid to infect the towns. But twentieth-century man has demonstrated superior technological skills. There is new scientific evidence that Germany experimented with anthrax weapons in Norway towards the end of the First World War.[100] In August 1942 Imperial Japanese technicians with armies conquering mainland China apparently used plague, dispersed from an aircraft, against the community of Congshan in Zhejiang Province. Two weeks after the spraying, rats began dying *en masse*, and then a quarter of the population died. Japan's technicians were on the scene, wearing protective clothing, and reportedly conducting medical experiments.[101]

Contemporary terrorists have sporadically produced or purchased biological weapons. In the 1970s, botulism culture was discovered growing in test tubes in a German Red Army Faction safehouse in Paris, and a now-forgotten American sect called the Order of the Rising Sun was found to possess typhoid bacteria for possible use against Midwestern city water supplies. Later, Japan's Aum Shinrikyo carried out two attacks with botulism and anthrax; neither succeeded and the failures have gone unpublicized.[102]

A castor bean by-product named ricin, was placed in special tiny pellets shot from 'umbrella guns' by would-be assassins in several European attacks against Eastern Bloc *émigrés*. This toxin infected and killed a Radio Liberty commentator, Bulgarian exile Georgi Markov, in London in 1978; the other victim was operated on swiftly and survived.[103] Today's terrorists remain interested in the potency of ricin: members of two different American 'militia' groups – in Arkansas and Minnesota – have been found with dangerous quantities. In the former case it was transported across the Canadian–US border; in the latter it was produced in a home. The Minnesotan reportedly intended to use the weapon against local officials. The other militiaman's intentions are unclear; imprisoned in Arkansas on possession charges, Thomas Lewis Lavy committed suicide in December 1995 before trial.[104]

State producers of biological weapons which might place them in terrorist hands are almost as numerous as chemical war producers. The Soviet Union had laboratories and an enormous scientific personnel pool at work in a project code-named 'Biopreparat'.[105] Research on infectious agents from animal, plant, and microbiological life was supplemented by Ministry of Defense-funded work on cloud physics, airborne infections, and other sciences with direct applicability to both offensive and defensive uses of biological warfare agents.[106] Post-Cold War defections have shown that the West underestimated the extent of the Soviet work; 70,000 scientists and technicians worked on germ weapons. Since there are now extreme personal pressures on these highly skilled Russians, who lack not only opportunity but often pay and food,[107] a long-standing concern has been that some personnel could easily be drafted away by radical states ready to pay huge salaries. The first public evidence of this is now out: Russian scientists have told of five colleagues known to have left for work in Iran, while more remain at work in the former Soviet Union while receiving Iranian salaries.[108] Iraq, for its part, until recently maintained a medical staff of hundreds at no less than five facilities that produced poisons, including the fiercely lethal diseases anthrax and botulinum toxin. Captured documents now indicate Iraqi plans for dispersing biological and chemical agents in missiles, drone aircraft, and airplanes such as crop-dusters.

The American military, taken aback by all this physical and documentary evidence of advanced production and deployment plans, has since carried out a war game at the Naval War College in Newport, Rhode Island, in which an enemy uses germ warfare. It did not proceed well; US carriers were 'attacked', and anthrax 'killed' a million civilians in Saudi Arabia.[109] By 1998 US armed forces were going ahead with plans for mass inoculations of service personnel against anthrax poisoning. Meanwhile, several American cities faced a flurry of phony anthrax weapon threats.

The nuclear weapon is the other category of weapons of mass destruction potentially available to terrorists. It has long been regarded as the ultimate weapon. But a nuclear bomb is far harder to obtain than a biological weapon. And it may not even necessarily be as lethal, given the 'small' yields of some modern tactical nuclear shells and missiles, as against the slow but growing devastation that a biological weapon could cause in advantageous weather. That said, there remain some portentous realities. Nuclear technology is familiar to scientists and graduate students in many countries. Nuclear weapons or enriched nuclear materials of various types lie in depots in at least these countries: China, England, France, Libya, India, Iran, Iraq (at least until recently), Israel, North Korea, Pakistan, Russia, South Africa, the Ukraine, the United States.[110] 'Bleeding' of nuclear technologies and materials into unauthorized hands has occurred frequently since the Warsaw Pact collapsed; most of its members used nuclear power plants. Dangerous states like Iran, Iraq, Libya, and North Korea all have 'dual use' (civilian and military) programs which are exceedingly difficult to distinguish and to control from afar.[111] Cuba plans nuclear power plants. Reactors in all these countries will use high-grade nuclear material and turn out large quantities of nuclear waste each year; both fuel and its byproducts could be useful to terrorists. And, finally, many radical states or radical groups all but lust for the power that even a single nuclear weapon bears. The totality of this means the first use since 1945 of a nuclear device for malevolent purposes is not only theoretically possible but practically possible. The two decisive issues are availability and will.

Availability is less of a problem than it was in the late 1980s. Nuclear technology is expensive and complex, yet it might be 'home-made'. While the traditional implosion device requires a delicately balanced sphere that is collapsed by explosive charges upon a central nuclear core, creating the primary explosion, there is a second, easier method: a nuclear 'gun', which may be more readily created by skilled technicians.[112] Or, existing weapons might be illicitly obtained. For example, nuclear mines were long available to NATO along the line through Europe opposite the Iron Curtain. Now there are even 'backpack' nuclear weapons. And some small, portable devices are exceedingly powerful.[113] Because many of the aforementioned nuclear program countries have a record of using international terrorism as a foreign policy tool, it is very possible that a state would help terrorists obtain a weapon or material for a weapon. It is also possible that such a state would use terrorists to carry out a limited nuclear strike prior to, or as an alternative to, initiating war itself with an enemy state. Such 'false flag' operations are common and serve to create ambiguity which, however temporary, can be an important advantage in military operations.

More disturbing is the possibility that perhaps no state *need* be involved. Since the demise of the Soviet nuclear weapons program, national security analysts have feared that a dissolving scientific superstructure would lead a minority of scientists to deal directly with overseas buyers, or to emigrate to foreign states where they might be offered important new posts in nascent nuclear programs. A few such high-level relocations could become a decisive link between a terrorist group or state willing to go to nuclear war, and the technical capacity to do so. This fear has led to an important and appropriate reallocation of resources within American intelligence services. Such linkages are not difficult to imagine, especially given decades of technical programs that saw Warsaw Pact country scientists and military advisors by the thousands in long-term employment in such states as Syria, Libya, Iran, and Iraq, Cuba, and China; many of those older contacts could become bridges to new contact.

The most likely nuclear terrorist threat of all is of the type that is the most technically practicable, yet one that is rarely publicly discussed. It would be a professional terrorist group's use of nuclear material valued not for its explosive power, but for its capacities to poison and to create fear. Plutonium or uranium can be obtained on the black market, or by theft from a state with a civilian or military nuclear program. Fortunately, most reported nuclear smuggling incidents or terror threats have been hoaxes, or have involved materials of insignificant strength. But late in 1995, Chechens placed a container of nuclear material in a Moscow park and then alerted authorities to protest Russian offensives in the war in Chechnya. Important incidents of theft include three kilos of enriched uranium in the Czech Republic in 1994,[114] and 50 kilograms taken in mid-1997 from a Lithuanian power station – but recovered later in a forest.[115]

Nuclear material of no real quality, even power plant waste, could be placed in a major air conditioning or water system. There are past cases of terror groups contemplating or attempting such actions in the United States. Another, very different scenario would involve nuclear waste, more easily obtainable and less potent than nuclear fuel. Several barrels of waste could be emplaced with conventional explosive in a city or near a military base. The upper reaches of a public building would make a promising location. Then the terrorists would issue a statement, presumably including evidence of planning and actual possession of the nuclear material. Any concessions would be a success. In the absence of political concessions, the cache would be blown up, disseminating poisonous nuclear waste. Public threat of such a detonation, if credible, could cause pervasive fear and a massive, possibly hysterical flight of population. On the other hand, exploding the nuclear waste would bring sickness to many over the long term. Either way, civil authorities would find the situation supremely difficult.[116]

Notes

1. US Department of State, *Patterns of Global Terrorism: 1996* (Washington, DC: GPD, April 1997), p. 70, and the subsequent *Patterns of Global Terrorism: 1997* (Washington, DC: GPO, April 1998).
2. The three wounded were Nicholas Starr, Calvin R. Morgan, and Stephen E. Williams. The shooting was on 25 January 1993; proceedings were in Fairfax County Circuit Court, Virginia during the latter half of 1997: *Washington Times* (2 July 1997).
3. An unknown group, the 'Amal Secret Committee', claimed credit for the assassination of four American businessmen in their car in Karachi. The *New York Times* (14 November 1997) reported that many Pakistanis were angered by the extradition of Kasi, and that some in Baluchistan had sworn revenge.
4. Article 27 of the Charter of Hamas speaks of close fraternal relations with the PLO but also states flatly: '... the PLO has adopted the idea of a Secular State ... Secular thought is diametrically opposed to religious thought'. Charter text as appearing in Raphael Israeli (trans.), 'The Charter of Allah: The Platform of the Islamic Resistance Movement (Hamas)', in Y. Alexander and H. Forman (eds), *The 1988–1989 Annual on Terrorism* (Netherlands: Kluwer, 1990), op. cit., p. 123. The Charter includes passages in which it intermingles its own religious emphasis with traditional Palestinian nationalism, as is suggested by another note below.
5. In past years some analysts, including a *New York Times* reporter, deprecated the idea that Colombian militants were involved in the drug trade. Now a typical news story from Colombia includes such details as this, from the 8 December 1996 *New York Times*: FARC had seized young army recruits and the suspicion was that the guerrillas would try to trade them back for an army commitment to vacate one coca-growing region of the south 'where the FARC collects protection money from growers and traffickers'. Pessimism now dominates most foreign reporters' assessments, as suggested by these titles: Robert D. Novak, 'Who Lost Colombia?', and Douglas F. Farah, 'Colombian Rebels Seen Winning War', *Washington Post* (9 and 10 April 1998).
6. The killing of demobilized Contras was ultimately the subject of an investigative report by a US Senate committee. The *New York Times* of 22 March 1997 covered one arms haul from a ranch owned by a retired Sandinista army officer: nearly two tons of dynamite, rifles, grenades, machine guns, rocket launchers, *plastique*, etc. Another find occurred in Managua in May 1993 after an explosion at a shop owned by a Basque of ETA.
7. Christopher C. Harmon, 'The Purposes of Terrorism Within Insurgency: Shining Path in Peru', *Small Wars and Insurgencies*, 3:2 (autumn 1992), pp. 170–90. A later article called 'Terrorism as a Strategy of Insurgency' appeared from Ariel Merari in *Terrorism and Political Violence*, 5:4 (winter 1993), pp. 213–51.
8. Expert foreign reporter Thomas A. Marks, however, argues in his 1996 book *Maoist Insurgency Since Vietnam* (London: Frank Cass), that the Maoist model has largely failed. I agree – with reservations; the world's biggest country has not been fully liberated from Maoism and on most continents Maoists challenge modern

political orders such as democracy, personalist despotism, and politicized Islam.

9. Many of the Palestinians of religious motives who are using terrorism have, in their own eyes, settled the dilemma of their nationalist interest in a homeland and the 'internationalism' of Islam. For example, Article 12 of the charter of Hamas begins:

> Hamas regards Nationalism (*Wataniyya*) as part and parcel of the religious faith. Nothing is loftier or deeper in Nationalism than waging Jihad against the enemy and confronting him when he sets foot on the land of the Muslims...
>
> While other nationalisms consist of material, human and territorial considerations, the nationality of Hamas also carries, in addition to all those, the all important divine factors ... [It] raises in the skies of the Homeland the Banner of the Lord, thus inexorably connecting earth with Heaven. (Charter text as repr. in Raphael Israeli, op. cit., p. 114; italics added).

10. An important monograph argues well that, in the post-communist age, many insurgencies are either more religious or more commercial and criminal in nature than were the older, more political insurgencies: Steven Metz, *The Future of Insurgency* (Carlisle Barracks, PA: US Army War College, 10 December 1993).

11. Kidnapping has become an industry in Latin America, and active or former leftist militants are involved; multiple sources, including a lengthy report by the *Los Angeles Times* (19 April 1998). Another illustration of communist interests giving way to criminal ones is the seepage of nuclear materials from the former Soviet Union. In 1994 the Russian intelligence service informed President Boris Yeltsin that in six months during the previous year there had been 900 thefts from military and nuclear plants. Most of the nuclear material incidents were attributable to 'insiders'. Making money – not political trouble – was deemed the primary motive. Security and risk analysts around the world recognize in this a shocking absence of effective state controls on what could be components of weapons of mass destruction. And if the former USSR's nuclear materials are ill-controlled, it is logical that the program in covert biological weapons production may be equally dangerous to the outside world.

12. One of the highest estimates, this is from Colombian and US intelligence sources, reports the *Washington Post* (27 December 1998).

13. Sources for this graphic are diverse, as are the parameters of each tally. For example, deaths in Palestine are for only a few years and were individually counted from an incident catalogue kept on the Internet site on 'Minorities at Risk' by Ted Robert Gurr. The Philippines/NPA tally is a government figure, courtesy of an AFP Army officer, but the Muslim-driven southern separatist movement figure is cumulative, covering more years, taken from a press source. The Basque tally reflects only ETA victims – not deaths from other terrorists, pro-state or anti-state. Many figures are running tallies from major US newspapers. Each statistic thus carries difficulties and comes with this analyst's reservations. Note as well the selective label; no attempt is made here to include all the world's conflict zones.

14. The PKK had been largely ignored by the American press for years, but the arrest and release of Ocalan in Italy prompted a wave of interest. Turkish press coverage included analysis by Middle East scholar Kamal Ali Beyoghlow, 'Ocalan's Italian Strategy', *Zaman*, repr. in English in the *Turkish Times* (Washington, DC: 15 December 1998).

15. See 'Russian Smuggling Ring Arms Kurd Rebels in Turkey', *Washington Times* (23 June 1997). By one published account, reporter Bill Gertz astonishes those in Washington charged with security of classified information.

16. *Washington Post* (9 February 1997).
17. The best-known thinker in this line is Harvard's Samuel Huntington, author of the celebrated 'Clash of Civilizations' article in *Foreign Affairs*. Dr Don Kagan of Yale University is among those opposing him.

   To accept Huntington's hypothesis and call the post-Cold War world one of battling civilizations would help to illuminate certain kinds of terrorism but also causes analytical problems. The thesis is of no help in understanding, for example, why American 'Patriots' would attack their federal government with truck bombs, since 'Western civilization' has a tradition of liberty but also one of limited elected government. A more likely example of Huntington's thesis is that of the Muslim gunmen, who I believe are operating as much on state impetus and with the aid of state governments as they are on spontaneous individual religious passion. One must not underestimate the role of states such as Iran and Sudan, and it remains to be seen just how 'autonomous' are such Muslim militant leaders as Sheik al Rahman of World Trade Center note.
18. According to Michael Kraft, legislation expert and congressional liaison at the State Department's Office of the Coordinator for Counterterrorism, as of January 1999 Bin Laden has not been placed on the United States list of 30 terrorist groups to whom Americans may not give any material aid. But such a ban on Bin Laden seems imminent. NBC News has reported that government sources say Bin Laden's operatives are in 50 countries world-wide and train in camps in 20 nations; Andrea Mitchell on 18 January 1999.
19. One source on these diverse efforts by outside powers to influence the internal affairs of the new central Asian states is the weekly *Foreign Report*. Jim Phillips, analyst at the Heritage Foundation, has been of great help via telephone. See Zbigniew Brzezinski, *Out of Control: Global Turmoil on the Eve of the 21st Century* (New York: Scribner's, 1993), p. 159, as quoted in the endnotes of Magnus Ranstorp and Gus Xhudo, 'A Threat to Europe? Middle East Ties with the Balkans and their Impact Upon Terrorist Activity throughout the Region', *Terrorism and Political Violence*, 6:2 (summer 1994), pp. 196–223.
20. *Foreign Report* (10 April 1997).
21. While that estimate seems high, one may consider that a more recent estimate by one German security official is 6,000, not 2,000.

   The Bosnian president pleaded for internationalist Muslim aid in September 1992 and, two months later, more than 50 guerrillas from Hezbollah and Islamic Tawheed arrived by sea from Lebanon: *Washington Times* (28 September and 10 November 1992). Many others would follow, including Egyptians trained by Pasdaran at Osama Bin Laden's expense; *Foreign Report* (13 August 1998).
22. *New York Times* (28 November 1996). Ranstorp and Xhudo, pp. 203–9, confirm in the Bosnian case many of the operational patterns of international terrorism I touch on in Chapter 3, e.g. drugs-for-guns trade along the Adriatic and eastern Mediterranean, use of Cyprus as one shipment point, efforts by Palestinians (Ahmad Jibril) to create forward bases in the former Yugoslavia, expenditure on weapons of funds raised from Islamic sources for humanitarian relief, and such expressions of internationalism as Hezbollah murals in Beirut depicting aspects of the Islamic struggle in Bosnia.
23. In America, both militias and 'eco-warriors' have recognized the operational advantages to semi-autonomy and decentralization; see Chapter 3. An Internet site where advice on this may be read is http://www.ANIMAL-LIBERATION.NET

   Considered internationally, note the view of the Secretary of Defense's Special Operations and Low Intensity Conflict office for the chapter on 'Unconventional

Military Instruments' in the annual volume *Strategic Assessment, 1996* (Washington, DC: National Defense University, 1996), Ch. 12: 'Increasingly, international terrorism has been marked by the appearance of less-organized groups, which coalesce around a leader for a specific operation or series of operations, receiving various kinds and levels of support from different governments and individuals. Such a group carried out the bombing of the World Trade Center.'

24. *New York Times* (29 October 1986), as cited by Bruce Hoffman, *Recent Trends and Future Prospects of Terrorism in the United States* (Santa Monica, CA: RAND, 1988), p. 43n.

25. Robert Sullivan, 'The Face of Eco-Terrorism', *New York Times Magazine* (20 December 1998).

26. Recently a British academic journal devoted an issue to international concerns over water. This is not surprising; what is notable is the subject and title of the journal: *Studies in Conflict and Terrorism.*

27. The White House, doubtless reflecting some of Vice President Al Gore's views, published *A National Security Strategy of Engagement and Enlargement* in 1995 which includes paragraphs on environmental matters, including: 'Increasing competition for the dwindling reserves of uncontaminated air, arable land, fisheries and other food sources, and water, once considered 'free' goods, is already a very real risk to regional stability around the world. The range of environmental risks serious enough to jeopardize international stability extends to massive population flight from man-made or natural catastrophes, such as Chernobyl or the East African drought, and to large-scale ecosystem damage caused by industrial pollution, deforestation, loss of biodiversity, ozone depletion, desertification, ocean pollution and ultimately climate change' (Washington, DC: GPO, February 1995), p. 18.

During a 1993 trip to Lithuania, I was intrigued to see in new (unclassified) drafts of the Ministry of National Defense's 'National Security Concept' paper, and hear from government officials, profound concern about Soviet damage to the Lithuanian environment during a half-century of occupation. The country was grappling with messes on evacuated military bases, chemical waste dumps, etc. One draft listing the nine 'most important National Security objects' placed 'Ecological status' even before 'Personal security of every citizen (and) freedom and rights for every person'. Another draft referred to 'Overspill of pollutants from neighboring countries', 'Ecological disasters', and even 'Covert burying of poisonous (radioactive) materials on the territory of Lithuania'.

28. There is still no evidence that the three Ethiopians were terrorists, but their motives are unclear; *Times* (16 May 1998).

29. Louis R. Mizell, Jr., *Target USA: The Inside Story of the New Terrorist War* (New York: John Wiley, 1998), p. 115. Mizell reports that from January 1976 to January 1996 a loose federation of anti-Castro paramilitaries 'committed nearly 250 acts of terrorism within US borders'.

In August 1998, activists including a prominent member of the Cuban American National Foundation were indicted by a federal grand jury for an elaborate plot to assassinate Fidel Castro when he visited the Isla Margarita off Venezuela in November 1997. The US coast guard intercepted the mercenaries in the Caribbean. *Washington Times* and *Washington Post* (26 August 1998).

30. In his written work, as well as a 1991 telephone interview, former RAND analyst Professor Gordon McCormick has argued that insurgents find political organization in city environments harder than they expect. Police presence is a

great problem, as are citizens willing to report subversion. Perhaps the 'class interests' of many city dwellers do not favor revolution. Shining Path has done poorly in Lima but well in the countryside.

However, some insurgencies perform well in cities: the Philippines' NPA was well organized in Manila in its better days of the 1980s; Rome and Turin were profoundly troubled by Red Brigade columns in the 1970s; Saigon was riddled by Viet Cong infrastructure during the Vietnam War, etc.

31. When terrorism struck the world in the face in the late 1960s and early 1970s, many forgiving journalists, academics, and political figures 'explained' terrorism as a natural derivative of poverty. Usually their argument was simplistic. It ignored the vital role of terror-group leadership. It could not explain such militants as the American and west European leftists, who were well-to-do and well educated. It could not explain why millions of poor people did *not* resort to terrorism. Today, when global economic differences are as deep as ever, and the population of the poor is expanding, one should not make the opposite mistake of assuming that the underclass will not support terrorists and other revolutionaries. As years of 'graduates' of the Palestinian refugee camps demonstrate, some will. And others among the poor, while not inclined to support terrorism, may find terrorist revolutionaries trying to use them or their cause.

32. Kevin D. Stringer, 'Border Control: A Key Component of National Strategy', *Strategic Review*, 24:3 (summer 1996), pp. 77–8. For one example – the flow into the United States of thousands of illegal Chinese through a single Indian reservation near the Canadian border – see the *New York Times* (20 December 1998).

33. 'Buck' Revelle, a recently retired FBI expert, says Hezbollah and Hamas are present within the United States, and have trained there with firearms and bombs, and are putting together arsenals in the United States. This view has been supported publicly by other authorities, and by the current FBI director before Congress. An important and initially neglected film documentary, 'Jihad in America' by Steven Emerson, detailed the training, money-collecting, and propaganda activities of radical Islamicists, many of whom are openly calling for violence in numerous parts of the world. Speakers for such interests made public appeals (which Emerson displayed on videotape) between 1988 and 1993 at rallies in half-a-dozen American cities, including Kansas City, Brooklyn, Atlanta, and Detroit. Emerson has continued to track Muslim extremists in the United States and to report on them, to the US Congress and in the journal *Security and Counterterrorism*.

Other foreign groups operate in the United States, especially to raise money and conduct propaganda. Actions, including planning and logistics for violent operations, occurred in the United States in the 1980s by the Japanese Red Army, Abu Nidal, the Syrian Socialist Nationalist Party, the Iranian Revolutionary Guards, etc. Some of the evidence was synopsized by Robert Kupperman and Jeff Kamen in *Final Warning: Averting Disaster in the New Age of Terrorism* (New York: Doubleday, 1989).

Swift to point to foreign-initiated violence against US citizens, the American government also has the duty to assure that its own citizens do not represent a threat to other countries. New Yorkers involved themselves illegally in a 'low-intensity conflict' as early as 1837. Certain American citizens were helping Canadian separatists, supplying them and even venturing across the Niagara River into Canadian territory. Canadian militia properly seized the Americans' steamer *Caroline*; they also set it on fire, and ran it over Niagara Falls so that it would carry no more contraband. Refusing to make a defense of selfish American interests, the US Secretary of State instead underscored a basic point in international law; he determined that these American partisans aiding rebellion in Canada had violated the sovereignty of that foreign state.

34. It is not important here to distinguish between the various and specialized types of intervening forces, although UN parlance on this grows ever more complicated.

35. A good example of the problem is the deployment of US Marines to Beirut in 1983. Ostensibly neutral, and given a mission to remain neutral, the battalion was harassed by factions of Lebanese and even Israelis. It understood that it could not afford to act belligerent or fire back; when it did so it became only more badly enmeshed. The battalion understood that it could not damage the delicate environment of restrained violence; when it acted accordingly, by keeping its defense minimal and many weapons unloaded, it was struck with one of the greatest tragedies in post World War Two deployments.

36. The most recent of the promised withdrawal dates was June 1998.

37. In 1997 there was a 'liberated zone' containing 60,000 Cambodians controlled by Khmer Rouge chieftains Khieu Samphan and Ta Mok, and another along an international border and controlled by Ieng Sary; maps and a long interview with Pol Pot appear in the 30 October 1997 *Far Eastern Economic Review*. But since that time events have reduced the powers of the Khmer Rouge.

38. While there is little question that Iran had, and has, connections to violent Lebanese Shiites, some regard Syria as having had a role in the Beirut bombing, to include control of the Bekaa Valley area in which Bulgarian experts helped Shiites assemble the truck bomb. I believe this point was advanced after the bombing, by Arnaud de Borchgrave in the *Washington Times*. See also Kupperman and Kamen, *Final Warning*, pp. 7–8. They argue that the Reagan administration and the Pentagon gave away subsequent opportunities for retaliation.

39. 'Poisoned Chalice Poses Problems: The Terrorist Threat to the World's Water', *International Defense Review* (1 January 1999), from the Internet courtesy of Lieutenant-Colonel Jim Cooney, USMC, who notes that the greatest threat to water stocks is probably chemical, not biological, given that water 'is a poor stand-alone medium to support microbial growth': Quantico, Virginia, 25 January 1999.

40. Navy Commander Marvin Butcher was in charge of the *USS Harlan County* in October 1993. Interviews in April 1995, by telephone and in Quantico, Virginia.

41. The United States was involved in 'Operation Provide Relief', an airlift of food supplies to Somalia and Somalian refugees in Kenya, from August 1992 through December, 'Operation Restore Hope', to establish security on the ground, from December 1992 to May 1993, and then 'Operation Continue Hope' through March 1994.

42. Ron Redmond, who served from 1992 to 1996 as chief spokesman for the Geneva-based UN High Commissioner for Refugees, wrote on these issues for the *Seattle Post-Intelligencer*, rpt. in the *Washington Times* (5 May 1997); he used the term 'peacekeeping overstretch' to describe how heavily involved, not always successfully, the UN Department of Peacekeeping Operations had become by the mid 1990s.

43. *New York Times* (18, 19, and 22 December 1996). These articles touch on why such attacks on aid workers might have occurred or made sense from the killers' unusual point of view. (An earlier abduction at the Red Cross site in Chechnya, for example, appeared to reflect a struggle between two Chechen factions; the innocent victim was 'caught between' them.) See also the cover story by Lee Hockstader, 'The Perils of Doing Good', *Washington Post Magazine* (17 August 1997).

Understanding this inhumane logic has also been a professional interest of my own, to include presenting a 28 April 1993 talk on terrorism and 'Emerging Humanitarian Missions: The Operational Environment', for a panel at the Marine Corps' School of Advanced Warfighting, Quantico, Virginia.

44. *New York Times* (17 April 1998). Withdrawal came after Ahmed Adley, a Daud family leader, took hostages that included a Belgian, a Norwegian, a South African, an American, and two Swiss, according to the *Washington Post* (16 April 1998). All were later released; *San Francisco Chronicle* (25 April 1998).

45. The term 'Zionist Occupied Government' appears in the aforementioned *Turner Diaries* by West Virginia activist William Pierce, and in the speeches, literature, and T-shirt logos of some like-minded American right-wingers. There are examples in such books as Morris Dees, *The Gathering Storm: America's Militia Threat* (New York: HarperCollins, 1996), and in Martinez and Gunther, *Brotherhood of Murder*.

46. One recent recrudescence occurred in Jaspar, Texas, where men reported to be white supremacists of the Confederate Knights of America chained a black man, James Byrd Jr, to a pick-up truck and dragged him to his death. One of the killers allegedly said: 'We're starting *The Turner Diaries* early.' Within days, a similar attack by other whites badly injured a black man in Bellevue, Illinois. *Washington Post* (13 and 14 June 1998).

47. Christian Identity is identified as the most dangerous white racist group by the 16 June 1998 report of the Southern Poverty Law Center: Reuters (17 June 1998), from the Internet.

48. As Chapter 1 indicated, Colonel Qaddafi is ready to exploit racial tensions or divisions in the United States. He offered millions in the mid 1980s to a Chicago street gang, El Rukns; subsequent arrests and convictions of gang members are the 'first instance in US history that American citizens had been found guilty of planning terrorist acts on behalf of a foreign government in return for money', according to the FBI.

49. Undated broadcast, quoted by James Corcoran, *Bitter Harvest. Gordon Kahl and the Posse Comitatus: Murder in the Heartland* (New York: Viking, 1990), p. 31. Corcoran's ch. 2, 'Sowers of Hate', is a good summary of anti-semitism among America's the group rightist militants in the 1980s. 'JDL' stands for Jewish Defense League, the group responsible for scores of attacks in the United States (and Israel) in the 1970s and 1980s, especially against Soviets.

50. The Hamas charter has been discussed above. Hezbollah's charter is its 'Open Letter Presented by Hizbollah to the Oppressed in Lebanon and the World'. It was published by Joint Publications Research Service (hereafter JPRS): *Near East/South Asia Report* (19 April 1985), and excerpted in *Hydra of Carnage*, ed. Uri Ra'anan *et al.*, pp. 488–91. Or see *Hezbollah's Vision*, Policy Paper no. 16 of the Washington Institute for Near East Policy, Washington, DC, 1989.

51. In 1990 there were 455 international terrorist incidents, of which 197 were directed at the United States. Next on the target list was Israel. Peter S. Probst, 'The Terrorist: Specter of the 1990s', *Defense '92* (Washington, DC: Department of Defense, January/February 1992), p. 20. In 1994, of 322 international incidents, 66 were aimed at the United States; in 1995, the numbers were 440 and 99 respectively, according to the State Department report *Patterns* for the year 1995. Numbers of international attacks against Israeli interests (by all parties including Palestinians, radical Jews, etc.) were unavailable in that report. About a third of all the international terror attacks that took place during 1997 were against targets in the United States.

52. In May 1998, for example, PFLP leader George Habash and Hamas leader Sheikh Ahmed Yassin were among those forming a new alliance to oppose the Oslo agreement on a settlement in Palestine; *Independent* (27 May 1998). There have been such explicit 'rejectionist' formations ever since Camp David.

53. The year 1998 brought reminders of how Iran terrorizes its own citizens, as well as foreigners. At least five noted regime opponents such as authors were simply murdered in the streets in Iran. And defector Ahmad Rezai, son of the last commander of the Islamic Revolutionary Guard, has reported torture and execution in Iranian prisons holding critics of the government; he says the 'moderates' are not in control but the clerics are, and speaks of Iran's continuing role in international terrorism. Associated Press (7 July 1998), from the Internet.

54. A *fatwa*, or religious edict, ordering Rushdie's death, appeared some years ago, and was renewed at the highest levels in Iran in 1997.

55. The best accounts of Syria's successful use of terror are in the work of Dr Daniel Pipes. See for example 'Why Asad's Terror Works and Qadhdhafi's Does Not', *Orbis*, 33 (autumn 1989), pp. 501–8, as well as *Syria Beyond the Peace Process*, Policy Paper no. 40 (Washington, DC: Washington Institute for Near East Policy, 1996).

56. Damascus Radio, 'National Struggle Legitimate,' *Ha'aretz* (17 March 1996), from the Internet, 14 November 1996 by Major Stephen W. Davis, USMC, in work on his April 1997 elective paper for Command and Staff College entitled 'What is Syria Doing with Terrorism Today?'

57. *Patterns of Global Terrorism: 1996*, p. 26. The *Independent* (27 May 1998) notes that the Habash–Yassin meeting to coordinate action against Oslo occurred in Damascus.

58. A superb article on PKK ground operations – and Turkish counter-insurgency – is Tammy Arbuckle, 'Stalemate in the Mountains', *Jane's International Defense Review* (January 1997), pp. 48–50.

59. See Adam Garfinkle's article in the *New Republic* (28 December 1998), pp. 18–20.

60. Sources for the inset on Ahmad Jibril's group include specialized journal literature and State Department reports such as the 15 November 1991 'Fact Sheet: The Iranians and the PFLP–GC: Early Suspects in the Pan Am 103 Bombing'. My most detailed source was Samuel M. Katz, *Israel Versus Jibril: The Thirty-Year War Against a Master Terrorist* (New York: Paragon House, 1993).

61. *Foreign Report* (13 August 1998). Al Venter, in 'North Africa Faces New Islamic threat', Jane's *Pointer* (March 1998), reports on the arrival of more Iranians, a naval bases lease to Tehran, and the arrival of many Arab 'Afghans' of extremist orientation.

62. Al-Turabi is frequently interviewed by the Western press; in 1996 there were major interviews by National Public Radio and the *Washington Post*, for example.

63. A detailed, nonscholarly account of Iraq's patronage of Abu Ibrahim, Adnan Awad, and other Palestinian terrorists is Stephen A. Emerson and Christina del Sesto, *Terrorist: The Inside Story of the Highest-Ranking Iraqi Terrorist Ever to Defect to the West* (New York: Villard Books, 1991). A principal in this group, Mohammed Rashid, was captured in Egypt and extradited to the United States in June 1998. He is charged with murder, sabotage, and other crimes in a 1992 airplane bombing.

64. This also happens to be the view of the State Department: *Patterns of Global Terrorism: 1995*, p. 24.

65. Such terrorism news is sometimes 'buried' in single small paragraphs of secondary

pages in United States newspapers, but an impressive exception is the long feature by William C. Rempel, 'Tale of Deadly Iranian Network Woven in Paris', *Los Angeles Times* (3 November 1994). Iran's clandestine networks are as good in some other parts of Europe. Credible accounts now number Iranian assassinations in Europe since 1979 at about 80: Al Venter, 'Iran Still Exporting Terrorism to Spread its Islamic Vision', *Jane's Intelligence Review*, from the Internet (20 November 1997). See also the latest *Patterns of Global Terrorism* (April 1998).

66. See my Chapter 3. The usual estimates of Hezbollah income from Tehran vary between 20 and 60 million dollars. There is also an estimate of 'over one hundred million per year in money and arms' by CIA director R. James Woolsey, testimony to the Senate Intelligence Committee, and an estimate of 'at least $100 million a year for [Hezbollah] activities in south Lebanon' by Israel's Major-General Yoram Yair, according to the November 1997 *Jane's Intelligence Review*.

67. Former CIA director James Woolsey, as cited by Venter, *Jane's Intelligence Review*.

68. 'NBC Race Marks Iraq–Iran–Libya Threat', in *Proliferation: Threat and Response* (Washington, DC: Department of Defense, April 1996), as reprinted in *Defense '96* (Washington, DC: Department of Defense, 3, 1996), pp. 33–42.

69. Terrorist-sponsoring states such as North Korea, the old Yugoslavia, Libya, and Iran have all possessed and trained with minisubmarines, which first proved their potency by sinking ships in World War Two. These vessels have had too little attention from low intensity conflict analysts, the US Navy, etc. Perhaps there will be some impact from the lengthy June 1998 *Jane's International Defense Review* report on minisubs. Minisubmarines are made by several states, including Russia and North Korea. A past *Jane's* article (by Al Venter, see above note 65) includes a few sentences about this problem: 'Underwater warfare and sea-borne activity is taught by the Pasdaran [Iranian Revolutionary Guards] at Bandar Abbas. It is here where Lebanese Hezbollah recruits are trained to use miniature two-man submarines. These North Korean-designed vessels are detailed in threat-identification posters at all Israeli operational bases in south Lebanon/north Galilee, although they are considered possibly more dangerous to their users than their intended targets at present.'

70. An estimate of Western intelligence services, as cited by the *New York Times* (31 December 1996); terrorism financier Osama Bin Laden is mentioned as having been seen during November 1996 in Jalalabad. He is known to have been in Afghanistan in 1998 as well.

The most disturbing account of terrorist training throughout Afghanistan appeared in 1994: Tim Weiner, 'Blowback from the Afghan Battlefield', *New York Times Sunday Magazine* (13 March 1994), pp. 52–5 speaks of the training of tens of thousands of foreigners over recent years, and reports that guerrilla leader Gulbuddin Hekmatyar speaks freely of world revolution and of training Algerians, Sudanese, Egyptians, and others for that revolution.

71. The best single review of Moscow's multifaceted work towards reconstituting its reach in the region is by Kevin D. Smith, 'The Soviet Re-Union', *Strategic Review*, 23:4 (autumn 1995), pp. 71–5.

72. For articles by Stephen J. Morris and others about the decline, but lingering, of the Khmer Rouge, see the *New York Times* (14–17 April and 24 July 1998).

73. June 1998 saw four royalist political workers murdered, including Thong Sophal, mutilated, killed, and discovered outside Phnom Penh a month before the mid-year elections: *New York Times* (30 June 1998).

74. A different angle on the potential problem between Tokyo and Moscow

manifested itself in June 1992, when an anonymous letter arrived at the Japanese Embassy in Moscow, threatening the Japanese with regards to materials it had been distributing on the northern territories problem: *Izvestiya* (Moscow) (25 June 1992), in JPRS, *Terrorism* (2 July 1992), p. 23.

75. When 14 cases of arson occurred on 13 October 1992, police attributed the attacks to leftist radicals opposed to the Japanese emperor's trip to China and to the dispatch of Japanese troops for peacekeeping in Cambodia; *Kyodo* (Tokyo) (13 October 1992), JPRS, *Terrorism* (16 October 1992), p. 2.

76. In their book *The Next War* (Washington, DC: Regnery, 1996), former Secretary of Defense Caspar Weinberger and co-writer Peter Schweitzer create six scenarios that they believe deserve consideration. The first of these is an invasion of South Korea, which includes use by North Korea of the anthrax virus outside a US military base in the south. Many others have feared a North Korean attack; United States experts talked of it steadily in 1995 and 1996.

77. *Patterns of Global Terrorism: 1996*, United States, p. 23.

78. In December 1996, for example, Cuba surprised the United States by turning over tons of cocaine seized in Cuban waters from a Latin fishing vessel destined for the United States. A sadder story surrounds General Ochoa, who became a war hero in Angola. Upon return to Cuba, he was emerging as a domestic political figure. Apparently threatened, the Castro regime set up General Ochoa on charges of trafficking in narcotics and had him executed amidst considerable publicity. The execution destroyed a political rival while making the pretense to the outside world of dealing with the notoriety surrounding Cuban narcotrafficking. For a fuller account of that Cuban business pattern see criminologist Rachel Ehrenfeld, *Narcoterrorism* (New York: Basic Books, 1990).

79. The long and very direct role that Cuba has played in Puerto Rican violence on the Commonwealth island and within the USA is well documented, as by congressional hearings of 1982. The latest powerful Puerto Rican group, Los Macheteros, were in part Cuban-trained. Cuba is suspected as the recipient country where the Macheteros deposited most of the $7.2 million they stole from Wells Fargo in Hartford, Connecticut in 1983. Most but not all of the Macheteros involved in that robbery are in jail. But a famous leader, Ojeda Rios, skipped bail and is at large, possibly in Cuba, and there is strong suspicion that the Wells Fargo employee most responsible for the theft, Victor Guerena, is living in Cuba.

80. Figures of the Committee to Protect Journalists, for 1976–92, *New York Times* (27 November 1996). One rarely sees press features on foreign terrorists' assassinations *within* the United States. I have noted those of two Palestinians, above. Other cases include that of David Belfield of Bay, New York. He became a radical Muslim; changed his name; on direction, murdered an opponent of the Iranian regime in Bethesda, Maryland, in 1980; and escaped to Tehran, where he still lives. David B. Ottaway, 'The Lone Assassin', *Washington Post Magazine* (25 August 1996), pp. 20–32. That case and some others appear briefly in Mizell, *Target USA*.

81. Virgilio Pablo Paz y Romero and his partner, Jose Dionisio Suarez y Esquivel, were both sentenced to 12 years in proceedings of 1990–91.

Another US case occurred in early 1989 when a van was blown up in California by a pipe bomb. Because the head of the owning family was a US Navy officer responsible for the ship that mistakenly shot down the Iranian airbus months before, killing 290 civilians, the act was first thought to be terrorism. But this later came to be doubted. Nearly all vehicle bombs in the United States have been 'punishment' killings or other nonpolitical crimes.

82. Clearly the size of bomb used, unexpected events, and other variables must be accounted for. No bomb is ever fully predictable, just as no carefully planned terrorist act can be completely 'discriminate'.

83. The LTTE Tigers have shown a capability to use their Russian SAM-7s – perhaps from fishing vessels – by destroying two Sri Lankan air force planes. So when 'Lionair' flight 602 disappeared into the Indian ocean not long after takeoff, on 29 September 1998, Sri Lankan authorities considered a SAM, as well as an on-board bomb or accidents; Jane's *Pointer* (1 November 1998). Months later the cause remained undetermined.

84. Reports are unclear. One implies that aircraft at Chicago airport were exactly what El Rukns had in mind when buying a missile. One FBI annual report of US terrorism refers to the item purchased as an (inert) 'anti-tank missile'. The latter could be used against aircraft at an airport. 'An aircraft spends 99 per cent of its operational life on the ground, where it is least maneuverable and most vulnerable … By their nature ports and airfields are fixed positions and not easily defended', according to Colonel Michael R. Lehnert, 'The End of the Attila the Hun Defense', *Marine Corps Gazette* (December 1997), pp. 62 and 63.

85. The two Colombian nationals were arrested in Tampa, Florida, on 5 May 1990, according to the FBI, *Terrorism in the United States: 1990* (Washington, DC: GPO, 1991).

86. *Diario 16* (Madrid; 16 March 1992), in FBIS, *Western Europe* (13 April 1992), p. 42.

87. FBI, *Terrorism in the United States: 1993* (Washington, DC: GPO, 1994). This pattern of IRA activity (anti-aircraft weapons procurement) has been described above in Chapter 3 under 'Weapons'.

88. The first 1994 incident involved Cuban exiles in an 18-foot boat off Key Biscayne with a cache of weapons and some 25,000 rounds of ammunition. While prosecutors did not press charges, the leader of the (Alpha 66) group admitted to the *Miami Herald* that they had tried to infiltrate Cuba. The second incident, involving one of the same men, a founder of Commandos F-4, was in June 1994 and included arrests of two Cuban exiles for trying to buy advanced weapons, including a Stinger: *New York Times* (4 June 1996). In this instance the information cited concerns arrests, not necessarily convictions.

89. The PKK's use was admitted by Akif Oktay, spokesman for the Turkish Embassy in Washington; *Washington Times* (23 June 1997). Also, the 'National Liberation Front of Kurdistan', ERNK, has openly acknowledged using SA-7B missiles against Turkish army efforts; press conference by European ERNK spokesman Dogan Cudi, The Hague, 12 June 1997, London MED Television, repr. in FBIS, *Terrorism* (17 June 1997).

90. The longest published article of late is probably by Thomas Hunter, 'Manportable SAMs: The Airline Anathema', *Jane's Intelligence Review* (October 1996), pp. 474–7). But other incidents involving various groups – especially terrorists – have received an occasional printed line or two in other publications. See for example: *New York Times* (27 April 1992 and 24 July 1993); *Foreign Report* (5 August 1993); *Washington Post* (7 March 1994); *Philippine Daily* (Manila; 3 January 1995), in JPRS, *Terrorism* (19 January 1995). An item referring to 'a rash of airliner shoot-downs' in the former Soviet Union and Georgia appeared in *Armed Forces Journal International* (February 1994), p. 41. On older instances of terror group acquisition and possession of SAMs, see Kupperman and Kamen, *Final Warning*, p. 91; and Christopher Dobson and Ronald Payne, *The Terrorists* (New York: Facts on File, 1979), p. 204, etc.

91. *Jane's Defense Weekly* (17 September 1994), p. 11.
92. A disturbing six-page statement by the CIA – released just after, not before, Congress renewed China's Most Favored Nation trade status – addresses Chinese and Russian sales of weapons and technology related to nuclear, biological, and chemical war to a host of radical states. The story appeared in the back pages of the *Washington Post* on 2 July 1997.
93. One of the newer models is the German-made Panzerfaust 3 LR, a shoulder-fired weapon with 800 meter range, a guidance unit, and laser illuminator; *International Defense Review* (October 1994), p. 22.
94. Full credit for tracking terrorists' use of very light aircraft goes to Jane's publications in England; there are virtually no details of these important matters in the world press. See 'A Novel Angle of Attack', *Jane's Defense Weekly* (12 May 1990), pp. 917–18, and 'Iran Still Exporting Terrorism to Spread its Islamic Vision', *Jane's Intelligence Review* (1 November 1997), from the Internet.
95. Most American gun groups have never engaged in organized violence, and scores of self-proclaimed 'militia' groups tracked by such authorities as Morris Dees and B'nai Brith have never killed. For example, the July 1996 arrests of members of the 'Viper Militia' in Arizona was accompanied by extensive allegations of plots to destroy federal buildings. But the only charges ultimately filed by prosecutors had to do with unlawful possession of unregistered machine guns and other destructive devices, giving instruction in the use of explosive devices, and other activities which, while dangerous, do not make a concrete plot; *Washington Post* (20 December 1996).

    The Amtrak derailment of 1995 in Arizona, however, has never been resolved and a message at the site suggests possible militia involvement. A West Virginia militia which was experimenting with explosives and had purchased blueprints to a nearby FBI building has been broken up by trials and convictions. In several cases – not limited to the Oklahoma City bombing – right-wing 'patriots' have indeed killed, as noted earlier.
96. In 1975, Brian Jenkins, formerly with the US Army, then RAND Corporation, and now Kroll Associates in Los Angeles, wrote the admirable essay 'Will Terrorists Go Nuclear', excerpted in *The Terrorism Reader*, ed. Walter Laqueur and Yonah Alexander, 2nd edn (New York: Meridian Books, 1987), pp. 350–57. For a reappraisal of his thesis, see the essay in Harvey W. Kushner (ed.), *The Future of Terrorism: Violence in the New Millennium* (Thousand Oaks, CA: SAGE Publications, 1998), pp. 225–49.
97. [Central Intelligence Agency], *The Biological & Chemical Warfare Threat* [Washington, DC: GPO, 1997; publisher and date not given], p. 24.
98. 'NBC Race Marks Iraq–Iran–Libya Threat', and Robert Waller, 'Libyan CW Raises the Issue of Pre-emption', *Jane's Intelligence Review* (November 1996), pp. 522–6.
99. In 1969 a United Nations expert estimated that the cost of producing mass casualties might be judged as follows for a given square kilometer of territory: for biological weapons, $1; for nerve agent (a chemical weapon), $600; for nuclear blast, $800; and for conventional blast damage, $2,000. Repeating this data in a recent speech, the Undersecretary of the Navy said that 'While these figures are outdated, the relative orders of magnitude they suggest are still quite valid.' 'Biological Warfare: A Nation at Risk – A Time to Act', speech by Richard Danzig at the National Defense University, as printed in *Strategic Forum*, a newsletter of the Institute for National Strategic Studies of NDU, no. 58, January 1996.

100. Live anthrax cells have just been found within sugar cubes in glass vials, probably intended for horses and/or reindeer. Killing such transport animals would have affected the critical logistical effort of moving British weapons across northern Norway, according to *Nature* magazine, as cited by the *New York Times* (25 June 1998).

101. See Patrick Tyler's story 'Germ War, a Current World Threat, is a Remembered Nightmare in China', *New York Times* (4 February 1997). I am unaware of other literature on biological warfare which mentions this usage in 1942, although Tyler notes that 'Historians say Congshan and other Chinese villages are the only confirmed targets of modern biological warfare'.

102. CIA, *Biological & Chemical Warfare Threat.*

103. The German terrorists' cultivation of botulism in their Paris safehouse has been widely cited in texts on terrorism. The 'Order of the Rising Sun' incident in the United States was reported without detail by the Office of Technology Assessment, *Technology Against Terrorism: Structuring Security* (Washington, DC: GPO, 1991), p. 40. The umbrella-gun attacks with the toxin ricin were described in a film by the BBC and in many publications.

104. An Associated Press wire story of late December 1995 by Brian MacIntyre refers to both ricin cases and to Lavy's suicide. Several cases I mention are also covered briefly in Jonathan B. Tucker, 'Chemical/Biological Terrorism: Coping with a New Threat', *Politics and the Life Sciences* (September 1996), pp. 167–83.

105. Joseph D. Douglass, Jr, 'Chemical and Biological Warfare Unmasked', *Wall Street Journal* (2 November 1995). Douglass was coauthor of one of the first noted studies of the problem: *CBW: The Poor Man's Atomic Bomb* (Philadelphia: Institute for Foreign Policy Analysis, 1984). Mention has already been made of his coauthored book on such threats, *America the Vulnerable.*

106. Defense Intelligence Agency, *Soviet Biological Warfare Threat* (Washington, DC: GPO, 1986), p. 1.

107. Recently the director of one of Russia's most prestigious nuclear weapons laboratories, Vladimir Nechal, shot himself in his office in Chelyabinsk-70, renamed Snezhinsk, weeks after writing to the prime minister that the lab's financial situation was a catastrophe; *Washington Post* (22 December 1996).

108. Kazakhstan, like Russia, has seen Iranian efforts to attract its bioweapons scientists; on these matters, see the pair of articles in the *New York Times* (8 December 1998).

109. *Army Times* (11 September 1995); William Safire, 'Iraq's Threat: Biological Warfare', *New York Times* (16 February 1995); *Time*, 4 September 1995. Among the many other useful articles, see Robert Wright, 'Be Very Afraid', *New Republic* (1 May 1995); an analysis of biological war risks in the December 1996 issue of *Scientific American*; and James Anderson, 'Microbes and Mass Casualties: Defending Against Bioterrorism', a Backgrounder for The Heritage Foundation (Washington, DC, 26 May 1998).

110. Belarus, Kazakhstan, and Ukraine possessed nuclear weapons when the Soviet Union existed, but have since been handing them back to Moscow or destroying them.
    Because many commentators qualify their words about whether Israel is a nuclear power, it should be noted here that the think tank for the US Joint Chiefs of Staff reports that Israel possesses 'at least several dozen weapons': Institute for National Strategic Studies, *Strategic Assessment, 1996* (Washington, DC: NDU, 1996), p. 91.

111. Admiral William O. Studeman, Acting Director of Central Intelligence, 'Threats

to the US and Its Interests Abroad', testimony before the US Senate, Armed Services Committee, 104th Congress, first session, 17 January 1995.

112. The nuclear 'gun' concept involves use of a high explosive like HMX to fire a small plug of highly enriched uranium down a barrel so that it impacts on and 'mates' with a larger supply of several pounds of uranium. The description in *Jane's Intelligence Review* (November 1997) continues: 'The bomb is crude. It has a yield of about two or three kilotonnes, with massive radioactive fallout. For the purposes for which it was intended, it is adequate, for it will kill many people and cause great destruction. It is known in the trade as the "suitcase nuke".'

113. Admiral William O. Studeman, Acting Director of Central Intelligence, testimony before the US House of Representatives, Judiciary Committee, 104th Congress, first session, 6 April 1995. He noted further: 'Even with no nuclear yield, such a device could cause significant radiological dispersion, contaminating the area of an attack and threatening survivors and rescue personnel.'

114. Studeman 'Threats to the US' has testified to this, so has R. James Woolsey, Director of CIA, statement for the record for the US Senate, Select Committee on Intelligence, 104th Congress, first session, 10 January 1995.

115. *Foreign Report* (26 June 1997).

116. One rarely sees this scenario described in print, but when I once spoke of it to a military officer from a Nordic country, he responded that his service had conducted exercises for dealing with such a potential act of terrorism.

5

Misconceptions

Introduction: five misconceptions

'Carlos the Jackal' – Ilich Ramirez Sanchez – committed acts of terror in 1972 and 1973 that astonished the world. His trial in France came only in 1998. The defendant was defiant: *'Vive la Revolucion!'* he proclaimed when convicted for the the human damage his acts had done. That trial closed one long chapter in international terrorism, making a good occasion for asking how well terrorism is understood today. After three decades in the public eye, is it less mysterious? Despite much experience and data in such fields as criminology, journalism, political science, and psychology, important misconceptions still obscure terrorism. Its nature as an implement of power and politics is often veiled. Some of its other characteristics remain unseen. The result is that some public discussions of terrorism are barren, and counter-terrorism policy at home and abroad is sometimes misdirected.

Of the five misconceptions explored in this chapter, the first is the set of common arguments that defend terrorism, or apologize for it, on moral grounds. Years of apparent lack of interest on the part of the United Nations – which still has not even defined terrorism – and such relativist notions as 'One man's terrorist is another man's freedom fighter', undercut the natural human antipathy for terrorist methods, and permit terrorist propaganda far more credence than it deserves. While the arguments may be impoverished, they have nonetheless obscured the fact that terrorist violence is abuse of human rights. Morally it touches all – whether or not one is targeted or injured oneself.

Because terrorism touches all, the misunderstanding of it is not only morally adverse but politically injurious as well. The second major misconception about terrorism is political; it is that the left and the right are true enemies. A Chicago newspaper editor spoke for many when he said in a televised discussion in 1978 that while the new subject of terrorism was bewildering, one could at least be certain that 'Fascists on the right are shooting Communists on the left; Communists on the left are shooting Fascists on the right.'[1] But it was not really true then. Nor is it now. Left and right are indeed rivals, but their true – and mutual – enemy is the existing system. Terrorists on the left and the right deliver their biggest impacts against the status quo, with its stability, moderation, and rule of law – qualities clearly varying in their proportions according to the country in question. This is key, because casualty figures show that terrorism's targets are far more often innocent civilians, establishment journalists, politicians, judges, and policemen than hated militants on the polar opposite. It is key to explaining why, when organizations dominated by terror rise to power, they remain antithetical to popular self-government. And it is key to a proper political posture against terrorism. As one scholar notes, repudiating the misconception that one man's terrorist is another man's freedom fighter, 'One democracy's terrorist is another democracy's terrorist'.[2]

If terrorism's amoral character and anti-democratic objective may be misperceived, so too can its strategies. The third misconception is that terrorism is 'mindless', to use the word favored by many senior political figures in the wake of an attack. In fact, terrorism is deliberate and often systematic; it is calculated, and sometimes precisely calibrated. Terrorist dramas, known for ending with casualties, very often also succeed in winning foreign supporters, distracting from or destroying a state's foreign policy, humbling a sovereign government, or driving a wedge between two close international allies. It is thus a dangerous underestimation of terrorism to call it mindlessness or insanity.

Even when terrorists are regarded as psychologically astute and smart strategists, their educations are routinely underestimated – a fourth important misconception. In fact, leaders of most terror groups, and many cadre and supporters too, are well educated. Like native intelligence, education aids them in designing their political platforms, making politically savvy choices, timing operations appropriately, and even influencing media coverage of their actions. Even a rampant nihilist like Sergey Nechaev, the Russian nineteenth-century anarchist who claimed that the true revolutionary knows 'only one science, the science of destruction', was quick to add that in order to destroy, the revolutionist 'will study mechanics, physics, chemistry, and perhaps medicine. To this end he will study day and night the living science: people, their characteristics and circumstances and all the features of the present social order at all possible levels.'[3] Different terrorists may seek to destroy, operate in, or change their environment; most study towards that end. Some are women and men of ideas who come into terrorist movements already well educated; they may become ideologists, or publicists, or rise to other positions of rank.

A final misconception about terrorists is that they are mostly male. Observers and analysts have usually neglected the large numbers of women in contemporary insurgent movements and small terror organizations. The typical voter in America, France, or Australia is aware of Abu Nidal or perhaps Abdullah Ocalan, but is unable to name any active female terrorist in the world. Yet scores of such political, violent women figure in police and newspaper reports every year. Scores of others are in jail, from Germany to Peru. As surely as women today seek political power in legitimate ways, they also seek it through violence against the innocent. Their presence in such numbers in most terror groups and insurgencies is a challenge to some suppositions about male/female differences in any number of societies, and it underestimates the powerful attachment of some women to political, economic, and social issues from anarchism to animal rights. The illusion that terrorists are males also deceives some security personnel, who fail to take women seriously despite their unique utility in reconnaissance and as couriers, and their other facility – shared with males – for politics, propaganda, and violent operations. Women have also carried and used weapons, in the time of the old Russian anarchism movement, and in the international terrorism of the 1960s and 1970s. Today, weapons are lighter and deadlier than ever before, and are easily managed by either sex.

We may now treat more fully each of the misconceptions sketched above.

Terrorism is never moral

It is not surprising that terrorist groups leaders advance arguments to justify the remarkable brutality of their actions. It takes all their imagination and intelligence to explain what good there could be in 'the deliberate and systematic murder, maiming, and menacing of the innocent to inspire fear for political ends'.[4] Many terrorists act as though they believe they are 'beyond good and evil', as free as Nietzschean supermen of the requirements of normal morality. And yet terrorist spokesmen tend to be articulate and persistent in arguing for the morality of their actions. There are a number of preferred arguments. The first, frankly relativist, is that 'One man's terrorist is another man's freedom fighter'. Put differently, terrorism is merely a name for revolutionary violence others do not like. Or, as one often hears, 'Terrorism is violence Westerners do not like'.

A *Fatwa* urging attacks on Americans

Fatwas are directives which derive authority from Islam. On occasion, a *fatwa* from a Muslim cleric has urged the faithful to violence when there was no recognized state of war. In late February 1998, six terror group leaders including ex-Saudi Osama Bin Laden released a *fatwa* supposedly originating with religious authorities in Lebanon, Jordan, and 'Palestine'. It urged all those faithful to Islam to 'kill the Americans and their allies – civilians and military…' This was declared to be 'an individual duty for every Muslim who can do it in any country…' This extraordinary document has been mentioned often but virtually never reproduced; following are lines purporting to justify the call for killing.[5]

First, for over seven years the United States has been occupying the lands of Islam in the holiest of places, the Arabian Peninsula, plundering its riches, dictating to its rulers, humiliating its people, terrorizing its neighbors …

Second, despite the great devastation inflicted on the Iraqi people by the crusader-Zionist alliance, and despite the huge number of those killed, which has exceeded 1 million … despite all this, the Americans are once again trying to repeat the horrific massacres …

Third, if the Americans' aims behind these wars are religious and economic, the aim is also to serve the Jews' petty state and divert attention from its occupation of Jerusalem and murder of Muslims there.

All these crimes and sins committed by the Americans are a clear declaration of war on God, his messenger, and Muslims. And *ulema* [clerics/holy men] have throughout Islamic history unanimously agreed that the *jihad* is an individual duty if the enemy destroys the Muslim countries.

But terrorism is violence which no moral person can like, or ethically approve. The essence of terrorism includes immoral kinds of calculations: singling out of victims who are innocent; and bloodying that innocence to shock and move a wider audience.[6] To this doubly immoral path of political action, terrorists sometimes add the deliberate use of weapons that are nonselective in their killing range. By attacking citizens in peacetime with such indiscriminate means as car bombs and grenades, terrorists become the moral equivalent of war criminals in time of war. They assuredly inflict, but cannot limit, their destruction; they cannot know how far their actions will reach; a bomb can in theory be well timed and well placed, but one never knows who or how many will be killed.[7] The terrorist admits of no contradiction between speaking warmly of 'the people' but also fighting 'for them' with bombs of compressed gas and nails that kill and burn passers-by. Such acts are abhorrent to nearly any civilization or any time and place. Indeed, one could well argue that if terrorism is not immoral, then nothing is immoral.

The second common argument by terrorists and their supporters is that terrorism is the only way the weak can fight against the strong. This is at best a half-truth. Reason dictates that the weak possess many natural rights. But how does this include a right to use terrorism? It is an odd argument that begins in moral regard for an aggrieved smaller party (e.g. the Shi'a in Lebanon) but then is used morally to justify abuse of a yet smaller and entirely apolitical group (e.g. the reporters and university teachers kidnapped by Lebanese Shi'a). Moreover, what is an aggrieved minority? In fact, aggrieved minorities are ubiquitous. They include small countries, and smaller nations within them, and narrow classes therein, and individuals representing no class but themselves, like the solitary Unabomber.[8] Under the logic of the terrorist and his outspoken attorneys, any and all of these may declare themselves aggrieved weaker parties and take up arms. If such self-awarded status as moral revolutionary alone justifies taking up arms, there could be anarchy, something even most terrorists do not want as a permanent condition. And if such self-awarded status is enough to justify not merely taking up arms but doing so against the innocent, systematically inflicting mayhem on them in a calculated attempt to draw attention to a cause, there *would* be anarchy. Instead of some injustice, the world would have no justice at all. Terrorist spokesmen never discuss this simple extension of their own logic, and reporters and social scientists usually fail to insist they discuss it.

There is no party, no movement, and no government which does not face dissatisfied minorities. For every Yasser Arafat, who did not blush at using terrorism against Israel when he was weak and aggrieved, there has been an Abu Nidal, also weak and aggrieved, who since 1974 has tried to kill Arafat and his senior lieutenants. Abu Nidal has hit so close that Arafat once indignantly declared to reporters that Nidal was after him with fanatical gunmen: 'He's a real terrorist', he said, wide-eyed. This is true, of course, but Yasser Arafat has no principled moral argument against Abu Nidal. Nor has he any against the more pressing threat of today, the aggrieved, unempowered religious Palestinians of Hamas and Islamic Jihad who want Arafat dead for being a secularist. The new terrorists use the old terrorists' arguments. There may be an international interest in preserving Arafat's life, but others must make the moral argument for him; Arafat has no credibility to make it himself. His power grew mainly from the barrel of a gun, a gun which was pointed at Israeli soldiers less often than it was at school busses, shoppers in Israeli public markets, innocent Arabs, foreign diplomats and international travelers. Ironically, the chapters of Arafat's career since 1974 thus raise the question of whether it is even in the interest of *terrorists* to rely upon terrorism. His overall success speaks in the affirmative, but his many problems, including legitimacy and security, cloud that success.

If terrorists are so obscure and undesirable that none support them, they may indeed feel they are without other options. But that hardly justifies killing to attract attention. Having no options may merely reveal eccentricity, or nihilism, or perhaps mental disorder, instead of legitimacy and injustice. Most groups with a narrow base of popular support act to broaden it, as well they ought if they are intent upon governing. There are dozens of methods of political organization and resistance which can gain popular support and engender change and which – unlike terrorism – are morally legitimate. These include formation of workers' unions and professional organizations, political parties, private appeals and public rallies, competition in local elections, and in every higher electoral tier. They include nonviolent resistance, agitation among foreign observers and foreign media, exploitation of the newest communications media, cooperation with the Church, etc. Such means may not be dismissed as naïve, for they have had a powerful impact when used by independent political parties of recent years in the Philippines, Burma, Pakistan, many Latin American states, and elsewhere.[9] Democratic orders are vulnerable – even undemocratic systems may be vulnerable – to these forms of political struggle. There are also clandestine methods of organization and struggle which may or may not be illegal but which can be effective and moral. Once a movement garners popular support, it is common to seek foreign support and perhaps even the approval of such foreign bodies as the UN General Assembly or lesser international alliances.

Beyond these means there is of course violence. Violence may be moral, judged by both ends and means. A just war may be conducted without the 'deliberate, systematic murder, maiming, and menacing of the innocent ... ' Under severe repression or with otherwise adequate cause, there may be nothing immoral about forming a guerrilla army of resistance – a guerrilla army *not* reliant upon terrorism. Even history's most repressive states have sometimes been resisted by clandestine organization and guerrilla war which used sabotage against military property and inflicted casualties on armed enemies or others in the chain of command. The French Resistance did not have a policy of taking hostages or murdering German women. In the 1980s the Afghan resistance sometimes broke the laws of war, yet they did not turn to bombings in Russian marketplaces, or kidnapping Soviet diplomats from international conferences, or any number of other crudely useful tactics.[10] If war knows certain restraints even when conducted against ruthless imperialism, it certainly knows limitations in fights against more humane regimes: the leadership of American revolutionaries of two centuries ago never adopted a policy of terrorism, despite the remarkable odds against them.

These cases remind us of a third argument of terrorists: that states rely upon violence and the violence of terrorists is no worse than that of soldiers and policemen. But a policeman is supposed to act within the law to restore the law, and with it the general welfare. The soldier, ideally, is expected to fight other soldiers in a recognized state of war. 'Just war' doctrine is recognized by most philosophers, and many theologians; without some such wars there would be no check on international aggression. Reasonable men, East and West, agree that some twentieth-century military efforts have been aimed against greater evils, and have sometimes defeated them. Legitimate wars may or may not be formally 'declared' today, but they *are* normally initiated and conducted by recognized legal and political authority. Legitimate wars may or may not involve whole nations, but they are prosecuted largely by fighting between armed forces.[11] Therefore, the normal soldier of a civilized state recognizes the differences between himself and the terrorist, by motives, by tactics and codes of armed conduct, and often by the end results. There is remarkably little moral similarity with terrorism.

In legitimate war, the norm is for soldiers to honor the age-old human distinction between a combatant and an innocent party. That distinction arises naturally from human instinct, and it is defensible by dispassionate moral judgment. But the terrorist deliberately destroys the distinction between the combatant, i.e. the perpetrator of harm, and the innocent party. Indeed, most of the motives and means of the terrorist lack parallels to those of the soldier in war. The terrorist calls himself part of an 'army' but many well-known groups comprise only a few dozen gunmen.[12] He may not reasonably claim to represent the will, let alone morals, of any humane culture or great people, and is sometimes repudiated by his own for that reason.[13] The terrorist is proud of his 'military' training and his 'military' tactics, but he attacks aircraft or vehicles that are civilian far more often than military.[14] He calls himself a 'guerrilla,' a word that means 'unconventional soldier,' but guerrillas attack other soldiers or military units in time of war, while the terrorist acts in peacetime more often than not, and deliberately chooses to murder a factory manager, or a policeman's family, precisely because such actions have more media impact.

It was a saying of Ramdane Abane, a commander of anti-French forces in Algeria in the 1950s, that 'One corpse in a [suit]jacket is always worth more than twenty in uniform.'[15] He helped move the FLN, which began mostly with guerrilla war, toward complementing that with systematic terrorism. The net result was strategic victory. A hundred subsequent groups have faced the same question. The Italian Red Brigades, for example, considered a written proposal by their Genoa column for 'targeting those in uniform, all those in uniform'. Instead they chose more general terrorism. They lost.[16] Terrorists kill civilians and the innocent for their own purposes, not because they are forced to.

A fourth argument used to defend terrorism is a legal one. Less often heard today, it echoed repeatedly through the last two decades, and still merits consideration. It derives from post-Second World War changes in modern international law which tended to legitimate national liberation struggles. At the General Assembly of the UN and at Geneva, where international conventions are reshaped and agreed to, the traditional power of a state government was slightly attenuated in favor of legitimate challengers. Laws of war were rewritten so that an armed guerrilla did not require a formal military uniform or a conventional style of organization. POW status, long the reserve of the armies of nation states, was expanded to include members of a legitimate revolutionary group under some circumstances.[18] A consistent procession of General Assembly votes of the 1970s drew attention to the right of a nation to oppose 'colonial' or 'racist' regimes. The legal and political environment is thus kinder to revolutionaries than before 1977. Apologists for terrorists, including some radical sovereign states, can point to the change.

What terrorism proponents leaning upon the new treaties do *not* add is

Abdullah Ocalan, leader of PKK, on the moral problem of terror

Even after his jailing in early 1999, Abdullah Ocalan remains the acknowledged head of PKK, the Kurdish Workers' Party. He has always been one to talk to the press about his cause. The following excerpts are from a conversation with a Turkish television reporter, in Ocalan's apartment in Damascus, Syria, in 1991:[17]

Ocalan: An armed struggle does not mean only firing weapons. As far as I am concerned, an armed struggle is the highest form of ideological consolidation. It is the truest form of political conscientiousness. This is probably a little more true for the Kurds, because no other option is given them to live like human beings...

TV reporter: A person in your situation must be very cruel, very removed from his feelings. At times, you send even your friends to be executed. Does this not disturb you?

Ocalan: If someone steps on a plant unnecessarily, I say: Do not do that. That is how sensitive I am.

TV reporter: The type of actions you carry out sometimes result in women and children also getting killed.

Ocalan: Do you know how I cope with the results of those actions? I consider those actions as a means of spreading our cause. A small group is eliminated, but a great humanity will be created in its place.

that contemporary laws of war still include absolute bans on the very kinds of activity terrorists most prefer. The accepted law of armed conflict first requires a state of war; most terror acts take place in peacetime when the advantages of surprise are greatest and the victims are most likely to be unarmed. Abu Sayyef's attacks on towns in the southern Philippines are examples; their campaigns went on even as negotiations for peace concluded successfully in 1996 between the Moro National Liberation Front and the central government in Manila. Next, law requires that a guerrilla soldier display some visible identification, at least at the point of using the weapon; terrorists specialize in operating unnoticed, killing while clothed as a civilian, and melding back into the civilian population. Filipino New People's Army 'Sparrow units' of two persons in everyday clothes carried out assassinations in the thronging streets of Manila for years. International law mandates discrimination between legitimate targets and innocent civilians; terrorist groups and even some militarily competent guerrilla leaders often select civilian targets while avoiding the armed security forces. The NPA preys less upon Filipino military bases than upon Filipino businessmen for cash contributions, using occasional killings and frequent threats to them and their families. The law of war also specially protects religious institutions, cultural artifacts, and charities – things precious to human beings and thus set apart from all political disputes; but terrorists often seek their congregated victims precisely there. Abu Sayyef has opened fire on worshippers in a cathedral, wounding dozens before fleeing into the jungle. Law mandates humane treatment of military captives; terrorists take non-belligerents as captives, and sometimes torture or kill them. The NPA has kidnapped innocent foreigners for ransom or other purposes, sometimes killing them later. Finally, military services have firm rules about reporting atrocities up the chain of command, so that they can be punished; the usual act of a terrorist is in response to chain of command. And after committing the crime, the group calls a newspaper, or mails a letter, taking credit and publicizing the potency of a given armed group. Abu Sayyef's communiqués are moralistic and politically inflammatory calls to arms amidst the relative general calm of an imperfect but free Filipino society.

The reality that terrorists and their apologists will not face is that a moralizing argument for immoral activity can be a useful lie, but only for the short term. Ultimately it is only by way of legitimate political principles and activity that any group, revolutionary or ruling, can exercise power morally and reasonably. Terrorism, once accepted, is not easily abandoned. It can be as self-destroying for an organization as it is soul-destroying for the individual.[19] If reliance upon terrorism were a moral man's route to power, then one could expect reason and peace in

The Armed Islamic Group:
A case study in moral issues and arguments

The most active Algerian terror organization is the Armed Islamic Group, GIA. It has committed many crimes in Algeria and France, accompanied by a fulsome propaganda campaign that includes personal letters to President Jacques Chirac.

GIA and other radicals rose in a popular reaction to the 'theft' of electoral results in 1992. The FLN government of the country denied explicitly Muslim parties the fruits of regional elections then,[20] and went further in 1996, changing the constitution to bar Islamic parties from a role in government. June 1997 brought new elections and unsurprising victory for the government. Clearly, Islamic parties and such armed wings as GIA have an argument to make about justice. But GIA gives up its moral force for a strategy of terrorism. Sympathetic observers of GIA try to ignore its terrorism, but the organization itself is anxious to demand proper credit, credit it fully deserves.

In 1994 a policeman was killed – a modest man of whom little is known. What placed this act in the international media is that the killers were from GIA and they murdered not only the policeman but his family. Their concept was apparently to use such deaths to intimidate others from joining the security forces. What man wants a job which costs him the lives of his family? This one incident in Haouch Gros, Algeria, illustrates the terrorist's way of relying upon moral half-truths. One must admit that taking a policeman's job is assuming personal risk. One might even be persuaded that, in a dictatorial regime, a uniformed security officer is a legitimate target for an insurrectionary popular force. But even if that were true, there can be no moral argument that the man's family should die, or that they can thus be used up in an effort to deter police recruiting. And yet such exploitation of innocents is central to the psychology of terrorism.

Late in 1994, an Air France passenger jet was hijacked by GIA. Its tanks were topped up with fuel, and explosives were brought on board. The concept was to liberate Muslim prisoners in French jails as well as terrorize the French nation. If the demands went unmet, GIA planned a suicide detonation in the skies over Paris, showering the City of Light with flaming debris. French counter-terrorist police foiled the attempt. Hostage-taking is illegitimate – absolutely banned by international law for centuries. It goes without saying that mass murder is also illegitimate.

In May 1996 the Group decapitated seven monks in Medea. This is part of a clear pattern of attacks on foreigners and foreign

Christians, intended to further racial and cultural divisions in Algeria as part of the drive for social and political revolution. (The pattern is also unfolding in Egypt where an Islamic group with a similar name is doing similar things.) The monks' offense was being French, living in Algeria, and bearing allegiance to the 'wrong' God. The act can not be dismissed as 'merely offensive to the West'. It violates multiple canons of military conduct, including those exempting undefended religious institutions from targeting. The act has been widely condemned, even by some radical Islamic groups in Libya and Egypt.

But GIA has pressed on. Its next assault in Paris was a gas and nail bomb explosion at the RER Port Royale train station. The concept for this indiscriminate attack was to undermine public morale, and to change French foreign policy, seen as too supportive of the FLN government in Algiers. GIA chief Antar Zouabri personally explained as much in a letter to President Jacques Chirac. His two pages of Arabic prose mixed proud admissions, threats of more violence, references to God, and a proposal for negotiations. Talks would be based on GIA demands: freedom for a named Muslim prisoner, payment of 'tribute' to the GIA, and absolute cessation of support for the government of Algeria, an 'infamous tyranny'.[21] This price was high. The prisoner, Abdelhaq Layada, is jailed for the shocking Air France hijacking. Payment of a 'tribute' upon the demand of an extortionist may be arguably 'practical' *in extremis*, but it is not 'moral'. And while Algeria is indeed a despotism, all GIA offers is civil war followed by unspeakable purges and then its own despotism. So while there may be reasons for GIA terrorism, they are not moral reasons.

The current dissidence within the Algerian terrorist movement – in that country and on French territory – is an illustration of why merely being the weaker party should not convey special moral privileges. GIA is rent by internal struggle; Antar Zouabri may even have risen to power at the point of a knife; his predecessor, Djamel Zitouni, was assassinated in July 1996.[22] A dispassionate observer can not make a moral argument why either of these men should have an advantage over the other. Moreover, GIA can not even claim to speak for the 'sacred cause of Algerian Islam'. The Front for Islamic Salvation, or FIS, is larger and less overtly brutal than GIA.

These minorities have every moral right to pursue power in Algeria. They have no moral right to make points against the government by murdering villagers by the half-dozen, as in 1996, or by the score, as in 1997 and 1998.

such regimes as Algeria, where the FLN insurgents took power three and a half decades ago after a lengthy campaign reliant upon terrorism. But in fact Algeria today is a nation of turmoil and dictatorship, of state reliance upon fear and of new terrorist groups rising against the state. The particulars vary for other regimes where terrorists triumphed, like the former Soviet Union, China, Cuba, and Iran. But all such states have at least this resemblance: they show that a strategy of using terrorism to gain political power is an intimation that the new regime will rely upon violence against the innocent to keep power. The moral arguments of terrorists and their supporters are thus emptier than spent cartridges.

Right and left: extremists but not enemies

The terrorists on the two political extremes of left and right are in truth apposites, more than opposites. Their mutual policy goal is usually some form of dictatorship. And during what is usually a lengthy period of struggle for power, each side tends silently to depend upon the other for an adequately inflammatory public response to its own terrorism. Ostensibly enemies, left and right spill more printer's ink than blood over their differences. Nearly all their violent acts are aimed at the democratic, peaceful center which lies between them; it is the legal government that is most hated by extremes of left and right. Governmental 'persecution' becomes a tool for propaganda, for recruitment, for mobilization.[23] Both extremes also detest the mass of civilians, even as they seek their support. The public is thought to be inadequate, unenlightened, and almost inhuman – 'the walking dead' is a phrase used by terrorists of the 1960s and 1970s and by philosophers favored by such groups, including Herbert Marcuse. In the 1980s and 1990s, readers of the right-wing novel *The Turner Diaries* receive the same impression of citizens who will not mobilize in support: they are pitilessly deprecated by the protagonist in terms invented by the left.[24] A final indicator of ambiguity between left and right extremes is that many militants switch sides, including the very founder of fascism, Benito Mussolini, originally a socialist who admired Lenin. The chief Bolshevik in turn admired Mussolini.[25] Trotsky spoke of the 'deadly similarity' between Soviet communism and fascism, while Adolph Hitler noted how much he had learned from Marxist methods.[26]

Such defiance of a common presumption is a pattern of the German underground. In Weimar Germany, Hitler's 'black' fascists and the 'red' communists battled in the streets but also collaborated against the broad, weak democratic center, as in the 1930 Berlin transit strike. Many militants switched from one extreme to the other. The Nazis' premier ideologist, Joseph Goebbels, had once been communist. Hitler boasted of attracting communists into his National Socialist German Workers' Party and had a standing order to admit them promptly, arguing that the Social Democrat and the 'petit bourgeois' will never make a National Socialist, 'but the communist always will'. They did, by the thousands. Storm-trooper chief Ernst Rohm called the converts 'beefsteaks – black outside but red in the middle'. The reverse was just as true: Germany's communist ranks included converts from Nazism, whom they called 'Black Bolsheviks'.[27]

In late 1970 anti-semitic sentiment in the German underground was rekindled by outside influences. The PLO was looking for international allies, because of the Arabs' defeat in the 1967 war, and the Jordanian army's battering of the PLO during 'Black September' of 1970. Munich's Nazi paper *National Zeitung* ran a PLO advertisement for 'courageous comrades' to come to the Middle East. The purpose was supposedly to allow favorably disposed German war correspondents to 'study the war of liberation of the Palestinian refugees', but there was special interest in anyone with 'tank experience'. With the summer of 1972 came the Munich Olympics' massacre of Jewish athletes, an event which won high praise from a subsequent rally of 600 neofascists in Munich.[28]

Abu Iyad, for decades a senior lieutenant to Arafat, admitted in 1981 that the 'leftist' PLO 'accommodated and protected' members of the 'Military Sports Group' of Karl-Heinz Hoffmann. Palestinian indulgence of a West German was not surprising; the PLO readily made its training camps and safe havens available to European terrorists. What was remarkable is that Hoffmann's group is neofascist. The PLO's protection and training of Hoffmann and 11 others of his group went on before – and for some of them, even after – the most infamous 'right-wing' bomb ever in Germany: the Munich Oktoberfest explosion of 1980. After police linked that bomb to a one-time Hoffmann group member, Abu Iyad was pressed by an interviewer as to how he could possibly ally himself with such neoNazis. He explained that his new trainees from the 'Military Sports Group' denied being fascists, insisting instead upon being a patriotic national liberation group. The PLO's Abu Iyad continued: 'We told him about other European groupings that also were patriots, progressive forces cooperating with us here … From Norway, Sweden, Denmark, and so on and so forth, a kind of association of Palestinians and forces supporting us. On that level, we explained to Hoffmann, we could also cooperate, if he was interested.'[29] He was.

Other threads in the story emerged.[30] A member of the Hoffmann group named Odfried Hepp, imprisoned for terrorism, co-authored a letter to a left-wing German newspaper calling for a truce between right and left so that both could fight the system in a unified struggle. Collaboration would be based on common 'overriding principles such as anti-imperialism, anti-racism, and anti-fascism'.[31] By then, the German right was as deeply involved in anti-American propaganda and attacks on US servicemen as the terrorists on the left had always been. This fabric of little-noticed information then grew again. In 1990 Germany discovered that Hepp and certain other German neoNazis had been dealing directly with the Stasi, the East German State Security Ministry. German rightist terrorists had been sheltered in East Berlin as part of a secret operation code-named 'Friedrich' designed to undermine West German democracy.[32]

In the neoNazi scene in Germany, there are always new variations on this pattern of left–right collusion – or at least ambiguity. For example there is Ingo Hasselbach of Berlin, born to East German communist parents, but rebellious; he was first a hippie, then a punk, and then he founded several neofascist groups, including National Alternative. Hasselbach's cohorts received training from soldiers from both East and West German armies, and Hasselbach declared after quitting the movement that 'The militant rightists have been reading the publications of the [communist] Red Army Faction for two or three years now.'[33] Steven Schar of the former East German city Hoyerswerda is a small-time neoNazi leader who favors street fighting and 'Heil Hitler' salutes, and feigns a 'balanced' view of the Holocaust, suspecting that the Nazi extermination program has been exaggerated, and proffers a convenient post-mortem alternative for dealing with the Jews: 'They could have deported them all.' But Schar says that he favors the socialist aspects of Nazism, criticizing Hitler as 'too close to the capitalists'.[34] In Munich, Ewald Althans, a tall, bright neoNazi leader, calls Hitler a hero. Althans is a writer and bookseller, and travels widely to keep up contacts in the movements abroad. He admits to needing punch-ups in the streets to keep his publicity machine going. His rhetoric against 'consumer-obsessed, television goggling society that is rotting away'[35] mirrors that of traditional leftist and rightist extremists. Althans says of his youth, 'I was always a rebel: I flirted with extreme political ideas of left and right just like every normal kid.' The German pattern of side-switching that dates back to Weimar street-fighting days is still holding: many of the active neoNazis of today were members of the East German communist youth organization until the Berlin Wall was dismantled.[36]

The Italian terrorist scene, now quiet, has had its own examples of left–right collaboration, and many more of mutual avoidance, even at the height of the savagery against the democratic state and its citizens. As of mid 1980, when there had been hundreds of Red Brigadist attacks throughout Italy, not a single one had ever been against a right-wing militant.[37] Terrorists of left and right were simply not killing one another. What Italian judicial and journalistic investigations of the time could show was direct physical support to both the Italian left and the right from outside powers – Assad's Syria, but especially Colonel Qaddafi's Libya.[38] Today, rightist separatists of authentic Italian stock are doing their own damage to the nation and the state by taking the positions of such political organizations as the Northern League. Psychologically the far right is no better prepared to lead government than is the far left; the right wing throughout Italy is badly divided between classical conservatism and the will to national revolution.[39]

Other extremists in Europe have attained state power in the post-communist world and some mirror this pattern of ideological ambiguity. Russia's hot-blooded 'black' nationalist Vladimir Zhirinovsky has talked openly of forming a front with the Russian 'red' Communist Party. Slovakia's Vladimir Meciar, Romania's Ion Iliescu, and Serbia's Slobodan Milosevic were all communists who have now become blood-and-soil nationalists. Some in the Serbian nationalist movement, the cutting edge of which is responsible for both terrorism and genocide, have simply switched their allegiance from the political collective and faith of Marxism, to the political collective and faith of Serb nationalism. This is true of many Serbs.[40]

Not mindless, but calculated

It is mostly on the surface that terrorism appears to be madness, or mindless. Behind the screaming and the blood there lies a controlling purpose, a motive, usually based in politics or something close to it, such as a drive for political and social change inspired by religion. However complex is human psychology, most terrorist crimes are comprehensible. The perpetrator is part of an organization, a political unit with publicly declared purposes; actions taken and bodies counted are intended to advance those purposes. The terrorist is not usually insane; he or she is more usually 'crazy like the fox'.

In June 1985, during the infamous hijacking of TWA flight 847, nothing must have seemed more completely irrational to the terrified passengers than the fact that one of the hijackers ranged up and down the aisle striking and abusing passengers, while another was later described by witnesses as soft-spoken.[41] Nine years earlier there had been two other cases of exactly this sort. At Entebbe, Uganda, where international terrorists opposed to Israel had taken an Air France flight from Tel Aviv, a German female hijacker came across as a wild animal, the open enemy. When one passenger was beaten, it was she who landed the most blows. In contrast, one of her male German counterparts struck people only by his pleasantness and reasonableness. He told jokes, and made promises that there was nothing to worry about.[42] A few months later, in a TWA flight originating in Chicago, early advocates of a free Croatia seized the aircraft. While one man apparently wired himself up as a suicide bomber and stalked the aisles acting insane, a pretty young woman on his Croatian team was equally active – assuring passengers in a warm tone that all would be right. The explanation for such a mix of dangerous and reassuring behavior is the aim of producing disorientation and despair in terror victims. Those debilitating psychological conditions lead rapidly to submission, and submissive passengers are the only safe kind, from the hijackers' point of view.

There are other cruel techniques. Passengers or hostages are separated by state of origin, as they were in three different actions over two decades: Entebbe in 1976, Beirut in 1985, and Lima in 1996. In all cases, the terrorists calculated that they would enhance the sense of isolation of a particular group – Jews at Entebbe and Beirut, Japanese in Lima. At Entebbe, all persons with Israeli passports or dual nationalities were held in a separate area of the airplane hanger the German–Palestinian team chose for staging the last act of its drama.[43] But Israeli commandos arrived to prevent it from happening. In Lima in 1996–97, the Japanese hostages were confined on the second floor of the embassy, instead of the lower floor from which groups of hostages were periodically released unharmed. Even the 'safer' group in such separations is the toy of the terrorists; they feel profound guilt at being vulnerable yet spared, while others on the same plane or at the same embassy party are singled out for murder. Psychologists are familiar with such guilt among survivors of natural disasters or lethal street crimes. Yet it is outside the scene of the crime – in the wider audience of public opinion and government circles – that the terrorists intend that the more important crisis will occur. Terrorism has rightly been called 'theater', and the public and government are the main audience, not the actual victims. When news of racial or religious separation is broadcast during the hostage situation, the fears, divisions, and hatreds engendered inside the barricades spread outward. The psychological divisions in the microcosm behind the barricades are intended to create parallel fracture lines in the macrocosm of the public and the government responsible for ending the disaster.

Consider the burdens placed on America and Israel by the TWA 847 hijacking of 1985. When seizing their prey – 153 innocent international travelers – the Shiite hijackers made a broadcast blaming their actions on American aid to Israel and US approval of the 1982 Israeli incursion into southern Lebanon. Their demands were closely related: they wanted freedom for hundreds of Shiite prisoners imprisoned for terrorism in Israeli jails. Their tactics in turn mirrored these policy claims and demands: they separated out all passengers with Israeli passports or Jewish-sounding names. They also drove home their willingness to kill by murdering an American aboard the plane. The net effect was exactly as calculated: prisoners were eventually released in Israel, in part because of tremendous pressures generated against the Washington–Tel Aviv relationship. News reports on the protracted crisis carried stories of the rise in those pressures. The number of American citizens favoring distancing US policies from Israel's rose to nearly half; poll results also showed that those who felt Israel had not done enough to resolve the crisis leapt to nearly two-thirds. Media referred to the 'clouds' and 'strains' appearing in American–Israeli relations.[44] Ultimately, a small gang proved that, with proper calculations, it could publicly murder a US citizen, terrorize a plane full of hostages, cause a mild rift in the relations of two sovereign democratic peoples, and force release of hundreds of Shiites from Israeli jails – all before escaping totally unharmed beneath the noses of the most anti-terrorist minded administration in US post-Second World War history.

The December 1996 Lima case ended better, but not before opening similar rifts, some within Peru, and some between Peru and foreign allies. MRTA used an embassy party guest list to separate the hostages. Then they confined most Peruvian civilians on the first floor of the embassy, and sent government officials, counter-terrorism experts, and Japanese up to the second floor. Having already fired its weapons in the seizure, MRTA now could play the other side of the psychological game: now they were warm, gentle partisans of the people. There was almost no shouting, or waving of guns. The terrorists chatted, joked, and permitted hostages such remarkable freedoms as use of cellular phones. In extended political discussions and speeches, they repeatedly underscored supposed differences between themselves – as 'politicians' – and the more violent, apocalyptic Shining Path,[45] notorious for its mass murders of villagers and its use of dynamite. By such words and actions, and by frequent releases of some of the hundreds of hostages, the group conveyed reasonableness and established an atmosphere in which negotiations might succeed, making MRTA the diplomatic equal of the elected government of millions of Peruvians. This solicited some embarrassingly generous remarks from hostages grateful to MRTA for being freed early.[46]

By singling out the Japanese Embassy, the terrorists also sought to drive a wedge between Peruvians and their tiny Japanese minority of 80,000 of which President Fujimori is the symbol. It was as in 1985: two democracies were the targets; both Japan and Peru found themselves in a crisis. Once again, playing the race card was the key to both the tactic of hostage separation and the larger strategy that aimed at terminating a wealthy country's aid to a poorer one. Japanese aid to Peru has been generous, despite its denunciation by an MRTA spokesman to Japanese television as 'ignoring the plight of thirty million hungry Peruvians'.[47] Japan, dogged by a deserved reputation for giving in to terrorists, worked hard not to criticize Fujimori's hard line on the embassy seizure. Only twice in the entire first month did Tokyo put distance between its views and those of Lima;[48] otherwise Japan forestalled trouble with its Latin ally and waited. Peruvian voters were similarly stalwart. Polls repeatedly showed support for their president and the shallowness of approval levels for Tupac Amaru. This rendered empty many of the terrorists' arguments about being a meaningful political force.[49]

Ironically, it was in American newspapers that MRTA saw the most progress in its declared desire to improve conditions for its comrades in Peruvian jails[50] – where some 400 members are confined as compared to less than a hundred still active in Peru. Stories by American columnists blossomed, especially in January 1997 in the third week of the siege, describing the dungeon-like conditions and freezing cold in which several thousand MRTA and Sendero convicts are held. Readers' letters printed by a major US paper said that Peru's prison conditions were evidence of 'state-sponsored terrorism'. Renewed media attention was also devoted to imprisoned MRTA member Lori Berenson of New York; an effort to get her a new trial drew many scores of supporters in the US Congress. Apparently displeased by the effect of such sympathetic coverage on public opinion, a Lima weekly magazine entered the debate. It published photographs of an underground brick cell in which Tupac Amaru had held kidnap victims, and wrote that since MRTA rebels ordered and carried out such illegal kidnappings, they have little to say now about the 'harshness' of lawful imprisonment.[51]

The selective holding (or murder) of a few, paired with the sparing or release of others, is a quintessential terrorist method of spreading disorientation and influence. It recurs repeatedly among villagers facing the members of a rural insurgency of the kind well known since the Second World War. A small team – sometimes called an 'armed propaganda squad' – singles out victims. The death of the immediate victim, and the terrorization of the village audience, serve the same purpose. Victim and audience are both expected to recognize the purpose of the drama, a demonstration of the guerrillas' organizational and lethal power, enhancing the submissiveness of the audience in the quaking aftermath and darkness. The same logic guides practice among insurgent groups world-wide. As with the more confined tactical situation of the hijacker, there is always more than the obvious ability to kill; there is an implied reasonableness – a willingness to negotiate something, or refrain from killing if behavior changes. A moral burden for righting a wrong situation is somehow transferred to the passengers, the villagers, or their government. There is a kind of choice, closely controlled. Choosing to resist the wrong of the situation will probably lead to death; yet choosing to submit and 'go along' leads to a kind of moral death, a death of spirit.[52]

For all the differences in their political objectives, pro-state terrorists rely upon much of the same psychology. Death squads, such as those which ravaged Argentina from 1976 to 1983,[53] may strike after warnings, or only with surprise. They may act at night to accentuate their fearfulness. They select their victim for his or her status as 'enemy of the state', but the political purpose goes well beyond that murder on that night. It is usually aimed at, and touches, a wider circle of related groups, be they labor unions, political parties, newspaper staffs, or violent revolutionary organizations. The single murderous act by pro-state terrorists thus 'terminates one problem' while sending a menacing message to the larger enemy groups. In realization of the old aphorism, with such a murder you 'kill one, frighten ten thousand'.

In India today, when there are occasional multiple murders of Sikh civilians, the killers are sometimes Hindu nationalists, perhaps in the extremes of the BJP (Bharatiya Janata Party) or sometimes zealous government security forces. Either way, the illegal killings drive more wedges between the Sikhs and Hindus, already religiously and ethnically divided. The political center is deeply harmed; the main beneficiaries are the advocates of Hindu power, on the one hand, and the advocates of Sikh independence on the other, no matter who was responsible for the murder. Extremists of both sides are satisfied by the fight and the sociopolitical polarization it yields.[54]

In Sri Lanka, where terrorism raged throughout the 1980s, an elected government was pitted against insurgents of the same majority ethnic-religious group: the democratic authorities and the revolutionaries were both Sinhalese (Sri Lankan Buddhists). The JVP, or People's Liberation Front, revolutionaries faced the somewhat ineffectual government and its all too effective death squads. The latter were largely from the army and police, serving at night in civilian clothes. By one account, these death squads killed at least 20,000 suspected militants, mostly between

1988 and 1990. They did so most often by execution-style shooting, burning the bodies with kerosene, decapitating them, or throwing them into the river so that the next day they would float slowly through the capital of Colombo.[55]

The educated terrorist

There is a popular impression, fostered by politicians and journalists and academics alike, that terrorists are ignorant people who do not know what they are doing. But take the Sri Lankan JVP example; many following Rohan Wijeweera were unemployed, but they were well educated – in a system befitting a nation tutored by Britain. The JVP leader had made further studies – of history and Marxism, during years spent in the Soviet Union. He read the works of Third World revolutionaries, and took a role in the inter-communist debate between Moscow and Beijing, ultimately declaring himself a Maoist. He declared himself an enemy of capitalism and a violent proponent of socialism. He justified his mass murders – which were to incite the Sri Lankan state death squads into lethal campaigns of their own – by declaring that 'Counter-revolutionaries resort to violence. Therefore to ensure the safe delivery of the new social system it becomes necessary to resort to revolutionary violence against the violence employed by the capitalist class.'[56]

Modern American terrorists of the left wing illustrate this. Unlike their skinhead or neoNazi counterparts in extremism, the left has consistently been led by adults with college education and often even graduate schooling, law degrees, and professorships. This has made their political arguments rational and often well-delivered, if not always successful, or truthful. It has assured them ready access to the media. And, in some cases, it has placed the would-be terrorist, former terrorist, outspoken ally of terrorism, or apologist for terrorism in the university classroom, where he or she can influence students.[57]

It is well enough known that in the Vietnam War era it was the universities which were the main source for not only peaceable opposition to the war but leftist militancy. The Students for a Democratic Society, and their terrorist offspring The Weathermen, were highly educated, including Chicago School of Law's Bernadine Dohrn, and Colombia University's Katherine Boudin and Mark Rudd. What has gone less noticed is that *most* of the leftist terrorist groups of that day and of successive decades have also been led by highly educated and professional people whose ideas can not be casually dismissed.

Exemplars of this pattern include the Palestinians, the Basque ETA, and a dozen other groups.[58]

Some Puerto Rican independence militants of the time, especially FALN, operated from Puerto Rican communities in Chicago and East Coast cities where many had been full- or part-time students in reputable schools. In the 1980s, with the FALN members jailed or dispersed, the movement passed to Los Macheteros, or 'Machete-wielders'. They were dominated by a strong Cuban connection (fugitive Filiberto Ojeda Rios)[59] and also by Juan Segarra Palmer, some of whose illegal activities were ongoing as he dropped out of Harvard, where he had held a scholarship. Segarra Palmer masterminded the $7.2 million robbery of Wells Fargo that landed many Macheteros in federal court in Hartford, Connecticut, in the late 1980s. The second tier of the Macheteros also had notable educational backgrounds; they were political activists, social workers, graduate students, etc., a pattern which was played up in oral arguments and formal submissions by defendants and their witnesses and defense attorneys. The explicit argument – easy to make – was that the defendants were political activists for Puerto Rican independence from the United States. The implicit argument – utterly without basis – was that one could not be so well educated and active in the community and also be a terrorist.

In fact, Ivonne H. Melendez Carrion, though president of a local parent–teacher association, was charged with possession of pistols and machine guns. Elias Castro-Ramos, alleged to a member of the Macheteros' Central Committee, is a former biology teacher whose wife holds an MA in counseling. Another Central Committee member, according to authorities, is Hilton Eduardo Fernandez Diamante, a writer for a leftist political magazine. Segarra Palmer's girlfriend, who laundered part of the stolen money, was Anne Gassin, a Harvard graduate, a teacher, and a performance artist. And Segarra Palmer's common-law wife, who also handled stolen cash, is a college graduate in occupational therapy who had devoted ten years of work to that admirable profession.[60]

Court proceedings of the last three decades indicate how well schooled many terrorists have been in such social sciences and professional fields as psychology, sociology, history, law, and journalism. The roster of Baader–Meinhof activists and supporters was full of lawyers, graduate students, and others of considerable learning, and so have been the ranks of subsequent leftist German terrorist groups. The pattern in America has been so similar that there is little peculiar about the education level of 'Unabomber' Theodore Kaczynski, who held a doctorate and a prestigious teaching post. He read widely, twice completing all the novels of Joseph Conrad (whose true name was Josef Teodor Konrad Korzeniowski, strikingly alike to that of the Unabomber). In the Conrad novel *The Secret Agent*, a professor turns terrorist out of hatred for modern science.[61] Both the novel and its modern re-enactor are indicators that liberal education is no guarantor of a gentle spirit. Instead it may be twisted into better arguments for violence.

Even religious education may be twisted towards terrorists' purposes, on occasion. Many of the recent international terrorist strikes by calculating individuals of *compos mentis* have been perpetrated by students or graduates of religious institutions which aim to blend the political with the more holy. A list of the well-educated Jewish militants with a record of terrorist attacks must include the Jewish Rabbi Meir Kahane, who founded the Jewish Defense League, and Kach, banned as a terrorist organization by Israel; Kahane's son Benjamin, founder of 'Kahane Lives', also banned; practising physician Baruch Goldstein, who managed to kill 30 Palestinian Muslims in a Hebron mosque before being bludgeoned with a pipe; and student Yigal Amir who assassinated Israel's Prime Minster Yitzak Rabin. There are many more examples on the Muslim side. And security analysts and journalists in the region can readily point to the schools which often 'graduate' new militants. For example, Gaza City's Islamic University has been called a breeding ground for Hamas, one of the two most violent anti-Israeli groups in the region.[63]

Religious institutions are very powerful in the countries of southwest Asia as well. A range of schools and school systems combine study of the Koran with the strongest forms of political mobilization and propaganda. Afghanistan, embroiled in clan warfare since the expulsion of the Soviet Red Army, has suddenly been swept by men for whom clans are tertiary concerns, well behind adherence to the Koran and political unification of the Muslim world. 'Taliban' is a militia named from the Pushtun word for 'student'. From its base in Sunni religious schools educating Afghan refugees in Pakistan, Taliban emerged in 1994 and took Kandahar, and then stretched its rule outward until holding nearly all of Afghanistan by the end of 1998. There is evidence the insurgents have inherited, rather than stopped, Afghanistan's thriving drug trade. Taliban is also doing nothing about the Afghans' training of international Islamic terrorists.[64]

Iran offers a similarly hot mix of religion, politics, education, and violence. This sovereign state of Shiite faith is also the world's leading supporter of international terrorists. Despite hopes that President Ali Hkbar Hashemi Rafsanjani might permit pragmatism a place within the

The liberal education of a bomber

American authorities spent 17 years hunting for the 'Unabomber', so named for initially targeting universities and airlines. Theodore Kaczynski was not a suspect. It was only when his anonymous 35,000-word manifesto was published that a family member recognized the ideas and language.

Raised in Chicago, Ted Kaczynski showed great intelligence. At twelve he could beat the neighborhood women in games of 'Scrabble'. He did very well in school, and skipped sixth grade, but was something of a bookish loner.

Ted's father left the two sons in the Kaczynski family with an early suspicion of technology and an admiration for nature. The father deeply admired the Amish people, still known for favoring horse and buggy. The Unabomber's later journals would express rage and lethal anger at noise-makers such as airliners and snowmobiles that penetrated his wild environs.

Early interest in chemicals led the schoolboy into minor trouble. He made small explosive packets and set them off. On one occasion he worked with a friend who made the mistake of substituting a pound of a chemical for a gram. The result blew up the lab.

Kaczynski's solitary lifestyle was underscored at Harvard, where he finished his degree in only three years. Next came a PhD in mathematics at the University of Michigan, where his dissertation was voted the best in math for the year. He then taught at the University of California at Berkeley, and published articles on mathematics in academic journals.

The 'Unabomber' initiated his attacks when a manuscript he had sent to the Northwestern University's math department was rejected and its written quality disparaged, according to one account. A bomb came later to the department through the mail. Subsequent attacks singled out individuals in high technology, computer science, etc. As Kaczynski wrote in a letter to one newspaper during the bombing campaign: 'people who willfully and knowingly promote economic growth and technical progress, in our eyes they are criminals, and if they get blown up they deserve it'. Journal entries repeatedly express a desire to kill or in some cases to maim.

'Industrial Society and its Future', Kaczynski's lengthy and literate manifesto, was typed in solitude in his now-famous Montana cabin, and mailed to the *New York Times* with the demand that it be published by that paper or the *Washington Post*. The two newspapers decided to do so by splitting the costs and releasing the manifesto as a special insert in the 19 September 1995 *Washington Post*.[62]

The propaganda reached millions (that day and subsequently on the Internet). But the readers included David Kaczynski, Ted's brother, who ultimately approached authorities. They arrested the Unabomber.

mullah-dominated regime, trends in Iran ran along normal channels through the end of his term. June 1997 elections yielded new speculation and hopes for successor Mohammed Khatemi, hopes rewarmed in June 1998 when the US Secretary of State proffered a hand to Tehran.[65] But an early cabinet appointment by the new president was Ms Massoumeh Ebtekar, two decades before the spokeswoman for militants holding hostages at the American Embassy.[66] The religious schools remain central to the continuing cultural revolution, whether from their own inclination or pressures from above; they are fostering the harder ideological lines. Campus publications have closed and publishers are fearful of releasing books – other than the safest of religious texts. There are ideological tests for graduate students, segregation of classes according to sex, and new examples of persecution of nonreligious or liberal professors by such radical organizations as Ansar Hezbollah, linked to the infamous Pasdaran Revolutionary Guards.[67] Such schools will invariably alienate some; just as inevitably they will produce students amenable to internationalist political organizing and possibly terrorist *jihad*.

Another, wholly different sort of education helps terrorists. The practical sciences have useful, direct application to explosives, communications, and other logistics required for making a clandestine movement a practical success. The backgrounds of Middle Eastern and southwest Asian terrorists,[68] for example, often include specialized technical training or advanced scientific schooling. Metallurgical engineer Marvam Rajavi of the People's Mujahideen is a good example. So are those responsible for the Luxor, Egypt, November 1997 attack. All six were students: several studied agricultural science at the university, while two others pursued medical and veterinary sciences. Terrorists know that engineering, chemistry, and computer science are all of use, and such schooling has been a common characteristic of terrorist captives interrogated by authorities in recent years.

In 1994 and 1995 Israel was rent by the bomb blasts of a Palestinian Hamas agent, Yahya Ayyash, head of the military wing and chief bomb-maker. Dubbed 'The Engineer' for his skills, he ran a shop that inflicted scores of casualties in Israeli public places until his death in early January 1996 in Gaza.[69] The education of another such engineer is known precisely: international Muslim and terrorist Ramzi Youssef of Pakistan, now jailed in New York, graduated in electrical engineering from Swansea University in Wales. This skilled technician was at the center of the band that carried out the New York Trade Towers bombing, plotted similar attacks in that city, and had other enterprises in the Philippines, including sophisticated airline bombings. Youssef could build a variety of explosive devices, some of which he disguised to pass through inspection points; he also built nitroglycerine bombs like the one that blew up inside a Philippines' Airline flight headed for Japan in 1994. He kept notebooks of chemical formulas and diagrams and directions to aid in his work. Competent in three languages, Ramzi Youssef defended himself in federal court in New York, even demonstrating a knowledge of legal jargon.[70]

Finally, there are terrorist movements or insurgencies using terrorism which have risen wholly from university grounds. This occurred in the early 1970s and did not die with Ulrike Meinhof, who committed suicide in German jail. Before Abimael Guzman became Peru's most famous captive, he built Sendero Luminoso from the ground up by organizational work in Peruvian universities. His first base was at Ayacucho where he was director of personnel, and thus able to influence hiring and ensure that his professorial colleagues were recruiting as enthusiastically as was he. When there were Shining Path organizations in many major upper schools, Guzman began organizing secondary schools. Sendero at its height was some 20,000 strong. It was led almost exclusively by educated adults, though its membership ranks included many workers and peasants. Peru's second terror group, Tupac Amaru, follows a different brand of communism but is also dominated by well educated cadres.

The most celebrated contemporary movement in Mexico is the Zapatistas, whose commander, 'Marcos', is thought to be a former university professor. After an introductory use of violence, which the Zapatista web site vehemently denies constituted 'terrorism',[71] the group has spent its next years using skills that require education much more than arms. They committed no terrorist attacks in 1996, for example, but they were negotiating, publishing communiqués, and posting verbose documents on the Internet. Another violent Mexican group is organized along nearly opposite lines: it is small and clandestine, as against the press-hungry Zapatistas. It is deeply enmeshed in violent ways of attracting attention, such as assassinations and hostage-taking. But there is one similarity, beyond its leftist ideology: it was founded by radical students led by a senior university administrator. Felipe Martinez Soriano was rector at the university in Oaxaca, on the Pacific Ocean side of southernmost Mexico. He was among the founders of the Clandestine Revolutionary Workers' Party–People's Union (Procup), which now two decades later has become the Popular Revolutionary Army, EPR. Felipe Martinez Soriano had to be moved to a higher security jail in the autumn of 1996 as his gunmen carried out attacks against power stations, public buildings, and security forces across Mexico.[72]

Clearly, terrorism is not mindless. Two striking patterns displayed above support this conclusion. First, a consideration of the psychology of hostage-taking shows how apparent disorder and insanity may be calibrated to produce certain psychological and political effects. Second, the high education level of leading terrorists indicates that the violence against the innocent on which terrorism relies is well considered violence, deployed in the service of a political purpose.[73]

The roles of the female terrorist

The general perception that nearly all terrorists are males is untrue. It cannot be supported by surveying the numbers of men versus women in the active contemporary insurgent and terrorist groups. Nor can it be supported by study of the decision-makers and leaders of the most dangerous and important groups of today. There are of course several facts which support the illusion: the males are more numerous, and some groups have few women members, or include them only in such roles as supporters and couriers (these include the IRA and European right-wing groups). But in reality there is no male 'norm'. By one estimate, more than 30 per cent of international terrorists are women,[74] and females are central to membership rosters and operational roles in nearly all insurgencies.

The single most wanted terrorist in Asia today may well be a woman: Fusako Shigenobu, head of the Japanese Red Army. She emerged from radical student politics like so many others around the world in the late 1960s. She helped found and build the JRA, responsible for crimes that include the Lod Airport massacre of 1972 and a pattern of attacks and attempted attacks on US consulates, embassies, and military personnel in the 1980s (Jakarta, 1986; Rome, 1987; New York, Naples, and Madrid, 1988).[75] For two decades, the group has lived and worked from exile (especially in the Bekaa Valley of Lebanon). Shigenobu may have personally conducted an occasional foreign operation during this time; by one account, she was sighted in Naples[76] in 1988 just prior to the bombing there of a US officers' club in mid-April, a retaliatory act marking the second anniversary of the US air raid on Libya, long a JRA patron.

There are other females among the two-dozen-strong membership of the Japanese Red Army. Some were figures in the radical student movements of that day. These include Nagata Hiroko, a top student who became politicized while at Kyoritsu Pharmaceutical College. She formed part of a radical feminist organization which itself then fused with other groups to form the JRA. Ms Hiroko ordered the murders of several JRA defectors. She was also a principal in the drama of the 'Snow Murders' of December 1972, when the JRA leadership, closeted in a rural home in the mountains of Japan, killed a number of its own in a purge. The 'charges' against the victims were of such things as sexual activity, or over-attentiveness to personal appearance. One person after another was singled out, psychologically brutalized in hours of shouting and Maoist-style 'self-criticism', and then forced outside and beaten, killed, or bound up and left to die in the freezing temperatures on the site. The 11 victims included three females, one of them eight months pregnant.[77]

Recent arrests of JRA cadre confirm the pattern of female participation in important roles. Yoshimura Kazue was connected to the 1974 embassy takeover in The Hague, an operation which successfully sprung from prison four JRA terrorists. Peru has arrested this JRA woman and deported her to Japan. A second case is Yukiko Ekita, picked up with a false passport by Romanian authorities in March 1995. She was involved in another violent action in which one tactical aim of the group was the release of fellow terrorists from jail. A JRA hijacking in 1977 had garnered $6 million in ransom and six comrades from prison, including Ekita, jailed years earlier for firebombing Japanese companies.[78] Yet another JRA woman, Mariko Yamamoto, was arrested in early 1997 in Lebanon, when she and four male JRA militants were picked up. Ultimately, however, all five were prosecuted only on innocuous charges such as document forgery and 'illegal entry'. Fusako Shigenobu was not arrested with them, although she too is believed to live in the Middle East – probably in Damascus. She no longer draws publicity to herself.[79]

Another celebrated Asian female terrorist is in custody and has told her own story: North Korean Kim Hyon Hui. The daughter of a diplomat, and a beautiful actress who starred in propaganda films, she assumed a new state-dictated role: airline bomber. In late 1987, with a male partner, she helped plant the bombs that destroyed Korean Air flight 858. The pair was on a mission explained to them by Kim Jong Il, the son of the North Korean dictator, who has since risen to take that senior position himself. In his words, the action was intended to 'block South Korea's attempts to perpetuate the [separation of the] two Koreas and also to host the 1988 Olympics on its own'. This project, continued Kim Jong Il, 'will pour cold water on the desire of all nations of the world to participate in the Olympics and will deal the South Korean puppet regime a fatal blow'.[80] The petite woman gladly accepted the job because she felt she was 'the Party's daughter'.[81]

Kim Hyon Hui and an older agent playing the role of her father traveled on false Japanese passports. From Pyongyang the pair flew to Moscow and then East Berlin, accompanied by control officers. To muddy the waters of their origins, they also went to Budapest, Vienna, and then Belgrade, where the North Korean station chief brought them prepared explosives. Flying from Yugoslavia to Baghdad, Kim Hyon Hui and her male partner boarded the targeted KAL flight, planting two bombs in the luggage bin above them. They exited the plane when it halted in Abu Dhabi and never reboarded. Flight 858 continued on towards Bangkok and its final destination, Seoul. The detonation over the Andaman Sea killed all 115 passengers and crew aboard, most of them South Koreans as befit the North's plan.

Another Asian woman has won celebrity only by her suicide. Called simply 'Dhanu' in formal reports, she assassinated Rajiv Gandhi, leader of India's largest political party. A lengthy investigation by Indian authorities has filled out the story she can no longer tell. Dhanu became a Tamil 'Tigress', a member of the LTTE group that marks its own determination by wearing cyanide capsules around their necks, ready for swallowing should they be captured by Sri Lankan authorities. Her attack was a rejoinder to the man who as prime minister had sent Indian peacekeeping troops across the Palk Strait to Sri Lanka to try to suppress the Tamil insurgency. The Tigers determined to assassinate him, and they planned well. The conspirators included both the LTTE intelligence chief and the movement's supreme leader, Velupillai Prabhakaran. Dhanu was selected to carry out the mission because she had been gang-raped by Indian troops during that peacekeeping exercise, and needed no convincing. There were two back-ups: a male, instructed to shoot the party leader on the spot should the suicide bombing fail; and another woman, 'Subha', who was prepared to become the next to destroy herself along with Gandhi should that prove necessary. Dry runs were made, both for approaching Rajiv Gandhi at public appearances, and for testing the explosive-laden belts at remote LTTE hideouts. On 21 May 1991, Dhanu approached Gandhi at a public rally, bowed before him, and detonated her bomb. Seventeen other innocent people also died.[82]

In many of these terrorism cases, women were not only well-trained and fiercely motivated killers, they were able to exploit their cultural environment. Women are simply more trusted. They are the least expected to be principals in political terror. A related explanation of their involvement begins at the same point: Asian women are raised in societies which treat them as subordinate, often wholly subservient. Some women have turned forcibly against this tradition and taken the path of militant politics, by joining the men and women of radical

Sri Lankan women lead rebel forces

The following are excerpts from an article by Inter Press Service in the Louis Farrakhan/Nation of Islam newspaper *Final Call*.[83] The news story emphasizes the female role in guerrilla war against the Sri Lankan army, rather than terrorism, in which women also play an important role in LTTE campaigns.

When Tamil rebels attacked government defense lines in northern Sri Lanka last month, they admitted to losing 130 cadre. Of these 40 were women Tigers.

Earlier, a specially trained force led by women rebels had paralyzed military operations for more than two weeks. In the final death count of that battle, the Liberation Tigers for Tamil Eelam (LTTE) admitted it had lost 140 fighters, 89 of them women.

There are an estimated 3,000 women in the ranks of the guerrilla group who are fighting for a separate state in the island's northeast for minority Tamils ...

In a speech on International Women's Day in 1992, LTTE leader Velupillai Prabhakaran said: 'Today, young women have taken up arms to liberate our land ... women can succeed in their struggle for emancipation only by mobilizing themselves behind a liberation organization. This will give them confidence, courage, determination and transform them as revolutionaries ...'

While the Vituthalai Pulikal Makalir Munani (Women's Front of the Liberation Tigers) was formed in 1983, it was not until two years later that they began training for the battlefront. The first batch were trained in Tamil Nadu in India in 1985 and their first battle was against the Sri Lankan forces in July 1986.

In October 1987 Prabhakaran set up the first training camp exclusively for women in Jaffna for ... successive batches ...

Nowadays, the women who join the LTTE are younger – barely into their teens and plucked straight out of school and for this reason, not as educated.

groups, forging their identities as part of groups that are driving to take political power. Far more women have taken an altogether different route, and have worked in pacific and democratic ways against cultures unfavorable to their rise in politics, succeeding in helping build political parties, and even coming to hold the elected premierships of such countries as Sri Lanka, India, Pakistan, and the Philippines.

The Latin experience mirrors that of Asia, in spite of all evident differences between cultures and continents. In the once-powerful Uruguayan Tupamaros, the Nicaraguan Sandinistas, and other modern Latin groups, hundreds of women have participated in terrorism or do so today. They often rise within their groups to positions of high authority which contrast with what they may feel to be low 'civilian' status, or uninteresting rural lives, or birth into a culture in which they feel held back by their sex.[84] Some are doubtless inspired by male friends or lovers to join. Many join for the same political reasons the males do: out of political principles, or from radicalization at the university. These women in Latin groups take all appropriate roles, from the clever courier who does not arouse suspicion, to reconnaissance agents strolling about prospective target areas, to unit commanders, to senior advisors. There is, however, no prominent Latin group whose top leader is female.

There are many Peruvian women in prison today among the some 400 persons convicted of association with MRTA, 'Tupac Amaru', the Castroite group active since 1983. MRTA's shockingly easy takeover of Japan's embassy and some 500 people underscored the proclivity of Latin groups for large-scale hostage-taking – a pattern that includes the M-19's seizure of the Dominican Republic's embassy in Bogota in February 1980 and 11 embassy takeovers in El Salvador in 1978–79.[85] It also included the pattern of female participation in Latin terrorism. One MRTA woman in Peruvian prison is the wife of group leader Nestor Cerpa Cartolini; she was among those he hoped to free in staging the hostage-taking at the Japanese embassy. Instead he and his terrorist team all perished, including several young MRTA women armed with assault rifles. Cartolini called the young women under his command 'Che's grandchildren'.[86]

The rival Peruvian group, Sendero Luminoso, has a larger profile, far more members, and a more ruthless spirit. Yet like MRTA it possesses a very high ratio of female members. These have included Catalina Andriansen (a Cusco regional leader), Edith Lagos Saenz (an Ayacucho leader), and Laura Zambrano Padilla (a Lima chief of operations, sentenced to prison in 1986).[87] Following the Latin pattern, no woman has ever been the foremost in command. But male Abimael Guzman, who built the Shining Path during years of organizational work, surrounded himself with senior female officers. His wife Augusta La

Torre was number two in Sendero until her death in late 1988.[88] By one account, she was succeeded – in her duties and in Guzman's heart – by Elena Albertina Iparraguirre Revoredo, later captured with the Sendero chief.[89]

After Dr Guzman's capture, the organization's leadership devolved to Oscar Ramirez Durand,[90] who was himself captured, along with female and male bodyguards, in July 1999. One female and historic founder, Jenny Rodriguez Neyra ('Rita'), was captured in 1998. But many senior positions may still be held by women, including Florella Montanez Castillo, an important Sendero military leader, and Margie Clavo Peralta, who as 'Nancy' has been the group's 'national coordinator'.[91] In the cell blocks, walls are decorated with political poems and posters laudatory of Abimael Guzman, Mao, and other heroes. The women pass their time in political studies and political conversation, neutralizing the common (unpolitical) prisoners, organizing their own relatives on the outside, and producing uniforms, political banners, and handicrafts. 'In this way, the black dungeons of the reaction [are transformed] into shining trenches of combat', notes Sendero Luminoso's underground newspaper El Diario.[92]

Foreign women sometimes join the struggle. Currently, the most famous is Lori Berenson, an American convicted in January 1996 by a Peruvian court for helping plan a hostage-taking in the Congress building in Lima. Berenson's incendiary courtroom speech in support of MRTA weakened her defense against these charges. So did her other Latin involvements, and the fact that MRTA soon thereafter took the Japanese Embassy in exactly the type of hostage seizure they were plotting for the Congress building in Lima. While that barricade situation continued on the last day of 1996, the Berenson case festered in New York, where her parents maintain a vigil and an Internet web site.[93] During 1998 the case was a reopened wound for Peru, where what to do about Berenson's imprisonment divided the president from his prime minister.[94]

The most female of all terror groups active today is that of Sunni Iranians and deracinated Arabs who go under the banner of the People's Mujahedeen of Iran, the Mujahedeen Khalq. This organization was shaped in the 1960s and opposed the Shah with its own secular ideas about the future of Iran. While it supported the 1979 hostage-taking at the US embassy in Tehran, the group was shouldered aside during the rise of Ayatollah Khomeini and his religious activists. Now based in Iraq, and possessing a long record of terrorist violence inside and outside Iran, the group also fields thousands of fighters[95] in what might fairly be called a semi-conventional army. This 'National Liberation Army' trains hard, is poised for an opportunity to retake Iran, and probes across the border occasionally. Maryam Rajavi and her husband rule the organization, but it is she who has been elected by the membership to be the future president of a renewed Iran. Once a student and then a metallurgical engineer, Mrs Rajavi is a strong leader. She is 'anathema to the Khomeini ideology, and that's why she is the cure', according to the chief of logistics at the army's Camp Ashraf, lying midway between Baghdad and the Iraqi border with Iran. There are both men and women in the populous lower ranks. Even members who were once married to each other now live separately and chastely. Most of the group's top officers are women.[96]

Northern European and American cultures differ from these, and usually offer immensely greater personal liberties and political opportunities to women. But the United States and the northern European countries are also home to terrorist groups that have innumerable females among their memberships and leaders. It thus appears that the factors which draw women into the ranks of militants are more political and personal than they are geographic or culture-specific. The 'first lady' of the movement must be found in fully legal politics: Alessandra Mussolini, granddaughter of the former dictator, is a legislator and leader of the legal rightist National Alliance, and she also attends such events as the May 1994 rally of the Italian Social Movement, the legal but far-right party.[97]

All the northern European organizations which coincidentally have the characteristics of revolutionary aims, terrorist records, and high numbers of females, are anarchist or communist. The once-powerful Italian Red Brigades were at least a third female, and the same may have been true of the French of 'Direct Action'. Since its founding in 1959, the Basque ETA has had hundreds of female members in the Spanish and French sections; these include members of many husband–wife teams as well as women joining independently.[98] One of the most important ETA leaders of the early 1990s has been Irene Idoia Lopez Riano, who served in Spain through 1991, crossed over into France for a time, and was subsequently believed to be back in Spain commanding a roving ETA unit.[99] To take another example: in January 1997, apparently in retaliation for arrests of ETA members, Basques assassinated Lieutenant-Colonel Jesus Cuesta as he stepped out of his car at home in Madrid. It was reportedly a young woman who fired the shots which killed Cuesta; her male accomplice missed in an attempt to shoot the victim's driver.[100]

The same pattern has been evident among Germany's violent leftists since the early 1970s. 'Red Zora', a group of German leftist women, attacked targets they considered to be sexist, like marriage offices which united German men with mail-order Asian brides. The Baader–Meinhof gang can be best understood not by studying Andreas Baader, who began as an ignorant and violent nihilist, but his educated and equally violent partner, Ulrike Meinhof, the intense and gifted student-turned-journalist, whose Marxism–Leninism and determination to overhaul West German society led her to take a leadership role. She wrote revolutionary literature while also committing armed robbery, assault, and bombing. The third principal in the gang was another woman, Gudrun Ensslin, a capable terrorist and the lover of Andreas Baader. She and Ms Meinhof organized the team that successfully sprung Andreas Baader from prison.[101] Like Baader–Meinhof, the successor groups of the left were also about half-female, including Second of June Movement, the Red Army Faction, and the minuscule Revolutionary Cells.

Red Army Faction's terrorists still make regular places in the news. Susan Albrecht of the RAF helped kill Dresden Bank head Jurgen Ponto and industrialist Martin Schleyer in the 1970s, but was not arrested until June 1990. She was in East Germany, which late in 1990 surrendered at least ten West Germans wanted for assassination and bombings; they were protected from Bonn's reach until reunification.[102] As of 1991, more than half of Germany's 22 most wanted terrorists were women. Five of the eight on Germany's 'Wanted Terrorists' poster were female, including Friedeike Krable and Barbara Meyer. There was as well Andrea Klump, who probably led an American soldier to his death in 1985.[103]

In February 1997, when Germany finally filed charges against defendants for the 1986 La Belle disco bombing in Berlin, two women were implicated along with three men. Verna Chanaa, and Andrea Haeussler, a younger sister, were indicted for placing the bomb. The older of the women was married to an East German secret police agent, Ali Chanaa, who was responding to an order from the Libyan government that arrived via the embassy in East Berlin. 'As many victims as possible' should die, according to the communiqué, because of US naval maneuvers off the Libyan coast (themselves the result of the terrorist attacks on Rome and Vienna airports). The German communists – East and West – and the Libyans accomplished their mutual objective with a 6.5 pound combination of *plastique* and shrapnel.[104] Two US servicemen died, and scores of Americans and Germans were injured.

German male terrorist 'Bommi' Baumann of the late Second of June Movement has observed that 'Women can get closer to the target. If a man in a high position, perhaps knowing that he may be a target for terrorists, is approached by a woman, he may think, she is a prostitute. Women can go straight to the target's doorstep; sometimes they do it in pairs, two women, saying they are lost. If two men approached him, he would be suspicious.'[105] Being less suspected, women are excellent couriers and intelligence agents for any underground. This has been portrayed in the film *The Battle of Algiers*,[106] and played out in reality by countless groups.[107] There is no inherent subservience in such roles; few terror group activities are as essential and as continuously pressing as work in reconnaissance and intelligence.

If the presence of women helps to illuminate the recruitment patterns of successful leftist groups, a relative absence of women in the active hard core is a revealing indicator of different recruitment patterns among neoNazis and similar rightist militant groups. The latter generally do not seek out and promote women members. That approach, the product of culture or ideology, may be one of the more decisive weaknesses of these groups, which remain stuck on the political margins and are also overwhelmingly male.[108] An analogy is suggested by the way some post-Second World War insurgencies devoted themselves mostly to work in the countryside, thus failing in the cities. Or, if well organized in the capital, they proved inattentive to their rural countrymen. Certain rightist terror groups of today which are all-male may be committing a similar blunder, ignoring fully half of their potential recruits.[109] That need not concern groups hypothetically concerned only with spreading chaos, or serving some government by 'death-squad' killings of its enemies and critics. But it may be decisive where the terror group's objective is seizing state power.

NeoNazism
and women

On the Internet, a 'National Socialism Primer' posted by Milton John Kleim, Jr outlines positions American neoNazis should take on various ideological, political, and social issues. Attempting to rebut some of the criticisms neofascists encounter in the 1990s, the document takes the form of questions and answers. From the '2nd edition', dated 17 April 1995 and still accessible, here is the section on the subject of women, according to Kleim's party, the 'American National Socialist Movement':[110]

'Why are you such male chauvinists?
Despite what Establishment academicians and the Jewish-controlled media insist you believe, male National Socialists consider our racial sisters partners in the struggle for racial survival, as activists, warriors, and mothers. The Creator intends for women and men to be complementary, not contradictory. While Marxist and Jewish 'Feminists' arrogantly reject women's uniqueness, attempting to 'liberate' women from their womanhood, National Socialists accept the slight differences between men and women as strengths, and demand an end to the gynophobia which is a consequence of centuries of pervasive ... Judeo-Christian tradition. Adolf Hitler, among his many revolutionary acts, broke the traditions of the highly androcentric German Armed Forces by awarding heroine test-pilot Hanna Reitsch the Iron Cross. Many capable, talented women, like Realm Women's Leader Gertrude Scholtz-Klink, assumed important roles in helping to rebuild German society, and later in the defense of Europe, often while tending their families in the face of great adversity.

Notes

1. James Hoge, editor-in-chief of the *Chicago Sun Times*, 'Terrorism: The World at Bay', WHYY Television (Philadelphia, PA: 21 March 1978).

2. Professor Paul Wilkinson, chair of the Centre for the Study of Terrorism and Political Violence, St Andrews University, Scotland, *Combating International Terrorism* (London: Institute of Jewish Affairs, 1995), p. 2, as quoted by Irwin Cotler, 'Toward a Counter-Terrorism Law and Policy', *Terrorism and Political Violence*, 10:2 (summer 1998), p. 3, n.10.

3. Sergey Nechaev, *Catechism of the Revolutionist* (1869), excerpted in *The Terrorism Reader: A Historical Anthology*, revised edn, Walter Laqueur and Yonah Alexander (New York: Meridian, 1987), p. 68.

4. As noted above in Chapter 1, this definition is in Benjamin Netanyahu (ed.), *Terrorism: How the West Can Win* (New York: Farrar, Straus, Giroux, 1986), p. 9. The article by Netanyahu himself in this collection, 'Defining Terrorism', is excellent on moral issues. For a longer treatment of 'Terrorism: A Matter for Moral Judgement', the reader could consider my essay of that title, prepared for the Naval Chaplains School in Newport, Rhode Island and published in *Terrorism and Political Violence*, 4:1 (spring 1992), pp. 1–21.

5. The *fatwa* was faxed to the Arabic-language newspaper *Al-Quds al-Arabi* in London, which printed it on 23 February 1998. Signatories, other than Bin Laden, were an amir of the Jihad Group, Egypt; a leader of the Islamic Group, also Egyptian; the secretary of the group, Jarniat-ul-Ulema-e-Pakistan; and the amir of the Jihad Movement, Bangladesh. Translated by the Foreign Broadcast Information Service (hereafter FBIS) and then released by Senator John Kyl of Arizona. The italics for foreign words are mine.

6. 'Terrorism, by definition, is aimed at a wider audience than its immediate victims', according to the US State Department's *Patterns of Global Terrorism: 1996* (Washington, DC: GPO, April 1997). One can well agree, while also insisting that terrorism's attack on the *innocent* is just as fundamental.

7. Terrorists are not always indiscriminate, and terrorism ought not be defined merely as 'indiscriminate violence'. Terrorists often target and then successfully assassinate particular persons, for example. The same group may then plan attacks to kill generally and indiscriminately.
   The IRA actually apologizes for unforeseen consequences of some of its attacks. This is intended to prove that 'the hard men' have a conscience, but it can as easily be seen as a remarkable admission of the essential immorality of a peacetime bombing campaign for political change.

8. The Unabomber especially hated technocrats, computer-makers, and business and government people. But his diaries show that his hatred spread to nearly all, because 'Almost anyone who holds steady employment is contributing his part in maintaining the technological society': handwritten journal entry of sometime between fall 1977 and August 1978, placed on the Internet at: http://www. dejanews.com/getdoc.xp?AN = 361598462. Downloaded from Deja News on 23 December 1998.

9. See Gregory A. Fossedal, *The Democratic Imperative: Exporting the American Revolution* (New York: New Republic Books, 1989).

10. I believe Lithuanian resistance to Soviet occupation after 1945 was both forceful and protracted, but without featuring Lithuanian attacks on, say, the wives of Soviet officers, or other terrorism.

11. The Second World War 'strategic bombing' became a moral issue that has never

been settled because it included the targeting of cities based less on their value as materiel producers or their other utility to military forces as upon the likelihood that such city bombing would break the morale of the enemy. Such a strategy was not then illegal; in 1922–23 The Hague had drafted a ban on the aerial bombardment of undefended population centers during war, but it was not ratified. I sought to address the question of whether area bombing was 'terrorism' in the monograph *Are We Beasts?: Churchill and the Moral Question of World War Two Area Bombing*, Newport Paper no. 1 (Newport, RI: Center for Naval Warfare Studies, December 1991).

12. One may contrast the German Red Army Faction of some two-dozen hard core operatives with the West German nation of 60 million, or today's even greater disparity: there are over 80 million citizens in the reunified Germany, and no hotly active leftist terrorist group. The Tupac Amaru group that captured 500 hostages and the attentions of the world in Lima in December 1996 then had at most a few hundred operatives not already jailed for terrorism; Peru's population is some 24 million. The Greek group 'November 17' is minuscule, while there are 11 million Greeks who are affected by their crimes.

A recent article makes a similar observation about a past terror group, the separatist militants of Quebec: 'the number of people who actually committed terrorist acts or gave material support numbered no more than several dozen', observe Saul Newman and Scott Piroth in 'Terror and Tolerance: The Use of Ballots, Bombs and Bullets by Ethnoregional Movements in Advanced Industrial Democracies', *Nationalism and Ethnic Politics*, 2:3 (autumn 1996), p. 386.

13. For example, polls of Basques in the 1990s always show that a majority reject the tactics of terrorism that ETA employs; these people prefer the nationalist parties using democratic means for support for their Basque cause.

14. The Tamil Tigers may be a formidable guerrilla force, but they get many of their best headlines from terror attacks. Two garnered great publicity in July 1996: an attack on a commuter train which left 70 passengers dead, and an attempt to kill the housing minister in Jaffna, which missed him but killed 25 others: *Patterns of Global Terrorism: 1996*, p. 6. Terror bombings in the capital are an LTTE standard.

15. Alistair Horne, *A Savage War of Peace: Algeria 1954–1962* (New York: Viking Press, 1978), p. 132; brackets are mine.

16. *Court Depositions of Three Red Brigadists*, ed. Sue Ellen Moran (Santa Monica, CA: RAND, February 1986), p. 195.

17. Show Television (Ankara: 18 May 1992), trans. and repr. in Joint Publications Research Service (hereafter JPRS), *Terrorism* (22 May 1992), p. 24.

18. In 1988 the United States brought to trial Marilyn Buck and Nutulu Shakur of the self-proclaimed 'Republic of New Africa' organization. They were charged with murdering police and other crimes. Their defense included the argument that they were 'at war' with the US government. They thus demanded POW rights under the 1949 Geneva Convention or its 1977 supplements, thinking it would make such acts as killing police 'acts of war' by legitimate combatants, protected by a state of war. But the United States never ratified Protocol 1 of the 1977 Geneva accords, in part because its widening of POW rights seemed unreasonable. And even if it had signed, there can be no POW rights without a state of war, as declared by at least one side and recognized internationally. Traditional international law has not recognized assassination, rioting, or other such acts as anything but common crime. Finally, even if the 'Republic of New Africa' were recognized as a legitimate belligerent under Protocol 1, they would

then be duty-bound to observe many traditional laws of armed conflict, which their murders and robberies contravene, such as protecting civilians. Police are not 'legitimate objects of attack' unless they are incorporated into the armed forces. See exhibit A of the affidavit of Assistant US Attorney Kerri L. Martin to the US District Court, Southern District of New York, in the case of *US* vs *Mutulu Shakur*, defendant, 23 March 1988 (SSS 82 Cr. 312 (CSH)).

19. One of the strangest facts of the French counter-insurgency effort in Algeria ending in 1962 is that some French soldiers who tortured terrorists and insurgents themselves became psychologically maimed for life in invisible ways by their own brutality to Algerians.

20. Graham E. Fuller, *Algeria: The Next Fundamentalist State?* (Santa Monica, CA: RAND, 1996), pp. xi, 37. This is a most intelligent monograph on present-day Algerian violence.

21. 'GIA: Le Djihad contra Chirac', and 'Antar Zouabri, Le Nouvel Emir Tueur', *L'Express* (2 January 1997), pp. 38–41.

22. This is the implication in the articles from *L'Express*, above.

23. For example, Frank Huebner, leader of the neoNazi 'German Alternative' declares that the banning of particular German extremist groups has 'already achieved quite a lot, especially regarding the coming together inside the politically radical right – that is, the borderlines between the parties have been abolished': ORF Television Network (Vienna), recording aired 9 December 1993, in repr. JPRS, *Terrorism* (15 December 1993), p. 38. Huebner's thinking is akin to that of many radical groups.

24. Those who do not love their race enough to fight for 'The Organization' are depicted as 'zombies', 'cows', 'slaves', 'brainwashed', etc. Andrew Macdonald (William Pierce), *The Turner Diaries*, 6th edn (Hillsboro, WV: National Vanguard Books, 1995), pp. 29, 33, 34, 101–2.

25. In part through conversations after 1978 with mentors Harry V. Jaffa and Harold W. Rood, I became aware of the unexpected similarities between radicals of the extremes of left and right, and sought parallels in European history and examples in contemporary terrorism. Findings appeared over many years. The best short, informal article on the apposite relationship of left and right may be Winston S. Churchill, 'The Creeds of the Devil', *Sunday Chronicle* (London), 27 June 1937, repr. in *The Collected Essays of Sir Winston Churchill*, ed. Michael Wolff (London: Library of Imperial History, 1975), vol. 2, *Churchill and Politics*, pp. 394–7. This article was kindly sent to me by Richard Langworth, President of the Churchill Center. The left–right apposition theme appears briefly in other Churchill writings and speeches.

26. The two references in this sentence are from Albert L. Weeks, 'The Current "Communazi" Phenomenon', *Global Affairs*, 2:2 (spring 1987), p. 141. It is an unusual and welcome article. But it is mistitled, since its focus is largely historical, and despite being historical, it makes no reference to the occasions on which Winston Churchill had taken up the theme.

27. See Nikolai Tolstoy, *Stalin's Secret War* (New York: Rinehart and Winston, 1981), pp. 85–8. When I mentioned the 'Beefsteaks' phenomenon to Professor James Gregor, an authority on fascism from the University of California at Berkeley, he noted that their German communist counterparts were called 'Black Bolsheviks'. Dr Gregor spoke on current events in Russia at the faculty of Command and Staff College, Marine Corps University, Quantico, Virginia, 25 September 1996.

28. The Nazi advertisement and the 1972 incident are cited by Claire Sterling, *The*

Terror Network (New York: Holt, Rinehart and Winston, 1981), pp. 113, 116.

29. The interview, *Der Spiegel*, printed 13 July 1981, rpt. in Uri Ra'anan *et al.*, *Hydra of Carnage* (Lexington, MA: Lexington Books, 1986). On the Hoffmann case as an instance of left–right collusion, see my article 'Terrorism: The Evidence of Collusion Between the Red and the Black', *Grand Strategy: Countercurrents* (Claremont, CA: Claremont Institute for the Study of Statesmanship and Political Philosophy), 2:4 (15 December 1982), pp. 1–7.

30. For example, there is the career of one Oedfried Hepp associate, Udo Albrecht. Albrecht began the 'Freikorps Adolf Hitler', fought in Jordan with the PLO, and subsequently became a connection between the West German neoNazis and leftist Palestinians.

31. Rainer Jogschies, 'Changing Political Mold of Terror Groupings', *Deutsches Allgemeines Sonntagsblatt* (12 June 1983), repr. *German Tribune* (3 July 1983), p. 15.

32. *Frankfurter Rundschau* (Frankfurt/Main) (6 September 1990), in JPRS, *Terrorism* (18 September 1990), p. 3. Six German rightists including Hepp and Udo Albrecht were taken care of by Stasi and then passed on to Arab countries. Hepp dealt directly with Department XXII, in charge of international terrorism, according to the newspaper, which confirmed parts of its story with a Stasi document and with Bonn's Federal Office for the Protection of the Constitution.

33. *New York Times* (2 February 1994). Since quitting, Ingo Hasselbach has published a memoir in German, *The Reckoning: A Neo-Nazi Drops Out*, which has appeared in America as *Fuhrer-Ex: Memoirs of a Former Neo-Nazi*, with Tom Reiss (New York: Random House, 1996). He admired Hitler less than he did the left-leaning Nazis such as the Strasser brothers. On left–right issues, see pp. viii, 18, 24, 34–7, 65, 79–81, 93, 106, 115, 131, and 161.

Another indicator that the left's militant writings are watched closely and imitated by the right is a report in the Vienna paper *Der Standard*. It notes that among readers of one neofascist newspaper, *Rechtskampf*, 'the example of the Red Army Faction' was warmed over again and presented as a positive example. An intensive debate on it is currently going on in Berlin Nazi circles': 7 December 1993, in JPRS, *Terrorism* (15 December 1993), p. 37.

34. *Wall Street Journal* (4 December 1991).

35. Interview with Ewald Althans, *Daily Telegraph* (2 March 1992), in FBIS, *Western Europe* (3 March 1992), pp. 14–15.

36. Stephen Kinzer, 'A Climate for Demagogues', *Atlantic Monthly* (February 1994), p. 33.

Consider other cases. Thomas Dienel of the 'German National Party' was publicly and repeatedly agitating in the early 1990s against Jews and Vietnamese, to include a Saalfeld speech in which he called for killing: Dienel had been a member of the East German Communist Party for the entire decade of the 1980s. *New York Times* (10 December 1992). Four members of the communist-era Stasi were arrested in Rostock in 1992 for plotting riots against refugees, according to a confidential report of the Bonn Interior Ministry obtained by the newspaper Bild, *San Francisco Chronicle* (3 September 1992).

'Anglo Saxon' neofascists have asserted themselves in Britain, and here too the ideological picture is more complicated than red versus black. Consider (only as a metaphor for terrorism) the ambiguous personalities of British 'football thugs'. Their lust for action and fighting has often attracted recruiters for leftist and rightist terrorist groups, but the football thugs' anarchism and preference for beer over politics have effectively prevented most such recruitment. There are exceptions. A journalist infiltrating the football thuggery movement found Phil Andrews, once trained as a policeman but since converted to the political view that the government is somehow responsible for football crowd violence. After his police stint, Andrews became a communist, only later to surrender that identity by joining the fascist Young National Front. When not brawling at sports matches or attending neofascist events, Andrews has been assigned to recruit from colleges and schools. Normally such institutions funnel youth into leftist groups, and Andrews' familiarity with methods from his communist days was judged especially valuable. A second thug talked to the journalist at a neofascist club, where the music included songs blaring against aliens and calls upon whites to 'take Britain back'. This member of the 'League of St George', which he declared to be more militant than the National Front, explained that his league favors agrarian socialism and disparages technology as a force that has uprooted man from his natural soil. Prompted that this sounded like the ideology of the 'red' Khmer Rouge, he readily agreed. Bill Buford, *Among the Thugs* (New York: W. W. Norton, 1991), pp. 146–7, 152–3.

Ingo Hasselbach's *The Reckoning* does not reflect anything but incidental contact between the 'thugs' and the political right's militants.

37.   *Los Angeles Times* (11 August 1980). In long depositions by Red Brigadists Massimo Cianfanelli and Enrico Fenzi, one reads nothing of attacks on neofascists or even loathing of the extreme right: Moran, *Court Depositions*. And on the rare occasions when Donatella della Porta's excellent essay on 'Left-Wing Terrorism in Italy' discusses Red Brigadist attacks on 'fascists', it emerges that these victims are factory supervisors or others, not persons identified by affiliation with rightist violence; see for example p. 131, *Terrorism in Context*, ed. Martha Crenshaw (University Park: Pennsylvania State University Press, 1995).

38.   Announcements of Italian Judge Ferdinando Imposimato in January 1982; see also my 'Left Meets Right in Terrorism: A Focus on Italy', *Strategic Review*, 13:1 (winter 1985), pp. 40–51.

39.   The last sentence – which actually refers to 'schizophrenia' – is suggested by leftist journalist Valerio Marchi, who believes this phenomenon is common to other western neofascists as well as the Italian; cited in 'The Ghost of Mussolini Keeps Rattling his Chains', *New York Times* (1 June 1994).

40.   *Washington Post* (6 December 1995); *Christian Science Monitor* (19 December 1995); *Sunday Independent*, staff editorial of 26 November 1995, repr. in *World Press Review* (February 1996), pp. 6–7; *New York Times* (10 December 1996; 1 November 1998).

Some East European and Russian communists also share neofascism's anti-semitism. When a senior communist, Albert Makashov, made racist remarks at a political rally southeast of Moscow, communist members of the Duma, including party boss Gennady Zyuganov, refused to vote for a resolution of censure: *Washington Post* (7 November 1998). Obviously not only rightist extremists in Russia may be anti-semitic.

41.   *Time Magazine* (24 June 1985). Some of the argument in this section is derived from earlier work done with Congressman Jim Courter of New Jersey, whose feature 'The TWA Case: Terrorists Put Into Practice What They Learned' appeared in the *Christian Science Monitor* (24 July 1985).

42.   William Stevenson, *90 Minutes at Entebbe* (New York: Bantam Books, 1976), pp. 24–36, 40, etc.

43.   Each person, selected by his or her passport, was ordered through a hole in the

wall of the hanger into a separate room. Of that passage, victims said later 'The feeling is like an execution'. Ibid., p. 27.

44. Congressman Courter twice mentioned this psychological/political issue in the House of Representatives, during and after the TWA 847 crisis; 'American–Israeli Bond and Terrorism', and 'Our Relations with Israel', repr. in his collection *Defending Democracy*, ed. Marc Lipsitz (Washington, DC: American Studies Center, 1986), pp. 209–10.

   A newer proof of the problem terrorism causes between allies is the case of PKK leader Abdullah Ocalan. When Italy held him at the end of 1998 but would not extradite him for trial to Turkey, it 'caused relations between Italy and Turkey to plummet ... The Turkish government was infuriated' according to the *New York Times* (17 January 1999).

45. 'Peru: Terror and Amiability Combine in Surreal Experience for Hostage', *Los Angeles Times* (21 December 1996).

46. A female contract worker for the Agency for International Development described one of the terrorists as 'young' and 'innocent'. Three Canadians spoke kindly; one said 'They are obviously professionals in what they do and believe in what they do deeply.' One Peruvian who was released, a political think-tank director, did not shrink from asking the smiling, chatty MRTA chief for his autograph; having done so, he did not shrink from writing about it immediately in the open press. Francisco Sagasti's 'Hostage Diary', *New York Times* (29 December 1996).

47. MRTA spokesman, quoted in *Los Angeles Times* (20 December 1996).

48. Seiroku Kajiyama, chief government spokesman, said after a few days that 'Japan and Peru are far apart' on ideas of how to solve the crisis; much later, Prime Minister Hashimoto also vaguely questioned the Fujimori government's management of the affair.

49. In age-old terrorist group fashion, the MRTA leader demonstrated a strong interest in what Peruvian polls show about his group. He questioned hostage Alfredo Torres, managing director of a polling agency. Once released, Torres said the polls' answer is 'Peru is not Central America, and we're not in a dictatorship, and they don't have a great popular support': *New York Times* (7 January 1997).

50. Initially, and several times thereafter, MRTA demanded the release of its comrades. But when the Peruvian government proved unyielding, another claim gained ascendancy: better treatment for the imprisoned.

51. The Peruvian magazine *Caretas* of 26 December 1996 is quoted in the next day's *Los Angeles Times*, 'Peruvian Prison Life is Backdrop to Hostage Crisis'. Other *Los Angeles Times* stories included material along such lines, noting for example on 6 January 1997: 'Convicted terrorists are held in cold, dark, dungeon-like settings that are blamed for disease, insanity and suicide.' On 5 January 1997 this paper also printed two letters to the editor on the crisis. Both placed the terrorists on the same moral level as the Fujimori government and accused the latter of state terrorism. Blase Bonpane of Los Angeles demanded 'immediate international investigations' of the Callao Marine Base prison, 'a living grave designed to physically and psychologically destroy prisoners'.

   The *Washington Post* ran frequent stories about conditions for terrorists in Peru's prisons. Substantial stories in the *New York Times* and a letter to the editor from the 'Committee to Support the Revolution in Peru' appeared 31 December 1996 and 4 and 9 January 1997. That same 'committee' keeps a web page on the Internet which sometimes includes expressions of solidarity with Berenson. In part because she is from New York, and in part because both her parents are PhDs who have become effective publicly in her defense, *Times* coverage of Berenson and the inhospitable character of Peruvian prisons has been frequent since her capture.

52. The film *Sophie's Choice* portrays the drama of such an instance. Unjustifiably holding a woman and her two children, the Nazi camp official orders her to choose which of the two children is to be spared; the other is to be killed. The mother is thus perversely ordered to participate in a 'free choice' to kill one of her own.

53. Somewhere between 9,000 and 30,000 were murdered during these years, according to varying Argentine estimates. Hundreds were Spanish nationals or close kin to Spanish nationals, provoking a recent inquiry by Madrid: *New York Times* (17 March 1998).

54. The latest wave of political violence in India is by Hindu extremists against Christians. Chapels have been torched, individuals have been terrorized; foreign diplomats and a new international passenger bus route have been threatened. Reportedly responsible is one of the small but established political parties, Shiv Sena, part of the BJP coalition; *Washington Post* (18 January 1999).

55. Steve Coll, 'Silence in the Killing Zone', *Washington Post Magazine* (16 January 1994), pp. 16–30, adapted from the book *On the Grand Trunk Road* (New York: Times Books, 1994). Coll argues that participation in the activities of the death squads was not entirely voluntary, as refusal to participate could lead to retaliatory deaths of members of the policeman's family.

For another personal account of the bloodied paradise, read William McGowan, *Only Man is Vile: The Tragedy of Sri Lanka* (New York: Farrar, Straus, Giroux, 1992).

56. Coll, 'Silence in the Killing Zone', p. 28.

57. As to the adult–youth point, and terrorism in Italy, 'the student movement was not rooted in youth counter-cultures but used the language of the two "adult" subcultures: Catholic and Communist'. Politicization and ideological training within the Italian leftist terrorist movement were relentless. Porta, 'Left-Wing Terrorism', pp. 112, 129, 132–4.

As to the potential for 'terrorist teachers', note one security expert's statement that 'about 260 educators in the United States were known to be members of extremist organizations': Louis R. Mizell, Jr, *Target USA: The Inside Story of the New Terrorist War* (New York: John Wiley, 1998), p. 34. Mizell was apparently referring to the late 1970s or early 1980s when he was with the Department of State, protecting foreign dignitaries and their families while they were in the United States.

58. For example, ETA 'emerged from a student group that opposed the PNV's [a nationalist legal party] lack of activism and its conservatism'. And the Corsican FNLC are 'mostly students and intellectuals'. Newman and Piroth, 'Terror and Tolerance', pp. 394, 410.

59. Filiberto Ojeda Rios has been described in a Congressional hearing as a Cuban intelligence agent who helped unify and lead the Puerto Rican militant movement on several occasions. A 1990 FBI report described him as the 'recognized leader' of Los Macheteros. Convicted for his role in the $7.2 million robbery of Wells Fargo in West Hartford, Connecticut, he is now a fugitive. US Senate, Committee on the Judiciary, *The Role of Cuba in International Terrorism and Subversion*, 97th Congress, 2nd session, 12 March 1982, pp. 164–9; Federal Bureau of Investigation, *Terrorism in the United States: 1990* (Washington, DC: GPO, 1991), p. 23.

60. Records at US Federal Court, Hartford, Connecticut, and reports in the *Hartford Courant*.

61. 'Mad Loner Builds Perfect Bomb', by Terry Teachout, *New York Times* (13 July 1996), led me to the Joseph Conrad novel *The Secret Agent*, which grew out of the actual 1894 attempt to blow up the Greenwich Observatory. Dan Fitz-Simons has directed me to another Conrad novel about terrorism: *Under Western Eyes*.

62. For several items about Kaczynski's past the author is indebted to a wide review of press sources done by Lieutenant-Colonel William Ritchie, USMC, spring 1997. For more recent and additional material, one can search the Internet under 'Unabomber' to find several sites with excerpts from Kaczynski's personal journals as submitted in court documents, a list of his mathematics publications, etc. There is an instructive, lengthy untitled document he allegedly wrote, 'The 1971 Essay', posted at http://www.cs.umass.edu/~ehaugsja/unabomb/docs/1971essay.html. The passage 'I hate people' *et al.* is from Kaczynski's journals, excerpted as part of government exhibits for the Sentencing Memorandum, 4 May 1998, transcribed for the web by Ellis Windham, and posted at: http:www.dejanews.com/getdoc.xp?AN = 361598462. All downloaded 23 December 1998.

63. Associated Press story in the *Washington Times* (20 October 1994).

64. *Patterns of Global Terrorism: 1996*, p. 3. A high-ranking US official reports that Taliban is directly involved in trafficking, according to Lally Weymouth, 'Drugs and Terror in Afghanistan', *Washington Post* (21 November 1996); see also *New York Times* (30 September and 9 December 1996). Afghanistan is now the second largest producer of opium in the world, according to the CIA, 'Major Coca and Opium Producing Nations: Cultivation and Production Estimates, 1993–1997' [undated: 1998]. What is at best 'neglect' of the drug export problem stands in contrast with Taliban's intensely controlling social behavior in other realms, like keeping girls out of school.

65. Madeleine K. Albright mentioned Iranian terrorism but offered warmer relations in a major address of 17 June 1998. President Clinton made related remarks the next day. This came only two months after their State Department report *Patterns of Global Terrorism* declared that 'The Government of Iran conducted at least 13 assassinations in 1997' and named Iran as the world's 'most active state sponsor of terrorism' (Washington, DC: GPO, 1998), pp. 1, 31.

66. *New York Times* (28 January 1998).

67. *Washington Post* (15 December 1996).

68. The best follow-up story on the perpetrators of the Luxor massacre in the American media was in the *New York Times* (11 January 1998). One notes the presence of two students of medicine, because any underground movement badly needs such knowledge; treating the wounded is an unrelenting challenge. From Che Guevara to George Habash, militants with medical backgrounds have been of great value to their comrades.

There is little published literature on the educations of terrorists. Three examples are Charles A. Russell and Bowman H. Miller, 'Profile of a Terrorist', *Terrorism: An International Journal*, 9:1 (1977); Leonard Weinberg and William Lee Eubank, 'Italian Women Terrorists', *Terrorism: An International Journal*, 9:3 (1987); and my 'Propaganda at Pistol-Point: The Use and Abuse of Education by Leftist Terrorists', *Political Communication: An International Journal*, 9:1 (1992).

69. *New York Times* (15 March 1996). The story provides other details: Ayyash survived the accidental detonation of one of his bomb factories. A few senior

Hamas men have studied or taught in the United States, including the engineer Mohammed Mousa Abu Marzook from Gaza, who was eventually imprisoned in the United States, and Ramadan Abdullah Shalah, now based in Syria. Yet another engineering-trained Hamas senior is Emad al-Alami, also of Gaza, and believed by intelligence to have discussed terrorism with the vice president of Iran in Tehran's embassy in Damascus.

70. *Washington Post* (30 August 1996); *New York Times* (14 August and 6 September 1996).

71. The Zapatista web page opens with Spanish and English, quoting both Marcos and Sonnet 23 by Shakespeare. The site includes a page on its 'army', the Ejercito Zapatista de Liberacion Nacional, with a claimed strength of 'around 12,000 troops, 2–3,000 of whom are fairly well-armed'. This web page has had half a million users since October 1996: http://www.ezln.org/. Their home page in English may be found at http://www.peak.org/~joshua/fzln.

72. *New York Times* (5 September 1996).

73. While terrorism's leaders are usually educated, every school has its failures, and even good 'students' may not be good practitioners. Bombings – the most common form of terrorist attack in the United States – often fail. This includes the non-detonation of a 2,000-pound truck bomb prepared by a California aerospace engineer angry at the Internal Revenue Service in 1990; Dean Harvey Hicks nearly leveled two city blocks. There is another level to failure: some bombs kill or injure their makers. The IRA has a phrase for the unwitting suicides: 'own goals', adopted from footballers' language for players' errors that let the ball slip into their own net. Just such an event spared Israelis one tragedy in April 1996, when an accountant-turned-Hamas bomber made a mistake in his East Jerusalem hotel. The bomb in his lap destroyed the room. Badly disfigured, the bomber did survive, becoming an intelligence asset of extraordinary value to Israel.

74. Mizell, *Target USA*, p. 67.

75. Department of Defense, *Terrorist Group Profiles* (Washington, DC: GPO, 1988), pp. 118–19. Many of the attacks of the 1980s were claimed by the 'Anti-Imperialist International Brigades', thought to be JRA.

76. The Defense Department's *Profiles* says only that 'two JRA members are the main suspects in the bombing' (p. 119). A foreign press account reprinted by JPRS suggests Shigenobu herself was spotted just prior to the attack in Naples: JPRS, *Terrorism* (26 May 1988), p. 1.

77. William R. Ferrell, *Blood and Rage: The Story of the Japanese Red Army* (Lexington, MA: Lexington Books, 1990), ch. 1. Some JRA women were more 'traditional' than the two discussed above.

78. *Pinkerton Risk Assessment Services Weekly* (Arlington, VA), 14:8 (21 February 1997).

79. *International Herald Tribune* (1 August 1997).

80. Eileen MacDonald, *Shoot the Women First* (New York: Random House, 1991), p. 51. MacDonald was interested in her subject after infiltrating a clandestine 'animal rights' group and discovering that it was the women, rather than the men, who were most committed to violence. Her book title is an alleged quotation from a German security official commenting on counter-terrorism tactics; Macdonald does not endorse the phrase. I noted a parallel quotation, from Palestinian female hijacker Leila Khaled: 'On some missions girls are better than men. We believe that women are more cold-blooded': Mizell, *Target USA*, p. 67.

81. Macdonald, *Shoot the Women First*, p. 60.

82. *The Hindu* (Madras: 14 May 1992), in JPRS, *Terrorism* (2 July 1992), p. 20, and the US State Department, *Patterns of Global Terrorism: 1991* (Washington, DC: GPO, 1992), p. 4. Many other LTTE members have committed suicide – in attacks or, more usually, to avoid capture by Indian security forces.

    Kurdish women have similarly killed and died for their cause recently. Two sisters and a brother, members of the PKK, carried out an attack against a Kurdish Democratic Party police station with explosives tied to their bodies: MED Television (London: 3 June 1997), in FBIS, *Terrorism* (24 May 1997). In late 1998 another PKK woman approached an army barracks in eastern Turkey and detonated a suicide bomb that wounded 22 people and killed one: *Washington Post* (25 December 1998).

83. *The Final Call* is published by the US organization Nation of Islam; this story by 'IPS' from Colombo, Sri Lanka appeared in the 26 August 1997 edition.

    Recently Tamil females took part in a speedboat attack on an Indian-owned freighter: Jane's Intelligence Review, *Pointer* (1 October 1998).

84. For example, Michael Radu and Vladimir Tismaneanu make this argument about many FSLN women in Nicaragua prior to the triumph of the Sandinista revolution: *Latin American Revolutionaries* (Washington, DC: Pergamon-Brassey's, 1990), p. 300.

85. Brian M. Jenkins, *Embassies Under Siege: A Review of 48 Embassy Takeovers, 1971–1980* (Santa Monica, CA: RAND, January 1981).

86. Interview with two MRTA women in the embassy by Phil Davison, *London Independent on Sunday* (5 January 1997), in FBIS, *Latin America* (5 January 1997), as well as *New York Times* (17 January 1997).

87. Radu and Tismaneanu, *Latin American Revolutionaries*, p. 327.

88. La Torre and Guzman were married in 1964 and stayed together until her death in November 1988. One faction of SL once accused Guzman of murdering his wife, but police have found letters which reportedly disprove this. Simon Strong, *Shining Path: The World's Deadliest Revolutionary Force* (London: HarperCollins, 1992), p. xvi.

89. *Expreso* (Lima: 17 September 1992), in JPRS, *Terrorism* (8 October 1992), p. 8.

90. By some indications he was SL leader. A few reports called him leader of only a dissident faction, Sendero Rojo (Red Path). *Expreso* (22 September 1996 and 24 February 1997), in FBIS, *Latin America*.

91. *El Comercio* (Lima: 15 September 1996), in FBIS, *Latin America*, on CD-ROM.

92. Quoted by Strong, *Shining Path*, p. 153; the bracketed words are Strong's; see p. 157 and the photos. *Time* magazine of 9 May 1988 noted that one-third of the hard core Sendero inmates at Canto Grande prison in Peru were female.

93. 'Lori's Page', web site http://www.geocites.com/Capitol Hill/9968/, had some 49,000 readers between May 1996 and December 1998. Related news items at other web sites have been common and supportive. Former Attorney General Ramsey Clark, ex-President Jimmy Carter, and William J. Clinton have all been involved in the Lori Berenson case. News coverage has included the *New York Times* of 9 December 1996: Ms Berenson admitted to taking part in Tupac Amaru, which she has described as 'a revolutionary organization and not a terrorist group'. While some revolutionary groups do not use terrorism, many others do, so the distinction Berenson made was inadequate. More importantly, Tupac Amaru has a long record of 'deliberate and systematic murder, maiming and menacing of the innocent to inspire fear and gain a political end', the definition of terrorism in Chapter 1. Participating in non-terrorist revolutionary activity within such a clandestine violent group cannot reasonably exempt her

from culpability for the other actions.

94. See the press for June 1998. In another recent instance of aid to Latin terrorism, three US women participated in a helicopter rescue of some jailed Chilean radicals. Hiring the aircraft at a Santiago airfield and departing with two Argentine helpers, they hovered over a top-security jail and lowered a basket for four convicts belonging to the Manuel Rodriguez Patriotic Front: *Washington Post* (1 January 1997).

95. The numbers in published accounts vary not widely but wildly. The *Wall Street Journal* of 30 December 1996 mentions 30,000, an unlikely estimate when compared with that of only 'several thousand' according to *Patterns of Global Terrorism: 1996*, p. 56.

96. *New York Times* (30 December 1996); *Wall Street Journal* (5 October 1994).

97. *New York Times* (1 June 1994; 2 March 1998).

98. ETA has proportionately fewer women members than most European leftist groups. Robert Clark's *The Basque Insurgents: ETA, 1952–1980* (Madison, WI: University of Wisconsin Press, 1984), portrays ETA as a group which does not attack women but also does not favor their membership. That said, Clark himself points to a history of many husband–wife teams, and includes other material about many women in active and supporting roles.

99. Once a lieutenant to Spain's most wanted man of the early 1990s, José Luis Urrusolo Sistiaga, she had differences with him, and began operating independently; *Foreign Report* (9 April 1992).

100. Reuter dispatch in the *Washington Post* (9 January 1997).

101. Jillian Becker, *Hitler's Children: The Story of the Baader–Meinhof Terrorist Gang*, (Philadelphia: J. B. Lippincott, 1977); see pp. 297–303 for 'A Selected List of Members and Associates of German Terrorist Groups (July 1976)'. The list does include several females who appear to have been involved only as friends or lovers of male group members. But it also displays an impressive range of committed or ideological activists in various German terror groups. And it is not exclusive: Susan Albrecht of RAF is excluded, for example. The generalization that about half the Red Army Faction members (and 80 per cent of others in support roles) are female may be found in MacDonald, *Shoot the Women First*, p. 198.

102. Greece decided in January 1997 to extradite a German woman suspected of involvement in the 1986 La Belle disco bombing in West Berlin which left three people dead and 200 wounded. Andrea Hausler went to Germany for trial, and two others were also arrested in Germany at that time (October 1996). Reuter dispatch in the *Washington Post* (9 January 1997). See the *Los Angeles Times* (8 February 1997).

103. MacDonald, *Shoot the Women First*, p. 198.

104. *Los Angeles Times* (8 February 1997); Bureau of Diplomatic Security, *Lethal Terrorist Actions Against Americans, 1973–1986* (Washington, DC: US Department of State, undated).

105. Quoted by MacDonald, *Shoot the Women First*, p. 208.

106. One portrayal of female couriers is the 1965 film *The Battle of Algiers*. Made by a French communist, Gillo Pontecorvo, and rather sympathetic to the rebellion, it has admirable qualities of verisimilitude. In one series of scenes, three Algerian FLN sympathizers or members, women chosen for appearances more French than Arab, deliver prepared bombs to three public targets. Their access to the targets, despite careful police surveillance and inspection stations, is shown to be much aided by the authorities' reluctance to delay, let alone search, the bags and

clothes of European-looking women.

107. One careful use of a woman for reconnaissance preceded The Order's assassination of radio broadcaster Alan Berg. In the spring of 1984 Ms Jean Craig traveled to Denver, Colorado and went to Berg's radio station posing as a student doing research. This allowed her to observe personnel, take notes, and make photographs. The murder followed on 18 June 1984, done by a male associate. Stephen Singular, *Talked to Death: The Life and Murder of Alan Berg* (New York: Beech Tree Books, 1987).

108. Ingo Hasselbach's memoir is one of many indicators that women are marginal figures in the German rightist groups. They seem absent from decision-making and largely absent from violent actions, with a few colorful exceptions; *The Reckoning*, pp. 110, 118, 150, 281, etc. One study of 1,400 German 'ethnoviolence' offenses found that less than 4 per cent involved females, and none of those had assaulted persons; cited by Peter H. Merkl, 'Why are they So Strong Now? Comparative Reflections on the Revival of the Radical Right in Europe', in Peter H. Merkl and Leonard Weinberg, eds, *The Revival of Right-Wing Extremism in the Nineties* (London: Frank Cass, 1997), pp. 45–6, n.56.

109. The new American militias – most of which are not terrorist – are predominately male. According to Major Jon Ross of the Marine Corps, 'The psychological and demographic profiles of members of radical right-wing organizations like militias are typically white Protestant males with limited education'; 'Arming for War: The Militia Threat to the US Military' (unpublished Master of Military Studies paper for Command and Staff College, Quantico, VA, 1998).

110. The document may be found under its author's name and also, as of 17 January 1999, it was available on a 'Stormfront' site at: http://www3.stormfront. org/ns/nsprimer.html.

6

Counter-terrorism

Introduction

Terrorism is an offense against humanity. In moral terms, though not in all other ways, it is akin to piracy, or war crime. And like those crimes, terrorism deserves to be dealt with by responsible authority anywhere and any time. The calculated way in which terrorism sheds innocent blood should be offensive and unforgettable to all, not only to the families and governments of the victims.

There is thoughtlessness in the commonly spoken arguments that 'one man's terrorist is another man's freedom fighter', or 'terrorism is only a Western obsession'. These are shallow reflections of relativism, inadequate for explaining anything. Arab terrorists with transnational sponsors have killed more Arab diplomats and other Arab civilians than they have Americans, so thoughtful Arabs understand that political murder differs from 'freedom fighting'. Palestinian terrorists who operated internationally to kill Israelis and their allies have taken a higher toll of innocent civilian life right at home, by killing other Palestinians derided as 'collaborators' – i.e. candidates daring to seek political office in elections in the West Bank before it came under Arafat's rule. The families of those dead Palestinian democrats may blame the PLO. The attempt to murder President Hosni Mubarak when he was on a state visit in Ethiopia in 1995 may have been forgotten by most because it failed, but Egyptians have not forgotten, for they must deal with the realities of Sudanese-trained terrorists.

Mr Mubarak, Arab summits, the UN General Assembly, and other official bodies have repudiated terrorism. Their argument is the stronger. They are not naive to insist that the principles of innocence, of non-belligerence, and of human rights deserve a central place amidst considerations of political violence. Principle always has a place in argument. Israel's Benjamin Netanyahu has been a leading writer and speaker for a principled stand against terrorism; but the same good arguments once led Britain's Winston Churchill to condemn terrorism when practised by Jewish zealots. Before 1948 Zionists had few truer life-long foreign allies than Churchill.[1] But when elements of the armed Jewish underground began targeting civilians in Palestine, and assassinated Britain's resident minister in the Middle East, Lord Moyne, Churchill rose in the House of Commons to denounce them as 'terrorists'. He compared them to Nazis, a shocking parallel for Jews to listen to in the year 1944.[2]

Terrorism is usually calibrated. It is intended to elicit certain public reactions, to include shock, horror, submissiveness, a change of opinion, or action on a particular issue, from release of prisoners to creation of a new national homeland. So too must counter-terrorism policy and strategy be calibrated and integrated. Force manifestly has a proper place, especially given that immoral use of force is a central characteristic of terrorism. But as in police work, or even the year-in-year-out deployments of nations' armed forces, gunfire is not the norm. Much more usual is detailed and demanding work on the fundamentals of civil law, international diplomacy, intelligence, public education and public diplomacy, and cooperation among police and military personnel. Those who favor stronger action against terrorism sometimes argue that 'terrorism is war'. They believe terrorism must not be treated as crime, to be pursued only by detectives and lawyers, because such a view weakens the public will for the harsher actions that terrorism invites and indeed requires. But the complicated phenomenon of modern terrorism is neither entirely 'war' nor entirely 'crime'; it is its own entity and has elements of both, their proportions varying with the given act, the terrorist, his intentions, his target, and the extent of his support, including state support.

If international terrorism were inherently and always 'war', every terrorist act would require a response at the highest level of state, ranging from international arbitration to military retaliation. In fact, some acts merit lesser responses. And some, which might merit the harshest response, remain obscure in their origins; the perpetrators successfully disguise their trails. It remains unclear whether Iran sponsored the Buenos Aires bombing that inflicted over 300 casualties at a Jewish cultural center in July 1994. Authorities still dispute whether Syria, in addition to Libya, had a role in the Pan Am 103 explosion that killed several hundred Americans and other travelers. Many terror acts are never claimed by the true sponsor. Acting with ambiguity is a leading feature of terrorism; part of the intent is to make retaliation difficult; often the strategy works.

When its roots and branches are domestic, most terrorism may be treated reasonably well under statutes on crime or criminal conspiracy. Where those using terror are engaged in a full armed rebellion, they might be charged with treason and other offenses. But again, it would be wrong to hold that all terrorism is war. That judgment would invite and indeed require sweeping and suppressive legislation which almost any democracy would find inimical, alienating not just professional civil libertarians but citizens generally. Many traditional liberties would be eroded; others would be virtually abandoned. The country might be more secure, but it would become a nation of 'order' when it should be one of law, order, and liberty. The principles of statesmanship, with their emphasis upon prudence, might allow for a different view under drastically worse circumstances. Abraham Lincoln properly dared to limit even so fundamental a right as *habeas corpus* when nationwide insurrection required it, but he would not have done so in the absence of such a threat. A contemporary Israeli might reasonably argue something an American cannot – that his small nation is continuously at war, with dictatorships looming nearby, with guerrillas and terrorists uncontrolled by the government in Lebanon, and with subversives internal to Israel, some of whom enjoy the patronage of the same outside dictators. But under present American conditions, such an argument by an American would be imprudent and insupportable.

Even when terrorism against Americans is foreign-born and foreign-sponsored – that is, when it runs the highest chance of being true war – counter-terrorist action must be calibrated and politically effective. The objective in the post-Cold War era should be more effective suppression of terrorism, not its 'extermination'. The latter is probably not possible even if the United States closed all its borders, which is itself not possible, and not desirable. Political figures and analysts will do well to avoid apocalyptic language and the making of impossible promises. Terrorism is a sophisticated form of political violence which enjoys many successes. But if it can not be eliminated, it can be resisted and fought and reduced, and it should be. The democracies can be more consistent and sometimes more forceful; thus they will make progress against terrorism.

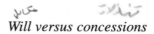

Will versus concessions

Political will, more than new laws or new direction in international politics, is the most important component of an enhanced effort against foreign-supported terrorism. This problem reveals itself in many ways.

Both corporations and governments frequently make decisions about whether to give in to extortion and kidnappers or to resist. It is exceedingly difficult to resist, but to do otherwise is to invite further terrorism. In Latin America today, where kidnapping is rampant, most foreign corporations pay the ransom demanded; even most middle-class Latins pay.[3] Such concessions are the proof of success that terrorists need to continue terrorizing. Western allies and indeed most sovereign states grant that international terrorism is reprehensible and that it should be opposed. The need for strong political will comes into play when coordinating desirable counter-terrorism measures with other equally desirable interests of such states. Economics often seem to dictate that capitals maintain relations with state terrorism sponsors, lest there be lost opportunities to enhance trade or sell arms. Any review of Italian policy toward Libya, or of German policy toward Iran, makes it evident that control of terrorism-sponsoring states requires greater political will – in Rome and Berlin, and in other capitals, which must nudge these allies towards actions their own business communities dislike.

A shortage of American and western European governmental will to fight back *with force* is evident from current official parlance and documents. The United States publishes a national security strategy which has forceful language about a state's rights to combat terrorism. But the annual report on terrorism from the State Department, which traditionally has held the lead in policy for counter-terrorism, carries no such language, although it did in previous administrations.[4] This change accurately suggests a weak governmental will to use force against nearly all sub-state enemies. Relative lack of action parallels the documents' words. The Clinton administration did strike at Iraq in 1993 for its attempt to assassinate former President George Bush, but only in the aftermath of an immensely popular conventional war against that same government and amidst continued sanctions imposed by UN air and naval power. It has also sent missiles into Afghanistan and Sudan to retaliate for vicious bombings in Africa in August 1998; Osama Bin Laden survived and has been giving press conferences about killing more Americans.

The current American administration's practice also seems to disdain most opportunities for milder uses of force, such as dispatching US personnel to 'snatch' unextraditable foreign terrorists and bring them in for trial. And even that lesser type of action, were it in frequent use, would not fully meet the terrorism problem. It is not always enough to 'solve particular cases' where terrorism is state-sponsored, because the actual killer may be only a pawn of larger political forces. Sovereign states could pluck innumerable arrows from their backs but never deal with the archers. Force must always be an active option of US counter-terrorism policy, as a warning and occasionally as an instrument of self-defense or reprisal. The options of force are never the first, and are always difficult and dangerous to implement, but they deserve to be used more often than they have been in recent years.

For the public to understand and support it, counter-terrorism policy must be consistent. That principle may seem obvious, yet it is not observed. The United States annually reaffirms that it makes no deals and submits to no blackmail.[5] But it has compromised its own position – and thus damaged its own position – under Republican and Democratic administrations. The worst cases of the past decade have all involved Iran, the most active of all state terrorism sponsors today. Iranians abused US diplomats in the Tehran embassy, bringing immense discredit to American prestige, and then, encouraged by the affair, prompted or at least allowed their Shiite allies in Lebanon to take other Americans hostage in Lebanon. The first American concessions came in the 'Iran–Contra' matter. American weapons and spare parts were shipped to Iran, then under the closest of American embargoes. Individual American hostages held in Lebanon were released, probably as a direct result of the arms deals and of subsequent resolution in the World Court of disputes over large monetary sums at issue between Washington and Tehran, a settlement attractive to Iran. President Reagan's failure was followed by one for President Clinton. Having helped the UN organize an arms embargo around Bosnia in the hope of weakening the forces of war, the White House then ignored, and probably tried to suppress, news of Iranian arms shipments to Bosnian Muslims. The third scandal emerged even as the second was holding back National Security Advisor Anthony Lake's confirmation as new CIA director.[6] It involved Iran's fervent Muslim ally Sudan, home to a score of training camps for foreign extremists, and the latest addition to the State Department's list of terrorism sponsors. The Sudan was selling oil to US-owned Occidental Petroleum, contrary to the special economic bans imposed by Washington only a year before. And a special provision excepts trade on one Sudanese food export to the United States. So instead of opposing Sudanese–Iranian support for international terrorism, the United States is indirectly helping to pay for it.

Every such break with declared policy has dual negative effects. It undermines the state's position, bringing suspicion upon all future dealings with both terrorist enemies and allied counter-terrorists. And it gives arms – or money which can be spent on arms and terrorism – to precisely those political entities which the victim state has most loudly condemned. Policy only has dignity and efficacy if it is observed by those who set it. The policy of consistently opposing terrorism is a sound and a moral one, and it deserves following.[7]

These dynamics occur almost anytime a terrorist kidnapping occurs, or when a campaign of bombings designed to free terrorist prisoners is underway. Any state will consider concessions which may halt the bloodshed. But while it is natural to consider concessions, it is reasonable subsequently to reject the arguments for them. The terror group's desire is to enter into negotiations with a sovereign government under the strain of pending death to compromise that state's power and prestige; the state risks much merely in negotiating; to make concessions amounts to a double undermining of legitimate government. Terrorists are delighted even with limited concessions, for they have not only placed themselves on the state's level of authority, but then gained something demonstrable in the negotiations. Tupac Amaru had little political presence in Lima, let alone the rest of Peru, when it seized the Japanese Embassy in December 1996. Yet within hours of doing so that small group, led by the self-confident Nestor Cerpa Cartolini, was the primary subject of governmental concern, and for months thereafter he dominated and strained bilateral relations between Tokyo and Lima.[8] He gave his life for his hours at center stage.

Concessions, made to free one captive, invite the capture of others while diminishing the entire policy and all its citizens, whose government is their agent. France has repeatedly and publicly been charged with 'deal-making' with terrorists in recent years, quietly making concessions to regimes and groups involved with international terrorism so as to protect Paris, to get hostages back from Lebanon, to retrieve the wanted 'Carlos the Jackal' from Sudan, and for other reasons.[9] Bargaining with extortionists can also be dangerous; it is widely believed that reneging on one deal in 1986 led directly to the dreadful bombing campaigns in Paris in August and September that year.[10] Even debasing business propositions by a government may not succeed, as the terrorists need not keep their word. A 1987 arrangement rumored to cost Paris $330 million for several Beirut captives left one hostage behind in terrorists' hands. Arguably, French 'deal-making' with Middle Eastern groups has probably prevented certain violent activities by particular individuals on French soil, but that is unimpressive: other terrorists are making their own continuous attacks on French soil, perhaps because they recognize a generous government when they see one, or perhaps because they hope to crown years of operating liberty in France with a cash deal to move elsewhere.[11] Making concessions thus solves little. In 1993, France released Iranian murderers from jail, doubtless expecting Tehran to moderate its campaign against Iranian *émigrés* living in Europe. But today Iran kills more Iranian *émigrés* in France than almost anywhere else.[12]

Sweden, with a reputation as a haven so gentle that it exceeds even that of liberal France, has become home to many Middle Eastern militants. They organize, raise money, and sometimes kill. Such an underground requires expensive attention by the Swedish police and government. Greece's Pan Hellenic Socialist Movement (PASOK) administrations have not always helped their western neighbors, as when rebuffing requests by Italy to extradite known terrorists (provoking an open complaint by the US State Department on behalf of Rome).[13] The Greek government did little to oppose Yasser Arafat's PLO when it was practising international terrorism, partly because of Athens' political stance and partly because it did not wish to be attacked. The reward of Greece has been that the PLO did not kill on Greek soil, but PLO enemy Abu Nidal did, attacking the passenger ship *City of Poros* in July 1988. Other groups have used the country with a frequency that brings unfavorable international attention and periodically hurts the tourist trade.

Israel has been the most surprising practitioner of occasional concessions. It does not bother to denounce such yielding, as most countries do; instead it hammers at terrorism with a fist, undercuts it with the nimble fingers of continuous intelligence and police work, and occasionally shakes a terrorist's hand in a bargain. On several notable occasions in the last decade and a half, Tel Aviv has decided upon prisoner releases or trades involving scores or even hundreds of Palestinians held on terrorism charges. Sometimes these are a response to international pressure, such as in the 1985 TWA hijacking case when several hundred Shia were let go. Sometimes they are a more internal matter, as when one or two Israeli armed services members held by guerrillas are traded for hundreds of Palestinians or Arabs. The latter cases probably cost the democratic state as much as the former in prestige, but both carry a side benefit: in cases of allied pressure, Israel protects foreign benefactors like the United States, as it did with its own prisoner release during the TWA 847 case. In the latter, purely domestic crises, while it may seem foolish to let a hundred terrorists go free, the Israeli nation may take satisfaction in the moral implication that so many Palestinians or Arabs weigh the same in a balance as one Israeli airman. Occasional deals are thus part of Israeli counter-terrorist strategy.[14]

The American, French, Swedish, Greek, and Israeli case-studies reveal how much action is required to protect the citizenry of these terrorism-plagued countries. Governments use unilateral maneuver but also continuous international cooperation in legal, political, and intelligence matters. Identifiable transnational attacks often point the finger of culpability at some sovereign state, be it the United States for permitting anti-Castro Cubans to do arms training in Florida or Georgia prior to forays into Cuban waters, or Greece for failing to extradite to the United States a Palestinian hijacker wanted there for crime. In such circumstances, the state from which the transgressor attacks has a recognized legal burden to act, as well as to prevent future international infractions by those using its territory. This is no platitude, but a principle of traditional international law.

Practical advantage, as well as righteous adherence to law and international norms, is at the foundation of such international rules. To take one representative example, early in 1997 Paris was trying to crack down on radical Islamicists in France who were connected to attacks in Spain made from bases in Morocco. This apparent international tangle is normal in contemporary terrorism. To help itself, France needed help from Spain and Morocco. Consider a related example: France was a refuge for Basque ETA members on 'holiday' from operations in Spain. Only when France realized this trammeling of its sovereignty by international fugitives was bad for its own interests did Paris begin adequate cooperation with Madrid, and only thereafter was Spain able to truly bring ETA to heel. Both countries have a Basque population, and it is in the interest of neither to foster criminality and political extremism among these citizens.

These have been observations on the ways in which contemporary terrorism is a human problem and an international problem. Earlier chapters demonstrated that it is likewise a direct political challenge to the stability and authority of legitimate states, and sometimes a threat to legitimate armed forces as well. Terrorism thus deserves close governmental attention and firm international action. But what in concrete terms is to be done? The types of contemporary terrorism are diverse. This chapter cannot deal properly with the disparate and complicated measures that may be taken against state-aided death squads, on the one hand, or deeply ingrained insurgency, on the other. The present chapter will confine itself to counter-measures against the most relevant terrorism problems for established democracies. It will include measures to counter purely domestic or indigenous terrorism, and also transnational terrorism by groups or individuals who attack citizens at home or abroad. The United States is consistently among the highest of countries on target lists of international terrorists, making it a suitable focus for discussion.[15]

Most of the options the United States requires for an effective counter-terrorism strategy exist in statutory law or are recognized as available foreign policy tools. They might be said to arrange themselves in four groups: options under domestic US law; actions abroad, including covert activities; paramilitary and military options; and international sanctions, both economic and political.

Options under domestic US law

A formidable array of existing US laws and agencies oppose terrorism. The Atlanta Olympic Park explosion, which may or may not have been politically motivated,[16] represented the only recent major bombing at a public event in the United States. Nothing interfered with the earlier summer Olympic Games, at Los Angeles in 1984, perhaps in part because of superb FBI advance work.[17] The same peace was evident at other international events hosted in the United States, such as the Lake Placid New York winter games, and the 1994 World Cup Soccer championships. There have been no terror actions at other kinds of public events in the United States, despite a profusion of attractive terrorist targets. October 1995 celebrations in New York of the 50th anniversary of the UN included 180 foreign heads of state. Annual 4th of July celebrations bring together hundreds of thousands of Americans at sites throughout the United States. Six thousand officers from ten law enforcement agencies were on duty at the second Clinton inaugural parade, backed up by Special Weapons and Tactics (SWAT) teams, helicopters, and anti-explosives experts with dogs and robots. Nothing occurred.[18]

The peace which almost routinely prevails at such events is due to a combination of many factors, including Americans' antipathy for the political strategy of terrorism, willingness of the various levels of government to spend money to protect human life, a large network of police and security forces extending up to the levels of the FBI and US military organizations, and successful pre-emptions of planned terror attacks. The latter, 'events that do not occur', are more common than is known; there were 23 successful pre-emptions by the FBI alone in the years 1989 through 1993.[19]

Military support to police is another tenet of counter-terrorism. The United States is more wary in this respect than are some democracies. In line with the early American opposition to standing armies, and to keep a check on governmental abuse of civil liberties, the principle of *posse comitatus* was written into US law in 1878. It blocks most uses of national military forces for routine policing operations within the country. In spite of this, the armed forces have been increasingly involved, due to race troubles, the drug war, and terrorism. US military forces under strict legal controls are today helping identify, track, and support arrest of drug-runners from south of the US border. They have even been active in this respect within the United States itself. Military units also retain their infrequent but traditional role of supporting police or National Guardsmen in extraordinary situations. Army and Marine Corps units are preparing to help handle chemical or biological incidents, and Marine Corps troops took a role against the arsonists, rioters, and armed urban gangs of Los Angeles in 1992. While the Los Angeles deployment was a remarkable success and had overwhelming public approval, there was grief several years later when a Marine unit hidden for nocturnal surveillance of the southern US border had an encounter with an armed shepherd and killed him.

There have been uglier scandals associated with the remarkable firepower federal forces can bring to bear. The sale of two sawn-off shotguns to an informer brought the Bureau of Alcohol, Tobacco and Firearms – and then the FBI – to Ruby Ridge, Idaho, in 1992. One engagement left fugitive Randy Weaver's son and one FBI man dead; another day saw an FBI sniper with remarkably permissive rules of engagement kill fugitive Weaver's wife, who was holding not a gun but a baby. The FBI followed up this dreadful error with an internal attempt to cover up the nature of the rules of engagement, harming its well-earned credibility and leading to the dismissal or reprimand of several government men.[20] The next year, on 19 April, in Waco, Texas, federal personnel, who might have been given training by army special forces,[21] broke into Mount Carmel Center, a heavily fortified compound of religious cult leader David Koresh, amidst an extraordinary fire fight. Eighty children, women, and men – many well armed – died in the fires that followed. The two cases had one theme: 'military'-style deployment of forces within the United States. They troubled Americans generally;[22] and their combination did more than any other events to popularize and recruit extremists and non-extremists alike for armed 'patriot' militias around the United States. The events led one determined terrorist directly to the symbol of federal power that was the Alfred Murrah Federal Building in Oklahoma City, blown up in 1995. The date chosen for that attack, 19 April, was a day of indignation for bomber Timothy McVeigh. It was the day scheduled for the execution of Richard Snell, a killer whose politics were favored by many in the extreme right wing; Snell had promised someone would retaliate; 19 April marked the second anniversary of the Waco fire; and, thirdly, the Oklahoma City bomber wanted a 'second American revolution' and he may well have known that 19 April was the 220th anniversary of the American engagement against British troops at Lexington, Massachusetts, 1775.

Federal excesses, and the heavily publicized investigations into them, temporarily checked the growing inclination to use national military forces to support local, county, and state police. But the need for such forces in some cases will not disappear. In the 1990s criminals and terrorists have a formidable array of conventional weapons. The Covenant, the Sword, and the Arm of the Lord, a religiously inspired violent white group, built homes and a church with stone walls, internal bunkers, and shooting ports. Some of the new 'militiamen' have served in the US armed forces and received formal training; they have little difficulty with such matters as wiring their defenses with Claymore mines. Given such redoubts of rural militiamen, and steel-doored drug-selling houses of big cities, there was little unusual about the situation at the fortified compound at Waco, Texas, and one cannot be surprised that local authorities wanted well armed support. No sheriff could have walked into Mount Carmel Center and arrested David Koresh, a man who had warned the FBI in a letter: 'I AM your God, and you will bow under my feet ... Do you think you have the power to stop My will?'[23]

The self-isolation of the cult in the Waco compound raises a second problem, one with only indirect relation to armaments or to *posse comitatus*, but a vital problem that managed to remain unexplored despite the tonnage of newspaper coverage of Waco. It is the constitutional issue of whether any group of citizens in the United States has the right to 'declare independence' from governmental authority. By selectively quoting from the American founding documents, and by exhortations to the age-old American sense of personal liberty, and with flags replicating the proclamation 'Don't Tread On Me', some militiamen and separatists such as the Montana Freemen and the 'Republic of Texas'[24] imagine that they may ignore court summons, print their own currency, refuse to pay taxes, break firearms laws, and, doubtless, ignore the registration of their youth for the military draft. The illegality of their acts is easily demonstrated in courts. But their proclamations have not been met with a thorough and public rebuttal by a statesman or jurist who can explain the destructive nihilism resident in individual secession from the social and political compact.

Superbly armed crime, recent terror attacks against buildings in Oklahoma City and New York City, and a grim appreciation for what happened in the subways of Tokyo in 1995 make it likely that public opinion and Congress will not entirely block military capabilities and units from potential engagements within the United States. No state police force can deal with a credible threat of a 'backpack' nuclear bomb; no city hospital is equipped to deal with an anthrax outbreak downtown.[25] Amidst wide concern about federal power, the countervailing fear of potential 'superterrorism' keeps alive the prospect of internal use of military forces. Some civil libertarians and senior military personnel alike fear that use by terrorists of a chemical or biological weapon could lead to a remarkable change of *posse comitatus*: the chief of staff of one US military service declared in a lecture in the mid-1990s that in his dispassionate judgment, the first time a group in America used a weapon like the sarin released in the Tokyo subways, '*posse comitatus* will go out the window'. That would be a national error.

Yet the Federal Emergency Management Agency has not yet come to grips with the scenarios of superterrorism.[26] Nor has the American medical establishment prepared. So, because a chemical or biological incident is probably the greatest single danger among prospects for terrorism incidents in the United States, very limited military plans and training programs for preventing or reacting to such terrorism are now being established. For a number of years, the 'Nuclear Emergency Search Team' with headquarters in Las Vegas, Nevada, has dealt with scares, threats, and problems related to the use of nuclear material for criminal or political purposes. Able to call upon scientists and a logistical structure built into US government and military capabilities, the NEST has fortunately never faced a true terrorist threat supported by actual fissile material. But the prospect for such an event is obvious, and there is as well the lesser chance of terrorists' use of an actual nuclear weapon. More dangerous and more likely is terrorism's use of a chemical or biological weapon, and for that eventuality there is as yet no equivalent of the NEST. The US Marine Corps has initiated a 'Chemical/Biological Incident Response Force' at Camp Lejeune, North Carolina, which aims at containing the consequences of an incident. The Army has an older program, to include a 'Technical Escort Unit' specializing in monitoring equipment and disarming weapons.[27]

There are also new US laws. A 1989 measure enhances authority for preventing biological weapons attacks, and it has been used.[28] Statutes applicable to conventional terrorist crime have been somewhat tightened up during the Clinton Administration. One example is the Supreme Court decision that permits the use of anti-racketeering statutes (RICO) against anti-abortion activists if they conspire to commit violence.[29] Another, with wider scope, are the new laws pushed through Congress with urgency in the wake of the Oklahoma City bombing. The draft bills offered strong measures against terrorism by conservatives chairing the two committees on the judiciary. But floor debate saw an unusual

US Marine Corps Commandant's Planning Guidance for chemical or biological warfare incidents

(published 31 August 1997)

The CPG [Commandant's Planning Guidance of 1 July 1995] called for the development of a strategic organization – manned, trained, and equipped – to manage the consequence of the growing chemical–biological threat. The Chemical, Biological, Incident Response Force (CBIRF), activated in April of 1996, grew from that initiative.

Status. The CBIRF has deployed to support the Olympic Games in Atlanta, the Presidential Inauguration, and the Summit of Eight in Denver, Colorado.

Future direction. The CBIRF must continue to forge ahead developing the concepts, doctrine, organization, tactics, techniques, and procedures to remain the nation's premier incident response force. This includes seeking out new detection and resolution technologies. Additionally, I would like the CBIRF to focus their efforts in two areas. First, on developing countermeasures and force-protection training and equipment support packages for deploying MEU(SOC)s [Marine Expeditionary Units/Special Operations-Capable]. Second, on assisting federal, state, and local response forces in developing their own training programs on how to manage the consequences of a chemical or biological incident.

coalition of liberals and conservatives – both concerned about overweening federal authority – strip some of the muscle out of the bills. The result, signed into law in April 1996, was modest, making limited additions to regulations already on the books.[30]

Authorities now possess slightly greater powers to expel aliens from the United States if they are believed to be involved with violent groups. The fullest federal guarantees, which for example include the right of the accused to face and answer his accusers, and to place the full burden of proof upon the accuser, no longer apply to aliens, but only to citizens. This will allow federal authorities to present summaries of evidence to sitting judges – a procedure which protects 'sources and methods' of intelligence gathering. The new law will also bar entry to persons on 'watch lists' for suspected terrorist activity, and it will make expulsions easier.[31] Conservatives and liberals alike prevented Congress from going further, concerned especially as to whether federal authorities would adequately protect civil liberties. The body did not, for example, reinstate the McCarren Walters Act, which long made it possible to expel or bar any alien who adheres to communism or other violently anti-democratic doctrines. Militant ideology alone is no longer a bar to entry to the United States; today, terrorist activity must be indicated. But any explicit exhortation to terrorism, even by someone not a member of the terror group, is enough to merit an alien's expulsion. The new law would have barred entry to the United States to Umar Abd al-Rahman, spiritual leader of the al-Gama'at terror group that probably murdered scores of tourists at Luxor, Egypt, in November 1997, and certainly carried out the New York City Trade Towers' bombing.

Fund-raising by terror groups is newly restricted under the Omnibus Counterterrorism Act, as well as an executive order signed by President Clinton in 1995. Foreigners in the United States, resident aliens, and American citizens are all affected; if active terrorist suspects are targeted by the new rules so too are Americans who are not group members but who contribute money or other material aid to their coffers or causes.[32] Enforcement begins with the October 1997 federal list of terror groups for whom fund-raising is proscribed. Responding to a White House directive issued under the International Emergency Economic Powers Act, the State and Justice Departments had already implemented use of another, narrower list banning 12 terror groups which aimed operations at destroying the Middle East peace process.[33] They have been moving money collected in the United States to violent operations in Palestine and Israel. The militant Jewish groups Kach and Kahane Lives, as well as Hamas and other Palestinian groups, are constricted by the new rules and are doubtless more closely watched than ever before. In 1998 the

Some highlights of new US counter-terrorism law
(Quoted from a summary by the Department of State
of the Act signed in April 1996.)

Designations The Secretary of State, in consultation with the Attorney-General, may designate an organization as a foreign terrorist organization if he finds that ... the organization engages in terrorist activity ... and the terrorist activity of the organization threatens the security of US nationals or the national security of the United States. [The latter includes] the national defense, foreign relations, or economic interests ... Section 303 makes the provision of material support to a designated terrorist organization a criminal offense, providing up to 10 years in prison as well as fines ...

Deportations Section 401 establishes the procedures for a special court to be established for deportation of alien terrorists cases while protecting classified information.

Terrorist states 'Financial transactions' with governments of countries on the terrorist list [are banned]. The new law currently affects primarily Syria and Sudan because the five other countries on the terrorism list – Cuba, Iran, Iraq, Libya, and North Korea – already are subject to embargoes under other laws administered by the Department of the Treasury.

Civil lawsuits Section 231 amends the Foreign Sovereign Immunities Act to permit US nationals to bring civil actions against countries the Secretary of State has design[ated] as terrorist supporting states ... if the lawsuit arises from aircraft sabotage, torture, extrajudicial killing or hostage-taking.

Nuclear matter Section 502 strengthens the existing prohibitions against possession of [or threats to use] nuclear materials by expanding the definition to include nuclear byproduct material.

Biological materials Section 511 expands existing prohibitions against possession of certain biological agents by broadening the definition of infectious substances to include biological products that may be engineered as a result of biotechnology, or any such micro-organism, virus, infectious substance or biological product.

Plastic explosives Section 601 [implements] the 1991 Convention on the Marking of Plastic Explosives For the Purposes of Detection [and] requires each manufacturing state to place specified chemical agents in plastic explosives to facilitate detection ...

'De-funding terrorism':
groups banned by the United States

In response to 1996 legislation (see p. 248) Congress made it a criminal act for individuals or groups to provide money or material support of most kinds to groups designated as foreign terrorist organizations. On 8 October 1997 the Office of the Coordinator for Counter-terrorism, Department of State, released the names of the 30 banned groups, shown here with this author's designation of the predominant nationality of group members.

Abu Nidal Organization (ANO)	Palestinian
Abu Sayyaf Group (ASG)	Filipino
Armed Islamic Group (GIA)	Algerian
Aum Shinrikyo (Aum)	Japanese
Euzkadi Ta Askatasuna (ETA)	Basque
Democratic Front for the Liberation of Palestine– Hawatmeh faction (DFLP)	Palestinian
HAMAS (Islamic resistance movement)	Palestinian
Harakat ul-Ansar (HUA)	Pakistani and Kashmiri
Hezbollah (Party of God)	Lebanese
Gama'a al-Islamiyya (Islamic Group: IG)	Egyptian
Japanese Red Army (JRA)	Japanese
al-Jihad	Egyptian
Kach	American and Jewish
Kahane Chai	American and Jewish
Khmer Rouge	Cambodian
Kurdistan Workers' Party (PKK)	Kurdish
Liberation Tigers of Tamil Eelam (LTTE)	Sri Lankan Tamils
Manuel Rodriguez Patriotic Front Dissidents (FPMR/D)	Chilean
Mujahedeen-e Khalq Organization (MEK, MKO)	Iranian
National Liberation Army (ELN)	Colombian
Palestine Islamic Jihad–Shaqaqi faction (PIJ)	Palestinian
Palestine Liberation Front–Abu Abbas faction (PLF)	Palestinian
Popular Front for the Liberation of Palestine (PFLP)	Palestinian
Popular Front for the Liberation of Palestine– General Command (PFLP–GC))	Palestinian
Revolutionary Armed Forces of Colombia (FARC)	Colombian
Revolutionary Organization 17 November (17 November)	Greek
Revolutionary People's Liberation Party/Front (DHKP/C)	Turkish
Revolutionary People's Struggle (ELA)	Greek
Shining Path (Sendero Luminoso, SL)	Peruvian
Tupac Amaru Revolutionary Movement (MRTA)	Peruvian

executive order permitted seizure of $1.4 million in assets from a
member of Hamas, his wife, and their 'Quranic Literary Institute' in
Chicago, Illinois. Osama Bin Laden and several comrades were added to
the list of banned Middle Eastern personnel immediately after their
August 1998 Africa bombings.[34]

Several apparent loopholes mar these useful new laws. By omission,
the IRA political front, Sinn Fein, enjoys protected legal status.[35]
Secondly, it may still be possible for suspicious groups in the United
States to collect funds if they can indicate that the specific moneys are
for the humanitarian programs run by such groups. For example, aid for
Hamas charities in Palestine might still be funded by private American
givers. Since money is fungible, any such monetary aid can still
effectively contribute to the power of an armed group and assist its
illegitimate violence.

Surveillance of terrorism suspects and radical groups within the
United States may only occur under set conditions. A variety of laws
designed to protect the civil liberties of citizens constrain police
surveillance. During drafting of the 1996 Act, the FBI had lobbied for
'roving' wire taps – the right to tap not just a phone used regularly by a
suspect but any phone used anywhere by that suspect. The FBI's
argument was that by merely using multiple or unusual phones, or by use
of new cell-phone technologies, terrorists and criminals could elude or
overly complicate legitimate wire tap operations. But Congress denied
this extension of authority, then changing its mind two years later. It did
add considerably to the FBI's budget, which in an era of government
'downsizing' has swelled year after year for over a decade. The Bureau's
$3 billion-plus budget is ten times higher than in 1960, and its manpower
has also grown dramatically – to about 27,000.[36] Domestic militias,
Americans aiding foreign terrorists, and non-American terror groups
eager to operate here face an increasingly vigorous and effective
deterrent. The FBI is not only casting its own nets wider over domestic
US incidents; it is aggressively working in tandem with state and local
law enforcement agencies. The overall result has been to hold terrorism
in America at low levels relative to the 1970s. This is true
notwithstanding important exceptions, especially the dramatic strikes in
Oklahoma and New York cities, and a general nation-wide increase in
pipe bombings, some of which have been politically motivated.

Operations abroad

Though little noted by the American people, FBI work in foreign
countries has doubled several times. Fifteen years ago there was one

minuscule program under which a handful of agents were posted in select key embassies overseas to help with international investigations. Today there is a new international division within the FBI, and the 'LEGAT' program of legal attachés, working with foreign police services to exchange information and coordinate casework, has expanded to include 23 foreign nations. Plans unveiled in 1996 aim at a total of 46 countries and 129 special agents, as well as supporting staff. The new operations overseas have occasionally strained relations between the FBI, the CIA, and the State Department; arrangements for delineating responsibilities, ultimate authority over particular foreign problem areas, and full sharing of intelligence, were still being worked out during 1997.

The explosion in organized crime, the problem of nuclear proliferation, and greater concern about terrorism, as well as a new sense of opportunity for focusing on such problems absent the Soviet threat, have all led to this expansion of FBI activity abroad. In 1996 for example the FBI was dealing with innumerable problems of international crime, such as helping Mexican authorities recover a kidnapped Japanese executive who is president of Sanyo's Video Component Corp, USA. That year the tiny Rome office was responsible for activities in 25 countries, including a major terrorism investigation in Saudi Arabia, and the effort to catch a Washington DC gang boss and drug-runner eventually apprehended in Tanzania. Other operations included efforts in Israel against Russian émigré organized criminals, detective work in China regarding Chinese gangs linked to US activities, terrorism and counterfeiting problems affecting the United States from Pakistan and Egypt, and the links to Alexandria, Egypt, suggested by a number of letter bombs arriving in the mail boxes of US recipients just before the New Year 1997.[37] In short, if the FBI now has more money, it also has many more problems of crime and violence to solve.

Extradition treaties are another facet of capability, and a natural answer to heightened need for dealing with terrorists and organized crime figures abroad and prosecuting them with all legal means. This is something the Justice Department, including the FBI, can do well with State Department support. Extradition is a conventional and usually calm form of action. Some 300 criminals a year are brought back to trial in the United States,[38] but until recent years only rarely has the same prospect threatened terrorists who kill or harm Americans overseas. Recent extraditions include cooperation with Pakistan to secure Ramzi Youssef, extradited to face trial and conviction on charges of New York terror plots, and cooperation with Israel in continuing efforts through 1996 and early 1997 to extradite a Hamas chief captured and held in

New York, Abu Marzook.[39] Mr Clinton's Democratic administration is committed to improvement and passage of new extradition treaties, and proudly notes that during the 3 years 1993–95, more terrorists were arrested and extradited to the United States than in the previous three Republican administrations added together.[40]

Some help is also obtained from Europe, so often the stage on which international terrorists choose to act. Many European states are proud of their records of offering asylum to the persecuted, and this has made them wary of binding extradition treaties, even with democratic neighbors. For example, a Belgian jurist noted in 1973 that his country had so little to fear from terrorism it should hesitate to change its own laws to suit outside states.[41] But then came the home-grown communist Combatant Cells, and their connections to the French of Action Direct and other European terrorists. Since the early 1970s, nearly all capitals have worked to tighten extradition treaties among themselves, even if each also has had its own list of reservations. The European Convention on the Suppression of Terrorism has been widely ratified, though Ireland took ten years to do so, and France, Italy, Norway, and Sweden all signed with express reservations that will protect some suspects and convicts claiming the traditional political exception. A 1979 follow-on, the Dublin Agreement, has helped advance the likelihood of extradition even among European Community members not party to the earlier convention.[42]

It was under public pressure from British Prime Minister Margaret Thatcher that President Reagan moved – against immediate US interests and tradition – to facilitate extradition of IRA members who had successfully hidden in the United States. A rewritten extradition treaty, much deprecated by civil libertarians and Irish-American activists, removed the 'political offense' exception to the extradition treaty which had traditionally been present to protect responsible political activism. The new position still protects the responsible, but it allows extradition of those charged with, or convicted earlier of, the murder, maiming, or menacing of the innocent to inspire fear and gain a political end. Many have since been deported to face justice in Northern Ireland or England. Maze prison escapee Jimmy Smyth, one of several deported from the San Francisco area, was sent back to Ireland in August 1996. And the next year brought US Congressional attention to four pending cases: Gabriel Megahey, Noel Gaynor, Kevin Crossan, and Matt Morrison.[43]

But even treaties among friends do not guarantee extradition. And all states jealously guard their sovereignty and their own citizens, assuring that disputes over extradition often arise. In 1998 Mexico was inflamed because US authorities ran a 'sting' operation on Mexican soil; it apparently netted millions in drug money and corrupt bankers who helped store and launder it; but for Mexico the real issue was the violation of its sovereignty[44] and the embarrassment of its government, which the United States probably did not trust enough to inform. For its part, Washington does not always extradite either. There is no extradition treaty with Cuba, and the United States does not give over to Cuba the anti-Castro activists it knows to have attempted or carried out international armed attacks. The rank despotism of the Cuban regime, and the certainty that a fair trial in a Cuban court is an astonishing rarity, can perhaps justify such reluctance by Washington. When the issue is between two governments more mutually dedicated to law – as against mere order and control – extraditions are hard to refuse, and ought to be.

Even when extradition laws allow no 'political exceptions' and are kept up to date by earnest NATO allies, there will remain differences between states' views. More than a decade ago, Rome and Washington completed a new treaty on such matters, and yet within a year the *Achille Lauro* crisis wedged itself between these two allies. Italy was unwilling to try, or even to send to the United States for trial, Abu Abbas, leader of the Palestine Liberation Front cell that murdered a New York retiree aboard the cruise ship. Abbas escaped[45] via Yugoslavia and thence to Tunisia: the former country supported Palestinian terrorists, while the latter, though friendly to the United States, was also the main headquarters of the PLO at the time. Washington was irritated by a similar case in the mid 1980s, in the wake of the TWA 847 hijacking. Paris coldly overlooked the embarrassment of perpetrator, Imad Mughniya, at liberty on French southern beaches, and declined to extradite him to the United States. In both cases there was a compelling national interest in effecting justice which a close ally helped foil for its own reasons. The incidents are reminders that more forcible and unilateral measures may sometimes be necessary in counter-terrorism, even though an ally's interests may be bruised. Certainly France found it in its own national interests to help arrange the abduction of the police-killer 'Carlos the Jackal' from the Sudan, bringing him in for a trial in 1998 in Paris.

Where normal extraditions are impossible, the United States may make use of 'long-arm' statutes. Relatively new to American jurisprudence, these additions to the US Code permit authorities to seize terrorists abroad for trial in America. Case law on the matter is sparse, but includes the instance in 1880s when private detectives went to Peru to seize a fugitive from American law. They brought him back to the United States for trial. The judge declared that he would overlook questions about the foreign arrest of a foreign national; what mattered was the fairness of the trial to the suspect.[46] Uncertainty about that common law precedent was transcended in the 1980s with legislation and other federal decisions, especially the 1986 Omnibus Counter-terrorism Act, explicitly granting long-arm powers to make foreign arrests under certain circumstances, including many acts by foreign terrorists.[47] These laws deserve further use.

Military and law enforcement capabilities to make such 'snatches' in appropriate circumstances have been proven. Several cases have involved gunmen who terrorized or killed Americans flying on international passenger airliners in 1985. A ruse tempted hijacker Fawaz Yunnis into international waters between Cyprus and the Lebanese coast in 1987, so that he could be plucked up by the FBI and flown to the United States from an aircraft carrier. Because of legal problems which could erupt if the party set down at any interim point, Yunnis was kept aloft with mid-air refueling and always in international air space. The Federal Court in Washington DC convicted Yunnis for air piracy and hostage-taking and sentenced him to 30 years.[48] This was the first 'trial' case of the new laws and procedures; it was a widely celebrated success, and a precedent too. The same year that Amal militiaman committed his hijacking, Abu Nidal gunmen, including Mohammed Ali Rezaq, hijacked an Egypt Air flight leaving Athens. Rezaq personally shot three Americans and two Israelis. Captured when the plane was stormed in Malta, Rezaq was convicted and jailed there, only to be released after serving eight years of a 'life sentence'. Rezaq went to Africa, but with the help of Nigeria and Ghana he was seized in 1993 and the FBI bundled him back to Maryland for trial.[49]

The judicial and political value of such public trials is enormous. What the civilized world sees is the same thing the terrorist underworld sees: a legitimate state acting with firmness but also due procedures of domestic law to run a fair trial of a foreign suspect, and to imprison someone convicted in such a trial. The political effects are greater than the legal. The citizenry is appropriately reassured that the government is willing to protect it, at home and abroad. Allied states recognize the capital's will on counter-terrorism is such that it may be of help on foreign terrorism problems, and that it is willing to act alone where other states do not help. Even the world community – so swift to criticize forceful unilateral acts – might profit. It acquires a formal court record of the convict's international movements and connections. And, less eagerly, it receives a pointed reminder that when it does defend against international terrorism, individual states may well defend themselves. In political and moral terms, the world is no more free to tolerate terrorists than it is pirates.

To be sure, there is potential for angering other states, and even allies, in the procedure of the international arrest without host country consent. The risk is evident in this maneuver, whatever it is called – sometimes a 'rendition' if there is no extradition treaty, sometimes an abduction or, popularly, a 'snatch'. Israel shocked many when in 1972 it kidnapped Adolph Eichmann from Argentina and brought him to Israel for trail, but few deny the justice in the matter.[50] The United States seized another, lesser murderer in a case that also generated headlines when authorities sent two Mexican bounty-hunters after the Mexican killer of Drugs Enforcement Agency agent, Enrique Camarena, for trial in California. The suspect, Dr Alvarez, was acquitted in 1992, embarrassing Washington.[51] But even substantial negative publicity need not bar future use of the tactic of the 'long-arm' arrest; one must ask what price a sovereign people pays for not punishing the killers of its citizens, especially when they live abroad at ease, continuing in activity that promises future international killings.

Probably few voters in democracies around the globe would have objected to a US 'snatch' of the two Libyans identified in a multi-million dollar international investigation into the destruction of Pan Am 103,[52] since the Lockerbie bomb murdered not only Americans but citizens of Argentina, Belgium, Bolivia, Britain, Canada, France, Germany, Hungary, India, Ireland, Israel, Italy, Jamaica, Japan, the Philippines, Scotland, South Africa, Spain, Sweden, Switzerland, and Trinidad. As it was, the two suspects were eventually handed over by the Libyan government to stand trial on neutral territory. The admitted dangers of covert or police operations abroad must also be weighed against the potential for far greater damage to life and property when the alternative is a military raid, such as that already carried out against Libya. Measured against this option, or against the alternative of doing nothing at all, covert actions may appear more responsible and useful.

Fear of retaliation is a major reason for doing nothing. And doing nothing is an option the United States has often taken. For four decades, terrorists have been seizing American hostages for financial and political reasons, especially in Latin America and the Middle East. Astonishingly few of these perpetrators have been seized for trial in the United States; there was no modern case at all until 1987. So while one must consider the problems of terrorist or foreign government retaliation, it must be granted that a gentle policy of general forbearance has not protected Americans. Nor have forbearance and pacific responses protected British and German citizens seized in the Levant.

Good intelligence must support all long-arm arrests, every successful extradition, and nearly every other counter-terrorism measure.

Intelligence is required to cut through the fog with which terrorists shroud their operations and their state connections. It was said to be inadequacy of intelligence about the Hezbollah of Lebanon that made it too difficult to retaliate for the 1983 bombings in Beirut, or to find and save the American hostages held there periodically throughout the mid 1980s. It was shortage of intelligence that stymied the United States in 1996 and 1997 as it wrestled with the damage done to civilians and military personnel by vehicle bombs at Riyadh and Dhahran, November 1995 and June 1996. The Saudis proved so protective of their sovereignty, and were doubtless embarrassed about their own intelligence and security failures which permitted the anti-American bombings, that they restricted US access to what was known about the perpetrators. The first bomb was attributed to four men who were swiftly executed without any interrogation by the United States. The next bomb[53] quickly led to promises of close cooperation, but soon the FBI and State Departments were again unable to get interviews with civilians who may have witnessed the terrorism in Dhahran.[54]

The US national security bureaucracy has gradually established special counter-terrorism offices within the CIA and the State Department.[55] However, few at the National Security Council – charged with coordinating all US security policies for the President – devote themselves full time to counter-terrorism issues.[56] Moreover, the United States experiences occasional internal bureaucratic problems which remind one of the international US–Saudi Arabian difference just noted. Charged by law to keep CIA surveillance of foreigners distinct from FBI case work against American suspects, the two agencies do not always share intelligence. The separation is sometimes a problem when foreign terrorists kill or injure Americans.[57] Both the CIA and the FBI must, and sometimes do, take proactive initiatives to assure cooperation such that each receives the other's intelligence. Otherwise, the legal, attitudinal, and bureaucratic barriers between them reduce exchange of information, or make them too slow to permit action.[58]

Most sovereign states are struggling with border-crossing terrorist groups, and they often encounter the spirits of friendly competition and of jealous self-protection about 'sources and methods' of intelligence,[59] spirits which limit adequate exchanges with other countries. There is no designated centerpiece of international intelligence collection on terrorists, unless one counts the International Criminal Police Organization based in Lyon, France. But INTERPOL's main divisions do not include one focused on terrorism, as there is for, say, Organized Crime.[60] INTERPOL has not always gratified victimized governments by the swift provision of key intelligence on a transnational attack. By its charter the organization has no enforcement powers; it merely issues arrest warrants which others may or may not use. The European states, more reliant than ever upon each other for security as external borders come down in the spirit of Maastricht, have established their own EUROPOL, based at The Hague and operating since February 1994 to overcome barriers to intelligence exchange.

No matter how well the unification of Europe continues, and how assiduously some countries pursue multilateral counter-terrorist actions, the need for aggressive unilateral pursuit of information, witnesses, and suspects will remain. There is boundless demand for better human intelligence – recommending improvements in it has become so predictable a cry from policy analysts that few now heed it.[61] But the repetition does not belie the need; better intelligence is expensive and is difficult to obtain and it is definitely needed. Two kinds of pressures, fiscal and moral, tend to keep the 'HUMINT' budget below what it ought to be. The Chinese theorist Sun Tzu dealt deftly with both in his classic *The Art of War*, and the argument merits application against powerful terrorist groups and their sponsors. Knowing the enemy's situation and action is so important, said Sun Tzu, that there can be no excuse for stinginess about spies. One who refuses to spend gold for reports from spies, reports which save lives, is not only unworthy as a general or assistant to a ruler; he is inhumane, says Sun Tzu; men die from his penury.[62]

'Pre-emption' is another category of covert action. It has a basis in US law, and some recognition in US policy. Under the Reagan and Bush administrations there came to be formally approved a principle of self-defensive action long used by sovereign states: pre-emption of terrorist acts. The means can be handled by intelligence professionals or the military or others. The US declaration was that its opposition to terrorists would include actions to 'disrupt their operations, and to destroy their networks'.[63] A classified intelligence finding was publicly reported to elaborate on the same strategy. The White House still occasionally declares a determination to 'prevent, disrupt and defeat terrorist operations before they occur ... '.[64] The Congressional bill on counter-terrorism which the president signed in April 1996 dictates that he 'use all necessary means, including covert action and military force, to disrupt, dismantle, and destroy international infrastructure used by international terrorists ...'[65] – the strongest language aimed at preventing terrorism the Clinton administration has ever been party to.

Pre-emption is a difficult route, and one heavily dependent upon human intelligence. But it is a route with great potential, deserving of use. An option too often limited to policy papers, pre-emption is commended by common sense. It should be apparent, after several decades of dealing with terrorism, that when a foreign group is the cause of a long train of abuses of innocent parties, that pattern of aggression merits, and may indeed require, a strong response. One form of such response is covert action that strikes at the cohesion, membership, political credibility, or operational capacity of the terrorist group.

In anarchy-prone regions of Lebanon, after Shia Muslim terrorists repeatedly took Western hostages, there was no reason in principle that the victim states' covert agencies and forces should not be deployed to disrupt or even wreck the terror operations of the groups Islamic Jihad and Hezbollah. Psychological operations, sabotage of property, and other strong measures short of outright military retaliation were fully appropriate. Yet there is little indication that more than one or two pre-emptive operations were launched in the hope of foiling future terrorism by known groups.[66] The present inaction recalls the dispiriting US attitude towards a French proposal for bilateral military action in 1983 after radical Muslims vehicle-bombed French and American facilities in Beirut; Paris offered and Washington declined.

When one considers the relatively small size of the family clans behind Hezbollah, the near-paranoia within the Abu Nidal Organization, or the flagrant unpopularity in and outside Peru of Tupac Amaru, it is hard to see only the political disadvantages to exploiting such vulnerabilities. Where law permits using powers of state to conduct covert activities against terror groups, the prospects for success deserve close consideration. Actions might be done with or without the cognizance of the foreign government with titular responsibility for control of its nationals. The barrier to such actions, against groups infamous for their criminal lethality, is mainly attitudinal. Democratic states should move forward, towards action, and deal with the other barriers to successful pre-emptive actions against long-known terror groups. Chief among these barriers are the stiff requirements for excellent intelligence, and the proximity of adept human agents able to carry out the required acts.

Paramilitary and military options

United States policy has long emphasized training foreign police and military forces. Besides offering an international way to work on an international problem, this program has the advantage of enhancing the indigenous internal capabilities of allied states, directly fulfilling a stated US interest in stability abroad. Aid may even forestall foreign crises which could be destructive and require UN or other foreign intervention.

The US training programs have varied with circumstance and need, as have their profile. For example, the training efforts were publicly discredited by incidents of foreign abuse of human rights, and media coverage of the same, yielding cutbacks in the 1970s, especially as pertaining to Latin America. The Reagan administration restored many training programs, and by 1987 could announce that in the three previous years over 4,000 officials from 40 countries had participated in the anti-terrorism assistance program, which covered bomb detection, security at airports, hostage rescue, and crisis management. The price tag, he noted, was a third of what one new jet fighter would cost.[67]

The Clinton administration continues, but does not advertise, such training programs. Even some of Yasser Arafat's Palestinian Authority police are now being trained by US intelligence in espionage, information-collection, and nonviolent interrogation techniques.[68] However, neither the State Department's leading public counter-terrorism document nor the White House *National Security Strategy* make but the briefest mention of training foreign counter-terrorist forces. Yet such programs are one bulwark of US defenses against international terrorism, as well as a useful ingredient of US bilateral relations with many important foreign states.[69]

The State Department's division of 'Anti-terrorism Training Assistance' helps the Pentagon help foreign military and police. It also offers a program – developed, put into practice, and eventually revealed publicly in mid-1995, called the 'Foreign Emergency Support Team'. Liaison with some 120 countries has already occurred to prepare for contingencies in which a foreign capital may seek US assistance in a hostage case or other terrorist attack. The FBI has its own international training programs, which emphasize police systems and crime control, rather than counter-terrorism. A new program in Budapest, Hungary, trains east European and Russian police officers. An older program at Quantico, Virginia, teaches a variety of foreign police organizations.[70] International classes of recent years have included two dozen Russians of the Ministry of the Interior, and ten officers of the Royal Ulster Constabulary, a pillar of the counter-terrorism structure in Northern Ireland. RUC participation has been denounced by some Irish-American activists opposing FBI help for 'a paramilitary force with a long history of human rights abuses in the North of Ireland'.[71]

Negative publicity still accompanies some bilateral counter-terror training; that political sentiment is not confined to the 1970s. When an Egyptian counter-terrorist force called Sa'iqa, or Thunderbolt, botched the take-down of an airliner held hostage by four Abu Nidal gunmen in Cyprus in November 1985, some media carried an assertion that Sa'iqa had had American coaching. But US training has in fact been of enormous help in many cases. Two of the long-forgotten are the US Army assistance to the Indonesian commandos who retook a hijacked airplane in Bangkok, Thailand, in March 1981, killing or wounding the four terrorists of the Muslim 'Kommando Jihad', and coaching for the 12 Venezuelans who tricked terrorists on a grounded airliner in Curaçao in July 1984, allowing them to kill the terrorists and free all hostages unharmed.

The practice of international exchange of counter-terrorism skills, a practice the United States now follows, was born in the needs of European Community states, which found themselves battered by domestic, Arab, and anti-NATO terrorism in the early 1970s. They sought to learn from the Second World War and post-war experience and studies by the British Special Air Service (SAS), which offered training to them in the knowledge that inter-European skill would mean better protection for the UK. This British specialty was digested and elaborated upon by other democratic states, especially Germany and France. The West Germans developed a superior border police unit, GSG-9, which established its credibility by recapturing a Lufthansa airliner forcibly taken to Mogadishu, Somalia, in 1977. Aimed at forcing Bonn to release terrorists from jail, the escapade failed so badly that some Baader–Meinhof prisoners committed suicide in their jail cells, and the organization never recovered psychologically. French commandos are as skilled as the Germans.[72] The Directorate of Territorial Security and 'Intervention Group' of the National Gendarmerie have captured innumerable foreign terrorists in France. By the account of one French counter-terrorism specialist, Paul Barril, French commandos were even summoned to handle a delicate Saudi problem – seizure of the Great Mosque in Mecca by armed Sunnis in 1979. The experts allegedly flew to Mecca, made their preparations, accomplished the recapture, and flew back to France with little of the world even aware of how the crisis had ended. Failures like Malta have been far fewer, and thus far less important, than the many successes by the world's counter-terrorist teams.[73]

Material aid to foreign organizations fighting terrorism is another kind of appropriate strategic option. Such donations might include communications gear, money, weapons, trucks, intelligence products, and conventional war *matériel*. Appropriate recipients might include not only legitimate state governments but democratic insurgent groups fighting against state terrorism sponsors. When countries are renowned for training terrorists and releasing them against the world community's wishes, as in the case of Iran, Syria, Libya, and the Sudan, and where diplomatic protests and attempts to organize UN or other world action have not succeeded, it may be appropriate to aid those regime's declared enemies. This can be a just and measured response to a pattern of international terrorism. It is best done only with friendly political or revolutionary groups that have made choices of ends and means which place them well above the moral level of the regime.

One response of the United States to Sudanese terrorism has been to increase aid to several of the more threatened neighbors: Eritrea, Ethiopia, and Uganda.[74] The same logic would permit aid to Iranians opposing theocratic despotism in Iran. Yet while it would be possible it would also be imprudent to extend aid to extremist nondemocratic bodies such as the Mujahedeen Khalq and its National Liberation Army, based across the border in Iraq. This organization has shown itself ready to use terrorism, and would if successful impose its own dictatorship upon the Iranian people.

Military strikes in self-defense can sometimes be appropriate. Nothing in international law and tradition forgives states that export terrorists. On the contrary, every right has attendant duties; the idea of the sovereignty of states only makes sense if international actions are appropriate to a community of other sovereign states. The recent decades of state sponsorship of international terrorism are not merely indefensible; they bear patterns of aggression that, at least under the traditional law of nations, permit reprisal actions by offended states. Although attenuated by the UN Charter, with its drive against retaliation and its favor for careful collective action, this older right of state has been persistently protected and restated by certain governments unwilling to rely completely for their security upon the will of the UN.

During the 1980s, when Prime Minister Margaret Thatcher dealt with Britain's allies she often emphasized the inherent right of a state to defend itself against foreign-sponsored attacks. Doubtless aware of UN tendencies, she argued that self-defense is so inviolable a right that it goes beyond the ability of foreigners to determine it.[75] The American position has often been worded differently, but is equally founded on the basis of self-defense. At the very post-war sessions which created the Charter of the UN, American negotiators repeatedly declared, orally and in written submissions for the record, that nothing could or would bar the United States from sober, well-directed military activities against flagrant aggressors. International terrorists and their state sponsors are among such aggressors – the Charter does not define 'aggression' as something only sovereign state armies do. The fact that this right is so rarely used suggests nothing about its importance as a right.

The US air raid on Libyan communication centers and training camps was justified by US officials as self-defense. A decade and a half of the most remarkable Libyan malfeasance had left dead and wounded throughout Europe and other regions. Given so long a train of abuses, and so solid the Colonel's governing position, any victimized states could have made such a strike, acting in self-defense with the reasonable and legitimate expectation that they were inhibiting further attacks in the near term. The same air raid can be fully justified as a legitimate reprisal. In the event, the unilateral US raid with air force and navy jets succeeded operationally, and is widely regarded as having effectively diminished Colonel Qaddafi's interest in strategic sponsorship of international low-intensity conflicts. Pro-Libyan groups sought to retaliate against the United States but generally failed. The marked decrease in Libyan-sponsored killings was notable, but so was a secondary effect, upon Syria. Under the diverse pressures of sanctions, diplomacy, and the raid on Libya, known incidents attributable to Damascus fell from numerous in the mid-1980s to none in 1988.[76]

However, military action need not mean an air raid or cruise missile attack. Many sovereign states today possess commando forces trained for direct action and forcible counter-terrorism missions as are required. Given sufficient national will, these small, human, potentially very discriminating forces, can deal with targeted groups and individuals known to be involved with international aggression of low-intensity kinds, or a radical state's factories preparing chemical or biological weapons contrary to international conventions. Germany, France, Britain, Israel, the United States, and many others possess such forces and have occasionally used them, as in dealing with hijackers holding country nationals abroad in the 1970s and 1980s.

States can act, together or individually, more often than they now do, to seek out and damage the offensive capabilities of identified terror groups. The terrorists, long-term students of fear, must themselves begin to fear the consequences of their own crimes. Experts at calculating the capacity of small arms and bombs to render human damage in public streets and meeting places, they must themselves be forced to recalculate their own chances of escaping justice. At present, most do not. Imad Mughniya of Hezbollah, Abu Nidal, and a dozen other principals of international terrorism are free. 'Afghani' financier Osama Bin Laden is overtly threatening US citizens with death; he made such threats four times between 1996 and December 1998.[77] Meanwhile hundreds of innocent victims and potential victims of these terrorists live in fear or under siege, including authors Salman Rushdie, groups of Iranian dissidents in Paris, and scores of Arab and European and American diplomats on government business in foreign capitals. That is ironic and unjust.

May states assassinate terrorists?

Terrorists kill civilians and innocents, sometimes randomly, often without warning, usually without a mutually acknowledged state of war. Thus their crimes are condemned by international law. But does that mean that a victimized state can track down a terrorist to kill him?

NO, according to some interpretations of the Hague Convention of 1907: 'It is especially forbidden ... to kill or wound treacherously individuals belonging to the hostile nation or army.'

NO, according to some American interpreters of legal language promulgated by President Ford and renewed (sometimes with changes) by all successive presidents; Executive Order 12333 states: 'No person employed by or acting on behalf of the United States Government shall engage in, or conspire to engage in, assassination.'

YES, say some leading American authorities: killing a known terrorist need not qualify as assassination. Two who think so are Dr Louis René Beres of Purdue University's political science faculty, and Hays Parks, the senior advisor on law of war to the US Army.[78] Following is a sketch of some of their arguments:

> 'Assassination' stands condemned, but how is it defined? Some kinds of purposeful killing are legal; they are not murderous.

> Reason can not deny a legitimate state its right to self-defense. Indeed, self-defense is encouraged by philosophical authorities as different as Cicero and Jeremy Bentham, and by traditional international law, current international law, and official US interpretations of the foregoing.

> Self-defense includes acting against (a) actual use of force; (b) imminent use of force; or (c) a continuing threat. Such threats from terrorists to citizens or national security are reasonable to conceive. This is especially true where the enemy is armed, financed, structured, and using illegal force.

> A President might thus authorize clandestine, low-visibility, or overt military force to kill an individual or a small group without violating laws against assassination. The objective of such an authorized killing would not be revenge or retaliation, but self-defense against a threat to citizens or the national security. For Dr Beres, there should also be a utilitarian or 'balance-of-harm calculation' that the killing would reduce overall violence and thus save lives.

> Repudiation of this reasoning may leave worse alternatives: (1) reliance upon broader, more destructive forms of force; or (2) doing nothing, which violates the ancient principle of criminal justice: 'No crime without a punishment'.

> Because assassination is discriminate and proportionate, it may be a reasonable option. Where terrorist crimes or other aggression are still ongoing, it may even be one to recommend.

Sanctions

While the international community rarely contemplates military reprisals it frequently uses an altogether different form of counter-terrorism: political and economic sanctions.

Political sanctions vary widely. Unilateral state action is often appropriate where a country's interests are affected. A simple ban on the activity and legal existence of a given terrorist party is one method often used in Europe, for example. Critics say declaring a group illegal merely forces it to change its name, or drives its activities underground – although neither of those changes of behavior is helpful to the terrorists. The concept of the ban has obvious advantages. It makes money collection extremely difficult. By 1994 both France and Germany had banned the Kurdish Worker's Party. But PKK has offices in many west European cities; it all but openly collects money in Holland and the UK, where no ban is in place, adding millions to the operating funds used for terrorism in other European countries. The ban also deprives a terror group of some political support. Front operations, rallies, the printing of leaflets, and the like become more difficult and dangerous, quite likely deterring help from marginal supporters such as religious groups, charities, and academic institutions. Belgium does not ban terror groups, and does not even have laws specifically making terrorism illegal; the other countries of Europe would be the better if it did, for international Muslim terrorists organize and operate in Belgium today as surely as international communist terrorists did 15 years ago.[79] It is only that bombs rarely detonate in Belgium.

The dramatic reduction of official contacts, or even the breaking off of diplomatic relations,[80] are traditional modes of political protest. These may include withdrawal of an ambassador, or closure of an embassy and conduct of relations through an intermediary country. When low-intensity conflicts stirred by the new Castro regime turned Havana's relations with its neighbors sour in the early 1960s, several countries broke relations. The United States was one of them; the State Department began communicating formally only through indirect channels and third governments, the Czech Embassy in Washington DC and an American Interests Section in the Swiss Embassy in Havana, and still does. During the late 1980s amidst debates over Sandinista Nicaragua (which harbored and trained Latin and European terrorists), members of the US House of Representatives unsuccessfully advanced a resolution calling for a formal break of relations with Managua; according to some opponents of Managua's policies, an open US embassy there was a good conduit for political and intelligence contacts with democratic Nicaraguans. In the 1990s the United States has formally protested Sudanese sponsorship of terrorism, and expelled from New York a Sudanese diplomat believed to have aided terrorist plots there by Sunni Muslim followers of Sheik al-Rahman.[81] Washington withdrew most, but not all, of its personnel in Khartoum; the embassy remains only minimally staffed, and the ambassador works in the country only at certain times. Uganda and Eritrea, neighbors of the Sudan, have formally broken state-to-state relations.

The expulsion of foreign diplomats or lesser consular staff without breaking relations is another measure that may be used to register a sharp protest and, just as importantly, to diminish the targeted country's opportunities to conduct offensive business on one's soil. Spies have often been expelled in this way, pulled out from under the cover of embassy duty and sent home for 'activities incompatible with official duties'. Terrorism-sponsoring countries have less often, but occasionally, faced this censure. Twenty Eastern Bloc officials on duties in Italian consulates and embassies were identified by the Italian secret service (SID) in 1972 as linked to Italian terrorism. Prime Minister Andreotti chose to overrule his intelligence organization's demand for their expulsion, although subsequent investigations, court cases, and Red Brigadist confessions confirmed the reality of the problem.[82] Italy did arrest an official who used his post as head of the Italian office of Bulgaria's state airlines to support the 1981 shooting of Pope John Paul, but a pair of accredited diplomats escaped the country and returned to Bulgaria before they too could be questioned about the attempted murder.[83]

Europe's most important counter-terrorist episode took place in 1986. With a clear pattern of Libyan support for a growing train of bloody attacks, the United States was urging action. European Community members on the other hand were reluctant. After quiet diplomatic efforts largely failed, the US bombed Libyan targets, supported only by Britain. Both democracies paid a price in some circles for their bold action.[84] Nonetheless, it is telling that in the aftermath of the air raid, all EC members did indeed join in sanctions against Tripoli's export of violence, reducing (but not terminating) their embassies there. European governments also sent more than 100 Libyans home from consulates and embassies and international businesses, a reprimand for years of terrorism in Europe and a direct strike against Colonel Qaddafi's network for intelligence operations and violent activities in Europe. The 12 states also took a belated vow to end sales of arms or military equipment to Libya.

In unusual cases the UN Security Council has taken political action to punish a terrorist-sponsoring state. Political sanctions were in place against Libya after the Pan Am 103 bombing, until the suspects were handed over for trial. There are sanctions against Sudan, because Sudanese nearly killed the President of Egypt in Ethiopia in 1995. The Council used a succession of three resolutions, several months apart, to raise the pressure on Khartoum to turn the suspects over for trial. Resolution 1044 demanded extradition and called on the Sudan to stop supporting and facilitating international terrorism; Resolution 1054 called on UN members to reduce Sudanese diplomatic posts and restrict their movements; Resolution 1070 imposed an air embargo against the country unless it swiftly complied with the previous resolutions.[85] Sudan has made no discernible change in its policies, however.

Economic sanctions are broadly directed against the material self-interest of a state. Almost by definition, they must be an extended multilateral enterprise, feasible only if collectively enforced. Otherwise they become a salve to the public conscience and little more, leaving many countries and businesses inconvenienced but terrorism unpunished; the targeted regime simply buys what it needs from countries not participating in the embargo. The multinational 'collective' can be a group of countries and firms possessing desperately needed supplies, such as food or petroleum or nuclear fuel, or it can be a large political alliance, such as NATO or the UN. The UN has imposed economic sanctions in many cases: in fact, both political and economic sanctions have been deployed against Iraq for its invasion of Kuwait and its brutality against the Kurds in its northern border regions, and Libya, prior to its handing over the two suspects in the Lockerbie bomb affair, was subject to embargoes on some trade and all international air traffic.

A range of thoughtful statesmen and analysts have spoken out in favour of sanctions.[86] As a policy, sanctions are a form of signaling, indicating resolution to stop an aggressor and permitting time for the perpetrator state to back down and reform its behavior. The predominant argument for sanctions, which is unexceptionable, is that these measures are nonmilitary and useful where the activity giving rise to them does not merit interstate war. Virtually every modern war is preceded by an attempt to use sanctions, from the unilateral US embargo of sales of oil and scrap iron to Imperial Japan in 1939, as a protest against the occupation of China, through the prolonged political dance before the Gulf War, to the arms embargo deployed against Serbia, then abusing its neighboring provinces from the old Yugoslavia. That record of attempted sanctions, usually followed by actual war (as in the case of Serbia) testifies to both the perennial appeal and the frequent failure of sanctions as a policy of deterrence.

During most of the 1990s, Libya, Syria, Iraq, and Cuba all operated under sanctions for promoting terrorism. For example, Syrian complicity in attacks in Europe was exposed by trials in London and West Berlin, leading West Germany to terminate development aid and the European Union to announce economic as well as other sanctions against Syrian terrorism. Today, while there is evidence that each of these states has moderated its behavior, none of the four has completely ceased supporting terrorists. All still harbor terrorists, and the Middle Eastern three permit them armed training, not mere propagandizing. Syria has proven adept at using terrorism sponsorship as a kind of currency of diplomacy: support is regulated like a faucet according to what Damascus is seeking from its neighbors.[87] And, since two of the four state sponsors have been bombed (Iraq and Libya) there is every reason to believe that military force, and not sanctions alone, deserve some credit for what progress can be discerned. The loss of Soviet encouragement and aid has also affected these four.

Unfortunately, in themselves, sanctions constitute a weak policy. Mild, nonmilitary measures are often as ineffectual as they are inoffensive to critics. They can be undermined in the two main ways noted just above. The first turns – as does so much else – upon will. Without serious and near-universal enforcement by all countries, they risk irrelevance as a strategy of deterrence. In late 1997 Americans, including Henry Kissinger and Assistant Secretary of State for Near East Affairs Martin Indyk, were justifiably indignant with European violators of the multilateral policy of isolating Iran. Especially irritating to them was France: the Total oil company made a $2 billion deal with Tehran that September. But by then American newspapers no longer recalled that US oil companies had been buying a limited amount of Iranian oil indirectly (on spot markets) throughout the 1990s, leaving a hole in otherwise tough US sanctions.[88] Political sanctions against Iran have been equally undermined. The European Union justly withdrew its ambassadors to Tehran in early 1997 after a Berlin court proved Iran had murdered dissidents. By November of that year, however, all the ambassadors but two had returned to embassies in Tehran.[89] Meanwhile, the Iranian government continued its extraordinary conventional arms buildup without abating in the slightest its external financial aid to radical regimes and groups.

A second problem with sanctions is moral and political: sanctions may or may not hurt dictators and the terrorists the dictators patronize, but they generally do hurt some innocent parties.[90] There is strong evidence that sanctions on Cuba and Iraq have made life hard for the average citizen, despite the existence of exemptions for medicines and

certain other goods. In both cases, meanwhile, the governments carry
on, troubled by popular restlessness but not undone. Castro has no
apparent rival, and struck down one popular commander and Angolan
war veteran, General Ochoa, whose political prestige was growing.
When Cubans complain of hunger, or a lack of goods, Castro points to
decades of sanctions and 'blames the Yankee'. Saddam Hussein, for his
part, has more economic troubles than before but remains in power by
force, as before. During the latter 1990s, while his secret services
murdered opponents, the dictator was furthering construction on a score
of palaces, and announcing new forms of mass conscription to prepare
for *jihad*. Overseas, his diplomats complain of the hunger ordinary
people face back home in Iraq.[91]

Sanctions as an alternative to high-risk troop deployments, or
outright war, also have had a disappointing record. As thoughtful a
general as Colin Powell, then senior military officer in America's armed
forces, argued publicly during 'Desert Shield' that the economic and
political sanctions imposed on Iraq by the UN must be allowed to work
much longer before war was ever dared. But a ruler like Saddam
Hussein, even with the world spotlight still upon him, did not back down
or withdraw from Kuwait. War came. The Iraqi dictator resumed a
variety of aggressive behaviors even after his armed forces were
devastated. He absorbed 70 hours of British and American air strikes in
December 1998, declared victory, and carries on. American debate has
also focused on sanctions against aggressors in Bosnia. Few wanted to
send American ground troops, hoping that international sanctions and
flight denial operations would deter Serbian aggression. Once again
Chairman of the Joint Chiefs Colin Powell argued for patience and
restraint (in part because he reasonably felt the rigorous Yugoslav terrain
would absorb more troops than America could afford to deploy). Again
the ground deployments and air actions – though not full war – proved
necessary to correct Serbian behavior towards Bosnia. The cases expose
the limits of sanctions. Regimes fierce enough to sponsor international
war and low-intensity conflict are difficult to deter. They may be
impossible to deter using only negative publicity, political censure, and
economic embargoes.

Secondary sanctions are a recent, innovative, and controversial
approach, currently being tried by Washington *vis-à-vis* Cuba. By the
means of secondary sanctions, a state declares that not only must its own
companies not trade with the targeted country, but foreign companies
and states trading with it will face embargoes on their own trade. Thus
the United States effectively ordered all its own trading partners, such as
Mexico and Canada, to cease commerce with Havana or face restrictions

on shipping into or trade with America. The double ban is doubly complicated; it automatically irritates any close commercial partner. Mexico, Canada, and NATO members in Europe have been opposed, sometimes strongly, to the secondary sanctions. Canada announced loudly that it will sooner surrender part of its US trade than abandon its relations with Cuba. It is too early to judge the new US effort, the latest in more than three decades of American attempts to reform or undermine the Castro regime. But among the certainties of economic sanctions is this: in most cases they take a long time to have an impact.

The greatest sovereign state terrorist threat of today is the combination of Iran and the Sudan. Years of accumulated intelligence reports, court records, and provocative rhetorical displays – from Khartoum, Tehran, and the foreign groups with bases in those two countries – point to their policies of educating, training, arming, financing, and exporting violent Muslim activists. Yet the two states have never been subjected to a sustained campaign by a strong collection of foreign powers determined to radically alter their calculations and their policies. As the last Prime Minister of Israel noted in his new book on fighting terrorism, the time for such a campaign has arrived.[92] Sanctions – both direct and secondary – are an appropriate step for all states to take against Sudan and Iran. These, at least, should be tried immediately. There are two other alternatives for statesmen facing this problem: serious paramilitary or military action on the one hand or flagrant neglect of common sense and common duties, on the other.

Conclusion

Terrorism is more than a persistent threat to the world community and to specific states' national interests. It is a moral challenge to legitimate political and social life. It requires a sober, consistent and sometimes forceful response by all nations, which should observe a policy of 'no concessions to terrorism'. A range of counter-measures are available, and all deserve use as appropriate. These include the legal punishments of international law and multilateral treaty, economic sanctions, and political sanctions. They include military strikes in unusual cases where these make sense as self-defense against further aggression. They include aggressive activity against known individuals, to include extradition and prosecution, 'snatching' of particular terrorists whom host states ignore or protect, and covert action to pre-empt and disrupt terror group activities. Those operations, in turn, depend upon expensive and laborious intelligence work. Obviously there are also the mild but partially effective defensive measures of hardening of targets and propagation of awareness of terrorist dangers on the part of such likely victims as diplomats and international businessmen. Ultimately, counter-terrorism must be infused by political will and shaped by political leadership.

In 1918 there was an obscure antecedent to the scores of similar abuses of diplomatically protected persons that would come to mar the late twentieth century. Bolsheviks broke into the British Embassy in Petrograd in the new Soviet Union, and murdered a Royal Navy attaché. The Minister of Munitions, Winston Churchill, wrote a memorandum for other officials in the British government to draw attention to the abnormal character of the act. He added these words of principle and sagacity: 'The exertions which a nation is prepared to make to protect its individual representatives or citizens from outrage is one of the truest measures of its greatness as an organized State.'[93]

Notes

1. See for example Matthew Spalding, 'Winston S. Churchill and the Middle East', in *Statecraft and Power: Essays in Honor of Harold W. Rood*, ed. Christopher C. Harmon and David Tucker (Lanham, MD: University Press of America, 1994), pp. 89–105.
2. A 7 November 1944 speech by Churchill referred to 'foul assassins', and a 17 November speech says 'terrorists', Winston S. Churchill, *The Dawn of Liberation*, ed. Charles Eade (London: Cassell, 1945), pp. 302–3; 322–3.
3. Published sources include a full page report by the *Los Angeles Times* (19 April 1998).
4. The State Department's *Patterns of Global Terrorism: 1988* (Washington, DC: GPO, March 1989) stated that an element of the strategy was 'to make state sponsors of terrorism pay a price for their actions', a concept 'graphically demonstrated by the April 1986 bombing raids'. The same section on policy and strategy in *Patterns of Global Terrorism: 1995* (Washington, DC: GPO, April 1996) says nothing of military action of any kind. Even in a passage about bringing 'maximum pressure on states that sponsor and support terrorists', the words that follow call only for 'economic, diplomatic, and political sanctions'. Compare p. iv of both reports.
5. See any issue of the aforementioned State Department annual, *Patterns of Global Terrorism*, or almost any speech by the ambassador who is coordinator for counter-terrorism at the department.
6. For this and other reasons, Lake was not confirmed, and the position went to George Tenet.
7. For an intelligent, original, and contrary view – i.e. one not always opposed to concessions – see David Tucker, *Skirmishes at the Edge of Empire* (Westport, CT: Praeger, 1997), pp. 73–80. Until late 1998 Tucker was acting director of policy at the Office of Special Operations and Low-Intensity Conflict, Office of the Secretary of Defense.

8. See for example Calvin Sims' articles in the *New York Times*, Sebastian Rotella's columns for the *Los Angeles Times*, and Gabriel Escobar's dispatches to the *Washington Post*.

9. In one 'trade' France reportedly made, 'Carlos the Jackal' was obtained from the Sudan, but a price was paid in French satellite imagery of southern positions of the Sudanese insurgents of the Sudanese People's Liberation Army. With the help of Iraqi imagery analysts, Sudan planned an air and ground offensive against the SPLA. Tony Worthington, a British MP, declared: 'Obviously we can understand that the French were keen to capture Carlos, but does it have to be at the expense of the Sudanese people who have been brutally murdered by the appalling regime in Khartoum whom the French have assisted by providing military intelligence to help the slaughter?' From research courtesy of Art Schoenwetter, February 1997. See also *La Stampa* (Turin: 7 January 1995), trans. and repr. by JPRS, *Terrorism* (30 January 1995), p. 28, which accuses France of feigning a hard line on terrorism while making deals with the Sudan and other sources of Islamic violence.

   Paul Wilkinson, perhaps Britain's leading counter-terrorism authority, argues that no concessions, combined with other good counter-terrorism strategies, is the best approach: 'The British model inevitably shows up the weaknesses and dangerously counter-productive aspects of the hostage deals pursued, for example, by successive French governments and the Reagan administration.' See 'British Policy on Terrorism: An Assessment', in Juliet Lodge, ed., *The Threat of Terrorism* (Boulder, CO: Westview Press, 1988), p. 53.

10. Juliet Lodge, 'The European Community and Terrorism: From Principles to Concerted Action', in Lodge, *The Threat*, p. 249.

11. Consider how Syria has profited from promoting terrorists, then profited from expelling them, and then letting terrorists return. Terrorists are a kind of currency in the bank for some states. Similarly, a supply of western hostages was held, paid out in small increments, and replenished by Hezbollah.

12. Ron Ben-Yishai, 'A Deal Between France and Iran', *Yediot Ahronot* (16 August 1994), from the Internet. Murderers of Shahpur Baktiar and another exile in Geneva were released for reasons of 'supreme national interest', according to President Mitterand. Older reports of French 'deal-making' have appeared in US reports (e.g. *Patterns: 1988*, p. 16). The most recent allegations have appeared since Chechen kidnappers – who may or may not have a political motive – seized six European hostages in July 1997. By November the French had been released, amidst rumors that $3.5 million had been given to the kidnappers. The two British, Jon James and Camilla Carr, remained in the hands of the kidnappers. The father of Mr James made a principled denunciation of deal-making as likely to spur further kidnappings. *Daily Mail* (29 November 1997).

13. An official US State Department report openly criticized quiet deal-making by Greece; *Patterns of Global Terrorism: 1988*, pp. 27, 29. Many critics have reported lax security in Greece: see Terrell E. Arnold and Neil C. Livingstone, 'Fighting Back', in *Fighting Back: Winning the War Against Terrorism* (Lexington, MA: Lexington Books, 1986), p. 237. Athens airport has often been on the high-risk list of the US State Department, being so designated in early 1996, for example.

14. One recent release was of 30 Palestinian women, of whom several were jailed for serious terrorism offenses. Promised as a confidence-building measure in its negotiations with the Palestine Authority, the release transpired in February 1997. Injunctions filed by a Jewish group, 'Victims of Arab Terror', were a cause of the delays; for example, the group holds that one of the female prisoners, Abir

Wahaidi, admits to heading the armed cell that is believed to have murdered Zvi Klein in a Jewish settlement at Ramallah in 1991. Yasser Arafat had called the prisoner release 'a great contribution to the peace process' but was angered by the delays; *Washington Post* (12 February 1997) and the same day's *New York Times*.

Prime Minister Netanyahu took unfavorable notice of the practice of Israeli 'deal-making', which releases jailed terrorists before they serve full sentences: 'This is a mistake that Israel, once the leader in anti-terror techniques, has made over and over again': *Fighting Terrorism: How Democracies can Defeat Domestic and International Terrorism* (New York: Farrar, Straus, Giroux, 1995), p. 144.

15. The *Los Angeles Times* reported on 9 August 1998 that about 40 per cent of international terrorist incidents are aimed at the United States. There are lower estimates.

16. As of March 1998 the leading suspect for the bombing is reportedly Eric Rudolph, said to be loosely associated with the anti-semitic and anti-federal 'Christian Identity' movement. The same right-winger may have carried out two other attacks in Alabama: bombing an Atlanta bar frequented by lesbians, and bombing a Birmingham abortion clinic. All three bombs inflicted casualties.

For another perspective on law enforcement preparations for Atlanta's games, see the FBI's *Terrorism in the United States: 1996* (Washington, DC: GPO, June 1998).

17. National police work at Los Angeles was undergirded and to a degree coordinated by the FBI, whose assets include the Hostage Rescue Team, based at Quantico, Virginia, and growing to nearly 100 personnel, including operators and administrators. The HRT has close links with city-based SWAT teams all over the United States. It trains with the best counter-terrorist forces in the world. Its 'raw material' is an impressive collection of former police officers and military men, nearly all of whom were first-class athletes; an average of 36 years' ensures a seasoned and careful operative. Training is intensive and so physically demanding that no woman has completed the course: included are innumerable physical challenges, including underwater training, rock- and ice-climbing, and night operations, as well as such classroom and field craft subjects as intelligence, firearms, breaching, sniping, and emergency medicine. Assault team armaments include the MP5 submachine gun, standard pistols, and 'flash-bang' grenades for stunning terrorists in a hostage situation. I am indebted to Loyd Sigler, an HRT member and subsequent administrator, who spoke annually to my (unclassified) elective course 'Terrorism Today' at Command and Staff College, Quantico, Virginia, 1994–96.

18. *Washington Post* (21 January 1997). Forcing governments into such enormous and expensive security efforts is one of the lesser-noted strategies of terrorism; security devours moneys for which there are many competing and worthy uses; see Chapter 2.

19. Federal Bureau of Investigation, *Terrorism in the United States: 1993* (Washington, DC: GPO, undated; 1994), p. 10. The annual report for 1988 lists preventions for the previous five-year period as numbering 49, of which there were 23 in 1985 alone. As I noted in a 1984 article, 'The Terrorist Acts That Weren't' (syndicated to newspapers by the Hoover Institution on War, Revolution and Peace in Stanford, California) these preventions get little press attention but represent a quiet chronicle of intense efforts by all levels of law enforcement in the United States. Such steady work is one reason why terrorism virtually disappeared in the United States in the late 1980s. In a nation of 260 million people there were only nine terrorist incidents in 1987, and seven in 1988; no one was injured or killed in these attacks.

20. Jerry Seper of the *Washington Times*, who has long reported on FBI issues and on domestic US terrorism and crime, unflinchingly reported what he saw as excesses of individual FBI officers in the Ruby Ridge case. Gradually his criticisms and those of the *Times* influenced others. This, and Congress, caused a self-examination within the bureau and several officers were censured.

21. *Soldier of Fortune* magazine and Carol Moore's book *The Davidian Massacre* are not endorsed here; however they are two of the sources alleging such training occurred. They describe off-site Army Green Berets training of Bureau of Alcohol, Tobacco, and Firearms agents planning the raid and allege that this was illegal under *posse comitatus*. Moore writes that the trial proved the existence of the training; BATF agent Bill Buford is said to have admitted it. Part of the justification for such possible training, and for the presence of National Guard helicopters and the Drug Enforcement Agency near Waco, was in allegations about drug production within the compound, allegations Moore sees as based on sketchy or false evidence. Carol Moore, *The Davidian Massacre* (Franklin, TN: Legacy Communications, 1995), pp. 98–104.

22. An ABC News poll of citizens supported the government's actions and held David Koresh, not the FBI, responsible for the burning of the compound; Ronald Kessler, *The FBI* (rev. edn; New York: Pocket Star Books, 1993), p. 514.

23. Letter by David Koresh, quoted ibid., p. 506.

24. In a 1996 separatist plot, 'Republic of Texas' Mr and Mrs Ronald McLaren and their comrades planned to illegally acquire as much as $1.8 billion by bilking credit card companies and banks in an effort to support their scheme for freeing Texas from the United States. In court, Evelyn McLaren declared: 'The nation of the Republic of Texas was stolen from you. We were taking it for the people of Texas'; *Washington Post* (6 March 1998).

25. While American agencies are working hard to develop a capability to deal with chem/bio incidents, the government is not yet prepared. The many admissions of that fact include the words of experts interviewed by the ABC News television program 'Prime Time Live' (25 February 1998); transcript from the Internet, courtesy of James Anderson. Or see the testimony before the Senate on 1 June 1998 by health experts; *New York Times* (3 June 1998).

26. Typical operations by FEMA include such efforts as work with communities and medical facilities located near the sites where the US armed forces are destroying their chemical weapons. The army and FEMA work together with eight (continental US) communities on that effort, called the Chemical Stockpile Emergency Preparedness Program. 'Destroying America's Chemical Weapons', *Defense '96* (Washington, DC: Department of Defense, 1996), no. 6, pp. 28–9.

27. State Department officer Tom Hastings of the Office of the Coordinator for Counter-terrorism, telephone interview of March 1998. Another source is 'Chemical and Biological Terrorism', *Jane's Defense Weekly* (14 August 1996). When a former white supremacist and another man were arrested with anthrax in February 1998, tests on their possession took place in the US Army Medical Research Institute of Infectious Diseases at Fort Detrick, Maryland: *Washington Post* (22 February 1998).

28. In 1995, two 'Patriot's Council' militiamen from Minnesota were convicted under this new law of illegally manufacturing ricin, the lethal toxin derived from castor beans; FBI, *Terrorism in the United States: 1995* (Washington, DC: GPO, undated; 1997), p. 6.

29. Mark D. W. Edington of the Institute for Foreign Policy Analysis, 'Terror Made Easy', in the *New York Times* (4 March 1994).

30. One House Member noted that there are already many counter-terrorism laws on the books and spoke of a list of their titles running to 17 pages, as compiled by the Congressional Research Service. Others noted gaps in current legislation, and argued for the bill, sponsored by Rep. Henry Hyde. In a critical vote, on an amendment to weaken the bill, conservatives such as California Reps. Dan Burton and Bob Dornan 'defected', voting with liberals against stronger federal authority on some key points. Thus, while the attenuated bill eventually did pass, its sponsors were disappointed. Congressman Hyde, referring to a conversation he overheard on the floor, expressed astonishment that some members could be more afraid of the federal government than they were of Hamas. House of Representatives, Congress of the United States, second session, 13 March 1996, *Congressional Record*, pp. H2137–91.

31. The political leader of Hamas, born in Gaza but a resident of northern Virginia for 15 years, was arrested in New York based on a watch list in 1995 and has sought to avoid extradition to Israel. Abu Marzook has argued against a deportation system that does not allow him the opportunity to call witnesses or to widen courtroom discussions from the strictly legal issues to the political nature of his dispute with Israel. At the end of January 1997, the Hamas leader decided to cease resisting deportation. But in Gaza, Hamas issued a threat to the United States 'that it will bear the whole responsibility of the status of unrest which will emerge as a result' of extradition. *New York Times* (29–30 January 1997); *Washington Post* (29–31 January 1997).

32. Section 103 of the House bill barred 'material support to terrorists', defining such support as meaning 'currency or other financial securities, financial services, lodging, training, safehouses, false documentation or identification, communications equipment, facilities, weapons, lethal substances, explosives, personnel, transportation, and other physical assets, except medicine or religious materials'. House of Representatives, 104th Congress, second session, 13 March 1996, *Congressional Record*, p. H2145.

33. According to congressional testimony of May 1995,

> On January 23rd of this year, President Clinton signed an Executive Order prohibiting transactions with terrorists who threaten to disrupt the Middle East peace process. This order is being enforced by OFAC [Office of Foreign Assets Control]. The order blocks the movement, sale, purchase, or transfer of property of certain terrorist organizations, or persons acting on their behalf, that threaten the Middle East peace process. The order also prohibits the transferring of any contribution of funds, goods, or services to or for the benefit of such persons. The order provides a new tool to combat fundraising in this country on behalf of organizations that use terror to undermine the Middle East peace process and cuts off their access to sources of support in the US and to the US financial system. Section 301 of the Omnibus Counterterrorism Act of 1995 … contains similar blocking provisions and prohibitions against the making or receiving of certain contributions to designated terrorists.
>
> (Testimony of Ronald K. Noble, Under-Secretary of the Treasury for Enforcement, before the Committee on Appropriations, Subcommittee on the Treasury, Postal Service, and General Government, US Senate, 104th Congress, first session, 1 May 1995).

The State Department has the lead on compiling the list of all terror groups barred by the new US law against fund-raising. Interview at the State Department with Michael Kraft, specialist on legislative measures for counter-terrorism with the Office for the Coordinator of Counterterrorism, 12 February, 1997.

34. These two 1998 actions are referenced in 'US Action on the 25 Recommendations from the [1996] Paris Terrorism Ministerial', via Lieutenant-Colonel Jim Cooney from the open US government web site in January 1999: http://www.state.gov/www/global/terrorism/25measures_oct98.html

35. The Clinton administration has overlooked the nature of Sinn Fein because it saw an opportunity to seek peace in Ireland; if the Good Friday 1998 accord holds, it will be held up in the United States as, among other things, an important feature of US foreign policy. Untroubled by visa problems he would face in different circumstances, Gerry Adams repeatedly tours the United States; he is drawing $30,000 per speech in January 1999; *Washington Times* (25 January 1999).

36. The FBI is a part of the Justice Department, whose overall budget is similarly rising. In fiscal 1996, Justice's budget rose about 12 per cent; the 1997 budget exceeded $3 billion: *Washington Post Magazine* (20 July 1997); *Washington Post* (20 August 1996).

37. *Washington Post* and *Los Angeles Times* for 20 August 1996; *New York Times* (3 July 1996 and 4 January 1997).

38. The Justice Department's Office of International Affairs coordinates the criminal extraditions; Kessler, *The FBI*, p. 423. Ch. 17 describes some of the international roles of the contemporary FBI.

39. On Abu Marzook and many significant US-based activities of Islamic radicals and terrorists, see the statement of Steven Emerson to the US Senate, Committee on the Judiciary, Subcommittee on Technology, Terrorism, and Government Information, hearings on 'Foreign Terrorists in America: Five Years After the World Trade Center', 105th Congress, second session, 24 February 1998; unpublished transcript courtesy of the office of Senator Jon Kyl.

40. The White House, *A National Security Strategy of Engagement and Enlargement* (Washington, DC: GPO, February, 1996), p. 16.

41. See David Laufer, 'The Evolution of Belgian Terrorism,' in Lodge, *The Threat*, p. 205.

42. Juliet Lodge, 'Introduction: Terrorism and Europe: Some General Considerations', in Lodge, *The Threat*, p. 23, citing to R. Crelinsten and other authors of *Terrorism and Criminal Justice* (Lexington, MA: Lexington Books, 1978), pp. 40–41.

43. *Irish People* (New York, 1 February 1997). Around the United States various Irish activists are demonstrating against each deportation. Their arguments are that the fugitive's initial conviction and imprisonment in the UK was unfair, that his life in the United States has been blameless, that to return to Ireland or the UK would be very dangerous. Activism by family, friends, and political allies such as American friends of the organization Sinn Fein have included fund-raising for political and legal activities. For example, a 'Matt Morrison Defense Fund' was the beneficiary of a gathering sponsored by the Richmond Irish Northern Aid Unit in January 1997 in Richmond, Virginia.

44. *Washington Post* (3 July 1998).

45. PLF boss Abu Abbas was not the only one of these terrorists to escape justice. In the early 1990s two other *Achille Lauro* hijackers fled, in separate instances of conditional parole. A third man, Youssef Magied Molqi, who pulled the trigger to kill Klinghoffer, took advantage of a good conduct leave in February 1996, and has never returned. This has left just one of the five terrorists behind bars. It has also left the United States indignant with Rome, which always refused efforts to

extradite these men. *Washington Times* (6 March 1996), and subsequent reports in that daily and in the *Washington Post* through March 1996. For further reading, consult Antonio Cassese, *Terrorism, Politics and Law: The* Achille Lauro *Affair* (Princeton, NJ: Princeton University Press, 1989).

46. The late nineteenth-century precedent is mentioned in literature on the legal aspects of terrorism; one recent reference in the popular press may be found on 5 February 1997 in the *Washington Post*.

47. The act of 1986 is well known. Less well known are several federal rulings or decision papers that clarified the policy allowing extraterritorial jurisdiction, even when the foreign country has not given permission. For example, according to Kessler, there was such a decision reached formally at the Department of Justice in 1989; *The FBI*, p. 424. See also 'Extraterritorial Jurisdiction' and 'Most Frequently Used Federal Statutes', in the FBI, *Terrorism in the United States: 1987* (Washington, DC: GPO, undated; 1988), pp. 29–30; 41–3.

48. Public accounts of the Yunnis 'snatch' include Diarmuid Jeffreys, *The Bureau: Inside the Modern FBI* (Boston: Houghton Mifflin, 1995), pp. 278–9.

49. Description by Tom Hastings of the State Department's Office of the Coordinator for Counter-terrorism, speaking on 25 March 1996, at Quantico, Virginia. See also the Department of Justice, *Terrorism in the United States: 1993* (Washington, DC: GPO, undated; 1994), p. 8.

50. Argentina's right to complain is somewhat mitigated by the fact that today, a quarter century after the abduction of Eichmann, former Nazis still dwell there; see *L'Express* (Paris, 9 April 1998).

51. *New York Times* (23 February 1997).

52. The two Libyan government agents suspected in the Pan Am case, which killed 259 people on board and another 11 on the ground in Scotland, are Abdel Basset Ali al-Megrahi, an intelligence agent, and Lamen Khalifa Fhimah, a former station manager in Malta for Libyan Arab Airlines. Accounts of the investigation include a brief one by Kessler, *The FBI*, pp. 428–32, and one of book-length by two reporters on national security affairs, Steven Emerson and Brian Duffy, *The Fall of Pan Am 103: Inside the Lockerbie Investigation* (New York: G. P. Putnum's, 1990). My list of victims' nationalities is from the unpublished Grand Jury indictment filed against the two principals in the District Court for the District of Columbia by US Attorney J. B. Stephens (undated), 29 pp.

53. Early on, US officials announced suspicions of Iranian support for the second bomb, against the US air base. An independent report – a lengthy review by the authoritative Jane's network – concludes that key players included Saudis, Osama Bin Laden and the state of Iran; sponsorship was 'tightly controlled by Tehran'. Chris Kozlow, 'The Bombing of Khobar Towers: Who Did It, and Who Funded It', *Jane's Intelligence Review* (1 December 1997). See also the *New York Times* (21 June 1998).

54. *Washington Post* (13 February 1997).

55. The CIA reportedly created a special unit for terrorism intelligence towards the end of the first Reagan administration. State's Office for the Coordinator for Counter-terrorism, which handles many dimensions of counter-terrorism policy, survived a bid by the first Clinton administration to fold it into a larger apparatus on global issues. Additionally, State has 'pressed ahead with a long overdue computer database so embassies abroad can share information on suspected members of terrorist groups seeking entry into the United States', according to Mark D. W. Edington, *New York Times* (4 March 1994).

56. This has been the case during the Clinton administration. In 1998, the White

House reportedly began considering an overhaul of counter-terrorist strategy to focus greater powers at the NSC; Richard Clarke is now key.

57. Working on terrorism matters for a member of Congress in the late 1980s, I once made brief inquiries to several federal agencies about a credible newspaper report that Puerto Rican terrorists were traveling to and probably receiving aid from Nicaragua, then ruled by the communist Sandinistas. While one US Marshall was helpful, the overall result was otherwise: the FBI told me they could not comment because they do not track Nicaraguan activities, while CIA told me any question about Puerto Ricans or other Americans placed the matter outside their legal arena. This came in the midst of an important congressional debate about Nicaragua which would determine levels of US aid to the Contras. I pursued the question in a different way, reading much of the open record on Los Macheteros suspects at federal court in Hartford, Connecticut, finding there further hints of Nicaraguan and Cuban connections. An inquiry to the FBI at this point was met with concern: any public discussion by the Bureau of its own evidence could conceivably sabotage elaborate and expensive trails of Machetero suspects then ongoing. So I did nothing but back-brief the Congressman.

I therefore read with interest the account by Dr Laurie Mylroie of her own investigation of the World Trade Center bombing. In an article and a book-length manuscript, she argues that the FBI's focus on successfully prosecuting the terrorists caused it to be overly protective of important evidence about the bombers, evidence needed for a proper understanding of the purpose and origins of this terrorist act, easily the largest ever carried out by foreigners on US soil. This difference of views points to the problem of how best to oppose terrorism: as crime, or war. Mylroie argues that treating terrorism as a purely law-enforcement matter allows the FBI to hold close all evidence for its proper release in due course in public trials, but that this approach effectively blocks other workings of the national security process and shelves for too long evidence that may point to involvement of a foreign state. Laurie Mylroie, 'The World Trade Center Bomb', *The National Interest*, 42 (winter 1995–96), pp. 3–15.

58. The CIA occasionally has its own internal problems of failure to share intelligence between its different departments. But CIA has been improving in this respect, according to Dr Tucker's book.

59. The French have several different intelligence departments which are concerned with terrorism and they do not always cooperate perfectly. The Republic of Ireland does not always render full assistance on cross-border traffic issues that include counter-terrorism, and Margaret Thatcher used to criticize the Republic for failures of will in dealing with terrorism. The United States is now involved too; the last US ambassador to Ireland, Ms Kennedy, has been called 'an ardent apologist for the IRA' by her predecessor Ray Seitz. The result, he charges, is that British authorities have interrupted some intelligence-sharing with Washington on terrorism. A final example of troubles between friends is the US–Israel relationship: leaks of intelligence have angered Israel occasionally, perhaps leading to reduced sharing by Tel Aviv at some times. Such problems have been discussed in: *New York Times* (19 January 1998); Christopher Dobson and Ronald Payne, *Counterattack: The West's Battle Against the Terrorists* (New York: Facts on File, Inc., 1982); and Richard Clutterbuck, *Terrorism and Guerrilla Warfare: Forecasts and Remedies* (London: Routledge, 1990).

60. INTERPOL world-wide web page, accessed 24 December 1998.

61. One of the most coherent addresses to this problem has been by then-Ambassador at Large for Counter-terrorism, L. Paul Bremer III, 'Terrorism and Intelligence',

remarks to the Texas Chapter of the Association of Former Intelligence Officers, at Houston, Texas, 26 May 1987, repr. in *Vital Speeches of the Day* (Mount Pleasant, SC: City News Publishing Co.), 53:19 (15 July 1987), pp. 578–81. Recently, Ambassador Bremer argued strongly for firmer counter-terrorism in 'Fight Plan For a Dirty War', *Washington Post* (24 August 1998).

62. Sun Tzu, *The Art of War*, trans. Ralph D. Sawyer (Boulder, CO: Westview Press, 1994), Ch. 13, 'Employing Spies'.
63. *Patterns of Global Terrorism: 1988*, p. iv.
64. The White House, *A National Security Strategy For a New Century* (Washington DC: GPO, May 1997), p. 10.
65. US Department of State, 'Counterterrorism Law: Highlights of the Counterterrorism Law of 1996', p. 4 of seven. Other excerpts from this summary appear as an inset in Chapter 6.
66. One possible rare case of 'pre-emption' was US training assistance to Lebanese Christian militiamen known to be themselves opposed to Shia terrorism in their country. The case gained notoriety when, without the approval of the American trainers, certain of these militiamen staged a car-bombing designed to kill Sheik Fadlallah, leader of the Hezbollah, well known for its terrorism and hostage-taking. The car bomb killed or injured some 280 people near Fadlallah's office and he survived. This 8 March 1985 incident – and the US indirect links to it – were reported in the open press 12 May 1985 and confirmed to me later by a former counter-terrorism official. While a congressional investigation concluded that there was no strong US link to this terrorism, others disagree; see for example Stansfield Turner, *Terrorism and Democracy* (Boston: Houghton Mifflin, 1991), pp. 182–7.
67. Bremer's speech (see note 61), p. 580.
68. This extraordinary revelation, and others about past US–Palestinian connections, appeared in a story by Tim Weiner in the inner pages of the *New York Times* (5 March 1998).
69. While older issues of *Patterns of Global Terrorism* referred to US training programs, that is untrue of the annual covering 1995. It was difficult to say how much Coordinator for Counter-terrorism Philip Wilcox orally dealt with US bilateral training; he made and published few speeches; his successor, Ambassador Chris Ross, lasted only a few months and was gone by January 1999. The toughest-sounding current policy statement on terrorism is the eight-paragraph section on 'Combating Terrorism' in the *National Security Strategy*, published in February 1996 by the White House.
     Investigative journalists have detailed many US army training operations (not necessarily tied directly to counter-terrorism) on several continents in the *Washington Post* (12–14 July and 14 December 1998).
70. The Budapest school is the result of a 5 December 1994 accord, according to a Reuter dispatch; *Gulf News* (Abu Dhabi: 15 December 1994). See also *New York Times* (8 December 1996); the Bureau hopes to open additional foreign academies in Latin America and Asia. The Quantico, Virginia, training program involving Russians was referred to by the *Washington Times* (25 February 1995).
71. Letter from two members of the Irish Action Coalition; *Irish People* (12 November 1994).
72. See for example Clutterbuck, *Terrorism and Guerrilla Warfare*, p. 194, and Dobson and Payne, *Counterattack*, pp. 123–8.
73. Some of these incidents of the retaking of hostages from terrorists are described in an article researched for Rep. Jim Courter, 'Protecting Our Citizens: When to Use

Force Against Terrorists', *Policy Review*, 36 (spring 1986), pp. 10–17. The journal issue was at press when the United States struck Libya, 15 April 1986.

74. *Washington Post* (10 November 1996). The UN (with US support) is also providing humanitarian aid directly to hungry southern Sudanese through 'Operation Lifeline Sudan', a program that invariably reflects ill upon the northern political regime while doing no harm to its enemy, the Christian-dominated Sudanese People's Liberation Army. The latter is a suggestion of the limits of the US program: John Garang's SPLA has not yet been able to garner direct military aid from the United States, apparently, despite common rumors to the contrary.

75. For example, in correspondence with Ronald Reagan after the 1983 Beirut bombings, both leaders emphasized not revenge but grounding 'military action on the right of self-defense which ultimately no outside body has the authority to question'. Margaret Thatcher, *The Downing Street Years* (New York: HarperCollins, 1993), pp. 333–5, 444–6.

76. *Patterns: 1988* attributes the decrease in Syrian violence to the sanctions. Damascus's aid to terror groups such as the PFLP–GC and the Kurdish PKK did continue.

77. *Washington Post* (25 February and 24 December 1998). See Chapter 5 for an excerpt of the February 1998 *fatwa*.

78. Louis René Beres, 'Assassination and the Law: A Policy Memorandum', *Studies in Conflict and Terrorism*, 18 (1995), pp. 299–315, as well as 'Assassination of Terrorists may be Law-Enforcing: A Brief According to International Law', unpublished essay (1997), courtesy of the author, who has written widely in law journals on this topic. Hays Parks, Special Assistant to the Judge Advocate-General of the Army, released an official, unclassified, 16-page opinion, coordinated with the Department of State, the National Security Council, the Department of Justice, and other federal agencies: 'Memorandum of Law: Executive Order 12333 and Assassination' (2 November 1989). Copy courtesy of the author.

79. For example, a number of militants of the Armed Islamic Group, which has been conducting terrorism in France and Algeria since 1992, were in Brussels when found by special forces in March, 1998; *New York Times* (6 March 1998).

80. For example, the United States broke relations with Libya in 1981, closing its 'Libyan People's Bureaus' in the US. Britain broke relations with Libya in 1984 after a Libyan gunman at a window in the embassy on St James Square fired on a crowd of anti-Libyan demonstrators, injuring several and killing a British policewoman, Yvonne Fletcher.

81. *Washington Post* (24 November 1996); FBI, *Terrorism: 1995*, p. 12.

82. Claire Sterling, *The Terror Network* (New York: Holt, Rinehart & Winston, 1981), pp. 35–6, and Ch. 16). She describes how as early as 1970 the Prefect of Milan had reported to Rome that Italians 'in alarming numbers' were going to Czechoslovakia for guerrilla training; his report, and many subsequent ones, were generally ignored.

83. Paul Henze, *The Plot to Kill the Pope* (New York: Charles Scribner's, 1983), p. 127, etc.

84. While the European governments seemed prepared to condemn Libyan terrorism in their countries, they had not taken credible action against it. Counter-terrorism Ambassador Robert Oakley visited one capital after another without getting support for retaliation or even harsh sanctions. He returned to Washington displeased. With British help, the United States then struck the Libyan targets. Ambassador Oakley later spoke on these issues in a talk before some House of

Representatives Members and aides in 1987 in the Rayburn House Office Building.

85. UN Resolution 1044 passed 31 January 1996; 1054 passed 29 April 1996; 1070 passed 16 August 1996; texts courtesy of Mr Art Schoenwetter.

86. See for example Netanyahu, *Fighting Terrorism*, Ch. 7. For another example, an argument that sanctions helped drive the junta out of Haiti in 1994, see David Weekman, 'Sanctions: The Invisible Hand of Statecraft', *Strategic Review*, 26:1 (winter 1998), pp. 39–45.

87. The simile is mine, but see Daniel Pipes' fine study, 'Why Asad's Terror Works and Qaddafi's Does Not', *Orbis,* 33 (autumn 1989), pp. 501–8. Dr Pipes appears to have underestimated the strategic success Arafat's PLO was garnering through terrorism, but it is otherwise a superb article by a veteran observer of Middle Eastern affairs.

88. *Washington Times* (31 December 1997). Dr Kissinger's essay 'The Oil Deal with Iran' appeared in the *Washington Post* (28 October 1997). He argued that the Total corporation deal proved lack of seriousness in Paris about Iran's support to such terrorists as Hezbollah, Hamas, and Palestine Islamic Jihad. The latter two 'regularly claim credit for attacks on Israeli civilians'.

89. *New York Times* (22 November 1997). By February of 1998 the European Union had formally terminated the sanctions against Iran; they had been in place less than one year.

90. See the well-considered argument of Patrick Clawson, 'Sanctions as Punishment, Enforcement, and Prelude to Further Action', *Ethics and International Affairs*, 7 (1993), pp. 17–37. In a more recent opinion piece for a newspaper, a former assistant administrator for the US Agency for International Development argues that even an anticommunist like President Ronald Reagan overruled his advisors and shipped food aid into communist-run Ethiopia, which was allowing the starvation of many of its own people: 'Though it may be in our interest to deplore a particular government, as we certainly did the Stalinist regime which ran Ethiopia in the 1980s, I have yet to see a member of the political elite or the military die in a famine anywhere.' Andrew Natsios, 'Feed North Korea', *Washington Post* (9 February 1997).

91. *Foreign Report* may have been the first English-language periodical to discuss the Iraqis' palace building amid sanctions. By early 1998, the private presidential estates had become suspect sites for development of weapons of mass production. As Pentagon plans for renewing punitive war against Iraq moved ahead, the dictator's palaces were increasingly discussed as targets; see for example 'UN Team Mapping Iraqi Leader's Palaces', *New York Times* (16 February 1998). See also *The Times* for 19 January 1998 *re.* the new conscription.

92. Netanyahu, *Fighting Terrorism*, p. 134.

93. Memorandum of 3 September 1918, quoted by Martin Gilbert, *Winston S. Churchill: The Stricken World, 1916–1922* (Boston: Houghton Mifflin, 1975), p. 225.

Glossary of Terrorist Groups

Selection of terrorist groups is based on current relevance, significant activity in the 1990s, or reference in this text. Bold print indicates the most common name(s) used in English language sources and/or terms separately glossed.

Abu Nidal Organization (**ANO**; Fatah – The Revolutionary Council) Nihilist and nationalist. Abu Nidal left the PLO in 1974 and has since been at war with mainline Palestinian groups as well as Israelis and Westerners. The target of a successful US intelligence effort of the latter 1980s, Nidal's group has become rather inactive, and he is rumored to be ill. Bases are in Libya and Lebanon.

Abu Sayyaf (Abu Sayyaf Group) Latest heirs to the long tradition of Muslim opposition to Manila and to foreign rule in the southern Philippine Islands. Training and funding from Libya and perhaps other Middle Easterners. Exceedingly violent against civilians, it emerged as a new peace pact quieted down the Moro National Liberation Front. Founder Abdurajik Abubakar Janjalani left the MNLF in 1991. Neither group is known for relations to another operating in Mindanao, the Moro Islamic Liberation Front.

African National Congress (**ANC**) Founded in the early twentieth century to oppose apartheid. In recent decades, aligned with the South African Communist Party, and making free use of terrorism, including assassination, 'necklacing' of black opponents, and car bombings. Led by Oliver Tambo while Nelson Mandela was imprisoned. Bases were in Tanzania and Zambia, and later also Angola and Mozambique. On his release, Mandela led the ANC to power, became President of the Republic of South Africa, and has worked for democracy as well as socialism.

al-Jihad (Islamic Group; Islamic Jihad) Seeks an Islamicized state in Egypt. Active for two decades, killing Anwar el-Sadat, Egyptian security officials, Coptic Christians, and Western tourists. One faction, al Gama'at, bombed the World Trade Center in New York City, for which Sheik Umar Abd-al Rahman and acolytes are now jailed in the United States. Another faction is led by Dr Ayman al-Zawahiri, currently at large.

Armed Islamic Group (GIA) Algerian Muslim zealots, fighting to overthrow the secular FLN regime. Operations are in rural northern Algeria, where they kill victims by the score with knives and small arms, but also in Paris, where they have struck with nail bombs in Metro stations and done other actions. On poor terms with a similar violent Algerian group, FIS. Extortion of Algerians in France is one source of funds.

Aum Shinrikyo (Aum; Supreme Truth) International religious cult founded in Japan by Shoko Asahara. After failed attempts to gain political offices, Aum prepared for apocalyptic war against the nation, acquiring Russian armaments and making huge supplies of chemical agents. Attacks include one with sarin gas in subway cars converging at political center of downtown Tokyo in 1995. Arrests did not destroy the organization.

Corsican National Liberation Front (FLNC; National Front for the Liberation of Corsica) A group working since the mid 1970s to secure Corsica's independence from France. Uses terrorism against French and other European interests, attempting to 'internationalize' the struggle. Banks and government buildings are targets, on the island and in Paris; so are all elements of the tourism industry. Attacks are usually non-lethal but numerous and persistent. Served by its political front A Cuncolta Naziunalista.

Democratic Front for the Liberation of Palestine (DFLP; DPFLP) A long-standing opponent of all peace accords with Israel, including those of Camp David and of 1993. Leader Naif Hawatmeh is Marxist–Leninist, was strongly pro-Soviet, and had international Communist support. Aided by Syria today and is based in Syria and Lebanon. Occasionally commits border raids against Israel.

Dev Sol (Devrimci Sol; Revolutionary Left) Turkish and Marxist–Leninist. Little known in the West but seasoned and effective at assassinations, etc. Targets conservative Turks or foreign military personnel (as during the Gulf War). Funding comes from throughout western Europe via robberies and extortion.

ELN see **National Liberation Army**.

Euzkadi to Askatasuna (ETA; Basque Fatherland and Liberty) Nationalist and Marxist–Leninist. One of Europe's most potent terror organizations, but presently troubled by internal difficulties, arrests, and a breach with their political front **Herri Batasuna** at a time of declining Basque support for militancy. Skilled and experienced, ETA's killers usually target police. World-wide contacts with some other groups.

EZLN see **Zapatista National Liberation Army**.

FARC see **Revolutionary Armed Forces of Columbia**.

Fatah An acronym for Palestine National Liberation Movement. The largest armed component of the PLO, personally led by Yasser Arafat and Saleh Khalaf until the latter's assassination in Tunis in 1991. A stable organization with decades of experience and many thousands of guerrillas. Conducted international terrorism under the guise of sub-groups such as Black September, Force 17, and the Hawari group. With Chairman Arafat now presiding over a growing statelet, Fatah could be the basis for a conventional army.

FIS see **Islamic Salvation Front**.

FLNC see **Corsican National Liberation Front**.

GIA see **Armed Islamic Group**.

Hamas (Movement of Islamic Resistance) Palestinian and largely Sunni, Hamas grew out of the *intifada* in territories controlled by Israel. Intensely religious and thus frequently in hostile contact with Yasser Arafat's **PLO**, as well as Israelis and Westerners. Began killing with knives and small arms, and now does car and bus bombings. Funded by Tehran and sympathetic American citizens.

Harakat ul-Ansar (HUA; renamed itself Harkat ul-Mujahideen) Pakistani militants who joined forces in 1993, merging two Islamic terrorist groups. One of many Pakistani-based and funded groups operating in Kashmir against Indian troops and civilians. US State Department believes HUA is connected to the 1995 kidnapping of six Western tourists in Kashmir; one US citizen escaped; one Norwegian was found beheaded. 'Al-Faran', perhaps a small subgroup, is reportedly associated with this crime. Banned by the United States, HUA recently modified its name.

Herri Batasuna (HB) Political front of **ETA**.

Hezbollah (Party of God; formerly Islamic Jihad) Lebanese Shiite organization whose main international patron is Iran. Initially reputed for its kidnappings of Western foreigners, especially in Beirut, today it is growing into an insurgency, attacking Israeli defense forces in southern Lebanon with skill, and marshaling candidates for parliament. Its own media outlets include a television station.

Irish National Liberation Army (INLA) The military arm of the Irish Republican Socialist Party. Conducts terrorism in urban areas of Northern Ireland to press for unification of all 32 counties. Has also had bouts of infighting. A small but strong rival of the **IRA**, INLA is not thought to keep formal connections to the **IRA** but sometimes follows its lead, as in the truce each made leading up to the Good Friday Accord of spring 1998.

Irish Republican Army (IRA; Provisionals; Provos) The most powerful Irish militant group. Remarkably well-armed and skilled, with a deep popular base and long record of foreign supporters including American citizens and the Libyan government. In 1998 the IRA and its political front **Sinn Fein** declared a truce, signing a pact with other Irish parties and Britain to commence a new legislature in Northern Ireland. Disarmament issues have slowed this progress. A few members, declaring themselves 'the Real IRA', continue with terrorism.

Islamic Salvation Front (FIS) One of two main Algerian religiopolitical groups angered by the FLN's cancellation of elections in 1992. The Front and its main armed force, the Islamic Salvation Army, have attacked government personnel and other civilians as well as security forces, but recently declared a ceasefire. Probably enjoys funding from Islamic states. Presence in western Europe.

Islami Inqilabi Mahaz Based in the Lahore area of Pakistan area. Veterans of the war in Afghanistan, and now prepared to kill those opposing their vision of Islam's rule on earth. Claims to have assassinated four American businessmen and their Pakistani driver in Karachi in 1998, in retaliation for the trial and conviction of Pakistani terrorist Mir Aimal Kasi, who shot people in Langley, Virginia, in 1993.

Janata Vimukti Peramuna (JVP; People's Liberation Army) Sri Lankan terrorist movement of ethnic Sinhalese practising 'terrorism of the majority' against their own, as well as Tamils and Muslims, in a drive for state power. Victims numbered several tens of thousands. Vigorously opposed by the democratic state. Leader Rohanna Wijeweera, whose ideology mixed communism and nationalism, was captured in late 1989 and soon died in police custody. No longer extant.

Japanese Red Army (JRA) A tiny Marxist–Leninist (and thus internationalist) group that cut a swath in the 1970s, as in the Lod Airport massacre in Israel. Remnants have lived in North Korea and the Bekaa Valley. Founded and still led by a woman named Fusako Shigenobu, who may live in Syria. Made a failed bombing attempt against a US Navy office in April 1988 on the second anniversary of the bombing of Libya. Recent operations include moving counterfeit currency in Asia. Several members were arrested in Lebanon in 1997.

Kach, Kahane Chai (Kach, 'Kahane Lives') Jewish supremacist groups. Rabbi Meir Kahane, an American, founded Kach, and later moved to Israel to carry out terrorism and also run for parliament. After his assassination, his son Benjamin formed the second group in his memory. Both groups terrorize Palestinians and Muslims and vocally support terrorism. Banned by the Israeli government, they operate in Israel and the West Bank, while receiving private American donations.

Khmer Rouge (Party of Democratic Kampuchea) Cambodian insurgency grounded in Maoist thought, and led by men who were highly educated. Accomplished a rise to power, and then the genocide of almost two million countrymen of noncommunist politics, before losing state power to Vietnamese invaders. Reverted to guerrilla status and 'liberated areas'. The late 1990s saw defections, military setbacks, the death of leader Pol Pot, arrests of most other leaders, and finally rampant defections.

Ku Klux Klan (KKK) From an innocuous birth after the American Civil War, the KKK grew violent, and spread through southern states. Seen as a champion of white supremacy. Terrorized and murdered blacks, and to a lesser extent Catholics and Jews. By the early twentieth century, a mass organization of men and women in America and also Canada. Numbers have dropped dramatically in recent decades. There are still occasional killings or terrorist crimes. Some members join other groups that use terror for similar ends.

Kurdish Workers' Party (PKK) Some 20 million Kurds live in diaspora, especially in Turkey and Iraq; PKK is the strongest violent group seeking a Kurdish homeland. Led by Abdullah Ocalan, who spent 1999 in jail in Turkey after Syria succumbed to pressures to turn him out. One of the world's largest insurgent groups and an experienced combatant against Turkish arms. A frequent employer of terrorism against other Kurds, Turkey's NATO partners, etc. Narcotics smuggling is a leading source of income.

Los Macheteros (The Machete-wielders) Puerto Rican heirs to the FLN of the 1970s and earlier militants opposed to US 'imperialism' and the island's status as a US commonwealth. Symbolic attacks on federal offices, and ambushes of US military personnel. Destroyed eight National Guard jets in one attack. Robberies include one of the largest in US history, in Hartford, Connecticut; some proceeds are believed to be in Cuba. Many members are now in US jails and others are fugitives.

LTTE see **Tamil Tigers**.

Manuel Rodriquez Patriotic Front (FPMR) Castroite group close to the Communist Party of Chile. One of the only surviving leftist terrorist groups in Latin America, but apparently no longer garnering Cuban aid. Favors attacks on US targets, from restaurant chains to Mormon missionaries. Several foreigners helped four members make a dramatic prison escape via helicopter in 1996.

MRTA See **Tupac Amaru**.

Mujahedeen Khalq (People's Holy Warriors) An organization of thousands – mostly Iranians – dedicated to replacing the mullahs' regime in Iran with a Marxist–Leninist one. Led by married couple Maryam and Massoud Rajavi. Based in Iraq and cooperative with Saddam Hussein's regime. Funds come from Iranian exiles and Iraq. Deploys armor and conventional forces in drills and border incursions. Terrorism includes bombs in public places inside Iran. Claimed the killing of a senior Iranian general at his home in Tehran in April 1999.

National Liberation Army (ELN) The second-ranked Colombian insurgent and terrorist group. Castro inspired its ideology and gave it aid. Largely on its own strengths, such as massive funding from extortion and other crimes against Colombians, ELN grew in personnel and wealth until 1997–98. Recently suffered the death of its founding leader, defrocked priest Manuel Perez Martinez. Hijacked an airplane with 46 passengers in April 1999. Like **FARC**, it now appears to focus less on national revolution than growing wealthy in its base areas.

New People's Army (NPA) A three-decade old Maoist group known for rural insurgency, terrorization of the populace, and murder or kidnapping of Americans for 'anti-imperialist' purposes. So powerful in the 1980s that some believed they would capture the Philippines. Now battered by internal discord, the replacement of the Marcos regime with democracy, and increased skills of the country's armed forces. Like the terrorists of the Alex Boncayao Brigade, NPA is an arm of the Communist Party.

Osama Bin Laden (Al-Qaeda) Scion of a Saudi family with a massive fortune from the construction business, Bin Laden helped Arab 'internationalists' fight the Red Army occupation of Afghanistan. When that war ended, he took his fight abroad, funding world-wide terror operations and militant Islam. Stripped of Saudi citizenship, he directed attacks on two US embassies in East Africa in 1998, prompting cruise missile attacks on parts of his infrastructure in Sudan and Afghanistan.

Palestine Islamic Jihad (PIJ) One of the newer, radical Islamic groups in the Palestinian underground. Predominantly Sunni. After its founder was killed in Malta, Ramadan Shallah has emerged as the leader. The group is based in Damascus and operates in Jordan, Lebanon, and especially the Israeli-occupied territories. Not just Israel but its foreign supporters, and moderate Arab governments, are among its targets. Acts include suicide bombings. Iran is a chief patron.

Palestine Liberation Front (PLF) One of many **PLO** factions which have remained loyal to Yasser Arafat. A small group, led by Abu Abbas, an articulate and cynical defender of terrorist strikes such as the PLF hijacking of the cruise ship *Achille Lauro* in which a tourist was shot and dumped overboard. Based in Iraq and has received support from Baghdad and from Tripoli.

Palestine Liberation Organization (PLO) Encompasses various

Palestinian resistance groups, including **Fatah**.

PKK see Kurdish Workers' Party.

Popular Front for the Liberation of Palestine (PFLP) George Habash
helped open the modern era of international hijacking and Palestinian
terrorism. His group has kept its Marxist–Leninist ideology and its
leading role among Middle Eastern 'rejectionists' of any peace with
Israel. Now stages few terror attacks or guerrilla contacts with Israeli
Defense Forces. Has been, and today remains, within the structure of the
PLO.

**Popular Front for the Liberation of Palestine – General Command
(PFLP–GCC)** A former Syrian army captain and **PFLP** member,
Ahmed Jibril broke away to found his own group. Fighting for an
independent Palestinian state. A sub-organization of the **PLO** but is a
'rejectionist' of accommodation with Israel. Still based in Syria. Known
for technical skills, as in airline bombings. Well armed and trained, from
conventional tactics to ultralight aircraft.

Red Army Faction (RAF) The German descendant of Andreas Baader
and Ulrike Meinhof. After stinging and bedeviling a West German nation
of 60 million throughout the late 1970s and the 1980s, these few dozen
armed Marxist–Leninists proved unable to expand their popular support
or to withstand the full response of the state. Published unusual public
confessions of failure in 1992 and formally disbanded six years later.

Revolutionary Armed Forces of Colombia (FARC) Strongest of the
Colombian insurgent movements. Practitioner of systematic terrorism
against Colombians and foreigners; holding a number of Americans
hostage in early 1999. An effective guerrilla force that often battles
Colombian army or shoots down its aircraft. President Pastrana in 1998
all but abdicated sovereignty over huge FARC-dominated areas. Rich
from extortion and drug income, FARC has larger annual receipts than
most Colombian corporations.

Revolutionary Organization 17 November (17 November) Marxist–
Leninist group, operating for 25 years, tiny but irrepressible.
Periodically kills Greeks or Americans, often with the same pistol.
Known for lengthy ideological statements. Recent targets include
multinational corporations. Incredibly, no member has ever been
brought to trial.

Shining Path (Sendero Luminoso) Founded by a Peruvian professor, Abimael Guzman, who believes himself to be 'the fourth sword of Marxism' – after Marx, Lenin, and Mao. The Sendero insurgency draws strength from poverty, the alienation of the country's Indian population, and the patient political work of a generation. Flagrant terrorism has been both a strength and a weakness. This powerful and growing movement was badly set back by the capture, in 1992, of its leader.

Sinn Fein ('We Ourselves') Political front of the **IRA**, currently led by Gerry Adams.

Tamil Tigers (Liberation Tigers of Tamil Eelam; **LTTE**) The best-known terrorists in an ethnic separatist movement against the state of Sri Lanka. Responsible for devastating urban bombings in Colombo and scores of terror attacks annually. Has a large guerrilla force that fights the Sri Lankan army, and **LTTE**'s 'navy' has hijacked, attacked, or sunk many Sri Lankan navy combat vessels. The founder and leader is Vellupillai Prabhakaran. The Tigers are no longer helped by the government of India.

Tupac Amaru (MRTA) Peruvian communists with a largely urban focus. In 1996, with several hundred cadres and the leader (Victor Polay Campos) in jail, 14 members in Lima led by Nestor Cerpa Cartolini seized the Japanese embassy and hundreds of dignitaries. After a prolonged stand-off, Peruvian commandos retook the embassy with dramatic success, killing all MRTA gunmen. Now an inconsequential group, especially as Peru's national prospects are improving.

Ulster Defence Association (UDA) Dedicated to retaining Protestant domination and British political authority in control of Northern Ireland. Formed three decades ago in Belfast. Copied some IRA methods and its military funeral ceremonies. Known for direct attacks on **IRA** members and meeting places, and some attacks south of the intra-Irish border. In 1973, spawned the Ulster Freedom Fighters, a smaller terrorist group. Both remain active.

Ulster Volunteer Force (UVF) A long-active militia, chiefly working class. Terrorizes Irish nationalists and **IRA** members on behalf of Protestantism and British authority in Ulster (Northern Ireland). Effectively, 'pro-state' terrorists, like the UDA, but like them, pursued by British authorities for their murders. Also, like the **UDA**, denounced by Irish nationalists for allegedly receiving clandestine help from British authorities and military units, especially in intelligence.

Zapatista National Liberation Army (Zapatistas; EZLN) Began on New Year's Day 1994, in the southern, poor Mexican state of Chiapas. Led by a publicity-wise adult male, 'Subcommandante Marcos', reportedly a former professor. Initial offensive swept over and captured several towns; there were shootings and hostage-taking. Thereafter, devoted to propaganda, within Mexico and 'on line' to the world. New offensives usually aim at publicity (and they get it) world-wide. No recent record of terrorism.

Select Bibliography

Journals and periodicals

Commentary	(occasional issues)
Foreign Affairs	(occasional issues)
Foreign Report	(1980–98)
Insight on the News	(occasional issues)
International Defense Review	(1993–98)
Jane's Defense Weekly	(1993–98)
Jane's Intelligence Review	(1994–98)
L'Express	(occasional issues)
Pinkerton Risk Assessment Services Weekly	(1996–97)
Small Wars and Insurgencies	(1991–98)
Strategic Review	(1984–98)
Studies in Conflict and Terrorism	(1992–97)
Terrorism and Political Violence	(1991–98)
TVI	(occasional issues)

Newspapers

Christian Science Monitor	(1993–97)
The Irish People	(1994–98)
Los Angeles Times	(1979–98)
Manchester Guardian Weekly	(occasional issues)
New York Times	(1988–98)
Wall Street Journal	(occasional issues)
Washington Post	(1985–98)
Washington Times	(1985–98)

Internet sites and paths

(*Note*: These examples are subject to change; they were accessed in January 1999).

Anarchism	http://flag.blackened.net/revolt/revolt/html.

Lori Berenson   http://www.freelori.org
                                      http.//www.geocities.com/CapitolHill/9968

LTTE   http://www.eelamweb.com/pirabha.html
                                      http://www.eelamweb.com/pirint.html
                                      http://members.tripod.com/~ltte/ourleaderin.html

Maoist Internationalist Movement http://www.etext.org/Politics/MIM

National Socialism Primer   http://www3.stormfront.org/ns/nsprimer.html

Republican Sinn Fein   http://members.tripod.com/~Republican
                                          _Sinn_Fein/index.html

Shining Path   http://www.csrp.org/

Sinn Fein   http://www.sinnfein.iel

Southern Poverty Law Center   http://www.splcenter.org

Stormfront   http://stormfront.org
                                      http://www.stormfront.org/dblack/

Unabomber   http://www.cs.umass.edu/~ehaugsja/unabomb/
                                          docs/1971essay.html
                                      http://www.dejanews.com/getdoc.xp?
                                          AN=361598462

Zapatistas   http://www.ezln.org/
                                      http://www.peak.org/~joshua/fzln
                                      http:www.autonomedia.org/zapatista.htm

Ernst Zundel   http://www.webcom.com/~ezundel/english/
                                          english/englishtoc.html.
                                      http://webcom.com/~ezundel/english/zgrams/zg
                                          1998/zg9809/980927-html

US government reports

Congressional Research Service reports	(occasional)
Department of State, *Patterns of Global Terrorism*	(annual)
Department of State, *Annual Report on Human Rights*	(occasional)
Department of State, *Significant Incidents of Political Violence Against Americans*	(occasional)
Federal Bureau of Investigation, *Terrorism in the US*	(annual)
Foreign Broadcast Information Service reports, including JPRS	(daily & periodic)
Institute for National Strategic Studies, *Strategic Assessment*	(1996, 1997)
The White House, *National Security Strategy*	(periodic)

Unpublished Papers and Court Documents

Herbert, Lieutenant-Commander Gretchen S. 'Information Warfare: An Alternative Weapon for Terrorists?', paper, Command and Staff College, Marine Corps University, Quantico, Virginia (1998).

Ross, Major Jon L. 'Arming for War: The Militia Threat to the US Military.' a master's paper, Command and Staff College, Marine Corps University, Quantico, Virginia (1998).

Schoenwetter, Arthur. 'Should the US Attack Sudan?' a master's paper, Command and Staff College, Marine Corps University, Quantico, Virginia (1997).

US Department of State. Office of Coordinator for Counter-terrorism. Highlights of the Counter-terrorism Law of 1996. Summary of Omnibus Counter-terrorism Bill signed into law 24 April (1996)

US Department of State. Office of Coordinator for Counter-terrorism. Designation of Foreign Terrorist Organizations, (10 August 1997).

US District Court. Hartford, Connecticut. Indictments against certain members of Los Macheteros (1987).

US District Court. New Jersey. Affidavit, briefs, and sentencing memorandum against Yu Kikumura of the Japanese Red Army (1988, 1989).

US District Court. New York City, Proceedings on Pan Am 103 claims (undated).

US District Court. Sacramento, California. Journal and Letter Exhibits to Sentencing Memorandum against Theodore John Kaczynski (1998).

US District Court. Southern District of New York. Papers *re* members of 'Republic of New Africa' (1988).

US Institute for Peace. Conference series on Covert Warfare (1990–91).

Woolsey, R. James (Director of CIA). Statement before US Congress. Select Committee on Intelligence. 104th Congress, 1st session (10 January (1995).

Books and monographs

Abbey, Edward. *The Monkey Wrench Gang*. New York: Avon Books, 1976.

Adams, James. *The Financing of Terror*. New York: Simon & Schuster, 1986.

Anti-Defamation League. *Danger: Extremism: The Major Vehicles and Voices on America's Far-Right Fringe*. New York: Anti-Defamation League, 1996.

Asprey, Robert B. *War in the Shadows: The Guerrilla In History*. Vol. 2. Garden City, New York: Doubleday, 1975.

Baumann, Michael [Bommi Baumann]. *How it All Began*. Vancouver: Pulp Press, 1977; repr., *Terror or Love? Bommi Baumann's Own Story of His Life as a West German Urban Guerrilla*. New York: Grove Press, 1978.

Becker, Jillian. *Hitler's Children: The Story of the Baader–Meinhof Terrorist Gang*. New York: J.B. Lippincott, 1977.

Blee, Kathleen M. *Women of the Klan: Racism and Gender in the 1920s*. Berkeley, CA: University of California Press, 1991.

Brackett, D. W. *Holy Terror: Armageddon in Tokyo*. Uncorrected proof. New York: Weatherhill, 1996.

Buford, Bill. *Among the Thugs*. New York: W. W. Norton, 1991.

Clark, Robert P. *The Basque Insurgents: ETA, 1952–1980*. Madison, WI: University of Wisconsin Press, 1984.

Cline, Ray S., and Yonah Alexander. *Terrorism: The Soviet Connection*. New York:

Crane Russak, 1984.

Cline, Ray S., and Yonah Alexander. *Terrorism as State-Sponsored Covert Warfare: What the Free World Must Do to Protect Itself.* Fairfax, VA: Hero Books, 1986.

Corcoran, James. *Bitter Harvest: Gordon Kahl and the Posse Comitatus: Murder in the Heartland.* New York: Viking Penguin, 1990.

Courter, Jim. *Defending Democracy.* ed. Mark Lipsitz. Foreword by the Hon. Richard N. Perle. Washington, DC: American Studies Center, 1986.

Crenshaw, Martha (ed.). *Terrorism in Context.* University Park, Pennsylvania: Pennsylvania State University Press, 1995.

Debray, Regis. *Revolution in the Revolution?* Librarie François Maspero, 1967; New York: Grove Press, 1967.

Dees, Morris, with James Corcoran. *Gathering Storm: America's Militia Threat.* New York: HarperCollins, Inc., 1996.

Dees, Morris, and Steve Fiffer. *Hate on Trial: The Case Against America's Most Dangerous Neo-Nazi.* New York: Villard Books, 1993.

Dillon, Martin. *25 Years of Terror: The IRA's War Against the British.* London: Bantam Books, 1997.

Dobson, Christopher, and Ronald Payne. *The Carlos Complex: A Study in Terror.* New York: Putnam's, 1977.

Dobson, Christopher, and Ronald Payne. *The Terrorists: Their Weapons, Leaders and Tactics.* New York: Facts On File, 1979.

Douglass, Joseph D., Jr *CBW: The Poor Man's Atomic Bomb.* Philadelphia: Institute for Foreign Policy Analysis, 1984.

Douglass, Joseph D., Jr, and Neil C. Livingstone. *America the Vulnerable: The Threat of Chemical and Biological Warfare.* Lexington, MA: Lexington Books, D.C. Heath, 1987.

Emerson, Steven, and Brian Duffy. *The Fall of Pan Am 103: Inside the Lockerbie Investigation.* New York: Putnam's, 1990.

Emerson, Steven, and Cristina Del Sesto. *Terrorist: The Inside Story of the Highest-Ranking Iraqi Terrorist Ever to Defect to the West.* New York: Villard Books, 1991.

Fanon, Frantz. *The Wretched of the Earth.* Preface by Jean-Paul Sartre. 1961; New York: Grove Press, 1968.

Fontaine, Roger W. *Terrorism: The Cuban Connection.* New York: Crane Russak, 1988.

Foreman, Dave. *Confessions of an Eco-Warrior.* New York: Harmony Books, 1991.

Godson, Roy and William. J. Olson. *International Organized Crime: Emerging Threat to US Security.* Washington, DC: National Strategy Information Center, 1993.

Goren, Roberta. *The Soviet Union and Terrorism,* ed. Jillian Becker, Introduction by Robert Conquest. London: George Allen & Unwin, 1984.

—— *The Diary of Che Guevara,* ed. Robert Scheer, Introduction by Fidel Castro. *Ramparts Magazine,* 1967; New York: Bantam, 1968.

Guevara, Che. *Guerrilla Warfare,* Prefatory note by I. F. Stone. New York: Vintage Books, 1969.

Hamas. *The Charter of Allah: The Platform of the Islamic Resistance Movement (Hamas).* Intro. and ed. by Raphael Israeli. *The 1988-89 Annual of Terrorism.* Yonah Alexander and H. Foxman (eds). Netherlands: Kluwer Academic Publishers, 1990.

Hearst, Patricia Campbell, with Alvin Moscow. *Every Secret Thing.* 1982; repr. *Patty Hearst: Her Own Story.* New York: Avon Books, 1988.

Henze, Paul. *The Plot to Kill the Pope.* New York: Charles Scribner's, 1983.

Herrington, Stuart A. *Silence Was a Weapon: The Vietnam War in the Villages.* 1982; New York: Ivy Books, 1987.

Hitler, Adolf. *Mein Kampf*, trans. and ed. Chamberlain *et al.* New York: Reynal & Hitchcock, 1939.

Hoffman, Bruce. *Recent Trends and Future Prospects of Terrorism in the United States.* Santa Monica, CA: RAND, 1988.

IRA. *Handbook for Volunteers of the Irish Republican Army: Notes on Guerrilla Warfare.* Eire: The Irish Republican Army, General Headquarters, 1956.

Janke, Peter, with Richard Sim. *Guerrilla and Terrorist Organizations: A World Directory and Bibliography.* New York: Macmillan, 1983.

Jeffreys, Diarmuid. *The Bureau: Inside the Modern FBI.* Boston: Houghton Mifflin, 1995.

Jenkins, Brian M. *Embassies Under Siege: A Review of 48 Embassy Takeovers, 1971–1980.* Santa Monica, CA: RAND, 1981.

Joll, James. *The Anarchists.* New York: The Universal Library, Grosset & Dunlap, 1966.

Jonas, George. *Vengeance.* Canada: Lester & Orpen Dennys and Collins, 1984; repr., New York: Bantam Books, 1985.

Kaczynski, Theodore John. *Industrial Society and its Future.* Washington, DC: *Washington Post* (19 September 1995). Special supplement.

Katz, Samuel M. *Israel Versus Jibril: The Thirty-Year War against a Master Terrorist.* New York: Paragon House, 1993.

Kessler, Ronald. *The FBI.* New York: Pocket Star Books, 1993.

Kleinknecht, William. *The New Ethnic Mobs: The Changing Face of Organized Crime in America.* New York: The Free Press, 1996.

Kramer, Martin. *Hezbollah's Vision of the West.* The Washington Institute Policy Papers Series (No. 16). Washington, DC: The Washington Institute for Near East Policy, 1989.

Kupperman, Robert, and Jeff Kamen. *Final Warning: Averting Disaster in the New Age of Terrorism.* New York: Doubleday, 1989.

Kushner, Harvey W. (ed.) *The Future of Terrorism: Violence in the New Millennium.* Thousand Oaks, CA: Sage, 1998.

Laffin, John. *The PLO Connections.* London: Corgi, 1982.

Laqueur, Walter. *The Age of Terrorism.* 2nd edn Boston: Little, Brown, 1987.

Laqueur, Walter, and Yonah Alexander (eds). *The Terrorism Reader.* 2nd edn, New York: Meridian Books, 1987.

Lenin, V.I. *'Left-Wing' Communism, an Infantile Disorder: A Popular Essay in Marxian Strategy and Tactics.* 1920; New York: International Publishers, 1940.

—— *State and Revolution.* 1917; New York: International Publishers, 1932, 1974.

—— *What is to be Done?* 1902; Beijing: Foreign Languages Press, 1975.

Lodge, Juliet (ed.). *The Threat of Terrorism.* Boulder, CO: Westview Press, 1988.

Macdonald, Andrew [William Pierce]. *The Turner Diaries.* 2nd edn, Hillsboro, West Virginia: National Vanguard Books, 1978.

MacDonald, Eileen. *Shoot the Women First.* New York: Random House, 1991.

Mao Tse-Tung. *Selected Military Writings of Mao Tse-Tung.* 2nd edn, Peking: Foreign Languages Press, 1963.

—— *Mao Tse-Tung on Guerrilla Warfare*, ed. Samuel B. Griffith. Washington, DC: United State Marine Corps, Department of the Navy, April 1989.

Marenches, Comte Alexandre de, and Christine Ockrent. *Dans le secret des princes*, Editions Stock, 1986; updated, adapted, and repr., Count de Marenches, and David A. Andelman. *The Fourth World War: Diplomacy and Espionage in the Age of*

Terrorism. New York: William Morrow, 1992.

Marighella, Carlos. *Urban Guerrilla Minimanual.* Vancouver: Pulp Press, 1974.

Martinez, Thomas, with John Guinther. *Brotherhood of Murder.* New York: McGraw-Hill, 1988.

McGurn, William. *Terrorist or Freedom Fighter? The Cost of Confusion.* United Kingdom: Institute for European Defense and Strategy, 1990.

Melman, Yossi. *The Master Terrorist: The True Story Behind Abu Nidal.* New York: Adama Books, 1986.

Mockaitis, Thomas Ross. 'The British Experience in Counterinsurgency, 1919–60'. PhD, University of Wisconsin, 1988. Ann Arbor, MI: UMI Dissertation Information Services, 1990.

Moore, Carol. *The Davidian Massacre: Disturbing Questions about Waco which Must be Answered.* Franklin, TN: Legacy Communications & Springfield, Virginia: Gun-Owners Foundation, 1995.

Moran, Sue Ellen (ed.). *Court Depositions of Three Red Brigadists.* Santa Monica, CA: RAND, February 1986. RAND Note, N-2391-RC.

Netanyahu, Benjamin. *Fighting Terrorism: How Democracies Can Defeat Domestic and International Terrorists.* New York: Farrar Straus Giroux, 1995.

—— (ed.). *Terrorism: How the West Can Win.* New York: Farrar Straus Giroux, 1986.

O'Neill, Bard E. *Insurgency and Terrorism: Inside Modern Revolutionary Warfare.* With a foreword by General Edward C. Meyer. New York: Brassey's, Maxwell Macmillan Pergamon Publishing Corp., 1990.

Paret, Peter. *French Revolutionary Warfare from Indochina to Algeria: The Analysis of a Political and Military Doctrine.* Princeton Studies in World Politics, No. 6. New York: Frederick A. Praeger, 1964.

Pipes, Daniel. *Syria Beyond the Peace Process.* Washington, DC: Washington Institute for Near East Policy, 1996.

Pisano, Vittorfranco S. *The Terrorist Threat to the US Army in Western Europe.* Carlisle Barracks, PA: US Army War College, 16 February 1988. Unpublished Military Studies Program Paper.

Potts, Mark, Nicholas Kochan and Robert Whittington. *Dirty Money: BCCI.* Washington, DC: National Press Books, 1992.

Powers, Thomas. *Diana: The Making of a Terrorist.* New York: Bantam Books and Houghton Mifflin, 1971.

Ra'anan, Uri, Robert L. Pfaltzgraff, Jr, Richard H. Shultz, Ernst Halperin and Igor Lukes. *Hydra of Carnage: The International Linkages of Terrorism and Other Low-Intensity Operations: The Witnesses Speak.* Lexington, MA: Lexington Books, D. C. Heath, 1986.

Rauschning, Hermann. *The Revolution of Nihilism: Warning to the West!* New York: Alliance Book Corporation, 1939.

Rood, Harold W. *Kingdoms of the Blind: How the Great Democracies have Resumed the Follies that So Nearly Cost them their Lives.* Durham, NC: Carolina Academic Press, 1980.

Ryan, Chris B. *Tourism, Terrorism, and Violence.* Conflict Studies no. 24. London: Research Institute for the Study of Conflict and Terrorism, September 1991.

Schmidt, Michael. *The New Reich: Violent Extremism in Unified Germany and Beyond.* New York: Pantheon Books, 1993.

Seale, Bobby. *Seize the Time: The Story of the Black Panther Party and Huey P. Newton.* New York: Random House, 1970.

Southern Poverty Law Center. *False Patriots.* Montgomery, AL: 1996.

Stanton, Bill. *Klanwatch: Bringing the Ku Klux Klan to Justice.* New York: Grove

Weidenfeld, 1991.

Sterling, Claire. *The Terror Network: The Secret War of International Terrorism.* New York: Holt, Rinehart & Winston and Reader's Digest, 1981.

—— *The Time of the Assassins.* New York: Holt, Rinehart & Winston, 1983.

Stevenson, William, with Uri Dan. *90 Minutes at Entebbe.* New York: Bantam Books, 1976.

Sun, Tzu. *The Art of War.* Trans. and intro. Samuel B. Griffith. Foreword B.H. Liddell Hart. Clarendon Press, 1963; repr., London: Oxford University Press, 1963.

'Tayacán', with Joanne Omang and Aryeh Neier. *Psychological Operations in Guerrilla Warfare.* New York: Vintage Books, 1985.

Taylor, Peter. *States of Terror: Democracy and Political Violence.* London: BBC Books, 1993.

Thompson, Jerry. *My Life in the Klan.* Intro. by John Seigenthaler. New York: Putnam's, 1982; repr. Nashville, TN: Rutledge Hill Press, 1988.

Trotsky, Leon. *Dictatorship vs Democracy.* 1920; New York: American Communists (Workers' Party), 1922; repr., *Terrorism and Communism: A Reply to Karl Kautsky.* Foreword Max Shachtman. Ann Arbor, MI: Ann Arbor Paperbacks for the Study of Communism and Marxism, The University of Michigan Press, 1961.

Tucker, David. *Skirmishes at the Edge of Empire: The United States and International Terrorism.* Westport, CT: Praeger, 1997.

US Central Intelligence Agency. *The Biological and Chemical Warfare Threat,* Washington, DC: US Government Printing Office, 1997.

US Congress. Senate. Committee on the Judiciary. Subcommittee on Security and Terrorism. *State-Sponsored Terrorism.* Report by Ray S. Cline and Yonah Alexander. 99th Congress, 1st session, 1985. Senate Print 99–56.

US Department of the Army. *Human Factors Considerations of Undergrounds in Insurgencies.* Washington, DC: Special Operations Research Office, The American University, 1966.

US Department of Defense. *Terrorist Group Profiles.* Washington, DC: US Government Printing Office, 1988.

US Department of Justice, Federal Bureau of Investigation. *Terrorism in the United States, 1982–1992.* Washington, DC: Terrorist Research and Analytical Center, Counter-terrorism Section, Intelligence Division, FBI, 1993.

US Department of State. *Libya's Continuing Responsibility for Terrorism.* Washington, DC: US Government Printing Office, November 1991.

US Government Accounting Office. *US Currency Abroad.* Washington, DC: US Government Printing Office, February 26, 1996.

von Clausewitz, Karl. *On War.* Ed. and trans. Michael Howard and Peter Paret. With introductory essays by Peter Paret, Michael Howard, and Bernard Brodie. Princeton, NJ: Princeton University Press, 1976.

Wardlaw, Grant. *Political Terrorism: Theory, Tactics, and Counter-measures.* 2nd edn, Cambridge: Cambridge University Press, 1989.

Weinberg, Leonard B. (ed.). *Political Parties and Terrorist Groups.* London: Frank Cass, 1992.

Weinberg, Leonard B. and Paul B. Davis. *Introduction to Political Terrorism.* New York: McGraw-Hill, 1989.

Wilkinson, Paul. *Terrorism and the Liberal State.* Rev. edn, London: Macmillan, 1986; New York: New York University Press, 1986.

Books of special regional interest

Asia

Farrell, William R. *Blood and Rage: The Story of the Japanese Red Army*. Lexington, MA: Lexington Books, D.C. Heath, 1990.
Kaplan, David E., and Andrew Marshall. *The Cult at the End of the World*. New York: Crown, 1996.
Marks, Thomas A. *Maoist Insurgency since Vietnam*. London: Frank Cass, 1996.
McGowan, William. *Only Man is Vile: The Tragedy of Sri Lanka*. New York: Farrar, Straus & Giroux, 1992.
Thompson, Robert. *Defeating Communist Insurgency: Experiences from Malaya and Vietnam*. Chatto & Windus, 1966; reprint, London: The Macmillan Press, Ltd., 1987.

North America

Fernandez, Ronald. *Los Macheteros: The Wells Fargo Robbery and the Violent Struggle for Puerto Rican Independence*. New York: Prentice Hall, 1987.
Holland, Jack. *The American Connection: US Guns, Money, and Influence in Northern Ireland*. New York: Viking Penguin, 1987.
Kinsella, Warren. *Web of Hate: Inside Canada's Far Right Network*. Toronto: HarperCollins, 1994; HarperPerennial, 1995.
Mizell, Louis R., Jr *Target USA: The Inside Story of the New Terrorist War*. New York: John Wiley, 1998.
Singular, Stephen. *Talked to Death: The Life and Murder of Alan Berg*. New York: Beech Tree Books, 1987.

Central and Latin America

Ehrenfeld, Rachel. *Narco-Terrorism: How Governments Around the World Have Used the Drug Trade to Finance and Further Terrorist Activities*. New York: Basic Books, 1990.
Metz, Steven. *The Future of Insurgency*. Carlisle Barracks, PA: US Army War College, 1993.
Radu, Michael, and Vladimir Tismaneanu. *Latin American Revolutionaries: Groups, Goals, Methods*. Washington, DC: Pergamon-Brassey's International Defense Publishers, 1990.
Strong, Simon. *Shining Path: The World's Deadliest Revolutionary Force*. London: HarperCollins, 1992.
US Congress. Senate. Committee on the Judiciary. Subcommittee on Security and Terrorism. *The Role of Cuba in International Terrorism and Subversion: Hearings Before the Subcommittee on Security and Terrorism*. 97th Congress, 2nd session, 26 February and 4, 11, and 12 March 1982.

Europe

Alexander, Yonah, and Dennis Pluchinsky. *Europe's Red Terrorists: The Fighting*

Communist Organizations. London: Frank Cass, 1992.

Cigar, Norman. *Genocide in Bosnia: The Policy of 'Ethnic Cleansing'*. College Station, TX: Texas A & M University Press, 1995.

Coogan, Tim Pat. *The IRA, A History*. Niwot, CO: Roberts Rinehart Publishers, 1993.

Hasselbach, Ingo, with Tom Reiss. *Fuhrer-Ex: Memoirs of a Former Neo-Nazi*. New York: Random House, 1996.

Merkl, Peter H., and Leonard Weinberg. *The Revival of Right-Wing Extremism in the Nineties*. London: Frank Cass, 1997.

The Middle East

Ciment, James. *The Kurds: State and Minority in Turkey, Iraq and Iran*. New York: Facts On File, 1996.

Hussain, Asaf. *Political Terrorism and the State in the Middle East*. London: Mansell, 1988.

Miller, Judith. *God has Ninety-Nine Names: Reporting from a Militant Middle East*. New York: Simon & Schuster, 1996.

O'Ballance, Edgar. *Islamic Fundamentalist Terrorism, 1979–95: The Iranian Connection*. New York: New York University Press, 1997.

Seale, Patrick. *Abu Nidal: A Gun for Hire: The Secret Life of the World's Most Notorious Arab Terrorist*. New York: Random House, 1992.

Index

Fortran 90/95
Explained

Second Edition

MICHAEL METCALF

Formerly of the
Information Technology Division
CERN, Geneva, Switzerland

JOHN REID

JKR Associates, Oxfordshire

OXFORD
UNIVERSITY PRESS

OXFORD
UNIVERSITY PRESS

Great Clarendon Street, Oxford OX2 6DP

Oxford University Press is a department of the University of Oxford.
It furthers the University's objective of excellence in research, scholarship,
and education by publishing worldwide in

Oxford New York

Auckland Bangkok Buenos Aires Cape Town Chennai
Dar es Salaam Delhi Hong Kong Istanbul Karachi Kolkata
Kuala Lumpur Madrid Melbourne Mexico City Mumbai Nairobi
São Paulo Shanghai Taipei Tokyo Toronto

Oxford is a registered trade mark of Oxford University Press
in the UK and in certain other countries

Published in the United States
by Oxford University Press Inc., New York

First published 1996
Second edition 1999

Reprinted 2000 (with corrections), 2002 (with corrections) (twice), 2003

A Catalogue record for this title is available from the British Library

Library of Congress Cataloging in Publication Data
(Data available)
ISBN 0 19 850558 2

Printed in Great Britain
on acid-free paper by
CPI Bath

100365 9693

Preface

Fortran has always been the principal language used in the fields of scientific, numerical, and engineering programming, and a series of revisions to the standard defining successive versions of the language has progressively enhanced its power and kept it competitive with several generations of rivals.

Beginning in 1978, the technical committee responsible for the development of Fortran standards, X3J3 (now called J3), laboured to produce a new, much-needed modern version of the language, Fortran 90. Its purpose is to "promote portability, reliability, maintainability, and efficient execution... on a variety of computing systems". The standard was published in 1991, and work began in 1993 on a minor revision, known informally as Fortran 95. Now this revised standard is in use, it seems appropriate to prepare a definitive informal description of the language it defines. This continues the series of editions of this book – the two editions of *Fortran 8x Explained* that described the two drafts of the standard (1987 and 1989), and *Fortran 90 Explained* that described the Fortran 90 standard (1990).

The whole of Fortran 77 is contained in Fortran 90, but certain of its features are labelled 'obsolescent' in the standard, and their use is not recommended. The obsolescent features of Fortran 90 have replacements in Fortran 77 and some have been removed from the Fortran 95 standard. Other Fortran 77 features, with replacements in Fortran 90, are labelled obsolescent in Fortran 95. We have relegated the description of all these Fortran 77 features to Appendix C. They are falling into disuse and an understanding of them is required only when dealing with old programs.

In this book, an initial chapter sets out the background to the work on the new standards, and the ten following chapters describe Fortran 90/95 less the obsolescent features in a manner suitable both for grasping the implications of the new features, and for writing programs. Features that are available in Fortran 95 only are labelled as such. Where the word 'Fortran' is used, it means 'common to both Fortran 90 and 95'. Some knowledge of programming concepts, although not necessarily of Fortran 77, is assumed. In order to reduce the number of forward references and also to enable, as quickly as possible, useful programs to be written based on material already absorbed, the order of presentation does not always follow that of the standard. In particular, we have chosen to defer to the final chapter the description of features that are redundant in Fortran 90 and whose use we deprecate. It would impair the flow of the exposition if we were to describe them in the main body of the text. They may be encountered in old programs, but are not needed in new ones.

This edition differs from the first edition in that descriptions of Fortran 95 features are integrated into the body instead of being confined to a separate chapter. This book is thus suitable for the reader who wishes to learn only Fortran 95 as well as for one who wishes to learn just Fortran 90 or even both Fortran 90 and Fortran 95.

We have chosen to use lower-case letters instead of upper-case letters for all the Fortran keywords and names, since this is the preferred style of many Fortran programmers and there are very few processors still in use that support only upper case. Also, we have switched to a different typesetting system (now LaTeX). These two changes give the book a very different (and in our opinion, improved) look.

This edition also differs from the first edition in that we have added two new chapters, 12 and 13, on official extensions of Fortran 95. Each is specified by an ISO Technical Report and WG5 has promised that the features of both will be included in the next revision of the language, apart from correcting defects found in the field. We expect Fortran 95 compilers increasingly to offer these features as extensions.

In order to make the book a complete reference work, it concludes with six appendices. They contain, successively, a list of the intrinsic procedures, a summary of Fortran statements, a description of the obsolescent and deleted features, an extended example illustrating the use of pointers and recursion, a glossary of Fortran terms, and solutions to most of the exercises.

It must be remembered that although the obsolescent features appear in an appendix, they were nevertheless an integral part of the Fortran 90 language, and some remain part of Fortran 95. However, the appendix includes advice on how to avoid their use, thereby enhancing the upwards compatibility of programs with respect to possible future standards. The same is true for the features whose use we deprecate, and which are described in Chapter 11.

It is our hope that this book, by providing a complete description of Fortran 90 and Fortran 95, will continue the helpful role that earlier editions played for the Fortran 90 standard, and will serve as a long-term reference work for Fortran 95 into the next decade.

Acknowledgements

The development of the Fortran 90 standard was a long procedure involving several hundred people in many countries. The main burden fell on the principal members of X3J3 (now called J3), and especially on its then chairman, Jeanne Adams, and on the then Convenor of WG5, Jeanne Martin. The work continued for Fortran 95 with Jerry Wagener as chairman of X3J3. We extend our thanks to them and all our colleagues on X3J3 and elsewhere for their devotion to this important but thankless task, and for creating such a friendly working atmosphere. We will long remember the week-long meetings held over such an extended period, as well as the personal contacts we made and valued. We have taken great pains to ensure that this book is a true and accurate representation of the final documents produced by the committee, and clearly any omissions or other errors or misrepresentations are entirely our responsibility.

We gratefully acknowledge the actual and former management of CERN and Harwell, and especially P. Zanella and D.O. Williams of CERN and the late A.E. Taylor of Harwell, for encouraging us to undertake this work, and for providing the necessary resources for its realization. JKR is also indebted to the Rutherford Appleton Laboratory for its subsequent support.

Conventions used in this book

Fortran displayed text is set in typewriter font:

```
integer :: i, j
```

and a line consisting of a colon indicates omitted lines:

```
subroutine sort
   :
end subroutine sort
```

Informal BNF terms are in italics:

```
if (scalar-logical-expr) action-stmt
```

Square brackets indicate optional items:

```
end if [name]
```

and an ellipsis represents an arbitrary number of repeated items:

```
[case selector [name]
         block] ...
```

The italic letter *b* signifies a blank character.

Contents

1. Whither Fortran?

This book is concerned with the Fortran programming language (Fortran 90 and Fortran 95), setting out a reasonably concise description of the whole language. The form chosen for its presentation is that of a textbook intended for use in teaching or learning the language. Its description occupies Chapters 2 to 11, which are written in such a way that simple programs can already be coded after the first three of these chapters (on language elements, expressions and assignments, and control) have been read. Successively more complex programs can be written as the information in each subsequent chapter is absorbed. Chapter 5 describes the important concept of the module and the many aspects of procedures, Chapter 6 completes the description of the powerful array features, Chapter 7 considers the details of specifying data objects and derived types, and Chapter 8 details the intrinsic procedures. Chapters 9 and 10 cover the whole of the input/output features in a manner such that the reader can also approach this more difficult area feature by feature, but always with a useful subset already covered. Finally, Chapter 11 describes those features that are redundant in the language, and whose use we choose to deprecate. Here we emphasize that this deprecation represents our own opinion, and is completely unofficial. In a concluding section of each of Chapters 2 to 10, we summarize the differences from Fortran 77. Chapters 12 and 13 describe official extensions to Fortran 95 that we expect increasingly to be present in Fortran 95 compilers.

Fortran 95 is a minor revision of Fortran 90, so most of this book applies to both. Features of Fortran 95 that are not part of Fortran 90 are usually described in separate subsections, but sometimes we use separate paragraphs. Every example that is not applicable to Fortran 90 is labelled as such. Features of Fortran 90 that are not part of Fortran 95 are obsolescent in Fortan 90 and are described only in Appendix C.

This introductory chapter has the task of setting the scene for those that follow. The first section presents the Fortran language and its considerable evolution since it was first introduced over thirty years ago. The second continues with a justification for preparing the Fortran 90 standard, summarizes the important new features, and outlines how standards are developed; the third looks at the mechanism that has been proposed to permit the language to evolve. The fourth section considers the development of Fortran 95 and the fifth some related issues.

The sixth concludes by considering the requirements on programs and processors for conformance with the standard.

1.1   Fortran history

Programming in the early days of computing was tedious in the extreme. Programmers required a detailed knowledge of the instructions, registers, and other aspects of the central processing unit (CPU) of the computer for which they were writing code. The *source code* itself was written in a numerical notation, so-called *octal code*. In the course of time mnemonic codes were introduced, a form of coding known as *machine* or *assembly code*. These codes were translated into the instruction words by programs known as *assemblers*. In the 1950s it became increasingly apparent that this form of programming was highly inconvenient, although it did enable the CPU to be used in a very efficient way.

These difficulties spurred a team led by John Backus of IBM to develop one of the earliest high-level languages, Fortran. Their aim was to produce a language which would be simple to understand but almost as efficient in execution as assembly language. In this they succeeded beyond their wildest dreams. The language was indeed simple to learn, as it was possible to write mathematical formulae almost as they are usually written in mathematical texts. (In fact, the name Fortran is a contraction of Formula Translation.) This enabled working programs to be written faster than before, for only a small loss in efficiency, as a great deal of care was devoted to the construction of the compiler.

But Fortran was revolutionary as well as innovatory. Programmers were relieved of the tedious burden of using assembler language, and were able to concentrate more on the problem in hand. Perhaps more important, however, was the fact that computers became accessible to any scientist or engineer willing to devote a little effort to acquiring a working knowledge of Fortran; no longer was it necessary to be an expert on computers to be able to write application programs.

Fortran spread rapidly as it fulfilled a real need. Inevitably dialects of the language developed, which led to problems in exchanging programs between computers, and so, in 1966 the then American Standards Association (later the American National Standards Institute, ANSI) brought out the first ever standard for a programming language, now known as Fortran 66.

Fortran brought with it several other advances, apart from its ease of learning combined with a stress on efficient execution of code. It was, for instance, a language which remained close to, and exploited, the available hardware rather than being an abstract concept. It also brought with it the possibility for programmers to control storage allocation in a simple way, a feature which was very necessary in those early days of small memories, even if it is now regarded as being potentially dangerous.

The proliferation of dialects remained a problem after the publication of the 1966 standard. There was a widespread implementation in compilers of features which were essential for large-scale programs, but which were ignored by the standard. Different compilers implemented such facilities in different ways.

These difficulties were partially resolved by the publication of a new standard, in 1978, known as Fortran 77. It included several new features that were based on vendor extensions or pre-processors and it was, therefore, not simply a common subset of existing dialects. By the mid-1980s, the changeover to Fortran 77 was in full swing. It was a relatively simple matter to write new code under the new standard, and converting old standard-conforming code was usually easy as there is a large measure of compatibility between the two standards.

1.2   The drive for the Fortran 90 standard

After thirty years' existence, Fortran was far from being the only programming language available on most computers. In the course of time new languages had been developed, and where they were demonstrably more suitable for a particular type of application they had been adopted in preference to Fortran for that purpose. Fortran's superiority had always been in the area of numerical, scientific, engineering, and technical applications and, in order that it be brought properly up-to-date, the ANSI-accredited technical committee J3 (then known as X3J3) working as a development body for the ISO committee ISO/IEC JTC1/SC22/WG5 (which we abbreviate to WG5), once again prepared a new standard, formerly known as Fortran 8x and now as Fortran 90.

J3 itself is a body composed of representatives of computer hardware and software vendors, users, and academia. It is accredited to ANSI, the body that publishes final American standards, but reports directly to its parent committee, X3 (computer systems), which is responsible for actually adopting, or rejecting, the proposed draft standards presented to it. In these decisions, it tries to ensure that the proposals really do represent a consensus of those concerned. J3 acts as the development body for the corresponding international group, WG5, consisting of international experts responsible for recommending that a draft standard become an international standard. J3 maintains other close contacts with the international community by welcoming foreign members, including both the present authors over several years.

What were the justifications for continuing to revise the definition of the Fortran language? As well as standardizing vendor extensions, there was a need to modernize it in response to the developments in language design which had been exploited in other languages, such as APL, Algol 68, Pascal, Ada, C and C++. Here, J3 could draw on the obvious benefits of concepts like data hiding. In the same vein was the need to begin to provide an alternative to dangerous storage association, to abolish the rigidity of the outmoded source form, and to improve further on the regularity of the language, as well as to increase the safety of programming in the language and to tighten the conformance requirements. To preserve the vast investment in Fortran 77 codes, the whole of Fortran 77 was retained as a subset. However, unlike the previous standard, which resulted almost entirely from an effort to standardize *existing practices*, the Fortran 90 standard is much more a *development* of the language, introducing features which are new to Fortran, but are based on experience in other languages.

The main features of Fortran 90 are, first and foremost, the array language and abstract data types. The former is built on whole array operations and assignments, array sections, intrinsic procedures for arrays, and dynamic storage. It was designed with optimization in mind. The latter is built on modules and module procedures, derived data types, operator overloading and generic interfaces, together with pointers. Also important are the new facilities for numerical computation including a set of numeric inquiry functions, the parametrization of the intrinsic types, new control constructs – select case and new forms of do, internal and recursive procedures and optional and keyword arguments, improved I/O facilities, and many new intrinsic procedures. Last but not least are the new free source form, an improved style of attribute-oriented specifications, the implicit none statement, and a mechanism for identifying redundant features for subsequent removal from the language. The requirement on compilers to be able to identify, for example, syntax extensions, and to report why a program has been rejected, are also significant. The resulting language is not only a far more powerful tool than its predecessor, but a safer and more reliable one too. Storage association, with its attendant dangers, is not abolished, but rendered unnecessary. Indeed, experience shows that compilers detect errors far more frequently than before, resulting in a faster development cycle. The array syntax and recursion also allow quite compact code to be written, a further aid to safe programming.

1.3 Language evolution

The procedures under which J3 works require that a period of notice be given before any existing feature is removed from the language. This means, in practice, a minimum of one revision cycle, which for Fortran means about five years. The need to remove features is evident: if the only action of the committee is to add new features, the language will become grotesquely large, with many overlapping and redundant items. The solution finally adopted by J3 was to publish as an appendix to a standard a set of two lists showing which items have been removed or are candidates for eventual removal.

One list contains the *deleted features*, those that have been removed. Since Fortran 90 contains the whole of Fortran 77, this list is empty for Fortran 90 but is not for Fortran 95 (see Appendix C).

The second list contains the *obsolescent features*, those considered to be outmoded and redundant, and which are candidates for deletion in the next revision. The Fortran 90 and Fortran 95 obsolescent features are described in Appendix C.

1.4 Fortran 95

Following the publication of the Fortran 90 standard in 1991, two further significant developments concerning the Fortran language occurred. The first was the
continued operation of the two Fortran standards committees, J3 and WG5, and
the second the founding of the High Performance Fortran Forum (HPFF).

Early on in their deliberations, the standards committees decided on a strategy
whereby a minor revision of Fortran 90 would be prepared by the mid-1990s and a
further revision by about the year 2000. The first revision, Fortran 95, is a subject
of this book.

The HPFF was set up in an effort to define a set of extensions to Fortran, such
that it would be possible to write portable code when using parallel computers for
handling problems involving large sets of data that can be represented by regular
grids. This version of Fortran was to be known as High Performance Fortran
(HPF), and it was quickly decided, given the array features of Fortran 90, that
it, and not Fortran 77, should be its base language. The final form of HPF[1] is of
a superset of Fortran 90, the main extensions being in the form of directives that
take the form of Fortran 90 comment lines, and are thus recognized as directives
only by an HPF processor. However, it did become necessary also to add some
additional syntax, as not all the desired features could be accommodated in the
form of such directives.

The work of J3 and WG5 went on at the same time as that of HPFF, and the
bodies liaised closely. It was evident that, in order to avoid the development of
divergent dialects of Fortran, it would be desirable to include the new syntax defined by HPFF in Fortran 95 and, indeed, the HPF features are the most significant
new features that Fortran 95 introduces. The other changes consist mainly of what
are known as corrections, clarifications and interpretations. These came about as
it was quickly discovered, as Fortran 90 compilers were written and used, that
the text of the Fortran 90 standard contained a few errors that required correction,
some obscure wording that required further textual clarification, and ambiguous
statements that required interpretation. (J3 and WG5 processed about 200 requests for interpretation.)   All the resulting changes have been included in the
Fortran 95 standard and, where appropriate, they have been incorporated at the
relevant places in this book. Apart from the HPF syntax and the corrections, only
a small number of other pressing but minor language changes were made and these
too are described.

Fortran 95 is backwards compatible with Fortran 90, apart from a minor change
in the definition of `sign` (Section 8.3.2) and the deletion of some Fortran 77
features declared obsolete in Fortran 90 (as described in Appendix C). However,
there are two new intrinsic procedures, `null` and `cpu_time`, which might also be
names of external procedures in an existing Fortran 90 program.

---

[1]*The High Performance Fortran Handbook*, C. Koebel et al., MIT Press, Cambridge, MA, 1994.

The details of Fortran 95 were finalized in November 1995, and the new ISO standard, replacing Fortran 90, was adopted in 1997, following successful ballots, as ISO/IEC 1539-1 : 1997.

1.5   Beyond Fortran 95

About the time of the publication of Fortran 95, another interesting development occurred. This was the specification of two (similar) subset versions of Fortran 90 that retain its modern features while casting aside its outmoded ones. The present authors were involved in the development of one of these, known as F, and that language's description can be found in *"The F programming language"* (OUP, 1996). These subsets can be regarded as important vehicles for the teaching of a safe and reliable style of modern programming.

At the same time, a formal standard, ISO/IEC 1539-2 : 1994, was developed for varying length strings. It defines the interface and semantics for a module that provides facilities for the manipulation of character strings of arbitrary and dynamically variable length. An annex contains a possible implementation in Fortran 90, which demonstrates its feasibility, but the intention was that vendors provide equivalent features that execute more efficiently. Unfortunately, none has done so. At the time of writing, this standard is being revised to take advantage of the Fortran 95 enhancements. In particular, this will allow a better implementation within the standard language.

Further, in 1995, WG5 decided that these three features:

i) handling floating point exceptions,

ii) permitting allocatable arrays as structure components, dummy arguments, and function results, and

iii) interoperability with C,

were so urgently needed in Fortran that it established development bodies to develop 'Technical Reports of Type 2'. The intent was that the material of these technical reports be integrated into the next revision of the Fortran standard, apart from any defects found in the field. It is essentially a beta-test facility for a language feature. In the event, the first two have been completed and are the subjects of Chapters 12 and 13. Difficulties were encountered with the third, so the report mechanism has therefore been abandoned for interoperability with C, but the intent of inclusion in the next standard remains.

Another auxiliary standard, ISO/IEC 1539-3 : 1998, has been developed to meet the need of programmers to maintain several versions of code to allow for different systems and different applications. Keeping several copies of the source code is error prone. It is far better to maintain a master code from which any of the versions may be selected. This standard is for a very simple form of conditional compilation, which selects some of the Fortran lines from the source and omits the rest or converts them to comments. The process is controlled by 'coco lines' in the source that are also omitted or converted to comments. It is hoped that the facilities will be built into compilers, but they may also be implemented by a preprocessor.

The next full language revision is planned for 2004 and is already being referenced as Fortran 2000, and the main features have been chosen:

- handling floating-point exceptions, as in TR15580,

- permitting allocatable arrays as structure components, dummy arguments, and function results, as in TR15581,

- interoperability with C,

- parameterized data types,

- object-orientation: constructors/destructors, inheritance, and polymorphism,

- derived type I/O,

- asynchronous I/O,

- procedure variables, and

- various minor enhancements.

All this activity provides a means of ensuring that Fortran remains a powerful and well-honed tool for numerical and scientific applications for the next decade and beyond.

1.6   Conformance

The standard is almost exclusively concerned with the rules for programs rather than processors. A processor is required to accept a standard-conforming program and to interpret it according to the standard, subject to limits that the processor may impose on the size and complexity of the program. The processor is allowed to accept further syntax and to interpret relationships that are not specified in the standard, provided they do not conflict with the standard. Of course, the programmer must avoid such syntax extensions if portability is desired.

The interpretation of some of the standard syntax is *processor dependent*, that is, may vary from processor to processor. For example, the set of characters allowed in character strings is processor dependent. Care must be taken whenever a processor-dependent feature is used in case it leads to the program not being portable to a desired processor.

A drawback of the Fortran 77 standard was that it made no statement about requiring processors to provide a means to detect any departure from the allowed syntax by a program, as long as that departure did not conflict with the syntax rules defined by the standard. The new standards are written in a different style to the old one. The syntax rules are expressed in a form of BNF with associated

constraints, and the semantics are described by the text. This semi-formal style is
not used in this book, so an example is perhaps helpful:

R609	*substring*	**is**	*parent-string (substring-range)*
R610	*parent-string*	**is**	*scalar-variable-name*
		or	*array-element*
		or	*scalar-structure-component*
		or	*scalar-constant*
R611	*substring-range*	**is**	[*scalar-int-expr*] : [*scalar-int-expr*]

Constraint: *parent-string* must be of type character.

The first *scalar-int-expr* in *substring-range* is called the **starting
point** and the second one is called the **ending point**. The length
of a substring is the number of characters in the substring and is
$\text{MAX}(\ell - f + 1, 0)$, where f and ℓ are the starting and ending points,
respectively.

Here, the three production rules and the associated constraint for a character
substring are defined, and the meaning of the length of such a substring explained.

The standard is written in such a way that a processor, at compile-time, may
check that the program satisfies all the constraints. In particular, the processor
must provide a capability to detect and report the use of any

- obsolescent feature,

- additional syntax,

- kind type parameter (Section 2.5) that it does not support,

- non-standard source form or character,

- name that is inconsistent with the scoping rules, or

- non-standard intrinsic procedure.

Furthermore, it must be able to report the reason for rejecting a program. These
capabilities are of great value in producing correct and portable code. They were
not required for Fortran 77 programs.

2. Language elements

2.1 Introduction

Written prose in a natural language, such as an English text, is composed firstly of basic elements – the letters of the alphabet. These are combined into larger entities, words, which convey the basic concepts of objects, actions, and qualifications. The words of the language can be further combined into larger units, phrases and sentences, according to certain rules. One set of rules defines the grammar. This tells us whether a certain combination of words is correct in that it conforms to the *syntax* of the language, that is those acknowledged forms which are regarded as correct renderings of the meanings we wish to express. Sentences can in turn be joined together into paragraphs, which conventionally contain the composite meaning of their constituent sentences, each paragraph expressing a larger unit of information. In a novel, sequences of paragraphs become chapters and the chapters together form a book, which usually is a self-contained work, largely independent of all other books.

2.2 Fortran character set

Analogies to these concepts are found in a programming language. In Fortran (Fortran 90 and Fortran 95), the basic elements, or character set, are the 26 letters of the English alphabet, the 10 Arabic numerals, 0 to 9, the underscore, _, and the so-called special characters listed in Table 2.1. The standard does not require the support of lower-case letters, but almost all computers nowadays support them. Within the Fortran syntax, the lower-case letters are equivalent to the corresponding upper-case letters; they are distinguished only when they form part of character sequences. In this book, syntactically significant characters will always be written in lower case. The letters, numerals, and underscore are known as *alphanumeric* characters.

Except for the currency symbol, whose graphic may vary (for example, to be £ in the United Kingdom), the graphics are fixed, though their styles are not fixed. The special characters $ and ? have no specific meaning within the Fortran language.

In the course of this and the following chapters, we shall see how further analogies with natural language may be drawn. The unit of Fortran information

Table 2.1. The special characters of the Fortran language

Character	Name	Character	Name
=	Equals sign	:	Colon
+	Plus sign		Blank
–	Minus sign	!	Exclamation mark
*	Asterisk	"	Quotation mark
/	Slash	%	Percent
(	Left parenthesis	&	Ampersand
)	Right parenthesis	;	Semicolon
,	Comma	<	Less than
.	Decimal point	>	Greater than
$	Currency symbol	?	Question mark
'	Apostrophe		

is the *lexical token*, which corresponds to a word or punctuation mark. Adjacent tokens are usually separated by spaces or the end of a line, but sensible exceptions are allowed just as for a punctuation mark in prose. Sequences of tokens form *statements*, corresponding to sentences. Statements, like sentences, may be joined to form larger units like paragraphs. In Fortran these are known as *program units*, and out of these may be built a *program*. A program forms a complete set of instructions to a computer to carry out a defined sequence of operations. The simplest program may consist of only a few statements, but programs of more than 100,000 statements are now quite common.

2.3 Tokens

Within the context of Fortran, alphanumeric characters (the letters, the under-score, and the numerals) may be combined into sequences that have one or more meanings. For instance, one of the meanings of the sequence 999 is a constant in the mathematical sense. Similarly, the sequence date might represent, as one possible interpretation, a variable quantity to which we assign the calendar date.

The special characters are used to separate such sequences and also have various meanings. We shall see how the asterisk is used to specify the operation of multiplication, as in x*y, and has also a number of other interpretations.

Basic significant sequences of alphanumeric characters or of special characters are referred to as *tokens;* they are labels, keywords, names, constants (other than complex literal constants), operators (listed in Table 3.4, Section 3.8), and *separators*, which are

$$/ \quad (\quad) \quad (/ \quad /) \quad , \quad = \quad => \quad : \quad :: \quad ; \quad \%$$

For example, the expression x*y contains the three tokens x, *, and y.

Apart from within a character string or within a token, blanks may be used freely to improve the layout. Thus, whereas the variable date may not be written as d a t e, the sequence x * y is syntactically equivalent to x*y. In this context, multiple blanks are syntactically equivalent to a single blank.

A name, constant, or label must be separated from an adjacent keyword, name, constant or label by one or more blanks or by the end of a line. For instance, in

```
      real x
      read 10
   30 do k=1,3
```

the blanks are required after real, read, 30, and do. Likewise, adjacent keywords must normally be separated, but some pairs of keywords, such as else if, are not required to be separated. Similarly, some keywords may be split; for example inout may be written in out. We do not use these alternatives in the main text, but the exact rules are given in the statement summaries in Appendix B.

2.4   Source form

Fortran 90/95 brings with it a new source form, well adapted to use at a terminal.[1] The statements of which a source program is composed are written on *lines*. Each line may contain up to 132 characters,[2] and usually contains a single statement. Since leading spaces are not significant, it is possible to start all such statements in the first character position, or in any other position consistent with the user's chosen layout. A statement may thus be written as

```
   x = (-y + root_of_discriminant)/(2.0*a)
```

In order to be able to mingle suitable comments with the code to which they refer, Fortran allows any line to carry a trailing comment field, following an exclamation mark (!). An example is

```
   x = y/a - b    ! Solve the linear equation
```

Any comment always extends to the end of the source line and may include processor-dependent characters (it is not restricted to the Fortran character set, Section 2.2). Any line whose first non-blank character is an exclamation mark, or contains only blanks, or which is empty, is purely commentary, and is ignored by the compiler. Such comment lines may appear anywhere in a program unit, including ahead of the first statement (but not after the final program unit). A *character context* (those contexts defined in Sections 2.6.4, 9.13.4, and C.3.5) is allowed to contain !, so the ! does not initiate a comment in this case; in all other cases it does.

---

[1]Some hints on maintaining compatibility between the old and the new source forms are given at the end of Section C.1.1.

[2]Lines containing characters of non-default kind (Sections 2.6.4) are subject to a processor-dependent limit.

Since it is possible that a long statement might not be accommodated in the 132 positions allowed in a single line, up to 39 additional continuation lines are allowed. The so-called *continuation mark* is the ampersand (&) character, and this is appended to each line that is followed by a continuation line. Thus, the first statement of this section (considerably spaced out) could be written as

```
x =                                                    &
   (-y + root_of_discriminant)                         &
   /(2.0*a)
```

In this book, the ampersands will normally be aligned to improve readability. On a non-comment line, if & is the last non-blank character or the last non-blank character ahead of the comment symbol !, the statement continues from the character immediately preceding the &. Normally, continuation is to the first character of the next non-comment line, but if the first non-blank character of the next non-comment line is &, continuation is to the character following the &. For instance, the above statement may be written

```
x =                                                    &
   &(-y + root_of_discriminant)/(2.0*a)
```

In particular, if a token cannot be contained at the end of a line, the first non-blank character on the next noncomment line must be an & followed immediately by the remainder of the token.

Comments are allowed to contain any characters, including &, so they cannot be continued since a trailing & is taken as part of the comment. However, comment lines may be freely interspersed among continuation lines and do not count towards the limit of 39 lines.

In a character context, continuation must be from a line without a trailing comment and to a line with a leading ampersand. This is because both ! and & are permitted both in character contexts and in comments.

No line is permitted to have & as its only non-blank character, or as its only non-blank character ahead of !. Such a line is really a comment and becomes a comment if & is removed.

When writing short statements one after the other, it can be convenient to write several of them on one line. The semi-colon (;) character is used as a *statement separator* in these circumstances, for example:

```
a = 0; b = 0; c = 0
```

Since commentary always extends to the end of the line, it is not possible to insert commentary between statements on a single line. In principle, it is possible to write even long statements one after the other in a solid block of lines, each 132 characters long and with the appropriate semi-colons separating the individual statements. In practice, such code is unreadable, and the use of multiple-statement lines should be reserved for trivial cases such as the one shown in this example.

Any Fortran statement (that is not part of a compound statement) may be labelled, in order to be able to identify it. For some statements a label is mandatory.

A statement *label* precedes the statement, and is regarded as a token. The label consists of from one to five digits, one of which must be nonzero. An example of a labelled statement is

```
100 continue
```

Leading zeros are not significant in distinguishing between labels. For example, 10 and 010 are equivalent.

2.5 Concept of type

In Fortran, it is possible to define and manipulate various types of data. For instance, we may have available the value 10 in a program, and assign that value to an integer scalar variable denoted by i. Both 10 and i are of type integer; 10 is a fixed or *constant* value, whereas i is a *variable* which may be assigned other values. Integer expressions, such as i+10, are available too.

A *data type* consists of a set of data values, a means of denoting those values, and a set of operations that are allowed on them. For the integer data type, the values are ..., −3, −2, −1, 0, 1, 2, 3, ... between some limits depending on the kind of integer and computer system being used. Such tokens as these are *literal constants*, and each data type has its own form for expressing them. Named scalar variables, such as i, may be established. During the execution of a program, the value of i may change to any valid value, or may become *undefined*, that is have no predictable value. The operations which may be performed on integers are those of usual arithmetic; we can write 1+10 or i-3 and obtain the expected results. Named constants may be established too; these have values that do not change during a given execution of the program.

Properties like those just mentioned are associated with all the data types of Fortran, and will be described in detail in this and the following chapters. The language itself contains five data types whose existence may always be assumed. These are known as the *intrinsic data types*, whose literal constants form the subject of the next section. Of each intrinsic type there is a default kind and a processor-dependent number of other kinds. Each kind is associated with a non-negative integer value known as the *kind type parameter*. This is used as a means of identifying and distinguishing the various kinds available.

In addition, it is possible to define other data types based on collections of data of the intrinsic types, and these are known as *derived data types*. The ability to define data types of interest to the programmer – matrices, geometrical shapes, lists, interval numbers – is a powerful feature of the language, one which permits a high level of *data abstraction*, that is the ability to define and manipulate data objects without being concerned about their actual representation in a computer.

2.6 Literal constants of intrinsic type

The intrinsic data types are divided into two classes. The first class contains three *numeric* types which are used mainly for numerical calculations – integer, real, and complex. The second class contains the two *non-numeric* types which are used for such applications as text-processing and control – character and logical. The numerical types are used in conjunction with the usual operators of arithmetic, such as + and -, which will be described in Chapter 3. Each includes a zero and the value of a signed zero is the same as that of an unsigned zero[3]. The non-numeric types are used with sets of operators specific to each type; for instance, character data may be concatenated. These too will be described in Chapter 3.

2.6.1   Integer literal constants

The first type of literal constant is the *integer literal constant*. The default kind is simply a signed or unsigned integer value, for example

```
1
0
-999
32767
+10
```

The *range* of the default integers is not specified in the language, but on a computer with a word size of n bits, is often from -2^{n-1} to $+2^{n-1} - 1$. Thus on a 32-bit computer the range is often from -2147483648 to $+2147483647$.

To be sure that the range will be adequate on any computer requires the specification of the kind of integer by giving a value for the kind type parameter. This is best done through a named integer constant. For example, if the range -999999 to 999999 is desired, k6 may be established as a constant with an appropriate value by the statement, fully explained later,

```
integer, parameter :: k6=selected_int_kind(6)
```

and used in constants thus:

```
-123456_k6
+1_k6
-2_k6
```

Here, selected_int_kind(6) is an intrinsic inquiry function call, and it returns a kind parameter value that yields the range -999999 to 999999 with the least margin (see Section 8.7.4).

On a given processor, it might be known that the kind value needed is 3. In this case, the first of our constants can be written

```
-123456_3
```

---

[3]Although the representation of data is processor dependent, for the numeric data types the standard defines model representations and means to inquire about the properties of those models. The details are deferred to Section 8.7.

but this form is less portable. If we move the code to another processor, this particular value may be unsupported, or might correspond to a different range.

Many implementations use kind values that indicate the number of bytes of storage occupied by a value, but the standard allows greater flexibility. For example, a processor might have hardware only for 4-byte integers, and yet support kind values 1, 2, and 4 with this hardware (to ease portability from processors that have hardware for 1-, 2-, and 4-byte integers). However, the standard makes no statement about kind values or their order, except that the kind value is never negative.

The value of the kind type parameter for a given data type on a given processor can be obtained from the `kind` intrinsic function (Section 8.2):

```
kind(1)        for the default value
kind(2_k6)     for the example
```

and the decimal exponent range (number of decimal digits supported) of a given entity may be obtained from another function (Section 8.7.2), as in

```
range(2_k6)
```

which in this case would return a value of at least 6.

In addition to the usual integers of the decimal number system, for some applications it is very convenient to be able to represent positive whole numbers in binary, octal, or hexadecimal form. Unsigned constants of these forms exist in Fortran, and are represented as illustrated in these examples:

```
binary (base 2):        b'01100110'
octal (base 8):         o'076543'
hexadecimal (base 16):  z'10fa'
```

In the hexadecimal form, the letters a to f represent the values beyond 9; they may be used also in upper case. The delimiters may be quotation marks or apostrophes. The use of these forms of constants is limited to their appearance as implicit integers in the `data` statement (Section 7.5.2). A binary, octal, or hexadecimal constant may also appear in an internal or external file as a digit string, without the leading letter and the delimiters (see Section 9.13.2).

Bits stored as an integer representation may be manipulated by the intrinsic procedures described in Section 8.8.

2.6.2   Real literal constants

The second type of literal constant is the *real literal constant*. The default kind is a floating-point form built of some or all of: a signed or unsigned integer part, a decimal point, a fractional part, and a signed or unsigned exponent part. One or both of the integer part and fractional part must be present. The exponent part is either absent or consists of the letter e followed by a signed or unsigned integer. One or both of the decimal point and the exponent part must be present. An example is

```
-10.6e-11
```

meaning -10.6×10^{-11}, and other legal forms are

```
1.
-0.1
1e-1
3.141592653
```

The default real literal constants are representations of a subset of the real numbers of mathematics, and the standard specifies neither the allowed range of the exponent nor the number of significant digits represented by the processor. Many processors conform to the IEEE standard for floating-point arithmetic and have values of 10^{-37} to 10^{+37} for the range, and a precision of six decimal digits.

To be sure to obtain a desired range and significance requires the specification of a kind parameter value. For example,

```
integer, parameter :: long = selected_real_kind(9, 99)
```

ensures that the constants

```
1.7_long
12.3456789e30_long
```

have a precision of at least nine significant decimals, and an exponent range of at least 10^{-99} to 10^{+99}. The number of digits specified in the significand has no effect on the kind. In particular, it is permitted to write more digits than the processor can in fact use.

As for integers, many implementations use kind values that indicate the number of bytes of storage occupied by a value, but the standard allows greater flexibility. It specifies only that the kind value is never negative. If the desired kind value is known it may be used directly, as in the case

```
1.7_4
```

but the resulting code is then less portable.

The processor must provide at least one representation with more precision than the default, and this second representation may also be specified as `double precision`. We defer the description of this alternative but outmoded syntax to Section 11.4.1.

The `kind` function is valid also for real values:

```
kind(1.0)        for the default value
kind(1.0_long)   for the example
```

In addition, there are two inquiry functions available which return the actual precision and range, respectively, of a given real·entity (see Section 8.7.2). Thus, the value of

```
precision(1.7_long)
```

would be at least 9, and the value of

    `range(1.7_long)`

would be at least 99.

2.6.3   Complex literal constants

Fortran, as a language intended for scientific and engineering calculations, has the advantage of having as third literal constant type the *complex literal constant*. This is designated by a pair of literal constants, which are either integer or real, separated by a comma and enclosed in parentheses. Examples are

    `(1., 3.2)`
    `(1, .99e-2)`
    `(1.0, 3.7_8)`

where the first constant of each pair is the real part of the complex number, and the second constant is the imaginary part. If one of the parts is integer, the kind of the complex constant is that of the other part. If both parts are integer, the kind of the constant is that of the default real type. If both parts are real and of the same kind, this is the kind of the constant. If both parts are real and of different kinds, the kind of the constant is that of one of the parts: the part with the greater decimal precision, or the part chosen by the processor if the decimal precisions are identical.

A default complex constant is one whose kind value is that of default real.

The `kind`, `precision`, and `range` functions are equally valid for complex entities.

Note that if an implementation uses the number of bytes needed to store a real as its kind value, the number of bytes needed to store a complex value of the corresponding kind is twice the kind value. For example, if the default real type has kind 4 and needs four bytes of storage, the default complex type has kind 4 but needs eight bytes of storage.

2.6.4   Character literal constants

The fourth type of literal constant is the *character literal constant*. The default kind consists of a string of characters enclosed in a pair of either apostrophes or quotation marks, for example

    `'Anything goes'`

    `"Nuts & bolts"`

The characters are not restricted to the Fortran set (Section 2.2). Any graphic character supported by the processor is permitted, but not control characters such as "newline". The apostrophes and quotation marks serve as *delimiters,* and are not part of the value of the constant. The value of the constant

```
'STRING'
```

is STRING. We note that in character constants the blank character is significant. For example

```
'a string'
```

is not the same as

```
'astring'
```

A problem arises with the representation of an apostrophe or a quotation mark in a character constant. Delimiter characters of one sort may be embedded in a string delimited by the other, as in the examples

```
'He said "Hello"'
"This contains an ' "
```

Alternatively, a doubled delimiter without any embedded intervening blanks is regarded as a single character of the constant. For example

```
'Isn''t it a nice day'
```

has the value Isn't it a nice day.

The number of characters in a string is called its *length,* and may be zero. For instance, ' ' and "" are character constants of length zero.

We mention here the particular rule for the source form concerning character constants that are written on more than one line (needed because constants may include the characters ! and &): not only must each line that is continued be without a trailing comment, but each continuation line must *begin* with a continuation mark. Any blanks following a trailing ampersand or preceding a leading ampersand are not part of the constant, nor are the ampersands themselves part of the constant. Everything else, including blanks, is part of the constant. An example is

```
long_string =                                                    &
          'Were I with her, the night would post too soon;       &
        & But now are minutes added to the hours;                &
        & To spite me now, each minute seems a moon;             &
        & Yet not for me, shine sun to succour flowers!          &
        &    Pack night, peep day; good day, of night now borrow: &
        &    Short, night, to-night, and length thyself tomorrow.'
```

On any computer, the characters have a property known as their *collating sequence.* One may ask the question whether one character occurs before or after another in the sequence. This question is posed in a natural form such as 'Does C precede M?', and we shall see later how this may be expressed in Fortran terms. Fortran requires the computer's collating sequence to satisfy the following conditions:

- A is less than B is less than C . . . is less than Y is less than Z;

- 0 is less than 1 is less than 2 . . . is less than 8 is less than 9;

- blank is less than A and Z is less than 0, or blank is less than 0 and 9 is less than A;

and, if the lower-case letters are available,

- a is less than b is less than c . . . is less than y is less than z;

- blank is less than a and z is less than 0, or blank is less than 0 and 9 is less than a.

Thus we see that there is no rule about whether the numerals precede or succeed the letters, nor about the position of any of the special characters or the underscore, apart from the rule that blank precedes both partial sequences. Any given computer system has a complete collating sequence, and most computers nowadays use the collating sequence of the ASCII standard (also known as ISO/IEC 646:1991). However, Fortran is designed to accommodate other sequences, notably EBCDIC, so for portability, no program should ever depend on any ordering beyond that stated above. Alternatively, Fortran provides access to the ASCII collating sequence on any computer through intrinsic functions (Section 8.5.1), but this access is not so convenient and is less efficient on some computers.

A processor is required to provide access to the default kind of character constant just described. In addition, it may support other kinds of character constants, in particular those of non-European languages, which may have more characters than can be provided in a single byte. For example, a processor might support Kanji with the kind parameter value 2; in this case, a Kanji character constant may be written

        2_'国内'
or
        kanji_"標準"

where kanji is an integer named constant with the value 2. We note that, in this case, the kind type parameter exceptionally *precedes* the constant. This is necessary in order to enable compilers to parse statements simply.

There is no requirement on a processor to provide more than one kind of character, and the standard does not require any particular relationship between the kind parameter values and the character sets and the number of bytes needed to represent them. In fact, all that is required is that each kind of character set includes a blank character. As for the other data types, the kind function gives the actual value of the kind type parameter, as in

        kind('ASCII')

Non-default characters are permitted in comments.

2.6.5 Logical literal constants

The fifth type of literal constant is the *logical literal constant.* The default kind has one of two values, `.true.` and `.false.`. These logical constants are normally used only to initialize logical variables to their required values, as we shall see in Section 3.6.

The default kind has a kind parameter value which is processor dependent. The actual value is available as `kind(.true.)`. As for the other intrinsic types, the kind parameter may be specified by an integer constant following an underscore, as in

```
.false._1
.true._long
```

Non-default logical kinds are useful for storing logical arrays compactly; we defer further discussion until Section 6.17.

2.7 Names

A Fortran program references many different entities by name. Such names must consist of between 1 and 31 alphanumeric characters (letters, underscores, and numerals) of which the first must be a letter. There are no other restrictions on the names; in particular there are no reserved words in Fortran. We thus see that valid names are, for example,

```
a
a_thing
x1
mass
q123
real
time_of_flight
```

and invalid names are

```
1a          First character is not alphabetic
a thing     Contains a blank
$sign       Contains a non-alphanumeric character
```

Within the constraints of the syntax, it is important for program clarity to choose names that have a clear significance – these are known as *mnemonic names.* Examples are `day`, `month`, and `year`, for variables to store the calendar date.

The use of names to refer to constants, already met in Section 2.6.1, will be fully described in Section 7.4.

2.8   Scalar variables of intrinsic type

We have seen in the section on literal constants that there exist five different intrinsic data types. Each of these types may have variables too. The simplest way by which a variable may be declared to be of a particular type is by specifying its name in a *type declaration statement* such as

```
integer   :: i
real      :: a
complex   :: current
logical   :: pravda
character :: letter
```

Here all the variables have default kind, and letter has default length, which is 1. Explicit requirements may also be specified through *type parameters*, as in the examples

```
integer(kind=4)            :: i
real(kind=long)            :: a
character(len=20, kind=1)  :: english_word
character(len=20, kind=kanji) :: kanji_word
```

Character is the only type to have two parameters, and here the two character variables each have length 20. Where appropriate, just one of the parameters may be specified, leaving the other to take its default value, as in the cases

```
character(kind=kanji) :: kanji_letter
character(len=20)     :: english_word
```

The shorter forms

```
integer(4)         :: i
real(long)         :: a
character(20, 1)   :: english_word
character(20, kanji) :: kanji_word
character(20)      :: english_word
```

are available, but note that

```
character(kanji) :: kanji_letter          ! Beware
```

is not an abbreviation for

```
character(kind=kanji) :: kanji_letter
```

because a single unnamed parameter is taken as the length parameter.

2.9   Derived data types

When programming, it is often useful to be able to manipulate objects that are more sophisticated than those of the intrinsic types. Imagine, for instance, that we wished to specify objects representing persons. Each person in our application is distinguished by a name, an age, and an identification number. Fortran allows us to define a corresponding data type in the following fashion:

```
type person
   character(len=10) :: name
   real              :: age
   integer           :: id
end type person
```

This is the *definition* of the type. A scalar object of such a type is called a *structure*. In order to create a structure of that type, we write an appropriate type declaration statement, such as

```
type(person) :: you
```

The scalar variable you is then a composite object of type person containing three separate components, one corresponding to the name, another to the age, and a third to the identification number. As will be described in Sections 3.8 and 3.9, a variable such as you may appear in expressions and assignments involving other variables or constants of the same or different types. In addition, each of the components of the variable may be referenced individually using the *component selector* character percent (%). The identification number of you would, for instance, be accessed as

```
you%id
```

and this quantity is an integer variable which could appear in an expression such as

```
you%id + 9
```

Similarly, if there were a second object of the same type:

```
type(person) :: me
```

the differences in ages could be established by writing

```
you%age - me%age
```

It will be shown in Section 3.8 how a meaning can be given to an expression such as

```
you - me
```

Just as the intrinsic data types have associated literal constants, so too may literal constants of derived type be specified. Their form is the name of the type followed by the constant values of the components, in order and enclosed in parentheses. Thus, the constant

```
person( 'Smith', 23.5, 2541)
```

may be written assuming the derived type defined at the beginning of this section, and could be *assigned* to a variable of the same type:

```
you = person( 'Smith', 23.5, 2541)
```

Any such *structure constructor* can appear only after the definition of the type.

A derived type may have a component that is of a previously defined derived type. This is illustrated in Figure 2.1. A variable of type triangle may be declared thus

```
type(triangle) :: t
```

and t has components t%a, t%b, and t%c all of type point, and t%a has components t%a%x and t%a%y of type real.

Figure 2.1

```
type point
   real :: x, y
end type point
type triangle
   type(point) :: a, b, c
end type triangle
```

2.10 Arrays of intrinsic type

Another compound object supported by Fortran is the *array*. An array consists of a rectangular set of elements, all of the same type and type parameters. There are a number of ways in which arrays may be declared; for the moment we shall consider only the declaration of arrays of fixed sizes. To declare an array named a of 10 real elements, we add the dimension attribute to the type declaration statement thus:

```
real, dimension(10) :: a
```

The successive elements of the array are a(1), a(2), a(3), ..., a(10). The number of elements of an array is called its *size*. Each array element is a scalar.

Many problems require a more elaborate declaration than one in which the first element is designated 1, and it is possible in Fortran to declare a lower as well as an upper *bound*:

```
real, dimension(-10:5) :: vector
```

This is a vector of 16 elements, vector(-10), vector(-9), ..., vector(5). We thus see that whereas we always need to specify the upper bound, the lower bound is optional, and by default has the value 1.

An array may extend in more than one dimension, and Fortran allows up to seven dimensions to be specified. For instance

```
real, dimension(5,4) :: b
```

declares an array with two dimensions, and

```
real, dimension(-10:5, -20:-1, 0:1, -1:0, 2, 2, 2) :: grid
```

declares seven dimensions, the first four with explicit lower bounds. It may be seen that the size of this second array is

$$16 \times 20 \times 2 \times 2 \times 2 \times 2 \times 2 = 10240,$$

and that arrays of many dimensions can thus place large demands on the memory of a computer. The number of dimensions of an array is known as its *rank*. Thus, grid has a rank of seven. Scalars are regarded as having rank zero. The number of elements along a dimension of an array is known as the *extent* in that dimension. Thus, grid has extents 16, 20, ...

The sequence of extents is known as the *shape*. For example, grid has the shape (16, 20, 2, 2, 2, 2, 2).

A derived type may contain an array component. For example, the following type

```
type triplet
    real                :: u
    real, dimension(3)  :: du
    real, dimension(3,3) :: d2u
end type triplet
```

might be used to hold the value of a variable in three dimensions and the values of its first and second derivatives. If t is of type triplet, t%du and t%d2u are arrays of type real.

Some statements treat the elements of an array one-by-one in a special order which we call the *array element order*. It is obtained by counting most rapidly in the early dimensions. Thus, the elements of grid in array element order are

```
grid(-10, -20, 0, -1, 1, 1, 1)
grid( -9, -20, 0, -1, 1, 1, 1)
      :
grid(  5,  -1, 1,  0, 2, 2, 2).
```

This is illustrated for an array of two dimensions in Figure 2.2. Most implementations actually store arrays in contiguous storage in array element order, but we emphasize that the standard does not require this.

We reference an individual element of an array by specifying, as in the examples above, its *subscript* values. In the examples we used integer constants, but in general each subscript may be formed of a *scalar integer expression,* that is, any arithmetic expression whose value is scalar and of type integer. Each subscript must be within the corresponding ranges defined in the array declaration and the number of subscripts must equal the rank. Examples are

---

Figure 2.2 The ordering of elements in the array b(5,4).

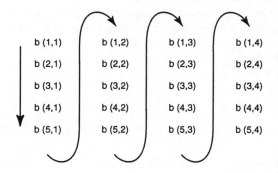

```
a(1)
a(i*j)              ! i and j are of type integer
a(nint(x+3.))       ! x is of type real
t%d2u(i+1,j+2)      ! t is of derived type triplet
```

where nint is an intrinsic function to convert a real value to the nearest integer (see Section 8.3.1). In addition subarrays, called *sections*, may be referenced by specifying a range for one or more subscripts. The following are examples of array sections:

```
a(i:j)              ! Rank-one array of size j-i+1
b(k, 1:n)           ! Rank-one array of size n
c(1:i, 1:j, k)      ! Rank-two array with extents i and j
```

We describe array sections in more detail in Section 6.13. An array section is itself an array, but its individual elements must not be accessed through the section designator. Thus, b(k, 1:n)(1) cannot be written; it must be expressed as b(k, 1).

A further form of subscript is shown in

```
a(ipoint)           ! ipoint is an integer array
```

where ipoint is an array of indices, pointing to array elements. It may thus be seen that a(ipoint), which identifies as many elements of a as ipoint has elements, is an example of another *array-valued object*, and ipoint is referred to as a *vector subscript*. This will be met in greater detail in Section 6.13.

It is often convenient to be able to define an array constant. In Fortran, a rank-one array may be constructed as a list of elements enclosed between the tokens (/ and /). A simple example is

```
(/ 1, 2, 3, 5, 10 /)
```

which is an array of rank one and size five. To obtain a series of values, the individual values may be defined by an expression that depends on an integer variable having values in a range, with an optional stride. Thus, the constructor

```
(/1, 2, 3, 4, 5/)
```

can be written as

```
(/ (i, i = 1,5) /)
```

and

```
(/2, 4, 6, 8/)
```

as

```
(/ (i, i = 2,8,2) /)
```

and

```
(/ 1.1, 1.2, 1.3, 1.4, 1.5 /)
```

as

```
(/ (i*0.1, i=11,15) /)
```

An array constant of rank greater than one may be constructed by using the function reshape (see Section 8.13.3) to reshape a rank-one array constant.

A full description of array constructors is reserved for Section 6.16.

2.11   Character substrings

It is possible to build arrays of characters, just as it is possible to build arrays of any other type:

```
character, dimension(80) :: line
```

declares an array, called line, of 80 elements, each one character in length. Each character may be addressed by the usual reference, line(i) for example. In this case, however, a more appropriate declaration might be

```
character(len=80) :: line
```

which declares a scalar data object of 80 characters. These may be referenced individually or in groups using a *substring* notation

```
line(i:j)   ! i and j are of type integer
```

which references all the characters from i to j in line. The colon is used to separate the two substring subscripts, which may be any scalar integer expressions. The colon is obligatory in substring references, so that referencing a single character requires line(i:i). There are default values for the substring subscripts. If the lower one is omitted, the value 1 is assumed; if the upper one is omitted, a value corresponding to the character length is assumed. Thus,

```
line(:i)    is equivalent to line(1:i)
line(i:)    is equivalent to line(i:80)
line(:)     is equivalent to line or line(1:80)
```

If i is greater than j in line(i:j), the value is a zero-sized string.

We may now combine the length declaration with the array declaration to build arrays of character objects of specified length, as in

```
character(len=80), dimension(60) :: page
```

which might be used to define storage for the characters of a whole page, with 60 elements of an array, each of length 80. To reference the line j on a page we may write page(j), and to reference character i on that line we could combine the array subscript and character substring notations into

```
page(j)(i:i)
```

A substring of a character constant or of a structure component may also be formed:

```
'ABCDEFGHIJKLMNOPQRSTUVWXYZ'(j:j)
you%name(1:2)
```

At this point we must note a limitation associated with character variables, namely that character variables must have a declared maximum length, making it impossible to manipulate character variables of variable length, unless they are defined appropriately as of a derived data type.[4] Nevertheless, this data type is adequate for most character manipulation applications.

2.12 Objects and subobjects

We have seen that derived types may have components that are arrays, as in

```
type triplet
   real, dimension(3) :: vertex
end type triplet
```

and arrays may be of derived type as in the example

```
type(triplet), dimension(10) :: t
```

---

[4]But see Section 1.5.

A single structure (for example, t(2)) is always regarded as a scalar, but it may
have a component (for example, t(2)%vertex) that is an array. Derived types may
have components of other derived types.

An object referenced by an unqualified name (up to 31 alphanumeric characters) is called a *named object* and is not part of a bigger object. Its subobjects have
designators that consist of the name of the object followed by one or more quali-
fiers (for example, t(1:7) and t(1)%vertex). Each successive qualifier specifies
a part of the object specified by the name or designator that precedes it.

Because of these possibilities, the terms *array* and *variable* are now used with a
more general meaning than in Fortran 77. The term 'array' is used for any object
that is not scalar, including an array section or an array-valued component of a
structure. The term 'variable' is used for any named object that is not specified to
be a constant and for any part of such an object, including array elements, array
sections, structure components, and substrings.

2.13   Pointers

In everyday language, nouns are often used in a way that makes their meaning
precise only because of the context. 'The chairman said that ...' will be understood precisely by the reader who knows that the context is the Fortran Committee
developing Fortran 90 and that its chairman was then Jeanne Adams.

Similarly, in a computer program it can be very useful to be able to use a name
that can be made to refer to different objects during execution of the program.
One example is the multiplication of a vector by a sequence of square matrices.
We might write code that calculates

$$y_i = \sum_{j=1}^{n} a_{ij} x_j, \quad i = 1, 2, \ldots, n$$

from the vector x_j, $j = 1, 2, \ldots, n$. In order to use this to calculate

$$BCz$$

we might first make x refer to z and A refer to C, thereby using our code to
calculate $y = Cz$, then make x refer to y and A refer to B so that our code
calculates the result vector we finally want.

An object that can be made to refer to other objects in this way is called a
pointer, and must be declared with the pointer attribute, for example

```
real, pointer                :: son
real, pointer, dimension(:)  :: x, y
real, pointer, dimension(:,:) :: a
```

In the case of an array, only the rank (number of dimensions) is declared, and
the bounds (and hence shape) are taken from that of the object to which it points.
Given such a declaration, the compiler arranges storage for a descriptor that will

later hold the address of the actual object (known as the *target*) and holds, if it is an array, its bounds and strides.

Besides pointing to existing variables, a pointer may be made explicitly to point at nothing:

```
nullify (son, x, y, a)    ! Further details are in Section 6.5.4
```

or may be given fresh storage by an allocate statement such as

```
allocate (son, x(10), y(-10:10), a(n, n))
```

In the case of arrays, the lower and upper bounds are specified just as for the dimension attribute (Section 2.10) except that any scalar integer expression is permitted. Permitting such expressions remedies one of the major deficiencies of Fortran 77, namely that areas of only static storage may be defined, and we will discuss this use further in Section 6.5.

In Fortran 90, pointers are initially undefined (see also Section 3.3). This is a very undesirable state since there is no way to test for it. In Fortran 95, it may be avoided by using the declaration:

```
real, pointer :: son => null()    ! Fortran 95 only
```

and we recommend that this always be employed. In Fortran 90, we recommend that pointers be defined as soon as they come into scope by execution of a nullify statement or a pointer assignment.

Components of derived types are permitted to have the pointer attribute. This enables a major application of pointers: the construction of linked lists. As a simple example, we might decide to hold a sparse vector as a chain of variables of the type shown in Figure 2.3, which allows us to access the entries one by one; given

```
type(entry), pointer :: chain
```

where chain is a scalar of this type and holds a chain that is of length two, its entries are chain%index and chain%next%index, and chain%next%next will have been nullified. Additional entries may be created when necessary by an appropriate allocate statement. We defer the details to Section 3.12.

Figure 2.3

```
    type entry
        real                  :: value
        integer               :: index
        type(entry), pointer  :: next
    end type entry
```

A subobject is not a pointer unless it has a final component selector for the name of a pointer component, for example, chain%next.

Pointers will be discussed in detail in later Chapters (especially Sections 3.12, 5.7.1, 6.14, 6.15, 7.5.3, 7.5.4, and 8.2) and a major application is given in Appendix D.

2.14   Summary

In this chapter, we have introduced the elements of the Fortran language. The character set has been listed, and the manner in which sequences of characters form literal constants and names explained. In this context, we have encountered the five intrinsic data types defined in Fortran, and seen how each data type has corresponding literal constants and named objects. We have seen how derived types may be constructed from the intrinsic types. We have introduced one method by which arrays may be declared, and seen how their elements may be referenced by subscript expressions. The concepts of the array section, character substring, and pointer have been presented, and some important terms defined. In the following chapter we shall see how these elements may be combined into expressions and statements, Fortran's equivalents of 'phrases' and 'sentences'.

With respect to Fortran 77, there are many changes in this area: the larger character set; a new source form; the significance of blanks; the parameterization of the intrinsic types; the binary, octal, and hexadecimal constants; the ability to obtain a desired precision and range; quotes as well as apostrophes as character constant delimiters; longer names; derived data types; new array subscript notations; array constructors; and last, but not least, pointers. Together they represent a substantial improvement in the ease of use and power of the language.

2.15   Exercises

1. For each of the following assertions, state whether it is true, false or not determined, according to the Fortran collating sequences:

```
b is less than m
8 is less than 2
* is greater than T
$ is less than /
blank is greater than A
blank is less than 6
```

2. Which of the Fortran lines in Figure 2.4 are correctly written according to the requirements of the Fortran source form? Which ones contain commentary? Which lines are initial lines and which are continuation lines?

3. Classify the following literal constants according to the five intrinsic data types of Fortran. Which are not legal literal constants?

Figure 2.4

```
    x = y
 3  a = b+c ! add
    word = 'string'
    a = 1.0; b = 2.0
    a = 15. ! initialize a; b = 22. ! and b
    song = "Life is just&
       & a bowl of cherries"
    chide = 'Waste not,
       want not!'
 0  c(3:4) = 'up"
```

```
-43                'word'
4.39               1.9-4
0.0001e+20         'stuff & nonsense'
4 9                (0.,1.)
(1.e3,2)           'I can''t'
'(4.3e9, 6.2)'     .true._1
e5                 'shouldn' 't'
1_2                "O.K."
z10                z'10'
```

4. Which of the following names are legal Fortran names?

```
name        name32
quotient    123
a182c3      no-go
stop!       burn_
no_go       long__name
```

5. What are the first, tenth, eleventh and last elements of the following arrays?

```
real, dimension(11)       :: a
real, dimension(0:11)     :: b
real, dimension(-11:0)    :: c
real, dimension(10,10)    :: d
real, dimension(5,9)      :: e
real, dimension(5,0:1,4)  :: f
```

Write an array constructor of eleven integer elements.

6. Given the array declaration

```
character(len=10), dimension(0:5,3) :: c
```

which of the following subobject designators are legal?

```
c(2,3)              c(4:3)(2,1)
c(6,2)              c(5,3)(9:9)
c(0,3)              c(2,1)(4:8)
c(4,3)(:)           c(3,2)(0:9)
c(5)(2:3)           c(5:6)
c(5,3)(9)           c(,)
```

7. Write derived type definitions appropriate for:

    a) a vehicle registration;

    b) a circle;

    c) a book (title, author, and number of pages).

Give an example of a derived type constant for each one.

8. Given the declaration for t in Section 2.12, which of the following objects and subobjects are arrays?

```
t                   t(4)%vertex(1)
t(10)               t(5:6)
t(1)%vertex         t(5:5)
```

9. Write specifications for these entities:

    a) an integer variable inside the range -10^{20} to 10^{20};

    b) a real variable with a minimum of 12 decimal digits of precision and a range of 10^{-100} to 10^{100};

    c) a Kanji character variable on a processor that supports Kanji with kind=2.

3. Expressions and assignments

3.1 Introduction

We have seen in the previous chapter how we are able to build the 'words' of Fortran — the constants, keywords, and names — from the basic elements of the character set. In this chapter we shall discover how these entities may be further combined into 'phrases' or *expressions,* and how these, in turn, may be combined into 'sentences', or *statements.*

In an expression, we describe a computation that is to be carried out by the computer. The result of the computation may then be assigned to a variable. A sequence of assignments is the way in which we specify, step-by-step, the series of individual computations to be carried out, in order to arrive at the desired result. There are separate sets of rules for expressions and assignments, depending on whether the operands in question are numeric, logical, character, or derived in type, and whether they are scalars or arrays. There are also separate rules for pointer assignments. We shall discuss each set of rules in turn, including a description of the relational expressions which produce a result of type logical and are needed in control statements (see next chapter). To simplify the initial discussion, we commence by considering expressions and assignments that are intrinsically defined and involve neither arrays nor entities of derived data types.

An expression in Fortran is formed of operands and operators, combined in a way which follows the rules of Fortran syntax. A simple expression involving a *dyadic* (or binary) operator has the form

operand *operator* operand

an example being

x+y

and a unary or *monadic* operator has the form

operator operand

an example being

-y

The operands may be constants, variables, or functions (see Chapter 5), and an expression may itself be used as an operand. In this way, we can build up more complicated expressions such as

> operand *operator* operand *operator* operand

where consecutive operands are separated by a single operator. Each operand must have a defined value and the result must be mathematically defined; for example, raising a negative real value to a real power is not permitted.

The rules of Fortran state that the parts of expressions without parentheses are evaluated successively from left to right for operators of equal precedence, with the exception of ** (see Section 3.2). If it is necessary to evaluate part of an expression, or *subexpression*, before another, parentheses may be used to indicate which subexpression should be evaluated first. In

> operand *operator* (operand *operator* operand)

the subexpression in parentheses will be evaluated, and the result used as an operand to the first operator.

If an expression or subexpression has no parentheses, the processor is permitted to evaluate an equivalent expression, that is an expression that always has the same value apart, possibly, from the effects of numerical round-off. For example, if a, b, and c are real variables, the expression

> a/b/c

might be evaluated as

> a/(b*c)

on a processor that can multiply much faster than it can divide. Usually, such changes are welcome to the programmer since the program runs faster, but when they are not (for instance because they would lead to more round-off) parentheses should be inserted because the processor is required to respect them.

If two operators immediately follow each other, as in

> operand *operator* *operator* operand

the only possible interpretation is that the second operator is unary. Thus, there is a general rule that a binary operator must not follow immmediately after another operator.

3.2   Scalar numeric expressions

A *numeric expression* is an expression whose operands are one of the three numeric types — integer, real, and complex — and whose operators are

**	exponentiation
* /	multiplication, division
+ -	addition, subtraction

These operators are known as *numeric intrinsic* operators, and are listed here in their order of precedence. In the absence of parentheses, exponentiations will be carried out before multiplications and divisions, and these before additions and subtractions.

We note that the minus sign (-) and the plus sign (+) can be used as a unary operators, as in

    -tax

Because it is not permitted in ordinary mathematical notation, a unary minus or plus must not follow immediately after another operator. When this is needed, as for x^{-y}, parentheses must be placed around the operator and its operand:

    x**(-y)

The type and kind type parameter of the result of a unary operation are those of the operand.

The exception to the left-to-right rule noted in Section 3.1 concerns exponentiations. Whereas the expression

    -a+b+c

will be evaluated from left to right as

    ((-a)+b)+c

the expression

    a**b**c

will be evaluated as

    a**(b**c)

For integer data, the result of any division will be truncated towards zero, that is to the integer value whose magnitude is equal to or just less than the magnitude of the exact result. Thus, the result of

    6/3   is 2
    8/3   is 2
    -8/3   is -2

This fact must always be borne in mind whenever integer divisions are written. Similarly, the result of

    2**3   is 8

whereas the result of

    2**(-3)   is 1/(2**3)

which is zero.

The rules of Fortran allow a numeric expression to contain numeric operands of differing types or kind type parameters. This is known as a *mixed-mode expression*. Except when raising a real or complex value to an integer power, the object of the weaker (or simpler) of the two data types will be converted, or *coerced*, into the type of the stronger one. The result will also be that of the stronger type. If, for example, we write a*i when a is of type real and i is of type integer, then i will be converted to a real data type before the multiplication is performed, and the result of the computation will also be of type real. The rules are summarized for each possible combination for the operations +, -, * and / in Table 3.1, and for the operation ** in Table 3.2. The functions real and cmplx that they reference are defined in Section 8.3.1. In both Tables, I stands for integer, R for real, and C for complex.

Table 3.1. Type of result of *a* .op. *b*, where .op. is +, -, * or /.

Type of *a*	Type of *b*	Value of *a* used	Value of *b* used	Type of result
I	I	a	b	I
I	R	real(a,kind(b))	b	R
I	C	cmplx(a,0,kind(b))	b	C
R	I	a	real(b,kind(a))	R
R	R	a	b	R
R	C	cmplx(a,0,kind(b))	b	C
C	I	a	cmplx(b,0,kind(a))	C
C	R	a	cmplx(b,0,kind(a))	C
C	C	a	b	C

If both operands are of type integer, the kind type parameter of the result is that of the operand with the greater decimal exponent range, or is processor dependent if the kinds differ but the decimal exponent ranges are the same. If both operands are of type real or complex, the kind type parameter of the result is that of the operand with the greater decimal precision, or is processor dependent if the kinds differ but the decimal precisions are the same. If one operand is of type integer and the other is of real or complex, the type parameter of the result is that of the real or complex operand.

Note that a literal constant in a mixed-mode expression is held to its own precision, which may be less than that of the expresssion. For example, given a variable a of kind long (Section 2.6.2), the result of a/1.7 will be less precise than that of a/1.7_long.

In the case of raising a complex value to a complex power, the principal value [1] is taken.

---

[1] The principal value of a^b is $\exp(b(\log|a| + i \arg a))$, with $-\pi < \arg a \leq \pi$.

Table 3.2. Type of result of $a**b$.

Type of a	Type of b	Value of a used	Value of b used	Type of result
I	I	a	b	I
I	R	$\mathrm{real}(a,\mathrm{kind}(b))$	b	R
I	C	$\mathrm{cmplx}(a,0,\mathrm{kind}(b))$	b	C
R	I	a	b	R
R	R	a	b	R
R	C	$\mathrm{cmplx}(a,0,\mathrm{kind}(b))$	b	C
C	I	a	b	C
C	R	a	$\mathrm{cmplx}(b,0,\mathrm{kind}(a))$	C
C	C	a	b	C

3.3 Defined and undefined variables

In the course of the explanations in this and the following chapters, we shall often refer to a variable becoming *defined* or *undefined*. In the previous chapter, we showed how a scalar variable may be called into existence by a statement like

```
real :: speed
```

In this simple case, the variable speed has, at the beginning of the execution of the program, no defined value. It is undefined. No attempt must be made to reference its value since it has none. A common way in which it might become defined is for it to be assigned a value:

```
speed = 2.997
```

After the execution of such an *assignment statement* it has a value, and that value may be referenced, for instance in an expression:

```
speed*0.5
```

For a compound object, all of its non-pointer subobjects must be individually defined before the object as a whole is regarded as defined. Thus, an array is said to be defined only when each of its elements is defined, an object of a derived data type is defined only when each of its non-pointer components is defined, and a character variable is defined only when each of its characters is defined.

A variable that is defined does not necessarily retain its state of definition throughout the execution of a program. As we shall see in Chapter 5, a variable that is local to a single subprogram usually becomes undefined when control is returned from that subprogram. In certain circumstances, it is even possible that a single array element becomes undefined: this causes the array considered as a whole to become undefined; a similar rule holds for entities of derived data type and for character variables.

A means to specify the initial value of a variable is explained in Section 7.5.

In the case of a pointer, the pointer association status may be *undefined* (its initial state), *associated* with a target, or *disassociated*, which means that it is not associated with a target but has a definite status that may be tested by the function associated (Section 8.2). Even though a pointer is associated with a target, the target itself may be defined or undefined. A means to specify the initial status of disassociated is provided by Fortran 95 (see Section 7.5.3).

3.4   Scalar numeric assignment

The general form of a scalar numeric assignment is

variable = expr

where *variable* is a scalar numeric variable and *expr* is a scalar numeric expression. If *expr* is not of the same type or kind as *variable*, it will be converted to that type and kind before the assignment is carried out, according to the set of rules given in Table 3.3 (the function int is defined in Section 8.3.1).

Table 3.3. Numeric conversion for assignment statement *variable* = *expr*

Type of *variable*	Value assigned
integer	int(*expr*, kind(*variable*))
real	real(*expr*, kind(*variable*))
complex	cmplx(*expr*, kind=kind(*variable*))

We note that if the type of *variable* is integer but *expr* is not, then the assignment will result in a loss of precision unless *expr* happens to have an integral value. Similarly, assigning a real expression to a real variable of a kind with less precision will also cause a loss of precision to occur, and the assignment of a complex quantity to a non-complex variable involves the loss of the imaginary part. Thus, the values in i and a following the assignments

```
i = 7.3                ! i of type default integer
a = (4.01935, 2.12372) ! a of type default real
```

are 7 and 4.01935, respectively. Also, if a literal constant is assigned to a variable of greater precision, the result will have the accuracy of the constant. For example, given a variable a of kind long (Section 2.6.2), the result of a = 1.7 will be less precise than that of a = 1.7_long.

3.5   Scalar relational operators

It is possible in Fortran to test whether the value of one numeric expression bears a certain relation to that of another, and similarly for character expressions. The relational operators are

.lt. or <	less than
.le. or <=	less than or equal
.eq. or ==	equal
.ne. or /=	not equal
.gt. or >	greater than
.ge. or >=	greater than or equal

If either or both of the expressions are complex, only the operators == and /= (or .eq. and .ne.) are available.

The result of such a comparison is one of the default logical values .true. or .false., and we shall see in the next chapter how such tests are of great importance in controlling the flow of a program. Examples of relational expressions (for i and j of type integer, a and b of type real, and char1 of type default character) are

i < 0	integer relational expression
a < b	real relational expression
a+b > i-j	mixed-mode relational expression
char1 == 'Z'	character relational expression

In the third expression above, we note that the two components are of different numeric types. In this case, and whenever either or both of the two components consist of numeric expressions, the rules state that the components are to be evaluated separately, and converted to the type and kind of their sum before the comparison is made. Thus, a relational expression such as

    a+b .le. i-j

will be evaluated by converting the result of (i-j) to type real.

For character comparisons, the kinds must be the same and the letters are compared from the left until a difference is found or the strings are found to be identical. If the lengths differ, the shorter one is regarded as being padded with blanks[2] on the right. Two zero-sized strings are considered to be identical.

No other form of mixed mode relational operator is intrinsically available, though such an operator may be defined (Section 3.8). The numeric operators take precedence over the relational operators.

3.6 Scalar logical expressions and assignments

Logical constants, variables, and functions may appear as operands in logical expressions. The logical operators, in decreasing order of precedence, are:

---

[2]Here and elsewhere, the blank padding character used for a non-default type is processor dependent.

unary operator:

> .not.   logical negation

binary operators:

.and.	logical intersection
.or.	logical union
.eqv. and .neqv.	logical equivalence and non-equivalence

If we assume a logical declaration of the form

```
logical i,j,k,l
```

then the following are valid logical expressions:

```
.not.j
j .and. k
i .or. l .and. .not.j
( .not.k .and. j .neqv. .not.l) .or. i
```

In the first expression we note the use of .not. as a unary operator. In the third expression, the rules of precedence imply that the subexpression l.and..not.j will be evaluated first, and the result combined with i. In the last expression, the two subexpressions .not.k.and.j and .not.l will be evaluated and compared for non-equivalence. The result of the comparison, .true. or .false., will be combined with i.

The kind type parameter of the result is that of the operand for .not., and for the others is that of the operands if they have the same kind or processor dependent otherwise.

We note that the .or. operator is an inclusive operator; the .neqv. operator provides an exclusive logical or (a.and..not.b .or. .not.a.and.b).

The result of any logical expression is the value true or false, and this value may then be assigned to a logical variable such as element 3 of the logical array flag in the example

```
flag(3) = ( .not. k .eqv. l) .or. j
```

The kind type parameter values of the variable and expression need not be identical.

A logical variable may be set to a predetermined value by an assignment statement:

```
flag(1) = .true.
flag(2) = .false.
```

In the foregoing examples, all the operands and results were of type logical – no other data type is allowed to participate in an intrinsic logical operation or assignment.

The results of several relational expressions may be combined into a logical expression, and assigned, as in

```
real    :: a, b, x, y
logical :: cond
:
cond = a>b .or. x<0.0 .and. y>1.0
```

where we note the precedence of the relational operators over the logical operators. If the value of such a logical expression can be determined without evaluating a subexpression, a processor is permitted not to evaluate the subexpression. An example is

```
i<=10 .and. ary(i)==0
```

when i has the value 11. However, the programmer must not rely on such behaviour. For example, when ary has size 10, an out-of-bounds subscript might be referenced if the processor chooses to evaluate the right-hand subexpression before the left-hand one. We return to this topic in Section 5.10.1.

3.7 Scalar character expressions and assignments

The only intrinsic operator for character expressions is the concatenation operator //, which has the effect of combining two character operands into a single character result. For example, the result of concatenating the two character constants AB and CD, written as

```
'AB'//'CD'
```

is the character string ABCD. The operands must have the same kind parameter values, but may be character variables, constants, or functions. For instance, if word1 and word2 are both of default kind and length 4, and contain the character strings LOOP and HOLE respectively, the result of

```
word1(4:4)//word2(2:4)
```

is the string POLE.

The length of the result of a concatenation is the sum of the lengths of the operands. Thus, the length of the result of

```
word1//word2//'S'
```

is 9, which is the length of the string LOOPHOLES.

The result of a character expression may be assigned to a character variable of the same kind. Assuming the declarations

```
character(len=4) :: char1, char2
character(len=8) :: result
```

we may write

```
char1 = 'any '
char2 = 'book'
result = char1//char2
```

In this case, `result` will now contain the string any book. We note in these examples that the lengths of the left- and right-hand sides of the three assignments are in each case equal. If, however, the length of the result of the right-hand side is shorter than the length of the left-hand side, then the result is placed in the left-most part of the left-hand side and the rest is filled with blank characters. Thus, in

```
character(len=5) :: fill
fill(1:4) = 'AB'
```

`fill(1:4)` will have the value AB*bb* (where *b* stands for a blank character). The value of `fill(5:5)` remains undefined, that is, it contains no specific value and should not be used in an expression. As a consequence, `fill` is also undefined. On the other hand, when the left-hand side is shorter than the result of the right-hand side, the right-hand end of the result is truncated. The result of

```
character(len=5) :: trunc8
trunc8 = 'TRUNCATE'
```

is to place in `trunc8` the character string TRUNC. If a left-hand side is of zero length, no assignment takes place.

The left-hand and right-hand sides of an assignment may overlap. In such a case, it is always the old values that are used in the right-hand side expression. For example, the assignment

```
result(3:5) = result(1:3)
```

is valid and if `result` began with the value ABCDEFGH, it would be left with the value ABABCFGH.

Other means of manipulating characters and strings of characters, via intrinsic functions, are described in Sections 8.5 and 8.6.

3.8   Structure constructors and scalar defined operators

No operators for derived types are automatically available, but a structure may be constructed from expressions for its components, just as a constant structure may be constructed from constants (Section 2.9). The general form of a *structure constructor* is

> *type-name (expr-list)*

where the *expr-list* specifies the values of the components. For example, given the type

```
type string
   integer          :: length
   character(len=10) :: value
end type string
```

and the variables

```
character(len=4) :: char1, char2
```

the following is a value of type string

```
string(8, char1//char2)
```

Each expression in *expr-list* corresponds to a component of the structure; if it is not a pointer component, the value is assigned to the component under the rules of intrinsic assignment; if it is a pointer component, the expression must be a valid target for it,[3] as in a pointer assignment statement (Section 3.12).

When a programmer defines a derived type and wishes operators to be available, he or she must define the operators, too. For a binary operator this is done by writing a function, with two intent in arguments, that specifies how the result depends on the operands, and an interface block that associates the function with the operator token (functions, intent, and interface blocks will be explained fully in Chapter 5). For example, given the type

```
type interval
    real :: lower, upper
end type interval
```

that represents intervals of numbers between a lower and an upper bound, we may define addition by a module (Section 5.5) containing the procedure

```
function add_interval(a,b)
    type(interval)               :: add_interval
    type(interval), intent(in) :: a, b
    add_interval%lower = a%lower + b%lower ! Production code
    add_interval%upper = a%upper + b%upper ! would allow for
end function add_interval                  ! roundoff.
```

and the interface block (Section 5.18)

```
interface operator(+)
    module procedure add_interval
end interface
```

This function would be invoked in an expression such as

```
y + z
```

to perform this programmer-defined add operation for scalar variables y and z of type interval. A unary operator is defined by an interface block and a function with one intent in argument.

The operator token may be any of the tokens used for the intrinsic operators or may be a sequence of up to 31 letters enclosed in decimal points other than .true. or .false. . An example is

---

[3] In particular, it must not be a constant.

```
.sum.
```

In this case, the header line of the interface block would be written as

```
interface operator(.sum.)
```

and the expression as

```
y.sum.z
```

If an intrinsic token is used, the number of arguments must be the same as for the intrinsic operation, the priority of the operation is as for the intrinsic operation, and a unary minus or plus must not follow immediately after another operator. Otherwise, it is of highest priority for defined unary operators and lowest priority for defined binary operators. The complete set of priorities is given in Table 3.4. Where another priority is required within an expression, parentheses must be used.

Table 3.4. Relative precedence of operators (in decreasing order)

Type of operation when intrinsic	Operator
—	monadic (unary) defined operator
Numeric	**
Numeric	* or /
Numeric	monadic + or −
Numeric	dyadic + or −
Character	//
Relational	.eq. .ne. .lt. .le. .gt. .ge. == /= < <= > >=
Logical	.not.
Logical	.and.
Logical	.or.
Logical	.eqv. or .neqv.
—	dyadic (binary) defined operator

Retaining the intrinsic priorities is helpful both to the readability of expressions and to the efficiency with which a compiler can interpret them. For example, if + is used for set union and * for set intersection, we can interpret the expression

```
i*j + k
```

for sets i, j, and k without difficulty.

If either of the intrinsic tokens .eq. and == is used, the definition applies to both tokens so that they are always equivalent. The same is true for the other equivalent pairs of relational operators.

Note that a defined unary operator not using an intrinsic token may follow immediately after another operator as in

```
y .sum. .inverse. x
```

Operators may be defined for any types of operands, except where there is an intrinsic operation for the operator and types. For example, we might wish to be able to add an interval number to an ordinary real, which can be done by adding the procedure

```
function add_interval_real(a,b)
    type(interval)                    add_interval_real
    type(interval), intent(in) :: a
    real, intent(in)           :: b
    add_interval_real%lower = a%lower + b ! Production code would
    add_interval_real%upper = a%upper + b ! allow for roundoff.
end function add_interval_real
```

and changing the interface block to

```
interface operator(+)
    module procedure add_interval, add_interval_real
end interface
```

The result of a defined operation may have any type. The type of the result, as well as its value, must be specified by the function.

Note that an operation that is defined intrinsically cannot be redefined; thus in

```
real :: a, b, c
   :
c = a + b
```

the meaning of the operation is always unambiguous.

3.9 Scalar defined assignments

Assignment of an expression of derived type to a variable of the same type is automatically available and takes place component by component. For example, if a is of the type interval defined at the start of Section 3.8, we may write

```
a = interval(0.0, 1.0)
```

(structure constructors were met in Section 3.8, too).

In other circumstances, however, we might wish to define a different action for an assignment involving an object of derived type, and indeed this is possible. An assignment may be redefined or another assignment may be defined by a subroutine with two arguments, the first having intent out or intent inout and corresponding to the variable and the second having intent in and corresponding to the expression (subroutines will also be dealt with fully in Chapter 5). In the case of an assignment involving an object of derived type and an object of a different type, such a definition must be provided. For example, assignment of reals to intervals and vice versa might be defined by a module containing the subroutines

```
subroutine real_from_interval(a,b)
    real, intent(out)          :: a
    type(interval), intent(in) :: b
    a = (b%lower + b%upper)/2
end subroutine real_from_interval
```

and

```
subroutine interval_from_real(a,b)
    type(interval), intent(out) :: a
    real, intent(in)            :: b
    a%lower = b
    a%upper = b
end subrcutine interval_from_real
```

and the interface block

```
interface assignment(=)
    module procedure real_from_interval, interval_from_real
end interface
```

Given this, we may write

```
type(interval) :: a
a = 0.0
```

A defined assignment must not redefine the meaning of an intrinsic assignment for intrinsic types, that is an assignment between two objects of numeric type, of logical type, or of character type with the same kind parameter, but may redefine the meaning of an intrinsic assignment for two objects of the same derived type. For instance, for an assignment between two variables of the type string (Section 3.8) that copies only the relevant part of the character component, we might write

```
subroutine assign_string (left, right)
    type(string), intent(out) :: left
    type(string), intent(in)  :: right
    left%length = right%length
    left%value(1:left%length) = right%value(1:right%length)
end subroutine assign_string
```

Intrinsic assignment for a derived-type object always involves intrinsic assignment for all its non-pointer components, even if a component is of a derived type for which assignment has been redefined.

3.10 Array expressions

So far in this chapter, we have assumed that all the entities in an expression are
scalar. However, any of the unary intrinsic operations may also be applied to
an array to produce another array of the same shape (identical rank and extents,
see Section 2.10) and having each element value equal to that of the operation
applied to the corresponding element of the operand. Similarly, binary intrinsic
operations may be applied to a pair of arrays of the same shape to produce an
array of that shape, with each element value equal to that of the operation applied
to corresponding elements of the operands. One of the operands to a binary
operation may be a scalar, in which case the result is as if the scalar had been
broadcast to an array of the same shape as the array operand. Given the array
declarations

```
real, dimension(10,20) :: a,b
real, dimension(5)     :: v
```

the following are examples of array expressions:

```
a/b         ! Array of shape (10,20), with elements a(i,j)/b(i,j)
v+1.        ! Array of shape (5), with elements v(i)+1.0
5/v+a(1:5,5) ! Array of shape (5), with elements 5/v(i)+a(i,5)
a.eq.b      ! Logical array of shape (10,20), with elements
            ! .true. if a(i,j).eq.b(i,j), and .false. otherwise
```

Two arrays of the same shape are said to be *conformable* and a scalar is conformable with any array.

Note that the correspondence is by position in the extent and not by subscript
value. For example,

```
a(2:9,5:10) + b(1:8,15:20)
```

has element values

```
a(i+1,j+4) + b(i,j+14), i=1,2,...,8, j=1,2,...,6.
```

This may be represented pictorially as in Figure 3.1.

The order in which the scalar operations in any array expression are executed
is not specified in the standard, thus enabling a compiler to arrange efficient
execution on a vector or parallel computer.

Any scalar intrinsic operator may be applied in this way to arrays and array-
scalar pairs. For derived operators, the programmer must define operators directly
for array operands, for each rank or pair of ranks involved. For example, the type

```
type matrix
   real :: element
end type matrix
```

might be defined to have scalar operations that are identical to the operations
for reals, but for arrays of ranks one and two the operator * defined to mean

Figure 3.1 The sum of two array sections.

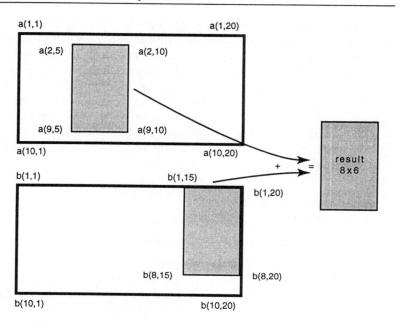

matrix multiplication. The type `matrix` would therefore be suitable for matrix arithmetic, whereas reals are not suitable because multiplication for real arrays is done element by element. This is further discussed in Section 6.7.

3.11   Array assignment

By intrinsic assignment, an array expression may be assigned to an array variable of the same shape, which is interpreted as if each element of the expression were assigned to the corresponding element of the variable. For example, with the declarations of the beginning of the last section, the assignment

```
a = a + 1.0
```

replaces $a(i,j)$ by $a(i,j)+1.0$ for $i = 1, 2, \ldots, 10$ and $j = 1, 2, \ldots, 20$. Note that, as for expressions, the element correspondence is by position within the extent rather than by subscript value. This is illustrated by the example

```
a(1,11:15) = v      ! a(1,j+10) is assigned from
                    ! v(j), j=1,2,...,5
```

A scalar expression may be assigned to an array, in which case the scalar value is broadcast to all the array elements.

If the expression includes a reference to the array variable or to a part of it, the expression is interpreted as being fully evaluated before the assignment commences. For example, the statement

```
v(2:5) = v(1:4)
```

results in each element v(i) for i = 2, 3, 4, 5 having the value that v(i-1) had prior to the commencement of the assignment. This rule exactly parallels the rule for substrings that was explained in Section 3.7. The order in which the array elements are assigned is not specified by the standard, to allow optimizations.

Sets of numeric and mathematical intrinsic functions, whose results may be used as operands in scalar or array expressions and in assignments, are described in Sections 8.3 and 8.4.

For a defined assignment (Section 3.9), a separate subroutine must be provided for each combination of ranks for which it is required. Intrinsic assignment is overridden only for those combinations of ranks for which a corresponding defined assignment is accessible.

A form of array assignment expressed with the help of indices is provided by Fortran 95 (Section 6.9). Also, elemental defined assignments are available in Fortran 95 (Section 6.11).

3.12   Pointers in expressions and assignments

A pointer may appear as a variable in the expressions and assignments that we have considered so far in this chapter, provided it has a valid association with a target. The target is accessed without any need for an explicit dereferencing symbol. In particular, if two pointers appear on opposite sides of an assignment statement, data are copied from one target to the other target.

Sometimes the need arises for another sort of assignment. We may want the left-hand pointer to point to another target, rather than that its current target acquire fresh data. That is, we want the descriptor to be altered. This is called *pointer assignment* and takes place in a pointer assignment statement:

   pointer => *target*

where *pointer* is the name of a pointer or the designator of a structure component that is a pointer, and *target* is usually a variable but may also be a reference to a pointer-valued function (see Section 5.10). For example, the statements

```
x => z
a => c
```

have variables as targets and are needed for the first matrix multiplication of Section 2.13, in order to make x refer to z and a to refer to c. In Fortran 95, the statement

```
x => null()    ! Fortran 95 only
```

nullifies x. Pointer assignment also takes place for a pointer component of a structure when the structure appears on the left-hand side of an ordinary assignment.
For example, suppose we have used the type entry of Section 2.13 to construct a
chain of entries and wish to add a fresh entry at the front. If first points to the
first entry and current is a scalar pointer of type entry, the statements

```
allocate (current)
current = entry(new_value, new_index, first)
first => current
```

allocate a new entry and link it into the top of the chain. The assignment statement
has the effect

```
current%next => first
```

and establishes the link. The pointer assignment statement gives first the new
entry as its target without altering the old first entry. An ordinary assignment
would be incorrect because the target would be copied, destroying the old first
entry, corresponding to the component assignments

```
first%value = current%value
first%index = current%index
first%next => current%next
```

In the case where the chain began with length two and consisted of

```
first :       (1.0, 10, associated)
first%next : (2.0, 15, null)
```

following the execution of the first set of statements it would have length 3 and
consist of

```
first :             (4.0, 16, associated)
first%next :        (1.0, 10, associated)
first%next%next : (2.0, 15, null)
```

If the *target* in a pointer assignment statement is a variable that is not itself a
pointer or a subobject of a pointer, it must have the target attribute. For example,
the statement

```
real, dimension(10), target :: y
```

declares y to have the target attribute. Any subobject of an object with the
target attribute also has the target attribute. The target attribute is required for
the purpose of code optimization by the compiler. It is very helpful to the compiler
to know that a variable that is not a pointer or a target may not be accessed by a
pointer.

The target in a pointer assignment statement may be a subobject of a pointer.
For example, given the declaration

```
character(len=80), dimension(:), pointer :: page
```

and an appropriate association, the following are all permitted targets:

```
page, page(10), page(2:4), page(2)(3:15)
```

Note that it is sufficient for any part of the subobject to have the pointer attribute. For example, given the declaration

```
type(entry) :: node ! This has a pointer component next,
                    ! see Section 2.13.
```

and an appropriate association, node%next%value is a permitted target.

If the *target* in a pointer assignment statement is itself a pointer, then a straightforward copy of the descriptor takes place. If the pointer association status is undefined or disassociated, this state is copied.

If the *target* is a pointer or a subobject of a pointer, the new association is with that pointer's target and is not affected by any subsequent changes to its pointer association status. This is illustrated by the following example. The sequence

```
b => c    ! c has the target attribute
a => b
nullify (b)
```

will leave a still pointing to c.

The type, type parameters, and rank of the *pointer* and *target* in a pointer assignment statement must each be the same. If the *pointer* is an array, it takes its shape and bounds from the *target*. The bounds are as would be returned by the functions lbound and ubound (Section 8.12.2) for the target, which means that an array section or array expression is always taken to have the value 1 for a lower bound and the extent for the corresponding upper bound.

Fortran is unusual in not requiring a special character for a reference to a pointer target, but requiring one for distinguishing pointer assignment from ordinary assignment. The reason for this choice was the expectation that most engineering and scientific programs will refer to target data far more often than they change targets.

3.13 Summary

In this chapter, we have seen how scalar and array expressions of numeric, logical, character, and derived types may be formed, and how the corresponding assignments of the results may be made. The relational expressions and the use of pointers have also been presented. We now have the information required to write short sections of code forming a sequence of statements to be performed one after the other. In the following chapter we shall see how more complicated sequences, involving branching and iteration, may be built up.

Features described in this chapter which are new since Fortran 77 are the use of the alternative representations <, <=, ... for the relational operators; the ability of the two sides of a character assignment to overlap; structure constructors; defined operators and assignment; array expressions and assignment; and the use of pointers in expressions and assignment.

3.14 Exercises

1. If all the variables are numeric scalars, which of the following are valid numeric expressions?

```
a+b              -c
a+-c             d+(-f)
(a+c)**(p+q)     (a+c)(p+q)
-(x+y)**i        4.((a-d)-(a+4.*x)+1)
```

2. In the following expressions, add the parentheses which correspond to Fortran's rules of precedence (assuming a, c-f are real scalars, i-n are logical scalars, and b is a logical array), for example

```
a+d**2/c      becomes      a+((d**2)/c)

c+4.*f
4.*g-a+d/2.
a**e**c**d
a*e-c**d/a+e
i .and. j .or. k
.not. 1 .or. .not. i .and. m .neqv. n
b(3).and.b(1).or.b(6).or..not.b(2)
```

3. What are the results of the following expressions?

```
3+4/2        6/4/2
3.*4**2      3.**3/2
-1.**2       (-1.)**3
```

4. A scalar character variable r has length 8. What are the contents of r after each of the following assignments?

```
r = 'ABCDEFGH'
r = 'ABCD'//'01234'
r(:7) = 'ABCDEFGH'
r(:6) = 'ABCD'
```

5. Which of the following logical expressions are valid if b is a logical array?

```
.not.b(1).and.b(2)      .or.b(1)
b(1).or..not.b(4)       b(2)(.and.b(3).or.b(4))
```

6. If all the variables are real scalars, which of the following relational expressions are valid?

```
d .le. c              p .lt. t > 0
x-1 /= y              x+y < 3 .or. > 4.
d.lt.c.and.3.0        q.eq.r .and. s>t
```

7. Write expressions to compute:

a) the perimeter of a square of side l;

b) the area of a triangle of base b and height h;

c) the volume of a sphere of radius r.

8. An item costs n cents. Write a declaration statement for suitable variables and assignment statements which compute the change to be given from a $1 bill for any value of n from 1 to 99, using coins of denomination 1, 5, 10, and 25 cents.

9. Given the type declaration for interval in Section 3.8, the definitions of + given in Section 3.8, the definitions of assignment given in Section 3.9, and the declarations

```
type(interval) :: a,b,c,d
real           :: r
```

which of the following statements are valid?

```
a = b + c
c = b + 1.0
d = b + 1
r = b + c
a = r + 2
```

10. Given the type declarations

```
real, dimension(5,6) :: a, b
real, dimension(5)   :: c
```

which of the following statements are valid?

```
a = b                 c = a(:,2) + b(5,:5)
a = c+1.0             c = a(2,:) + b(:,5)
a(:,3) = c            b(2:,3) = c + b(:5,3)
```

4. Control constructs

4.1 Introduction

We have learnt in the previous chapter how assignment statements may be written, and how these may be ordered one after the other to form a sequence of code which is executed step-by-step. In most computations, however, this simple sequence of statements is by itself inadequate for the formulation of the problem. For instance, we may wish to follow one of two possible paths through a section of code, depending on whether a calculated value is positive or negative. We may wish to sum 1000 elements of an array, and to do this by writing 1000 additions and assignments is clearly tedious; the ability to iterate over a single addition is required instead. We may wish to pass control from one part of a program to another, or even stop processing altogether.

For all these purposes, we have available in Fortran various facilities to enable the logical flow through the program statements to be controlled. The facilities contained in Fortran correspond to those now widely regarded as being the most appropriate for a modern programming language. Their general form is that of a *block* construct, that is a construct which begins with an initial keyword statement, may have intermediate keyword statements, and ends with a matching terminal statement, and that may be entered only at the initial statement. Each sequence of statements between keywords is called a *block*. A block may be empty, though such cases are rare.

Block constructs may be *nested*, that is a block may contain another block construct. In such a case, the block must contain the whole of the inner construct. Execution of a block always begins with its first statement.

However, we begin by describing the simple go to statement.

4.2 The go to statement

In this section, we consider the most disputed statement in programming languages – the go to statement. It is generally accepted that it is difficult to understand a program which is interrupted by many branches, especially if there is a large number of backward branches – those returning control to a statement preceding the branch itself. At the same time there are certain occasions, especially when dealing with error conditions, when go to statements are required in even the most advanced languages.

The form of the unconditional go to statement is

go to *label*

where *label* is a statement label. This statement label must be present on an *executable statement* (a statement which can be executed, as opposed to one of an informative nature, like a declaration). An example is

```
  x = y+3.0
  go to 4
3 x = x+2.0
4 z = x+y
```

in which we note that after execution of the first statement, a branch is taken to the last statement, labelled 4. This is a *branch target statement*. The statement labelled 3 is jumped over, and can be executed only if there is a branch to the label 3 somewhere else. If the statement following an unconditional go to is unlabelled it can never be reached and executed, creating *dead code,* normally a sign of incorrect coding.

A go to statement must never specify a branch into a block, though it may specify a branch

- from within a block to another statement in the block,

- to the terminal statement of its construct, or

- to a statement outside its construct.

4.3   The if statement and construct

The if statement and if construct provide a mechanism for branching depending on a condition. They are powerful tools, the if construct being a generalized form of the if statement.

4.3.1   The if statement

In the if statement, the value of a scalar logical expression is tested, and a single statement executed if its value is true. The general form is

if (*scalar-logical-expr*) *action-stmt*

where *scalar-logical-expr* is any scalar logical expression, and *action-stmt* is any executable statement other than one that marks the beginning or end of a block (for instance, if, else if, else, end if, see next subsection), another if statement, or an end statement (see Chapter 5). Examples are

```
if (flag) go to 6
if (x-y > 0.0) x = 0.0
if (cond .or. p<q .and. r<=1.0) s(i,j) = t(j,i)
```

The if statement is normally used either to perform a single assignment depending on a condition, or to branch depending on a condition. The *action-stmt* may not be labelled separately.

4.3.2 The if construct

The if construct allows either the execution of a sequence of statements (a block) to depend on a condition, or the execution of alternative sequences of statements (blocks) to depend on alternative conditions. The simplest of its three forms is

> [*name:*] if (*scalar-logical-expr*) then
>   *block*
>   end if [*name*]

where *scalar-logical-expr* is any scalar logical expression and *block* is any sequence of executable statements (except an end statement or an incomplete construct). The *block* is executed if *scalar-logical-expr* evaluates to the value true, and is not executed if it evaluates to the value false. The if construct may be optionally named: the first and last statements may bear the same name, which may be any valid and distinct Fortran name (see Section 5.15 for a discussion on the scope of names). The fact that the name is optional is indicated here by the square brackets, a convention that will be followed throughout the book.

We notice that the if construct is a compound statement, the beginning being marked by the if...then, and the end by the end if. An example is

```
swap: if (x < y) then
         temp = x
         x = y
         y = temp
      end if swap
```

in which we notice also that the block inside the if construct is indented with respect to its beginning and end. This is not obligatory, but makes the logic easier to understand, especially in nested if constructs as we shall see at the end of this section.

In the second form of the if construct, an alternative block of statements is executable, for the case where the condition is false. The general form is

> [*name:*]   if (*scalar-logical-expr*) then
>   *block1*
>   else [*name*]
>   *block2*
>   end if [*name*]

in which the first block of statements (*block1*) is executed if the condition is true and the second block (*block2*), following the else statement, is executed if the condition is false. An example is

```
if (x < y) then
    x = -x
else
    y = -y
end if
```

in which the sign of x is changed if x is less than y, and the sign of y is changed if x is greater than or equal to y.

The third and most general type of if construct uses the else if statement to make a succession of tests, each of which has its associated block of statements. The tests are made one after the other until one is fulfilled, and the associated statements of the relevant if or else if block are executed. Control then passes to the end of the if construct. If no test is fulfilled, no block is executed, unless there is a final 'catch-all' else clause. The general form is shown in Figure 4.1. Here, and later in the book, we use the notation [ ] to indicate an optional item and [ ]... to indicate an item that may occur any number of times (including zero). There can be any number (including zero) of else if statements, and zero or one else statements. An else or else if statement may be named only if the corresponding if and end if statements are named, and must be given the same name.

Figure 4.1

```
[name:] if (scalar-logical-expr) then
            block
        [else if (scalar-logical-expr) then [name]
            block]...
        [else [name]
            block]
        end if [name]
```

The statements within an if construct may be labelled, but the labels must never be referenced in such a fashion as to pass control into the range of an if construct from outside it, to an else if or else statement, or into a block of the construct from outside the block. For example, the following if construct is illegal:

```
    if (temp > 100.0) then
        go to 1                      ! illegal branch
        boil = .true.
        steam = .true.
    else
1       boil = .false.
        liquid = .true.
    end if
```

It is permitted to pass control to an end if statement from within its construct. execution of an end if statement has no effect.

It is permitted to nest if constructs within one another to an arbitrary depth, as shown to two levels in Figure 4.2, in which we see again the necessity to indent the code in order to be able to understand the logic easily. For even deeper nesting, naming is to be recommended. The constructs must be properly nested, that is each construct must be wholly contained in a block of the next outer construct.

Figure 4.2

```
if (i < 0) then
    if (j < 0) then
        x = 0.0
        y = 0.0
    else
        z = 0.0
    end if
else if (k < 0) then
    z = 1.0
else
    x = 1.0
    y = 1.0
end if
```

4.4   The case construct

Fortran provides another means of selecting one of several options, rather similar to that of the if construct. The principal differences between the two constructs are that, for the case construct, only *one* expression is evaluated for testing, and the evaluated expression may belong to no more than one of a series of pre-defined sets of values. The form of the case construct is shown by:

```
[name:]  select case (expr)
            [case selector [name]
                block] ...
         end select [name]
```

As for the if construct, the leading and trailing statements must either both be unnamed or both bear the same name; an intermediate statement may be named only if the leading statement is named and bears the same name. The expression *expr* must be scalar and of type character, logical, or integer, and the specified values in each *selector* must be of this type. In the character case, the lengths are permitted to differ, but not the kinds. In the logical and integer cases, the kinds may differ. The simplest form of *selector* is a scalar initialization expression[1] in parentheses, such as in the statement

    case(1)

For character or integer *expr*, a range may be specified by a lower and an upper scalar initialization expression separated by a colon:

    case (*low:high*)

Either *low* or *high*, but not both, may be absent; this is equivalent to specifying that the case is selected whenever *expr* evaluates to a value that is less than or equal to *high*, or greater than or equal to *low*, respectively. An example is shown in Figure 4.3.

Figure 4.3

```
select case (number)      ! number is of type integer
case (:-1)                ! all values below 0
   n_sign = -1
case (0)                  ! only 0
   n_sign = 0
case (1:)                 ! all values above 0
   n_sign = 1
end select
```

The general form of *selector* is a list of non-overlapping values and ranges, all of the same type as *expr*, enclosed in parentheses, such as

    case (1, 2, 7, 10:17, 23)

The form

    case default

is equivalent to a list of all the possible values of *expr* that are not included in the other selectors of the construct. Though we recommend that the values be in order, as in this example, this is not required. Overlapping values are not permitted within one *selector*, nor between different ones in the same construct.

There may be only a single case default *selector* in a given case construct as shown in Figure 4.4. The case default clause does not necessarily have to be the last clause of the case construct.

Since the values of the selectors are not permitted to overlap, at most one selector may be satisfied; if none is satisfied, control passes to the next executable statement following the end select statement.

---

[1]An initialization expression is a restricted form of constant expression (the restrictions being chosen for ease of implementation). The details are tedious and are deferred to Section 7.4. In this section, all examples employ the simplest form of initialization expression: the literal constant.

Figure 4.4

```
    select case (ch)          ! ch of type character
    case ('c', 'd', 'r':)
       ch_type = .true.
    case ('i':'n')
       int_type = .true.
    case default
       real_type = .true.
    end select
```

Like the if construct, case constructs may be nested inside one another. Branching to a statement in a case block is permitted only from another statement in the block, it is not permitted to branch to a case statement, and any branch to an end select statement must be from within the case construct which it terminates.

4.5 The do construct

Many problems in mathematics require, for their representation in a programming language, the ability to *iterate*. If we wish to sum the elements of an array a of length 10, we could write

```
    sum = a(1)
    sum = sum+a(2)
    :
    sum = sum+a(10)
```

which is clearly laborious. Fortran provides a facility known as the do construct which allows us to reduce these ten lines of code to

```
    sum = 0.0
    do  i = 1,10 ! i is of type integer
       sum = sum+a(i)
    end do
```

In this fragment of code we first set sum to zero, and then require that the statement between the do statement and the end do statement shall be executed ten times. For each iteration there is an associated value of an index, kept in i, which assumes the value 1 for the first iteration through the loop, 2 for the second, and so on up to 10. The variable i is a normal integer variable, but is subject to the rule that it must not be explicitly modified within the do construct.

The do statement has more general forms. If we wished to sum the fourth to ninth elements we would write

```
    do  i = 4, 9
```

thereby specifying the required first and last values of i. If, alternatively, we wished to sum all the odd elements, we would write

        do i = 1, 9, 2

where the third of the three loop *parameters,* namely the 2, specifies that i is to be incremented in steps of 2, rather than by the default value of 1, which is assumed if no third parameter is given. In fact, we can go further still, as the parameters need not be constants at all, but integer expressions, as in

        do i = j+4, m, -k(j)**2

in which the first value of i is j+4, and subsequent values are decremented by k(j)**2 until the value of m is reached. Thus, do constructs may run 'backwards' as well as 'forwards'. If any of the three parameters is a variable or is an expression that involves a variable, the value of the variable may be modified within the loop without affecting the number of iterations, as the *initial* values of the parameters are used for the control of the loop.

The general form of this type of bounded do construct control clause is

  [*name:*]   do [,] *variable* = *expr1, expr2* [*,expr3*]
                  block
          end do [*name*]

where *variable* is a named scalar integer variable, *expr1, expr2,* and *expr3* (*expr3* is optional but must be nonzero when present) are any valid scalar integer expressions, and *name* is the optional construct name. The do and end do statements must either both bear the same *name*, or both be unnamed.

The number of iterations of a do construct is given by the formula

    max((*expr2-expr1+expr3*)/*expr3*, 0)

where max is a function which we shall meet in Section 8.3.2 and which returns either the value of the expression or zero, whichever is the larger. There is a consequence following from this definition, namely that if a loop begins with the statement

        do i = 1, n

then its body will not be executed at all if the value of n on entering the loop is zero or less. This is an example of the *zero-trip loop,* and results from the application of the max function.

A very simple form of the do statement is the unbounded

        [*name:*] do

which specifies an endless loop. In practice, a means to exit from an endless loop is required, and this is provided in the form of the exit statement:

        exit [*name*]

where *name* is optional and is used to specify from which construct the exit should be taken in the case of nested constructs. Execution of an exit statement causes control to be transferred to the next executable statement after the end do statement to which it refers. If no name is specified, it terminates execution of the innermost do construct in which it is enclosed. As an example of this form of the do, suppose we have used the type entry of Section 2.13 to construct a chain of entries in a sparse vector, and we wish to find the entry with index 10, known to be present. If first points to the first entry, the code in Figure 4.5 is suitable.

Figure 4.5

```
type(entry), pointer :: first, current
  :
current => first
do
    if (current%index == 10) exit
    current => current%next
end do
```

The exit statement is also useful in a bounded loop when all iterations are not always needed.

A related statement is the cycle statement

```
cycle [name]
```

which transfers control to the end do statement of the corresponding construct. Thus, if further iterations are still to be carried out, the next one is initiated.

The value of a do construct index (if present) is incremented at the end of every loop iteration for use in the subsequent iteration. As the value of this index is available outside the loop after its execution, we have three possible situations, each illustrated by the following loop:

```
do  i = 1, n
    :
    if (i==j) exit
    :
end do
l = i
```

The situations are:

i) If, at execution time, n has the value zero or less, i is set to 1 but the loop is not executed, and control passes to the statement following the end do statement.

ii) If n has a value which is greater than or equal to j, an exit will be taken at the if statement, and l will acquire the last value of i, which is of course j.

iii) If the value of n is greater than zero but less than j, the loop will be executed
    n times, with the successive values of i being 1, 2, . . . *etc.* up to n. When
    reaching the end of the loop for the *nth* time, i will be incremented a final
    time, acquiring the value n+1, which will then be assigned to 1.

We see how important it is to make careful use of loop indices outside the do block,
especially when there is the possibility of the number of iterations taking on the
boundary value of the maximum for the loop.

The do block, just mentioned, is the sequence of statements between the do
statement and the end do statement. From anywhere outside a do block, it is
prohibited to jump into the block or to its end do statement. The following
sequence is thus illegal:

```
      go to 2           ! illegal branch
      :
      do i = 1, n
      :
   2     a = b + c
      :
      end do
```

It is similarly illegal for the block of a do construct (or an if, case, or where
construct, see Section 6.8), to be only partially contained in a block of another
construct. The construct must be completely contained in the block. The following two sequences are thus legal:

```
      if (scalar-logical-expr) then
         do i = 1, n
         :
         end do
      else
      :
      end if
```

and

```
      do i = 1, n
         if (scalar-logical-expr) then
         :
         end if
      end do
```

but this third sequence is not:

```
      if (scalar-logical-expr) then
         do i = 1, 10
         :
      end if   ! illegal position of if construct termination
      :
      end do
```

Any number of do constructs may be nested provided that the range of each nested loop is completely contained within the range of another. We may thus write a matrix multiplication as shown in Figure 4.6.

Figure 4.6

```
do  i = 1, n
   do  j = 1, m
      a(i,j) = 0.0
      do  l = 1, k
         a(i,j) = a(i,j)+b(i,l)*c(l,j)
      end do
   end do
end do
```

Another example is the summation loop in Figure 4.7.

Figure 4.7

```
do  i = 1, n
   sum = 0.0
   do  j = 1,i
      sum = sum+b(j,i)
   end do
   a(i) = sum
end do
```

A final form of the do construct makes use of a statement label to identify the end of the construct. In this case, the terminating statement may be either a labelled end do statement or a labelled continue ('do nothing') statement[2]. The label is, in each case, the same as that on the do statement itself. Simple examples are

```
   do 10 i = 1, n
      :
10 end do
```

and

```
   do 20 i = 1, j
      do 10 k = 1, l
         :
10    continue
20 continue
```

[2]The continue statement is not limited to being the last statement of a do construct; it may appear anywhere among the executable statements.

As shown in the second example, each loop must have a separate label. Additional, but redundant, do syntax is described in Section 11.3.2 (and Appendix C.2.2 and C.3.1). The full do construct syntax is given in Appendix B.

Finally, it should be noted that many short do-loops can be expressed alternatively in the form of array expressions and assignments. However, this is not always possible, and a particular danger to watch for is where one iteration of the loop depends upon a previous one. Thus, the loop

```
do i = 2, n
   a(i) = a(i-1) + b(i)
end do
```

cannot be replaced by the statement

```
a(2:n) = a(1:n-1) + b(2:n)          ! Beware
```

4.6   Summary

In this chapter we have introduced the four main features by which the control in Fortran code may be programmed – the go to statement, the if statement and construct, the case construct and the do construct. The effective use of these features is the key to sound code. Of these features, the case construct is new to Fortran, and the do construct was formerly limited to the labelled form ending on a continue statement.

We have touched upon the concept of a *program unit* as being like the chapter of a book. Just as a book may have just one chapter, so a complete program may consist of just one program unit, which is known as a *main program.* In its simplest form it consists of a series of statements of the kinds we have been dealing with so far, and terminates with an end statement, which acts as a signal to the computer to stop processing the current program. In order to test whether a program unit of this type works correctly, we need to be able to output, to a terminal or printer, the values of the computed quantities. This topic will be fully explained in Chapter 9, and for the moment we need to know only that this can be achieved by a statement of the form

```
print * , ' var1 = ', var1 , ' var2 = ', var2
```

which will output a line such as

```
var1 = 1.0   var2 = 2.0
```

Similarly, input data can be read by statements like

```
read *, val1, val2
```

Figure 4.8

```
!   Print a conversion table of the Fahrenheit and Celsius
!   temperature scales between specified limits.
!
    real      :: celsius, fahrenheit
    integer   :: low_temp, high_temp, temperature
    character :: scale
!
read_loop: do
!
!   Read scale and limits
       read *, scale, low_temp, high_temp
!
!   Check for valid data
       if (scale /= 'C' .and. scale /= 'F') exit read_loop
!
!   Loop over the limits
       do  temperature = low_temp, high_temp
!
!   Choose conversion formula
          select case (scale)
          case ('C')
             celsius = temperature
             fahrenheit = 9.0/5.0*celsius + 32.0
          case ('F')
             fahrenheit = temperature
             celsius = 5.0/9.0*(fahrenheit-32.0)
          end select
!
!   Print table
          print *, celsius, ' degrees C correspond to',  &
                   fahrenheit, ' degrees F'
       end do
    end do read_loop
!
!   Termination
print *, ' End of valid data'
    end
C  90    100
F  20    32
*  0     0
```

This is sufficient to allow us to write simple programs like that in Figure 4.8, which outputs the converted values of a temperature scale between specified limits. Valid inputs are shown at the end of the example.

4.7 Exercises

1. Write a program which

    a) defines an array to have 100 elements;

    b) assigns to the elements the values 1, 2, 3, ..., 100;

    c) reads two integer values in the range 1 to 100;

    d) reverses the order of the elements of the array in the range specified by the two values.

2. The first two terms of the Fibonacci series are both 1, and all subsequent terms are defined as the sum of the preceding two terms. Write a program which reads an integer value limit and which computes and prints the coefficients of the first limit terms of the series.

3. The coefficients of successive orders of the binomial expansion are shown in the normal Pascal triangle form as

$$1$$
$$1\ \ 1$$
$$1\ \ 2\ \ 1$$
$$1\ \ 3\ \ 3\ \ 1$$
$$1\ \ 4\ \ 6\ \ 4\ \ 1$$
etc.

Write a program which reads an integer value limit and prints the coefficients of the first limit lines of this Pascal triangle.

4. Define a character variable of length 80. Write a program which reads a value for this variable. Assuming that each character in the variable is alphabetic, write code which sorts them into alphabetic order, and prints out the frequency of occurrence of each letter.

5. Write a program to read an integer value limit and print the first limit prime numbers, by any method.

6. Write a program which reads a value x, and calculates and prints the corresponding value x/(1.+x). The case x=-1. should produce an error message and be followed by an attempt to read a new value of x.

7. Given a chain of entries of the type entry of Section 2.13, modify the code in Figure 4.5 (Section 4.5) so that it removes the entry with index 10, and makes the previous entry point to the following entry.

5. Program units and procedures

5.1 Introduction

As we saw in the previous chapter, it is possible to write a complete Fortran program as a single unit, but it is preferable to break the program down into manageable units. Each such *program unit* corresponds to a program task that can be readily understood and, ideally, can be written, compiled, and tested in isolation. We will discuss the three kinds of program unit, the main program, external subprogram, and module.

A complete program must, as a minimum, include one *main program*. This may contain statements of the kinds that we have met so far in examples, but normally its most important statements are invocations or *calls* to subsidiary programs known as *subprograms*. A subprogram defines a *function* or a *subroutine*[1]. They differ in that a function returns a single object and usually does not alter the values of its arguments (so that it represents a function in the mathematical sense), whereas a subroutine usually performs a more complicated task, returning several results through its arguments and by other means. Functions and subroutines are known collectively as *procedures*.

There are various kinds of subprograms. A subprogram may be a program unit in its own right, in which case it is called an *external subprogram* and defines an *external procedure*. External procedures may also be defined by means other than Fortran (usually assembly language). A subprogram may be a member of a collection in a program unit called a *module*, in which case we call it a *module subprogram* and it defines a *module procedure*. A subprogram may be placed inside a module subprogram, an external subprogram, or a main program, in which case we call it an *internal subprogram* and it defines an *internal procedure*. Internal subprograms may not be nested, that is they may not contain further subprograms, and we expect them normally to be short sequences of code, say up to about twenty lines. We illustrate the nesting of subprograms in program units in Figure 5.1. If a program unit or subprogram contains a subprogram, it is called the *host* of that subprogram.

---

[1] It is possible to write a subprogram that defines more than one function or more than one subroutine (see Section 11.2.6), but we do not recommend this practice.

Figure 5.1 Nesting of subprograms in program units.

Besides containing a collection of subprograms, a module may contain data definitions, derived type definitions, interface blocks (Section 5.11), and namelist groups (Section 7.15). This collection may be expected to provide facilities associated with some particular task, such as providing matrix arithmetic, a library facility, or a data base. It may sometimes be large.

In this chapter, we will describe program units and the statements that are associated with them. Within a complete program, they may appear in any order, but many compilers require a module to precede other program units that use it.

5.2 Main program

Every complete program must have one, and only one, main program. Optionally, it may contain calls to subprograms. A main program has the following form:

        [program *program-name*]
            [*specification-stmts*]
            [*executable-stmts*]
        [contains
            internal-subprograms]
        end [program [*program-name*]]

The program statement is optional, but we recommend its use. The *program-name* may be any valid Fortran name such as model. The only non-optional statement is the end statement which has two purposes. It acts as a signal to the compiler that it has reached the end of the program unit and, when executed, it causes the complete program to stop. If it includes *program-name*, this must be the name on the program statement. We recommend using the full form so that it is clear both to the reader and to the compiler exactly what is terminated by the end statement.

A main program without calls to subprograms is usually used only for short tests, as in

```
program test
   print *, 'Hello world!'
end program test
```

The specification statements define the environment for the executable statements. So far, we have met the type declaration statement (integer, real, complex, logical, character, and type(*type-name*)) that specifies the type and other properties of the entities that it lists, and the type definition block (bounded by type *type-name* and end type statements). We will meet other specification statements in this and the next two chapters.

The executable statements specify the actions that are to be performed. So far, we have met the assignment statement, the pointer assignment statement, the go to statement, the if statement and construct, the do and case constructs, and the read and print statements. We will meet other executable statements in this and later chapters. Execution of a program always commences with the first executable statement of the main program.

The contains statement flags the presence of one or more internal subprograms. We will describe internal subprograms in Section 5.6. If the execution of the last statement ahead of the contains statement does not result in a branch, control passes over the internal subprograms to the end statement and the program stops. The end statement may be labelled and may be the target of a branch from one of the executable statements. If such a branch is taken, again the program stops.

5.3   The stop statement

Another way to stop program execution is to execute a stop statement. This statement may be labelled, may be part of an if statement, and is an executable statement that may appear in the main program or any subprogram. A well-designed program normally returns control to the main program for program termination, so the stop statement should appear there. However, in applications where several stop statements appear in various places in a complete program, it is possible to distinguish which of the stop statements has caused the termination by adding to each one an *access code* consisting of a default character constant or a string of up to five digits whose leading zeros are not significant. This might be used by a given processor to indicate the origin of the stop in a message. Examples are

```
stop
stop 'Incomplete data. Program terminated.'
stop 12345
```

5.4   External subprograms

External subprograms are called from a main program or elsewhere, usually to perform a well-defined task within the framework of a complete program. Apart from the leading statement, they have a form that is very like that of a main program:

> *subroutine-stmt*
>   [*specification-stmts*]
>   [*executable-stmts*]
> [contains
>   *internal-subprograms*]
> end [subroutine [*subroutine-name*]]

or

> *function-stmt*
>   [*specification-stmts*]
>   [*executable-stmts*]
> [contains
>   *internal-subprograms*]
> end [function [*function-name*]]

The contains statement plays exactly the same role as within a main program (see Section 5.2). The effect of executing an end statement in a subprogram is to return control to the caller, rather than to stop execution. As for the end program statement, we recommend using the full form for the end statement so that it is clear both to the reader and to the compiler exactly what it terminates.

The simplest form of external subprogram defines a subroutine without any arguments and has a *subroutine-stmt* of the form

> subroutine *subroutine-name*

Such a subprogram is useful when a program consists of a sequence of distinct phases, in which case the main program consists of a sequence of call statements that invoke the subroutines as in the example

```
program game      ! Main program to control a card game
   call shuffle    ! First shuffle the cards.
   call deal       ! Now deal them.
   call play       ! Play the game.
   call display    ! Display the result.
end program game   ! Cease execution.
```

But how do we handle the flow of information between the subroutines? How does play know which cards deal has dealt? There are, in fact, two methods by which information may be passed. The first is via data held in a module (Section 5.5) and accessed by the subprograms, and the second is via arguments (Section 5.7) in the procedure calls.

5.5 Modules

The third type of program unit, the module, provides a means of packaging global data, derived types and their associated operations, interface blocks (Section 5.11), and namelist groups (Section 7.15). Everything associated with some task (such as interval arithmetic, see later in this section) may be collected into a module and accessed whenever it is needed. Those parts that are associated with the internal working and are of no interest to the user may be made 'invisible' to the user, which allows the internal design to be altered without the need to alter the program that uses it and prevents accidental alteration of internal data. We expect Fortran 90/95 libraries to consist of sets of modules.

The module has the form

```
module module-name
    [specification-stmts]
[contains
    module-subprograms]
end [module [module-name]]
```

As for the `end program`, `end subroutine`, and `end function` statements, we recommend using the full form for the end statement.

In its simplest form, the body consists only of data specifications. For example

```
module state
    integer, dimension(52) :: cards
end module state
```

might hold the state of play of the game of Section 5.4. It is accessed by the statement

```
use state
```

appearing at the beginnings of the main program game and subprograms `shuffle`, `deal`, `play`, and `display`. The array `cards` is set by `shuffle` to contain the integer values 1 to 52 in a random order, where each integer value corresponds to a pre-defined playing card. For instance, 1 might stand for the ace of clubs, 2 for the two of clubs, etc. up to 52 for the king of spades. The array `cards` is changed by the subroutines `deal` and `play`, and finally accessed by subroutine `display`.

A further example of global data in a module would be the definitions of the values of the kind type parameters that might be required throughout a program (Sections 2.6.1 and 2.6.2). They can be placed in a module and used wherever they are required. On a processor that supports all the kinds listed, an example might be:

```
module numeric_kinds
   ! named constants for 4, 2, and 1 byte integers:
   integer, parameter ::                                  &
        i4b = selected_int_kind(9),                       &
        i2b = selected_int_kind(4),                       &
        i1b = selected_int_kind(2)
   ! and for single, double and quadruple precision reals:
   integer, parameter ::                                  &
        sp = kind(1.0),                                   &
        dp = selected_real_kind(2*precision(1.0_sp)),     &
        qp = selected_real_kind(2*precision(1.0_dp))
end module numeric_kinds
```

A very useful role for modules is to contain definitions of types and their associated operators. For example, a module might contain the type interval of Section 3.8, as shown in Figure 5.2. Given this module, any program unit needing this type and its operators need only include the statement

```
use interval_arithmetic
```

at the head of its specification statements.

Figure 5.2

```
module interval_arithmetic
   type interval
      real :: lower, upper
   end type interval
   interface operator(+)
      module procedure add_intervals
   end interface
   :
contains
   function add_intervals(a,b)
      type(interval)                :: add_intervals
      type(interval), intent(in) :: a, b
      add_intervals%lower = a%lower + b%lower
      add_intervals%upper = a%upper + b%upper
   end function add_intervals
   :
end module interval_arithmetic
```

A module subprogram has exactly the same form as an external subprogram, except that function or subroutine *must* be present on the end statement, so there is no need for a separate description. It always has access to other entities of the module, including the ability to call other subprograms of the module, rather as if it contained a use statement for its module.

A module may contain use statements that access other modules. It must not access itself directly or indirectly through a chain of use statements, for example a accessing b and b accessing a. No ordering of modules is required by the standard, but normal practice is to require each module to precede its use. We recommend this practice, which will make it impossible for a module to access itself through other modules. It is required by many compilers.

It is possible within a module to specify that some of the entities are private to it and cannot be accessed from other program units. Also there are forms of the use statement that allow access to only part of a module and forms that allow renaming of the entities accessed. These features will be explained in Sections 7.6 and 7.10. For the present, we assume that the whole module is accessed without any renaming of the entities in it.

Besides data definitions, type definitions, subprograms, and interface blocks, a module may contain namelist groups (Section 7.15). The ability to make single definitions of interface blocks will be seen to be important in the context of constructing large libraries of reusable software.

5.6 Internal subprograms

We have seen that internal subprograms may be defined inside main programs and external subprograms, and within module subprograms. They have the form

> *subroutine-stmt*
>   [*specification-stmts*]
>   [*executable-stmts*]
> end subroutine [*subroutine-name*]

or

> *function-stmt*
>   [*specification-stmts*]
>   [*executable-stmts*]
> end function [*function-name*]

that is, the same form as a module subprogram, except that they may not contain further internal subprograms. Note that function or subroutine must be present on the end statement. An internal subprogram automatically has access to all the host's entities, including the ability to call its other internal subprograms. Internal subprograms must be preceded by a contains statement in the host.

In the rest of this chapter, we describe several properties of subprograms that apply to external, module, and internal subprograms. We therefore do not need to describe internal subprograms separately. An example is given in Figure 5.10 (Section 5.15).

5.7 Arguments of procedures

Procedure arguments provide an alternative means for two program units to access the same data. Returning to our card game example, instead of placing the array cards in a module, we might declare it in the main program and pass it as an actual argument to each subprogram, as shown in Figure 5.3.

Figure 5.3

```
program game        ! Main program to control a card game
   integer, dimension(52) :: cards
   call shuffle(cards)       ! First shuffle the cards.
   call deal(cards)          ! Now deal them.
   call play(cards)          ! Play the game.
   call display(cards)       ! Display the result.
end program game             ! Cease execution.
```

Each subroutine receives cards as a dummy argument. For instance, shuffle has the form shown in Figure 5.4.

Figure 5.4

```
subroutine shuffle(cards)
   ! Subroutine that places the values 1 to 52 in cards
   ! in random order.
   integer, dimension(52) :: cards
   ! Statements that fill cards
   :
end subroutine shuffle   ! Return to caller.
```

We can, of course, imagine a card game in which deal is going to deal only three cards to each of four players. In this case, it would be a waste of time for shuffle to prepare a deck of 52 cards when only the first 12 cards are needed. This can be achieved by requesting shuffle to limit itself to a number of cards that is transmitted in the calling sequence thus:

```
call shuffle(3*4, cards(1:12))
```

Inside shuffle, we would define the array to be of the given length and the algorithm to fill cards would be contained in a do construct with this number of iterations, as shown in Figure 5.5.

We have seen how it is possible to pass an array and a constant expression between two program units. An actual argument may be any variable or expression (or a procedure name, see Section 5.12). Each dummy argument of the called procedure must agree with the corresponding actual argument in type, type parameters, and shape (the requirements on character length and shape agreement

Figure 5.5

```
subroutine shuffle(ncards, cards)
   integer                    :: ncards, icard
   integer, dimension(ncards) :: cards
   do icard = 1, ncards
      :
      cards(icard) = ...
   end do
end subroutine shuffle
```

are relaxed in Chapter 12). However, the names do not have to be the same. For instance, if two decks had been needed, we might have written the code thus:

```
program game
   integer, dimension(52) :: acards, bcards
   call shuffle(acards)        ! First shuffle the a deck.
   call shuffle(bcards)        ! Next shuffle the b deck.
   :
end program game
```

The important point is that subprograms can be written independently of one another, the association of the dummy arguments with the actual arguments occurring each time the call is executed. We can imagine shuffle being used in other programs which use other names. In this manner, libraries of subprograms may be built up.

Being able to have different names for actual and dummy arguments provides a useful flexibility, but it should only be used when it is actually needed. When the same name can be used, the code is more readable.

As the type of an actual argument and its corresponding dummy argument must agree, care must be taken when using component selection within an actual argument. Thus, supposing the type definitions point and triangle of Figure 2.1 (Section 2.9) are available in a module def, we might write

```
use def
type(triangle) :: t
:
call sub(t%a)
:
contains
   subroutine sub(p)
      type(point) :: p
```

5.7.1 Pointer arguments

A dummy argument is permitted to have the attribute pointer. In this case, the actual argument must also have the attribute pointer. When the subprogram is invoked, the rank of the actual argument must match that of the dummy argument, and its pointer association status is passed to the dummy argument. On return, the actual argument normally takes its pointer association status from that of the dummy argument, but it becomes undefined if the dummy argument is associated with a target that becomes undefined when the return is executed (for example, if the target is a local variable that does not have the save attribute, Section 7.9). The intent attribute (Section 5.9) would be ambiguous in this context, since it might refer to the pointer association status alone or to both the pointer association status and the value of its target; it is not allowed to be specified.

In the case of a module or internal procedure, the compiler knows when the dummy argument is a pointer. In the case of an external or dummy procedure, the compiler assumes that the dummy argument is not a pointer unless it is told otherwise in an interface block (Section 5.11).

A pointer actual argument is also permitted to correspond to a non-pointer dummy argument. In this case, the pointer must have a target and the target is associated with the dummy argument, as in

```
    real, pointer :: a(:,:)
    :
    allocate ( a(80,80) )
    call find (a)
    :
subroutine find (c)
    real :: c(:,:) ! Assumed-shape array, see Section 6.3
```

5.7.2 Restrictions on actual arguments

There are two important restrictions on actual arguments, which are designed to allow the compiler to optimize on the assumption that the dummy arguments are distinct from each other and from other entities that are accessible within the procedure. For example, a compiler may arrange for an array to be copied to a local variable on entry, and copied back on return. While an actual argument is associated with a dummy argument:

i) Action that affects the allocation status or pointer association status of the argument or any part of it (any pointer assignment, allocation, deallocation, or nullification) must be taken through the dummy argument. If this is done, then throughout the execution of the procedure, the argument may be referenced only through the dummy argument.

ii) Action that affects the value of the argument or any part of it must be taken through the dummy argument unless

   a. the dummy argument has the pointer attribute,

   b. the part is all or part of a pointer subobject, or

   c. the dummy argument has the target attribute, the dummy argument does not have intent in, the dummy argument is scalar or an assumed-shape array, and the actual argument is a target other than an array section with a vector subscript.

If the value of the argument or any part of it is affected through a dummy argument for which neither a., b., or c. holds, then throughout the execution of the procedure, the argument may be referenced only through that dummy argument.

An example of i) is a pointer that is nullified (Section 6.5.4) while still associated with the dummy argument. As an example of ii), consider

```
call modify(a(1:5), a(3:9))
```

Here, a(3:5) may not be changed through either dummy argument since this would violate the rule for the other argument. However, a(1:2) may be changed through the first argument and a(6:9) may be changed through the second. Another example is an actual argument that is an object being accessed from a module; here, the same object must not be accessed from the module by the procedure and redefined. As a third example, suppose an internal procedure call associates a host variable h with a dummy argument d. If d is defined during the call, then at no time during the call may h be referenced directly.

5.7.3 Arguments with the target attribute

In most circumstances, an implementation is permitted to make a copy of an actual argument on entry to a procedure and copy it back on return. This may be desirable on efficiency grounds, particularly when the actual argument is not held in contiguous storage. In any case, if a dummy argument has neither the target nor pointer attribute, any pointers associated with the actual argument do not become associated with the corresponding dummy argument but remain associated with the actual argument.

However, copy in / copy out is not allowed when

   i) a dummy argument has the target attribute and is either scalar or is an assumed-shaped array, and

   ii) the actual argument is a target other than an array section with a vector subscript.

In this case, the dummy and actual arguments must have the same shape, any pointer associated with the actual argument becomes associated with the dummy argument on invocation, and any pointer associated with the dummy argument on return remains associated with the actual argument.

When a dummy argument has the target attribute, but the actual argument is not a target or is an array section with a vector subscript, any pointer associated with the dummy argument obviously becomes undefined on return.

In other cases where the dummy argument has the target attribute, whether copy in / copy out occurs is processor dependent. No reliance should be placed on the pointer associations with such an argument after the invocation.

5.8 The return statement

We saw in Section 5.2 that if the last executable statement in a main program is executed and does not cause a branch, the end statement is executed and the program stops. Similarly, if the last executable statement in a subprogram is executed and does not cause a branch, the end statement is executed and control returns to the point of invocation. Just as the stop statement is an executable statement that provides an alternative means of stopping execution, so the return statement provides an alternative means of returning control from a subprogram. It has the form

```
return
```

Like the stop statement, this statement may be labelled, may be part of an if statement, and is an executable statement. It must not appear among the executable statements of a main program.

5.9 Argument intent

In Figure 5.5, the dummy argument cards was used to pass information out from shuffle and the dummy argument ncards was used to pass information in. A third possibility is for a dummy argument to be used for both. We can specify the intent on the type declaration statement for the argument, for example:

```
subroutine shuffle(ncards, cards)
   integer, intent(in)                    :: ncards
   integer, intent(out), dimension(ncards) :: cards
```

For input-output arguments, intent inout may be specified.

If a dummy argument is specified with intent in, it (or any part of it) must not be redefined by the procedure, say by appearing on the left-hand side of an assignment or by being passed on as an actual argument to a procedure that redefines it. For the specification intent inout, the corresponding actual argument must be a variable because the expectation is that it will be redefined by the procedure. For the specification intent out, the corresponding actual argument must again be a variable; in this case, it becomes undefined on entry to the procedure because the intention is that it be used only to pass information out.

If a function specifies a defined operator (Section 3.8), the dummy arguments must have intent in. If a subroutine specifies defined assignment (Section 3.9), the first argument must have intent out or inout, and the second argument must have intent in.

If a dummy argument has no intent, the actual argument may be a variable or an expression, but the actual argument must be a variable if the dummy argument is redefined. It has been traditional for Fortran compilers not to check this rule, since they usually compile each program unit separately. Breaching the rule can lead to program errors at execution time that are very difficult to find. We recommend that all dummy arguments be given a declared intent. Not only is this good documentation, but it allows compilers to make more checks at compile time.

If a dummy argument has the pointer attribute, its intent is not allowed to be specified. This is because of the ambiguity of whether the intent applies to the target data object or to the pointer association.

If a dummy argument is of a derived type with pointer components, its intent attribute also refers to the pointer association status of those components. For example, if the intent is in, no pointer assignment, allocation, or deallocation is permitted.

5.10 Functions

Functions are similar to subroutines in many respects, but they are invoked within an expression and return a value that is used within the expression. For example, the subprogram in Figure 5.6 returns the distance between two points in space and the statement

```
if (distance(a, c) > distance(b, c) ) then
```

invokes the function twice in the logical expression that it contains.

Figure 5.6

```
function distance(p, q)
   real                          :: distance
   real, intent(in), dimension(3) :: p, q
   distance = sqrt( (p(1)-q(1))**2 + (p(2)-q(2))**2 +    &
                    (p(3)-q(3))**2 )
   ! The intrinsic function sqrt is defined in Section 8.4.
end function distance
```

Note the type declaration for the function result. The result behaves just like a dummy argument with intent out. It is initially undefined, but once defined it may appear in an expression and it may be redefined. The type may also be defined on the function statement thus:

```
real function distance(p, q)
```

It is permissible to write functions that change the values of their arguments, modify values in modules, rely on saved local data (Section 7.9), or perform input-output operations. However, these are known as *side-effects* and conflict with good programming practice. Where they are needed, a subroutine should be used. It is reassuring to know that when a function is called, nothing else goes on 'behind the scenes', and it may be very helpful to an optimizing compiler, particularly for internal and module subprograms. A formal mechanism for avoiding side-effects is provided by Fortran 95, but we defer its description to Section 6.10.

A function result may be an array, in which case it must be declared as such. It may also be a pointer,[2] which is very useful when the size of the result depends on a calculation in the function itself. The result is initially undefined. Within the function, it must become associated or defined as disassociated. We expect the function reference usually to be such that a pointer assignment takes place for the result, that is, the reference occurs as the right-hand side of a pointer assignment (Section 3.12) or as a pointer component of a structure constructor. For example, the statements

```
use data_handler
real        :: x(100)
real, pointer :: y(:)
:
y => compact(x)
```

might be used to reference the pointer function

```
function compact(x) ! a procedure to remove duplicates from
                    ! the array x
   real, pointer :: compact(:)
   real          :: x(:) ! Assumed-shape array, see Section 6.3
   integer       :: n
   :                     ! find the number of distinct values, n
   allocate(compact(n))
   :                     ! copy the distinct values into compact
end function compact
```

in the module data_handler. The reference may also occur as a primary of an expression or as the right-hand side of an ordinary assignment, in which case the result must be associated with a target that is defined and the value of the target is used. We do not recommend this practice, however, since it is likely to lead to memory leakage, discussed at the end of Section 6.5.3.

The value returned by a non-pointer function must always be defined.

As well as being a scalar or array value of intrinsic type, a function result may also be a scalar or array value of a derived type, as we have seen already in Section 3.8. When the function is invoked, the function value must be used as a whole, that

---

[2]However, it is not possible for a pointer to have a function as its target. In other words, *dynamic binding*, or association of a pointer with a function at run time, is not available.

is, it is not permitted to be qualified by substring, array-subscript, array-section, or structure-component selection.

Although this is not very useful, a function is permitted to have an empty argument list. In this case, the brackets are obligatory both within the function statement and at every invocation.

5.10.1   Prohibited side-effects

In order to assist an optimizing compiler, the standard prohibits reliance on certain side-effects. It specifies that it is not necessary for a processor to evaluate all the operands of an expression, or to evaluate entirely each operand, if the value of the expression can be determined otherwise. For example, in evaluating

```
x>y .or. l(z)   ! x, y, and z are real; l is a logical function
```

the function reference need not be made if x is greater than y. Since some processors will make the call and others will not, any variable (for example z) that is redefined by the function becomes undefined following such expression evaluation. Similarly, it is not necessary for a processor to evaluate any subscript or substring expressions for an array of zero size or character object of zero character length.

Another prohibition is that a function reference must not redefine the value of a variable that appears in the same statement or affect the value of another function reference in the same statement. For example, in

```
d = max(distance(p,q), distance(q,r))
```

distance is required not to redefine its arguments. This rule allows any expressions that are arguments of a single procedure call to be evaluated in any order. With respect to this rule, an if statement,

```
if (lexpr) stmt
```

is treated as the equivalent if construct

```
if (lexpr) then
    stmt
end if
```

and the same is true for the where statement (Section 6.8).

5.11   Explicit and implicit interfaces

A call to an internal subprogram must be from a statement within the same program unit. It may be assumed that the compiler will process the program unit as a whole and will therefore know all about any internal subprogram. In particular, it will know about its *interface*, that is whether it defines a function or a subroutine, the names and properties of the arguments, and the properties of the result if it defines a function. This, for example, permits the compiler to check whether the actual and dummy arguments match in the way that they should. We say that the interface is *explicit*.

A call to a module subprogram must either be from another statement in the module or from a statement following a use statement for the module. In both cases, the compiler will know all about the subprogram, and again we say that the interface is explicit. Similarly, intrinsic procedures (Chapter 8) always have explicit interfaces.

When compiling a call to an external or dummy procedure (Section 5.12), the compiler normally does not have a mechanism to access its code. We say that the interface is *implicit*. To specify that a name is that of an external or dummy procedure, the external statement is available. It has the form

>   external *external-name-list*

and appears with other specification statements, after any use or implicit statements (Section 7.2) and before any executable statements. The type and type parameters of a function with an implicit interface are usually specified by a type declaration statement for the function name; an alternative is by the rules of implicit typing (Section 7.2) applied to the name, but this is not available in a module unless the function has the private attribute (see Section 7.6).

The external statement merely specifies that each *external-name* is the name of an external or dummy procedure. It does not specify the interface, which remains implicit. However, a mechanism is provided for the interface to be specified. It may be done through an interface block of the form

>   interface
>   *interface-body*
>   end interface

Normally, the *interface-body* is an exact copy of the subprogram's header, the specifications of its arguments and function result, and its end statement. However,

- the names of the arguments may be changed;

- other specifications may be included (for example, for a local variable), but not internal procedures, data or format statements;

- the information may be given by a different combination of statements [3]; and

- in the case of an array argument or function result, the expressions that specify a bound may differ as long as their values can never differ.

---

[3] A practice that is permitted by the standard, but which we do not recommend, is for a dummy argument to be declared implicitly as a procedure by invoking it in an executable statement. If the subprogram has such a dummy procedure, the interface will need an external statement for that dummy procedure.

An *interface-body* may be provided for a call to an external procedure defined by means other than Fortran (usually assembly language).

Naming a procedure in an `external` statement or giving it an interface body (doing both is not permitted) ensures that it is an external or dummy procedure. We strongly recommend the practice for external procedures, since otherwise the processor is permitted to interpret the name as that of an intrinsic procedure. It is needed for portability since processors are permitted to provide additional intrinsics. Naming a procedure in an `external` statement makes all versions of an intrinsic procedure having the same name unavailable. The same is true for giving it an interface body in the way described in the next section (but not when the interface is generic, Section 5.18).

The interface block is placed in a sequence of specification statements and this suffices to make the interface explicit. Perhaps the most convenient way to do this is to place the interface block among the specification statements of a module and then use the module. We imagine subprogram libraries being written as sets of external subprograms together with modules holding interface blocks for them. This keeps the modules of modest size. Note that if a procedure is accessible in a scoping unit, its interface is either explicit or implicit there. An external procedure may have an explicit interface in some scoping units and an implicit interface in others.

Interface blocks may also be used to allow procedures to be called as defined operators (Section 3.8), as defined assignments (Section 3.9), or under a single generic name. We therefore defer description of the full generality of the interface block until Section 5.18, where overloading is discussed.

An explicit interface is required to invoke a procedure with a pointer or target dummy argument or a pointer function result, and is required for several useful features that we will meet later in this and the next chapter. It is needed so that the processor can make the appropriate linkage. Even when not strictly required, it gives the compiler an opportunity to examine data dependencies and thereby improve optimization. Explicit interfaces are also desirable because of the additional security that they provide. It is straightforward to ensure that all interfaces are explicit and we recommend the practice.

5.12   Procedures as arguments

So far, we have taken the actual arguments of a procedure invocation to be variables and expressions, but another possibility is for them to be procedures. Let us consider the case of a minimization subprogram to perform function minimization. It needs to receive the user's function, just as the subroutine `shuffle` in Figure 5.5 needs to receive the required number of cards. The minimization code might look like the code in Figure 5.7. Notice the way the procedure argument is declared by an interface block playing a similar role to that of the type declaration statement for a data object. Although such an interface block is not required, we recommend its use.

Figure 5.7

```
real function minimum(a, b, func) ! Returns the minimum
        ! value of the function func(x) in the interval (a,b)
   real, intent(in) :: a, b
   interface
      real function func(x)
         real, intent(in) :: x
      end function func
   end interface
   real :: f,x
   :
   f = func(x)    ! invocation of the user function.
   :
end function minimum
```

Just as the type and shape of actual and dummy data objects must agree, so must the properties of the actual and dummy procedures. The agreement is exactly as for a procedure and an interface body for that procedure (see Section 5.11). It would make no sense to specify an `intent` attribute (Section 5.9) for a dummy procedure, and this is not permitted.

On the user side, the code may look like that in Figure 5.8. Notice that the structure is rather like a sandwich: user-written code invokes the minimization code which in turn invokes user-written code. Again, we recommend the use of an interface block. As a minimum, the procedure name must be declared in an `external` statement.

Figure 5.8

```
program main
   real :: a, b, f
   interface
      real function fun(x)
         real, intent(in) :: x
      end function fun
   end interface
   f = minimum(1.0, 2.0, fun)
   :
end program main
real function fun(x)
   :
end function fun
```

The procedure that is passed must be an external or module procedure and its specific name must be passed when it also has a generic name (Section 5.18). Internal procedures are not permitted because it is anticipated that they may be implemented quite differently (for example, by in-line code), and because of the need to identify the depth of recursion when the host is recursive (Section 5.16) and the procedure involves host variables.

5.13 Keyword and optional arguments

In practical applications, argument lists can get long and many of the arguments may often not be needed. For example, a subroutine for constrained minimization might have the form

```
subroutine mincon(n, f, x, upper, lower,                    &
              equalities, inequalities, convex, xstart)
```

On many calls, there may be no upper bounds, or no lower bounds, or no equalities, or no inequalities, or it may not be known whether the function is convex, or a sensible starting point may not be known. All the corresponding dummy arguments may be declared optional (see also Section 7.8). For instance, the bounds might be declared by the statement

```
real, optional, dimension(n) :: upper,lower
```

If the first four arguments are the only wanted ones, we may use the statement

```
call mincon(n, f, x, upper)
```

but usually the wanted arguments are scattered. In this case, we may follow a (possibly empty) ordinary positional argument list for leading arguments by a keyword argument list, as in the statement

```
call mincon(n, f, x, equalities=q, xstart=x0)
```

The keywords are the dummy argument names and there must be no further positional arguments after the first keyword argument.

This example also illustrates the merits of both positional and keyword arguments as far as readability is concerned. A small number of leading positional arguments (for example, n, f, x) are easily linked in the reader's mind to the corresponding dummy arguments. Beyond this, the keywords are very helpful to the reader in making these links. We recommend their use for long argument lists even when there are no gaps caused by optional arguments that are not present.

A non-optional argument must appear exactly once, either in the positional list or in the keyword list. An optional argument may appear at most once, either in the positional list or in the keyword list. An argument must not appear in both lists.

The called subprogram needs some way to detect whether an argument is present so that it can take appropriate action when it is not. This is provided by the intrinsic function present (see Section 8.2). For example

```
present(xstart)
```

returns the value .true. if the current call has provided a starting point and .false. otherwise. When it is absent, the subprogram might use a random number generator to provide a starting point.

A slight complication occurs if an optional dummy argument is used within the subprogram as an actual argument in a procedure invocation. For example, our minimization subroutine might start by calling a subroutine that handles the corresponding equality problem by the call

```
call mineq(n, f, x, equalities, convex, xstart)
```

In such a case, an absent optional argument is also regarded as absent in the second-level subprogram. For instance, when convex is absent in the call of mincon, it is regarded as absent in mineq too. Such absent arguments may be propagated through any number of calls, provided the dummy argument is optional in each case. An absent argument further supplied as an actual argument must be specified as a whole, and not as a subobject. Furthermore, an absent pointer is not permitted to be associated with a non-pointer dummy argument (the target is doubly absent).

Since the compiler will not be able to make the appropriate associations unless it knows the keywords (dummy argument names), the interface must be explicit (Section 5.11) if any of the dummy arguments are optional or keyword arguments are in use. Note that an interface block may be provided for an external procedure to make the interface explicit. In all cases where an interface block is provided, it is the names of the dummy arguments in the block that are used to resolve the associations.

5.14   Scope of labels

Execution of the main program or a subprogram always starts at its first executable statement and any branching always takes place from one of its executable statements to another. Indeed, each subprogram has its own independent set of labels. This includes the case of a host subprogram with several internal subprograms. The same label may be used in the host and the internal subprograms without ambiguity.

This is our first encounter with *scope*. The scope of a label is a main program or a subprogram, excluding any internal subprograms that it contains. The label may be used unambiguously anywhere among the executable statements of its scope. Notice that the host end statement may be labelled and be a branch target from a host statement, that is the internal subprograms leave a hole in the scope of the host (see Figure 5.9).

5.15   Scope of names

In the case of a named entity, there is a similar set of statements within which the name may always be used to refer to the entity. Here, type definitions and interface blocks as well as subprograms can knock holes in scopes. This leads us to regard each program unit as consisting of a set of non-overlapping scoping units. A *scoping unit* is one of the following:

- a derived-type definition,

- a procedure interface body, excluding any derived-type definitions and interface bodies contained within it, or

- a program unit or subprogram, excluding derived-type definitions, interface bodies, and subprograms contained within it.

An example containing five scoping units is shown in Figure 5.9.

Figure 5.9
```
module scope1              ! scope 1
    :                      ! scope 1
contains                   ! scope 1
    subroutine scope2      ! scope 2
        type scope3        ! scope 3
            :              ! scope 3
        end type scope3    ! scope 3
        interface          ! scope 2
            :              ! scope 4
        end interface      ! scope 2
        :                  ! scope 2
    contains               ! scope 2
        function scope5(...) ! scope 5
            :              ! scope 5
        end function scope5 ! scope 5
    end subroutine scope2  ! scope 2
end module scope1          ! scope 1
```

Once an entity has been declared in a scoping unit, its name may be used to refer to it in that scoping unit. An entity declared in another scoping unit is always a different entity even if it has the same name and exactly the same properties[4]. Each is known as a *local* entity. This is very helpful to the programmer, who does not have to be concerned about the possibility of accidental name clashes. Note that this is true for derived types, too. Even if two derived types have the same

---
[4] Apart from the effect of storage association, which is not discussed until Chapter 11 and whose use we strongly discourage.

name and the same components, entities declared with them are treated as being of different types[5].

A use statement of the form

   use *module-name*

is regarded as a re-declaration of all the module entities inside the local scoping unit, with exactly the same names and properties. The module entities are said to be accessible by *use association*. Names of entities in the module may not be used to declare local entities (but see Section 7.10 for a description of further facilities provided by the use statement when greater flexibility is required).

In the case of a derived-type definition, a module subprogram, or an internal subprogram, the name of an entity in the host (including an entity accessed by use association) is similarly treated as being automatically re-declared with the same properties, provided no entity with this name is declared locally, is a local dummy argument or function result, or is accessed by use association. The host entity is said to be accessible by *host association*. For example, in the subroutine inner of Figure 5.10, x is accessible by host association, but y is a separate local variable and the y of the host is inaccessible. We note that inner calls another internal procedure that is a function, f; it must not contain a type specification for that function, as the interface is already explicit. Such a specification would, in fact, declare a different, *external* function of that name. The same remark applies to a module procedure calling a function in the same module.

Figure 5.10

```
subroutine outer
   real :: x, y
   :
contains
   subroutine inner
      real :: y
      y = f(x) + 1.
      :
   end subroutine inner
   function f(z)
      real            :: f
      real, intent(in) :: z
      :
   end function f
end subroutine outer
```

Note that the host does not have access to the local entities of any subroutine that it contains.

---

[5] Apart from storage association effects (Chapter 11)

Host association does not extend to interface blocks. This allows an interface body to be constructed mechanically from the specification statements of an external procedure. Note, however, that if a derived type needed for the interface is accessed from a module, the interface block constructed from the procedure cannot be placed in the module that defines the type since a module is not permitted to access itself. For example, the following is not permitted:

```
module m
    type t
        integer :: i, j, k
    end type t
    interface g
        subroutine s(a)
            use m          ! Illegal module access.
            type(t) :: a
        end subroutine s
    end interface
end module m
```

Within a scoping unit, each named data object, procedure, derived type, named construct, and namelist group (Section 7.15) must have a distinct name, with the one exception of generic names of procedures (to be described in Section 5.18). Note that this means that any appearance of the name of an intrinsic procedure in another rôle makes the intrinsic procedure inaccessible by its name (the renaming facility described in Section 7.10 allows an intrinsic procedure to be accessed from a module and renamed). Within a type definition, each component of the type, each intrinsic procedure referenced, and each derived type or named constant accessed by host association, must have a distinct name. Apart from these rules, names may be re-used. For instance, a name may be used for the components of two types, or the arguments of two procedures referenced with keyword calls.

The names of program units and external procedures are *global*, that is available anywhere in a complete program. Each must be distinct from the others and from any of the local entities of the program unit.

At the other extreme, the do variable of an implied-do in a data statement (Section 7.5.2) or an array constructor (Section 6.16) has a scope that is just the implied-do. It is different from any other entity with the same name.

5.16   Direct recursion

Normally, a subprogram may not invoke itself, either directly or indirectly through a sequence of other invocations. However, if the leading statement is prefixed recursive, this is allowed. Where the subprogram is a function that calls itself directly in this fashion, the function name cannot be used for the function result and another name is needed. This is done by adding a further clause to the function statement as in Figure 5.11, which illustrates the use of a recursive function to calculate $n! = n(n-1)\ldots(1)$.

Figure 5.11

```
recursive function factorial(n) result(res)
   integer, intent(in) :: n
   integer             :: res
   if(n==1) then
      res = 1
   else
      res = n*factorial(n-1) ! Beware - few computers check for
   end if                    ! integer overflow.
end function factorial
```

The type of the function (and its result) may be specified on the function statement, either before or after the token `recursive`:

    integer recursive function factorial(n) result(res)

or

    recursive integer function factorial(n) result(res)

or in a type declaration statement for the result name (as in Figure 5.11). In fact, the result name, rather than the function name, must be used in any specification statement. In the executable statements, the function name refers to the function itself and the result name must be used for the result variable. If there is no `result` clause, the function name is used for the result, and is not available for a recursive function call.

The `result` clause may also be used in a non-recursive function.

Just as in Figure 5.11, any recursive procedure that calls itself directly must contain a conditional test that terminates the sequence of calls at some point, otherwise it will call itself indefinitely.

Each time a recursive procedure is invoked, a fresh set of local data objects is created, which ceases to exist on return. They consist of all data objects declared in its specification statements or declared implicitly (see Section 7.2), but excepting those with the `data` or `save` attribute (see Sections 7.5 and 7.9) and any dummy arguments. The interface is explicit within the procedure.

5.17 Indirect recursion

A procedure may also be invoked by indirect recursion, that is, it may call itself through calls to other procedures. To illustrate that this may be useful, suppose we wish to perform a two-dimensional integration but have only the procedure for one-dimensional integration shown in Figure 5.12. For example, suppose that it is desired to integrate a function f of x and y over a rectangle. We might write a Fortran function in a module to receive the value of x as an argument and the value of y from the module itself by host association, as shown in Figure 5.13.

Figure 5.12

```
recursive function integrate(f, bounds)
   ! Integrate f(x) from bounds(1) to bounds(2)
   real :: integrate
   interface
      function f(x)
          real             :: f
          real, intent(in) :: x
      end function f
   end interface
   real, dimension(2), intent(in) :: bounds
   :
end function integrate
```

Figure 5.13

```
module func
   real                :: yval
   real, dimension(2) :: xbounds, ybounds
contains
   function f(xval)
      real             :: f
      real, intent(in) :: xval
      f = ...        ! Expression involving xval and yval
   end function f
end module func
```

We can then integrate over x for a particular value of y, as shown in Figure 5.14, where integrate might be as shown in Figure 5.12. We may now integrate over the whole rectangle thus

```
volume = integrate(fy, ybounds)
```

Note that integrate calls fy, which in turn calls integrate.

5.18   Overloading and generic interfaces

We saw in Section 5.11 how to use a simple interface block to provide an explicit interface to an external or dummy procedure. Another use is for overloading, that is being able to call several procedures by the same generic name. Here

Figure 5.14

```
function fy(y)
   use func
   real                :: fy
   real, intent(in) :: y
   yval = y
   fy = integrate(f, xbounds)
end function fy
```

the interface block contains several interface bodies and the interface statement specifies the generic name. For example,

```
interface gamma
   function sgamma(x)
      real (selected_real_kind( 6))                :: sgamma
      real (selected_real_kind( 6)), intent(in) :: x
   end function sgamma
   function dgamma(x)
      real (selected_real_kind(12))                :: dgamma
      real (selected_real_kind(12)), intent(in) :: x
   end function dgamma
end interface
```

permits both the functions sgamma and dgamma to be invoked using the generic name gamma.

A specific name for a procedure may be the same as its generic name. For example, the procedure sgamma could be renamed gamma without invalidating the interface block.

Furthermore, a generic name may be the same as another accessible generic name. In such a case, all the procedures that have this generic name may be invoked through it. This capability is important, since a module may need to extend the intrinsic functions such as sin to a new type such as interval (Section 3.8).

If it is desired to overload a module procedure, the interface is already explicit so it is inappropriate to specify an interface body. Instead, the statement

module procedure *procedure-name-list*

is included in the interface block in order to name the module procedures for overloading: if the functions sgamma and dgamma above were defined in a module, the interface block becomes

```
interface gamma
   module procedure sgamma, dgamma
end interface
```

It is probably most convenient to place such a block in the module itself.

Fortran 95 allows any generic specification on an `interface` statement to be repeated on the corresponding end `interface` statement, for example,

    end interface gamma   ! Fortran 95 only

As for other end statements, we recommend use of this fuller form.

Another form of overloading occurs when an interface block specifies a defined operation (Section 3.8) or a defined assignment (Section 3.9) to *extend* an intrinsic operation or assignment. The scope of the defined operation or assignment is the scoping unit that contains the interface block, but it may be accessed elsewhere by use or host association. If an intrinsic operator is extended, the number of arguments must be consistent with the intrinsic form (for example, it is not possible to define a unary `*`).

The general form of the interface block is

    interface [generic-spec]
        [interface-body]...
        [module procedure procedure-name-list]...
            ! In Fortran 95, interface bodies and
            ! module procedure statements may appear in any order.
    end interface [generic-spec] ! Only in Fortran 95 is
                        ! generic-spec allowed here

where *generic-spec* is

    generic-name, operator(defined-operator), or assignment(=).

A `module procedure` statement is permitted only when a *generic-spec* is present, and all the procedures must be accessible module procedures (as shown in the complete module in Figure 5.16 below). No procedure name may be given a particular *generic-spec* more than once in the interface blocks accessible within a scoping unit. An interface body must be provided for an external or dummy procedure.

If `operator` is specified on the interface statement, all the procedures in the block must be functions with one or two non-optional arguments having intent `in`[6]. If `assignment` is specified, all the procedures must be subroutines with two non-optional arguments, the first having intent `out` or `inout` and the second intent `in`. In order that invocations are always unambiguous, if two procedures have the same generic operator and the same number of arguments or both define assignment, one must have a dummy argument that corresponds by position in the argument list to a dummy argument of the other that has a different type, different kind type parameter, or different rank.

All procedures that have a given generic name must be subroutines or all must be functions, including the intrinsic ones when an intrinsic procedure is extended. Any two non-intrinsic procedures with the same generic name must have arguments that differ sufficiently for any invocation to be unambiguous. The rule is that either

---

[6]Since intent must not be specified for a pointer dummy argument (Section 5.7.1), this implies that if an operand of derived data type also has the pointer attribute, it is the value of its target that is passed to the function defining the operator, and not the pointer itself. The pointer status is inaccessible within the function.

i) one of them has more non-optional dummy arguments of a particular data type, kind type parameter, and rank than the other has dummy arguments (including optional dummy arguments) of that data type, kind type parameter, and rank; or

ii) at least one of them must have a non-optional dummy argument that both

- corresponds by position in the argument list to a dummy argument that is not present in the other, is present with a different type or kind type parameter, or is present with a different rank, and

- corresponds by name to a dummy argument that is not present in the other, is present with a different type or kind type parameter, or is present with a different rank.

For case (ii), both rules are needed in order to cater for both keyword and positional dummy argument lists. For instance, the interface in Figure 5.15 is invalid because the two functions are always distinguishable in a positional call, but not on a keyword call such as f(i=int, x=posn). If a generic invocation is ambiguous between a non-intrinsic and an intrinsic procedure, the non-intrinsic procedure is invoked.

Figure 5.15

```
!  Example of a broken overloading rule
   interface f
      function fxi(x,i)
         real            :: fxi
         real, intent(in) :: x
         integer         :: i
      end function fxi
      function fix(i,x)
         real            :: fix
         real, intent(in) :: x
         integer         :: i
      end function fix
   end interface
```

Note that the presence or absence of the pointer attribute is insufficient to ensure an unambiguous invocation since a pointer actual argument may be associated with a non-pointer dummy argument, see Section 5.7.1.

There are many scientific applications in which it is useful to keep a check on the sorts of quantities involved in a calculation. For instance, in dimensional analysis, whereas it might be sensible to divide length by time to obtain velocity, it is not sensible to add time to velocity. There is no intrinsic way to do this, but we conclude this section with an outline example, Figures 5.16 & 5.17, of how it might be achieved using derived types.

Figure 5.16

```
module sorts
   type time
      real :: seconds
   end type time
   type velocity
      real :: metres_per_second
   end type velocity
   type length
      real :: metres
   end type length
   type length_squared
      real :: metres_squared
   end type length_squared
   interface operator(/)
      module procedure length_by_time
   end interface
   interface operator(+)
      module procedure time_plus_time
   end interface
   interface sqrt
      module procedure sqrt_metres_squared
   end interface
contains
   function length_by_time(s, t)
      type(length), intent(in) :: s
      type(time), intent(in)   :: t
      type(velocity)           :: length_by_time
      length_by_time%metres_per_second = s%metres / t%seconds
   end function length_by_time
   function time_plus_time(t1, t2)
      type(time), intent(in)   :: t1, t2
      type(time)               :: time_plus_time
      time_plus_time%seconds = t1%seconds + t2%seconds
   end function time_plus_time
   function sqrt_metres_squared(l2)
      type(length_squared), intent(in) :: l2
      type(length)                     :: sqrt_metres_squared
      sqrt_metres_squared%metres = sqrt(l2%metres_squared)
   end function sqrt_metres_squared
end module sorts
```

Figure 5.17

```
program test
   use sorts
   type(length)          :: s  = length(10.0), l
   type(length_squared)  :: s2 = length_squared(10.0)
   type(velocity)        :: v
   type(time)            :: t  = time(3.0)
   v = s / t
! Note: v = s + t    or    v = s * t  would be illegal
   t = t + time(1.0)
   l = sqrt(s2)
   print *, v, t, l
end program test
```

Note that definitions for operations between like entities are also required, as shown by time_plus_time. Similarly, any intrinsic function that might be required, here sqrt, must be overloaded appropriately. Of course, this can be avoided if the components of the variables are referenced directly, as in

```
t%seconds = t%seconds + 1.0
```

5.19 Assumed character length

A character dummy argument may be declared with an asterisk for the value of the length type parameter, in which case it automatically takes the value from the actual argument. For example, a subroutine to sort the elements of a character array might be written thus

```
subroutine sort(n,chars)
   integer, intent(in)                          :: n
   character(len=*), dimension(n), intent(in) :: chars
   :
end subroutine sort
```

If the length of the associated actual argument is needed within the procedure, the intrinsic function len (Section 8.6) may be invoked, as in Figure 5.18.

An asterisk must not be used for a kind type parameter value. This is because a change of character length is analogous to a change of an array size and can easily be accommodated in the object code, whereas a change of kind probably requires a different machine instruction for every operation involving the dummy argument. A different version of the procedure would need to be generated for each possible kind value of each argument. The overloading feature (previous section) gives the programmer an equivalent functionality with explicit control over which versions are generated.

Figure 5.18

```
    integer function count (letter, string)
        character (1), intent(in) :: letter
        character (*), intent(in) :: string
!       Count the number of occurrences of letter in string
        count = 0
        do i = 1, len(string)
            if (string(i:i) == letter) count = count + 1
        end do
    end function count
```

5.20 The subroutine and function statements

We finish this chapter by giving the full syntax of the Fortran 90 subroutine and function statements, which have so far been explained through examples. It is

> [recursive]   &
> subroutine *subroutine-name* [([*dummy-argument-list*])]

and

> [*prefix*] function *function-name* ([*dummy-argument-list*]) &
> [result(*result-name*)]

where *prefix* is

> *type* [recursive]

or

> recursive [*type*]

(for details of *type* see Section 7.13).

Each feature has been explained separately and the meanings are the same in the combinations allowed by the syntax. The syntax has been extended in Fortran 95 to allow pure and elemental procedures to be specified (Sections 6.10 and 6.11).

5.21 Summary

A program consists of a sequence of program units. It must contain exactly one main program but may contain any number of modules and external subprograms. We have described each kind of program unit. Modules contain data definitions, type definitions, namelist groups, interface blocks, and module subprograms, all of which may be accessed in other program units with the use statement. The program units may be in any order, but many compilers require modules to precede their use.

Subprograms define procedures, which may be functions or subroutines. They may also be defined intrinsically (Chapter 8) and external procedures may be defined by means other than Fortran. We have explained how information is passed between program units and to procedures through argument lists and through the use of modules. Procedures may be called recursively provided they are correspondingly specified.

The interface to a procedure may be explicit or implicit. If it is explicit, keyword calls may be made, and the procedure may have optional arguments. Interface blocks permit procedures to be invoked as operations or assignments, or by a generic name. The character lengths of dummy arguments may be assumed.

We have also explained about the scope of labels and Fortran names, and introduced the concept of a scoping unit.

Many of the features are new since Fortran 77: the internal subprogram, modules, the interface block, optional and keyword arguments, argument intent, pointer dummy arguments and function results, recursion, and overloading. These are powerful additions to the language, particularly in the construction of large programs and libraries.

5.22 Exercises

1. A subroutine receives as arguments an array of values, x, and the number of elements in x, n. If the mean and variance of the values in x are estimated by

$$\text{mean} = \frac{1}{n} \sum_{i=1}^{n} x(i)$$

and

$$\text{variance} = \frac{1}{n-1} \sum_{i=1}^{n} (x(i) - \text{mean})^2$$

write a subroutine which returns these calculated values as arguments. The subroutine should check for invalid values of n (≤ 1).

2. A subroutine matrix_mult multiplies together two matrices A and B, whose dimensions are $i \times j$ and $j \times k$, respectively, returning the result in a matrix C dimensioned $i \times k$. Write matrix_mult, given that each element of C is defined by

$$C(m, n) = \sum_{\ell=1}^{J} (A(m, \ell) \times B(\ell, n))$$

The matrices should appear as arguments to matrix_mult.

3. the subroutine random_number (Section 8.16.3) returns a random number in the range 0.0 to 1.0, that is

```
call random_number(r)    ! 0≤r<1
```

Using this function, write the subroutine shuffle of Figure 5.4.

4. A character string consists of a sequence of letters. Write a function to return that letter of the string which occurs earliest in the alphabet, for example, the result of applying the function to 'DGUMVETLOIC' is 'C'.

5. Write an internal procedure to calculate the volume of a cylinder of radius r and length ℓ, $\pi r^2 \ell$, using as the value of π the result of acos(-1.0), and reference it in a host procedure.

6. Choosing a simple card game of your own choice, and using the random number procedure (Section 8.16.3), write subroutines deal and play of Section 5.4, using data in a module to communicate between them.

7. Objects of the intrinsic type character are of a fixed length. Write a module containing a definition of a variable length character string type, of maximum length 80, and also the procedures necessary to:

i) assign a character variable to a string;

ii) assign a string to a character variable;

iii) return the length of a string;

iv) concatenate two strings.

6. Array features

6.1 Introduction

In an era when many computers have the hardware capability for efficient processing of array operands, it is self-evident that a numerically based language such as Fortran should have matching notational facilities. Such facilities provide not only a notational convenience for the programmer, but provide an opportunity to extend the power of the language. However, new optimization techniques are required, for instance the ability to recognize that two or more consecutive array statements may, in some cases, be processed in a single loop at the object code level. These techniques are being progressively introduced.[1]

Arrays were introduced in Sections 2.10 to 2.13, their use in simple expressions and in assignments was explained in Sections 3.10 and 3.11, and they were used as procedure arguments in Chapter 5. These descriptions were deliberately restricted because Fortran contains a very full set of array features whose complete description would have unbalanced those chapters. The purpose of this chapter is to describe the array features in detail, but without anticipating the descriptions of the array intrinsic procedures of Chapter 8; the rich set of intrinsic procedures should be regarded as an integral part of the array features.

6.2 Zero-sized arrays

It might be thought that an array would always have at least one element. However, such a requirement would force programs to contain extra code to deal with certain natural situations. For example, the code in Figure 6.1 solves a lower-triangular set of linear equations. When i has the value n, the sections have size zero, which is just what is required.

Fortran allows arrays to have zero size in all contexts. Whenever a lower bound exceeds the corresponding upper bound, the array has size zero.

There are few special rules for zero-sized arrays because they follow the usual rules, though some care may be needed in their interpretation. For example, two zero-sized arrays of the same rank may have different shapes. One might have shape (0,2) and the other (0,3) or (2,0). Such arrays of differing shape are not

---

[1] A fuller discussion of this topic can be found in *Optimizing Supercompilers for Supercomputers*, M. Wolfe (Pitman, 1989).

Figure 6.1

```
do i = 1,n
   x(i) = b(i) / a(i, i)
   b(i+1:n) = b(i+1:n) - a(i+1:n, i) * x(i)
end do
```

conformable and therefore may not be used together as the operands of a binary operation. However, an array is always conformable with a scalar so the statement

zero-sized-array = scalar

is valid and the scalar is 'broadcast to all the array elements', making this a 'do nothing' statement.

A zero-sized array is regarded as being defined always, because it has no values that can be undefined.

6.3 Assumed-shape arrays

Outside Chapter 11, we require that the shapes of actual and dummy arguments agree, and so far we have achieved this by passing the extents of the array arguments as additional arguments. However, it is possible to require that the shape of the dummy array be taken automatically to be that of the corresponding actual array argument. Such an array is said to be an *assumed-shape* array. When the shape is declared by the dimension clause, each dimension has the form

[*lower-bound*] :

where *lower-bound* is an integer expression that may depend on module data or the other arguments (see Section 7.14 for the exact rules). If *lower-bound* is omitted, the default value is 1. Note that it is the shape that is passed, and not the upper and lower bounds. For example, if the actual array is a, declared thus:

```
real, dimension(0:10, 0:20) :: a
```

and the dummy array is da, declared thus:

```
real, dimension(:, :) :: da
```

then a(i,j) corresponds to da(i+1,j+1); to get the natural correspondence, the lower bound must be declared:

```
real, dimension(0:, 0:) :: da
```

In order that the compiler knows that additional information is to be supplied, the interface must be explicit (Section 5.11) at the point of call. A dummy array with the pointer attribute is not regarded as an assumed-shape array because its shape is not necessarily assumed.

6.4 Automatic objects

A procedure with dummy arguments that are arrays whose size varies from call to
call may also need local arrays whose size varies. A simple example is the array
work in the subroutine to interchange two arrays that is shown in Figure 6.2.

Figure 6.2

```
subroutine swap(a, b)
   real, dimension(:), intent(inout) :: a, b
   real, dimension(size(a))          :: work
            ! size provides the size of an array,
            ! and is defined in Section 8.12.2.
   work = a
   a = b
   b = work
end subroutine swap
```

Arrays whose extents vary in this way are called *automatic arrays*, and are
examples of *automatic data objects*. These are data objects whose declarations
depend on the value of non-constant expressions, and are not dummy arguments.
Implementations are likely to bring them into existence when the procedure is
called and destroy them on return, maintaining them on a stack[2]. The non-
constant expressions are limited to be specification expressions (Section 7.14).

The other way that automatic objects arise is through varying character length.
The variable word2 in

```
subroutine example(word1)
   character(len = *), intent(inout) :: word1
   character(len = len(word1))        :: word2
```

is an example. If a function result has varying character length, the interface must
be explicit at the point of call because the compiler needs to know this, as shown
in Figure 6.3.

An array bound or the character length of an automatic object is fixed for the
duration of each execution of the procedure and does not vary if the value of the
specification expression varies or becomes undefined.

Some small restrictions on the use of automatic data objects appear in Sections
7.5, 7.9, and 7.15.

---

[2]A stack is a memory management mechanism whereby fresh storage is established and old storage
is discarded on a 'last in, first out' basis within contiguous memory.

Figure 6.3

```
program loren
    character (len = *), parameter :: a = 'just a simple test'
    print *, double(a)
contains
    function double(a)
        character (len = *), intent(in) :: a
        character (len = 2*len(a))      :: double
        double = a//a
    end function double
end program loren
```

6.5   Heap storage

There is an underlying assumption in Fortran that the processor supplies a mechanism for managing heap [3] storage. The statements described in this section are the user interface to that mechanism.

6.5.1   Allocatable arrays

Sometimes an array is required to be of a size that is known only after some data have been read or some calculations performed. An array with the `pointer` attribute might be used for this purpose, but this is really not appropriate if the other properties of pointers are not needed. Instead, an array that is not a dummy argument or function result may be given the `allocatable` attribute by a statement such as

```
real, dimension(:, :), allocatable :: a
```

Such an array is called *allocatable*. Its rank is specified when it is declared, but the bounds are undefined until an `allocate` statement such as

```
allocate(a(n, 0:n+1))      ! n of type integer
```

has been executed for it. Its initial allocation status is 'not currently allocated' and it becomes allocated following successful execution of an `allocate` statement.

An important example is shown in Figure 6.4. The array `work` is placed in a module and is allocated at the beginning of the main program to a size that depends on input data. The array is then available throughout program execution in any subprogram that has a `use` statement for `work_array`.

When an allocatable array `a` is no longer needed, it may be deallocated by execution of the statement

---

[3] A heap is a memory management mechanism whereby fresh storage may be established and old storage may be discarded in any order. Mechanisms to deal with the progressive fragmentation of the memory are usually required.

Figure 6.4

```
module work_array
   integer                              :: n
   real, dimension(:,:,:), allocatable :: work
end module work_array
program main
   use work_array
   read *, n
   allocate(work(n, 2*n, 3*n))
   :
```

```
deallocate (a)
```

following which the array is 'not currently allocated'. The deallocate statement is described in more detail in Section 6.5.3.

If it is required to make any change to the bounds of an allocatable array, the array must be deallocated and then allocated afresh. Allocating an allocatable array that is already allocated, or deallocating an allocatable array that is not currently allocated, is an error.

If a variable-sized array component of a structure is required, unfortunately, an array pointer must be used (see Section 6.14). The prohibition on allocatable arrays here was made to keep the feature simple, but this is now recognized as a mistake that will be corrected in Fortran 2000 (see Sections 1.5 and 13.4).

In Fortran 90, an allocatable array that does not have the save attribute (Section 7.9) may have a third allocation state: undefined. Since an undefined allocatable array may not be referenced in any way, not even an enquiry about its status using the allocated intrinsic function, we recommend avoiding this state. It occurs on return from a subprogram if the array is local to the subprogram or local to a module that is currently accessed only by the subprogram, and the array is allocated. To avoid this situation, such an allocatable array must be explicitly deallocated before such a return.

In Fortran 95, the undefined allocation status cannot occur. On return from a subprogram, an allocated allocatable array without the save attribute is automatically deallocated if it is local to the subprogram, and it is processor dependent as to whether it remains allocated or is deallocated if it is local to a module and is accessed only by the subprogram. This automatic deallocation not only avoids inadvertent memory leakage, but prevents the very undesirable undefined allocation status.

6.5.2 The allocate statement

We mentioned in Section 2.13 that the allocate statement can also be used to give fresh storage for a pointer target directly. A pointer becomes associated

(Section 3.3) following successful execution of the statement. The general form of the allocate statement is

allocate(*allocation-list* [,stat=*stat*])

where *allocation-list* is a list of allocations of the form

allocate-object [(*array-bounds-list*)]

each *array-bound* has the form

[*lower-bound*:] *upper-bound*

and *stat* is a scalar integer variable that must not be part of an object being allocated.

If the stat= specifier is present, *stat* is given either the value zero after a successful allocation or a positive value after an unsuccessful allocation (for example, if insufficient storage is available). After an unsuccessful execution, each array that was not successfully allocated retains its previous allocation or pointer association status. If stat= is absent and the allocation is unsuccessful, program execution stops.

Each *allocate-object* is an allocatable array or a pointer. It may have zero character length and in the case of a pointer may be a structure component.

Each *lower-bound* and each *upper-bound* is a scalar integer expression. The default value for the lower bound is 1. The number of *array-bounds* in a list must equal the rank of the *allocate-object*. They determine the array bounds, which do not alter if the value of a variable in one of the expressions changes subsequently. An array may be allocated to be of size zero.

The bounds of all the arrays being allocated are regarded as undefined during the execution of the allocate statement, so none of the expressions that specify the bounds may depend on any of the bounds. For example,

allocate (a(size(b)), b(size(a)))   ! illegal

or even

allocate (a(n), b(size(a)))   ! illegal

is not permitted, but

allocate (a(n))
allocate (b(size(a)))

is valid. This restriction allows the processor to perform the allocations in a single allocate statement in any order.

In contrast to the case with an allocatable array, a pointer may be allocated a new target even if it is currently associated with a target. In this case, the previous association is broken. If the previous target was created by allocation, it becomes inaccessible unless another pointer is associated with it. We expect linked lists normally to be created by using a single pointer in an allocate statement for each node of the list, using pointer components of the allocated object at the node to hold the links from the node. We illustrate this by the addition of an extra nonzero element to the sparse vector held as a chain of entries of the type

```
type entry
   real                 :: value
   integer              :: index
   type(entry), pointer :: next
end type entry
```

of Section 2.13. The code in Figure 6.5 adds the new entry at the front of the chain. Note the importance of the last statement being a pointer assignment: the assignment

```
first = current
```

would overwrite the old leading entry by the new one.

Figure 6.5

```
type(entry), pointer :: first, current
real    :: fill
integer :: fill_index
:
allocate (current)
current = entry (fill, fill_index, first)
first => current
```

6.5.3 The deallocate statement

When an allocatable array or pointer target is no longer needed, its storage may be recovered by using the deallocate statement. Its general form is

```
deallocate ( allocate-object-list [,stat=stat] )
```

where each *allocate-object* is an allocatable array that is allocated or a pointer that is associated with the whole of a target that was allocated through a pointer in an allocate statement. Here *stat* is a scalar integer variable that must not be deallocated by the statement nor depend on an object that is deallocated by the statement. If stat= is present, *stat* is given either the value zero after a successful execution or a positive value after an unsuccessful execution (for example, if a pointer is disassociated). After an unsuccessful execution, each array that was not successfully deallocated retains its previous allocation or pointer association status. If stat= is absent and the deallocation is unsuccessful, program execution stops.

A pointer becomes disassociated (Section 3.3) following successful execution of the statement. If there is more than one object in the list, there must be no dependencies among them, to allow the processor to deallocate the objects one by one in any order.

A danger in using the deallocate statement is that storage may be deallocated while pointers are still associated with the targets it held. Such pointers are left 'dangling' in an undefined state, and must not be reused until they are again associated with an actual target.

In order to avoid an accumulation of unused and unusable storage, all explicitly allocated storage should be explicitly deallocated when it is no longer required (although, as noted at the end of Section 6.5.1, in Fortran 95, for allocatable arrays, there are circumstances in which this is automatic). This explicit management is required in order to avoid a potentially significant overhead on the part of the processor in handling arbitrarily complex allocation and reference patterns.

Note also that the standard does not specify whether the processor recovers storage allocated through a pointer but no longer accessible through this or any other pointer. This might be important where, for example, a pointer function is referenced within an expression — the programmer cannot rely on the compiler to arrange for deallocation. To ensure that there is no memory leakage, it is necessary to use functions on the right-hand side of pointer assignments, as in the example compact in Section 5.10, or as pointer component values in structure constructors, and to deallocate the pointer (y in Section 5.10) when it is no longer needed (but see also Section 13.3).

6.5.4   The nullify statement

A pointer may be explicitly disassociated from its target by executing a nullify statement. Its general form is

    nullify(*pointer-object-list*)

There must be no dependencies among the objects, in order to allow the processor to nullify the objects one by one in any order. The statement is also useful for giving the disassociated status to an undefined pointer. An advantage of nullifying pointers rather than leaving them undefined is that they may then be tested by the intrinsic function associated (Section 8.2). For example, the end of the chain of Figure 6.5 will be flagged as a disassociated pointer if the statement

    nullify(first)

is executed initially to create a zero-length chain. Because often there are other ways to access a target (for example, through another pointer), the nullify statement does not deallocate the targets. If deallocation is also required, a deallocate statement should be executed instead.

6.6   Elemental operations and assignments

We saw in Section 3.10 that an intrinsic operator can be applied to conformable operands, to produce an array result whose element values are the values of the operation applied to the corresponding elements of the operands. Such an operation is called *elemental*.

It is not essential to use operator notation to obtain this effect. Many of the intrinsic procedures (Chapter 8) are elemental and have scalar dummy arguments that may be called with array actual arguments provided all the array arguments have the same shape. For a function, the shape of the result is the shape of the array arguments. For example, we may find the square roots of all the elements of a real array thus:

```
a = sqrt(a)
```

For a subroutine, if any argument is array-valued, all the arguments with intent out or inout must be arrays. If a procedure that references an elemental function has an optional array-valued dummy argument that is absent, that dummy argument must not be used in the elemental reference unless another array of the same rank is associated with an non-optional argument of the elemental procedure (to ensure that the rank does not vary from call to call).

Similarly, an intrinsic assignment may be used to assign a scalar to all the elements of an array, or to assign each element of an array to the corresponding element of an array of the same shape (Section 3.11). Such an assignment is also called *elemental*.

If a similar effect is desired for a defined operator, a function must be provided for each rank or pair of ranks for which it is needed (but this is not necessary in Fortran 95, see Section 6.11). For example, the module in Figure 6.6 provides summation for scalars and rank-one arrays of intervals (Section 3.8). We leave it as an exercise for the reader to add definitions for mixing scalars and rank-one arrays.

Similarly, elemental versions of defined assignments must be provided explicitly (but, again, this is not necessary in Fortran 95, see Section 6.11).

6.7   Array-valued functions

We mentioned in Section 5.10 that a function may have an array-valued result, and have used this language feature in Figure 6.6 where the interpretation is obvious.

In order that the compiler should know the shape of the result, the interface must be explicit (Section 5.11) whenever such a function is referenced. The shape is specified within the function definition by the dimension attribute for the function name. Unless the function result is a pointer, the bounds must be explicit expressions and they are evaluated on entry to the function. For another example, see the declaration of the function result in Figure 6.7.

An array-valued function is not necessarily elemental. For example, at the end of Section 3.10 we considered the type

Figure 6.6

```
module interval_addition
   type interval
      real :: lower, upper
   end type interval
   interface operator(+)
      module procedure add00, add11
   end interface
contains
   function add00 (a, b)
      type (interval)             :: add00
      type (interval), intent(in) :: a, b
      add00%lower = a%lower + b%lower  ! Production code would
      add00%upper = a%upper + b%upper  ! allow for roundoff.
   end function add00
   function add11 (a, b)
      type (interval), dimension(:), intent(in)       :: a
      type (interval), dimension(size(a))             :: add11
      type (interval), dimension(size(a)), intent(in) :: b
      add11%lower = a%lower + b%lower  ! Production code would
      add11%upper = a%upper + b%upper  ! allow for roundoff.
   end function add11
end module interval_addition
```

```
type matrix
   real :: element
end type matrix
```

Its scalar and rank-one operations might be as for reals, but for multiplying a rank-two array by a rank-one array, we might use the module function shown in Figure 6.7 to provide matrix by vector multiplication.

6.8   The where statement and construct

It is often desired to perform an array operation only for certain elements, say those whose values are positive. The where statement provides this facility. A simple example is

```
where ( a > 0.0 ) a = 1.0/a     ! a is a real array
```

which reciprocates the positive elements of a and leaves the rest unaltered. The general form is

```
where (logical-array-expr) array-variable = expr
```

Figure 6.7

```
function mult(a, b)
!
    type(matrix), dimension(:, :)        :: a
    type(matrix), dimension(size(a, 2)) :: b
                    ! size is defined in Section 8.12
    type(matrix), dimension(size(a, 1)) :: mult
    integer                              :: j, n
!
    mult = 0.0      ! A defined assignment from a real
                    ! scalar to a rank-one matrix.
    n = size(a, 1)
    do j = 1, size(a, 2)
       mult = mult + a(1:n, j) * b(j)
                ! Uses defined operations for addition of
                ! two rank-one matrices and multiplication
                ! of a rank-one matrix by a scalar matrix.
    end do
end function mult
```

The logical array expression *logical-array-expr* must have the same shape as *array-variable*. It is evaluated first and then just those elements of *expr* that correspond to elements of *logical-array-expr* that have the value true are evaluated and are assigned to the corresponding elements of *array-variable*. All other elements of *array-variable* are left unaltered. **In Fortran 90**, the assignment must not be a defined assignment (this restriction is relaxed in Fortran 95, see Section 6.8.1).

A single logical array expression may be used for a sequence of array assignments all of the same shape. The general form of this construct is

```
where (logical-array-expr)
    array-assignments
end where
```

The logical array expression *logical-array-expr* is first evaluated and then each array assignment is performed in turn, under the control of this mask. If any of these assignments affect entities in *logical-array-expr*, it is always the value obtained when the where statement is executed that is used as the mask.

Finally, the where construct may take the form

```
where (logical-array-expr)
    array-assignments
elsewhere
    array-assignments
end where
```

Here, the assignments in the first block of assignments are performed in turn under the control of *logical-array-expr* and then the assignments in the second block are performed in turn under the control of .not.*logical-array-expr*. Again, if any of these assignments affect entities in *logical-array-expr*, it is always the value obtained when the where statement is executed that is used as the mask. No array assignment in a where construct may be a branch target statement.

A simple example of a where construct is

```
where (pressure <= 1.0)
    pressure = pressure + inc_pressure
    temp = temp + 5.0
elsewhere
    raining = .true.
end where
```

where pressure, inc_pressure, temp, and raining are arrays of the same shape.

If a where statement or construct masks an elemental function reference, the function is called only for the wanted elements. For example,

```
where ( a > 0 ) a = log(a)      ! log is defined in Section 8.4
```

would not lead to erroneous calls of log for negative arguments.

This masking applies to all elemental function references except any that are within an argument of a non-elemental function reference. The masking does not extend to array arguments of such a function. In general, such arguments have a different shape so that masking would not be possible, but the rule applies in such a case as

```
where (a > 0) a = a/sum(log(a)) ! sum is defined in Section 8.11
```

Here the logarithms of each of the elements of a are summed, and the statement will fail if they are not all positive.

If a non-elemental function reference or an array constructor is masked, it is fully evaluated before the masking is applied.

6.8.1   Some where construct extensions (Fortran 95 only)

In Fortran 95, it is permitted to mask not only the where statement of the where construct (Section 6.8), but also any elsewhere statement that it contains. The masking expressions involved must be of the same shape. A where construct may contain any number of masked elsewhere statements but at most one elsewhere statement without a mask, and that must be the final one. In addition, where constructs may be nested within one another; the masking expressions of the nested constructs must be of the same shape, as must be the array variables on the left-hand sides of the assignments.

A simple where statement such as that at the start of Section 6.8 is permitted within a where construct and is interpreted as if it were the corresponding where construct containing one array assignment.

A where assignment statement is permitted to be a defined assignment, provided that it is elemental (Section 6.11).

Finally, a where construct may be named in the same way as other constructs. These extensions allow sequences like those in Figure 6.8.

Figure 6.8

```
assign_1: where (cond_1)        ! Fortran 95
             :                   ! masked by cond_1
          elsewhere (cond_2)
             :                   ! masked by
             :                   ! cond_2.and..not.cond_1
  assign_2:    where (cond_4)
                :                ! masked by
                :                ! cond_2.and..not.cond_1.and.cond_4
             elsewhere
                :          ! masked by
                :          ! cond_2.and..not.cond_1.and..not.cond_4
             end where assign_2
             :
          elsewhere (cond_3) assign_1
             :             ! masked by
             :             ! cond_3.and..not.cond_1.and..not.cond_2
          elsewhere assign_1
             :       ! masked by
             :       ! not.cond_1.and..not.cond_2.and..not.cond_3
          end where assign_1
```

All the statements of a where construct are executed one by one in sequence, including the where and elsewhere statements. The logical array expressions in the where and elsewhere statements are evaluated once and control of subsequent assignments is not affected by changes to the values of these expressions. Throughout a where construct there is a control mask and a pending mask which change after the evaluation of each where, elsewhere, and end where statement, as illustrated in Figure 6.8.

6.9 The forall statement and construct (Fortran 95 only)

When elements of an array are assigned values by a do construct such as

```
do i = 1, n
    a(i, i) = 2.0 * x(i)      ! a is rank-2 and x rank-1
end do
```

the processor is required to perform each successive iteration in order and one after the other. This represents a potentially severe impediment to optimization on a parallel processor so, for this purpose, Fortran 95 has the forall statement. The above loop can be written as

```
forall(i = 1:n) a(i, i) = 2.0 * x(i)        ! Fortran 95
```

which specifies that the set of expressions denoted by the right-hand side of the assignment is first evaluated in any order, and the results are then assigned to their corresponding array elements, again in any order of execution. The forall statement may be considered to be an array assignment expressed with the help of indices. In this particular example, we note also that this operation could not otherwise be represented as a simple array assignment. Other examples of the forall statement are

```
            ! Fortran 95
forall(i = 1:n, j = 1:m)              a(i, j) = i + j
forall(i = 1:n, j = 1:n, y(i, j) /= 0.) x(j, i) = 1.0/y(i, j)
```

where, in the second statement, we note the masking condition — the assignment is not carried out for zero elements of y.

The forall construct also exists. The forall equivalent of the array assignments

```
a(2:n-1, 2:n-1) = a(2:n-1, 1:n-2) + a(2:n-1, 3:n)   &
                + a(1:n-2, 2:n-1) + a(3:n, 2:n-1)
b(2:n-1, 2:n-1) = a(2:n-1, 2:n-1)
```

is

```
forall(i = 2:n-1, j = 2:n-1)          ! Fortran 95
    a(i, j) = a(i, j-1) + a(i, j+1) + a(i-1, j) + a(i+1, j)
    b(i, j) = a(i, j)
end forall
```

This sets each internal element of a equal to the sum of its four nearest neighbours and copies the result to b. The forall version is more readable. Note that each assignment in a forall is like an array assignment; the effect is as if all the expressions were evaluated in any order, held in temporary storage, then all the assignments performed in any order. The first statement must fully complete before the second can begin.

A forall statement or construct may contain pointer assignments. An example is

```
type element
   character(32), pointer :: name
end type element
type(element)           :: chart(200)
character(32), target :: names(200)
   :                    ! define names
forall(i =1:200)                    ! Fortran 95
   chart(i)%name => names(i)
end forall
```

Note that there is no array syntax for performing, as in this example, an array of pointer assignments.

As with all constructs, forall constructs may be nested. The sequence

```
forall (i = 1:n-1)              ! Fortran 95
   forall (j = i+1:n)
      a(i, j) = a(j, i)         ! a is a rank-2 array
   end forall
end forall
```

assigns the transpose of the lower triangle of a to the upper triangle of a.

A forall construct can include a where statement or construct. Each statement of a where construct is executed in sequence. An example with a where statement is

```
forall (i = 1:n)               ! Fortran 95
   where ( a(i, :) == 0) a(i, :) = i
   b(i, :) = i / a(i, :)
end forall
```

Here, each zero element of a is replaced by the value of the row index and, following this complete operation, the elements of the rows of b are assigned the reciprocals of the corresponding elements of a multiplied by the corresponding row index.

The complete syntax of the forall construct is

```
[name:]  forall (index = lower: upper [:stride] & ! Fortran 95
          [, index = lower: upper [:stride]]... [,scalar-logical-expr] )
              [body]
          end forall [name]
```

where *index* is a named integer scalar variable. Its scope is that of the construct; that is, other variables may have the name but are separate and not accessible in the forall. The *index* may not be redefined within the construct. Within a nested construct, each *index* must have a distinct name. The expressions *lower, upper,* and *stride* (*stride* is optional but must be nonzero when present) are scalar integer expressions and form a sequence of values as for a section subscript (Section 6.13); they may not reference any *index* of the same statement but may reference an *index* of an outer forall. Once these expressions have been evaluated, the *scalar-logical-expr*, if present, is evaluated for each combination of index values. Those for which it has the value .true. are active in each statement of the construct. The *name* is the optional construct name; if present, it must appear on both the forall and the end forall statements. The blank between the keywords end and forall is optional.

The *body* itself consists of one or more: assignment statements, pointer assignment statements, where statements or constructs, and further forall statements or constructs. The subobject on the left-hand side of each assignment in the *body* should reference each *index* of the constructs it is contained in as part of the identification of the subobject, whether it be a non-pointer variable or a pointer object.[4] None of the statements in the *body* may be a branch target, for instance for a go to statement.

In the case of a defined assignment statement, the subroutine that is invoked must not reference any variable that becomes defined by the statement, nor any pointer object that becomes associated.

A forall construct whose body is a single assignment or pointer assignment statement may be written as a single forall statement.

Procedures may be referenced within the scope of a forall, both in the logical scalar expression that forms the optional mask or, directly or indirectly (for instance as a defined operation or assignment), in the body of the construct. *All such procedures must be pure* (see Section 6.10)

As in assignments to array sections (Section 6.13), it is not allowed to make a many-to-one assignment. The construct

```
forall (i = 1:10)          ! Fortran 95
   a(index(i)) = b(i)      ! a, b and index are arrays
end forall
```

is valid if and only if index(1:10) contains no repeated values. Similarly, it is not permitted to associate more than one target with the same pointer.

6.10   Pure procedures (Fortran 95 only)

In the description of functions in Section 5.10, we noted the fact that, although it is permissible to write functions with side-effects, this is regarded as undesirable. In fact, used within forall statements or constructs (Section 6.9), the possibility that a function or subroutine reference might have side-effects is a severe impediment to optimization on a parallel processor – the order of execution of the assignments could affect the results. In order to control this situation, it is possible for the

---

[4]This is not actually a requirement, but any missing *index* would need to be restricted to a single value to satisfy the requirements of the final paragraph of this section. For example, the statement

```
forall (i = i1:i2, j = j1:j2) a(j) = a(j) + b(i, j)
```

is valid only if i1 and i2 have the same value.

programmer to assert that a procedure has no side-effects by adding the pure keyword to the subroutine or function statement. In practical terms, this is an assertion that the procedure

   i) if a function, does not alter any dummy argument;

   ii) does not alter any part of a variable accessed by host or use association;

   iii) contains no local variable with the save attribute;

   iv) performs no operation on an external file (Chapters 9 and 10); and

   v) contains no stop statement.

To ensure that these requirements are met and that a compiler can easily check that this is so, there are the following further rules:

   i) any dummy argument that is a procedure and any procedure referenced must be pure and have an explicit interface;

   ii) the intent of a dummy argument must be declared unless it is a procedure or a pointer, and this intent must be in in the case of a function;

   iii) any procedure internal to a pure procedure must be pure; and

   iv) a variable that is accessed by host or use association or is an intent in dummy argument or any part of such a variable must not be the target of a pointer assignment statement; it must not be the right-hand side of an intrinsic assignment if the left-hand side is of derived type with a pointer component at any level of component selection; and it must not be associated as an actual argument with a dummy argument that is a pointer or has intent out or inout.

This last rule ensures that a local pointer cannot cause a side effect but unfortunately prevents benign uses such as aliasing (Section 6.15) for use within an expression.

The function in Figure 5.6 (Section 5.10) is pure, and this could be specified explicitly:

```
pure function distance(p, q)      ! Fortran 95
```

An external or dummy procedure that is used as a pure procedure must have an interface block that specifies it as pure. However, the procedure may be used in other contexts without the use of an interface block or with an interface block that does not specify it as pure. For example, this allows library procedures to be specified as pure without limiting them to be used as such.

The main reason for allowing pure subroutines is to be able to use a defined assignment in a forall statement or construct and so, unlike pure functions, they may have dummy arguments that have intent out or inout or the pointer attribute. Their existence also gives the possibility of making subroutine calls from within pure functions.

All the intrinsic functions (Chapter 8) are pure, and can thus be referenced freely within pure procedures. In addition, the elemental intrinsic subroutine mvbits (Section 8.8.3) is pure.

The pure attribute is given automatically to any procedure that has the elemental attribute (next section).

The complete set of options for the *prefix* of a function statement (Section 5.20) is

```
prefix-spec [ prefix-spec ] ...     ! Fortran 95
```

where *prefix-spec* is *type*, recursive, pure, or elemental. A *prefix-spec* must not be repeated. A subroutine statement is permitted a similar prefix, except of course that *type* must not be present.

6.11   Elemental procedures (Fortran 95 only)

We have met already the notion of elemental intrinsic procedures (Section 6.6 and, later, Chapter 8) — those with scalar dummy arguments that may be called with array actual arguments provided that the array arguments have the same shape (that is, provided all the arguments are conformable). For a function, the shape of the result is the shape of the array arguments. Fortran 95 extends this to non-intrinsic procedures. This requires the elemental prefix on the function or subroutine statement. For example, we could make the function add_intervals of Section 3.8 elemental, as shown in Figure 6.9. This is enormously useful to the programmer who can get the same effect in Fortran 90 only by writing 22 versions, for ranks 0-0, 0-1, 1-0, 1-1, 0-2, 2-0, 2-2, ... 0-7, 7-0, 7-7, and is an aid to optimization on parallel processors.

Figure 6.9

```
elemental function add_intervals(a,b)      ! Fortran 95
   type(interval)                :: add_intervals
   type(interval), intent(in) :: a, b
   add_intervals%lower = a%lower + b%lower ! Production code
   add_intervals%upper = a%upper + b%upper ! would allow for
end function add_intervals                 ! roundoff.
```

A procedure is not permitted to be both elemental and recursive.

An elemental procedure must satisfy all the requirements of a pure procedure (previous section); in fact, it automatically has the pure attribute. In addition, all dummy arguments and function results must be scalar variables without the pointer attribute. A dummy argument or its subobject may be used in a specification expression only as an argument to the intrinsic functions bit_size, kind, len or numeric inquiry functions of Section 8.7.2. An example is

```
elemental real function f(a)      ! Fortran 95
   real, intent(in)                            :: a
   real(selected_real_kind(precision(a)*2)) :: work
   :
end function f
```

This restriction prevents character functions yielding an array result with elements of varying character lengths and permits implementations to create array-valued versions that employ ordinary arrays internally. A simple example that would break the rule is

```
elemental function c(n)           ! Fortran 95
   character (len=n)   :: c        ! Invalid
   integer, intent(in) :: n
   real                :: work(n) ! Invalid
   :
end function c
```

If this were allowed, a rank-one version would need to hold work as a ragged-edge array of rank two.

An interface block for an external procedure is required if the procedure itself is non-intrinsic and elemental. The interface must specify it as elemental. This is because the compiler may use a different calling mechanism in order to accommodate the array case efficiently. It contrasts with the case of pure procedures, where more freedom is permitted (see previous section).

For an elemental subroutine, if any argument is array valued, all the arguments with intent inout or out must be arrays. For example, we can make the subroutine swap of Figure 6.2 (Section 6.4) perform its task on arrays of any shape or size, as shown in Figure 6.10. Calling swap with an array and a scalar argument is obviously erroneous and is not permitted.

Figure 6.10

```
elemental subroutine swap(a, b)      ! Fortran 95
   real, intent(inout)  :: a, b
   real                 :: work
   work = a
   a = b
   b = work
end subroutine swap
```

If a generic procedure reference (Section 5.18) is consistent with both an elemental and a non-elemental procedure, the non-elemental procedure is invoked. For example, we might write versions of add_intervals (Figure 6.9) for arrays of rank one and rely on the elemental function for other ranks. In general, one must expect the elemental version to execute more slowly for a specific rank than the corresponding non-elemental version.

We note that a non-intrinsic elemental procedure may not be used as an actual argument.

6.12   Array elements

In Section 2.10, we restricted the description of array elements to simple cases. In general, an array element is a scalar of the form

> *part-ref* [*%part-ref*] ...

where *part-ref* is

> *part-name*[(*subscript-list*)]

The last *part-ref* must have a *subscript-list*. The number of subscripts in each list must be equal to the rank of the array or array component, and each subscript must be a scalar integer expression whose value is within the bounds of its dimension of the array or array component. To illustrate this, take the type

```
type triplet
    real                :: u
    real, dimension(3)   :: du
    real, dimension(3,3) :: d2u
end type triplet
```

which was considered in Section 2.10. An array may be declared of this type:

```
type(triplet), dimension(10,20,30) :: tar
```

and

```
tar(n,2,n*n)          ! n of type integer
```

is an array element. It is a scalar of type `triplet` and

```
tar(n, 2, n*n)%du
```

is a real array with

```
tar(n, 2, n*n)%du(2)
```

as one of its elements.

If an array element is of type character, it may be followed by a substring reference:

> (*substring-range*)

for example,

```
page (k*k) (i+1:j-5) ! i, j, k of type integer.
```

By convention, such an object is called a substring rather than an array element.

Notice that it is the array *part-name* that the subscript list qualifies. It is not permitted to apply such a subscript list to an array designator unless the designator terminates with an array *part-name*. An array section, a function reference, or an array expression in parentheses must not be qualified by a subscript list.

6.13 Array subobjects

Array sections were introduced in Section 2.10 and provide a convenient way to access a regular subarray such as a row or a column of a rank-two array:

```
a(i, 1:n)   ! Elements 1 to n of row i
a(1:m, j)   ! Elements 1 to m of column j
```

For simplicity of description, we did not explain that one or both bounds may be omitted when the corresponding bound of the array itself is wanted, and that a stride other than one may be specified:

```
a(i, :)      ! The whole of row i
a(i, 1:n:3)  ! Elements 1, 4, ... of row i
```

Another form of section subscript is a rank-one integer expression. All the elements of the expression must be defined with values that lie within the bounds of the parent array's subscript. For example,

```
v( (/ 1, 7, 3, 2 /) )
```

is a section with elements $v(1)$, $v(7)$, $v(3)$, and $v(2)$, in this order. Such a subscript is called a *vector subscript*. If there are any repetitions in the values of the elements of a vector subscript, the section is called a *many-one section* because more than one element of the section is mapped onto a single array element. For example

```
v( (/ 1, 7, 3, 7 /) )
```

has elements 2 and 4 mapped onto $v(7)$. A many-one section must not appear on the left of an assignment statement because there would be several possible values for a single element. For instance, the statement

```
v( (/ 1, 7, 3, 7 /) ) = (/ 1, 2, 3, 4 /)     ! Illegal
```

is not allowed because the values 2 and 4 cannot both be stored in $v(7)$. The extent is zero if the vector subscript has zero size.

When an array section with a vector subscript is an actual argument, it is regarded as an expression and the corresponding dummy argument must not be defined or redefined and must not have intent out or inout. We expect compilers to make a copy as a temporary regular array on entry but to perform no copy back on return. Also, an array section with a vector subscript is not permitted to be a pointer target, since allowing them would seriously complicate the mechanism that compilers would otherwise have to establish for pointers. For similar reasons, such an array section is not permitted to be an internal file (Section 9.6).

In addition to the regular and irregular subscripting patterns just described, the intrinsic circular shift function cshift (Section 8.13.5) provides a mechanism that manipulates array sections in a 'wrap-round' fashion. This is useful in handling the boundaries of certain types of periodic grid problems, although it is subject to

similar restrictions to those on vector subscripts. If an array v(5) has the value
[1,2,3,4,5], then cshift(v, 2) has the value [3,4,5,1,2].

The general form of a subobject is

part-ref[%*part-ref*] ... [(*substring-range*)]

where *part-ref* now has the form

part-name [(*section-subscript-list*)]

where the number of section subscripts in each list must be equal to the rank of
the array or array component. Each *section-subscript* is either a *subscript* (Section
6.12), a rank-one integer expression (vector subscript), or a *subscript-triplet* of the
form

[*lower*] : [*upper*] [: *stride*]

where *lower*, *upper*, and *stride* are scalar integer expressions. If *lower* is omitted,
the default value is the lower bound for this subscript of the array. If *upper* is
omitted, the default value is the upper bound for this subscript of the array. If
stride is omitted, the default value is one. The stride may be negative so that it is
possible to take, for example, the elements of a row in reverse order by specifying
a section such as

a(i, 10:1:-1)

The extent is zero if *stride*>0 and *lower*>*upper*, or if *stride*<0 and *lower*<*upper*.
The value of *stride* must not be zero.

Normally, we expect the values of both *lower* and *upper* to be within the bounds
of the corresponding array subscript. However, all that is required is that each
value actually used to select an element is within the bounds. Thus,

a(1, 2:11:2)

is legal even if the upper bound of the second dimension of a is only 10.

The *subscript-triplet* specifies a sequence of subscript values,

*lower, lower + stride, lower + 2*stride,...*

going as far as possible without going beyond *upper* (above it when *stride* > 0 or
below it when *stride*< 0). The length of the sequence for the i-th *subscript-triplet*
determines the i-th extent of the array that is formed.

The rank of a *part-ref* with a *section-subscript-list* is the number of vector
subscripts and subscript triplets that it contains. So far in this section, all the
examples have been of rank one; by contrast, the ordinary array element

a(1,7)

is an example of a *part-ref* of rank zero, and the section

a(:,1:7)

is an example of a *part-ref* of rank two. The rank of a *part-ref* without a *section-subscript-list* is the rank of the object or component. A *part-ref* may be an array; for example,

```
tar%du(2)
```

for the array `tar` of Section 6.12 is an array section with elements `tar(1)%du(2)`, `tar(2)%du(2)`, `tar(3)%du(2)`, ... Being able to form sections in this way from arrays of derived type, as well as by selecting sets of elements, is a very useful feature of the language. A more prosaic example, given the specification

```
type(person), dimension(1:50) :: my_group
```

for the type `person` of Section 2.9, is the subobject `my_group%id` which is an integer array section of size 50.

Unfortunately, it is not permissible for more than one *part-ref* to be an array; for example, it is not permitted to write

```
tar%du    ! Illegal
```

for the array `tar` of Section 6.12. The reason for this is that if `tar%du` were considered to be an array, its element (1,2,3,4) would correspond to

```
tar(2,3,4)%du(1)
```

which would be too confusing a notation.

The *part-ref* with nonzero rank determines the rank and shape of the subobject. If any of its extents is zero, the subobject itself has size zero. It is called an array section if the final *part-ref* has a *section-subscript-list* or another *part-ref* has a nonzero rank.

A *substring-range* may be present only if the last *part-ref* is of type character and is either a scalar or has a *section-subscript-list*. By convention, the resulting object is called a section rather than a substring. It is formed from the unqualified section by taking the specified substring of each element. Note that, if c is a rank-one character array,

```
c(i:j)
```

is the section formed from elements i to j; if substrings of all the array elements are wanted, we may write the section

```
c(:)(k:1)
```

An array section that ends with a component name is also called a *structure component*. Note that if the component is scalar, the section cannot be qualified by a trailing subscript list or section subscript list. Thus, using the example of Section 6.12,

```
tar%u
```

is such an array section and

```
tar(1, 2, 3)%u
```

is a component of a valid element of `tar`. The form

```
tar%u(1, 2, 3)   ! not permitted
```

is not allowed.

Additionally, a *part-name* to the right of a *part-ref* with nonzero rank must not have the `pointer` attribute. This is because such an object would represent an array of pointers and require a very different implementation mechanism from that needed for an ordinary array. For example, consider the array

```
type(entry), dimension(n) :: rows   ! n of type integer
```

for the type `entry` defined near the end of Section 6.5.2. If we were allowed to write the object `rows%next`, it would be interpreted as another array of size n and type `entry`, but its elements are likely to be stored without any regular pattern (each having been separately given storage by an `allocate` statement) and indeed some will be null if any of the pointers are disassociated. Note that there is no problem over accessing individual pointers such as `rows(i)%next`.

6.14   Arrays of pointers

Although arrays of pointers as such are not allowed in Fortran, the equivalent effect can be achieved by creating a type containing a pointer component. For example, a lower-triangular matrix may be held by using a pointer for each row. Consider the type

```
type row
    real, dimension(:), pointer :: r
end type row
```

and the arrays

```
type(row), dimension(n) :: s, t     ! n of type integer
```

Storage for the rows can be allocated thus

```
do i = 1, n                 ! i of type integer.
    allocate (t(i)%r(1:i)) ! Allocate row i of length i.
end do
```

The array assignment

```
s = t
```

would then be equivalent to the pointer assignments

```
s(i)%r => t(i)%r
```

for all the components.

A type containing just a pointer component is useful also when constructing a linked list that is more complicated than the chain described in Section 2.13. For instance, if a variable number of links are needed at each entry, the recursive type entry of Figure 2.3 might be expanded to the pair of types:

```
type ptr
   type(entry), pointer :: point
end type ptr
type entry
   real                 :: value
   integer              :: index
   type(ptr), pointer   :: children(:)
end type entry
```

After appropriate allocations and pointer associations, it is then possible to refer to the index of child j of node as

```
node%children(j)%point%index
```

This extra level of indirection is necessary because the individual elements of children do not, themselves, have the pointer attribute – this is a property only of the whole array. For example, we can take two existing nodes, say a and b, each of which is a tree root, and make a big tree thus

```
tree%children(1)%point => a
tree%children(2)%point => b
```

which would not be possible with the original type entry.

6.15 Pointers as aliases

If an array section without vector subscripts, such as

```
table(m:n, p:q)
```

is wanted frequently while the integer variables m, n, p, and q do not change their values, it is convenient to be able to refer to the section as a named array such as

```
window
```

Such a facility is provided in Fortran by pointers and the pointer assignment statement. Here window would be declared thus

```
real, dimension(:, :), pointer :: window
```

and associated with table, which must of course have the target or pointer attribute, by the execution of the statement

```
window  => table(m:n, p:q)
```

If, later on, the size of `window` needs to be changed, all that is needed is another pointer assignment statement. Note, however, that the subscript bounds for `window` in this example are (1:n-m+1, 1:q-p+1) since they are as provided by the functions `lbound` and `ubound` (Section 8.12.2).

The facility provides a mechanism for subscripting or sectioning arrays such as

    tar%u

where `tar` is an array and `u` is a scalar component, discussed in Section 6.13. Here we may perform the pointer association

    taru => tar%u

if `taru` is a rank-three pointer of the appropriate type. Subscripting as in

    taru(1, 2, 3)

is then permissible. Here the subscript bounds for `taru` will be those of `tar`.

6.16 Array constructors

The syntax that we introduced in Section 2.10 for array constants may be used to construct more general rank-one arrays. The general form of an *array-constructor* is

    (/ array-constructor-value-list /)

where each *array-constructor-value* is one of *expr* or *constructor-implied-do*. The array thus constructed is of rank one with its sequence of elements formed from the sequence of scalar expressions and elements of the array expressions in array element order. A *constructor-implied-do* has the form

    (array-constructor-value-list, variable = expr1, expr2 [,expr3])

where *variable* is a named integer scalar variable, and *expr1*, *expr2*, and *expr3* are scalar integer expressions. Its interpretation is as if the *array-constructor-value-list* had been written

    max ((expr2 - expr1 + expr3)/expr3, 0)

times, with *variable* replaced by *expr1*, *expr1*+*expr3*, . . ., as for the do construct (Section 4.5). A simple example is

    (/ (i,i=1,10) /)

which is equal to

    (/ 1, 2, 3, 4, 5, 6, 7, 8, 9, 10 /)

Note that the syntax permits nesting of one *constructor-implied-do* inside another, as in the example

```
(/ ((i,i=1,3), j=1,3) /)
```

which is equal to

```
(/ 1, 2, 3, 1, 2, 3, 1, 2, 3 /)
```

and the nesting of structure constructors within array constructors (and vice versa), for instance, for the type in Section 6.7,

```
(/ (matrix(0.0), i = 1, 100) /)
```

The sequence may be empty, in which case a zero-sized array is constructed. The scope of the *variable* is the *constructor-implied-do*. Other statements, or even other parts of the array constructor, may refer to another variable having the same name. The value of the other variable is unaffected by execution of the array constructor and is available except within the *constructor-implied-do*.

The type and type parameters of an array constructor are those of the first *expr*, and each *expr* must have the same type and type parameters. If every *expr, expr1, expr2,* and *expr3* is a constant expression, the array constructor is a constant expression.

An array of rank greater than one may be constructed from an array constructor by using the intrinsic function reshape (Section 8.13.3). For example,

```
reshape( source = (/ 1,2,3,4,5,6 /), shape = (/ 2,3 /) )
```

has the value

```
1   3   5
2   4   6
```

6.17　Mask arrays

Logical arrays are needed for masking in where statements and constructs (Section 6.8), and they play a similar role in many of the array intrinsic functions (Chapter 8). Often, such arrays are large, and there may be a worthwhile storage gain from using non-default logical types, if available. For example, some processors may use bytes to store elements of logical(kind=1) arrays, and bits to store elements of logical(kind=0) arrays. Unfortunately, there is no *portable* facility to specify such arrays, since there is no intrinsic function comparable to selected_int_kind and selected_real_kind.

Logical arrays are formed implicitly in certain expressions, usually as compiler-generated temporary variables. In

```
where (a > 0.0) a = 2.0 * a
```

or

```
if (any(a > 0.0)) then    ! any is described in Section 8.11.1.
```

the expression a > 0.0 is a logical array. In such a case, an optimizing compiler can be expected to choose a suitable kind type parameter for the temporary array.

6.18   Summary

We have explained that arrays may have zero size and that no special rules are needed for them. A dummy array may assume its shape from the corresponding actual argument. Storage for an array may be allocated automatically on entry to a procedure and automatically deallocated on return, or the allocation may be controlled in detail by the program. Functions may be array-valued either through the mechanism of an elemental reference that performs the same calculation for each array element (in Fortran 90, for intrinsic functions only), or through the truly array-valued function. Array assignments may be masked through the use of the where statement and construct. Structure components may be arrays if the parent is an array or the component is an array, but not both. A subarray may either be formulated directly as an array section, or indirectly by using pointer assignment to associate it with a pointer. An array may be constructed from a sequence of expressions. A logical array may be used as a mask.

Basically, the whole of the contents of this chapter represents features new since Fortran 77, and is a hallmark of Fortran 90/95. The intrinsic functions are an important part of the array features and will be described in Chapter 8.

We conclude this chapter with a complete program, Figures 6.12 & 6.13, that illustrates the use of array expressions, array assignments, allocatable arrays, automatic arrays, and array sections. The module linear contains a subroutine for solving a set of linear equations, and this is called from a main program that prompts the user for the problem and then solves it.

Figure 6.12

```
module linear
    integer, parameter, public :: kind=selected_real_kind(10)
    public :: solve

contains
    subroutine solve(a, piv_tol, b, ok)
    ! arguments
        real(kind), intent(inout), dimension(:,:) :: a
                        ! The matrix a.
        real(kind), intent(in) :: piv_tol
                        ! Smallest acceptable pivot.
        real(kind), intent(inout), dimension(:) :: b
                        ! The right-hand side vector on
                        ! entry. Overwritten by the solution.
        logical, intent(out)       :: ok
                        ! True after a successful entry
                        ! and false otherwise.

    ! Local variables
        integer :: i     ! Row index.
        integer :: j     ! Column index.
        integer :: n     ! Matrix order.
        real(kind), dimension(size(b)) :: row
                        ! Automatic array needed for workspace;
                        ! size is described in Section 8.12.2.
        real(kind) :: element ! Workspace variable.

        n = size(b)
        ok = size(a, 1) == n .and. size(a, 2) == n
        if (.not.ok) then
            return
        end if

        do j = 1, n

!       Update elements in column j.
            do i = 1, j - 1
                a(i+1:n, j) = a(i+1:n, j) - a(i,j) * a(i+1:n, i)
            end do

!       Find pivot and check its size (using maxval just to
!       obtain a scalar).
            i = maxval(maxloc(abs(a(j:n, j)))) + j - 1
                ! maxval and maxloc are in Sections 8.11.1 and 8.14.
            if (abs(a(i, j)) < piv_tol) then
                ok = .false.
                return
            end if
```

Figure 6.13

```
!      If necessary, apply row interchange
          if (i/=j) then
              row = a(j, :); a(j, :) = a(i, :); a(i, :) = row
              element = b(j); b(j) = b(i); b(i) = element
          end if

!      Compute elements j+1 : n of j-th column.
          a(j+1:n, j) = a(j+1:n, j)/a(j, j)
          end do

!   Forward substitution
          do i = 1, n-1
              b(i+1:n) = b(i+1:n) - b(i)*a(i+1:n, i)
          end do

!    Back-substitution
          do j = n, 1, -1
              b(j) = b(j)/a(j, j)
              b(1:j-1) =  b(1:j-1) - b(j)*a(1:j-1, j)
          end do
      end subroutine solve
end module linear

program main
    use linear
    integer :: i, n
    real(kind), allocatable :: a(:, :), b(:)
    logical :: ok

    print *, ' Matrix order?'
    read *,  n
    allocate ( a(n, n), b(n) )
    do i = 1, n
        write(*,'(a, i2, a)') ' Elements of row ', i, ' of a?'
              ! Edit descriptors are described in Section 9.13
        read *, a(i,:)
        write(*,'(a, i2, a)') ' Component ', i, ' of b?'
        read *, b(i)
    end do

    call solve(a, maxval(abs(a))*1.0e-10, b, ok)
    if (ok) then
        write(*, '(/,a,/,(5f12.4))') ' Solution is', b
    else
        print *, ' The matrix is singular'
    end if
end program main
```

6.19 Exercises

1. Given the array declaration

```
real, dimension(50,20) :: a
```

write array sections representing

    i) the first row of a;

    ii) the last column of a;

    iii) every second element in each row and column;

    iv) as for (iii) in reverse order in both dimensions;

    v) a zero-sized array.

2. Write a where statement to double the value of all the positive elements of an array z.

3. Write an array declaration for an array j which is to be completely defined by the statement

```
j = (/ (3, 5, i=1,5), 5,5,5, (i, i =  5,3,-1 ) /)
```

4. Classify the following arrays:

```
subroutine example(n, a, b)
   real, dimension(n, 10) :: w
   real                :: a(:), b(0:)
   real, pointer       :: d(:, :)
```

5. Write a declaration and a pointer assignment statement suitable to reference as an array all the third elements of component du in the elements of the array tar having all three subscript values even (Section 6.12).

6. Given the array declarations

```
integer, dimension(100, 100), target :: l, m, n
integer, dimension(:, :), pointer    :: ll, mm, nn
```

rewrite the statements

```
l(j:k+1, j-1:k) = l(j:k+1, j-1:k) + l(j:k+1, j-1:k)
l(j:k+1, j-1:k) = m(j:k+1, j-1:k) + n(j:k+1, j-1:k) + n(j:k+1, j:k+1)
```

as they could appear following execution of the statements

```
ll => l(j:k+1, j-1:k)
mm => m(j:k+1, j-1:k)
nn => n(j:k+1, j-1:k)
```

7. Complete Exercise 1 of Chapter 4 using array syntax instead of do constructs.

8. Write a module to maintain a data structure consisting of a linked list of integers, with the ability to add and delete members of the list, efficiently.

9. Write a module that contains the example in Figure 6.7 (Section 6.7) as a module procedure and supports the defined operations and assignments that it contains.

7. Specification statements

7.1 Introduction

In the preceding chapters we have learnt the elements of the Fortran language, how they may be combined into expressions and assignments, how we may control the logic flow of a program, how to divide a program into manageable parts, and have considered how arrays may be processed. We have seen that this knowledge is sufficient to write programs, when combined with a rudimentary print statement and with the end statement.

Already in Chapters 2 to 6, we met some specification statements when declaring the type and other properties of data objects, but to ease the reader's task we did not always explain all the available options. In this chapter we fill this gap. To begin with, however, it is necessary to recall the place of specification statements in a programming language. A program is processed by a computer in (usually) three stages. In the first stage, *compilation*, the source code (text) of the program is read and processed by a program known as a *compiler* which analyses it, and generates a file containing *object code*. Each program unit of the complete program is usually processed separately. The object code is a translation of the source code into a form which can be understood by the computer hardware, and contains the precise instructions as to what operations the computer is to perform. In the second stage of processing, the object code is placed in the relevant part of the computer's storage system by a program often known as a loader which prepares it for the next stage; during this second stage, the separate program units are linked to one another, that is joined to form a complete executable program. The third stage consists of the *execution*, whereby the coded instructions are performed and the results of the computations made available.

During the first stage, the compiler requires information about the entities involved. This information is provided at the beginning of each program unit or subprogram by specification statements. The description of most of these is the subject of this chapter. The specification statements associated with procedure interfaces, including interface blocks and the interface statement and also the external statement, were explained in Chapter 5. The intrinsic statement is explained in Chapter 8. The statements connected with storage association (common, equivalence, and sequence) are deferred to Chapter 11.

7.2　Implicit typing

Many programming languages require that all typed entities have their types specified explicitly. Any data entity that is encountered in an executable statement without its type having been declared will cause the compiler to indicate an error. This, and a prohibition on mixing types, is known as *strong typing*. In the case of Fortran, an entity appearing in the code without having been explicitly typed is normally *implicitly* typed, being assigned a type according to its initial letter. The default in a program unit or an interface block is that entities whose names begin with one of the letters i,j,...,n are of type default integer, and variables beginning with the letters a,b,...,h or o,p,...,z are of type default real. This absence of strong typing can lead to program errors; for instance, if a variable name is misspelt, the misspelt name will give rise to a separate variable. For this reason, we recommend that implicit typing be avoided.

Implicit typing does not apply to an entity accessed by use or host association because its type is the same as in the module or the host.

If a different rule for implicit typing is desired in a given scoping unit, the implicit statement may be employed. For no implicit typing whatsoever, the statement

```
implicit none
```

is available (our recommendation), and for changing the mapping between the letters and the types, statements such as

```
implicit integer (a-h)
implicit real(selected_real_kind(10)) (r,s)
implicit type(entry) (u,x-z)
```

are available. The letters are specified as a list in which a set of adjacent letters in the alphabet may be abbreviated, as in a-h. No letter may appear twice in the implicit statements of a scoping unit and if there is an implicit none statement, there must be no other implicit statement in the scoping unit. For a letter not included in the implicit statements, the mapping between the letter and a type is the default mapping.

In the case of a scoping unit other than a program unit or an interface block, for example a module subprogram, the default mapping for each letter in an inner scoping unit is the mapping for the letter in the immediate host. If the host contains an implicit none statement, the default mapping is null and the effect may be that implicit typing is available for some letters, because of an additional implicit statement in the inner scope, but not for all of them. The mapping may be to a derived type even when that type is not otherwise accessible in the inner scoping unit because of a declaration there of another type with the same name.

Figure 7.1 provides a comprehensive illustration of the rules of implicit typing.

Figure 7.1

```
module example_mod
   implicit none
   :
   interface
      function fun(i)      ! i is implicitly
         integer :: fun    ! declared integer.
      end function fun
   end interface
contains
   function jfun(j)        ! All data entities must
      integer :: jfun, j   ! be declared explicitly.
      :
   end function jfun
end module example_mod
subroutine sub
   implicit complex (c)
   c = (3.0,2.0)           ! c is implicitly declared complex.
   :
contains
   subroutine sub1
      implicit integer (a,c)
      c = (0.0,0.0) ! c is host associated and of type complex
      z = 1.0        ! z is implicitly declared real.
      a = 2          ! a is implicitly declared integer.
      cc = 1.0       ! cc is implicitly declared integer.
      :
   end subroutine sub1
   subroutine sub2
      z = 2.0              ! z is implicitly declared real and is
                           ! different from the variable z in sub1.
      :
   end subroutine sub2
   subroutine sub3
   use example_mod         ! Access the integer function fun.
      q = fun(k)           ! q is implicitly declared real and
                           ! k is implicitly declared integer.
      :
   end subroutine sub3
end subroutine sub
```

The general form of the implicit statement is

```
implicit none
```

or

```
implicit type (letter-spec-list) [,type (letter-spec-list)]...
```

where *type* specifies the type and type parameters (Section 7.13) and each *letter-spec* is *letter* [- *letter*].

The implicit statement may be used for a derived type. For example, given access to the type

```
type posn
    real    :: x, y
    integer :: z
end type posn
```

and given the statement

```
implicit type(posn) (a,b), integer (c-z)
```

variables beginning with the letters a and b are implicitly typed posn and variables beginning with the letters c,d,...,z are implicitly typed integer.

An implicit none statement may be preceded within a scoping unit only by use (and format) statements, and other implicit statements may be preceded only by use, parameter, and format statements. We recommend that all implicit statements be at the start of the specifications, immediately following any use statements.

7.3   Declaring entities of differing shapes

So far, we have used separate type declaration statements such as

```
integer                 :: a, b
integer, dimension(10)  :: c, d
integer, dimension(8,7) :: e
```

to declare several entities of the same type but differing shapes. In fact, Fortran permits the convenience of using a single statement. Whether or not there is a dimension attribute present, arrays may be declared by placing the shape information after the name of the array:

```
integer :: a, b, c(10), d(10), e(8, 7)
```

If the dimension attribute is present, it provides a default shape for the entities that are not followed by their own shape information, and is ignored for those that are:

```
integer, dimension(10) :: c, d, e(8, 7)
```

7.4 Named constants and constant expressions

Inside a program, we often need to define a constant or set of constants. For instance, in a program requiring repeated use of the speed of light, we might use a real variable c that is given its value by the statement

```
c = 2.99792458
```

A danger in this practice is that the value of c may be overwritten inadvertently, for instance because another programmer re-uses c as a variable to contain a different quantity, failing to notice that the name is already in use.

It might also be that the program contains specifications such as

```
real    :: x(10), y(10), z(10)
integer :: mesh(10, 10), ipoint(100)
```

where all the dimensions are 10 or 10^2. Such specifications may be used extensively, and 10 may even appear as an explicit constant, say as a parameter in a do-construct which processes these arrays:

```
do i = 1, 10
```

Later, it may be realised that the value 20 rather than 10 is required, and the new value must be substituted everywhere the old one occurs, an error-prone undertaking.

Yet another case was met in Section 2.6, where named constants were needed for kind type parameter values.

In order to deal with all of these situations, Fortran contains what are known as *named constants*. These may never appear on the left-hand side of an assignment statement, but may be used in expressions in any way in which a literal constant may be used, except within a complex constant (Section 2.6.3). A type declaration statement may be used to specify such a constant:

```
real, parameter :: c = 2.99792458
```

The value is protected, as c is now the name of a constant and may not be used as a variable name in the same scoping unit. Similarly, we may write

```
integer, parameter :: length = 10
real               :: x(length), y(length), z(length)
integer            :: mesh(length, length), ipoint(length**2)
:
do i = 1, length
```

which has the clear advantage that in order to change the value of 10 to 20 only a single line need be modified, and the new value is then correctly propagated.

In this example, the expression length**2 appeared in one of the array bound specifications. This is a particular example of a constant expression. A *constant expression* is an expression in which each operation is intrinsic, and each primary is

i) a constant or a subobject of a constant,

ii) an array constructor whose expressions (including bounds and strides) have primaries that are constant expressions,

iii) a structure constructor whose components are constant expressions,

iv) an elemental intrinsic function reference whose arguments are constant expressions,

v) a transformational intrinsic function reference whose arguments are constant expressions,

vi) a reference to an inquiry function (Section 8.1.2) other than `present`, `associated`, or `allocated`, where each argument is either a constant expression or a variable whose type parameters or bounds inquired about are neither assumed, defined by an expression that is not constant, defined by an `allocate` statement, nor defined by a pointer assignment,

vii) an implied-do variable with constant expressions as bounds and strides, or

viii) a constant expression enclosed in parentheses,

and where each subscript, section subscript, and substring bound is a constant expression. In Fortran 95, v) includes `null`.

Because the values of named constants are expected to be evaluated at compile time, the expressions permitted for their definition are restricted in their form. An *initialization expression* is a constant expression in which

i) the exponentiation operator must have an integer power,

ii) an elemental intrinsic function must have arguments and results of type integer or character, and

iii) of the transformational functions, only `null` (Fortran 95 only), `repeat`, `reshape`, `selected_int_kind`, `selected_real_kind`, `transfer`, and `trim` are permitted.

If an initialization expression invokes an inquiry function for a type parameter or an array bound of an object, the type parameter or array bound must be specified in a prior specification statement or to the left in the same specification statement.

In the definition of a named constant we may use any initialization expression, and the constant becomes defined with the value of the expression according to the rules of intrinsic assignment. This is illustrated by the example:

```
integer, parameter :: length=10, long=selected_real_kind(12)
real, parameter    :: lsq = length**2
```

Note from this example that it is possible in one statement to define several named constants, in this case two, separated by commas.

A named constant may be an array, as in the case

```
real, dimension(3), parameter :: field = (/ 0.0, 10.0, 20.0 /)
```

For an array of rank greater than one, the reshape function described in Section 8.13.3 must be applied.

A named constant may be of derived type, as in the case

```
type(posn), parameter :: a = posn(1.0,2.0,0)
```

for the type defined at the end of Section 7.2. Note that a subobject of a constant need not necessarily have a constant value. For example, if i is an integer variable, field(i) may have the value 0.0, 10.0, or 20.0. Note also that a constant may not be a pointer, allocatable array, dummy argument, or function result, since these are always variables. However, in **Fortran 95**, a constant may be of a derived type with a pointer component that is disassociated (Section 7.5.4):

```
type(entry), parameter :: e = entry(0.0, null()) ! Fortran 95
```

Clearly, since such a pointer component is part of a constant, it is not permitted to be allocated or pointer assigned.

Any named constant used in an initialization expression must either be accessed from the host, be accessed from a module, be declared in a preceding statement, or be declared to the left of its use in the same statement. An example using a constant expression including a named constant that is defined in the same statement is

```
integer, parameter :: apple = 3, pear = apple**2
```

Finally, there is an important point concerning the definition of a scalar named constant of type character. Its length may be specified as an asterisk and taken directly from its value, which obviates the need to count the length of a character string, making modifications to its definition much easier. An example of this is

```
character(len=*), parameter :: string = 'No need to count'
```

Unfortunately, there *is* a need to count when a character array is defined using an array constructor, since all the elements must be of the same length:

```
character(len=7), parameter, dimension(2) ::            &
                  c=(/'Metcalf', 'Reid    '/)
```

would not be correct if the three blanks in 'Reid   ' were removed.

The parameter attribute is an important means whereby constants may be protected from overwriting, and programs modified in a safe way. It should be used for these purposes on every possible occasion.

7.5 Initial values for variables

7.5.1 Initialization in type declaration statements

A variable may be assigned an initial value in a type declaration statement, simply by following the name of the variable by an initialization expression (Section 7.4), as in the examples:

```
real              :: a = 0.0
real, dimension(3) :: b = (/ 0.0, 1.2, 4.5 /)
```

The initial value is defined by the value of the corresponding expression according to the rules of intrinsic assignment. The variable automatically acquires the save attribute (Section 7.9). It must not be a dummy argument, a pointer, an allocatable array, an automatic object, or a function result.

7.5.2 The data statement

An alternative way to specify an initial value for a variable is by the data statement. It has the general form

> data *object-list* /*value-list*/ [[,] *object-list* /*value-list*/] . . .

where *object-list* is a list of variables and *implied*-do *loops*; and *value-list* is a list of scalar constants and structure constructors. A simple example is

```
real    :: a, b, c
integer :: i, j, k
data       a,b,c/1.,2.,3./, i,j,k/1,2,3/
```

in which a variable a acquires the initial value 1., b the value 2., etc.

If any part of a variable is initialized in this way, the variable automatically acquires the save atribute. The variable must not be a dummy argument, an allocatable array, an automatic object, or a function result. It may be a pointer only in Fortran 95, and the correspnding value must be null().

After any array or array section in *object-list* has been expanded into a sequence of scalar elements in array element order, there must be as many constants in each *value-list* as scalar elements in the corresponding *object-list*. Each scalar element is assigned the corresponding scalar constant.

Constants which repeat may be written once and combined with a scalar integer *repeat count* which may be a named or literal constant:

```
data i,j,k/3*0/
```

The value of the repeat count must be positive or zero. As an example consider the statement

```
data r(1:length)/length*0./
```

where r is a real array and length is a named constant which might take the value zero.

Arrays may be initialized in three different ways: as a whole, by element, or by an implied-do loop. These three ways are shown below for an array declared by

```
real :: a(5, 5)
```

Firstly, for the whole array, the statement

```
data a/25*1.0/
```

sets each element of a to 1.0.

Secondly, individual elements and sections of a may be initialized, as in

```
data a(1,1), a(3,1), a(1,2), a(3,3) /2*1.0, 2*2.0/
data a(2:5,4) /4*1.0/
```

in each of which only the four specified elements and the section are initialized. Each array subscript must be an initialization expression, as must any character substring subscript.

When the elements to be selected fall into a pattern which can be represented by do-loop indices, it is possible to write data statements a third way, like

```
data ((a(i,j), i=1,5,2), j=1,5) /15*0./
```

The general form of an implied-do loop is

(*dlist, do-var = expr, expr*[, *expr*])

where *dlist* is a list of array elements, scalar structure components, and implied-do loops, *do-var* is a named integer scalar variable, and each *expr* is a scalar integer expression. It is interpreted as for a do construct (Section 4.5) except that the do variable has the scope of the implied-do as in an array constructor (Section 6.16). A variable in an *expr* must be a *do-var* of an outer implied-do:

```
integer            :: j, k
integer, parameter :: l=5, l2=((l+1)/2)**2
real               :: a(l,l)
data ((a(j,k), k=1,j), j=1,l,2) / l2 * 1.0 /
```

This example sets to 1.0 the first element of the first row of a, the first three elements of the third row, and all the elements of the last row, as shown in Figure 7.2.

Figure 7.2 Result of an implied-do loop in a data statement.

1.0	.	.	.	.
.	.	.	.	.
1.0	1.0	1.0	.	.
.	.	.	.	.
1.0	1.0	1.0	1.0	1.0

The only variables permitted in subscript expressions in data statements are do indices of the same or an outer level loop, and all operations must be intrinsic.

An object of derived type may appear in a data statement. In this case, the corresponding value must be a structure constructor having an initialization expression for each component. Using the type definition of posn in Section 7.2, we can write

```
type(posn) :: position1, position2
data position1 /posn(2., 3., 0)/, position2%z /4/
```

In the examples given so far, the types and type parameters of the constants in a *value-list* have always been the same as the type of the variables in the *object-list*. This need not be the case, but they must be compatible for intrinsic assignment since the entity is initialized following the rules for intrinsic assignment. It is thus possible to write statements such as

```
data q/1/, i/3.1/, b/(0.,1.)/
```

(where b and q are real and i is integer). Integer values may be binary, octal, or hexadecimal constants (Section 2.6.1).

Each variable must either have been typed in a previous type declaration statement in the scoping unit, or its type is that associated with the first letter of its name according to the implicit typing rules of the scoping unit. In the case of implicit typing, the appearance of the name of the variable in a subsequent type declaration statement in the scoping unit must confirm the type and type parameters. Similarly, any array variable must have previously been declared as such.

No variable or part of a variable may be initialized more than once in a scoping unit.

We recommend using the type declaration statement rather than the data statement, but the data statement *must* be employed when only part of a variable is to be initialized.

7.5.3 Pointer initialization and the function null (Fortran 95 only)

In Fortran 90, the initial status of a pointer is always undefined.   This is a most undesirable status since such a pointer cannot even be tested by the intrinsic function associated (Section 8.2). Fortran 95 allows pointers to be given the initial status of disassociated in a type declaration statement such as

```
real, pointer, dimension(:) :: vector => null()   ! Fortran 95
```

or a data statement

```
real, pointer, dimension(:) :: vector
data vector/ null() /                              ! Fortran 95
```

This, of course, implies the save attribute, which applies to the pointer association status. The pointer must not be a dummy argument or function result.

Our recommendation is that all pointers be so initialized to reduce the risk of bizarre effects from the accidental use of undefined pointers. This is an aid too in writing code that avoids memory leaks.

The function null is a new intrinsic function (Section 8.15), whose simple form null(), as used in the above example, is almost always suitable since the attributes are immediately apparent from the context. For example, given the type entry of Section 6.5.2, the structure constructor

```
entry (0.0, 0, null())                          ! Fortran 95
```

is available. Also, for a pointer vector, the statement

```
vector => null()                                ! Fortran 95
```

is equivalent to

```
nullify(vector)
```

The form with the argument is needed when null is an actual argument in a reference to a generic procedure and the type, type parameter, or rank is needed to resolve the reference (Section 5.18).

As in Fortran 90, there is no mechanism to initialize a pointer as associated.

7.5.4   Default initialization of components (Fortran 95 only)

Means are available in Fortran 95 to specify that any object of a derived type is given a default initial value for a component. The value must be specified when the component is declared as part of the type definition (Section 2.9). If the component is not a pointer, this is done in the usual way (Section 7.5.1) with the equal sign followed by an initialization expression and the rules of intrinsic assignment apply (including specifying a scalar value for all the elements of an array component). If the component is a pointer, the only initialization allowed is the pointer assignment symbol followed by null().

Initialization does not have to apply to all components of a given derived type. An example for the type defined in Section 6.5.2 is

```
type entry
   real                 :: value = 2.0
   integer              :: index
   type(entry), pointer :: next => null()    ! Fortran 95
end type entry
```

Given an array declaration such as

```
type(entry), dimension(100) :: matrix
```

subobjects such as matrix(3)%value will have the initial value 2.0, and the reference associated(matrix(3)%next) will return the value false.

For an object of a nested derived type, the initializations associated with components at all levels are recognized. For example, given the specifications

```
type node
   integer     :: counter
   type(entry) :: element
end type node
type (node) :: n
```

the component n%element%value will have the initial value 2.0.

Unlike explicit initialization in a type declaration or data statement, default initialization does not imply that the objects have the save attribute. However, an object of such a type that is declared in a module is required to have the save attribute unless it is a pointer or an allocatable array. This is because of the difficulty that some implementations would have with determining when a non-saved object would need to be re-initialized.

Objects may still be explicitly initialized in a type declaration statement, as in

```
type(entry), dimension(100) :: matrix=entry(huge(0.0),   &
                               huge(0),null()) ! Fortran 95
```

in which case the default initialization is ignored. Similarly, default initialization may be overridden in a nested type definition such as

```
type node
   integer    :: counter
   type(entry) :: element=entry(0.0, 0 , null()) ! Fortran 95
end type node
```

However, no part of a non-pointer object with default initialization is permitted in a data statement (subsection 7.5.2).

As well as applying to the initial values of static data, default initialization also applies to any data that is dynamically created during program execution. This includes allocation with the allocate statement. For example, the statement

```
allocate (matrix(1)%next)
```

creates a partially initialized object of type entry. It also applies to automatic objects and to dummy arguments with intent out. It applies even if the type definition is private or the components are private.

7.6   The public and private attributes

Modules (Section 5.5) permit specifications to be 'packaged' into a form that allows them to be accessed elsewhere in the program. So far, we have assumed that all the entities in the module are to be accessible, that is have the public attribute, but sometimes it is desirable to limit the access. For example, several procedures in a module may need access to a work array containing the results of calculations that they have performed. If access is limited to only the procedures of the module, there is no possibility of an accidental corruption of these data by another procedure and design changes can be made within the module without affecting the rest of the program. In cases where entities are not to be accessible outside their own module, they may be given the private attribute.

These two attributes may be specified with the public and private attributes on type declaration statements in the module, as in

```
real, public     :: x, y, z
integer, private :: u, v, w
```

or in public and private statements, as in

```
public  :: x, y, z, operator(.add.)
private :: u, v, w, assignment(=), operator(*)
```

which have the general forms

```
public [ [ :: ] access-id-list]
private [ [ :: ] access-id-list]
```

where *access-id* is a name or a *generic-spec* (Section 5.18).

Note that if a procedure has a generic identifier, the accessibility of its specific name is independent of the accessibility of its generic identifier. One may be public while the other is private, which means that it is accessible only by its specific name or only by its generic identifier.

If a public or private statement has no list of entities, it confirms or resets the default. Thus the statement

```
public
```

confirms public as the default value, and the statement

```
private
```

sets the default value for the module to private accessibility. For example,

```
private
public :: means
```

gives the entity means the public attribute whilst all others are private. There may be at most one accessibility statement without a list in a scoping unit.

The entities that may be specified by name in public or private lists are named variables, procedures (including generic procedures), derived types, named constants, and namelist groups. Thus, to make a generic procedure name accessible but the corresponding specific names inaccessible, we might write

```
module example
    private specific_int, specific_real
    interface generic_name
        module procedure specific_int, specific_real
    end interface
contains
    subroutine specific_int(i)
        :
    subroutine specific_real(a)
        :
end module example
```

An entity with a type must not have the public attribute if its type is declared with the private attribute (because there is virtually nothing one can do with such an entity without access to its type). However, a type that is accessed from a module may be given the private attribute in the accessing module (see Section 7.10). If an entity of this type has the public attribute, a subsequent use statement for it may be accompanied by a use statement for the type from the original module. Therefore, the restriction in the first sentence of this paragraph refers only to types originally declared to be private.

For similar reasons, if a module procedure has a dummy argument or function result of a type declared with the private attribute, the procedure must be given the attribute private and must not have a generic identifier that is public.

The use of the private statement for components of derived types in the context of defining an entity's access within a module will be described in Section 7.11.

The public and private attributes may appear only in the specifications of a module.

7.7   The pointer, target, and allocatable statements

For the sake of regularity in the language, there are statements for specifying the pointer, target, and allocatable attributes of entities. They take the forms:

```
pointer [::]  object-name[(array-spec)]
                    [,object-name [(array-spec)]]...
target [::]  object-name[(array-spec)]
                    [,object-name [(array-spec)]]...
```

and

```
allocatable [::]  array-name[(array-spec)]
                    [,array-name [(array-spec)]]...
```

as in

```
real         ::a, son, y
allocatable :: a(:,:)
pointer      :: son
target       :: a, y(10)
```

We believe that it is much clearer to specify these attributes on the type declaration statements, and therefore do not use these forms.

7.8   The intent and optional statements

The intent attribute (Section 5.9) for a dummy argument that is not a dummy procedure or pointer may be specified in a type declaration statement or in an intent statement of the form

```
intent( inout ) [::] dummy-argument-name-list
```

where *inout* is in, out, or inout. Examples are

```
subroutine solve (a, b, c, x, y, z)
   real         :: a, b, c, x, y, z
   intent(in)   :: a, b, c
   intent(out)  :: x, y, z
```

The optional attribute (Section 5.13) for a dummy argument may be specified in a type declaration statement or in an optional statement of the form

```
optional [::] dummy-argument-name-list
```

An example is

```
optional :: a, b, c
```

The optional attribute is the only attribute which may be specified for a dummy argument that is a procedure.

Note that the intent and optional attributes may be specified only for dummy arguments.

7.9 The save attribute

Let us suppose that we wish to retain the value of a local variable in a subprogram, for example to count the number of times the subprogram is entered. We might write a section of code as in Figure 7.3. In this example, the local variables, a and counter, are initialized to zero, and it is assumed that their current values are available each time the subroutine is called. This is not necessarily the case. Fortran allows the computer system being used to 'forget' a new value, the variable becoming undefined on each return unless it has the save attribute. In Figure 7.3, it is sufficient to change the declaration of a to

```
real, save :: a
```

to be sure that its value is always retained between calls. This may be done for counter, too, but is not necessary as all variables with initial values acquire the save attribute automatically (Section 7.5).

A similar situation arises with the use of variables in modules (Section 5.5). On return from a subprogram that accesses a variable in a module, the variable becomes undefined unless the main program accesses the module, another subprogram in execution accesses the module, or the variable has the save attribute.

If a variable that becomes undefined has a pointer associated with it, the pointer's association status becomes undefined.

The save attribute must not be specified for a dummy argument, a function result, or an automatic object (Section 6.4). It may be specified for a pointer, in which case the pointer association status is saved. It may be specified for an

Figure 7.3

```
subroutine anything(x)
    real    :: a, x
    integer :: counter = 0 ! Initialize the counter
    :
    counter = counter + 1
    if (counter==1) then
        a = 0.0
    else
        a = a + x
    end if
    :
```

allocatable array, in which case the allocation status and value are saved. A saved variable in a recursive subprogram is shared by all instances of the subprogram.

An alternative to specifying the save attribute on a type declaration statement is the save statement:

save [[::] *variable-name-list*]

A save statement with no list is equivalent to a list containing all possible names, and in this case the scoping unit must contain no other save statements and no save attributes in type declaration statements. Our recomendation is against this form of save. If a programmer tries to give the save attribute explicitly to an automatic object, a diagnostic will result. On the other hand, he or she might think that save without a list would do this too, and not get the behaviour intended. Also, there is a loss of efficency associated with save on some processors, so it is best to restrict it to those objects for which it is really needed.

The save statement or save attribute may appear in the declaration statements in a main program but has no effect.

7.10   The use statement

In Section 5.5, we introduced the use statement in its simplest form

use *module-name*

which provides access to all the public named data objects, derived types, interface blocks, procedures, generic identifiers, and namelist groups in the module named. Any use statements must precede other specification statements in a scoping unit. The only attribute of an accessed entity that may be specified afresh is public or private (and this only in a module), but the entity may be included in one or more namelist groups (Section 7.15).

If access is needed to two or more modules that have been written independently, the same name may be used in more than one module. This is the main reason for permitting accessed entities to be renamed by the use statement. Re-naming is also available to resolve a name clash between a local entity and an entity accessed from a module, though our preference is to use a text editor or other tool to change the local name. With renaming, the use statement has the form

   use *module-name, rename-list*

where each *rename* has the form

   local-name => *use-name*

and refers to a public entity in the module that is to be accessed by a different local name.

   As an example,

   use stats_lib, sprod => prod
   use maths_lib

makes all the public entities in both stats_lib and maths_lib accessible. If maths_lib contains an entity called prod, it is accessible by its own name while the entity prod of stats_lib is accessible as sprod.

   Renaming is not needed if there is a name clash between two entities that are not required. A name clash is permitted if there is no reference to the name in the scoping unit.

   A name clash is also permissible for a generic name that is required. Here, all generic interfaces accessed by the name are treated as a single concatenated interface block. This is true also for defined operators and assignments, where no renaming facility is available. In all these cases, any two procedures having the same generic identifier must differ as explained in Section 5.18. We imagine that this will usually be exactly what is needed. For example, we might access modules for interval arithmetic and matrix arithmetic, both needing the functions sqrt, sin, etc., the operators +, -, etc., and assignment, but for different types.

   For cases where only a subset of the names of a module is needed, the only option is available, having the form

   use *module-name,* only : [*only-list*]

where each *only* has the form

   access-id

or

   [*local-name* =>] *use-name*

where each *access-id* is a public entity in the module, and is either a *use-name* or a *generic-spec* (Section 5.18). This provides access to an entity in a module only if the entity is public and is specified as a *use-name* or *access-id*. Where a *use-name* is preceded by a *local-name*, the entity is known locally by the *local-name*. An example of such a statement is

```
use stats_lib, only : sprod => prod, mult
```

which provides access to prod by the local name sprod and to mult by its own name.

We would recommend that only one use statement for a given module be placed in a scoping unit, but more are allowed. If there is a use statement without an only qualifier, all public entities in the module are accessible and the *rename-lists* and *only-lists* are interpreted as if concatenated into a single *rename-list* (with the form *use-name* in an only list being treated as the rename *use-name* => *use-name*). If all the statements have the only qualification, only those entities named in one or more of the *only-lists* are accessible, that is all the *only-lists* are interpreted as if concatenated into a single *only-list*.

The form

```
use module-name, only :
```

might appear redundant. It is provided for the situation where a scoping unit calls a set of procedures that communicate with each other through shared data in a module. It ensures that the data are available throughout the execution of the scoping unit.

An only list will be rather clumsy if almost all of a module is wanted. The effect of an 'except' clause can be obtained by renaming unwanted entities. For example, if a large program (such as one written in Fortran 77) contains many external procedures, a good practice is to collect interface blocks for them all into a module that is referenced in each program unit for complete mutual checking. In an external procedure, we might then write:

```
use all_interfaces, except_this_one => name
```

to avoid having two explicit interfaces for itself (where all_interfaces is the module name and name is the procedure name).

When a module contains use statements, the entities accessed are treated as entities in the module. They may be given the private or public attribute explicitly or through the default rule in effect in the module.

An entity may be accessed by more than one local name. This is illustrated in Figure 7.4, where module b accesses s of module a by the local name bs; if a subprogram such as c accesses both a and b, it will access s by both its original name and by the name bs. Figure 7.4 also illustrates that an entity may be accessed by the same name by more than one route (see variable t).

A more direct way for an entity to be accessed by more than one local name is for it to appear more than once as a *use-name*. This is not a practice that we recommend.

Of course, all the local names of entities accessed from modules must differ from each other and from names of local entities. If a local entity is accidentally given the same name as an accessible entity from a module, this will be noticed at compile time if the local entity is declared explicitly (since no accessed entity may given any attribute locally, other than private or public, and that only in a

Figure 7.4

```
module a
   real :: s, t
   :
end module a
module b
   use a, bs => s
   :
end module b
subroutine c
   use a
   use b
   :
end subroutine c
```

module). However, if the local entity is intended to be implicitly typed (Section 7.2) and appears in no specification statements, then each appearance of the name will be taken, incorrectly, as a reference to the accessed variable. To avoid this, we recommend the use of

```
implicit none
```

in a scoping unit containing one or more use statements. For greater safety, the only option may be employed on a use statement to ensure that all accesses are intentional.

7.11   Derived-type definitions

When derived types were introduced in Section 2.9, some simple example definitions were given, but the full generality was not included. An example illustrating more features is

```
type, public :: lock
   private
   integer, pointer :: key(:)
   logical          :: state
end type lock
```

The general form (apart from redundant features, see Sections 11.2 and C.1.3) is

```
type [[,access]:: ] type-name
    [ private ]
    component-def-stmt
    [component-def-stmt] ...
end type [ type-name ]
```

Each *component-def-stmt* has the form

> *type* [[,*component-attr-list*] ::]*component-decl-list*

where *type* specifies the type and type parameters (Section 7.13), each *component-attr* is either pointer or dimension(*bounds-list*), and each *component-decl* is

> *component-name* [(*bounds-list*)][**char-len*]

or (Fortran 95 only)

> *component-name* [(*bounds-list*)][**char-len*] [*comp-int*]

The meaning of **char-len* is explained in Section 7.13 and *comp-int* represents component initialization, as explained in Section 7.5.4. If the *type* is a derived type and the pointer attribute is not specified, the type must be previously defined in the host scoping unit or accessible there by use or host association.   If the pointer attribute is specified, the type may also be the one being defined (for example, the type entry of Section 2.13), or one defined elsewhere in the scoping unit.

A *type-name* must not be the same as the name of any intrinsic type or a derived type accessed from a module.

The bounds of an array component are declared by a *bounds-list* where each *bounds* is

> :

for a pointer component (see example in Section 6.14) or

> [*lower-bound*:] *upper-bound*

for a non-pointer component, and *lower-bound* and *upper-bound* are constant expressions that are restricted to specification expressions (Section 7.14). Similarly, the character length of a component of type character must be a constant specification expression. If there is a *bounds-list* attached to the *component-name*, this defines the bounds. If a dimension attribute is present in the statement, its *bounds-list* applies to any component in the statement without its own *bounds-list*.

Only if the host scoping unit is a module may the *access* qualifier or private statement appear. The *access* qualifier on a type statement may be public or private and specifies the accessibility of the type. If it is private, then the type name, the structure constructor for the type, any entity of the type, and any procedure with a dummy argument or function result of the type are all inaccessible outside the host module. The accessibility may also be specified in a private or public statement in the host. In the absence of both of these, the type takes the default accessibility of the host module. If a private statement appears for a type with public accessibility, the components of the type are inaccessible in any scoping unit accessing the host module, so that neither component selection nor structure construction are available there. Also, if any component is of a derived type that is private, the type being defined must be private or have private components.

We can thus distinguish three levels of access:

i) all public, where the type and all its components are accessible, and the components of any object of the type are accessible wherever the object is accessible;

ii) a public type with private components, where the type is accessible but its components are hidden;

iii) all private, where both the type and its components are used only within the host module, and are hidden to an accessing procedure.

Case ii) has, where appropriate, the advantage of enabling changes to be made to the type without in any way affecting the code in the accessing procedure. Case iii) offers this advantage and has the additional merit of not cluttering the name space of the accessing procedure. The use of private accessibility for the components or for the whole type is thus recommended whenever possible.

We note that even if two derived-type definitions are identical in every respect except their names, that entities of those two types are *not* equivalent and are regarded as being of different types. Even if the names, too, are identical, the types are different (unless they have the sequence attribute, a feature that we do not recommend and whose description is left to Section 11.2.1). If a type is needed in more than one program unit, the definition should be placed in a module and accessed by a use statement wherever it is needed. Having a single definition is far less prone to errors.

7.12   The type declaration statement

We have already met many simple examples of the declarations of named entities by integer, real, complex, logical, character, and type(*type-name*) statements. The general form is

type [[, *attribute*]... ::] *entity-list*

where *type* specifies the type and type parameters (Section 7.13), *attribute* is one of the following

parameter	dimension(*bounds-list*)
public	intent(*inout*)
private	optional
pointer	save
target	external
allocatable	intrinsic

and each *entity* is

object-name [(*bounds-list*)] [**char-len*] [=*initialization-expr*]

or

function-name [**char-len*]

or (Fortran 95 only)

> *pointer-name* [(*bounds-list*)] [**char-len*] [=>null()]

The meaning of **char-len* is explained in Section 7.13; a *bounds-list* specifies the rank and possibly bounds of array-valued entities.

No attribute may appear more than once in a given type declaration statement. The double colon :: need not appear in the simple case without any *attributes* and without any =*initialization-expr*; for example

```
real a, b, c(10)
```

If the statement specifies a parameter attribute, =*initialization-expr* must appear.

If a pointer attribute is specified, the target, intent, external, and intrinsic attributes must not be specified. The target and parameter attributes may not be specified for the same entity, and the pointer and allocatable attributes may not be specified for the same array. If the target attribute is specified, neither the external nor the intrinsic attribute may also be specified.

If an object is specified with the intent or parameter attribute, this is shared by all its subobjects. The pointer attribute is not shared in this manner, but note that a derived-data type component may itself be a pointer. However, the target attribute is shared by all its subobjects, except for any that are pointer components.

The allocatable, parameter, or save attribute must not be specified for a dummy argument or function result.

The intent and optional attributes may be specified only for dummy arguments.

For a function result, specifying the external attribute is an alternative to the external statement (Section 5.11) for declaring the function to be external, and specifying the intrinsic attribute is an alternative to the intrinsic statement (Section 8.1.3) for declaring the function to be intrinsic. These two attributes are mutually exclusive.

Each of the attributes may also be specified in statements (such as save) that list entities having the attribute. This leads to the possibility of an attribute being specified explicitly more than once for a given entity, but this is not permitted. Our recommendation is to avoid such statements because it is much clearer to have all the attributes for an entity collected in one place.

7.13   Type and type parameter specification

We have used *type* to represent one of the following

```
integer [( [kind=] kind-value)]
real   [( [kind=] kind-value)]
complex  [( [kind=] kind-value)]
character [(actual-parameter-list)]
logical [([kind=] kind-value) ]
type ( type-name )
```

in the `function` statement (Section 5.20), the `implicit` statement (Section 7.2), the component definition statement (Section 7.11), and the type declaration statement (Section 7.12). A *kind-value* must be an initialization expression (Section 7.4) and must have a value that is valid on the processor being used.

For `character`, each *actual-parameter* has the form

> `[len=]` *len-value*

or

> `[kind=]` *kind-value*

and provides a value for one of the parameters. It is permissible to omit `kind=` from a kind *actual-parameter* only when `len=` is omitted and *len-value* is both present and comes first, just as for an actual argument list (Section 5.13). Neither parameter may be specified more than once.

For a scalar named constant or for a dummy argument of a subprogram, a *len-value* may be specified as an asterisk, in which case the value is assumed from that of the constant itself or the associated actual argument. In both cases, the `len` intrinsic function (Section 8.6.1) is available if the actual length is required directly, for instance as a do construct iteration count. A combined example is

```
character(len=len(char_arg)) function line(char_arg)
   character(len=*)             :: char_arg
   character(len=*), parameter :: char_const = 'page'
   if ( len(char_arg) < len(char_const) ) then
   :
```

A *len-value* that is not an asterisk must be a specification expression (Section 7.14). Negative values declare character entities to be of zero length.

In addition, it is possible to attach an alternative form of *len-value* to individual entities in a type declaration statement using the syntax *entity*char-len*, where *char-len* is either (*len-value*) or *len* and *len* is a scalar integer literal constant which specifies a length for the entity. The constant *len* must not have a kind type parameter specified for it. An illustration of this form is

```
character(len=8) :: word(4), point*1, text(20)*4
```

here, `word`, `point` and `text` have character length 8, 1, and 4, respectively. Similarly, the alternative form may be used for individual components in a component definition statement.

7.14   Specification expressions

Non-constant scalar integer expressions may be used to specify the array bounds (examples in Section 6.4) and character lengths of data objects in a subprogram, and of function results. Such an expression may depend only on data values that are defined on entry to the subprogram. It must not depend on an optional argument, even if present. Any variable referenced must not have its type and type parameters specified later in the same sequence of specification statements, unless they are those implied by the implicit typing rules.

Array constructors and derived-type constructors are permitted. The expression may reference an inquiry function for an array bound or for a type parameter of an entity which either is accessed by use or host association, or is specified earlier in the same specification sequence, but not later in the sequence[1]. An element of an array specified in the same specification sequence can be referenced only if the bounds of the array are specified earlier in the sequence[2]. Such an expression is called a *specification expression*.

An array whose bounds are declared using specification expressions is called an *explicit-shape array*.

A variety of possibilities are shown in Figure 7.5.

Figure 7.5

```
subroutine sample(arr, value, string)
   use definitions  ! Contains the real a
   real, dimension(:,:), intent(out) :: arr ! Assumed-shape array
   integer, intent(in)               :: value
   character(len=*), intent(in)      :: string ! Assumed length
   real, dimension(ubound(arr, 1)+5) :: x     ! Automatic array
   character(len=value+len(string))  :: cc    ! Automatic object
   integer, parameter :: pa2 =   &
                         selected_real_kind(2*precision(a))
   real(kind=pa2) :: z   ! Precision of z is at least twice
                         ! the precision of a
   :
```

The bounds and character lengths are not affected by any redefinitions or undefinitions of variables in the expressions during execution of the procedure.

7.14.1   Specification expression restrictions (Fortran 90 only)

In Fortran 90, references to non-intrinsic procedures are not permitted and intrinsic function references are limited to:

- an elemental function reference for which the arguments and result are of type integer or character,

---

[1]This avoids such a case as

```
character (len=len(a)) ::  fun
character (len=len(fun)) ::  a
```

[2]This avoids such a case as

```
integer, parameter, dimension (j(1):j(1)+1) ::  i = (/0,1/)
integer, parameter, dimension (i(1):i(1)+1) ::  j = (/1,2/)
```

- a reference to repeat, trim, transfer, or reshape for which the arguments are of type integer or character,

- a reference to selected_int_kind or selected_real_kind,

- a reference to an inquiry function other than present, associated, or allocated, provided the quantity inquired about does not depend on an allocation or on a pointer assignment.

7.14.2 Specification functions (Fortran 95 only)

In Fortran 95, any of the intrinsic functions defined by the standard may be used in a specification expression. In addition, a non-intrinsic pure function may be used provided that such a function is neither an internal function nor recursive, it does not have a dummy procedure argument, and the interface is explicit. Functions that fulfil these conditions are termed *specification functions*. The arguments of a specification function when used in a specification expression are subject to the same restrictions as those on specification expressions themselves, except that they do not necessarily have to be scalar.

As the interfaces of specification functions must be explicit yet they cannot be internal functions,[3] such functions are probably most conveniently written as module procedures.

This feature will be a great convenience for specification expressions that cannot be written as simple expressions. Here is an example,

```
function solve (a, ...          ! Fortran 95
   use matrix_ops
   type(matrix), intent(in) :: a
   :
   real                     :: work(wsize(a))
   :
```

where matrix is a type defined in the module matrix_ops and intended to hold a sparse matrix and its LU factorization:

```
type matrix      ! Fortran 95
   integer :: n  ! Matrix order.
   integer :: nz ! Number of nonzero entries.
   logical :: new = .true. ! Whether this is a new,
                           ! unfactorized matrix.
      :
end type matrix
```

and wsize is a module procedure that calculates the required size of the array work:

---

[3]This prevents them enquiring, via host association, about objects being specified in the set of statements in which the specification function itself is referenced.

```
pure integer function wsize(a)   ! Fortran 95
   type(matrix), intent(in) :: a
   wsize = 2*a%n + 2
   if(a%new) wsize = a%nz + wsize
end function wsize
```

7.15   The namelist statement

It is sometimes convenient to gather a set of variables into a single group, in order to facilitate input/output (I/O) operations on the group as a whole. The actual use of such groups is explained in Section 9.10. The method by which a group is declared is via the namelist statement which in its simple form has the syntax

namelist *namelist-spec*

where *namelist-spec* is

/namelist-group-name/ variable-name-list

The *namelist-group-name* is the name given to the group for subsequent use in the I/O statements. A variable named in the list must not be a dummy array with a non-constant bound, a variable with non-constant character length, an automatic object, an allocatable array, a pointer, or have a component at any depth of component selection that is a pointer or is inaccessible. An example is

```
real :: carpet, tv, brushes(10)
namelist /household_items/ carpet, tv, brushes
```

It is possible to declare several namelist groups in one statement, with the syntax

namelist *namelist-spec* [[,] *namelist-spec*] . . .

as in the example

```
namelist /list1/ a, b, c /list2/ x, y, z
```

It is possible to continue a list within the same scoping unit by repeating the namelist name on more than one statement. Thus,

```
namelist /list/ a, b, c
namelist /list/ d, e, f
```

has the same effect as a single statement containing all the variable names in the same order. A namelist group object may belong to more than one namelist group.

If the type, type parameters, or shape of a namelist variable is specified in a specification statement in the same scoping unit, the specification statement must either appear before the namelist statement, or be a type declaration statement that confirms the implicit typing rule in force in the scoping unit for the initial letter of the variable. Also, if the namelist group has the public attribute, no variable in the list may have the private attribute or have private components.

Figure 7.6

```
module sort              ! To sort postal addresses by zip code.
   implicit none
   private
   public :: selection_sort
   integer, parameter :: string_length = 30
   type, public :: address
      character(len = string_length) :: name, street, town, &
                                        state*2
      integer                        :: zip_code
   end type address
contains
   recursive subroutine selection_sort (array_arg)
      type (address), dimension (:), intent (inout)        &
                                        :: array_arg
      integer                           :: current_size
      integer, dimension (1)            :: big
         ! Result of maxloc (Section 8.14) is array valued
      current_size = size (array_arg)
      if (current_size > 0) then
         big = maxloc (array_arg(:)%zip_code)
         call swap (big(1), current_size)
         call selection_sort (array_arg(1: current_size - 1))
      end if
   contains
      subroutine swap (i, j)
         integer, intent (in) :: i, j
         type (address)       :: temp
         temp = array_arg(i)
         array_arg(i) = array_arg(j)
         array_arg(j) = temp
      end subroutine swap
   end subroutine selection_sort
end module sort
```

Figure 7.7

```
program zippy
   use sort
   implicit none
   integer, parameter                      :: array_size = 100
   type (address), dimension (array_size) :: data_array
   integer                                 :: i, n
   do i = 1, array_size
      read  (*, '(/a/a/a/a2,i8)', end=10) data_array(i)
                          ! For end= see Section 9.7;
      write (*, '(/a/a/a/a2,i8)')          data_array(i)
   end do                 ! for editing see Section 9.13.
10 n = i - 1
   call selection_sort (data_array(1: n))
   write(*, '(//a)') 'after sorting:'
   do i = 1, n
      write (*, '(/a/a/a/a2,i8)') data_array(i)
   end do
end program zippy
```

7.16 Summary

In this chapter most of the specification statements of Fortran have been described. The following concepts have been introduced: implicit typing and its attendant dangers, named constants, constant expressions, data initialization, control of the accessibility of entities in modules, saving data between procedure calls, selective access of entities in a module, renaming entities accessed from a module, specification expressions that may be used when specifying data objects and function results, and the formation of variables into namelist groups. We have also explained alternative ways of specifying attributes.

The features described here that are new since Fortran 77 are implicit none; initialization and specification expressions; a much extended type declaration statement; data statement extended to include derived types, subobjects, and binary, octal, and hexadecimal constants; new attributes and statements: public, private, pointer, allocatable, target, intent, and optional; and the use and namelist statements.

We conclude this chapter with a complete program, Figures 7.6 and 7.7, that uses a module to sort US-style addresses (name, street, town, and state with a numerical zip code) by order of zip code. It illustrates the interplay between many of the features described so far, but note that it is not a production code since the sort routine is not very efficient and the full range of US addresses is not handled. Suitable test data are:

Prof. James Bush,
206 Church St. SE,
Minneapolis,
MN 55455

J. E. Dougal,
Rice University,
Houston,
TX 77251

Jack Finch,
104 Ayres Hall,
Knoxville,
TN 37996

7.17 Exercises

1. Write suitable type statements for the following quantities:

   i) an array to hold the number of counts in each of the 100 bins of a histogram numbered from 1 to 100;

   ii) an array to hold the temperature to two significant decimal places at points, on a sheet of iron, equally spaced at 1cm intervals on a rectangular grid 20cm square, with points in each corner (the melting point of iron is 1530° C);

   iii) an array to describe the state of 20 on/off switches;

   iv) an array to contain the information destined for a printed page of 44 lines each of 70 letters or digits.

2. Explain the difference between the following pair of declarations

    real :: i = 3.1

and

    real, parameter :: i = 3.1

What is the value of i in each case?

3. Write type declaration statements which initialize:

   i) all the elements of an integer array of length 100 to the value zero.

   ii) all the odd elements of the same array to 0 and the even elements to 1.

   iii) the elements of a real 10×10 square array to 1.0 .

   iv) a character string to the digits 0 to 9.

4. In the following module, identify all the scoping units and list the mappings for implicit typing for all the letters in all of them:

```
module mod
   implicit character(10, 2) (a-b)
   :
contains
   subroutine outer
      implicit none
      :
   contains
      subroutine inner(fun)
         implicit complex (z)
         interface
            function fun(x)
               implicit real (f, x)
               :
            end function fun
         end interface
      end subroutine inner
   end subroutine outer
end module mod
```

5.

i) Write a type declaration statement that declares and initializes a variable of derived type person (Section 2.9).

ii) Either

    a. write a type declaration statement that declares and initializes a variable of type entry (Section 2.13), or

    b. write a type declaration statement for such a variable and a data statement to initialize its non-pointer components.

6. Which of the following are initialization expressions:

i) kind(x), for x of type real

ii) selected_real_kind(6, 20)

iii) 1.7**2

iv) 1.7**2.0

v) (1.7, 2.3)**(-2)

vi) (/ (7*i, i=1, 10) /)

vii) person("Reid", 25*2.0, 22**2)

viii) entry(1.7, 1, null_pointer)

8. Intrinsic procedures

8.1 Introduction

In a language that has a clear orientation towards scientific applications there is an obvious requirement for the most frequently required mathematical functions to be provided as part of the language itself, rather than expecting each user to code them afresh. When provided with the compiler, they are normally coded to be very efficient and will have been well tested over the complete range of values that they accept. It is difficult to compete with the high standard of code provided by the vendors.

The efficiency of the intrinsic procedures when handling arrays is likely to be particularly marked because a single call may cause a large number of individual operations to be performed, during the execution of which advantage may be taken of the specific nature of the hardware.

Another feature of a substantial number of the intrinsic procedures is that they extend the power of the language by providing access to facilities that are not otherwise available in the language. Examples are inquiry functions for the presence of an optional argument, the parts of a floating-point number, and the length of a character string.

There are over a hundred intrinsic procedures in all, a particularly rich set. They fall into distinct groups, which we describe in turn. A list in alphabetical order, with one-line descriptions, is given in Appendix A. Some processors may offer additional intrinsic procedures. Note that a program containing references to such procedures is portable only to other processors that provide those same procedures. In fact, it does not conform to the standard unless the access is through use association.

8.1.1 Keyword calls

The procedures may be called with keyword actual arguments, using the dummy argument names as keywords. This facility is not very useful for those with a single non-optional argument, but is useful for those with several optional arguments. For example

```
call date_and_time (date=d)
```

returns the date in the scalar character variable d. The rules for positional and keyword argument lists were explained in Section 5.13. In this chapter, the dummy arguments that are optional are indicated with square brackets. We have taken some 'poetic licence' with this notation, which might suggest to the reader that the positional form is permitted following an absent argument (this is not the case).

8.1.2   Categories of intrinsic procedures

There are four categories of intrinsic procedures:

i) *Elemental procedures* are specified for scalar arguments, but may also be applied to conforming array arguments. In order that the rank always be known at compile time, at least one of the array arguments must correspond to a non-optional argument of the elemental procedure. In the case of an elemental function, each element of the result, if any, is as would have been obtained by applying the function to corresponding elements of each of the array arguments. In the case of an elemental subroutine with an array argument, each argument of intent out or inout must be an array, and each element is as would have resulted from applying the subroutine to corresponding elements of each of the array arguments.

ii) *Inquiry functions* return properties of their principal arguments that do not depend on their values; indeed, for variables, their values may be undefined.

iii) *Transformational functions* are functions that are neither elemental nor inquiry; they usually have array arguments and an array result whose elements depend on many of the elements of the arguments.

iv) *Non-elemental subroutines.*

8.1.3   The intrinsic statement

A name may be specified to be that of an intrinsic procedure in an intrinsic statement, which has the general form

   intrinsic [::] *intrinsic-name-list*   ! :: in Fortran 95 only

where *intrinsic-name-list* is a list of intrinsic procedure names. A name must not appear more than once in the intrinsic statements of a scoping unit and must not appear in an external statement there (but may appear as a generic name on an interface block if an intrinsic procedure is being extended, see Section 5.18). We believe that it is good programming practice to include such a statement in every scoping unit that contains references to intrinsic procedures, because this makes the use clear to the reader. We particularly recommend it when referencing intrinsic procedures that are not defined by the standard, for then a clear diagnostic message should be produced if the program is ported to a processor that does not support the extra intrinsic procedures.

8.1.4 Argument intents

The functions do not change the values of their arguments. In fact, the non-pointer arguments all have the intent in. For the subroutines, the intents vary from case to case (see the descriptions given later in the chapter).

8.2 Inquiry functions for any type

The following are inquiry functions whose arguments may be of any type:

associated (pointer [,target]), when target is absent, returns the value true if the pointer pointer is associated with a target and false otherwise. The pointer association status of pointer must not be undefined. If target is present, it must have the same type, type parameters, and rank as pointer. The value is true if pointer is associated with target, and false otherwise. In the array case, true is returned only if the shapes are identical and corresponding array elements, in array element order, are associated with each other. If the character length or array size is zero, false is returned. A different bound, as in the case of associated(p,a) following the pointer assignment p => a(:) when lbound(a) = 0, is insufficient to cause false to be returned. The argument target may itself be a pointer, in which case its target is compared with the target of pointer; the pointer association status of target must not be undefined and if either pointer or target is disassociated, the result is false .

present (a) may be called in a subprogram that has an optional dummy argument a or accesses such a dummy argument from its host. It returns the value true if the corresponding actual argument is present in the current call to it, and false otherwise. If an absent dummy argument is used as an actual argument in a call of another subprogram, it is regarded as also absent in the called subprogram.

There is an inquiry function whose argument may be of any intrinsic type:

kind (x) has type default integer and value equal to the kind type parameter value of x.

8.3 Elemental numeric functions

There are 17 elemental functions for performing simple numerical tasks, many of which perform type conversions for some or all permitted types of arguments.

8.3.1 Elemental functions that may convert

If kind is present in the following elemental functions, it must be a scalar integer initialization expression and provide a kind type parameter that is supported on the processor.

abs (a) returns the absolute value of an argument of type integer, real, or complex. The result is of type integer if a is of type integer and otherwise it is real. It has the same kind type parameter as a.

aimag (z) returns the imaginary part of the complex value z. The type is real and the kind type parameter is that of z.

aint (a [,kind]) truncates a real value a towards zero to produce a real that is a whole number. The value of the kind type parameter is the value of the argument kind if it is present, or that of a otherwise.

anint (a [,kind]) returns a real whose value is the nearest whole number to the real value a. The value of the kind type parameter is the value of the argument kind, if it is present, or that of a otherwise.

ceiling (a [,kind]) returns the least integer greater than or equal to its real argument. The optional argument kind is available in **Fortran 95 only**. If kind is present, the value of the kind type parameter of the result is the value of kind, otherwise it is that of the default integer type.

cmplx (x [,y][,kind]) converts x or (x, y) to complex type with the value of the kind type parameter being the value of the argument kind if it is present or that of default complex otherwise. If y is absent, x may be of type integer, real, or complex. If y is present, it must be of type integer or real and x must be of type integer or real.

floor (a [,kind]) returns the greatest integer less than or equal to its real argument. The optional argument kind is available in **Fortran 95 only**. If kind is present, the value of the kind type parameter of the result is the value of kind, otherwise it is that of the default integer type.

int (a [,kind]) converts to integer type with the value of the kind type parameter being the value of the argument kind, if it is present, or that of the default integer otherwise. The argument a may be

- integer, in which case int(a)=a,
- real, in which case the value is truncated towards zero, or
- complex, in which case the real part is truncated towards zero.

nint (a [,kind]) returns the integer value that is nearest to the real a. If kind is present, the value of the kind type parameter of the result is the value of kind, otherwise it is that of the default integer type.

real (a [,kind]) converts to real type with the value of the kind type parameter being that of kind if it is present. If kind is absent, the kind type parameter is that of default real when a is of type integer or real, and is that of a when a is type complex. The argument a may be of type integer, real, or complex. If it is complex, the imaginary part is ignored.

8.3.2   Elemental functions that do not convert

The following are elemental functions whose result is of type and kind type parameter that are those of the first or only argument. For those having more than one argument, all arguments must have the same type and kind type parameter.

conjg (z) returns the conjugate of the complex value z.

dim (x, y) returns max(x-y, 0.) for arguments that are both integer or both real.

max (a1, a2 [,a3,...]) returns the maximum of two or more integer or real values.

min (a1, a2 [,a3,...]) returns the minimum of two or more integer or real values.

mod (a, p) returns the remainder of a modulo p, that is a-int(a/p)*p. The value of p must not be zero; a and p must be both integer or both real.

modulo (a, p) returns a modulo p when a and p are both integer or both real, that is a-floor(a/p)*p in the real case, and a-floor(a÷p)*p in the integer case, where ÷ represents ordinary mathematical division. The value of p must not be zero.

sign (a, b) returns the absolute value of a times the sign of b. The arguments a and b must be both integer or both real. If b is zero, its sign is taken as positive. **In Fortran 95 only**, however, if b is real with the value zero and the processor can distiguish between a negative and a positive real zero, the result has the sign of b (see also Section 8.7.1).

8.4   Elemental mathematical functions

The following are elemental functions that evaluate elementary mathematical functions. The type and kind type parameter of the result are those of the first argument, which is usually the only argument.

acos (x) returns the arc cosine (inverse cosine) function value for real values x such that $|x| \leq 1$, expressed in radians in the range $0 \leq \mathrm{acos}(x) \leq \pi$.

asin (x) returns the arc sine (inverse sine) function value for real values x such that $|x| \leq 1$, expressed in radians in the range $-\frac{\pi}{2} \leq \mathrm{asin}(x) \leq \frac{\pi}{2}$.

atan (x) returns the arc tangent (inverse tangent) function value for real x, expressed in radians in the range $-\frac{\pi}{2} \leq \text{atan}(x) \leq \frac{\pi}{2}$.

atan2 (y, x) returns the arc tangent (inverse tangent) function value for pairs of reals, x and y, of the same type and type parameter. The result is the principal value of the argument of the complex number (x, y), expressed in radians in the range $-\pi < \text{atan2}(y, x) \leq \pi$. The values of x and y must not both be zero.

cos (x) returns the cosine function value for an argument of type real or complex that is treated as a value in radians.

cosh (x) returns the hyperbolic cosine function value for a real argument x.

exp (x) returns the exponential function value for a real or complex argument x.

log (x) returns the natural logarithm function for a real or complex argument x. In the real case, x must be positive. In the complex case, x must not be zero, and the imaginary part w of the result lies in the range $-\pi < w \leq \pi$.

log10 (x) returns the common (base 10) logarithm of a real argument whose value must be positive.

sin (x) returns the sine function value for a real or complex argument that is treated as a value in radians.

sinh (x) returns the hyperbolic sine function value for a real argument.

sqrt (x) returns the square root function value for a real or complex argument x. If x is real, its value must be not be negative. In the complex case, the real part of the result is not negative, and when it is zero the imaginary part of the result is not negative.

tan (x) returns the tangent function value for a real argument that is treated as a value in radians.

tanh (x) returns the hyperbolic tangent function value for a real argument.

8.5   Elemental character and logical functions

8.5.1   Character-integer conversions

The following are elemental functions for conversions from a single character to an integer, and vice-versa.

achar (i) is of type default character with length one and returns the character in the position in the ASCII collating sequence that is specified by the integer i. i must be in the range $0 \leq i \leq 127$, otherwise the result is processor dependent.

char (i[,kind]) is of type character and length one, with a kind type parameter value that of the value of kind if present, or default otherwise. It returns the character in position i in the processor collating sequence associated with the relevant kind parameter. The value of i must be in the range $0 \leq i \leq n-1$, where n is the number of characters in the processor's collating sequence. If kind is present, it must be a scalar integer initialization expression and provide a kind type parameter that is supported on the processor.

iachar (c) is of type default integer and returns the position in the ASCII collating sequence of the default character c. If c is not in the sequence, the result is processor dependent.

ichar (c) is of type default integer and returns the position of the character c in the processor collating sequence associated with the kind parameter of c.

8.5.2   Lexical comparison functions

The following elemental functions accept default character strings as arguments, make a lexical comparison based on the ASCII collating sequence, and return a default logical result. If the strings have different lengths, the shorter one is padded on the right with blanks.

lge (string_a, string_b) returns the value true if string_a follows string_b in the ASCII collating sequence or is equal to it, and the value false otherwise.

lgt (string_a, string_b) returns the value true if string_a follows string_b in the ASCII collating sequence, and the value false otherwise.

lle (string_a, string_b) returns the value true if string_b follows string_a in the ASCII collating sequence or is equal to it, and the value false otherwise.

llt (string_a, string_b) returns the value true if string_b follows string_a in the ASCII collating sequence, and false otherwise.

8.5.3   String-handling elemental functions

The following are elemental functions that manipulate strings. The arguments string, substring, and set are always of type character, and where two are present have the same kind type parameter. The kind type parameter value of the result is that of string.

adjustl (string) adjusts left to return a string of the same length by removing all leading blanks and inserting the same number of trailing blanks.

adjustr (string) adjusts right to return a string of the same length by removing all trailing blanks and inserting the same number of leading blanks.

index (string, substring [,back]) has type default integer and returns the starting position of substring as a substring of string, or zero if it does not occur as a substring. If back is absent or present with value false, the starting position of the first such substring is returned; the value 1 is returned if substring has zero length. If back is present with value true, the starting position of the last such substring is returned; the value len(string)+1 is returned if substring has zero length.

len_trim (string) returns a default integer whose value is the length of string without trailing blank characters.

scan (string, set [,back]) returns a default integer whose value is the position of a character of string that is in set, or zero if there is no such character. If the logical back is absent or present with value false, the position of the leftmost such character is returned. If back is present with value true, the position of the rightmost such character is returned.

verify (string, set [,back]) returns the default integer value 0 if each character in string appears in set, or the position of a character of string that is not in set. If the logical back is absent or present with value false, the position of the left-most such character is returned. If back is present with value true, the position of the rightmost such character is returned.

8.5.4   Logical conversion

The following elemental function converts from a logical value with one kind type parameter to another.

logical (l [,kind]) returns a logical value equal to the value of the logical l. The value of the kind type parameter of the result is the value of kind if it is present or that of default logical otherwise. If kind is present, it must be a scalar integer initialization expression and provide a kind type parameter that is supported on the processor.

8.6   Non-elemental string-handling functions

8.6.1   String-handling inquiry function

len (string) is an inquiry function that returns a scalar default integer holding the number of characters in string if it is scalar, or in an element of string if it is array valued. The value of string need not be defined.

8.6.2   String-handling transformational functions

There are two functions that cannot be elemental because the length type parameter of the result depends on the value of an argument.

repeat (string, ncopies) forms the string consisting of the concatenation of ncopies copies of string, where ncopies is of type integer and its value must not be negative. Both arguments must be scalar.

trim (string) returns string with all trailing blanks removed. The argument string must be scalar.

8.7   Numeric inquiry and manipulation functions

8.7.1   Models for integer and real data

The numeric inquiry and manipulation functions are defined in terms of a model set of integers and a model set of reals for each kind of integer and real data type implemented. For each kind of integer, it is the set

$$i = s \times \sum_{k=1}^{q} w_k \times r^{k-1}$$

where s is ± 1, q is a positive integer, r is an integer exceeding one (usually 2), and each w_k is an integer in the range $0 \le w_k < r$. For each kind of real, it is the set

$$x = 0$$

and

$$x = s \times b^e \times \sum_{k=1}^{p} f_k \times b^{-k}$$

where s is ± 1, p and b are integers exceeding one, e is an integer in a range $e_{\min} \le e \le e_{\max}$, and each f_k is an integer in the range $0 \le f_k < b$ except that f_1 is also nonzero.

Values of the parameters in these models are chosen for the processor so as best to fit the hardware with the proviso that all model numbers are representable. Note that it is quite likely that there are some machine numbers that lie outside the model. For example, many computers represent the integer $-r^q$, and the IEEE standard for Binary Floating-point Arithmetic (IEEE 754-1985 or IEC 60559:1989) contains reals with $f_1 = 0$ (called denormalized numbers) and register numbers with increased precision and range.

In Section 2.6, we noted that the value of a signed zero is regarded as being the same as that of an unsigned zero. However, many processors distinguish at the hardware level between a negative real zero value and a positive real zero value, and the IEEE standard makes use of this where possible. For example, when the exact result of an operation is nonzero but the rounding produces a zero, the sign is retained.

In Fortran 95, the two zeros are still treated identically in all relational operations, as input arguments to all intrinsic functions (except sign), or as the scalar expression in the arithmetic if-statement (Appendix C.2.1). However, the function sign (Section 8.3.2) has been generalized such that the sign of the second argument may be taken into account even if its value is zero. On a processor that has IEEE arithmetic, the value of sign(2.0, -0.0) is -2.0. Also, a Fortran 95 processor is required to represent all negative numbers on output, including zero, with a minus sign.

8.7.2 Numeric inquiry functions

There are nine inquiry functions that return values from the models associated with their arguments. Each has a single argument that may be scalar or array-valued and each returns a scalar result. The value of the argument need not be defined.

digits (x), for real or integer x, returns the default integer whose value is the number of significant digits in the model that includes x, that is p or q.

epsilon (x), for real x, returns a real result with the same type parameter as x that is almost negligible compared with the value one in the model that includes x, that is b^{1-p}.

huge (x), for real or integer x, returns the largest value in the model that includes x. It has the type and type parameter of x. The value is

$$(1 - b^{-p})b^{e_{max}}$$

or

$$r^{q-1}$$

maxexponent (x), for real x, returns the default integer e_{max}, the maximum exponent in the model that includes x.

minexponent (x), for real x, returns the default integer e_{min}, the minimum exponent in the model that includes x.

precision (x), for real or complex x, returns a default integer holding the equivalent decimal precision in the model representing real numbers with the same type parameter value as x. The value is

$$\text{int}((p - 1) * \text{log10}(b)) + k,$$

where k is 1 if b is an integral power of 10 and 0 otherwise.

radix (x), for real or integer x, returns the default integer that is the base in the model that includes x, that is b or r.

range (x), for integer, real, or complex x, returns a default integer holding the equivalent decimal exponent range in the models representing integer or real numbers with the same type parameter value as x. The value is int(log10(*huge*)) for integers and

$$\text{int}(\text{min}(\text{log10}(huge), -\text{log10}(tiny)))$$

for reals, where *huge* and *tiny* are the largest and smallest positive numbers in the models.

tiny (x), for real x, returns the smallest positive number

$$b^{e_{min}-1}$$

in the model that includes x. It has the type and type parameter of x.

8.7.3   Elemental functions to manipulate reals

There are seven elemental functions whose first or only argument is of type real and that return values related to the components of the model values associated with the actual value of the argument.

exponent (x) returns the default integer whose value is the exponent part *e* of x when represented as a model number. If x=0, the result has value zero.

fraction (x) returns a real with the same type parameter as x whose value is the fractional part of x when represented as a model number, that is x b^{-e}.

nearest (x, s) returns a real with the same type parameter as x whose value is the nearest different machine number in the direction given by the sign of the real s. The value of s must not be zero.

rrspacing (x) returns a real with the same type parameter as x whose value is the reciprocal of the relative spacing of model numbers near x, that is $| x\, b^{-e} | b^{p}$.

scale (x, i) returns a real with the same type parameter as x, whose value is x b^{i}, where *b* is the base in the model for x, and i is of type integer.

set_exponent (x, i) returns a real with the same type parameter as x, whose fractional part is the fractional part of the model representation of x and whose exponent part is i, that is x b^{i-e}.

spacing (x) returns a real with the same type parameter as x whose value is the absolute spacing of model numbers near x. It is b^{e-p} if x is nonzero and this result is within range; otherwise, it is tiny(x).

8.7.4   Transformational functions for kind values

There are two functions that return the least kind type parameter value that will meet a given numeric requirement. They have scalar arguments and results, so are classified as transformational.

selected_int_kind (r) returns the default integer scalar that is the kind type
parameter value for an integer data type able to represent all integer values *n*
in the range $-10^r < n < 10^r$, where r is a scalar integer. If more than one is
available, a kind with least decimal exponent range is chosen (and least kind
value if several have least decimal exponent range). If no corresponding
kind is available, the result is -1.

selected_real_kind ([p][, r]) returns the default integer scalar that is the
kind type parameter value for a real data type with decimal precision (as
returned by the function precision) at least p, and decimal exponent range
(as returned by the function range) at least r. If more than one is available,
a kind with the least decimal precision is chosen (and least kind value if
several have least decimal precision). Both p and r are scalar integers;
at least one of them must be present. If no corresponding kind value is
available, the result is -1 if sufficient precision is unavailable, -2 if sufficient
exponent range is unavailable, and -3 if both are unavailable.

8.8   Bit manipulation procedures

There are eleven procedures for manipulating bits held within integers. They are
based on those in the US Military Standard MIL-STD 1753. They differ only in
that here they are elemental, where appropriate, whereas the original procedures
accepted only scalar arguments.

   These intrinsics are based on a model in which an integer holds *s* bits w_k,
$k = 0, 1, \ldots, s - 1$, in a sequence from right to left, based on the non-negative
value

$$\sum_{k=0}^{s-1} w_k \times 2^k$$

This model is valid only in the context of these intrinsics. It is identical to the
model for integers in Section 8.7.1 when $r = 2$ and $w_{s-1} = 0$, but when $r \neq 2$
or $w_{s-1} = 1$ the models do not correspond, and the value expressed as an integer
may vary from processor to processor.

8.8.1   Inquiry function

bit_size (i) returns the number of bits in the model for bits within an integer
of the same type parameter as i. The result is a scalar integer having the
same type parameter as i.

8.8.2   Elemental functions

btest (i, pos) returns the default logical value true if bit pos of the integer i
has value 1 and false otherwise. pos must be an integer with value in the
range $0 \leq pos < bit\_size(i)$.

iand (i, j) returns the logical and of all the bits in i and corresponding bits in j, according to the truth table

i	1	1	0	0
j	1	0	1	0
iand(i, j)	1	0	0	0

The arguments i and j must have the same type parameter value, which is the type parameter value of the result.

ibclr (i, pos) returns an integer, with the same type parameter as i, and value equal to that of i except that bit pos is cleared to 0. The argument pos must be an integer with value in the range $0 \le pos < bit\_size(i)$.

ibits (i, pos, len) returns an integer, with the same type parameter as i, and value equal to the len bits of i starting at bit pos right adjusted and all other bits zero. The arguments pos and len must be integers with non-negative values such that $pos+len \le bit\_size(i)$.

ibset (i, pos) returns an integer, with the same type parameter as i, and value equal to that of i except that bit pos is set to 1. The argument pos must be an integer with value in the range $0 \le pos < bit\_size(i)$.

ieor (i, j) returns the logical exclusive or of all the bits in i and corresponding bits in j, according to the truth table

i	1	1	0	0
j	1	0	1	0
ieor(i, j)	0	1	1	0

The arguments i and j must have the same type parameter value, which is the type parameter value of the result.

ior (i, j) returns the logical inclusive or of all the bits in i and corresponding bits in j, according to the truth table

i	1	1	0	0
j	1	0	1	0
ior(i, j)	1	1	1	0

The arguments i and j must have the same type parameter value, which is the type parameter value of the result.

ishft (i, shift) returns an integer, with the same type parameter as i, and value equal to that of i except that the bits are shifted shift places to the left (-shift places to the right if shift is negative). Zeros are shifted in from the other end. The argument shift must be an integer with value satisfying the inequality $|shift| \le bit\_size(i)$.

ishftc (i, shift [, size]) returns an integer, with the same type parameter as i, and value equal to that of i except that the size rightmost bits (or all the bits if size is absent) are shifted circularly shift places to the left (-shift places to the right if shift is negative). The argument shift must be an integer with absolute value not exceeding the value of size (or bit_size(i) if size is absent).

not (i) returns the logical complement of all the bits in i, according to the truth table

i	0	1
not(i)	1	0

8.8.3   Elemental subroutine

call mvbits (from, frompos, len, to, topos) copies the sequence of bits in from that starts at position frompos and has length len to to, starting at position topos. The other bits of to are not altered. The arguments from, frompos, len, and topos are all integers with intent in, and they must have values that satisfy the inequalities: frompos+len ≤ bit_size(from), len ≥ 0, frompos ≥ 0, topos+len ≤ bit_size(to), and topos ≥ 0. The argument to is an integer with intent inout; it must have the same kind type parameter as from. The same variable may be specified for from and to.

8.9   Transfer function

The transfer function allows data of one type to be transferred to another without the physical representation being altered. This would be useful, for example, in writing a data storage and retrieval system. The system itself could be written for one type, default integer say, and other types handled by transfers to and from that type, for example:

```
integer         :: store
character(len=4) :: word        ! To be stored and retrieved
:
store = transfer(word, store)   ! Before storage
:
word  = transfer(store, word)   ! After retrieval
:
```

transfer (source, mold [,size]) returns a result of type and type parameters those of mold. When size is absent, the result is scalar if mold is scalar, and it is of rank one and size just sufficient to hold all of source if mold is array-valued. When size is present, the result is of rank one and size size. If the physical representation of the result is as long as or longer than that

that of source, the result contains source as its leading part and the value of the rest is processor dependent; otherwise the result is the leading part of source. As the rank of the result can depend on whether or not size is specified, the corresponding actual argument must not itself be an optional dummy argument.

8.10   Vector and matrix multiplication functions

There are two transformational functions that perform vector and matrix multi-plications. They each have two arguments that are both of numeric type (integer, real, or complex) or both of logical type. The result is of the same type and type parameter as for the multiply or and operation between two such scalars. The functions sum and any, used in the definitions, are defined in Section 8.11.1.

dot_product (vector_a, vector_b) requires two arguments each of rank one and the same size. If vector_a is of type integer or type real, it returns sum(vector_a * vector_b); if vector_a is of type complex, it returns sum(conjg(vector_a) * vector_b); and if vector_a is of type logical, it returns any(vector_a .and. vector_b).

matmul (matrix_a, matrix_b) performs matrix multiplication. For numeric arguments, three cases are possible:

 i) matrix_a has shape (n, m) and matrix_b has shape (m, k). The result has shape (n, k) and element (i, j) has the value
  sum(matrix_a(i, :) * matrix_b(:, j)).

 ii) matrix_a has shape (m) and matrix_b has shape (m, k). The result has shape (k) and element (j) has the value
  sum(matrix_a * matrix_b(:, j)).

 iii) matrix_a has shape (n,m) and matrix_b has shape (m). The result has shape (n) and element (i) has the value
  sum(matrix_a(i, :) * matrix_b).

For logical arguments, the shapes are as for numeric arguments and the values are determined by replacing 'sum' and '*' in the above expressions by 'any' and '.and.'.

8.11   Transformational functions that reduce arrays

There are seven transformational functions that perform operations on arrays such as summing their elements.

8.11.1   Single argument case

In their simplest form, these functions have a single array argument and return a scalar result. All except count have a result of the same type and type parameter as the argument. The mask array mask, used as an argument in any, all, count, and optionally in others, is described also in Section 6.17.

all (mask) returns the value true if all elements of the logical array mask are true or mask has size zero, and otherwise returns the value false.

any (mask) returns the value true if any of the elements of the logical array mask is true, and returns the value false if no elements are true or if mask has size zero.

count (mask) returns the default integer value that is the number of elements of the logical array mask that have the value true.

maxval (array) returns the maximum value of an element of an integer or real array. If array has size zero, it returns the negative value of largest magnitude supported by the processor.

minval (array) returns the minimum value of an element of an integer or real array. If array has size zero, it returns the largest positive value supported by the processor.

product (array) returns the product of the elements of an integer, real, or complex array. It returns the value one if array has size zero.

sum (array) returns the sum of the elements of an integer, real, or complex array. It returns the value zero if array has size zero.

8.11.2   Optional argument dim

All these functions have an optional second argument dim that is a scalar integer. If this is present, the operation is applied to all rank-one sections that span right through dimension dim to produce an array of rank reduced by one and extents equal to the extents in the other dimensions. For example, if a is a real array of shape (4,5,6), sum(a,dim=2) is a real array of shape (4,6) and element (i, j) has value sum(a(i,:,j)).

As the rank of the result depends on whether dim is specified, the corresponding actual argument must not itself be an optional dummy argument.

8.11.3   Optional argument mask

The functions maxval, minval, product, and sum have a third optional argument, a logical array mask. If this is present, it must have the same shape as the first argument and the operation is applied to the elements corresponding to true elements of mask; for example, sum(a, mask = a>0) sums the positive elements of the array a. The argument mask affects only the value of the function and does not affect the evaluation of arguments that are array expressions. In **Fortran 95 only**, mask is permitted as the second positional argument when dim is absent.

8.12   Array inquiry functions

There are five functions for inquiries about the bounds, shape, size and allocation status of an array of any type. Because the result depends only the array properties, the value of the array need not be defined.

8.12.1   Allocation status

allocated (array) returns, when the allocatable array array is currently allocated, the value true; otherwise it returns the value false. If the allocation status of array is undefined, the result is undefined.

8.12.2   Bounds, shape, and size

The following functions enquire about the bounds of an array. In the case of an allocatable array, it must be allocated; and in the case of a pointer, it must be associated with a target. An array section or an array expression is taken to have lower bounds 1 and upper bounds equal to the extents (like an assumed-shape array with no specified lower bounds). If a dimension has size zero, the lower bound is taken as 1 and the upper bound is taken as 0.

lbound (array [,dim]), when dim is absent, returns a rank-one default integer array holding the lower bounds. When dim is present, it must be a scalar integer and the result is a scalar default integer holding the lower bound in dimension dim. As the rank of the result depends on whether dim is specified, the corresponding actual argument must not itself be an optional dummy argument.

shape (source) returns a rank-one default integer array holding the shape of the array or scalar source. In the case of a scalar, the result has size zero.

size (array [,dim]) returns a scalar default integer that is the size of the array array or extent along dimension dim if the scalar integer dim is present.

ubound (array [,dim]) is similar to lbound except that it returns upper bounds.

8.13   Array construction and manipulation functions

There are eight functions that construct or manipulate arrays of any type.

8.13.1   The merge elemental function

merge (tsource, fsource, mask) is an elemental function. The argument tsource may have any type and fsource must have the same type and type parameters. The argument mask must be of type logical. The result is tsource if mask is true and fsource otherwise.

The principal application of merge is when the three arguments are arrays having the same shape, in which case tsource and fsource are merged under the control of mask. Note, however, that tsource or fsource may be scalar in which case the elemental rules effectively broadcast it to an array of the correct shape.

8.13.2 Packing and unpacking arrays

The transformational function pack packs into a rank-one array those elements of an array that are selected by a logical array of conforming shape, and the transformational function unpack performs the reverse operation. The elements are taken in array element order.

pack (array, mask [,vector]), when vector is absent, returns a rank-one array containing the elements of array corresponding to true elements of mask in array element order; mask may be scalar with value true, in which case all elements are selected. If vector is present, it must be a rank-one array of the same type and type parameters as array and size at least equal to the number t of selected elements; the result has size equal to the size n of vector; if $t < n$, elements i of the result for $i > t$ are the corresponding elements of vector.

unpack (vector, mask, field) returns an array of the type and type parameters of vector and shape of mask. The argument mask must be a logical array and vector must be a rank-one array of size at least the number of true elements of mask. field must be of the same type and type parameters as vector and must either be scalar or be of the same shape as mask. The element of the result corresponding to the ith true element of mask, in array element order, is the ith element of vector; all others are equal to the corresponding elements of field if it is an array or to field if it is a scalar.

8.13.3 Reshaping an array

The transformational function reshape allows the shape of an array to be changed, with possible permutation of the subscripts.

reshape (source, shape [,pad][,order]) returns an array with shape given by the rank-one integer array shape, and type and type parameters those of the array source. The size of shape must be constant, and its elements must not be negative. If pad is present, it must be an array of the same type and type parameters as source. If pad is absent or of size zero, the size of the result must not exceed the size of source. If order is absent, the elements of the result, in array element order, are the elements of source in array element order followed by copies of pad in array element order. If order is present, it must be a rank-one integer array with a value that is a permutation of $(1,2,...,n)$; the elements $r(s_1, \ldots, s_n)$ of the result, taken in subscript order for the array having elements $r(s_{order(1)}, \ldots, s_{order(n)})$, are those of source in array element order followed by copies of pad in array element order. For example, if order has the value (/3,1,2/), the elements $r(1,1,1)$, $r(1,1,2)$, ..., $r(1,1,k)$, $r(2,1,1)$, $r(2,1,2)$, ... correspond to the elements of source and pad in array element order.

8.13.4 Transformational function for replication

spread (source, dim, ncopies) returns an array of type and type parameters those of source and of rank increased by one. The argument source may be scalar or array-valued. The arguments dim and ncopies are integer scalars. The result contains max(ncopies, 0) copies of source, and element $(r_1, \ldots, r_{n+1})$ of the result is source$(s_1, \ldots, s_n)$ where $(s_1, \ldots, s_n)$ is $(r_1, \ldots, r_{n+1})$ with subscript dim omitted (or source itself if it is scalar).

8.13.5 Array shifting functions

cshift (array, shift [,dim]) returns an array of the same type, type parameters, and shape as array. The argument shift is of type integer and must be scalar if array is of rank one. If shift is scalar, the result is obtained by shifting every rank-one section that extends across dimension dim circularly shift times. The argument dim is an integer scalar and, if it is omitted, it is as if it were present with the value 1. The direction of the shift depends on the sign of shift, being to the left for a positive value and to the right for a negative value. Thus, for the case with shift=1 and array of rank one and size m, the element i of the result is array(i+1), where $i = 1, 2, \ldots, m-1$, and element m is array(1). If shift is an array, it must have the same shape as that of array with dimension dim omitted, and it supplies a separate value for each shift. For example, if array is of rank three and shape (k, l, m) and dim has the value 2, shift must be of shape (k, m) and supplies a shift for each of the $k \times m$ rank-one sections in the second dimension of array.

eoshift (array, shift [,boundary][,dim]) is identical to cshift except that an end-off shift is performed and boundary values are inserted into the gaps so created. The argument boundary may be omitted when array has intrinsic type, in which case the value zero is inserted for the integer, real, and complex cases; false in the logical case; and blanks in the character case. If boundary is present, it must have the same type and type parameters as array; it may be scalar and supply all needed values or it may be an array whose shape is that of array with dimension dim omitted and supply a separate value for each shift.

8.13.6 Matrix transpose

The transpose function performs a matrix transpose for any array of rank two.

transpose (matrix) returns an array of the same type and type parameters as the rank-two array matrix. Element (i, j) of the result is matrix(j, i).

8.14   Transformational functions for geometric location

There are two transformational functions that find the locations of the maximum and minimum values of an integer or real array.

maxloc (array [,mask]) returns a rank-one default integer array of size equal to the rank of array. Its value is the sequence of subscripts of an element of maximum value (among those corresponding to true values of the conforming logical array mask if it is present), as though all the declared lower bounds of array were 1. If there is more than one such element, the first in array element order is taken.

maxloc (array, dim [,mask]) is available in **Fortran 95 only**. It returns a default integer array of shape equal to the that of array with dimension dim omitted, where dim is a scalar integer with value in the range $1 \leq \text{dim} \leq \text{rank(array)}$. The value of each element of the result is the position of the first element of maximum value in the corresponding rank-one section spanning dimension dim, among those elements corresponding to true values of the conforming logical array mask when it is present.

minloc (array [,mask]) is identical to maxloc (array [,mask]) except that the position of an element of minimum value is obtained.

minloc (array, dim [,mask]) (available in **Fortran 95 only**) is identical to maxloc (array, dim [,mask]) except that positions of elements of minimum value are obtained.

8.15   Transformational function for pointer disassociation (Fortran 95)

In Fortran 95, the function null is available to give the disassociated status to pointer entities.

null ([mold]) returns a disassociated pointer. The argument mold is a pointer of any type and may have any association status, including undefined. The type, type parameter, and rank of the result are those of mold if it is present and otherwise are those of the object with which it is associated. In an actual argument associated with a dummy argument of assumed character length, mold must be present.

8.16   Non-elemental intrinsic subroutines

There are also in Fortran non-elemental intrinsic subroutines, which were chosen to be subroutines rather than functions because of the need to return information through the arguments.

8.16.1   Real-time clock

There are two subroutines that return information from the real-time clock, the first based on the ISO standard IS 8601 (Representation of dates and times). It is assumed that there is a basic system clock that is incremented by one for each clock count until a maximum count_max is reached and on the next count is set to zero. Default values are returned on systems without a clock. All the arguments have intent out.

call date_and_time ([date] [,time] [,zone] [,values]) returns the following (with default values blank or -huge(0), as appropriate, when there is no clock):

   date is a scalar character variable holding the date in the form *ccyymmdd*, corresponding to century, year, month, and day.

   time is a scalar character variable holding the time in the form *hhmmss.sss*, corresponding to hours, minutes, seconds, and milliseconds.

   zone is a scalar character variable that is set to the difference between local time and Coordinated Universal Time (UTC, also known as Greenwich Mean Time) in the form *Shhmm*, corresponding to sign, hours, and minutes. For example, a processor in New York in winter would return the value -0500.

   values is a rank-one default integer array of size at least 8 holding the sequence of values: the year, the month of the year, the day of the month, the time difference in minutes with respect to UTC, the hour of the day, the minutes of the hour, the seconds of the minute, and the milliseconds of the second.

call system_clock ([count] [,count_rate] [,count_max]) returns the following:

   count is a scalar default integer holding a processor-dependent value based on the current value of the processor clock, or -huge(0) if there is no clock. On the first call, the processor may set an initial value that may be zero.

   count_rate is a scalar default integer holding the number of clock counts per second, or zero if there is no clock.

   count_max is a scalar default integer holding the maximum value that count may take, or zero if there is no clock.

8.16.2   CPU time (Fortran 95 only)

In Fortran 95, there is a non-elemental intrinsic subroutine that returns the processor time.

call cpu_time (time) returns the following:

> time is a scalar real that is assigned a processor-dependent approximation
> to the processor time in seconds, or a processor-dependent negative
> value if there is no clock.

The exact definition of time is left imprecise because of the variability in what
different processors are able to provide. The primary purpose is to compare
different algorithms on the same computer or discover which parts of a calculation
on a computer are the most expensive.

The start time is left imprecise because the purpose is to time sections of code,
as in the example

```
real :: t1, t2
  :
call cpu_time(t1)    ! Fortran 95
  :                  ! Code to be timed.
call cpu_time(t2)
write (*,*) 'Time taken by code was ', t2-t1, ' seconds'
```

8.16.3   Random numbers

A sequence of pseudorandom numbers is generated from a seed that is held as
a rank-one array of integers. The subroutine random_number returns the pseudorandom numbers and the subroutine random_seed allows an inquiry to be made
about the size or value of the seed array, and the seed to be reset. The subroutines
provide a portable interface to a processor-dependent sequence.

call random_number (harvest) returns a pseudorandom number from the uniform distribution over the range $0 \leq x < 1$ or an array of such numbers.
harvest has intent out, may be a scalar or an array, and must be of type
real.

call random_seed ([size] [put] [get]) has the following arguments:

> size has intent out and is a scalar default integer that the processor sets to
> the size n of the seed array.

> put has intent in and is a default integer array of rank one and size n that is
> used by the processor to reset the seed. A processor may set the same
> seed value for more than one value of put.

> get has intent out and is a default integer array of rank one and size n that
> the processor sets to the current value of the seed.

> No more than one argument may be specified; if no argument is specified,
> the seed is set to a processor-dependent value.

8.17 Summary

In this chapter, we introduced the four categories of intrinsic procedures, explained the `intrinsic` statement, and gave detailed descriptions of all the procedures. The procedures of Sections 8.2, 8.6.2, and 8.7 to 8.16 are all new since Fortran 77. Within Sections 8.3 to 8.5 the procedures `ceiling`, `floor`, `modulo`, `achar`, `iachar`, `adjustl`, `adjustr`, `len_trim`, `scan`, `verify`, and `logical` are new; the remaining functions were present in Fortran 77, have been generalized to handle all kind type parameters, have become elemental, and several have been given additional optional arguments. The function `len` has become an inquiry function.

Of the many new intrinsic procedures, some have names that might also be names of external functions in existing Fortran 77 programs. Appendix B15 of the Fortran 77 standard recommended that external procedures be identified as such by using the `external` statement. For any external procedure with a name contained in the following list, it is essential to provide an interface body or to use the `external` statement.

achar	all	any	btest	count	cshift
digits	floor	huge	iachar	iand	ibclr
ibits	ibset	ieor	ior	ishft	ishftc
kind	lbound	matmul	maxloc	maxval	merge
minloc	minval	modulo	mvbits	not	null
pack	radix	range	repeat	scale	scan
shape	size	spread	sum	tiny	trim
ubound	unpack	verify			

Note: `null` is **Fortran 95 only**.

8.18 Exercises

1. Write a program to calculate the real roots or pairs of complex-conjugate roots of the quadratic equation $ax^2 + bx + c = 0$ for any real values of a, b, and c. The program should read these three values and print the results. Use should be made of the appropriate intrinsic functions.

2. Repeat Exercise 1 of Chapter 5, avoiding the use of do constructs.

3. Given the rules explained in Sections 3.12 and 8.2, what are the values printed by the following program?

```
program main
    real, target  :: a(3:10)
    real, pointer :: p1(:), p2(:)
    p1 => a(3:9:2)
    p2 => a(9:3:-2)
    print *, associated(p1, p2)
    print *, associated(p1, p2(4:1:-1))
end program main
```

4. In the following program, two pointer assignments, one to an array the other to an array section, are followed by a subroutine call. Bearing in mind the rules given in Sections 3.12, 6.3, and 8.12.2, what values does the program print?

```
program main
   real, target  :: a(5:10)
   real, pointer :: p1(:), p2(:)
   p1 => a
   p2 => a(:)
   print *, lbound (a), lbound (a(:))
   print *, lbound (p1), lbound (p2)
   call what (a, a(:))
contains
   subroutine what (x, y)
      real, intent (in) :: x(:), y(:)
      print *, lbound (x), lbound (y)
   end subroutine what
end program main
```

9. Data transfer

9.1 Introduction

Fortran has, in comparison with most other high-level programming languages, a particularly rich set of facilities for input/output (I/O). The Fortran 77 standard brought with it important new features including direct-access files, internal files, execution-time format specification, list-directed input/output, file inquiry, and some new edit descriptors. By contrast, the only significant new features in the latest standards are non-advancing I/O, namelist, and some new edit descriptors. In addition, there are a number of detailed changes to support new facilities in other areas.

Input/output is an area of Fortran into which not all programmers need to delve very deeply. For most small-scale programs it is sufficient to know how to read a few data records containing input variables, and how to transmit to a terminal or printer the results of a calculation. In large-scale data processing, on the other hand, the programs often have to deal with huge streams of data to and from many disc, tape, and cartridge files; in these cases it is essential that great attention be paid to the way in which the I/O is designed and coded, as otherwise both the execution time and the real time spent in the program can suffer dramatically. The term *file* is used for a collection of data on one of these devices and a file is always organized into a sequence of *records*.

This chapter begins by discussing the various forms of formatted I/O, that is I/O which deals with records that do not use the internal number representation of the computer, but rather a character string which can be displayed for visual inspection by the human eye. It is also the form usually needed for transmitting data between different kinds of computers. The so-called *edit descriptors*, which are used to control the translation between the internal number representation and the external format, are then explained. Finally, the topics of unformatted (or binary) I/O and direct-access files are covered.

9.2 Number conversion

The ways in which numbers are stored internally by a computer are the concern of neither the Fortran standard nor this book. However, if we wish to output values – to display them on a terminal or to print them – then their internal representations must be converted into a character string which can be read in a normal way. For instance, the contents of a given computer word may be (in hexadecimal) be1d7dbf and correspond to the value -0.000450 . For our particular purpose, we may wish to display this quantity as -.000450, or as -4.5E-04, or rounded to one significant digit as -5e-04. The conversion from the internal representation to the external form is carried out according to the information specified by an edit descriptor contained in a *format specification*. These will both be dealt with fully later in this chapter; for the moment, it is sufficient to give a few examples. For instance, to print an integer value in a field of 10 characters width, we would use the edit descriptor i10, where i stands for integer conversion, and 10 specifies the width of the output field. To print a real quantity in a field of 10 characters, five of which are reserved for the fractional part of the number, we specify f10.5. The edit descriptor f stands for floating-point (real) conversion, 10 is the total width of the output field and 5 is the width of the fractional part of the field. If the number given above were to be converted according to this edit descriptor, it would appear as *bb*-0.00045, where *b* represents a blank. To print a character variable in a field of 10 characters, we would specify a10, where a stands for alphanumeric conversion.

A format specification consists of a list of edit descriptors enclosed in parentheses, and can be coded either as a default character expression, for instance

```
'(i10, f10.3, a10)'
```

or as a separate format statement, referenced by a statement label, for example

```
10 format(i10, f10.3, a10)
```

To print the scalar variables j, b, and c, of types integer, real, and character respectively, we may then write either

```
print '(i10, f10.3, a10)', j,b,c
```

or

```
    print 10, j,b,c
10 format(i10, f10.3, a10)
```

The first form is normally used when there is only a single reference in a scoping unit to a given format specification, the second when there are several or when the format is complicated. The part of the statement designating the quantities to be printed is known as the *output list* and forms the subject of the following section.

9.3 I/O lists

The quantities to be read or written by a program are specified in an I/O list. For output, they may be expressions but for input must be variables. In both cases, list items may be implied-do lists of quantities. Examples are shown in Figure 9.1, where we note the use of a *repeat count* in front of those edit descriptors that are required repeatedly. A repeat count must be a positive integer literal constant and not have a kind type parameter. Function references are permitted in an I/O list, provided they do not themselves cause further I/O to occur.

Figure 9.1

```
      integer             :: i
      real, dimension(10) :: a
      character(len=20)   :: word
      print '(i10)',      i
      print '(10f10.3)', a
      print '(3f10.3)',  a(1),a(2),a(3)
      print '(a10)',      word(5:14)
      print '(5f10.3)',  (a(i), i=1,9,2)
      print '(2f10.3)',  a(1)*a(2)+i, sqrt(a(3))
```

In all these examples, except the last one, the expressions consist of single variables and would be equally valid in input statements using the read statement, for example

```
      read '(i10)', i
```

Such statements may be used to read values which are then assigned to the variables in the input list.

If an array appears as an item, it is treated as if the elements were specified in array element order. For example, the third of the print statements in Figure 9.1 could have been written

```
      print '(3f10.3)', a(1:3)
```

However, no element of the array may appear more than once in an input item. Thus, the case in Figure 9.2 is not allowed.

Figure 9.2

```
      integer :: j(10), k(3)
      :
      k = (/ 1, 2, 1 /)
      read '(3i10)', j(k)       ! Illegal because j(1) appears twice
```

If an allocatable array appears as an item, it must be currently allocated.

Any pointers in an I/O list must be associated with a target, and transfer takes place between the file and the targets.

An item of derived type is treated as if the components were specified in the same order as in the type declaration. This rule is applied repeatedly for components of derived type, so that it is as if we specified the list of items of intrinsic type that constitute its ultimate components. For example, if p and t are of the types point and triangle of Figure 2.1, the statement

```
read '(8f10.5)', p, t
```

has the same effect as the statement

```
read '(8f10.5)', p%x, p%y, t%a%x, t%a%y, t%b%x,        &
                 t%b%y, t%c%x, t%c%y
```

Each ultimate component must be accessible (not, for example, be a private component of a public type).

An object in an I/O list is not permitted to be of a derived type that has a pointer component at any level of component selection. One reason for this restriction is because of the problems associated with recursive data structures. For example, supposing chain is a data object of the type entry of Figure 2.3 (in Section 2.13) and is set up to hold a chain of length three, then it has as its ultimate components chain%index, chain%next%index, chain%next%next%index, and chain%next%next%next, the last of which is a disassociated pointer. Another reason is the intention to add defined edit descriptors for data structures to Fortran 2000. Programmers will be able to write procedures that are called as part of the I/O processing. Such a procedure will be much better able to handle structures whose size and composition vary dynamically, the usual case for pointer components.

An I/O list may include an implied-do list, as illustrated by the fifth print statement in Figure 9.1. The general form is

(*do-object-list*, *do-var* = *expr*, *expr* [, *expr*])

where each *do-object* is a variable (for input), an expression (for output), or is itself an implied-do list; *do-var* is a named scalar integer variable; and each *expr* is a scalar integer expression. The loop initialization and execution is the same as for a (possibly nested) set of do constructs (Section 4.5). In an input list, a variable that is an item in a *do-object-list* must not be a *do-var* of any implied-do list in which it is contained, nor be associated[1] with such a *do-var*. In an input or output list, no *do-var* may be a *do-var* of any implied-do list in which it is contained or be associated with such a *do-var*.

Note that a zero-sized array, or an implied-do list with a zero iteration count, may occur as an item in an I/O list. Such an item corresponds to no actual data transfer.

9.4   Format definition

In the print and read statements of the previous section, the format specification was given each time in the form of a character constant immediately following the keyword. In fact, there are three ways in which a format specification may be given. They are:

---

[1]Such an illegal association could be established by pointer association.

i) As a statement label referring to a format statement containing the relevant specification between parentheses:

```
    print 100, q
    :
100 format(f10.3)
```

The format statement must appear in the same scoping unit, before the contains statement if it has one. It is customary either to place each format statement immediately after the first statement which references it, or to group them all together just before the contains or end statement. It is also customary to have a separate sequence of numbers for the statement labels used for format statements. A given format statement may be used by any number of formatted I/O statements, whether for input or for output.

ii) As a default character expression whose value commences with a format specification in parentheses:

```
    print '(f10.3)', q
```

or

```
    character(len=*), parameter :: form='(f10.3)'
    :
    print form, q
```

or

```
    character :: carray(7)=(/ '(','f','1','0','.','3',')' /)
    :
    print carray, q ! Elements of an array expression
                    ! are concatenated.
```

or

```
    character(4) :: carr1(10)
    character(3) :: carr2(10)
    integer      :: i, j
    :
    carr1(10) = '(f10'
    carr2(3) = '.3)'
    :
    i = 10
    j = 3
    :
    print carr1(i)//carr2(j), q
```

From these examples it may be seen that it is possible to program formats in a flexible way, and particularly that it is possible to use arrays, expressions and also substrings in a way which allows a given format to be built up dynamically at execution-time from various components. Any character data which might follow the trailing right parenthesis are ignored and may be undefined. In the case of an array, its elements are concatenated in array element order. However, on input *no* component of the format specification may appear also in the input list, or be associated with it. This is because the standard requires that the whole format specification be established *before* any I/O takes place. Further, no redefinition or undefinition of any characters of the format is permitted during the execution of the I/O statement.

iii) As an asterisk. This is a type of I/O known as *list-directed* I/O, in which the format is defined by the computer system at the moment the statement is executed, depending on both the type and magnitude of the entities involved. This facility is particularly useful for the input and output of small quantities of values, especially in temporary code which is used for test purposes, and which is removed from the final version of the program:

```
print *, 'Square-root of q = ', sqrt(q)
```

This example outputs a character constant describing the expression which is to be output, followed by the value of the expression under investigation. On the terminal screen, this might appear as

```
Square-root of q = 4.392246
```

the exact format being dependent on the computer system used. Character strings in this form of output are normally undelimited, as if an a edit descriptor were in use, but an option in the open statement (Section 10.3) may be used to require that they be delimited by apostrophes or quotation marks. Except for adjacent undelimited strings, values are separated by spaces or commas. Logical variables are represented as T for true and F for false. The processor may represent a sequence of r identical values c by the form $r * c$. Further details of list-directed input/output are deferred until Section 9.9.

Blank characters may precede the left parenthesis of a format specification, and may appear at any point within a format specification with no effect on the interpretation, except within a character string edit descriptor (Section 9.13.4).

9.5   Unit numbers

Input/output operations are used to transfer data between the variables of an executing program, as stored in the computer, and an external medium. There are many types of external media: the terminal, printer, disc drive, and CD are perhaps the most familiar. Whatever the device, a Fortran program regards each one from which it reads or to which it writes as a *unit*, and each unit, with two exceptions, has associated with it a *unit number*. This number must not be negative and is often in the range 1 to 99. Thus we might associate with a disc drive from which we are reading the unit number 10, and to a hard disc drive to which we are writing the unit number 11. All program units of an executable program that refer to a particular unit number are referencing the same file.

There are two I/O statements, print and a variant of read, that do not reference any unit number; these are the statements that we have used so far in examples, for the sake of simplicity. A read statement without a unit number will normally expect to read from the terminal, unless the program is working in batch (non-interactive) mode in which case there will be a disc file with a reserved name from which it reads. A print statement will normally expect to output to the terminal, unless the program is in batch mode in which case another disc file with a reserved name will be used. Such files are usually suitable for subsequent output on a physical output device. The system may implicitly associate unit numbers to these default units.

Apart from these two special cases, all I/O statements must refer explicitly to a unit in order to identify the device to which or from which data are to be transferred. The unit may be given in one of three forms. These are shown in the following examples which use another form of the read containing a unit specifier, *u*, and format specifier, *fmt*, in parentheses and separated by a comma, where *fmt* is a format specification as described in the previous section:

    read (u, fmt) list

The three forms of *u* are:

i) As a scalar integer expression that gives the unit number:

```
read (4, '(f10.3)') q
read (nunit, '(f10.3)') q
read (4*i+j, 100) a
```

where the value may be any nonnegative integer allowed by the system for this purpose.

ii) As an asterisk:

```
read (*, '(f10.3)') q
```

where the asterisk implies the standard input unit designated by the system, the same as that used for read without a unit number.

iii) As a default character variable identifying an *internal file* (see next section).

9.6 Internal files

Internal files allow format conversion between various representations to be carried out by the program in a storage area defined within the program itself. There are two particularly useful applications, one to read data whose format is not properly known in advance, and the other to prepare output lists containing mixed character and numerical data, all of which has to be prepared in character form, perhaps to be displayed as a caption on a graphics display. The character data must be of default kind. The first application will now be described; the second will be dealt with in Section 9.8.

Imagine that we have to read a string of 30 digits, which might correspond to 30 one-digit integers, 15 two-digit integers or 10 three-digit integers. The information as to which type of data is involved is given by the value of an additional digit, which has the value 1, 2, or 3, depending on the number of digits each integer contains. An internal file provides us with a mechanism whereby the 30 digits can be read into a character buffer area. The value of the final digit can be tested separately, and 30, 15, or 10 values read from the internal file, depending on this value. The basic code to achieve this might read as follows (no error recovery or data validation is included, for simplicity):

```
integer      :: ival(30), key, i
character(30):: buffer
character(6) :: form(3) = (/ '(30i1)', '(15i2)', '(10i3)' /)
read (*, '(a30,i1)')      buffer, key
read (buffer, form (key)) (ival(i), i=1,30/key)
```

Here, ival is an array which will receive the values, buffer a character variable of a length sufficient to contain the 30 input digits, and form a character array containing the three possible formats to which the input data might correspond. The first read statement reads 30 digits into buffer as character data, and a final digit into the integer variable key. The second read statement reads the data from buffer into ival, using the appropriate conversion as specified by the edit descriptor selected by key. The number of variables read from buffer to ival is defined by the implied-do loop, whose second specifier is an integer expression depending also on key. After execution of this code, ival will contain 30/key values, their number and exact format not having been known in advance.

If an internal file is a scalar, it has a single record whose length is that of the scalar. If it is an array, its elements, in array element order, are treated as successive records of the file and each has length that of an array element. It may not be an array section with a vector subscript.

A record becomes defined when it is written. The number of characters sent must not exceed the length of the record. It may be less, in which case the rest of the record is padded with blanks. For list-directed output (Section 9.4), character constants are not delimited. A record may be read only if it is defined (which need not only be by an output statement). Records are padded with blanks, if necessary.

An internal file is always positioned at the beginning of its first record prior to data transfer (the array section notation may be used to start elsewhere in an array). Of course, if an internal file is an allocatable array or pointer, it must be allocated or associated with a target. Also, no item in the input/output list may be in the file or associated with the file.

An internal file must be of default character type and non-default character items are not permitted in input/output lists. It may be used for list-directed I/O (Section 9.9), but not for namelist I/O (Section 9.10).

9.7 Formatted input

In the previous sections we have given complete descriptions of the ways that formats and units may be specified, using simplified forms of the read and print statements as examples. There are, in fact, two forms of the formatted read statement. Without a unit, it has the form

read *fmt* [,*list*]

and with a unit it may take the form

read ([unit=]*u*, [fmt=]*fmt* [,iostat=*ios*]   &
        [, err=*error-label*] [,end=*end-label*]) [*list*]

where *u* and *fmt* are the unit and format specifiers described in Sections 9.4 and 9.5; iostat=, err=, and end= are optional specifiers which allow a user to specify how a read statement shall recover from various exceptional conditions; and *list* is a list of variables and implied-do lists of variables. The keyword items may be specified in any order, although it is usual to keep the unit number and format specification as the first two. The unit number must be first if it does not have its keyword. If the format does not have its keyword, it must be second, following the unit number without its keyword. Note that this parallels the rules for keyword calls of procedures, except that the positional list is limited to two items.

For simplicity of exposition, we have so far limited ourselves to formats that correspond to a single record in the file, but we will meet later in this chapter cases that lead to the input of a part of a record or of several successive records.

The meanings of the optional specifiers are as follows. If the iostat= is specified, then *ios* must be a scalar integer variable of default kind which, after execution of the read statement, has a negative value if an end-of-record condition is encountered during non-advancing input (Section 9.12), a different negative value if an endfile condition was detected on the input device (Section 10.2.3), a positive value if an error was detected (for instance a formatting error), or the value zero otherwise. The actual values assigned to *ios* in the event of an exception occurring are not defined by the standard, only the signs.

If the end= is specified, then *end-label* must be a statement label of a statement in the same scoping unit, to which control will be transferred in the event of the end of the file being reached.

If the err= is specified, then *error-label* is a statement label in the same scoping unit, to which control will be transferred in the event of any other exception occurring. The labels *error-label* and *end-label* may be the same. If they are not specified and an exception occurs, execution will stop, unless iostat is specified. An example of a read statement with its associated error recovery is given in Figure 9.3, in which error and last_file are subroutines to deal with the exceptions. They will normally be system dependent.

Figure 9.3

```
      read (nunit, '(3f10.3)', iostat=ios, err=110, end=120) a,b,c
   !
   !   Successful read - continue execution.
      :
      :
   !
   !   Error condition - take appropriate action.
  110 call error (ios)
      go to 999
   !
   !   End-of-file condition - test whether more
   !   files follow.
  120 call last_file
      :
  999 end
```

If an error or end-of-file condition occurs on input, the statement terminates and all list items and any implied-do variables become undefined. If an end-of-file condition occurs for an external file, the file is positioned following the endfile record (Section 10.2.3); if there is otherwise an error condition, the file position is indeterminate. An end-of-file condition occurs also if an attempt is made to read beyond the end of an internal file.

It is a good practice to include some sort of error recovery in all read statements which are included permanently in a program. On the other hand, input for test purposes is normally sufficiently well handled by the simple form of read without unit number, and without error recovery.

9.8 Formatted output

There are two types of formatted output statements, the print statement which has appeared in many of the examples so far in this chapter, and the write statement whose syntax is similar to that of the read statement:

   print *fmt* [, *list*]

and

```
write ([unit=]u, [fmt=]fmt [,iostat=ios]                    &
             [,err=error-label] ) [list]
```

where all the components have the same meanings as described for the read
statement (Section 9.7). An asterisk for *u* specifies the standard output unit, as
used by print. If an error condition occurs on output, execution of the statement
terminates, any implied-do variables become undefined, and the file position
becomes indeterminate.

An example of a write statement is

```
write (nout, '(10f10.3)', iostat=ios, err=110) a
```

An example using an internal file is given in Figure 9.4, which builds a character
string from numeric and character components. The final character string might
be passed to another subroutine for output, for instance as a caption on a graphics
display.

Figure 9.4

```
integer        :: day
real           :: cash
character(len=50) :: line
:
!   write into line
write (line,'(a, i2, a, f8.2, a)')                          &
      'Takings for day ', day, ' are ', cash, ' dollars'
```

In this example, we declare a character variable that is long enough to contain
the text to be transferred to it. (The write statement contains a format specification with a edit descriptors without a field width. These assume a field width
corresponding to the actual length of the character strings to be converted.) After
execution of the write statement, line might contain the character string

```
Takings for day  3 are  4329.15 dollars
```

and this could be used as a string for further processing.

The number of characters written to line must not exceed its length.

9.9 List-directed I/O

In Section 9.4, the list-directed output facility using an asterisk as format specifier
was introduced. We assumed that the list was short enough to fit into a single
record, but for long lists the processor is free to output several records. Character
constants may be split between records, and complex constants that are as long as,
or longer than, a record may be split after the comma that separates the two parts.
Apart from these cases, a value always lies within a single record. For the sake of
carriage control (which is described in Section 9.11), the first character of each

record is blank unless a delimited character constant is being continued. Note that when an undelimited character constant is continued, the first character of the continuation record is blank. The only blanks permitted in a numeric constant are within a split complex constant after the comma.

This facility is equally useful for input, especially of small quantities of test data. On the input record, the various constants may appear in any of their usual forms, just as if they were being read under the usual edit descriptors, as defined in Section 9.13. Exceptions are that complex values must be enclosed in parentheses, character constants may be delimited, a blank must not occur except in a delimited character constant or in a complex constant before or after a numeric field, blanks are never interpreted as zeros, and the optional characters which are allowed in a logical constant (those following t or f, see Section 9.13.2) must include neither a comma nor a slash.

Character constants that are enclosed in apostrophes or quotation marks may be spread over as many records as necessary to contain them, except that a doubled quotation mark or apostrophe must not be split between records. Delimiters may be omitted for a default character constant if

- it is of nonzero length;

- the constant does not contain a blank, comma, or slash;

- it is contained in one record;

- the first character is neither a quotation mark nor an apostrophe; and

- the leading characters are not numeric followed by an asterisk.

In this case, the constant is terminated when a blank, comma, slash, or end of record is encountered, and apostrophes or quotation marks appearing within the constant must not be doubled.

Whenever a character value has a different length from the corresponding list item, the value is truncated or padded on the right with blanks, as in the character assignment statement.

It is possible to use a repeat count for a given constant, for example 6*10 to specify six occurrences of the integer value 10. If it is possible to interpret the constant as either a literal constant or an undelimited character constant, the first corresponding list item determines which it is.

The (optionally repeated) constants are separated in the input by *separators*. A separator is one of the following, appearing other than in a character constant:

- a comma, optionally preceded and optionally followed by one or more contiguous blanks,

- a slash (/), optionally preceded and optionally followed by one or more contiguous blanks, or

- one or more contiguous blanks between two non-blank values or following the last non-blank value.

An end of record not within a character constant is regarded as a blank and, therefore, forms part of a separator. A blank embedded in a complex constant or delimited character constant is not a separator. An input record may be terminated by a slash separator, in which case all the following values in the record are ignored, and the input statement terminates.

If there are no values between two successive separators, or between the beginning of the first record and the first separator, this is taken to represent a *null value* and the corresponding item in the input list is left unchanged, defined or undefined as the case may be. A null value must not be used for the real or imaginary part of a complex constant, but a single null value may be used for the whole complex value. A series of null values may be represented by a repeat count without a constant: `,6*,`. When a slash separator is encountered, null values are given to any remaining list items.

An example of this form of the `read` statement is:

```
integer           :: i
real              :: a
complex           :: field(2)
logical           :: flag
character (len=12) :: title
character (len=4)  :: word
:
read *, i, a, field, flag, title, word
```

If this reads the input record

10*b*6.4*b*(1.,0.)*b*(2.,0.)*b*t*b*test/

(in which *b* stands for a blank, and blanks are used as separators), then i, a, field, flag, and title will acquire the values 10, 6.4, (1.,0.) and (2.,0.), .true. and test respectively, while word remains unchanged. For the input records

```
10,.64e1,2*,.true.
'histogramb10'/val1
```

(in which commas are used as separators), the variables i, a, flag, and title will acquire the values 10, 6.4, .true., and histogram*b*10 respectively. The variable field and word remain unchanged, and the input string val1 is ignored as it follows a slash. (Note the apostrophes, which are required as the string contains a blank. Without delimiters, this string would appear to be a string followed by the integer value 10.) Because of this slash, the read statement does not continue with the next record and the list is thus not fully satisfied.

9.10 Namelist I/O

It can be useful, especially for program testing, to input or output an annotated list of values. The values required are specified in a `namelist` group (Section 7.15), and the I/O is performed by a `read` or `write` statement that does not have an I/O list, and in which either

- the format is replaced by a namelist-group name as the second positional parameter, or

- the `fmt=` specifier is replaced by a `nml=` specifier with that name.

When reading, only those objects which are specified in the input record and which do not have a null value become defined. All other list items remain in their existing state of definition or undefinition. It is possible to define the value of an array element or section without affecting the other portions of the array. When writing, all the items in the group are written to the file specified. This form of I/O is not available for internal files.

The value for a scalar object or list of values for an array is preceded in the records by the name or designator and an equals sign which may optionally be preceded or followed by blanks. The form of the list of values and null values in the input and output records is as that for list-directed I/O (Section 9.9), except that character constants must *always* be delimited in input records and logical constants must not contain an equals sign. A `namelist` input statement terminates on the appearance of a slash in the list outside a character constant. A simple example is

```
integer   ::  no_of_eggs, litres_of_milk, kilos_of_butter
namelist/food/no_of_eggs, litres_of_milk, kilos_of_butter
read (5, nml=food)
```

to read the record

```
&food litres_of_milk=5, no_of_eggs=12 /
```

where we note that the order of the two values given is not the same as their order in the `namelist` group — the orders need not necessarily match. The value of `kilos_of_butter` remains unchanged. The first non-blank item in the record is an ampersand followed without an intervening blank by the group name. The slash is obligatory as a terminator. On output, a similar annotated list of values is produced, starting with the name of the group and ending with a slash. Here the order is that of the `namelist` group. Thus, the statements

```
integer   :: number, list(10)
namelist/out/number, list
write (6, nml=out)
```

might produce the record

```
&OUT NUMBER=1, LIST=14, 9*0 /
```

On output, the names are always in upper case.

Where a subobject designator appears in an input record, all substring expressions, subscripts, and strides must be scalar integer literal constants without specified kind parameters. All group names, object names, and component names are interpreted without regard to case. Blanks may precede or follow the name or designator, but must not appear within it.

If the object is scalar and of intrinsic type, the equals sign must be followed by one value. If it is of derived type or is an array, the equals sign must be followed by a list of values of intrinsic type corresponding to the replacement of each derived-type value by its ultimate components and each array by its elements in array element order.

The list of values must not be too long, but it may be too short, in which case trailing null values are regarded as having been appended. If an object is of type character, the corresponding item must be of the same kind.

Zero-sized objects must not appear in a namelist input record. In any multiple occurrence of an object in a sequence of input records, the final value is taken.

9.10.1   Comments in namelist input (Fortran 95 only)

In Fortran 95, input records for namelist input may bear a comment following an object name/value separator other than a slash. This allows programers to document the structure of a namelist input file line-by-line. The comment is in the usual format for comments. Taking the input record of Section 9.10, it may be documented thus:

```
&food litres_of_milk=5,    ! Fortran 95
no_of_eggs=12 /
```

A comment line, with ! as the first non-blank character in an input record, is also permitted, but may not occur in a character context.

9.11   Carriage control

Fortran's formatted output statements were originally designed for line-printers, with their concept of lines and pages of output. On such a device, the first character of each output record must be of default kind. It is not printed but interpreted as a *carriage control character*. If it is a blank, no action is taken, and it is good practice to insert a blank as the first character of each record, either explicitly as ' ' or using the t2 edit descriptor (described in Section 9.13.5), in order to avoid inadvertent generation of spurious carriage control characters. This can happen when the first character in an output record is non-blank, and might occur, for instance, when printing integer values with the format '(i5)'. Here all output values between -999 and 9999 will have a blank in the first position, but all others will generate a character there which may be used mistakenly for carriage control.

The carriage control characters defined by the standard are:

     b   to start a new line

     +   to remain on the same line (overprint)

     0   to skip a line

     1   to advance to the beginning of the next page

As a precaution, the first character of each record produced by list-directed and namelist output is a blank, unless it is the continuation of a delimited character constant.

In this context, we note that execution of a print statement does not imply that any printing will actually occur, and nor does execution of a write statement imply that printing will not occur.

9.12 Non-advancing I/O

So far we have considered each read or write statement to perform the input or output of a complete record. There are, however, many applications, especially in screen management, where this would become an irksome restriction. What is required is the ability to read and write without always advancing the file position to ahead of the next record. This facility is provided by *non-advancing* I/O. To gain access to this facility, the optional advance= specifier must appear in the read or write statement and be associated with a scalar default character expression *advance* which evaluates, after suppression of any trailing blanks and conversion of any upper-case letters to lower case, to the value no. The only other allowed value is yes which is the default value if the specifier is absent; in this case normal (advancing) I/O occurs.

The following optional specifiers are available for a non-advancing read statement:

    eor=*eor-label*
    size=*size*

where *eor-label* is a statement label in the same scoping unit and *size* is a default integer scalar variable. The *eor-label* may be the same as an *end-label* or *error-label* of the read statement.

An advancing I/O statement always repositions the file after the last record accessed, but a non-advancing I/O statement usually leaves the file positioned within the record. However, if a non-advancing input statement attempts to transfer data from beyond the end of the *current* record, an end-of-record condition occurs and the file is repositioned to follow the record. The iostat variable, if present, will acquire a different negative value to the one indicating an end-of-file condition; and, if the eor= specifier is present, control is transferred to the statement specified by its associated *eor-label*. In order to provide a means of controlling this process, the size= specifier, when present, sets *size* to the number of characters actually read. A full example is thus

```
    character(len=3) :: key
    integer          :: unit, size
    read (unit, '(a3)', advance='no', size=size, eor=66) key
    :
  ! key is not in one record
66  key(size+1:) = ''
    :
```

As for error and end-of-file conditions, the program terminates when an end-of-record condition occurs if neither eor= nor iostat= is specified.

If encountering an end-of-record on reading results in the input list not being satisfied, the pad= specifier described in Section 10.3 will determine whether any padding with blank characters occurs. Blanks inserted as padding are not included in the size= count.

It is possible to perform normal and non-advancing I/O on the same record or file. For instance, a non-advancing read might read the first few characters of a record and a normal read the remainder.

A particular application of this facility is to write a prompt to a terminal screen and to read from the next character position on the screen without an intervening line-feed:

```
write (*, '(a)', advance='no') 'enter next prime number:'
read  (*, '(i10)') prime_number
```

Non-advancing I/O may be performed only on an external file, and may not be used for namelist or list-directed I/O. Note that, as for advancing input/output, several records may be processed by a single statement.

9.13 Edit descriptors

In the description of the possible forms of a format specification in Section 9.4, a few examples of the edit descriptors were given. As mentioned there, edit descriptors give a precise specification of how values are to be converted into a character string on an output device or internal file, or converted from a character string on an input device or internal file to internal representations.

With certain exceptions noted in the following text, edit descriptors in a list are separated by commas, and only in the case where an input/output list is empty or specifies only zero-sized arrays may there be no edit descriptor at all in the format specification.

On a processor that supports upper- and lower-case letters, edit descriptors are interpreted without regard to case. This is also true for numerical and logical input fields; an example is 89AB as a hexadecimal input value.

9.13.1 Repeat counts

Edit descriptors fall into three classes: *data, control,* and *character-string.* The data edit descriptors may be preceded by a repeat count (a nonzero unsigned default integer literal constant), as in the example

        10f12.3

Of the remaining edit descriptors, only the slash edit descriptor (Section 9.13.5) may have an associated repeat count. A repeat count may be applied to a group of edit descriptors, enclosed in parentheses:

    print '(4(i5,f8.2))', (i(j), a(j), j=1,4)

(for integer i and real a). This is equivalent to writing

    print '(i5,f8.2,i5,f8.2,i5,f8.2,i5,f8.2)', (i(j), a(j), j=1,4)

Repeat counts such as this may be nested:

    print '(2(2i5,2f8.2))', i(1),i(2),a(1),a(2),i(3),i(4),a(3),a(4)

If a format specification without components in parentheses is used with an I/O list that contains more elements than the number of edit descriptors, taking account of repeat counts, then a new record will begin, and the format specification repeated. Further records begin in the same way until the list is exhausted. To print an array of 100 integer elements, 10 elements to a line, the following statement might be used:

    print '(10i8)', (i(j), j=1,100)

Similarly, when reading from an input file, new records would be read until the list is satisfied, a new record being taken from the input file each time the specification is repeated *even if the individual records contain more input data than specified by the format specification.* These superfluous data would be ignored. For example, reading the two records (*b* again stands for a blank)

    *bbb*10*bbb*15*bbb*20
    *bbb*25*bbb*30*bbb*35

under control of the read statement

        read '(2i5)', i,j,k,l

would result in the four integer variables i, j, k and l acquiring the values 10, 15, 25 and 30, respectively.

If a format contains components in parentheses, as in

        '(2i5, 3(i2,2(i1,i3)), 2(2f8.2,i2))'

whenever the format is exhausted, a new record is taken and format control reverts to the repeat factor preceding the left parenthesis corresponding to the last-but-one right parenthesis, here 2(2f8.2,i2), or to the parenthesis itself if it has no repeat factor. This we call *reversion.*

9.13.2 Data edit descriptors

Values of all the intrinsic data types may be converted by the g edit descriptor. However, for reasons of clarity, it is described last.

Integer values may be converted by means of the i edit descriptor. This comes in a basic form, iw, where w is a nonzero unsigned default integer literal constant that defines the width of the field. The integer value will be read from or written to this field, adjusted to its right-hand side. If we again designate a blank position by b then the value -99 printed under control of the edit descriptor i5 will appear as bb-99, the sign counting as one position in the field.

For output, an alternative form of this edit descriptor allows the number of digits that are to be printed to be specified exactly, even if some are leading zeros. The form i$w.m$ specifies the width of the field, w, and that at least m digits are to be output, where m is an unsigned default integer literal constant. The value 99 printed under control of the edit descriptor i5.3 would appear as bb099. The value of m is even permitted to be zero, and the field will be then filled with blanks if the value printed is 0. On input, i$w.m$ is interpreted in exactly the same way as iw.

For the i and all other numeric edit descriptors, if the output field is too narrow to contain the number to be output, it is filled with asterisks.

Integer values may also be converted by the bw, b$w.m$, ow, o$w.m$, zw, and z$w.m$ edit descriptors. These are similar to the i form, but are intended for integers represented in the binary, octal, and hexadecimal number systems, respectively (Section 2.6.1). The external form does not contain the leading letter (b, o, or z) or the delimiters.

Real values may be converted by either e, en, es, or f edit descriptors. The f descriptor we have met in earlier examples. Its general form is f$w.d$, where w and d are unsigned default integer literal constants which define, respectively, the field width and the number of digits to appear after the decimal point in the output field. The decimal point counts as one position in the field. On input, if the input string has a decimal point, the value of d is ignored. Reading the input string b9.3729b with the edit descriptor f8.3 would cause the value 9.3729 to be transferred. All the digits are used, but roundoff may be inevitable because of the actual physical storage reserved for the value on the computer being used.

There are, in addition, two other forms of input string that are acceptable to the f edit descriptor. The first is an optionally signed string of digits without a decimal point. In this case, the d rightmost digits will be taken to be the fractional part of the value. Thus b-14629 read under control of the edit descriptor f7.2 will transfer the value -146.29. The second form is the standard default real form of literal constant, as defined in Section 2.6.2, and the variant in which the exponent is signed and e is omitted. In this case, the d part of the descriptor is again ignored. Thus the value 14.629e-2 (or 14.629-2), under control of the edit descriptor f9.1, will transfer the value 0.14629. The exponent letter may also be written in upper case.

Values are rounded on output following the normal rules of arithmetic. Thus, the value 10.9336, when output under control of the edit descriptor f8.3, will appear as bb10.934, and under the control of f4.0 as b11.

The e edit descriptor has two forms, ew.d and ew.dee, and is more appropriate for numbers with a magnitude below about 0.01, or above 1000. The rules for these two forms for input are identical to those for the fw.d edit descriptor. For output with the ew.d form of the descriptor, a different character string will be transferred, containing a significand with absolute value less than 1 and an exponent field of four characters that consists of either E followed by a sign and two digits or of a sign and three digits. Thus, for $1.234 * 10^{23}$ converted by the edit descriptor e10.4, the string b.1234E+24 or b.1234+024 will be transferred. The form containing the exponent letter E is not used if the magnitude of the exponent exceeds 99. For instance, e10.4 would cause the value $1.234 * 10^{-150}$ to be transferred as b.1234-149. Some processors print a zero before the decimal point.

In the second form of the e edit descriptor, ew.dee, e is an unsigned, nonzero default integer literal constant that determines the number of digits to appear in the exponent field. This form is obligatory for exponents whose magnitude is greater than 999. Thus the value $1.234 * 10^{1234}$ with the edit descriptor e12.4e4 is transferred as the string b.1234E+1235. An increasing number of computers are able to deal with these very large exponent ranges. It can also be used if only one exponent digit is desired. For example, the value 1.211 with the edit descriptor e9.3e1 is transferred as the string b0.121E+1.

The en (*engineering*) edit descriptor is identical to the e edit descriptor except that on output the decimal exponent is divisible by three, a nonzero significand is greater than or equal to 1 and less than 1000, and the scale factor (Section 9.13.5) has no effect. Thus, the value 0.0217 transferred under an en9.2 edit descriptor would appear as 21.70E-03 or 21.70-003.

The es (*scientific*) edit descriptor is identical to the e edit descriptor, except that on output the absolute value of a nonzero significand is greater than or equal to 1 and less than 10 and the scale factor (Section 9.13.5) has no effect. Thus, the value 0.0217 transferred under an es9.2 edit descriptor would appear as 2.17E-02 or 2.17-002.

Complex values may be edited under control of pairs of f, e, en, or es edit descriptors. The two descriptors do not need to be identical. The complex value (0.1,100.) converted under control of f6.1,e8.1 would appear as bbb0.1b0.1E+03. The two descriptors may be separated by character string and control edit descriptors (to be described in Sections 9.13.4 and 9.13.5).

Logical values may be edited using the lw edit descriptor. This defines a field of width w which on input consists of optional blanks, optionally followed by a decimal point, followed by t or f (or T or F), optionally followed by additional characters. Thus a field defined by l7 permits the strings .true. and .false. to be input. The characters t or f will be transferred as the values true or false respectively. On output, the character T or F will appear in the right-most position in the output field.

Character values may be edited using the a edit descriptor in one of its two forms, either a or aw. In the first of the two forms, the width of the input or output field is determined by the actual width of the item in the I/O list, measured in number of characters of whatever kind. Thus, a character variable of length 10, containing the value STATEMENTS, when written under control of the a edit descriptor would appear in a field 10 characters wide, and the non-default character variable of length 4 containing the value 国際標準 would appear in a field 4 characters wide. If, however, the first variable were converted under an a11 edit descriptor, it would be printed with a leading blank, *b*STATEMENTS. Under control of a8, the eight left-most characters only would be written: STATEMEN.

Conversely, with the same variable on input, an a11 edit descriptor would cause the 10 right-most characters in the 11 character-wide input field to be transferred: *b*STATEMENTS would be transferred as STATEMENTS. The a8 edit descriptor would cause the eight characters in the field to be transferred to the eight left-most positions in the variable, and the remaining two would be filled with blanks: STATEMEN would be transferred as STATEMEN*bb*.

All characters transferred under the control of an a or aw edit descriptor have the kind of the I/O list item, and we note that this edit descriptor is the *only* one which can be used to transmit non-default characters to or from a record. In the non-default case, the blank padding character is processor dependent.

The g$w.d$ and g$w.dee$ (*general*) edit descriptor may be used for any intrinsic data type. When used for real or complex types, it is identical to the e edit descriptor except that an output value with magnitude n in the range

$$0.1 - 0.5 \times 10^{-d-1} \leq n < 10^d - 0.5$$

or zero when $d = 0$ are converted as if by an f edit descriptor, and followed by the same number of blanks as the e edit descriptor would have used for the exponent part. The equivalent f edit descriptor is f$w'.d'$, where $w' = w - 4$ for g$w.d$ or w-e-2 for g$w.dee$, and $d' = d - k$ when n lies in the range

$$10^{k-1}(1 - 0.5 \times 10^{-d}) \leq n < 10^k(1 - 0.5 \times 10^{-d})$$

for $k = 0, 1, \ldots, d$ and $d' = d - 1$ when $n = 0$ and $d > 0$. This form is useful for printing values whose magnitudes are not well known in advance, and where an f conversion is preferred where possible, and an e otherwise.

When the g edit descriptor is used for integer, logical, or character types, it follows the rules of the iw, lw, and aw edit descriptors, respectively.

Finally, values of *derived types* are edited by the appropriate sequence of edit descriptors corresponding to the intrinsic types of the ultimate components of the derived type. An example is:

```
type string
   integer           :: length
   character(len=20) :: word
end type string
type(string) :: text
read(*, '(i2, a)') text
```

9.13.3 Minimal field width editing (Fortran 95 only)

In order to allow output records to contain as little unused space as possible, the i, f, b, o, and z edit descriptors (Section 9.13.2) may specify, in Fortran 95, a field width of zero, as in i0 or f0.3. This does not denote a zero-width field, but a field that is of the minimum width necessary to contain the output value in question. The programmer does not need to worry that a field with too narrow a width will cause output values to overflow and contain only asterisks.

9.13.4 Character string edit descriptor

A *default character* literal constant without a specified kind parameter can be transferred to an output file by embedding it in the format specification itself, as in the example

```
print "(' This is a format statement')"
```

The string will appear each time the statement is executed. In this descriptor, case is significant. Character string edit descriptors must not be used on input.

9.13.5 Control edit descriptors

It is sometimes necessary to give other instructions to an I/O device than just the width of fields and how the contents of these fields are to be interpreted. For instance, it may be that one wishes to position fields at certain columns or to start a new record without issuing a new write command. For this type of purpose, the control edit descriptors provide a means of informing the processor which action has to be taken. Some of these edit descriptors contain information that is used as it is processed; others are like switches, which change the conditions under which I/O takes place from the point where they are encountered, until the end of the processing of the I/O statement containing them (including reversions, Section 9.13.1). These latter descriptors we shall deal with first.

Control edit descriptors setting conditions

Embedded blanks in numeric input fields are treated in one of two ways, either as zero, or as null characters that are squeezed out by moving the other characters in the input field to the right, and adding leading blanks to the field (unless the field is totally blank, in which case it is interpreted as zero). The default is given by the blank= specifier (Section 10.3) currently in effect for the unit or is null for an internal file. Whatever the default may then be for a file, it may be overridden during a given format conversion by the bn (blanks null) and bz (blanks zero) edit descriptors. Let us suppose that the mode is that blanks are treated as zeros. The input string $bb1b4$ converted by the edit descriptor i5 would transfer the value 104. The same string converted by bn, i5 would give 14. A bn or bz edit descriptor switches the mode for the rest of that format specification, or until another bn or bz edit descriptor is met. The bn and bz edit descriptors have no effect on output.

Negative numerical values are always written with *leading signs* on output. For positive quantities other than exponents, whether the signs are written depends on the processor. The ss (sign suppress) edit descriptor suppresses leading plus signs, that is the value 99 printed by i5 is *bbb*99 and 1.4 is printed by e10.2 as *bb*0.14E+01. To switch on plus sign printing, the sp (sign print) edit descriptors may be used: the same numbers written by sp,i5,e10.2 become *bb*+99 and *b*+0.14E+01. The s edit descriptor restores the option to the processor. An ss, sp, or s will remain in force for the remainder of the format specification, unless another ss, sp, or s edit descriptor is met. These edit descriptors provide complete control over sign printing, and are useful for producing coded outputs which have to be compared automatically, on two different computers.

Scale factors apply to the input of real quantities under the e, f, en, es, and g edit descriptors, and are a means of scaling the input values. Their form is kp, where k is a default integer literal constant specifying the scale factor. The value is zero at the beginning of execution of the statement. The effect is that any quantity which does not have an exponent field will be reduced by a factor 10^k. Quantities with an exponent are not affected.

The scale factor kp also affects output with e, f or g editing, but has no effect with en or es editing. Under control of an f edit descriptor, the quantity will be multiplied by a factor 10^k. Thus, the number 10.39 output by an f6.0 edit descriptor following the scale factor 2p will appear as *b*1039.. With the e edit descriptor, and with g where the e style editing is taken, the quantity is transferred with the exponent reduced by k, and the significand multiplied by 10^k. Thus $0.31 * 10^3$, written after a 2p edit descriptor under control of e9.2, will appear as 31.00E+01. This gives a better control over the output style of real quantities which otherwise would have no significant digits before the decimal point.

The comma between a scale factor and an immediately following f, e, en, es, or g edit descriptor may be omitted, but we do not recommend that practice since it suggests that the scale factor applies only to the next edit descriptor, whereas in fact it applies throughout the format until another scale factor is encountered.

Control edit descriptors for immediate processing

Tabulation in an input or output field can be achieved using the edit descriptors tn, tr$n$ (and nx), and tl$n$, where n is a positive default integer literal constant. These state, respectively, that the next part of the I/O should begin at position n in the current record (where the *left tab limit* is position 1), or at n positions to the right of the current position, or at n positions to the left of the current position (the left tab limit if the current position is less than or equal to n). Let us suppose that, following an advancing read, we read an input record *bb*9876 with the following statement:

```
read (*, '(t3, i4, tl4, i1, i2)') i, j, k
```

The format specification will move a notional pointer firstly to position 3, whence i will be read. The variable i will acquire the value 9876, and the notional pointer is then at position 7. The edit descriptor t14 moves it left four positions, back to position 3. The quantities j and k are then read, and they acquire the values 9 and 87, respectively. These edit descriptors cause replacement on output, or multiple reading of the same items in a record on input. On output, any gaps ahead of the last character actually written are filled with spaces. If any character that is skipped by one of the descriptors is of other than default type, the positioning is processor dependent.

If the current record is the first one processed by the I/O statement and follows non-advancing I/O that left the file positioned within a record, the next character is the left tab limit; otherwise, the first character of the record is the left tab limit.

The *n*x edit descriptor is equivalent to the t*rn* edit descriptor. It is often used to place spaces in an output record. For example, to start an output record with a blank by this method, one writes

        fmt= '(1x,....)'

Spaces such as this can precede a data edit descriptor, but 1x,i5 is not, for instance, exactly equivalent to i6 on output, as any value requiring the full six positions in the field will not have them available in the former case.

The t and x edit descriptors never cause replacement of a character already in an output record, but merely cause a change in the position within the record such that such a replacement might be caused by a subsequent edit descriptor.

New records may be started at any point in a format specification by means of the slash (/) edit descriptor. This edit descriptor, although described here, may in fact have repeat counts; to skip, say, three records one can write either /,/,/ or 3/. On input, a new record will be started each time a / is encountered, even if the contents of the current record have not all been transferred. Reading the two records

        *bbb*99*bbb*10
        *bb*100*bbb*11

with the statement

        read '(bz,i5,i3,/,i5,i3,i2)', i, j, k, l, m

will cause the values 99, 0, 100, 0 and 11 to be transferred to the five integer variables, respectively. This edit descriptor does not need to be separated by a comma from a preceding edit descriptor, unless it has a repeat count; it does not ever need to be separated by a comma from a succeeding edit descriptor.

The result of writing with a format containing a sequence of, say, four slashes, as represented by

        print '(i5,4/,i5)', i, j

is to separate the two values by three blank records (the last slash starts the record containing j); if i and j have the values 99 and 100, they would appear as

> *bbb*99
> *b*
> *b*
> *b*
> *bb*100

A slash edit descriptor written to an internal file will cause the following values to be written to the next element of the character array specified for the file. Each such element corresponds to a record, and the number of characters written to a record must not exceed its length.

Colon editing is a means of terminating format control if there are no further items in an I/O list. In particular, it is useful for preventing further output of character strings used for annotation if the output list is exhausted. Consider the following output statement, for an array l(3):

```
print '(" 11 = ", i5, :, " 12 = ", i5, :," 13 = ", i5)', &
      (l(i) ,i=1,n)
```

If n has the value 3, then three values are printed. If n has the value 1 then, without the colons, the following output string would be printed:

```
11 = 59 12 =
```

The colon, however, stops the processing of the format, so that the annotation for the absent second value is not printed. This edit descriptor need not be separated from a neighbour by a comma. It has no effect if there are further items in the I/O list.

9.14 Unformatted I/O

The whole of this chapter has so far dealt with formatted I/O. The internal representation of a value may differ from the external form, which is always a character string contained in an input or output record. The use of formatted I/O involves an overhead for the conversion between the two forms, and often a roundoff error too. There is also the disadvantage that the external representation usually occupies more space on a storage medium than the internal representation. These three actual or potential drawbacks are all absent when unformatted I/O is used. In this form, the internal representation of a value is written exactly as it stands to the storage medium, and can be read back directly with neither roundoff nor conversion overhead. Here, a value of derived type is treated as a whole and is not equivalent to a list of its ultimate components. This is another reason for the rule (Section 9.3) that it must not have a pointer component at any level of component selection.

This type of I/O should be used in all cases where the records are generated by a program on one computer, to be read back on the same computer or another computer using the same internal number representations. Only when this is not the case, or when the data have to be visualized in one form or another, should formatted I/O be used. The records of a file must all be formatted or all be unformatted (apart from the endfile record).

Unformatted I/O has the incidental advantage of being simpler to program since no complicated format specifications are required. The forms of the read and write statements are the same as for formatted I/O, but without any fmt= or nml= specifier:

```
read(4) q
write(nout, iostat=ios, err=110) a
```

Non-advancing I/O is not available (in fact, an advance= specifier is not allowed).

Each read or write statement transfers exactly one record. The file must be an external file. The number of values specified by the input list of a read statement must not exceed the number of values available in the current record.

On output to a file connected for sequential access, a record of sufficient length is created. On input, the type and type parameters of each entity in the list must agree with those of the value in the record, except that two reals may correspond to one complex when all three have the same kind parameter.

9.15   Direct-access files

The only type of file organization that we have so far dealt with is the sequential file, which has a beginning and an end, and which contains a sequence of records, one after the other. Fortran permits another type of file organization known as *direct access* (or sometimes as random access or indexed). All the records have the same length, each record is identified by an index number, and it is possible to write, read, or re-write any specified record without regard to position. (In a sequential file, only the last record may be rewritten without losing other records; in general, records in sequential files cannot be replaced.) The records are either all formatted or all unformatted.

By default, any file used by a Fortran program is a sequential file, unless declared to be direct access. This declaration has to be made using the access= 'direct' and recl=*rl* specifiers of the open statement, which is described in the next chapter, (*rl* is the length of a record in the file). Once this declaration has been made, reading and writing, whether formatted or unformatted, proceeds as described for sequential files, except for the addition of a rec=*i* specifier to the read and write statements, where *i* is a scalar integer expression whose value is the index number of the record concerned. An end= specifier is not permitted. Usually, a data transfer statement for a direct-access file accesses a single record, but during formatted I/O any slash edit descriptor increases the record number by one and causes processing to continue at the beginning of this record. A sequence of statements to write, read, and replace a given record is given in Figure 9.5.

The file must be an external file and namelist formatting, list-directed formatting, and non-advancing I/O are all unavailable.

Figure 9.5

```
      integer, parameter :: nunit=2, len=100
      integer            :: i, length
      real               :: a(len), b(len+1:2*len)
      :
      inquire (iolength=length) a          ! See Section 10.5
      open (nunit, access='direct', recl=length)
                                           ! See Section 10.3
      :
 !   Write array B to direct-access file in record 14
     write (nunit, rec=14) b
      :
 !
 !   Read the array back into array a
     read (nunit, rec=14) a
      :
     do i = 1, len/2
        a(i) = i
     end do
 !
 !   Replace modified record
     write (nunit, rec=14) a
```

Direct-access files are particularly useful for applications which involve lots of hopping around inside a file, or where records need to be replaced, for instance in data base applications. A weakness is that the length of all the records must be the same, though on formatted output, the record is padded with blanks if necessary. For unformatted output, if the record is not filled, the remainder is undefined.

This simple and powerful facility allows much clearer control logic to be written than is the case for a sequential file which is repeatedly read, backspaced, or rewound. Only when direct-access files become large may problems of long access times become evident on some computer systems, and this point should always be investigated before heavy investments are made in programming large direct-access file applications.

Some computer systems allow the same file to be regarded as sequential or direct access according to the specification in the open statement or its default. The standard, therefore, regards this as a property of the connection rather than of the file. In this case, the order of records, even for sequential I/O, is that determined by the direct-access record numbering.

9.16   Execution of a data transfer statement

So far, we have used simple illustrations of data transfer statements without dependencies. However, some forms of dependency are permitted and can be very useful. For example, the statement

```
read (*, *) n, a(1:n)                ! n is an integer
```

allows the length of an array section to be part of the data.

With dependencies in mind, the order in which operations are executed is important. It is as follows:

i) identify the unit;

ii) establish the format (if any);

iii) position the file ready for the transfer (if required);

iv) transfer data between the file and the I/O list or namelist;

v) position the file following the transfer (if required);

vi) cause the iostat and size variables (if present) to become defined.

The order of transfer of namelist input is that in the input records. Otherwise, the order is that of the I/O list or namelist. Each input item is processed in turn, and may affect later subobjects and implied-do indices. All expressions within an I/O list item are determined at the beginning of processing of the item. If an entity is specified more than once during execution of a namelist input statement, the later value overwrites the earlier value. Any zero-sized array or zero-length implied-do list is ignored.

When an input item is an array, no element of the array is permitted to affect the value of an expression within the item. For example, the cases shown in Figure 9.6 are not permitted. This prevents dependencies occurring within the item itself.

Figure 9.6

```
integer :: j(10)
:
read *, j(j)                      ! Not permitted
read *, j(j(1):j(10))             ! Not permitted
```

In the case of an internal file, an I/O item must not be in the file or associated with it. Nor may an input item contain or be associated with any portion of the established format.

Finally, a function reference must not appear in an expression anywhere in an I/O statement if it causes another I/O statement or a stop statement to be executed.

9.17 Summary

This chapter has begun the description of Fortran's extensive I/O facilities. It has covered the formatted I/O statements, and their associated format specifications, and then turned to unformatted I/O and direct-access files.

The syntax of the read and write statements has been introduced gradually. The full syntax is

> read (*control-list*) [*input-list*]

and

> write (*control-list*) [*output-list*]

where *control-list* contains one or more of the following:

[unit=] *u*,
[fmt=] *fmt*,
[nml=] *nml-name*,
rec= *i*,
iostat= *ios*,
err= *error-label*,
end= *end-label*,
advance= *advance*,
size= *size*,
eor= *eor-label*.

A *control-list* must include a unit specifier and must not include any specifier more than once. The iostat and size variables must not be associated with each other (for instance be identical), nor with any entity being transferred, nor with any *do-var* of an implied-do list of the same statement. If either of these variables is an array element, the subscript value must not be affected by the data transfer, implied-do processing, or the evaluation of any other specifier in the statement.

There are many detailed changes with respect to Fortran 77, often to support new features in other parts of the language, such as derived types. Other new features are namelist, non-advancing I/O, the b, o, z, en and es edit descriptors, and the generalization of the g edit descriptor. In Fortran 95, minimal field width editing is new.

9.18 Exercises

1. Write suitable print statements to print the name and contents of each of the following arrays:

    a) real :: grid d(10,10), 10 elements to a line (assuming the values are between 1.0 and 100.0);

    b) integer :: list(50), the odd elements only;

   c) `character(len=10) ::  titles(20)`, two elements to a line;

   d) `real ::  power(10)`, five elements to a line in engineering notation;

   e) `logical ::  flags(10)`, on one line;

   f) `complex ::  plane(5)`, on one line.

2. Write statements to output the state of a game of tic-tac-toe (noughts-and-crosses) to a unit designated by the variable `unit`.

3. Write a program which reads an input record of up to 132 characters into an internal file and classifies it as a Fortran comment line with no statement, an initial line without a statement label, an initial line with a statement label, a continuation line, or a line containing multiple statements.

4. Write separate list-directed input statements to fill each of the arrays of Exercise 1. For each statement write a sample first input record.

5. Write the function `get_char`, to read single characters from a formatted, sequential file, ignoring any record structure.

10. Operations on external files

10.1 Introduction

So far we have discussed the topic of external files in a rather superficial way. In the examples of the various I/O statements in the previous chapter, an implicit assumption has always been made that the specified file was actually available, and that records could be written to it and read from it. For sequential files, the file control statements described in the next section further assume that it can be positioned. In fact, these assumptions are not necessarily valid. In order to define explicitly and to test the status of external files, three file status statements are provided: open, close, and inquire. Before beginning their description, however, two new definitions are required.

A computer system contains, among other components, a CPU and a storage system. Modern storage systems are usually based on some form of disc, which is used to store files for long or short periods of time. The execution of a computer program is, by comparison, a transient event. A file may exist for years, whereas programs run for only seconds or minutes. In Fortran terminology, a file is said to *exist* not in the sense we have just used, but in the restricted sense that it exists as a file *to which the program might have access*. In other words, if the program is prohibited from using the file because of a password protection system, or because some necessary action has not been taken in the job control language which is controlling the execution of the program, the file 'does not exist'.

A file which exists for a running program may be empty and may or may not be *connected* to that program. The file is connected if it is associated with a unit number known to the program. Such connection is usually made by executing an open statement for the file, but many computer systems will *pre-connect* certain files which any program may be expected to use, such as terminal input and output. Thus we see that a file may exist but not be connected. It may also be connected but not exist. This can happen for a pre-connected new file. The file will only come into existence (be *created*) if some other action is taken on the file: executing an open, write, print, or endfile statement. A unit must not be connected to more than one file at once, and a file must not be connected to more than one unit at once.

There are a number of other points to note with respect to files:

- The set of allowed names for a file is processor dependent.

- Both sequential and direct access may be available for some files, but normally a file is limited to one or the other.

- A file never contains both formatted and unformatted records.

Finally, we note that no statement described in this chapter applies to internal files.

10.2   File positioning statements

When reading or writing an external file that is connected for sequential access, whether formatted or unformatted, it is sometimes necessary to perform other control functions on the file in addition to input and output. In particular, one may wish to alter the current position, which may be within a record, between records, ahead of the first record (at the *initial point*), or after the last record (at its *terminal point*). The following three statements are provided for these purposes.

10.2.1   The backspace statement

It can happen in a program that a series of records is being written and that, for some reason, the last record written should be replaced by a new one, that is be overwritten. Similarly, when reading records, it may be necessary to reread the last record read, or to check-read a record which has just been written. For this purpose, Fortran provides the backspace statement, which has the syntax

    backspace *u*

or

    backspace ([unit=]*u* [,iostat=*ios*] [,err=*error-label*])

where *u* is a scalar integer expression whose value is the unit number, and the other optional specifiers have the same meaning as for a read statement. Again, keyword specifiers may be in any order, but the unit specifier must come first as a positional specifier.

The action of this statement is to position the file before the current record if it is positioned within a record, or before the preceding record if it is positioned between records. An attempt to backspace when already positioned at the beginning of a file results in no change in the file's position. If the file is positioned after an endfile record (Section 10.2.3), it becomes positioned before that record. It is not possible to backspace a file that does not exist, nor to backspace over a record written by a list-directed or namelist output statement (Sections 9.9 and 9.10). A series of backspace statements will backspace over the corresponding number of records. This statement is often very costly in computer resources and should be used as little as possible.

10.2.2 The rewind statement

In an analogous fashion to rereading, rewriting, or check-reading a record, a similar operation may be carried out on a complete file. For this purpose the rewind statement,

> rewind *u*

or

> rewind ([unit=]*u* [,iostat=*ios*] [,err=*error-label*])

may be used to reposition a file, whose unit number is specified by the scalar integer expression *u*. Again, keyword specifiers may be in any order, but the unit specifier must come first as a positional specifier. If the file is already at its beginning, there is no change in its position. The statement is permitted for a file that does not exist, and has no effect.

10.2.3 The endfile statement

The end of a file connected for sequential access is normally marked by a special record which is identified as such by the computer hardware, and computer systems ensure that all files written by a program are correctly terminated by such an *endfile record*. In doubtful situations, or when a subsequent program step will reread the file, it is possible to write an endfile record explicitly using the endfile statement:

> endfile *u*

or

> endfile ([unit=]*u* [,iostat=*ios*] [,err=*error-label*])

where *u*, once again, is a scalar integer expression specifying the unit number. Again, keyword specifiers may be in any order, but the unit specifier must come first as a positional specifier. The file is then positioned after the endfile record. This endfile record, if subsequently read by a program, must be handled using the end=*end-label* specifier of the read statement, otherwise program execution will normally terminate. Prior to data transfer, a file must not be positioned after an endfile record, but it is possible to backspace or rewind across an endfile record, which allows further data transfer to occur. An endfile record is written automatically whenever either a backspace or rewind operation follows a write operation as the next operation on the unit, or the file is closed by execution of a close statement (Section 10.4), by an open statement for the same unit (Section 10.3), or by normal program termination.

If the file may also be connected for direct access, only the records ahead of the endfile record are considered to have been written and only these may be read during a subsequent direct-access connection.

Note that if a file is connected to a unit but does not exist for the program, it will be made to exist by executing an endfile statement on the unit.

10.2.4   Data transfer statements

Execution of a data transfer statement (read, write, or print) also affects the file position. If it is between records, it is moved to the start of the next record. Data transfer then takes place, which usually moves the position. No further movement occurs for non-advancing access. For advancing access, the position finally moves to follow the last record transferred.

10.3   The open statement

The open statement is used to connect an external file to a unit, create a file that is preconnected, create a file and connect it to a unit, or change certain properties of a connection. The syntax is

> open ([unit=]*u* [,*olist*])

where *u* is a scalar integer expression specifying the external file unit number, and *olist* is a list of optional specifiers. If the unit is specified with unit=, it may appear in *olist*. A specifier must not appear more than once. In the specifiers, all entities are scalar and all characters are of default kind. In character expressions, any trailing blanks are ignored and, except for file=, any upper-case letters are converted to lower case. The specifiers are

iostat= *ios*, where *ios* is a default integer variable which is set to zero if the statement is correctly executed, and to a positive value otherwise.

err= *error-label*, where *error-label* is the label of a statement in the same scoping unit to which control will be transferred in the event of an error occurring during execution of the statement.

file= *fln*, where *fln* is a character expression that provides the name of the file. If this specifier is omitted and the unit is not connected to a file, the status= specifier must be specified with the value scratch and the file connected to the unit will then depend on the computer system. Whether the interpretation is case sensitive varies from system to system.

status= *st*, where *st* is a character expression that provides the value old, new, replace, scratch, or unknown. The file= specifier must be present if new or replace is specified or if old is specified and the unit is not connected; the file= specifier must not be present if scratch is specified. If old is specified, the file must already exist; if new is specified, the file must not already exist, but will be brought into existence by the action of the open statement. The status of the file then becomes old. If replace is specified and the file does not already exist, the file is created; if the file does exist, the file is deleted, and a new file is created with the same name. In each case the status is changed to old. If the value scratch is specified, the file is created and becomes connected, but it cannot be kept after completion of the program or execution of a close statement (Section 10.4). If unknown is specified, the status of the file is system dependent. This is the default value of the specifier, if it is omitted.

access= *acc*, where *acc* is a character expression that provides one of the values sequential or direct. For a file which already exists, this value must be an allowed value. If the file does not already exist, it will be brought into existence with the appropriate access method. If this specifier is omitted, the value sequential will be assumed.

form= *fm*, where *fm* is a character expression that provides the value formatted or unformatted, and determines whether the file is to be connected for formatted or unformatted I/O. For a file which already exists, the value must be an allowed value. If the file does not already exist, it will be brought into existence with an allowed set of forms that includes the specified form. If this specifier is omitted, the default is formatted for sequential access and unformatted for direct-access connection.

recl= *rl*, where *rl* is an integer expression whose value must be positive. For a direct-access file, it specifies the length of the records, and is obligatory. For a sequential file, it specifies the maximum length of a record, and is optional with a default value that is processor dependent. For formatted files, the length is the number of characters for records that contain only default characters; for unformatted files it is system dependent but the inquire statement (Section 10.5) may be used to find the length of an I/O list. In either case, for a file which already exists, the value specified must be allowed for that file. If the file does not already exist, the file will be brought into existence with an allowed set of record lengths that includes the specified value.

blank= *bl*, where *bl* is a character expression that provides the value null or zero. This connection must be for formatted I/O. This specifier sets the default for the interpretation of blanks in numeric input fields, as discussed in the description of the bn and bz edit descriptors (Section 9.13.5). If the value is null, such blanks will be ignored (except that a completely blank field is interpreted as zero). If the value is zero, such blanks will be interpreted as zeros. If the specifier is omitted, the default is null.

position= *pos*, where *pos* is a character expression that provides the value asis, rewind, or append. The access method must be sequential, and if the specifier is omitted the default value asis will be assumed. A new file is positioned at its initial point. If asis is specified and the file exists and is already connected, the file is opened without changing its position; if rewind is specified the file is positioned at its initial point; if append is specified and the file exists, it is positioned ahead of the endfile record if it has one (and otherwise at its terminal point). For a file which exists but is not connected, the effect of the asis specifier on the file's position is unspecified.

action= *act*, where *act* is a character expression that provides the value read, write, or readwrite. If read is specified, the write, print and endfile statements must not be used for this connection; if write is specified, the read statement must not be used (and backspace and position='append' may fail on some systems); if readwrite is specified, there is no restriction. If the specifier is omitted, the default value is processor dependent.

delim= *del* where *del* is a character expression that provides the value quote, apostrophe, or none. If apostrophe or quote is specified, the corresponding character will be used to delimit character constants written with list-directed or namelist formatting, and it will be doubled where it appears within such a character constant; also, non-default character values will be preceded by kind values. No delimiting character is used if none is specified, nor does any doubling take place. The default value if the specifier is omitted is none. This specifier may appear only for formatted files.

pad= *pad*, where *pad* is a character expression that provides the value yes or no. If yes is specified, a formatted input record will be regarded as padded out with blanks whenever an input list and the associated format specify more data than appear in the record. (If no is specified, the length of the input record must not be less than that specified by the input list and the associated format, except in the presence of an advance='no' specifier and either an eor= or an iostat= specification.) The default value if the specifier is omitted is yes. For non-default characters, the blank padding character is processor dependent.

An example of an open statement is

```
open (2, iostat=ios, err=99, file='cities',                    &
      status='new', access='direct', recl=100)
```

which brings into existence a new, direct-access, unformatted file named cities, whose records have length 100. The file is connected to unit number 2. Failure to execute the statement correctly will cause control to be passed to the statement labelled 99, where the value of ios may be tested.

The open statements in a program are best collected together in one place, so that any changes which might have to be made to them when transporting the program from one system to another can be carried out without having to search for them. Regardless of where they appear, the connection may be referenced in any program unit of the program.

The purpose of the open statement is to connect a file to a unit. If the unit is, however, already connected to a file then the action may be different. If the file= specifier is omitted, the default is the name of the connected file. If the file in question does not exist, but is pre-connected to the unit, then all the properties specified by the open statement become part of the connection. If the file is already connected to the unit, then of the existing attributes only the blank=, delim=, pad=, err=, and iostat= specifiers may have values different from those already in effect. If the unit is already connected to another file, the effect of the open statement includes the action of a prior close statement on the unit (without a status= specifier, see next section).

A file already connected to one unit must not be specified for connection to another unit.

In general, by repeated execution of the open statement on the same unit, it is possible to process in sequence an arbitrarily high number of files, whether they exist or not, as long as the restrictions just noted are observed.

10.4   The close statement

The purpose of the close statement is to disconnect a file from a unit. Its form is

close ([unit=]*u* [,iostat=*ios*] [,err=*error-label*] [,status=*st*])

where *u, ios,* and *error-label* have the same meanings as described in the previous section for the open statement. Again, keyword specifiers may be in any order, but the unit specifier must come first as a positional specifier.

The function of the status= specifier is to determine what will happen to the file once it is disconnected. The value of *st*, which is a scalar default character expression, may be either keep or delete, ignoring any trailing blanks and converting any upper-case letters to lower case. If the value is keep, a file that exists continues to exist after execution of the close statement, and may later be connected again to a unit. If the value is delete, the file no longer exists after execution of the statement. In either case, the unit is free to be connected again to a file. The close statement may appear anywhere in the program, and if executed for a non-existing or unconnected unit, acts as a 'do nothing' statement. The value keep must not be specified for files with the status scratch.

If the status= specifier is omitted, its default value is keep unless the file has status scratch, in which case the default value is delete. On normal termination of execution, all connected units are closed, as if close statements with omitted status= specifiers were executed.

An example of a close statement is

close (2, iostat=ios, err=99, status='delete')

10.5   The inquire statement

The status of a file can be defined by the operating system prior to execution of the program, or by the program itself during execution, either by an open statement or by some action on a pre-connected file which brings it into existence. At any time during the execution of a program it is possible to inquire about the status and attributes of a file using the inquire statement. Using a variant of this statement, it is similarly possible to determine the status of a unit, for instance whether the unit number exists for that system (that is, whether it is an allowed unit number), whether the unit number has a file connected to it and, if so, which attributes that file has. Another variant permits an inquiry about the length of an output list when used to write an unformatted record.

Some of the attributes that may be determined by use of the inquire statement are dependent on others. For instance, if a file is not connected to a unit, it is not meaningful to inquire about the form being used for that file. If this is nevertheless attempted, the relevant specifier is undefined.

The three variants are known as inquire by file, inquire by unit, and inquire by output list. In the description of the inquire statement which follows, the first two variants will be described together. Their forms are

> inquire ([unit=]*u, ilist*)

for inquire by unit, where *u* is a scalar integer expression specifying an external unit, and

> inquire (file=*fln, ilist*)

for inquire by file, where *fln* is a scalar character expression whose value, ignoring any trailing blanks, provides the name of the file concerned. Whether the interpretation is case sensitive is system dependent. If the unit or file is specified by keyword, it may appear in *ilist*. A specifier must not occur more than once in the list of optional specifiers, *ilist*. All assignments occur following the usual rules, and all values of type character, apart from that for the name= specifier, are in upper case. The specifiers, in which all variables are scalar and of default kind, are

iostat= *ios* and err= *error-label*, have the meanings described for them in the open statement in Section 10.3. The iostat= variable is the only one which is defined if an error condition occurs during the execution of the statement.

exist= *ex*, where *ex* is a logical variable. The value true is assigned to *ex* if the file (or unit) exists, and false otherwise.

opened= *open*, where *open* is a logical variable. The value true is assigned to *open* if the file (or unit) is connected to a unit (or file), and false otherwise.

number= *num*, where *num* is an integer variable that is assigned the value of the unit number connected to the file, or -1 if no unit is connected to the file.

named= *nmd* and name= *nam*, where *nmd* is a logical variable that is assigned the value true if the file has a name, and false otherwise. If the file has a name, the character variable *nam* will be assigned the name. This value is not necessarily the same as that given in the file specifier, if used, but may be qualified in some way. However, in all cases it is a name which is valid for use in a subsequent open statement, and so the inquire can be used to determine the actual name of a file before connecting it. Whether the file name is case sensitive is system dependent.

access= *acc*, where *acc* is a character variable that is assigned one of the the values SEQUENTIAL or DIRECT depending on the access method for a file that is connected, and UNDEFINED if there is no connection.

sequential= *seq* and direct= *dir*, where *seq* and *dir* are character variables that are assigned the value YES, NO, or UNKNOWN, depending on whether the file *may* be opened for sequential or direct access respectively, or whether this cannot be determined.

form= *frm*, where *frm* is a character variable that is assigned one of the values FORMATTED or UNFORMATTED, depending on the form for which the file is actually connected, and UNDEFINED if there is no connection.

formatted= *fmt* and unformatted= *unf*, where *fmt* and *unf* are character variables that are assigned the value YES, NO, or UNKNOWN, depending on whether the file *may* be opened for formatted or unformatted access, respectively, or whether this cannot be determined.

recl= *rec*, where *rec* is an integer variable that is assigned the value of the record length of a file connected for direct access, or the maximum record length allowed for a file connected for sequential access. The length is the number of characters for formatted records containing only characters of default type, and system dependent otherwise. If there is no connection, *rec* becomes undefined.

nextrec= *nr*, where *nr* is an integer variable that is assigned the value of the number of the last record read or written, plus one. If no record has been yet read or written, it is assigned the value 1. If the file is not connected for direct access or if the position is indeterminate because of a previous error, *nr* becomes undefined.

blank= *bl*, where *bl* is a character variable that is assigned the value NULL or ZERO, depending on whether the blanks in numeric fields are by default to be interpreted as null fields or zeros, respectively, and UNDEFINED if there is either no connection, or if the connection is not for formatted I/O.

position= *pos*, where *pos* is a character variable that is assigned the value REWIND, APPEND, or ASIS, as specified in the corresponding open statement, if the file has not been repositioned since it was opened. If there is no connection, or if the file is connected for direct access, the value is UNDEFINED. If the file has been repositioned since the connection was established, the value is processor dependent (but must not be REWIND or APPEND unless that corresponds to the true position).

action= *act*, where *act* is a character variable that is assigned the value READ, WRITE, or READWRITE, according to the connection. If there is no connection, the value assigned is UNDEFINED.

read= *rd*, where *rd* is a character variable that is assigned the value YES, NO or UNKNOWN according to whether read is allowed, not allowed, or is undetermined for the file.

write= *wr*, where *wr* is a character variable that is assigned the value YES, NO or UNKNOWN according to whether write is allowed, not allowed, or is undetermined for the file.

readwrite= *rw*, where *rw* is a character variable that is assigned the value YES, NO or UNKNOWN according to whether read/write is allowed, not allowed, or is undetermined for the file.

delim= *del*, where *del* is a character variable that is assigned the value QUOTE, APOSTROPHE, or NONE, as specified by the corresponding open statement (or by default). If there is no connection, or if the file is not connected for formatted I/O, the value assigned is UNDEFINED.

pad= *pad*, where *pad* is a character variable that is assigned the value YES or NO as specified by the corresponding open statement (or by default). If there is no connection, or if the file is not connected for formatted I/O, the value assigned is UNDEFINED.

A variable that is a specifier in an inquire statement or is associated with one must not appear in another specifier in the same statement.

The third variant of the inquire statement, inquire by I/O list, has the form

```
inquire (iolength=length) olist
```

where *length* is a scalar integer variable of default kind and is used to determine the length of an unformatted output list in processor-dependent units, and might be used to establish whether, for instance, an output list is too long for the record length given in the recl= specifier of an open statement, or be used as the value of the length to be supplied to a recl= specifier, (see Figure 9.5 in Section 9.15).

An example of the inquire statement, for the file opened as an example of the open statement in Section 10.3, is

```
logical            :: ex, op
character (len=11) :: nam, acc, seq, frm
integer            :: irec, nr
inquire (2, err=99, exist=ex, opened=op, name=nam, access=acc, &
    sequential=seq, form=frm, recl=irec, nextrec=nr)
```

After successful execution of this statement, the variables provided will have been assigned the following values:

```
ex        .true.
op        .true.
nam       citiesbbbbb
acc       DIRECTbbbbb
seq       NObbbbbbbbb
frm       UNFORMATTED
irec      100
nr        1
```

(assuming no intervening read or write operations).

The three I/O status statements just described are perhaps the most indigestible of all Fortran statements. They provide, however, a powerful and portable facility for the dynamic allocation and deallocation of files, completely under program control, which is far in advance of that found in any other programming language suitable for scientific applications.

10.6 Summary

This chapter has completed the description of the input/output features begun in the previous chapter, and together they provide a complete reference to all the facilities available. The features new since Fortran 77 are inquire by I/O list and the additional specifiers for the open and inquire statements: position, action, delim, pad, read, write, and readwrite. There have also been detailed changes to accommodate other features of the language.

10.7 Exercises

1. A direct-access file is to contain a list of names and initials, to each of which there corresponds a telephone number. Write a program which opens a sequential file and a direct-access file, and copies the list from the sequential file to the direct-access file, closing it for use in another program.

Write a second program which reads an input record containing either a name or a telephone number (from a terminal if possible), and prints out the corresponding entry (or entries) in the direct-access file if present, and an error message otherwise. Remember that names are as diverse as Wu, O'Hara and Trevington-Smythe, and that it is insulting for a computer program to corrupt or abbreviate people's names. The format of the telephone numbers should correspond to your local numbers, but the actual format used should be readily modifiable to another.

11. Other features

11.1 Introduction

This chapter describes features that are redundant within Fortran 90 and whose use we deprecate. They might become obsolescent in a future revision, but this is a decision that can be made only within the standardization process. We note again that this decision to group certain features into a final chapter and to deprecate their use is ours alone, and does not have the actual or implied approval of either WG5 or J3.

Our deprecated features fall into three groups:

- those linked to storage association;

- those introduced into Fortran 90 because of strong public pressure, but for which there are better ways to achieve the same effects; and

- those which are made redundant by newer features.

Each description mentions how the feature concerned may be effectively replaced by a newer feature or features.

11.2 Storage association

11.2.1 Storage units

Storage units are the fixed units of physical storage allocated to certain data. There is a storage unit called *numeric* for any non-pointer scalar of the default real, default integer, and default logical types, and a storage unit called *character* for any non-pointer scalar of type default character and character length 1. Non-pointer scalars of type default complex or double precision real (Section 11.4.1) occupy two contiguous numeric storage units. Non-pointer scalars of type default character length *len* occupy *len* contiguous character storage units.

As well as numeric and character storage units, there are a large number of *unspecified* storage units. A non-pointer scalar object of type non-default integer, real other than default or double precision, non-default logical, non-default complex, or non-default character of any particular length occupies a single unspecified storage unit that is different for each case. An object with the `pointer` attribute has an unspecified storage unit, different from that of any non-pointer object and different for each combination of type, type parameters, and rank. The standard makes no statement about the relative sizes of all these storage units and permits storage association to take place only between objects with the same category of storage unit.

An array of intrinsic type occupies a sequence of storage units, one for each element, in array element order.

Objects of derived type have no storage association, each occupying an unspecified storage unit that is different in each case, except where a given type contains a sequence statement making it a *sequence type*:

```
type storage
   sequence
   integer i          ! First numeric storage unit;
   real a(0:999)      ! subsequent 1000 numeric storage units.
end type storage
```

Should any other derived types appear in such a definition, they too must be sequence types. A scalar of sequence type occupies a storage sequence that consists of the concatenation of the storage sequences of its components. An array of sequence type occupies a storage sequence that consists of the concatenation of the storage sequences of its elements.

A sequence type whose ultimate components are non-pointers of type default integer, default real, double precision real, default complex and default logical has *numeric storage association*. Similarly, a sequence type whose ultimate components are non-pointers of type default character has *character storage association*.

A derived type with the sequence attribute may have private components:

```
type storage
   private
   sequence
   integer i
   real a(0:999)
end type storage
```

The `private` and `sequence` statements may be interchanged but must be the second and third statements of the type definition.

Two type definitions in different scoping units define the same data type if they have the same name[1], both have the `sequence` attribute, and they have components that are not `private` and agree in order, name, and attributes. However, such a practice is prone to error and offers no advantage over having a single definition in a module and accessed by use association.

---

[1] If one or both types have been accessed by use association and renamed, it is the original names that must agree.

11.2.2 The equivalence statement

The `equivalence` statement specifies that a given storage area may be shared by two or more objects. For instance

```
real aa, angle, alpha, a(3)
equivalence (aa, angle), (alpha, a(1))
```

allows aa and angle to be used interchangeably in the program text, as both names now refer to the same storage location. similarly, alpha and a(1) may be used interchangeably.

It is possible to equivalence arrays together. In

```
real a(3,3), b(3,3), col1(3), col2(3), col3(3)
equivalence (col1, a, b), (col2, a(1,2)), (col3, a(1,3))
```

the two arrays a and b are equivalenced, and the columns of a (and hence of b) are equivalenced to the arrays col1, etc. We note in this example that more than two entities may be equivalenced together, even in a single declaration.

It is possible to equivalence variables of the same intrinsic type and kind type parameter or of the same derived type having the sequence attribute. It is also possible to equivalence variables of different types if both have numeric storage association or both have character storage association (see Section 11.2.1). Default character variables need not have the same length, as in

```
character(len=4) a
character(len=3) b(2)
equivalence (a, b(1)(3:))
```

where the character variable a is equivalenced to the last four characters of the six characters of the character array b. Zero character length is not permitted. An example for different types is

```
integer i(100)
real x(100)
equivalence (i, x)
```

where the arrays i and x are equivalenced. This might be used, for instance, to save storage space if i is used in one part of a program unit and x separately in another part. This is a highly dangerous practice, as considerable confusion can arise when one storage area contains variables of two or more data types, and program changes may be made very difficult if the two uses of the one area are to be kept distinct.

Types with default initialization (Fortran 95 only) are permitted, provided each initialized component has the same type, type parameters, and value in any pair of equivalenced objects.

All the various combinations of types that may be equivalenced have been described. No other is allowed. Also, apart from double precision real and the default numeric types, equivalencing objects that have different kind type parameters is not allowed. The general form of the statement is equivalence (*object, object-list*) [, (*object, object-list*)]...

where each *object* is a variable name, array element, or substring. An object must be a variable and must not be a dummy argument, a function result, a pointer, an object with a pointer component at any level of component selection, an allocatable array, an automatic object, a function, a structure component, or a subobject of such an object. Each array subscript and character substring range must be an initialization expression. The interpretation of an array name is identical to that of its first element. An equivalence object must not have the target attribute.

The objects in an equivalence set are said to be *storage associated*. Those of nonzero length share the same first storage unit. Those of zero length are associated with each other and with the first storage unit of those of nonzero length. equivalence statements may cause other parts of the objects to be associated, but not such that different subobjects of the same object share storage. For example

```
real a(2), b
equivalence (a(1), b), (a(2), b)   ! Prohibited.
```

is not permitted. Also, objects declared in different scoping units must not be equivalenced. For example

```
use my_module, only : xx
real bb
equivalence(xx, bb)                ! Prohibited.
```

is not permitted.

The various uses to which the equivalence was put are replaced by automatic arrays, allocatable arrays, and pointers (reuse of storage, Sections 6.4 and 6.5), pointers as aliases (storage mapping, Section 6.15), and the transfer function (mapping of one data type onto another, Section 8.9).

11.2.3 The common block

We have seen in Chapter 5 how two program units are able to communicate by passing variables, or values of expressions between them via argument lists or by using modules. It is also possible to define areas of storage known as common blocks. Each has a storage sequence and may be either named or unnamed, as shown by the simplified syntax of the common specification statement,

common [/[*cname*]/] *vlist*

in which *cname* is an optional name, and *vlist* is a list of variable names, each optionally followed by an array bounds specification. An unnamed common block is known as a *blank* common block. Examples of each are

```
common /hands/ nshuff, nplay, nhand, cards(52)
```

and

```
common // buffer(10000)
```

in which the named common block hands defines a data area containing the quantities which might be required by the subroutines of a card playing program, and the blank common defines a large data area which might be used by different routines as a buffer area.

The name of a common block has global scope and must differ from that of any other global entity (external procedure, program unit, or common block). It may, however, be the same as that of a local entity other than a named constant or intrinsic procedure.

No object in a common block may have the parameter attribute or be a dummy argument, an automatic object, an allocatable array, or a function. An array may have its bounds declared either in the common statement or in a type declaration or dimension statement. If it is a non-pointer array, the bounds must be declared explicitly and with constant specification expressions. If it is a pointer array, however, the bounds may not be declared in the common statement itself. An object of derived type must have the sequence attribute and (Fortran 95 only) the type must not have default initialization.

In order for a subroutine to access the variables in the data area, it is sufficient to insert the common definition in each scoping unit which requires access to one or more of the entities in the list. In this fashion, the variables nshuff, nplay, nhand and cards are made available to the those scoping units. No variable may appear more than once in all the common blocks in a scoping unit.

Usually, a common block contains identical variable names in all its appearances, but this is not necessary. In fact, the shared data area may be partitioned in quite different ways in different routines, using different variable names. They are said to be storage associated. It is thus possible for one subroutine to contain a declaration

```
common /coords/ x, y, z, i(10)
```

and another to contain a declaration

```
common /coords/ i, j, a(11)
```

This means that a reference to $i(1)$ in the first routine is equivalent to a reference to $a(2)$ in the second. Through multiple references via use or host association, this can even happen in a single routine. This manner of coding is both untidy and dangerous, and every effort should be made to ensure that all declarations of a given common block declaration are identical in every respect. In particular, the presence or absence of the target attribute is required to be consistent, since otherwise a compiler would have to assume that everything in common has the target attribute in case it has it in another program unit.

A further practice that is permitted but which we do not recommend is to mix different storage units in the same common block. When this is done, each position in the storage sequence must always be occupied by a storage unit of the same category.

The total number of storage units must be the same in each occurrence of a named common block, but blank common is allowed to vary in size and the longest definition will apply for the complete program.

Yet another practice to be avoided is to use the full syntax of the common statement,

common [/[*cname*]/] *vlist* [[,]/[*cname*]/*vlist*] ...

which allows several common blocks to be defined in one statement, and a single common block to be declared in parts. A combined example is

common /pts/x,y,z /matrix/a(10,10),b(5,5) /pts/i,j,k

which is equivalent to

```
common /pts/ x, y, z, i, j, k
common /matrix/ a(10,10), b(5,5)
```

which is certainly a more understandable declaration of two shared data areas. The only need for the piece-wise declaration of one block is when the limit of 39 continuation lines is otherwise too low.

The common statement may be combined with the equivalence statement, as in the example

```
real a(10), b
equivalence (a,b)
common /change/ b
```

In this case, a is regarded as part of the common block, and its length is extended appropriately. Such an equivalence must not cause data in two different common blocks to become storage associated, it must not cause an extension of the common block except at its tail, and two different objects or subobjects in the same common block must not become storage associated. In Fortran 95, it must not cause an object of a type with default initialization to become associated with an object in a common block.

A common block may be declared in a module, and its variables accessed by use association. Variable names in a common block in a module may be declared to have the private attribute, but this does not prevent associated variables being declared elsewhere through other common statements.

An individual variable in a common block may not be given the save attribute, but the whole block may. If a common block has the save attribute in any scoping unit other than the main program, it must have the save attribute in all such scoping units. The general form of the save statement is

save [[::] *saved-entity-list*]

where *saved-entity* is *variable-name* or *common-block-name*. A simple example is

```
save /change/
```

Blank common always has the save attribute.

Data in a common block without the save attribute become undefined on return from a subprogram unless the block is also declared in the main program or in another subprogram that is in execution.

Use of modules (section 5.5) obviates the need for common blocks.

11.2.4 The block data program unit

Non-pointer variables in named common blocks may be initialized in data statements, but such statements must be collected into a special type of program unit, known as a block data program unit. It must have the form

```
block data [block-data-name]
    [specification-stmt] . . .
end [block data [block-data-name]]
```

where each *specification-stmt* is an implicit, use, type declaration (including double precision), intrinsic, pointer, target, common, dimension, data, equivalence, parameter, or save statement or derived-type definition. A type declaration statement must not specify the allocatable, external, intent, optional, private, or public attributes. An example is

```
block data
    common /axes/ i,j,k
    data i,j,k /1,2,3/
end block data
```

in which the variables in the common block axes are defined for use in any other scoping unit which accesses them.

It is possible to collect many common blocks and their corresponding data statements together in one block data program unit. However, it may be a better practice to have several different block data program units, each containing common blocks which have some logical association with one another. To allow for this eventuality, block data program units may be named in order to be able to distinguish them. A complete program may contain any number of block data program units, but only one of them may be unnamed. A common block must not appear in more than one block data program unit. It is not possible to initialize blank common.

The name of a block data program unit may appear in an external statement. When a processor is loading program units from a library, it may need such a statement in order to load the block data program unit.

Use of modules (Section 5.5) obviates the need for block data.

11.2.5   Shape and character length disagreement

In Fortran 77, it was often convenient, when passing an array, not to have to specify the size of the dummy array. For this case, the *assumed-size* array declaration is available, where the last *bounds* in the *bounds-list* is

[*lower-bound*:] *

and the other bounds (if any) must be declared explicitly. Such an array must not be a function result.

Since an assumed-size array has no bounds in its last dimension, it does not have a shape and, therefore, must not be used as a whole array in an executable statement, except as an argument to a procedure that does not require its shape. However, if an array section is formed with an explicit upper bound in the last dimension, this has a shape and may be used as a whole array.

An object of one size or rank may be passed to an explicit-shape or assumed-size dummy argument array that is of another size or rank, except when the dummy argument has the target attribute and the actual argument is a target other than an array section with a vector subscript. If an array element is passed to an array, the actual argument is regarded as an array with elements that are formed from the parent array from the given array element onwards, in array element order. Figure 11.1 illustrates this. Here only the last 49 elements of a are available to sub, as the first array element of a which is passed to sub is a(52). Within sub, this element is referenced as b(1).

Figure 11.1

```
real a(100)
:
call sub (a(52), 49)
:
subroutine sub(b,n)
:
real b(n)
:
```

In the same example, it would also be perfectly legitimate for the declaration of b to be written as

```
real b(7, 7)
```

and for the last 49 elements of a to be addressed as though they were ordered as a 7×7 array. The converse is also true. An array dimensioned 10×10 in a calling subroutine may be dimensioned as a singly-dimensioned array of size 100 in the called subroutine. Within sub, it is illegal to address b(50) in any way, as that would be beyond the declared length of a in the calling routine. In all cases, the association is by storage sequence, in array element order.

In the case of default character type, agreement of character length is not required. For a scalar dummy argument of character length *len*, the actual argument may have a greater character length and its leftmost *len* characters are associated with the dummy argument. For example, if chasub has a single dummy argument of character length 1,

```
call chasub(word(3:4))
```

is a valid call statement. For an array dummy argument, the restriction is on the total number of characters in the array. An array element or array element substring is regarded as a sequence of characters from its first character to the last character of the array. For an assumed-size array, the size is the number of characters in the sequence divided by the character length of the dummy argument.

Shape or character length disagreement of course cannot occur when the dummy argument is assumed-shape (by definition the shape is assumed from the actual argument). It can occur for explicit-shape and assumed-size arrays. Implementations are likely to receive explicit-shape and assumed-size arrays in contiguous storage, but permit any uniform spacing of the elements of an assumed-shape array. They will need to make a copy of any array argument that is not stored contiguously (for example, the section a(1:10:2)), unless the dummy argument is assumed shape. To avoid unnecessary copies of this kind, a scalar actual argument is permitted to be associated with an array only if the actual argument is an element of an array that is not an assumed-shaped array, an array pointer, a dummy argument with the target attribute, or is a subobject of such an element.

When a procedure is invoked through a generic name, as a defined operation, or as a defined assignment, rank agreement between the actual and the dummy arguments is required. Note also that only a scalar dummy argument may be associated with a scalar actual argument.

Assumed-shape arrays (Section 6.3) supplant this feature.

11.2.6 The entry statement

A subprogram usually defines a single procedure, and the first statement to be executed is the first executable statement after the header statement. In some cases it is useful to be able to define several procedures in one subprogram, particularly when wishing to share access to some saved local variables or to a section of code. This is possible for external and module subprograms (but not for internal subprograms) by means of the entry statement. This is a statement that has the form

```
entry entry-name [([dummy-argument-list]) [result(result-name)]]
```

and may appear anywhere between the header line and contains (or end if it has no contains) statement of a subprogram, except within a construct. The entry statement provides a procedure with an associated dummy argument list, exactly as does the subroutine or function statement, and these arguments may be different from those given on the subroutine or function statement. Execution commences with the first executable statement following the entry statement.

In the case of a function, each entry defines another function, whose characteristics (that is, shape, type, type parameters, and whether a pointer) are given by specifications for the *result-name* (or *entry-name* if there is no result clause). If the characteristics are the same as for the main entry, a single variable is used for both results; otherwise, they must not be pointers, must be scalar, and must both be one of the default integer, default real, double precision real (Section 11.4.1), or default complex types, and they are treated as equivalenced. The result clause plays exactly the same rôle as for the main entry.

Each entry is regarded as defining another procedure, with its own name. The names of all these procedures and their result variables (if any) must be distinct. The name of an entry has the same scope as the name of the subprogram. It must not be the name of a dummy argument of any of the procedures defined by the subprogram. An entry statement is not permitted in an interface block; there must be another body for each entry whose interface is wanted, using a subroutine or function statement, rather than an entry statement.

An entry is called in exactly the same manner as a subroutine or function, depending on whether it appears in a subroutine subprogram or a function subprogram. An example is given in Figure 11.2 which shows a search function with two entry points. We note that looku and looks are synonymous within the function, so that it is immaterial which value is set before the return.

None of the procedures defined by a subprogram is permitted to reference itself, unless the keyword recursive is present on the subroutine or function statement. For a function, such a reference must be indirect unless there is a result clause on the function or entry statement. If a procedure may be referenced directly in the subprogram that defines it, the interface is explicit in the subprogram.

The name of an entry dummy argument that appears in an executable statement preceding the entry statement in the subprogram must also appear in a function, subroutine, or entry statement that precedes the executable statement. Also, if a dummy argument is used to define the array size or character length of an object, the object must not be referenced unless the argument is present in the procedure reference that is active.

During the execution of one of the procedures defined by a subprogram, a reference to a dummy argument is permitted only if it is a dummy argument of the procedure referenced.

The entry statement is made unnecessary by the use of modules (Section 5.5), with each procedure defined by an entry becoming a module procedure. Its presence has substantially complicated the standard because the reader has to remember that a subprogram may define several procedures.

Figure 11.2

```
       function looku(list, member)
       integer looku, list(:), member, looks
!
!      To locate member in an array list.
!      If list is unsorted, entry looku is used;
!      if list is sorted, entry looks is used.
!
!      list is unsorted
       do looku = 1, size(list)
          if list(looku) .eq. member) go to 9
       end do
       go to 3
!
!       entry for sorted list
       entry looks(list, member)
!
       do looku = 1, size(list)
          if (list(looku) .ge. member) go to 2
       end do
       go to 3
!
!       is member at position looku?
     2 if (list(looku) .eq. member) go to 9
!
!       member not in list
     3 looku = 0
!
     9 end function looku
```

11.3 New redundant features

11.3.1 The include line

It is sometimes useful to be able to include source text from somewhere else into the source stream presented to the compiler. This facility is possible using an include line:

    include *char-literal-constant*

where *char-literal-constant* must not have a kind parameter that is a named constant. This line is not a Fortran statement and must appear as a single source line where a statement may occur. It will be replaced by material in a processor-dependent way determined by the character string *char-literal-constant*. The included text may itself contain include lines, which are similarly replaced. An include line must not reference itself, directly or indirectly. When an include line is resolved, the first included line must not be a continuation line and the last line must not be continued. An include line may have a trailing comment, but may not be labelled nor, when expanded, may it contain incomplete statements.

The include line was available as an extension to many Fortran 77 systems and was often used to ensure that every occurrence of global data in common was identical. In Fortran 90, the same effect is better achieved by placing global data in a module (Section 5.5). This cannot lead to accidental declarations of local variables in each procedure.

This feature is useful when identical executable statements are needed for more than one type, for example in a set of procedures for sorting data values of various types. The executable statements can be maintained in an include file that is referenced inside each instance of the sort procedure.

11.3.2 The do while form of loop control

In Section 4.5, a form of the do construct was described that may be written as

```
do
    if (scalar-logical-expr) exit
    :
end do
```

An alternative, but redundant, form of this is its representation using a do while statement:

```
do [label] [,] while (.not.scalar-logical-expr)
```

We prefer the form that uses the exit statement because this can be placed anywhere in the loop, whereas the do while statement always performs its test at the loop start. If the *scalar-logical-expr* becomes false in the middle of the loop, the rest of the loop is still executed. Potential optimization penalties that the use of the do while entails are fully described in Chapter 10 of *Optimizing Supercompilers for Supercomputers*, M. Wolfe (Pitman, 1989).

11.4 Old redundant features

11.4.1 Double precision real

Another *type* that may be used in a type declaration, function, implicit, or component declaration statement is double precision which specifies double precision real. The precision is greater than that of default real.

Literal constants written with the exponent letter d (or D) are of type double precision real by default; no kind parameter may be specified if this exponent letter is used. Thus, 1d0 is of type double precision real. If dp is an integer named constant with the value kind(1d0), double precision is synonymous with real(kind=dp).

There is a d (or D) edit descriptor that was originally intended for double precision quantities but, in Fortran 90, it is identical to the e edit descriptor except that the output form may have a D instead of an E as its exponent letter. A double precision real literal constant, with exponent letter d, is acceptable on input whenever any other real literal constant is acceptable.

There are two elemental intrinsic functions which were not described in Chapter 8 because they have result of type double precision real:

dble (a) for a of type integer, real, or complex returns the double precision real value real(a, kind(0d0)).

dprod (x, y) returns the product x*y for x and y of type default real as a double precision real result.

The double precision real data type has been replaced by the real type of kind kind(0.d0).

11.4.2 The dimension and parameter statements

To declare entities, we normally use type specifications. However, if all the entities involved are arrays, they may be declared *without* type specifications in a dimension statement:

```
dimension i(10), b(50,50), c(n,m) ! n and m are dummy integer
                                  ! arguments or named constants.
```

The general form is

```
dimension [::] array-name(array-spec) [,array-name(array-spec)]...
```

Here, the type may either be specified in a type declaration statement such as

```
integer i
```

that does not specify the dimension information, or be specified implicitly. Our view is that neither of these is sound practice: the type declaration statement looks like a declaration of a scalar and we explained in Section 7.2 that we regard implicit typing as dangerous. Therefore, the use of the dimension statement is not recommended.

An alternative way to specify a named constant is by the parameter statement. It has the general form

```
parameter ( named-constant-definition-list )
```

where each *named-constant-definition* is

```
constant-name = initialization-expr
```

Each constant named must either have been typed in a previous type declaration statement in the scoping unit, or take its type from the first letter of its name according to the implicit typing rule of the scoping unit. In the case of implicit typing, the appearance of the named constant in a subsequent type declaration statement in the scoping unit must confirm the type and type parameters, and there must not be an implicit statement for the letter subsequently in the scoping unit. Similarly, the shape must have been specified previously or be scalar. Each named constant in the list is defined with the value of the corresponding expression according to the rules of intrinsic assignment.

An example using implicit typing and a constant expression including a named constant that is defined in the same statement is

```
implicit integer (a, p)
parameter (apple = 3, pear = apple**2)
```

For the same reasons as for dimension, we recommend avoiding the parameter statement.

11.4.3   Specific names of intrinsic procedures

There are a number of intrinsic functions that may have arguments that are all of one type and type parameters or all of another. For instance, we may write

```
a = sqrt(b)
```

and the appropriate square-root function will be invoked, depending on whether the variable b is real or complex and on its type parameters. In this case, the name sqrt is known as a *generic name*, meaning that the appropriate function is supplied, depending on the type and type parameters of the actual arguments of the function, and that a single name may be used for what are, probably, different specific functions.

Some of the intrinsic functions have *specific names* and are specified by the standard. They are listed in Tables 11.1 and 11.2. In the Tables, 'Character' stands for default character, 'Integer' stands for default integer, 'Real' stands for default real, 'Double' stands for double precision real, and 'Complex' stands for default complex. Those in Tables 11.2 may be passed as actual arguments to a subprogram, provided they are specified in an intrinsic statement (Section 8.1.3).

All the procedures that we described in Chapter 8 are regarded as generic, even where there is only one version.

Table 11.1. Specific intrinsic functions not available as actual arguments

Description	Generic Form	Specific Name	Argument Type	Function Type
Conversion	`int(a)`	`int`	Real	Integer
to integer		`ifix`	Real	Integer
		`idint`	Double	Integer
Conversion	`real(a)`	`real`	Integer	Real
to real		`float`	Integer	Real
		`sngl`	Double	Real
max(a1,a2,...)	`max(a1,a2,...)`	`max0`	Integer	Integer
		`amax1`	Real	Real
		`dmax1`	Double	Double
		`amax0`	Integer	Real
		`max1`	Real	Integer
min(a1,a2,...)	`min(a1,a2,...)`	`min0`	Integer	Integer
		`amin1`	Real	Real
		`dmin1`	Double	Double
		`amin0`	Integer	Real
		`min1`	Real	Integer

Table 11.2. Specific intrinsic functions available as actual arguments

Description	Generic Form	Specific Name	Argument Type	Function Type
absolute value of a times sign of b	sign(a,b)	isign	Integer	Integer
		sign	Real	Real
		dsign	Double	Double
max(x-y,0)	dim(x,y)	idim	Integer	Integer
		dim	Real	Real
		ddim	Double	Double
x*y	dprod(x,y)		Real	Double
truncation	aint(a)	aint	Real	Real
		dint	Double	Double
nearest whole number	anint(a)	anint	Real	Real
		dnint	Double	Double
nearest integer	nint(a)	nint	Real	Integer
		idnint	Double	Integer
absolute value	abs(a)	iabs	Integer	Integer
		abs	Real	Real
		dabs	Double	Double
		cabs	Complex	Real
remainder modulo p	mod(a,p)	mod	Integer	Integer
		amod	Real	Real
		dmod	Double	Double
square root	sqrt(x)	sqrt	Real	Real
		dsqrt	Double	Double
		csqrt	Complex	Complex
exponential	exp(x)	exp	Real	Real
		dexp	Double	Double
		cexp	Complex	Complex
Natural logarithm	log(x)	alog	Real	Real
		dlog	Double	Double
		clog	Complex	Complex
Common logarithm	log10(x)	alog10	Real	Real
		dlog10	Double	Double
Sine	sin(x)	sin	Real	Real
		dsin	Double	Double
		csin	Complex	Complex

Cosine	cos(x)	cos	Real	Real
		dcos	Double	Double
		ccos	Complex	Complex
Tangent	tan(x)	tan	Real	Real
		dtan	Double	Double
Arcsine	asin(x)	asin	Real	Real
		dasin	Double	Double
Arccosine	acos(x)	acos	Real	Real
		dacos	Double	Double
Arctangent	atan(x)	atan	Real	Real
		datan	Double	Double
	atan2(y,x)	atan2	Real	Real
		datan2	Double	Double
Hyperbolic sine	sinh(x)	sinh	Real	Real
		dsinh	Double	Double
Hyperbolic cosine	cosh(x)	cosh	Real	Real
		dcosh	Double	Double
Hyperbolic tangent	tanh(x)	tanh	Real	Real
		dtanh	Double	Double
Imaginary part	aimag(z)	aimag	Complex	Real
Complex conjugate	conjg(z)	conjg	Complex	Complex
Character length	len(s)	len	Character	Integer
Starting position	index(s,t)	index	Character	Integer

12. Floating-point exception handling

12.1 Introduction

Exception handling is required for the development of robust and efficient numerical software, a principal application of Fortran. Indeed, the existence of such a facility makes it possible to develop more efficient software than than would otherwise be possible. The clear need for exception handling, something that had been left out of the standards so far, led to a facility being developed on a 'fast track' as a Technical Report[1], suitable for immediate implementation as an extension to existing Fortran compilers (Section 1.5).

The subject of this chapter is this extension of Fortran 95. WG5 has promised that it will be included in the next revision of the Fortran standard, apart from correcting any defects found in the field. The intention is that this promise will encourage vendors to implement the feature in their compilers, confident that their efforts will have a secure future.

Similarly, programmers are encouraged to use the feature if it is available to them. Their code may have limited portability initially, but it will eventually become fully portable. This is why we feel that a book on Fortran 95 needs to include its description. This chapter is written with exactly the same aims as the rest of the book: to provide a complete description of all the facilities and provide some explanation of the choices the committees made in their design.

Most computers nowadays have hardware based on the IEEE standard for binary floating-point arithmetic[2], which later became an ISO Standard[3]. Therefore, the Fortran exception handling features are based on the ability to test and set the five flags for floating-point exceptions that the IEEE standard specifies. However, non-IEEE computers have not been ignored; they may provide support for some of the features and the programmer is able to find out what is supported or state that certain features are essential.

---

[1] Technical Report ISO/IEC 15580: 1998(E).
[2] IEEE 754-1985, Standard for binary floating-point arithmetic.
[3] IEC 559:1989, Binary floating-point arithmetic for microprocessor systems.

Few (if any) computers support every detail of the IEEE standard. This is because considerable economies in construction and increases in execution performance are available by omitting support for features deemed to be necessary to few programmers. It was therefore decided to include inquiry facilities for the extent of support of the standard, and for the programmer to be able to state which features are essential.

The mechanism finally chosen by the committees is based on a set of procedures for setting and testing the flags and inquiring about the features, collected in an intrinsic module called ieee_exceptions. An alternative that was seriously considered is described in the next subsection.

Given that procedures were being provided for the IEEE flags, it seemed sensible to provide procedures for other aspects of the IEEE standard. These are collected in a separate intrinsic module, ieee_arithmetic, which contains a use statement for ieee_exceptions.

To provide control over which features are essential, there is a third intrinsic module, ieee_features containing named constants corresponding to the features. If a named constant is accessible in a scoping unit, the corresponding feature must be available there.

12.1.1 Abandoned alternative

An alternative approach to providing exception handling that was seriously considered [4] [5] was based on a construct of the form

```
enable [(exceptions)]
    [enable block]
[handle [(exceptions)]
    handle block]
end enable
```

The idea was that certain exceptions are 'enabled' during execution of the enable block and, if any signals, control is transferred to the handle block. The enable block would contain fast code that is usually successful, and slower but more reliable alternative code in the handle block would be executed only if needed. The transfer is imprecise, so the compiler can use all its optimization features within the enable block. If the programmer needed precision, this could be obtained by using short enable blocks, but that may have inhibited optimization. If an exception led to slow execution, the programmer could limit its use to places where it is really needed.

Everyone was attracted to the enable construct, but there were serious difficulties associated with scoping. If a procedure is called in an enable block, it cannot

---

[4] Reid, J. K. (1995). Exception handling in Fortran. ACM Fortran Forum, 14, 9-15.

[5] Reid, J. K. (1997). Two approaches to exception handling in Fortran 90. In *The quality of numerical software: assessment and enhancement*, Ed R. F. Boisvert, Chapman and Hall (1997), 210-223.

be assumed that the enabled conditions are enabled within the procedure. If a condition signals but there is no local handler, is the condition handled somewhere else in the call chain? If so, what happens in an intermediate scope with no condition enabling? Maintaining good optimization properties when conditions do not signal, while defining precisely what happens when they do, proved to be difficult and confusing. For these reasons the procedures approach, whose effect is easier for everyone to understand, was adopted.

12.2   Intrinsic modules

Fortran 95 does not have the concept of an intrinsic module. This has been introduced as part of this feature. New syntax on the use statement provides control over whether it is intended to access an intrinsic or a non-intrinsic module:

```
use, intrinsic     :: ieee_arithmetic
use, non_intrinsic :: my_ieee_arithmetic
```

For the old form of the syntax:

```
use ieee_arithmetic
```

the processor looks first for a non-intrinsic module. The double colon is obligatory when one of the new keywords is present and is permitted when neither is there:

```
use :: ieee_arithmetic
```

All other aspects of the use statement, including renaming and the only option (see Section 7.10) are unchanged. The intrinsic statement itself is not extended.

12.3   The IEEE standard

In this section, we explain those aspects of the IEEE standard that the reader needs to know in order to understand the features of this extension of Fortran 95. We do not attempt to give a complete description of the standard.

Two floating-point data formats are specified, one for real and one for double precision arithmetic. They are supersets of the Fortran model, repeated here (see Section 8.7.1),

$$x = 0$$

and

$$x = s \times b^e \times \sum_{k=1}^{p} f_k \times b^{-k}$$

where s is ± 1, p and b are integers exceeding one, e is an integer in a range $e_{\min} \le e \le e_{\max}$, and each f_k is an integer in the range $0 \le f_k < b$ except that f_1 is also nonzero. Both IEEE formats are binary, with $b = 2$. The precisions are $p = 24$ and $p = 53$, and the exponent ranges are $-125 \le e \le 128$ and $-1021 \le e \le 1024$, for real and double precision, respectively.

In addition, there are numbers with $e = e_{min}$ and $f_1 = 0$, which are known as *denormalized* numbers; note that they all have absolute values less than that returned by the intrinsic tiny since it considers only numbers within the Fortran model. Also, zero has a sign and both 0 and -0 have inverses, ∞ and $-\infty$. Within Fortran 95, -0 is treated as the same as a zero in all intrinsic operations and comparisons, but it can be detected by the sign function and is respected on formatted output.

The IEEE standard also specifies that some of the binary patterns that do not fit the model be used for the results of exceptional operations, such as 0/0. Such a number is known as a *NaN* (Not a Number). A NaN may be *signaling* or *quiet*. Whenever a signaling NaN appears as an operand, the invalid exception signals and the result is a quiet NaN. Quiet NaNs propagate through almost every arithmetic operation without signaling an exception.

The standard specifies four rounding modes:

nearest rounds the exact result to the nearest representable value.

to-zero rounds the exact result towards zero to the next representable value.

up rounds the exact result towards $+\infty$ to the next representable value.

down rounds the exact result towards $-\infty$ to the next representable value.

Some computers perform division by inverting the denominator and then multiplying by the numerator. The additional roundoff that this involves means that such an implementation does not conform with the IEEE standard. The IEEE standard also species that sqrt properly rounds the exact result and returns -0 for $\sqrt{-0}$. The Fortran facilities include inquiry functions for IEEE division and sqrt.

The presence of -0, ∞, $-\infty$, and the NaNs allows IEEE arithmetic to be closed, that is, every operation has a result. This is very helpful for optimization on modern hardware since several operations, none needing the result of any of the others, may actually be progressing in parallel. If an exception occurs, execution continues with the corresponding flag signaling, and the flag remains signaling until explicitly set quiet by the program. The flags are therefore called *sticky*.

There are five flags:

overflow occurs if the exact result of an operation with two normal values is too large for the data format. The stored result is ∞, huge(x), -huge(x), or $-\infty$, according to the rounding mode in operation, always with the correct sign.

divide_by_zero occurs if a finite nonzero value is divided by zero. The stored result is ∞ or $-\infty$ with the correct sign.

invalid occurs if the operation is invalid, for example, $\infty \times 0$, 0/0, or when an operand is a signaling NaN.

underflow occurs if the result of an operation with two finite nonzero values cannot be represented exactly and is too small to represent with full precision. The stored result is the best available, depending on the rounding mode in operation.

inexact occurs if the exact result of an operation cannot be represented in the data format without rounding.

The standard specifies the possibility of exceptions being trapped by user-written handlers, but this inhibits optimization and is not supported by the Fortran feature. Instead it supports the possibility of halting program execution after an exception signals. For the sake of optimization, such halting need not occur immediately.

The standard specifies several functions which are implemented in this Fortran extension as `ieee_copy_sign`, `ieee_logb`, `ieee_next_after`, `ieee_rem`, `ieee_rint`, `ieee_scalb`, and `ieee_unordered`, and which are described in Section 12.9.3.

12.4 Access to the features

To access the features of this chapter, we recommend that the user employ use statements for one or more of the intrinsic modules `ieee_exceptions`, `ieee_arithmetic` (which contains a use statement for `ieee_exceptions`), and `ieee_features`. If the processor does not support a module accessed in a use statement, the compilation must, of course, fail.

If a scoping unit does not access `ieee_exceptions` or `ieee_arithmetic`, the level of support is processor dependent, and need not include support for any exceptions. If a flag is signaling on entry to such a scoping unit, the processor ensures that it is signaling on exit. If a flag is quiet on entry to such a scoping unit, whether it is signaling on exit is processor dependent.

The module `ieee_features` contains the derived type:

    ieee_features_type

for identifying a particular feature. The only possible values objects of this type may take are those of named constants defined in the module, each corresponding to an IEEE feature. If a scoping unit has access to one of these constants, the compiler must support the feature in the scoping unit or reject the program. For example, some hardware is much faster if denormalized numbers are not supported and instead all underflowed values are flushed to zero. In such a case, the statement

    use, intrinsic :: ieee_features, only: ieee_denormal

will ensure that the scoping unit is compiled with (slower) code supporting denormalized numbers.

The module is unusual in that all a code ever does is to access it with use statements, which affect the way the code is compiled in the scoping units with access to one or more of the module's constants. There is no purpose in declaring data of type ieee_features_type, though it is permitted; the components of the type are private, no operation is defined for it, and only intrinsic assignment is available for it. In a scoping unit containing a use statement, the effect is that of a compiler directive, but the other properties of use make the feature more powerful than would be possible with a directive.

The complete set of named constants in the module and the effect of their accessibility is:

ieee_datatype The scoping unit must provide IEEE arithmetic for at least one kind of real.

ieee_denormal The scoping unit must support denormalized numbers for at least one kind of real.

ieee_divide The scoping unit must support IEEE divide for at least one kind of real.

ieee_halting The scoping unit must support control of halting for each flag supported.

ieee_inexact_flag The scoping unit must support the inexact exception for at least one kind of real.

ieee_inf The scoping unit must support ∞ and $-\infty$ for at least one kind of real.

ieee_invalid_flag The scoping unit must support the invalid exception for at least one kind of real.

ieee_nan The scoping unit must support NaNs for at least one kind of real.

ieee_rounding The scoping unit must support control of the rounding mode for all four rounding modes on at least one kind of real.

ieee_sqrt The scoping unit must support IEEE square root for at least one kind of real.

ieee_underflow_flag The scoping unit must support the underflow exception for at least one kind of real.

Execution may be slowed on some processors by the support of some features. If ieee_exceptions is accessed but ieee_features is not accessed, the vendor is free to choose which subset to support. The processor's fullest support is provided when all of ieee_features is accessed:

```
use, intrinsic :: ieee_arithmetic
use, intrinsic :: ieee_features
```

but execution may then be slowed by the presence of a feature that is not needed. In all cases, the extent of support may be determined by the inquiry functions of Sections 12.8.2 and 12.9.2.

12.5 The Fortran flags

There are five Fortran exception flags, corresponding to the five IEEE flags. Each has a value that is either quiet or signaling. The value may be determined by the function `ieee_get_flag` (Section 12.8.3). Its initial value is quiet and it signals when the associated exception occurs in a real or complex operation. Its status may also be changed by the subroutine `ieee_set_flag` (Section 12.8.3) or the subroutine `ieee_set_status` (Section 12.8.4). Once signaling, it remains signaling unless set quiet by an invocation of the subroutine `ieee_set_flag` or the subroutine `ieee_set_status`.

If a flag is signaling on entry to a procedure, the processor will set it to quiet on entry and restore it to signaling on return. This allows exception handling within the procedure to be independent of the state of the flags on entry, while retaining their 'sticky' properties: within a scoping unit, a signaling flag remains signaling until explicitly set quiet. Evaluation of a specification expression may cause an exception to signal.

If a scoping unit has access to `ieee_exceptions` and references an intrinsic procedure that executes normally, the values of the overflow, divide-by-zero and invalid flags are as on entry to the intrinsic procedure, even if one or more signals during the calculation. If a real or complex result is too large for the intrinsic procedure to handle, overflow may signal. If a real or complex result is a NaN because of an invalid operation (for example, `log(-1.0)`), invalid may signal. Similar rules apply to format processing and to intrinsic operations: no signaling flag shall be set quiet and no quiet flag shall be set signaling because of an intermediate calculation that does not affect the result.

An implementation may provide alternative versions of an intrinsic procedure; for example, one might be rather slow but be suitable for a call from a scoping unit with access to `ieee_exceptions`, while an alternative faster one might be suitable for other cases.

If it is known that an intrinsic procedure will never need to signal an exception, there is no requirement for it to be handled – after all, there is no way that the programmer will be able to tell the difference. The same principle applies to a sequence of in-line code with no invocations of `ieee_get_flag`, `ieee_set_flag`, `ieee_get_status`, `ieee_set_status`, or `ieee_set_halting`. If the code, as written, includes an operation that would signal a flag, but after execution of the sequence no value of a variable depends on that operation, whether the exception signals is processor dependent. Thus, an implementation is permitted to optimize such an operation away. For example, when y has the value zero, whether the code

```
x = 1.0/y
x = 3.0
```

signals divide-by-zero is processor dependent. Another example is:

```
real, parameter :: x=0.0, y=6.0
:
if (1.0/x == y) print *,'Hello world'
```

where the processor is permitted to discard the if statement since the logical expression can never be true and no value of a variable depends on it.

An exception does not signal if this could arise only during execution of code not required or permitted by the standard. For example, the statement

```
if (f(x) > 0.0) y = 1.0/z
```

must not signal divide-by-zero when both f(x) and z are zero and the statement

```
where(a > 0.0) a = 1.0/a
```

must not signal divide-by-zero. On the other hand, when x has the value 1.0 and y has the value 0.0, the expression

```
x > 0.00001 .or. x/y > 0.00001
```

is permitted to cause the signaling of divide-by-zero.

The processor need not support the invalid, underflow, and inexact exceptions. If an exception is not supported, its flag is always quiet. The function ieee_support_flag (Section 12.8.2) may be used to inquire whether a particular flag is supported. If invalid is supported, it signals in the case of conversion to an integer (by assignment or an intrinsic procedure) if the result is too large to be representable.

12.6   Halting

Some processors allow control during program execution of whether to abort or continue execution after an exception has occurred. Such control is exercised by invocation of the subroutine ieee_set_halting_mode (Section 12.8.3). Halting is not precise and may occur any time after the exception has occurred. The function ieee_support_halting (Section 12.8.2) may be used to inquire whether this facility is available. The initial halting mode is processor dependent.

In a procedure other than ieee_set_halting_mode, the processor does not change the halting mode on entry, and on return ensures that the halting mode is the same as it was on entry.

12.7   The rounding modes

Some processors support alteration of the rounding mode during execution. In this case, the subroutine ieee_set_rounding_mode (Section 12.9.4) may be used to alter it. The function ieee_support_rounding (Section 12.9.2) may be used to inquire whether this facility is available for a particular mode.

In a procedure other than ieee_set_rounding_mode, the processor does not change the rounding mode on entry, and on return ensures that the rounding mode is the same as it was on entry.

Note that the value of a literal constant is not affected by the rounding mode.

12.8   The module ieee_exceptions

When the module ieee_exceptions is accessible, the overflow and divide-by-zero flags are supported in the scoping unit for all available kinds of real and complex data. This minimal level of support has been designed to be possible also on a non-IEEE computer. Which other exceptions are supported may be determined by the function ieee_support_flag, see Section 12.8.2. Whether control of halting is supported may be determined by the function ieee_support_halting, see Section 12.8.2. The extent of support of the other exceptions may be influenced by the accessibility of the named constants ieee_inexact_flag, ieee_invalid_flag, and ieee_underflow_flag of the module ieee_features, see Section 12.4.

The module contains two derived types (Section 12.8.1), named constants of these types (Section 12.8.1), and a collection of generic procedures (Sections 12.8.2, 12.8.3, and 12.8.4). None of the procedures is permitted as an actual argument.

12.8.1   Derived types

The module ieee_exceptions contains two derived types:

ieee_flag_type for identifying a particular exception flag. The only possible values that can be taken by objects of this type are those of named constants defined in the module:

```
ieee_overflow    ieee_divide_by_zero   ieee_invalid
ieee_underflow   ieee_inexact
```

and these are used in the module to define the named array constants

```
type(ieee_flag_type), parameter ::                      &
ieee_usual(3) =                                         &
     (/ieee_overflow, ieee_divide_by_zero, ieee_invalid/), &
ieee_all(5) = (/ieee_usual, ieee_underflow, ieee_inexact/)
```

These array constants are convenient for inquiring about the state of several flags at once by using elemental procedures. Besides convenience, such elemental calls may be more efficient than a sequence of calls for single flags.

ieee_status_type for saving the current floating-point status, which includes the values of all the flags supported. It also includes the current rounding mode if dynamic control of rounding is supported and the halting mode if dynamic control of halting is supported.

The components of both types are private. No operation is defined for them and only intrinsic assignment is available for them.

12.8.2 Inquiry functions for IEEE exceptions

The module ieee_exceptions contains two inquiry functions, both of which are pure. Their argument flag must be of type type(ieee_flag_type) with one of the values ieee_invalid, ieee_overflow, ieee_divide_by_zero, ieee_inexact, and ieee_underflow. The inquiries are in terms of reals, but the same level of support is provided for the corresponding kinds of complex type.

ieee_support_flag (flag [,x]) returns .true. if the processor supports the exception flag for all reals (x absent) or for reals of the same kind type parameter as the real argument x. Otherwise, it returns .false..

ieee_support_halting (flag) returns .true. if the processor supports the ability to change the mode by call ieee_set_halting(flag). Otherwise, it returns .false..

12.8.3 Elemental subroutines

The module ieee_exceptions contains the following elemental subroutines:

call ieee_get_flag (flag, flag_value) where:

flag is of type type(ieee_flag_type) and has intent in. It specifies a flag.

flag_value is of type default logical and has intent out. If the value of flag is ieee_invalid, ieee_overflow, ieee_divide_by_zero, ieee_underflow, or ieee_inexact, flag_value is given the value true if the corresponding exception flag is signaling and false otherwise.

call ieee_get_halting_mode (flag, halting) where:

flag is of type type(ieee_flag_type) and has intent in. It must have one of the values ieee_invalid, ieee_overflow, ieee_divide_by_zero, ieee_underflow, or ieee_inexact.

halting is of type default logical has intent out. If the exception specified by flag will cause halting, halting is given the value true; otherwise, it is given the value false.

`call ieee_set_flag (flag, flag_value)` where:

> `flag` is of type `type(ieee_flag_type)` and has intent in. It specifies a flag.

> `flag_value` is of type default logical and has intent in. If the value of `flag` is `ieee_invalid`, `ieee_overflow`, `ieee_divide_by_zero`, `ieee_underflow`, or `ieee_inexact`, the corresponding flag is set to be signaling if `flag_value` has the value true, and to be quiet if `flag_value` has the value false.

`call ieee_set_halting_mode (flag, halting)` where:

> `flag` is of type `type(ieee_flag_type)` and has intent in. It must have one of the values `ieee_invalid`, `ieee_overflow`, `ieee_divide_by_zero`, `ieee_underflow`, or `ieee_inexact`.

> `halting` is of type default logical has intent in. If the value is true, the exception specified by `flag` will cause halting. Otherwise, execution will continue after this exception. The value returned by `ieee_support_halting(flag)` must be true.

12.8.4 Non-elemental subroutines

The module `ieee_exceptions` contains the following non-elemental subroutines:

`call ieee_get_status (status_value)` where:

> `status_value` is scalar and of type `type(ieee_status_type)` and has intent out. It returns the floating-point status, including all the exception flags, the rounding mode, and the halting mode.

`call ieee_set_status (status_value)` where:

> `status_value` is scalar and of type `type(ieee_status_type)` and has intent in. Its value must have been set in a previous invocation of `ieee_get_status`. The floating-point status, including all the exception flags, the rounding mode, and the halting mode, is reset to as it was then.

These subroutines have been included for convenience and efficiency when a subsidiary calculation is to be performed, and one wishes to resume the main calculation with exactly the same environment, as shown in Figure 12.1. There are no facilities for finding directly the value held within such a variable of a particular flag, of the rounding mode, or of the halting mode.

Figure 12.1

```
use, intrinsic         :: ieee_exceptions
type(ieee_status_type) :: status_value
    :
call ieee_get_status(status_value)   ! Get the flags
call ieee_set_flag(ieee_all,.false.) ! Set the flags quiet.
    :  ! Calculation involving exception handling
call ieee_set_status(status_value)   ! Restore the flags
```

12.9   The module ieee_arithmetic

The module ieee_arithmetic behaves as if it contained a use statement for
the module ieee_exceptions, so all the features of ieee_exceptions are also
features of ieee_arithmetic.

The module contains two derived types (Section 12.9.1), named constants of
these types (Section 12.9.1), and a collection of generic procedures (Sections
12.9.2, 12.9.3, 12.9.4 and 12.9.5). None of the procedures is permitted as an actual
argument.

12.9.1   Derived types

The module ieee_arithmetic contains two derived types:

ieee_class_type for identifying a class of floating-point values. The only pos-
    sible values objects of this type may take are those of the named constants
    defined in the module:

```
ieee_signaling_nan    ieee_quiet_nan
ieee_negative_inf     ieee_negative_normal
ieee_negative_denormal ieee_negative_zero
ieee_positive_zero    ieee_positive_denormal
ieee_positive_normal  ieee_positive_inf
```

ieee_round_type for identifying a particular rounding mode. The only possible
    values objects of this type may take are those of the named constants defined
    in the module:

```
ieee_nearest ieee_to_zero
ieee_up      ieee_down
```

for the IEEE modes and

```
ieee_other
```

for any other mode.

The components of both types are private. The only operations defined for them are == and /= for comparing values of one of the types; they return a value of type default logical. Intrinsic assignment is also available.

12.9.2   Inquiry functions for IEEE arithmetic

The module ieee_arithmetic contains the following inquiry functions, all of which are pure. The inquiries are in terms of reals, but the same level of support is provided for the corresponding kinds of complex type.

ieee_support_datatype ([x]) returns .true. if the processor supports IEEE arithmetic for all reals (x absent) or for reals of the same kind type parameter as the real argument x. Otherwise, it returns .false.. Complete conformance with the IEEE standard is not required for .true. to be returned, but the normalized numbers must be exactly those of IEEE single or IEEE double; the binary arithmetic operators +, -, and * must be implemented with at least one of the IEEE rounding modes; and the functions ieee_copy_sign, ieee_scalb, ieee_logb, ieee_next_after, ieee_rem, and ieee_unordered must implement the corresponding IEEE functions.

ieee_support_denormal ([x]) returns .true. if the processor supports the IEEE denormalized numbers for all reals (x absent) or for reals of the same kind type parameter as the real argument x. Otherwise, it returns .false..

ieee_support_divide ([x]) returns .true. if the processor supports divide with the accuracy specified by the IEEE standard for all reals (x absent) or for reals of the same kind type parameter as the real argument x. Otherwise, it returns .false..

ieee_support_inf ([x]) returns .true. if the processor supports the IEEE infinity facility for all reals (x absent) or for reals of the same kind type parameter as the real argument x. Otherwise, it returns .false..

ieee_support_nan ([x]) returns .true. if the processor supports the IEEE Not-A-Number facility for all reals (x absent) or for reals of the same kind type parameter as the real argument x. Otherwise, it returns .false..

ieee_support_rounding (round_value [,x]) for a round_value of the type ieee_round_type returns .true. if the processor supports that rounding mode for all reals (x absent) or for reals of the same kind type parameter as the argument x. Otherwise, it returns .false.. Here, support includes the ability to change the mode by the invocation

```
call ieee_set_rounding_mode (round_value)
```

ieee_support_sqrt ([x]) returns .true. if sqrt implements IEEE square root
   for all reals (x absent) or for reals of the same kind type parameter as the
   real argument x. Otherwise, it returns .false..

ieee_support_standard ([x]) returns .true. if the processor supports all the
   IEEE facilities defined in this chapter for all reals (x absent) or for reals of
   the same kind type parameter as the real argument x. Otherwise, it returns
   .false..

12.9.3   Elemental functions

The module ieee_arithmetic contains the following elemental functions for
the reals x and y for which the values of ieee_support_datatype(x) and
ieee_support_datatype(y) are true. If x or y is an infinity or a NaN, the behaviour is consistent with the general rules of the IEEE standard for arithmetic
operations. For example, the result for an infinity is constructed as the limiting
case of the result with a value of arbitrarily large magnitude, when such a limit
exists.

ieee_class (x) is of type type(ieee_class_type) and returns the IEEE class
   of the real argument x. The possible values are explained in Section 12.9.1.

ieee_copy_sign (x, y) returns a real with the same type parameter as x, holding the value of x with the sign of y. This is true even for the IEEE special
   values, such as NaN and ∞ (on processors supporting such values).

ieee_is_finite (x) returns the value .true. if ieee_class (x) has one of the
   values

         ieee_negative_normal   ieee_negative_denormal
         ieee_negative_zero   ieee_positive_zero
         ieee_positive_denormal ieee_positive_normal

   and .false. otherwise.

ieee_is_nan (x) returns the value .true. if the value of x is an IEEE NaN and
   .false. otherwise.

ieee_is_negative (x) returns the value .true. if ieee_class (x) has one of
   the values

         ieee_negative_normal ieee_negative_denormal
         ieee_negative_zero   ieee_negative_inf

   and .false. otherwise.

ieee_is_normal (x) returns the value .true. if ieee_class (x) has one of the
   values

```
ieee_negative_normal   ieee_negative_zero
ieee_positive_zero     ieee_positive_normal
```

and .false. otherwise.

ieee_logb (x) returns a real with the same type parameter as x. If x is neither zero, infinity, nor NaN, the value of the result is the unbiased exponent of x, that is, exponent(x)-1. If x==0, the result is $-\infty$ if ieee_support_inf(x) is true and -huge(x) otherwise; ieee_divide_by_zero signals.

ieee_next_after (x, y) returns a real with the same type parameter as x. If x==y, the result is x, without an exception ever signaling. Otherwise, the result is the neighbour of x in the direction of y. The neighbours of zero (of either sign) are both nonzero. If either x or y is a NaN, the result is one of the input NaNs. Overflow is signaled when x is finite but ieee_next_after (x, y) is infinite; underflow is signaled when ieee_next_after (x, y) is denormalized; in both cases, ieee_inexact signals.

ieee_rem (x, y) returns a real with the type parameter of whichever argument has the greater precision and value exactly x-y*n, where n is the integer nearest to the exact value x/y; whenever $|n - x/y| = 1/2$, n is even. If the result value is zero, the sign is that of x.

ieee_rint (x, y) returns a real with the same type parameter as x whose value is that of x rounded to an integer value according to the current rounding mode.

ieee_scalb (x, i) returns a real with the same type parameter as x whose value is 2^ix if this is within the range of normalized numbers. If 2^ix is too large, ieee_overflow signals; if ieee_support_inf(x) is true, the result value is infinity with the sign of x; otherwise, it is sign(huge(x),x). If 2^ix is too small and cannot be represented exactly, ieee_underflow signals; the result is the nearest representable number with the sign of x.

ieee_unordered (x, y) returns .true. if x or y is a NaN or both are, and .false. otherwise.

ieee_value (x, class) returns a real with the same type parameter as x and a value specified by class. The argument class may have value

ieee_signaling_nan or ieee_quiet_nan if ieee_support_nan(x) is true,

ieee_negative_inf or ieee_positive_inf if ieee_support_inf(x) is true,

ieee_negative_denormal or ieee_positive_denormal if the value of ieee_support_denormal(x) is true, or ieee_negative_normal, ieee_negative_zero, ieee_positive_zero, or ieee_positive_normal.

Although in most cases the value is processor dependent, it does not vary between invocations for any particular kind type parameter of x and value of class.

12.9.4   Non-elemental subroutines

The module ieee_arithmetic contains the following non-elemental subroutines:

call ieee_get_rounding_mode (round_value) where:

> round_value is scalar and of type type(ieee_round_type) and has intent out. It returns the floating-point rounding mode, with value ieee_nearest, ieee_to_zero, ieee_up, or ieee_down if one of the IEEE modes is in operation, and ieee_other otherwise.

call ieee_set_rounding_mode (round_value) where:

> round_value is scalar, of type type(ieee_round_type), and has intent in. It specifies the mode to be set. The value of ieee_support_rounding (round_value, x) must be true for some x such that the value of ieee_support_datatype(x) is true.

The example in Figure 12.2 shows the use of these subroutines to store all the exception flags, perform a calculation involving exception handling, and restore them later.

Figure 12.2

```
use, intrinsic :: ieee_arithmetic
type(ieee_round_type) round_value
    :
call ieee_get_rounding_mode(round_value) ! Store the rounding
                                         ! mode
call ieee_set_rounding_mode(ieee_nearest)
    :  ! Calculation with round to nearest
call ieee_set_rounding_mode(round_value) ! Restore the
                                         ! rounding mode
```

12.9.5   Transformational function for kind value

The module ieee_arithmetic contains the following transformational function that is permitted in an initialization expression (Section 7.4):

ieee_selected_real_kind ([p][, r]) is just like selected_real_kind (Section 8.7.4) except that the result is the kind value of a real x for which ieee_support_datatype(x) is true.

12.10   Examples

12.10.1   Dot product

Our first example, Figure 12.3, is of a module for the dot product of two real arrays of rank 1. It contains a logical scalar dot_error, which acts as an error flag. If the sizes of the arrays are different, an immediate return occurs with dot_error true. If overflow occurs during the actual calculation, the overflow flag will signal and dot_error is set true. If all is well, its value is unchanged.

Figure 12.3

```
module dot ! Module for dot product of two real rank-1 arrays.
  ! The caller must ensure that exceptions do not cause halting.
    use, intrinsic :: ieee_exceptions
    implicit none
    private        :: mult
    logical        :: dot_error = .false.
    interface operator(.dot.)
       module procedure mult
    end interface
contains
    real function mult(a,b)
       real, intent(in) :: a(:), b(:)
       integer        :: i
       logical        :: overflow
       if (size(a)/=size(b)) then
          dot_error = .true.
          return
       end if
! The processor ensures that ieee_overflow is quiet
       mult = 0.0
       do i = 1, size(a)
          mult = mult + a(i)*b(i)
       end do
       call ieee_get_flag(ieee_overflow,overflow)
       if (overflow) dot_error = .true.
    end function mult
end module dot
```

12.10.2   Calling alternative procedures

Suppose the function fast_inv is a code for matrix inversion that 'lives danger-ously' and may cause a condition to signal. The alternative function slow_inv is far less likely to cause a condition to signal, but is much slower. The follow-ing code, Figure 12.4, tries fast_inv and, if necessary, makes another try with slow_inv. If this still fails, a message is printed and the program stops. Note, also, that it is important to set the flags quiet before the second try. The state of all the flags is stored and restored.

Figure 12.4

```
use, intrinsic :: ieee_exceptions
use, intrinsic :: ieee_features, only: ieee_invalid_flag
! The other exceptions of ieee_usual (ieee_overflow and
! ieee_divide_by_zero) are always available with ieee_exceptions
type(ieee_status_type) :: status_value
logical, dimension(3)  :: flag_value
     :
call ieee_get_status(status_value)
call ieee_set_halting_mode(ieee_usual,.false.) ! Needed in case the
!             default on the processor is to halt on exceptions.
call ieee_set_flag(ieee_usual,.false.)         ! Elemental
! First try the "fast" algorithm for inverting a matrix:
matrix1 = fast_inv(matrix) ! This must not alter matrix.
call ieee_get_flag(ieee_usual,flag_value)      ! Elemental
if (any(flag_value)) then
! "Fast" algorithm failed; try "slow" one:
   call ieee_set_flag(ieee_usual,.false.)
   matrix1 = slow_inv(matrix)
   call ieee_get_flag(ieee_usual,flag_value)
   if (any(flag_value)) then
      write (*, *) 'Cannot invert matrix'
      stop
   end if
end if
call ieee_set_status(status_value)
```

12.10.3   Calling alternative in-line code

This example, Figure 12.5, is similar to the inner part of the previous one, but here the code for matrix inversion is in line, we know that only overflow can signal, and the transfer is made more precise by adding extra tests of the flag.

Figure 12.5

```
use, intrinsic :: ieee_exceptions
logical         :: flag_value
   :
call ieee_set_halting_mode(ieee_overflow,.false.)
call ieee_set_flag(ieee_overflow,.false.)
! First try a fast algorithm for inverting a matrix.
do k = 1, n
   :
   call ieee_get_flag(ieee_overflow,flag_value)
   if (flag_value) exit
end do
if (flag_value) then
! Alternative code which knows that k-1 steps have
! executed normally.
:
end if
```

12.10.4   Reliable hypotenuse function

The most important use of a floating-point exception handling facility is to make possible the development of much more efficient software than is otherwise possible. The code in Figure 12.6 for the 'hypotenuse' function, $\sqrt{x^2 + y^2}$, illustrates the use of the facility in developing efficient software.

An attempt is made to evaluate this function directly in the fastest possible way. This will work almost every time, but if an exception occurs during this fast computation, a safe but slower way evaluates the function. This slower evaluation may involve scaling and unscaling, and in (very rare) extreme cases this unscaling can cause overflow (after all, the true result might overflow if x and y are both near the overflow limit). If the overflow or underflow flag is signaling on entry, it is reset on return by the processor, so that earlier exceptions are not lost.

12.10.5   Access to IEEE arithmetic values

The program in Figure 12.7 illustrates how the ieee_arithmetic module can be used to test for special IEEE values. It repeatedly doubles a and halves b, testing for overflowed, denormalized, and zero values. It uses ieee_set_halting_mode to prevent halting. The beginning and end of a sample output are shown. Note the warning messages; the processor is required to produce some such output if any exceptions are signalling at termination.

Figure 12.6

```
  real function hypot(x, y)
  implicit none
! In rare circumstances this may lead to the signaling of
! ieee_overflow.
! The caller must ensure that exceptions do not cause halting.
  use, intrinsic :: ieee_exceptions
  use, intrinsic :: ieee_features, only: ieee_underflow_flag
! ieee_overflow is always available with ieee_exceptions
  real               :: x, y
  real               :: scaled_x, scaled_y, scaled_result
  logical, dimension(2) :: flags
  type(ieee_flag_type), parameter, dimension(2) ::        &
        out_of_range = (/ ieee_overflow, ieee_underflow /)
  intrinsic :: sqrt, abs, exponent, max, digits, scale
! The processor clears the flags on entry
  call ieee_set_halting_mode(out_of_range, .false.) ! Needed in
!     case the default on the processor is to halt on exceptions.
! Try a fast algorithm first
  hypot = sqrt( x**2 + y**2 )
  call ieee_get_flag(out_of_range, flags)
  if ( any(flags) ) then
    call ieee_set_flag(out_of_range, .false.)
    if ( x==0.0 .or. y==0.0 ) then
      hypot = abs(x) + abs(y)
    else if ( 2*abs(exponent(x)-exponent(y)) > digits(x)+1 ) then
      hypot = max( abs(x), abs(y) )! We can ignore one of x and y
    else      ! Scale so that abs(x) is near 1
      scaled_x = scale( x, -exponent(x) )
      scaled_y = scale( y, -exponent(x) )
      scaled_result = sqrt( scaled_x**2 + scaled_y**2 )
      hypot = scale(scaled_result, exponent(x)) ! May cause
    end if                                      ! overflow
  end if
! The processor resets any flag that was signaling on entry
end function hypot
```

Figure 12.7

```
program test
   use ieee_arithmetic; use ieee_features
   real    :: a=1.0, b=1.0
   integer :: i
   call ieee_set_halting_mode(ieee_overflow, .false.)
   do i = 1,1000
      a = a*2.0
      b = b/2.0
      if(.not. ieee_is_finite(a)) then
         write(*,*) '2.0**',i,' is infinite'
         a = 0.0
      end if
      if(.not. ieee_is_normal(b)) write(*,*) '0.5**', i,   &
                                    ' is denormal'
      if(b==0.0) exit
   end do
   write(*,*) '0.5**',i,' is zero'
end program test


 0.5** 127  is denormal
 2.0** 128  is infinite
 0.5** 128  is denormal
 0.5** 129  is denormal
 :
 0.5** 148  is denormal
 0.5** 149  is denormal
 0.5** 150  is zero
Warning: Floating overflow occurred during execution
Warning: Floating underflow occurred during execution
```

13. Allocatable array extensions

13.1 Introduction

The subject of this chapter is another extension[1] of Fortran 95. It involves the use of allocatable arrays as dummy arguments, function results, and components of structures. Pointer arrays may be used instead in Fortran 90/95, but there are significant advantages for memory management and execution speed in using allocatable arrays when the added functionality of pointers is not needed.

This is another extension that WG5 has promised will be included in the next revision of the Fortran standard, apart from correcting any defects found in the field. Again, the intention is that this promise will encourage vendors to implement the feature in their compilers, confident that their efforts will have a secure future (Section 1.5).

Why is this extension needed? Firstly, code for a pointer array is likely to be less efficient because allowance has to be made for strides other than unity. For example, its target might be the section vector(1:n:2) or the section matrix(i,1:n) with non-unit strides, whereas most computers hold allocatable arrays in contiguous memory.

Secondly, if a defined operation involves a temporary variable of a derived type with a pointer component, the compiler will probably be unable to deallocate its target when storage for the variable is freed. Consider, for example, the statement

```
a = b + c*d       ! a, b, c, and d are of the same derived type
```

This will create a temporary for c*d, which is not needed once b + c*d has been calculated. The compiler is unlikely to be sure that no other pointer has the component or part of it as a target, so is unlikely to deallocate it.

Thirdly, intrinsic assignment is often unsuitable for a derived type with a pointer component because the assignment

```
a = b
```

will leave a and b sharing the same target for their pointer component. Therefore, a defined assignment that allocates a fresh target and copies the data will be used instead. However, this is very wasteful if the right-hand side is a temporary such as that of the assignment of the previous paragraph.

---

[1] Technical Report ISO/IEC 15581: 1998(E).

Fourthly, similar considerations apply to a function invocation within an expression. The compiler will be unlikely to be able to deallocate the pointer after the expression has been calculated.

Although the Fortran standard does not mention descriptors, it is very helpful to think of an allocatable array as being held as a descriptor that records whether it is allocated and, if so, its address and its bounds in each dimension. This is like a descriptor for a pointer, but no strides need be held since these are always unity. As for pointers, the expectation is that the array itself is held separately.

13.2   Allocatable dummy arguments

A dummy argument is permitted to have the allocatable attribute. In this case, the corresponding actual argument must be an allocatable array of the same type, kind parameters, and rank; also, the interface must be explicit. The dummy argument always receives the allocation status (descriptor) of the actual argument on entry and the actual argument receives that of the dummy argument on return. In both cases, this includes the bounds and may be 'not currently allocated'.

Our expectatation is that some compilers will perform copy in / copy out of the descriptor. Rule i) of Section 5.7.2 is applicable and is designed to permit compilers to do this. In particular, this means that no reference to the actual argument (for example, through it being a module variable) is permitted from the invoked procedure if the dummy array is allocated or deallocated there.

For the array itself, the situation is just like the case when the actual and dummy arguments are both explicit-shaped arrays (see Section 6.7.3). Copy in / copy out is permitted unless both arrays have the target attribute.

An allocatable dummy argument is permitted to have intent and this applies both to the allocation status (the descriptor) and to the array itself. If the intent is in, the array is not permitted to be allocated or deallocated and the value is not permitted to be altered. If the intent is out and the array is allocated on entry, it becomes deallocated. An example of the application of an allocatable dummy argument to reading arrays of variable bounds is shown in Figure 13.1.

Figure 13.1

```
subroutine load(array, unit)
   real, allocatable, intent(out), dimension(:,:,:) :: array
   integer, intent(in)          :: unit
   integer                      :: n1, n2, n3
   read(unit) n1, n2, n3
   allocate(array(n1, n2, n3))
   read(unit) array
end subroutine load
```

13.3 Allocatable functions

A function result is permitted to have the allocatable attribute. The allocation status on each entry to the function is 'not currently allocated'. The result may be allocated and deallocated any number of times during execution of the procedure, but it must be allocated and have a defined value on return.

The interface must be explicit in any scoping unit in which the function is referenced. The result array is automatically deallocated after execution of the statement in which the reference occurs, even if it has the target attribute. We can thus recast the example in Section 5.10, and safely use the function result in an expression as shown in Figure 13.2, without fearing a memory leak.

Figure 13.2

```
program no_leak
   real, dimension(100) :: x, y
   :
   y(:size(compact(x)) = compact(x)**2
   :
contains
   function compact(x) ! To remove duplicates from the array x
      real, allocatable, dimension(:) :: compact
      real, dimension(:), intent(in)  :: x
      integer                         :: n
      :                  ! Find the number of distinct values, n
      allocate(compact(n))
      :                        ! Copy the distinct values into compact
   end function compact
end program no_leak
```

13.4 Allocatable components

Components of derived type are permitted to have the allocatable attribute. For example, for each scalar variable of type type(stack) with the type declaration

```
type stack
   integer :: index
   integer, allocatable :: content(:)
end type stack
```

the bounds of component content are determined by an allocate statement, by assignment, or by argument association.

In Section 9.3, we used the term *ultimate component* when a sequence of component selections involves no pointer components of derived type and ends with an intrinsic type. It is convenient to extend the term to include the case that ends with a component of derived type that is allocatable or is a pointer. For example, if the components called alloc are allocatable and the components called point are pointers, the components obj%point and obj%alloc are ultimate components, but obj%point%comp and obj%alloc%comp are not. The parent object (obj in our example) may be allocatable or a pointer.

Just as for an ordinary allocatable array, the initial state of an allocable component is 'not currently allocated'. This is also true for an ultimate allocatable component of an object created by an allocate statement. Hence, there is no need for default initialization of allocatable components. In fact, initialization in a derived type definition (Section 7.11) of an allocatable component is not permitted.

In a structure constructor (Section 3.8), an expression corresponding to an allocatable component must be an array or null(). If it is an allocatable array, the component takes the same allocation status and, if allocated, the same bounds and value. If it is an array, but not an allocatable array, the component is allocated with the same bounds and is assigned the same value. If it is null(), the component receives the allocation status of 'not currently allocated'.

Allocatable components are illustrated in Figure 13.3, where code to manipulate polynomials with variable numbers of terms is shown.

Just as an allocatable array is not permitted to have the parameter attribute (be a constant), so an object with an ultimate allocatable component is not permitted to have the parameter attribute. An array constructor of such a type cannot be a constant and cannot participate in an initialization expression (Section 7.4). To correspond with this, a variable of such a type is not permitted to be initialized.

In an array subobject (Section 6.13), a *part-ref* to the right of a *part-ref* with nonzero rank must not be an element of an allocatable component, for example,

```
type(stack) :: a(10)    ! The type was declared at the
  :                     ! start of this section.
... a(:)%content(1)     ! Not permitted.
```

This is because such an object would not be an ordinary array – its elements are likely to be stored without any regular pattern, each having been separately given storage by an allocate statement.

When a variable of derived type is deallocated, any ultimate allocatable component that is currently allocated is also deallocated, as if by a deallocate statement. The variable may be a pointer or an allocatable array, and the rule applies recursively, so that all allocated allocatable components at all levels (apart from any lying beyond pointer components) are deallocated. Such deallocations of components also occur when a variable is associated with an intent(out) dummy argument. Note the convenience to the programmer of this feature; to avoid memory leakage with pointer components, the programmer would need to deallocate each one explicitly and be careful to order the deallocations correctly.

Intrinsic assignment

$$variable = expr$$

Figure 13.3

```
module real_polynomial_module
    type real_polynomial
        real, allocatable, dimension(:) :: coeff
    end type real_polynomial
    interface operator(+)
        module procedure rp_add_rp
    end interface operator(+)
contains
    function rp_add_rp(p1, p2)
        type(real_polynomial)                :: rp_add_rp
        type(real_polynomial), intent(in) :: p1, p2
        integer                              :: m, m1, m2
        m1 = ubound(p1%coeff,1)
        m2 = ubound(p2%coeff,1)
        allocate(rp_add_rp%coeff(max(m1,m2)))
        m = min(m1,m2)
        rp_add_rp%coeff(:m) = p1%coeff(:m) +p2%coeff(:m)
        if (m1 > m) rp_add_rp%coeff(m+1:) = p1%coeff(m+1:)
        if (m2 > m) rp_add_rp%coeff(m+1:) = p2%coeff(m+1:)
    end function rp_add_rp
end module real_polynomial_module
program example
    use real_polynomial_module
    type(real_polynomial) :: p, q, r
    p = real_polynomial((/4.0, 2.0, 1.0/))  ! Set p to 4+2x+x**2
    q = real_polynomial((/-1.0, 1.0/))
    r = p + q
    print *, 'Coefficients are: ', r%coeff
end program example
```

for a type with an ultimate allocatable component consists of the following steps for each such component:

i) If the component of *variable* is currently allocated, it is deallocated.

ii) If the component of *expr* is currently allocated, the component of *variable* is allocated with the same bounds and the value is then transferred using intrinsic assignment.

If the allocatable component of *expr* is 'not currently allocated', nothing happens in step ii), so the component of *variable* is left 'not currently allocated'. Note that if the component of *variable* is already allocated with the same shape, the compiler may chose to avoid the overheads of deallocation and reallocation. Note also that if the compiler can tell that there will be no subsequent reference to *expr*, because it is a function reference or a temporary variable holding the result of expression evaluation, no allocation or assignment is needed – all that has to happen is the deallocation of any allocated ultimate allocatable components of *variable* followed by copying of the descriptor.

If an actual argument and the corresponding dummy argument have an ultimate allocatable component, rule i) of Section 5.7.2 is applicable and requires all allocations and deallocations of the component to be performed through the dummy argument, in case copy in / copy out is in effect.

If a statement contains a reference to a function whose result is of a type with an ultimate allocatable component, any allocated ultimate allocatable components of the function result are deallocated after execution of the statement. This parallels the rule for allocatable function results (Section 13.3).

Just as for pointer components (see Section 9.3), a structure with an ultimate allocatable component is not permitted in an I/O list. The reason is the intention to add defined edit descriptors for data structures to Fortran 2000. Programmers will be able to write procedures that are called as part of the I/O processing. Such a procedure will be much better able to handle structures whose size and composition vary dynamically, the usual case with allocatable components.

Similarly, such a structure is not permitted in a namelist group (Section 7.15). This is entirely consistent with not permitting allocatable arrays or structures with pointer components here.

A sequence type (Section 11.2.1) is permitted to have an allocatable component, which permits independent declarations of the same type in different scopes, but such a type has an unspecified storage unit, that is, does not have numeric or character storage association (as for a type with a pointer component).

This dynamic feature is ill adapted to the fixed storage model implied by storage association, and so, just as for pointer components (see Section 11.2.2), a structure with an ultimate allocatable component is not permitted as an `object` in an `equivalence` statement. Just as for allocatable arrays (see Section 11.2.3), a structure with an ultimate allocatable component is not permitted in a `common` block. Thus, such a structure is not permitted at all in a storage association context.

A. Intrinsic procedures

Name	Section	Description
abs (a)	8.3.1	Absolute value.
achar (i)	8.5.1	Character in position i of ASCII collating sequence.
acos (x)	8.4	Arc cosine (inverse cosine) function.
adjustl (string)	8.5.3	Adjust left, removing leading blanks and inserting trailing blanks.
adjustr (string)	8.5.3	Adjust right, removing trailing blanks and inserting leading blanks.
aimag (z)	8.3.1	Imaginary part of complex number.
aint (a [,kind])	8.3.1	Truncate to a whole number.
all (mask [,dim])	8.11	True if all elements are true.
allocated (array)	8.12.1	True if the array is allocated.
anint (a [,kind])	8.3.1	Nearest whole number.
any (mask [,dim])	8.11	True if any element is true.
asin (x)	8.4	Arcsine (inverse sine) function.
associated (pointer [,target])	8.2	True if pointer is associated with target.
atan (x)	8.4	Arctangent (inverse tangent) function.
atan2 (y, x)	8.4	Argument of complex number (x, y).
bit_size (i)	8.8.1	Maximum number of bits that may be held in an integer.
btest (i, pos)	8.8.2	True if bit pos of integer i has value 1.

ceiling (a [, kind])	8.3.1	Least integer greater than or equal to its argument (kind permitted only in Fortran 95).
char (i [,kind])	8.5.1	Character in position i of the processor collating sequence.
cmplx (x [,y] [,kind])	8.3.1	Convert to complex type.
conjg (z)	8.3.2	Conjugate of a complex number.
cos (x)	8.4	Cosine function.
cosh (x)	8.4	Hyperbolic cosine function.
count (mask [,dim])	8.11	Number of true elements.
cpu_time (time)	8.16.2	Processor time (Fortran 95 only)
cshift (array, shift [,dim])	8.13.5	Perform circular shift.
call date_and_time ([date] [,time] [,zone] [,values])	8.16.1	Real-time clock reading date and time.
dble (a)	11.4.1	Convert to double precision real.
digits (x)	8.7.2	Number of significant digits in the model for x.
dim (x, y)	8.3.2	$\max(x-y,\ 0)$.
dot_product (vector_a, vector_b)	8.10	Dotproduct.
dprod (x, y)	11.4.1	Double precision real product of two default real scalars.
eoshift (array, shift [,boundary][,dim])	8.13.5	Perform end-off shift.
epsilon (x)	8.7.2	Number that is almost negligible compared with one in the model for numbers like x.
exp (x)	8.4	Exponential function.
exponent (x)	8.7.3	Exponent part of the model for x.
floor (a [, kind])	8.3.1	Greatest integer less than or equal to its argument (kind permitted only in Fortran 95).
fraction (x)	8.7.3	Fractional part of the model for x.
huge (x)	8.7.2	Largest number in the model for numbers like x.
iachar (c)	8.5.1	Position of character c in ASCII collating sequence.

iand (i, j)	8.8.2	Logical and on the bits.
ibclr (i, pos)	8.8.2	Clear bit pos to zero.
ibits (i, pos, len)	8.8.2	Extract a sequence of bits.
ibset (i, pos)	8.8.2	Set bit pos to one.
ichar (c)	8.5.1	Position of character c in the processor collating sequence.
ieor (i, j)	8.8.2	Exclusive or on the bits.
index (string, substring [,back])	8.5.3	Starting position of substring within string.
int (a [,kind])	8.3.1	Convert to integer type.
ior (i, j)	8.8.2	Inclusive or on the bits.
ishft (i, shift)	8.8.2	Logical shift on the bits.
ishftc (i, shift [,size])	8.8.2	Logical circular shift on a set of bits on the right.
kind (x)	8.2	Kind type parameter value.
lbound (array [,dim])	8.12.2	Array lower bounds.
len (string)	8.6.1	Character length.
len_trim (string)	8.5.3	Length of string without trailing blanks.
lge (string_a, string_b)	8.5.2	True if string_a equals or follows string_b in ASCII collating sequence.
lgt (string_a, string_b)	8.5.2	True if string_a follows string_b in ASCII collating sequence.
lle (string_a, string_b)	8.5.2	True if string_a equals or precedes string_b in ASCII collating sequence.
llt (string_a, string_b)	8.5.2	True if string_a precedes string_b in ASCII collating sequence.
log (x)	8.4	Natural (base e) logarithm function.
logical (1, [,kind])	8.5.4	Convert between kinds of logicals.
log10 (x)	8.4	Common (base 10) logarithm function.
matmul (matrix_a, matrix_b)	8.10	Matrix multiplication.
max (a1, a2 [,a3,...])	8.3.2	Maximum value.

maxexponent (x)	8.7.2	Maximum exponent in the model for numbers like x.
maxloc (array [,mask])　or maxloc (array, dim 　[,mask])	8.14	Location of maximum array element (dim in Fortran 95 only).
maxval (array [,mask])　or maxval (array, dim 　[,mask])	8.11	Value of maximum array element (mask as second positional argument in Fortran 95 only).
merge (tsource, fsource, 　mask)	8.13.1	tsource when mask is true and fsource otherwise.
min (a1, a2 [,a3,...])	8.3.2	Minimum value.
minexponent (x)	8.7.2	minimum exponent in the model for numbers like x.
minloc (array [,mask])　or minloc (array, dim 　[,mask])	8.14	Location of minimum array element (dim in Fortran 95 only).
minval (array [,mask])　or minval (array, dim 　[,mask])	8.11	Value of minimum array element (mask as second positional argument in Fortran 95 only).
mod (a, p)	8.3.2	Remainder modulo p, that is a-int(a/p)*p.
modulo (a, p)	8.3.2	a modulo p.
call mvbits (from, 　frompos, len, to, 　topos)	8.8.3	Copy bits.
nearest (x, s)	8.7.3	Nearest different machine number in the direction given by the sign of s.
nint (a [,kind])	8.3.1	Nearest integer.
not (i)	8.8.2	Logical complement of the bits.
null([mold])	8.15	Disassociated pointer (Fortran 95 only).
pack (array, mask 　[,vector])	8.13.2	Pack elements corresponding to true elements of mask into rank-one result.
precision (x)	8.7.2	Decimal precision in the model for x.
present (a)	8.2	True if optional argument is present.

product (array [,mask]) or product (array, dim [,mask])	8.11	Product of array elements (mask as second positional argument in Fortran 95 only).
radix (x)	8.7.2	Base of the model for numbers like x.
call random_number (harvest)	8.16.3	Random numbers in range $0 \le x < 1$.
call random_seed ([size] [put] [get])	8.16.3	Initialize or restart random number generator.
range (x)	8.7.2	Decimal exponent range in the model for x.
real (a [,kind])	8.3.1	Convert to real type.
repeat (string, ncopies)	8.6.2	Concatenates ncopies of string.
reshape (source, shape [,pad] [,order])	8.13.3	Reshape source to shape shape.
rrspacing (x)	8.7.3	Reciprocal of the relative spacing of model numbers near x.
scale (x, i)	8.7.3	$x \times b^i$, where b=radix(x).
scan (string, set [,back])	8.5.3	Index of left-most (right-most if back is true) character of string that belongs to set; zero if none belong.
selected_int_kind (r)	8.7.4	Kind of type parameter for specified exponent range.
selected_real_kind ([p] [,r])	8.7.4	Kind of type parameter for specified precision and exponent range.
set_exponent (x, i)	8.7.3	Model number whose sign and fractional part are those of x and whose exponent part is i.
shape (source)	8.12.2	Array (or scalar) shape.
sign (a, b)	8.3.2	Absolute value of a times sign of b.
sin (x)	8.4	Sine function.
sinh (x)	8.4	Hyperbolic sine function.
size (array [,dim])	8.12.2	Array size.
spacing (x)	8.7.3	Absolute spacing of model numbers near x.
spread (source, dim, ncopies)	8.13.4	ncopies copies of source forming an array of rank one greater.

sqrt (x)	8.4	Square root function.
sum (array [,mask]) or sum(array, dim [,mask])	8.11	Sum of array elements (mask as second positional argument in Fortran 95 only).

call system_clock ([count]
   [,count_rate]
   [,count_max])
	8.16.1	Integer data from real-time clock.

tan (x)	8.4	Tangent function.
tanh (x)	8.4	Hyperbolic tangent function.
tiny (x)	8.7.2	Smallest positive number in the model for numbers like x.
transfer (source, mold [,size])	8.9	Same physical representation as source, but type of mold.
transpose (matrix)	8.13.6	Matrix transpose.
trim (string)	8.6.2	Remove trailing blanks from a single string.
ubound (array [,dim])	8.12.2	Array upper bounds.
unpack (vector, mask, field)	8.13.2	Unpack elements of vector corresponding to true elements of mask.
verify (string, set [,back])	8.5.3	Zero if all characters of string belong to set or index of left-most (right-most if back true) that does not.

B. Fortran 90/95 statements

Notes:

- Obsolescent features (see Appendix C) have not been included in this list.
- Where no optional blank is indicated between two adjacent keywords, the blank is mandatory.

Statement	Section
NON-EXECUTABLE STATEMENTS	
Program Units and Subprograms	
program *program-name*	5.2
module *module-name*	5.5
end[ ][module [*module-name*]]	5.5
use *module-name* [,*rename-list*]	7.10
use *module-name*, only: [*only-list*]	7.10
private [[::] *access-id-list*]	7.6 & 7.11
public [[::] *access-id-list*]	7.6
external *external-name-list*	5.11
intrinsic [::] *intrinsic-name-list* (:: in Fortran 95 only)	8.1.3
[*prefix*] subroutine *subroutine-name* [([*dummy-argument-list*])]	5.20
where *prefix* is recursive or, for Fortran 95, pure or elemental	
[*prefix*] function *function-name* ([*dummy-argument-list*]) [result(*result-name*)]	5.20
where *prefix* is type [recursive] or recursive [*type*] or also, for Fortran 95, pure or elemental	
entry *entry-name* [([*dummy-argument-list*]) [result(*result-name*)]]	11.2.6
intent (*inout*) [::] *dummy-argument-name-list*	7.8
where *inout* is in, out, or in[ ]out	
optional [::] *dummy-argument-name-list*	7.8
save [[::] *saved-entity-list*]	7.9

where *saved-entity* is *variable-name* or */common-block-name/*

`contains`	5.2
`interface` [*generic-spec*]	5.18

where *generic-spec* is *generic-name*, `operator`(*defined-operator*), or `assignment`(=)

`end[ ]interface` [*generic-spec*] (*generic-spec* in Fortran 95 only)	5.18
`module procedure` *procedure-name-list*	5.18

Data Specification

type [[, *attribute*]... ::] *entity-list*	7.12
where *type* is `integer`[([`kind=`]*kind-value*)],	7.13

`real`[(([`kind=`]*kind-value*)],
`logical`[(([`kind=`]*kind-value*)],
`complex`[(([`kind=`]*kind-value*)],
`character`[*actual-parameter-list*],
`double`[ ]`precision`, or
`type`(*type-name*)

and *attribute* is `parameter`, `public`, `private`, `pointer`, `target`, `al-` `locatable`, `dimension`(*bounds-list*), `intent`(*inout*), `external`, `in-` `trinsic`, `optional` or `save`	7.12
`implicit none`	7.2
`implicit` *type*(*letter-spec-list*) [,*type*(*letter-spec-list*)]...	7.2
`type` [[, *access*]::] *type-name*	7.11
where *access* is `public` or `private`	7.6
type[[,*component-attr*]... ::] *component-decl-list*	7.11

where *component-attr* is `pointer` or `dimension`(*bounds-list*) and *component-decl* is *component-name*[(*bounds-list*)] [**char-len*] [*comp-init*] and *comp-init* (Fortran 95 only) is = *expr* or => `null`()

`end[ ]type` [*type-name*]	7.11
`sequence`	11.2.1
`data` *object-list*/*value-list*/ [[,] *object-list*/*value-list*/]...	7.5.2
`block[ ]data` [*block-data-name*]	11.2.4
`end[[ ]block[ ]data` [*block-data-name*]]	11.2.4
`parameter` (*named-constant-definition-list*)	11.4.2
`namelist` */namelist-group-name/* *variable-name-list* [[,]/*namelist-group-name/* *variable-name-list*]...	7.15
`dimension` [::] *array-name*(*array-spec*) [, *array-name*(*array-spec*)]...	11.4.2
`allocatable` [::] *array-name* [(*array-spec*)] [,*array-name* [(*array-spec*)]]...	7.7

pointer [::] *object-name* [(*array-spec*)]   7.7
[,*object-name* [(*array-spec*)]]...

target [::] *object-name* [(*array-spec*)]   7.7
[,*object-name* [(*array-spec*)]]...

equivalence (*object, object-list*) [, (*object, object-list*)]...   11.2.2

common [/[*cname*]/]*vlist* [[,]/[*cname*]/ *vlist*]...   11.2.3

EXECUTABLE STATEMENTS
Assignment

variable = expr

where *variable* may be an array and may be a subobject   Chap. 3

pointer => target   3.12

if (*scalar-logical-expr*) *action-stmt*   4.3.1

where (*logical-array-expr*) *array-variable = expr*   6.8

forall(*index = lower: upper* [:*stride*] [, *index = lower: upper*   6.9
[:*stride*]]... [,*scalar-logical-expr*]) *assignment* (Fortran 95)

Program Units and Subprograms

call *subroutine-name* [(([*actual-argument-list*])]   5.13

return   5.8

end[ ][*unit* [*unit-name*]]   Chap. 5

where *unit* is program, subroutine, or function.

Dynamic Storage Allocation

allocate (*allocation-list* [, stat=*stat*])   6.5.2

deallocate (*allocate-object-list* [, stat=*stat*])   6.5.3

nullify (*pointer-object-list*)   6.5.4

Control Constructs

[*do-name*:] do [*label*] [[,] *do-variable = scalar-integer-expr, scalar-*   4.5
integer-expr [,*scalar-integer-expr*]]

[*do-name*:] do [*label*] [,] while(*scalar-logical-expr*)   11.3.2

cycle [*do-name*]   4.5

exit [*do-name*]   4.5

continue   4.5

end[ ]do [*do-name*]   4.5

[*if-name*:] if (*scalar-logical-expr*) then   4.3.2

else[[ ]if (*scalar-logical-expr*) then] [*if-name*]   4.3.2

end[ ]if [*if-name*]	4.3.2
[*select-name*:] select[ ]case (*scalar-expr*)	4.4
case (*case-value-list*) [*select-name*]	4.4
case default [*select-name*]	4.4
end[ ]select [*select-name*]	4.4
go[ ]to *label*	4.2
stop [*access-code*]	5.3
[*where-name*:] where (*logical-array-expr*)	6.8
elsewhere [*where-name*]	6.8
elsewhere (*logical-array-expr*) [*where-name*] (Fortran 95)	6.8.1
end[ ]where [*where-name*]	6.8
[*forall-name*:] forall(*index = lower: upper* [:*stride*] [, *index = lower: upper* [:*stride*]]... [,*scalar-logical-expr*]) (Fortran 95)	6.9
end[ ]forall [*forall-name*] (Fortran 95)	6.9

Input-Output

read (*control-list*) [*input-list*]	9.17
read *format* [, *input-list*]	9.7
write (*control-list*) [*output-list*]	9.17
print *format* [, *output-list*]	9.8
rewind *external-file-unit*	10.2.2
rewind (*position-list*)	10.2.2
end[ ]file *external-file-unit*	10.2.3
end[ ]file (*position-list*)	10.2.3
backspace *external-file-unit*	10.2.1
backspace (*position-list*)	10.2.1
open (*connect-list*)	10.3
close (*close-list*)	10.4
inquire (*inquire-list*)	10.5
inquire (iolength = *length*) *olist*	10.5
format ([*format-list*]) (this statement is actually non-executable).	9.4

C. Obsolescent features

C.1 Obsolescent in Fortran 95 only

The features of this section were of first-class status in Fortran 90. However, the Fortran 95 standard defines them to be obsolescent, and they are thus, in a Fortran 95 context, part of this Appendix. Their replacements are described in the relevant subsections.

C.1.1 Fixed source form

The fixed source form has been replaced by the free source form (Section 2.4). In the old form, each statement consists of one or more *lines* exactly 72 characters long,[1] and each line is divided into three *fields*. The first field consists of positions 1 to 5 and may contain a *statement label*. A Fortran statement may be written in the second fields of up to 20 consecutive lines. The first line of a multi-line statement is known as the *initial line* and the succeeding lines as *continuation lines*.

A non-comment line is an initial line or a continuation line depending on whether there is a character, other than zero or blank, in position 6 of the line, which is the second field. The first field of a continuation line must be blank. The ampersand is not used for continuation.

The third field, from positions 7 to 72, is reserved for the Fortran statements themselves. Note that if a construct is named, the name must be placed here and not in the label field.

Except in a character context, blanks are insignificant.

The presence of an asterisk (*) or a character c in position 1 of a line indicates that the whole line is commentary. An exclamation mark indicates the start of commentary, except in position 6, where it indicates continuation.

Several statements separated by a semi-colon (;) may appear on one line. The semi-colon may not, in this case, be in column 6, where it would indicate continuation. Only the first of the statements on a line may be labelled. A semi-colon that is the last non-blank character of a line, or the last non-blank character ahead of commentary, is ignored.

---

[1] This limit is processor dependent if the line contains characters other than those of the default type.

A program unit end statement must not be continued, and any other statement with an initial line that appears to be a program unit end statement must not be continued.

A processor may restrict the appearance of its defined control characters, if any, in the fixed source form.

In applications where a high degree of compatibility between the old and the new source forms is required, for instance in code to be included into several programs which might exist in different forms, observance of the following rules can be of great help:

- confine statement labels to positions 1 to 5 and statements to positions 7 to 72;

- treat blanks as being significant;

- use only ! to indicate a comment (but not in position 6);

- for continued statements, place an ampersand in both position 73 of a continued line and position 6 of a continuing line.

Also, a tool to facilitate the conversion of Fortran 77 code to the free source form can be obtained by anonymous ftp to *ftp.numerical.rl.ac.uk*; the directory is */pub/MandR* and the file name is *convert.f90*. The tool has a number of other features, such as the ability to indent code.

C.1.2   Computed go to

A form of branch statement is the computed go to, which enables one path among many to be selected, depending on the value of a scalar integer expression. The general form is

> go to (*sl1, sl2, sl3,...*) [,] *intexpr*

where *sl1, sl2, sl3* etc. are labels of statements in the same scoping unit, and *intexpr* is any scalar integer expression. The same statement label may appear more than once. An example is

> go to (6,10,20) i(k)**2+j

which references three statement labels. When the statement is executed, if the value of the integer expression is 1, the first branch will be taken, and control is transferred to the statement labelled 6. If the value is 2, the second branch will be taken, and so on. If the value is less than 1, or greater than 3, no branch will be taken, and the next statement following the go to will be executed.

This statement is replaced by the case construct (Section 4.4).

C.1.3 Character length specification character*

Alternatives to

`character([len=]`*len-value*`)`

as a *type* in a type declaration, `function`, `implicit`, or component definition statement are

`character*(`*len-value*`)[,]`

and

`character*`*len*`[,]`

where *len* is an integer literal constant without a specified kind value and the optional comma is permitted only in a type declaration statement and only when `::` is absent:

`character*20 word, letter*1`

Note that these alternative forms are provided only for default characters.

C.1.4 Data statements among executables

The `data` statement may be placed among the executable statements, but such placement offers no extra advantage and is rarely used and not recommended, since data initialization properly belongs with the specification statements.

C.1.5 Statement functions

It may happen that within a single program unit there are repeated occurrences of a computation which can be represented as a single statement. For instance, to calculate the parabolic function represented by

$$y = a + bx + cx^2$$

for different values of x, but with the same coefficients, there may be references to

```
y1 = 1. + x1*(2. + 3.*x1)
 :
y2 = 1. + x2*(2. + 3.*x2)
 :
```

etc. In Fortran 77, it was more convenient to invoke a so-called *statement function* (now better coded as an internal subroutine, Section 5.6), which must appear after any `implicit` and other relevant specification statements and before the executable statements. The example above would become

```
parab(x) = 1. + x*(2. + 3.*x)
:
y1 = parab(x1)
:
y2 = parab(x2)
```

Here, x is a dummy argument, which is used in the definition of the statement function. The variables x1 and x2 are actual arguments to the function.

The general form is

$$\textit{function-name}\,(\,[\textit{dummy-argument-list}]\,) \; = \; \textit{scalar-expr}$$

where the *function-name* and each *dummy-argument* must be specified, explicitly or implicitly, to be scalar data objects. To make it clear that this is a statement function and not an assignment to a host array element, we recommend declaring the type by placing the *function-name* in a type declaration statement; this is *required* whenever a host entity has the same name. The *scalar-expr* must be composed of constants, references to scalar variables, references to functions, and intrinsic operations. If there is a reference to a function, the function must not be a transformational intrinsic nor require an explicit interface, the result must be scalar, and any array argument must be a named array. A reference to a non-intrinsic function must not require an explicit interface. A named constant that is referenced or an array of which an element is referenced must be declared earlier in the scoping unit or be accessed by use or host association. A scalar variable referenced may be a dummy argument of the statement function or a variable that is accessible in the scoping unit. A dummy argument of the host procedure must not be referenced unless it is a dummy argument of the main entry or of an entry that precedes the statement function. If any entity is implicitly typed, a subsequent type declaration must confirm the type and type parameters. The dummy arguments are scalar and have a scope of the statement function statement only.

A statement function always has an implicit interface and may not be supplied as a procedure argument. It may appear within an internal procedure, and may reference other statement functions appearing before it in the same scoping unit, but not itself nor any appearing after. A function reference in the expression must not redefine a dummy argument. A statement function is pure (Section 6.10) if it references only pure functions.

A statement function statement is not permitted in an interface block.

Note that statement functions are irregular in that use and host association are not available.

C.1.6   Assumed character length of function results

A non-recursive external function whose result is scalar, character, and non-pointer may have assumed character length as in Figure C.1. Such a function is not permitted to specify a defined operation. In a scoping unit that invokes such a function, the interface must be implicit and there must be a declaration of the length, as in Figure C.2, or such a declaration must be accessible by use or host association.

Figure C.1

```
function copy(word)
   character(len=*) copy, word
   copy = word
end function copy
```

Figure C.2

```
program main
   external copy                ! Interface block not allowed.
   character(len=10) copy
   write(*, *) copy('This message will be truncated')
end program main
```

This facility is included only for compatibility with Fortran 77 and is completely at variance with the philosophy of Fortran 90/95 that the attributes of a function result depend only on the actual arguments of the invocation and on any data accessible by the function through host or use association.

This facility may be replaced by use of a subroutine whose arguments correspond to the function result and the function arguments.

C.2 Obsolescent in Fortran 90 and 95

The features of this section are obsolescent in both Fortran 90 and Fortran 95. Their replacements are described in the relevant subsections.

C.2.1 Arithmetic if statement

The arithmetic if provides a three-way branching mechanism, depending on whether an arithmetic expression has a value which is less than, equal to, or greater than zero. It is replaced by the if statement and construct (Section 4.3). Its general form is

    if (*expr*) *sl1, sl2, sl3*

where *expr* is any scalar expression of type integer or real, and *sl1, sl2,* and *sl3* are the labels of statements in the same scoping unit. If the result obtained by evaluating *expr* is negative then the branch to *sl1* is taken, if the result is zero the branch to *sl2*, and if the result is greater than zero the branch to *sl3*. An example is

```
      if (p-q) 1,2,3
   1  p = 0.
      go to 4
   2  p = 1.
      q = 1.
      go to 4
   3  q = 0.
   4  ...
```

in which a branch to 1, 2 or 3 is taken depending on the value of p-q. The arithmetic if may be used as a two-way branch when two of the labels are identical:

```
      if (x-y) 1,2,1
```

C.2.2   Shared do loop termination

A do-loop may be terminated on a labelled statement other than an end do or continue. Such a statement must be an executable statement other than go to, return or an end statement of a subprogram, stop or an end statement of a main program, exit, cycle, arithmetic-if, or assigned go to statement. Nested do-loops may share the same labelled terminal statement, in which case all the usual rules for nested blocks hold, but a branch to the label must be from within the innermost loop. Thus we may write a matrix multiplication as

```
      a(1:n, 1:n) = 0.
      do 1 i = 1,n
        do 1 j = 1,n
          do 1 l = 1,n
   1          a(i,j) = a(i,j)+b(i,l)*c(l,j)
```

Execution of a cycle statement restarts the loop without execution of the terminal statement. This form of do-loop offers no additional functionality but considerable scope for unexpected mistakes.

C.2.3   Alternate return

When calling certain types of subroutines, it is possible that specific exceptional conditions will arise, which should cause a break in the normal control flow. It is possible to anticipate such conditions, and to code different flow paths following a subroutine call, depending on whether the called subroutine has terminated normally, or has detected an exceptional or abnormal condition. This is achieved using the alternate return facility which uses the argument list in the following manner. Let us suppose that a subroutine deal receives in an argument list the number of cards in a shuffled deck, the number of players and the number of cards to be dealt to each hand. In the interests of generality, it would be a reasonable precaution for the first executable statement of deal to be a check that there is at least one player and that there are, in fact, enough cards to satisfy each player's requirement. If there are no players or insufficient cards, it can signal this to the main program which should then take the appropriate action. This may be written in outline as

```
call deal(nshuff, nplay, nhand, cards, *2, *3)
call play
:
2  ........    ! Handle no-player case.
:
3  ........    ! Handle insufficient-cards case.
:
```

If the cards can be dealt, normal control is returned, and the call to play executed. If an exception occurs, control is passed to the statement labelled 2 or 3, at which point some action must be taken — to stop the game or shuffle more cards. The relevant statement label is defined by placing the statement label preceded by an asterisk as an actual argument in the argument list. It must be a label of an executable statement of the same scoping unit. Any number of such alternate returns may be specified, and they may appear in any position in the argument list. Since, however, they are normally used to handle exceptions, they are best placed at the end of the list.

In the called subroutine, the corresponding dummy arguments are asterisks and the alternate return is taken by executing a statement of the form

```
return intexpr
```

where *intexpr* is any scalar integer expression. The value of this expression at execution time defines an index to the alternate return to be taken, according to its position in the argument list. If *intexpr* evaluates to 2, the second alternate return will be taken. If *intexpr* evaluates to a value which is less than 1, or greater than the number of alternate returns in the argument list, a normal return will be taken. Thus, in deal, we may write simply

```
subroutine deal(nshuff, nplay, nhand, cards, *, *)
:
if (nplay.le.0) return 1
if (nshuff .lt. nplay*nhand) return 2
```

This feature is also available for subroutines defined by entry statements. It is not available for functions or elemental subroutines.

This feature is replaced by use of an integer argument holding a return code used in a computed go to following the call statement. A following case construct is now an even better alternative.

C.3   Obsolescent in Fortran 90, deleted in Fortran 95

The features of this section are obsolescent in Fortran 90 and are deleted from the Fortran 95 language entirely. They should thus be regarded, in a Fortran 95 context, as being absent from this book. Although it can be expected that compilers will continue to support these features for some period, their use should be completely avoided to ensure very long-term portability and to avoid unnecessary compiler warning messages. Their replacements are described in the relevant subsections.

C.3.1   Non-integer do indices

The do variable and the expressions that specify the limits and stride of a do-construct or an implied-do in an I/O statement may be of type default real or double precision real. We may therefore write a loop such as

        do 1 a = 1, 15.7, 2.1

in which the real variable a will assume the initial value of 1.0 (note the conversion), and will subsequently have the values 3.1, 5.2, etc. up to 15.7.

   There are, however, serious problems associated with do-loops with real indices, and in order to understand them we recall how the number of iterations of a do-loop is actually determined:

$$\texttt{max(int(}(\textit{expr2-expr1+expr3})\texttt{/}\textit{expr3}\texttt{),0)}$$

   A consequence of this formula is rather insidious, and results from the application of the int function. Consider the statement

        do 1 a = -0.3, -2.1, -0.3

which we would normally expect to result in seven iterations of the loop it controls. The number of iterations is obtained from the result of a computation whose intermediate value may not be 7.00000.. but 6.99999.., due to rounding errors. After applying the int function we then have the integer 6 as the number of iterations. Whether or not this rounding error will occur for a given loop on a given computer is difficult to foresee, and this is the reason for avoiding the use of real do-loop parameters. A similar problem can arise with a long loop: the repeated addition of the one to the other can lead to an unexpected loss of precision.

C.3.2   Assigned go to and assigned formats

Another form of branch statement is actually written in two parts, an assign statement and an assigned go to statement. The form is

        assign *sl1* to *intvar*
        :

```
assign sl2 to intvar
:
go to intvar [[,] (sl1,sl2,... )]
```

where *sl1, sl2* etc. are labels of statements in the same scoping unit, and *intvar* is a named scalar default integer variable (so cannot be an array element or structure component). When an assign statement is executed, *intvar* acquires a representation of a statement label. Different labels may be assigned in different parts of the scoping unit. When the assigned go to is executed, then depending on the value of *intvar*, the appropriate path is taken. If the optional statement label list in the go to statement is present, it must contain the label in *intvar*, and permits a check that *intvar* has acquired an expected value during program execution. A label may appear more than once in the list.

The assigned go to's main purpose is to control logic flow in a scoping unit having a number of paths which come together at one point at which some common code is executed, and from which a new branch is taken depending on the path taken before. This is shown in Figure C.3, where we see three paths joining before the go to, and three after. For this type of application, an internal subprogram (Section 5.6) is more appropriate.

Figure C.3

```
      :
      x = y+1.
      assign 4 to jump
      go to 3
  4   :
  1   x = y+2.
      assign 5 to jump
      go to 3
  5   :
  2   x = y+3.
      assign 6 to jump
  6   :
  3   z = x**2
      :
      go to jump (4,5,6)
      :
```

A default integer variable to which a statement label has been assigned in an assign statement may also be used to specify a format statement:

```
      assign 10 to key
      :
      print key, q
 10   format(f10.3)
```

The label must be that of a format statement in the same scoping unit as the I/O statement.

This use of the assign statement is replaced by character expressions to define format specifiers (Section 9.4). This feature is not part of Fortran 95.

C.3.3   Branching to an end if statement

It is permissible to branch to an end if statement from outside the construct that it terminates. A branch to the following statement is a replacement for this practice, which is not part of Fortran 95.

C.3.4   The pause statement

At certain points in the execution of a program it might be useful to pause, in order to allow some possible external intervention in the running conditions to be made, for instance for an operator to activate a peripheral device required by the program. This can be achieved by executing a pause statement which may also contain a default character constant, or a string of up to five digits, for example

```
pause 'Please mount the next disc pack'
pause 1234
```

Execution is resumed by some form of external command, for instance one given by an operator. The effect may be achieved with a read statement that awaits data. This feature is not part of Fortran 95.

C.3.5   H edit descriptor

The H (or h) edit descriptor provides an alternative character string edit descriptor: the output string is preceded by an nH edit descriptor, where n is the number of default characters in the following string (blanks being significant):

```
100   format(23HI must count characters)
```

The value n must be an integer literal constant without a kind parameter. If the Hollerith string occurs within a character constant delimited by apostrophes and contains an apostrophe, the apostrophe must be represented by two apostrophes, but counts as only one in the nH character count, as in the example

```
print '(7H Don''t, a)', caution
```

and similarly for quotes.

The H edit descriptor provides the same functionality as the character string edit descriptor but is prone to error as it is easy to miscount the number of characters in the string. The feature is not part of Fortran 95.

D. Pointer example

A recurring problem in computing is the need to manipulate a linked data structure. This might be a simple linked list like the one encountered in Section 2.13, but often a more general tree structure is required.

The example in this Appendix consists of a module that establishes and navigates one or more such trees, organized as a 'forest', and a short test program for it. Here, each node is identified by a name and has any number of children, any number of siblings, and (optionally) some associated real data. Each root node is regarded as having a common parent, the 'forest root' node, whose name is 'forest_root'. Thus, every node has a parent. The module provides facilities for adding a named node to a specified parent, for enquiring about all the nodes that are offspring of a specified node, for removing a tree or subtree, and for performing I/O operations on a tree or subtree.

The user-callable interfaces are:

start: must be called to initialize a forest.

add_node: stores the data provided at the node whose parent is specified and sets up pointers to the parent and siblings (if any).

remove_node: deallocates all the storage occupied by a complete tree or subtree.

retrieve: retrieves the data stored at a specified node and the names of the parent and children.

dump_tree: writes a complete tree or subtree.

restore_tree: reads a complete tree or subtree.

finish: deallocates all the storage occupied by all the trees of the forest.

The source code can be obtained by anonymous ftp to *ftp.numerical.rl.ac.uk*. When prompted for a userid, reply with

    anonymous

and give your name as password. The directory is */pub/MandR* and the file name is *pointer.f90*.

```
module directory
!
! Strong typing imposed
   implicit none
!
! Only subroutine interfaces, the length of the character
! component, and the I/O unit number are public
   public  :: start, add_node, remove_node, retrieve,              &
              dump_tree, restore_tree, finish
   private :: find, remove
!
! Module constants
   character(len=*), private, parameter :: eot = "End-of-Tree....."
   integer, parameter, public :: unit = 4,  & ! I/O unit number
                                 max_char = 16 ! length of character
                                               ! component
!
! Define the basic tree type
   type, private :: node
      character(len=max_char)      :: name        ! name of node
      real, pointer, dimension(:) :: y            ! stored real data
      type(node), pointer         :: parent       ! parent node
      type(node), pointer         :: sibling      ! next sibling node
      type(node), pointer         :: child        ! first child node
   end type node

!
! Module variables
   type(node), pointer, private   :: current     ! current node
   type(node), pointer, private   :: forest_root ! the root of the forest
   integer,private                :: max_data    ! max size of data array
   character(len=max_char), private, allocatable, target, dimension(:)  &
                                                 :: names
                                  ! for returning list of names
! The module procedures

contains

   subroutine start ()
! Initialize the tree.
      allocate (forest_root)
      current => forest_root
      forest_root%name = "forest_root"
      nullify(forest_root%parent, forest_root%sibling, forest_root%child)
      allocate(forest_root%y(0))
      max_data = 0
      allocate (names(0))
   end subroutine start
```

```
  subroutine find(name)
      character(len=*), intent(in) :: name
! Make the module variable current point to the node with given name,
! or be null if the name is not there.
      type(node), pointer    :: root
! For efficiency, we search the tree rooted at current, and if this
! fails try its parent and so on until the forest root is reached.
      if (associated(current)) then
          root => current
          nullify (current)
      else
          root => forest_root
      end if
      do
          call look(root)
          if (associated(current)) then
              return
          end if
          root => root%parent
          if (.not.associated(root)) then
              exit
          end if
      end do
  contains
      recursive subroutine look(root)
          type(node), pointer    :: root
! (type(node), intent(in), target :: root   is standard conforming too)
! Look for name in the tree rooted at root. If found, make the
! module variable current point to the node
          type(node), pointer    :: child
!
          if (root%name == name) then
              current => root
          else
              child => root%child
              do
                  if (.not.associated(child)) then
                    exit
                  end if
                  call look(child)
                  if (associated(current)) then
                    return
                  end if
                  child => child%sibling
              end do
          end if
      end subroutine look
  end subroutine find
```

```
      subroutine add_node(name, name_of_parent, data)
         character(len=*), intent(in)              :: name, name_of_parent
! For a root, name_of_parent = ""
         real, intent(in), optional, dimension(:) :: data
! Allocate a new tree node of type node, store the given name and
! data there, set pointers to the parent and to its next sibling
! (if any). If the parent is not found, the new node is treated as
! a root. It is assumed that the node is not already present in the
! forest.
         type(node), pointer :: new_node
!
         allocate (new_node)
         new_node%name = name
         if (present(data)) then
            allocate(new_node%y(size(data)))
            new_node%y = data
            max_data = max(max_data, size(data))
         else
            allocate(new_node%y(0))
         end if
!
! If name of parent is not null, search for it.
! If not found, print message.
         if (name_of_parent == "") then
            current => forest_root
         else
            call find (name_of_parent)
            if (.not.associated(current)) then
               print *, "no parent ", name_of_parent, " found for ", name
               current => forest_root
            end if
         end if
         new_node%parent => current
         new_node%sibling => current%child
         current%child => new_node
         nullify(new_node%child)
      end subroutine add_node

      subroutine remove_node(name)
         character(len=*), intent(in) :: name
! Remove node and the subtree rooted on it (if any),
! deallocating associated pointer targets.
         type(node), pointer :: parent, child, sibling
!
         call find (name)
         if (associated(current)) then
            parent => current%parent
            child => parent%child
            if (.not.associated(child, current)) then
```

```
! Make it the first child, looping through the siblings to find it
! and resetting the links
            parent%child => current
            sibling => child
            do
               if (associated (sibling%sibling, current)) then
                 exit
               end if
               sibling => sibling%sibling
            end do
            sibling%sibling => current%sibling
            current%sibling => child
         end if
         call remove(current)
      end if
   end subroutine remove_node

   recursive subroutine remove (old_node)
! Remove a first child node and the subtree rooted on it (if any),
! deallocating associated pointer targets.
      type(node), pointer :: old_node
      type(node), pointer :: child, sibling
!
      child => old_node%child
      do
         if (.not.associated(child)) then
            exit
         end if
         sibling => child%sibling
         call remove(child)
         child => sibling
      end do
! remove leaf node
      if (associated(old_node%parent)) then
         old_node%parent%child => old_node%sibling
      end if
      deallocate (old_node%y)
      deallocate (old_node)
   end subroutine remove

   subroutine retrieve(name, data, parent, children)
      character(len=*), intent(in)           :: name
      real, pointer, dimension(:)            :: data
      character(len=*), intent(out)          :: parent
      character(len=*), pointer, dimension(:) :: children
! Returns a pointer to the data at the node, the name of the
! parent, and a pointer to the names of the children.
      integer :: counter, i
      type(node), pointer :: child
```

```
!
      call find (name)
      if (associated(current)) then
         data => current%y
         parent = current%parent%name
! Count the number of children
         counter = 0
         child => current%child
         do
            if (.not.associated(child)) then
              exit
            end if
            counter = counter + 1
            child => child%sibling
         end do
         deallocate (names)
         allocate (names(counter))
! and store their names
         children => names
         child => current%child
         do i = 1, counter
            children(i) = child%name
            child => child%sibling
         end do
      else
         nullify(data)
         parent = ""
         nullify(children)
      end if
   end subroutine retrieve

   subroutine dump_tree(root)
      character(len=*), intent(in) :: root
! Write out a complete tree followed by an end-of-tree record
! unformatted on the file unit.
      call find (root)
      if (associated(current)) then
         call tree_out(current)
      end if
      write(unit = unit) eot, 0, eot
   contains
      recursive subroutine tree_out (root)
! Traverse a complete tree or subtree, writing out its contents
         type(node), intent(in) :: root      ! root node of tree
! Local variable
         type(node), pointer    :: child
!
         write(unit = unit) root%name, size(root%y), root%y, &
                            root%parent%name
```

```
                child => root%child
                do
                    if (.not.associated(child)) then
                      exit
                    end if
                    call tree_out (child)
                    child => child%sibling
                end do
            end subroutine tree_out
        end subroutine dump_tree

    subroutine restore_tree ()
! Reads a subtree unformatted from the file unit.
        character(len=max_char)          :: name
        integer :: length_y
        real, allocatable, dimension(:) :: y
        character(len=max_char)          :: name_of_parent
!
        allocate(y(max_data))
        do
            read (unit= unit) name, length_y, y(:length_y), name_of_parent
            if (name == eot) then
              exit
            end if
            call add_node( name, name_of_parent, y(:length_y) )
        end do
        deallocate(y)
    end subroutine restore_tree

    subroutine finish ()
! Deallocate all allocated targets.
        call remove (forest_root)
        deallocate(names)
    end subroutine finish

end module directory

module tree_print

    use  directory
    implicit none
    private
    public :: print_tree

contains

    recursive subroutine print_tree(name)
! To print the data contained in a subtree
        character(len=*), intent(in)                          :: name
```

```
      integer                                      :: i
      real, pointer, dimension(:)                  :: data
      character(len=max_char)                      :: parent, self
      character(len=max_char), pointer, dimension(:)      :: children
      character(len=max_char), allocatable, dimension(:) :: siblings
!
      call retrieve(name, data, parent, children)
      if (.not.associated(data)) then
        return
      end if
      self = name
      write(unit=*,fmt=*) self, data
      write(unit=*,fmt=*) "    parent:    ", parent
      if (size(children) > 0 ) then
         write(unit=*,fmt=*)  "   children: ", children
      end if
      allocate(siblings(size(children)))
      siblings = children
      do i = 1, size(children)
         call print_tree(siblings(i))
      end do
      deallocate(siblings)
   end subroutine print_tree
end module tree_print

program test
   use directory
   use tree_print
   implicit none
!
! Initialize a tree
   call start ()
! Fill it with some data
   call add_node("ernest","",(/1.0,2.0/))
   call add_node("helen","ernest",(/3.0,4.0,5.0/))
   call add_node("douglas","ernest",(/6.0,7.0/))
   call add_node("john","helen",(/8.0/))
   call add_node("betty","helen",(/9.0,10.0/))
   call add_node("nigel","betty",(/11.0/))
   call add_node("peter","betty",(/12.0/))
   call add_node("ruth","betty")
! Manipulate subtrees
   open(unit=unit, form="unformatted", status="scratch",    &
        action="readwrite", position="rewind")
   call dump_tree("betty")
   call remove_node("betty")
   write(unit=*,fmt=*)
   call print_tree("ernest")
   rewind (unit=unit)
```

```
    call restore_tree ()
    rewind (unit=unit)
    write(unit=*,fmt=*)
    call print_tree("ernest")
    call dump_tree("john")
    call remove_node("john")
    write(unit=*,fmt=*)
    call print_tree("ernest")
    rewind (unit=unit)
    call restore_tree ()
    write(unit=*,fmt=*)
    call print_tree("ernest")
! Return storage
    call finish ()

end program test
```

E. Fortran terms

The following is a list of the principal technical terms used in this book and their definitions. To facilitate reference to the standard, we have kept closely to the meanings used there. Where the definition uses a term that is itself defined in this glossary, the first occurrence of the term is printed in italics. Some terms used in Fortran 77 have a different meaning here and we draw the reader's attention to each such term by marking it with a bold asterisk *****. We make no reference to obsolescent or deleted features (Appendix C) in this Appendix.

Actual argument An *expression*, a *variable*, or a *procedure* that is specified in a procedure *reference*.

Allocatable array A *named array* having the allocatable *attribute*. Only when it has space allocated for it does it have a *shape* and may it be *referenced* or *defined*.

Argument An *actual argument* or a *dummy argument*.

Argument association The relationship between an *actual argument* and a *dummy argument* during the execution of a *procedure reference*.

Argument keyword A *dummy argument name*. It may used in a *procedure reference* ahead of the equals symbol provided the procedure has an *explicit interface*.

Array * A set of *scalar data*, all of the same *type* and *type parameters*, whose individual elements are arranged in a rectangular pattern. It may be a *named* array, an *array section*, a *structure component*, a *function* value, or an *expression*. Its *rank* is at least one. [In Fortran 77, arrays were always named and never constants.]

Array element One of the *scalar data* that make up an *array* that is either *named* or is a *structure component*.

Array pointer A *pointer* that is an *array*.

Array section A *subobject* whose *designator* contains a *subscript triplet*, a *vector subscript*, or an *array component selector* that is followed by one or more further component selectors.

Array-valued Having the property of being an *array*.

Assignment statement A *statement* of the form '*variable = expression*'.

Assignment token The *lexical token* = used in an *assignment statement*.

Association *Name association, pointer association,* or *storage association*.

Assumed-size array A *dummy array* whose *size* is assumed from the associated *actual argument*. Its last upper bound is specified by an asterisk.

Attribute A property of a *data object* that may be specified in a *type declaration statement*.

Belong If an exit or a cycle *statement* contains a *construct name*, the statement **belongs** to the do construct using that name. Otherwise, it **belongs** to the innermost do construct in which it appears.

Block A sequence of *executable constructs* embedded in another executable construct, bounded by *statements* that are particular to the construct, and treated as an integral unit.

Block data program unit A *program unit* that provides initial values for *data objects* in *named common blocks*.

Bounds For a *named array*, the limits within which the values of the *subscripts* of its *array elements* must lie.

Character A letter, digit, or other symbol.

Character storage unit The unit of storage for holding a *scalar* of *type* default character and character length one that is not a *pointer*.

Character string A sequence of *characters* numbered from left to right 1, 2, 3,...

Characteristics

> i) Of a *procedure*, its classification as a *function* or *subroutine*, the characteristics of its *dummy arguments*, and the characteristics of its *function result* if it is a function.

> ii) Of a *dummy argument*, whether it is a *data object*, is a *procedure*, or has the optional *attribute*.

> iii) Of a *data object*, its *type, type parameters, shape*, the exact dependence of an array bound or the character length on other entities, *intent*, whether it is optional, whether it is a *pointer* or a *target*, and whether the *shape, size*, or *character length* is assumed.

> iv) Of a *dummy procedure*, whether the interface is explicit, its characteristics as a procedure if the interface is explicit, and whether it is optional.

v) Of a *function result*, its type, type parameters, whether it is a pointer, rank if it is a pointer, shape if it is not a pointer, the exact dependence of an array bound or the character length on other entities, and whether the character length is assumed.

Collating sequence An ordering of all the different *characters* of a particular *kind type parameter*.

Common block A block of physical storage that may be accessed by any of the *scoping units* in an *executable program*.

Component A constituent of a *derived type*.

Conformable Two *arrays* are said to be **conformable** if they have the same *shape*. A *scalar* is **conformable** with any array.

Conformance An *executable program* conforms to the standard if it uses only those forms and relationships described therein and if the executable program has an interpretation according to the standard. A *program unit* conforms to the standard if it can be included in an executable program in a manner that allows the executable program to be standard conforming. A *processor* conforms to the standard if it executes standard-conforming programs in a manner that fulfills the interpretations prescribed in the standard.

Connected

i) For an *external unit*, the property of referring to an *external file*.

ii) For an *external file*, the property of having an *external unit* that refers to it.

Constant * A *data object* whose value must not change during execution of an *executable program*. It may be a *named constant* or a *literal constant*.

Constant expression An *expression* satisfying rules that ensure that its value does not vary during program execution.

Construct A sequence of *statements* starting with a select case, do, if, or where statement and ending with the corresponding terminal statement.

Data Plural of *datum*.

Data entity An *entity* that has or may have a data value. It may be a *constant*, a *variable*, an *expression*, or a *function result*.

Data object A *datum* of *intrinsic* or *derived type* or an *array* of such *data*. It may be a *literal constant*, a *named* data object, a *target* of a *pointer*, or it may be a *subobject*.

Data type A *named* category of *data* that is characterized by a set of values, together with a way to denote these values and a collection of *operations* that interpret and manipulate the values. For an *intrinsic* data type, the set of data values depends on the values of the *type parameters*.

Datum A single quantity that may have any of the set of values specified for its *data type*.

Definable A *variable* is **definable** if its value may be changed by the appearance of its *name* or *designator* on the left of an *assignment statement*. A *allocatable array* that has not been allocated is an example of a *data object* that is not definable. An example of a *subobject* that is not definable is c(i) when c is an *array* that is a *constant* and i is an integer variable.

Defined For a *data object*, the property of having or being given a valid value.

Defined assignment statement An *assignment statement* that is not an *intrinsic* assignment statement and is defined by a *subroutine subprogram* and an *interface block*.

Defined operation An *operation* that is not an *intrinsic* operation and is defined by a *function subprogram* and an *interface block*.

Deleted feature A feature in Fortran 77 that has been deleted from Fortran 95. No features in Fortran 77 have been deleted from Fortran 90. Note that a feature designated as an *obsolescent feature* may become a deleted feature in a future revision.

Derived type A *type* whose *data* have *components* each of which is either of *intrinsic* type or of another derived type.

Designator See *subobject designator*.

Disassociated A *pointer* is **disassociated** following execution of a deallocate or nullify *statement*.

Dummy argument An *entity* whose *name* appears in the parenthesized list following the *procedure* name in a function *statement*, a subroutine statement, an entry statement, or a *statement function* statement.

Dummy array A *dummy argument* that is an *array*.

Dummy pointer A *dummy argument* that is a *pointer*.

Dummy procedure A *dummy argument* that is specified or *referenced* as a *procedure*.

Elemental An adjective applied to an *intrinsic operation, procedure*, or *assignment statement* that is applied independently to the elements of an *array* or corresponding elements of a set of *conformable* arrays and *scalars*.

Entity The term used for any of the following: a *program unit*, a *procedure*, an *operator*, an *interface block*, a *common block*, an *external unit*, a *statement function*, a *type*, a *data entity*, a *statement label*, a *construct*, or a namelist group.

Executable construct A case, do, if, or where *construct*.

Executable program A set of *program units* that includes exactly one *main program*.

Executable statement An instruction to perform or control one or more computational actions.

Explicit interface For a *procedure referenced* in a *scoping unit*, the property of being an *internal procedure*, a *module procedure*, an *intrinsic procedure*, an *external procedure* that has an *interface block* or is defined by the scoping unit and is recursive, or a *dummy procedure* that has an interface block.

Explicit-shape array A *named array* that is declared with *explicit bounds*.

Expression A sequence of *operands*, *operators*, and parentheses. It may be a *variable*, a *constant*, a *function reference*, or may represent a computation.

Extent The size of one dimension of an *array*.

External file A sequence of *records* that exists in a medium external to the *executable program*.

External procedure A *procedure* that is defined by an *external subprogram* or by a means other than Fortran.

External subprogram * A *subprogram* that is not contained in a *main program*, *module*, or another subprogram. [In Fortran 77, a *block data program unit* is called a subprogram.]

External unit A mechanism that is used to refer to an *external file*. It is identified by a nonnegative integer.

File An *internal file* or an *external file*.

Function A *procedure* that is invoked in an *expression*.

Function result The *data entity* that returns the value of a *function*.

Function subprogram A sequence of *statements* beginning with a function statement that is not in an *interface block* and ending with the corresponding end statement.

Generic identifier A *name*, *operator*, or *assignment token* specified in an interface *statement* to provide an alternative means of invoking any of the *procedures* in the *interface block*.

Global entity An *entity* identified by a *lexical token* whose *scope* is an *executable program*. It may be a *program unit*, a *common block*, or an *external procedure*.

Host A *main program* or *subprogram* that contains an *internal subprogram* is called the **host** of the internal subprogram. A *module* that contains a *module subprogram* is called the **host** of the module subprogram.

Host association The process by which a *subprogram* or a *derived type* definition accesses *entities* of its *host*.

Implicit interface A *procedure referenced* in a *scoping unit* is said to have an **implicit interface** if the procedure does not have an *explicit interface* there.

Inquiry function An *intrinsic function* whose result depends on properties of the principal *argument* other than the value of the argument.

Instance of a subprogram The copy of a *subprogram* that is created when a *procedure* defined by the subprogram is *invoked*.

Intent Of a *dummy argument* that is a neither a *procedure* nor a *pointer*, whether it is intended to transfer data into the procedure, out of the procedure, or both.

Interface block A sequence of *statements* beginning with an `interface` statement and ending with the corresponding end `interface` statement.

Interface body A sequence of *statements* in an *interface block* beginning with a `function` or `subroutine` statement and ending with the corresponding end statement.

Interface of a procedure See *procedure interface*.

Internal file A character *variable* that is used to transfer and convert *data* from internal storage to internal storage.

Internal procedure A *procedure* that is defined by an *internal subprogram*.

Internal subprogram A *subprogram* contained in a *main program* or another subprogram.

Intrinsic An adjective applied to *types, operations, assignment statements*, and *procedures* that are defined in the standard and may be used in any *scoping unit* without further definition or specification.

Invoke

   i) To call a *subroutine* by a `call` *statement* or by a *defined assignment statement*.

ii) To call a *function* by a *reference* to it by *name* or *operator* during the evaluation of an *expression*.

Keyword *Statement keyword* or *argument keyword*.

Kind type parameter A parameter whose values label the available kinds of an *intrinsic type*.

Label See *statement label*.

Length of a character string The number of *characters* in the *character string*.

Lexical token A sequence of one or more characters with an indivisible interpretation.

Line A source-form *record* containing from 0 to 132 *characters*.

Literal constant A *constant* without a *name*. [In Fortran 77, this was called a constant.]

Local entity An *entity* identified by a *lexical token* whose *scope* is a *scoping unit*.

Main program A *program unit* that is not a *module, external subprogram*, or *block data program unit*.

Many-one array section An *array section* with a *vector subscript* having two or more elements with the same value.

Module A *program unit* that contains or accesses definitions to be accessed by other program units.

Module procedure A *procedure* that is defined by a *module subprogram*.

Module subprogram A *subprogram* that is contained in a *module* but is not an *internal subprogram*.

Name * A *lexical token* consisting of a letter followed by up to 30 alphanumeric characters (letters, digits, and underscores). [In Fortran 77, this was called a symbolic name.]

Name association *Argument association, use association*, or *host association*.

Named Having a *name*.

Named constant * A *constant* that has a *name*. [In Fortran 77, this was called a symbolic constant.]

Numeric storage unit The unit of storage for holding a *scalar* of *type* default real, default integer, or default logical that is not a *pointer*.

Numeric type Integer, real, or complex *type*.

Object *Data object*.

Obsolescent feature A feature that is considered to be redundant but that is still in frequent use. It may be deleted in a future revision of the standard.

Operand An *expression* that precedes or succeeds an *operator*.

Operation A computation involving one or two *operands*.

Operator A *lexical token* that specifies an *operation*.

Pointer A *data object* that has the `pointer` *attribute*. It may not be *referenced* or *defined* unless it is *pointer associated* with a *target*. If it is an *array*, it does not have a *shape* unless it is pointer associated.

Pointer assignment The *pointer association* of a *pointer* with a *target* by the execution of a *pointer assignment statement* or the execution of an *assignment statement* for a *data object* of *derived type* having the pointer as a *subobject*.

Pointer assignment statement A *statement* of the form '*pointer => target*'.

Pointer associated The relationship between a *pointer* and a *target* following a *pointer assignment* or a valid execution of an `allocate` *statement*.

Pointer association The process by which a *pointer* becomes *pointer associated* with a *target*.

Present A *dummy argument* or an entity that is host associated with a dummy argument is not **present** if the dummy argument is not associated with an actual argument or is associated with an actual argument that is not present. Otherwise, it is **present**.

Procedure A computation that may be *invoked* during program execution. It may be a *function* or a *subroutine*. It may be an *intrinsic procedure*, an *internal procedure*, an *external procedure*, a *module procedure*, a *dummy procedure*, or a *statement function*. A *subprogram* may define more than one procedure if it contains `entry` *statements*.

Procedure interface The *characteristics* of a *procedure*, the *name* of the procedure, the name of each *dummy argument*, and the *generic identifiers* (if any) by which it may be *referenced*.

Processor The combination of a computing system and the mechanism by which *executable programs* are transformed for use on that computing system.

Program See *executable program* and *main program*.

Program unit The fundamental component of an *executable program*. A sequence of *statements* and comment lines. It may be a *main program*, a *module*, an *external subprogram*, or a *block data program unit*.

Rank The number of dimensions of an *array*. Zero for a *scalar*.

Record A sequence of values that is treated as a whole within a *file* .

Reference The appearance of a *data object name* or *subobject designator* in a context requiring the value at that point during execution, or the appearance of a *procedure* name, its *operator* symbol, or a *defined assignment statement* in a context requiring execution of the procedure at that point. Note that neither the act of defining a *variable* nor the appearance of the name of a procedure as an *actual argument* is regarded as a reference.

Scalar

    i) A single *datum* that is not an *array*.

    ii) Not having the property of being an *array*.

Scope That part of an *executable program* within which a *lexical token* has a single interpretation. It may be an *executable program*, a *scoping unit*, a single *statement*, or a part of a statement.

Scoping unit One of the following:

    i) A *derived-type* definition,

    ii) An *interface body*, excluding any derived-type definitions and interface bodies contained within it, or

    iii) A *program unit* or *subprogram*, excluding derived-type definitions, interface bodies, and subprograms contained within it.

Section subscript A *subscript, subscript triplet*, or *vector subscript* in an *array section selector*.

Selector A syntactic mechanism for designating

    i) Part of a *data object*. It may designate a *substring*, an *array element*, an *array section*, or a *structure component*.

    ii) The set of values for which a case *block* is executed.

Shape For an *array*, the *rank* and *extents*. The shape may be represented by the rank-one array whose elements are the extents in each dimension.

Size For an *array*, the total number of elements.

Standard module A *module* standardized as a separate collateral standard.

Statement A sequence of *lexical tokens*. It usually consists of a single line, but the ampersand symbol may be used to continue a statement from one line to another and the semicolon symbol may be used to separate statements within a line.

Statement entity An *entity* identified by a *lexical token* whose *scope* is a single *statement* or part of a statement.

Statement function A *procedure* specified by a single *statement* that is similar in form to an *assignment statement*.

Statement keyword A word that is part of the syntax of a *statement* and that may be used to identify the statement.

Statement label A *lexical token* consisting of up to five digits that precedes a *statement* and may be used to refer to the statement.

Storage association The relationship between two *storage sequences* if a storage unit of one is the same as a storage unit of the other.

Storage sequence A sequence of contiguous *storage units*.

Storage unit A *character storage unit*, a *numeric storage unit*, or an *unspecified storage unit*.

Stride The increment specified in a *subscript triplet*.

Structure A *scalar data object* of *derived type*.

Structure component The part of an *object* of *derived-type* corresponding to a *component* of its type.

Subobject Of a *named data object* or *target* of a *pointer*, a portion that may be *referenced* or *defined* independently of other portions. It may be an *array element*, an *array section*, a *structure component*, or a *substring*.

Subobject designator A *name*, followed by one or more *component selectors*, *array section* selectors, *array element* selectors, and *substring* selectors.

Subprogram * A *function subprogram* or a *subroutine subprogram*. [In Fortran 77, a *block data program unit* was called a subprogram.]

Subroutine A *procedure* that is *invoked* by a `call` *statement* or by a *defined assignment statement*.

Subroutine subprogram A sequence of *statements* from a `subroutine` statement that is not in an *interface block* to the corresponding end statement.

Subscript * One of the list of *scalar* integer *expressions* in an *array element selector*. [In Fortran 77, the whole list was called the subscript.]

Subscript triplet An item in the list of an *array section selector* that contains a colon and specifies a regular sequence of integer values.

Substring A contiguous portion of a *scalar character string*. Note that an *array section* can include a *substring selector*; the result is called an array section and not a substring.

Target A *named data object* specified in a *type declaration statement* containing the `target` *attribute*, a data object created by an `allocate` statement for a *pointer*, or a *subobject* of such an object.

Transformational function An *intrinsic function* that is neither an *elemental* function nor an *inquiry function*. It usually has *array arguments* and an array result whose elements have values that depend on the values of many of the elements of the arguments.

Type *Data type*.

Type declaration statement An `integer`, `real`, `double precision`, `complex`, `character`, `logical`, or `type(`*type-name*`)` *statement*.

Type parameter A parameter of an *intrinsic data type*.

Type parameter values The values of the *type parameters* of a *data entity* of an *intrinsic data type*.

Ultimate component For a *derived type* or a *structure*, a *component* that is of *intrinsic type*, has the *allocatable* or *pointer attribute*, or is an *ultimate component* of a component that is of derived type and does not have the allocatable or pointer attribute.

Undefined For a *data object*, the property of not having a determinate value.

Unspecified storage unit A unit of storage for holding a *pointer* or a *scalar object* of non-default *intrinsic type* that is not a pointer.

Use association The relationship specified by a `use` *statement* between two *names* in different *scoping units*.

Variable * A *data object* whose value can be *defined* and redefined during the execution of an *executable program*. It may be a *named* data object, an *array element*, an *array section*, a *structure component*, or a *substring*. [In Fortran 77, a variable was always *scalar* and named.]

Vector subscript A *section subscript* that is an integer *expression* of *rank* one.

F. Solutions to exercises

Note: A few exercises have been left to the reader.

Chapter 2

1.

B is less than M	true
8 is less than 2	false
* is greater than T	not determined
$ is less than /	not determined
blank is greater than A	false
blank is less than 6	true

2.

```
   x = y                      correct
 3 a = b+c ! add              correct, with commentary
   word = 'string'            correct
   a = 1.0; b = 2.0           correct
   a = 15. ! initialize a; b = 22. ! and b
                              incorrect (embedded commentary)
   song = "Life is just&      correct, initial line
      & a bowl of cherries"   correct, continuation
   chide = 'Waste not,        incorrect, trailing & missing
      want not!'              incorrect, leading & missing
 0 c(3:4) = 'up"              incorrect (invalid statement
                                 label; invalid form of
                                 character constant)
```

3.

-43	integer	'word'	character
4.39	real	1.9-4	not legal
0.0001e+20	real	'stuff & nonsense'	character
4 9	not legal	(0.,1.)	complex
(1.e3,2)	complex	'I can''t'	character
'(4.3e9, 6.2)'	character	.true._1	legal logical
			provided kind=1 available
e5	not legal	'shouldn' 't'	not legal

```
1_2              legal integer    "O.K."           character
  provided kind=2 available
z10              not legal        z'10'            hexadecimal
```

4.

```
name       legal        name32       legal
quotient   legal        123          not legal
a182c3     legal        no-go        not legal
stop!      not legal    burn_        legal
no_go      legal        long__name   legal
```

5.

```
real, dimension(11)      :: a    a(1), a(10), a(11), a(11)
real, dimension(0:11)    :: b    b(0), b(9), b(10), b(11)
real, dimension(-11:0)   :: c    c(-11), c(-2), c(-1), c(0)
real, dimension(10,10)   :: d    d(1,1), d(10,1), d(1,2), d(10,10)
real, dimension(5,9)     :: e    e(1,1), e(5,2), e(1,3), e(5,9)
real, dimension(5,0:1,4) :: f    f(1,0,1), f(5,1,1), f(1,0,2),
                                           f(5,1,4)
```

Array constructor: (/ (i, i = 1,11) /)

6.

```
c(2,3)      legal        c(4:3)(2,1)   not legal
c(6,2)      not legal    c(5,3)(9:9)   legal
c(0,3)      legal        c(2,1)(4:8)   legal
c(4,3)(:)   legal        c(3,2)(0:9)   not legal
c(5)(2:3)   not legal    c(5:6)        not legal
c(5,3)(9)   not legal    c(,)          not legal
```

7.

a) ```
    type vehicle_registration
        character(len=3) :: letters
        integer   :: digits
    end type vehicle_registration
    ```

b)  ```
    type circle
        real             ::   radius
        real, dimension(2) :: centre
    end type circle
    ```

c) ```
    type book
        character(len=20)   :: title
        character(len=20), dimension(2) :: author
        integer   :: no_of_pages
    end type book
    ```
    ```

Derived type constants:

```
vehicle_registration('PQR', 123)
circle(15.1, (/ 0., 0. /))
book("Pilgrim's Progress", (/ 'John  ', 'Bunyan' /), 250 )
```

8.

t	array	t(4)%vertex(1)	scalar
t(10)	scalar	t(5:6)	array
t(1)%vertex	array	t(5:5)	array (size 1)

9.

a)
```
integer, parameter ::  twenty = selected_int_kind(20)
integer (kind = twenty) :: counter
```
b)
```
integer, parameter :: high = selected_real_kind(12,100)
real(kind = high)  :: big
```
c)
```
character(kind=2)  :: sign
```

Chapter 3

1.

a+b	valid	-c	valid
a+-c	invalid	d+(-f)	valid
(a+c)**(p+q)	valid	(a+c)(p+q)	invalid
-(x+y)**i	valid	4.((a-d)-(a+4.*x)+1)	invalid

2.

```
c+(4.*f)
((4.*g)-a)+(d/2.)
a**(e**(c**d))
((a*e)-((c**d)/a))+e
(i .and. j) .or. k
((.not. l) .or. ((.not. i) .and. m)) .neqv. n
((b(3).and.b(1)).or.b(6)).or.(.not.b(2))
```

3.

```
3+4/2   = 5      6/4/2   = 0
3.*4**2 = 48.    3.**3/2 = 13.5
-1.**2  = -1.    (-1.)**3 = -1.
```

4.

```
ABCDEFGH
ABCD0123
ABCDEFGu          u = unchanged
ABCDbbuu          b = blank
```

5.

```
.not.b(1).and.b(2)  valid    .or.b(1)                    invalid
b(1).or..not.b(4)   valid    b(2)(.and.b(3).or.b(4))     invalid
```

6.

```
d .le. c        valid        p .lt. t > 0       invalid
x-1 /= y        valid        x+y < 3 .or. > 4.  invalid
d.lt.c.and.3.0  invalid      q.eq.r .and. s>t   valid
```

7.

a) 4*1
b) b*h/2.
c) 4./3.*pi*r**3

             (assuming pi has value π)

8.

```
integer :: n, one, five, ten, twenty_five
twenty_five = (100-n)/25
ten         = (100-n-25*twenty_five)/10
five        = (100-n-25*twenty_five-10*ten)/5
one         = 100-n-25*twenty_five-10*ten-5*five
```

9.

```
a = b + c       valid
c = b + 1.0     valid
d = b + 1       invalid
r = b + c       valid
a = r + 2       valid
```

10.

```
a = b          valid        c = a(:,2) + b(5,:5)    valid
a = c+1.0      invalid      c = a(2,:) + b(:,5)     invalid
a(:,3) = c     valid        b(2:,3) = c + b(:5,3)   invalid
```

Chapter 4

1.

```
integer                    :: i, j, k, temp
integer, dimension(100) :: reverse
do i = 1,100
   reverse(i) = i
end do
read *, i, j
do k= i, i+(j-i-1)/2
   temp = reverse(k)
   reverse(k) = reverse(j-k+i)
```

```
          reverse(j-k+i) = temp
       end do
       end
```

Note: A simpler method for performing this operation will become apparent in Section 6.13.

2.

```
       integer :: limit, f1, f2, f3
       read *, limit
       f1 = 1
       if (limit.ge.1) print *, f1
       f2 = 1
       if (limit.ge.2) print *, f2
       do i = 3, limit
          f3 = f1+f2
          print *, f3
          f1 = f2
          f2 = f3
       end do
       end
```

6.

```
       real x
       do
          read *, x
          if (x.eq.-1.) then
             print *, 'input value -1. invalid'
          else
             print *, x/(1.+x)
             exit
          end if
       end do
       end
```

7.

```
    type(entry), pointer :: first, current, previous
    current => first
    if (current%index == 10) then
       first => first%next
    else
       do
          previous => current
          current => current%next
          if (current%index == 10) exit
       end do
       previous%next => current%next
    end if
```

Chapter 5

1.

```fortran
subroutine calculate(x, n, mean, variance, ok)
   integer, intent(in)         :: n
   real, dimension(n), intent(in) :: x
   real, intent(out)           :: mean, variance
   logical :: ok
   integer :: i
   mean = 0.
   variance = 0.
   ok = n > 1
   if (ok) then
      do i = 1, n
         mean = mean + x(i)
      end do
      mean = mean/n
      do i = 1, n
         variance = variance + (x(i) - mean)**2
      end do
      variance = variance/(n-1)
   end if
end subroutine calculate
```

Note: A simpler method will become apparent in Chapter 8. **2.**

```fortran
subroutine matrix_mult(a, b, c, i, j, k)
   integer, intent(in)            :: i, j, k, l, m, n
   real, dimension(i,j), intent(in)  :: a
   real, dimension(j,k), intent(in)  :: b
   real, dimension(i,k), intent(out) :: c
   c(1:i, 1:k) = 0.
   do n = 1, k
      do l = 1, j
         do m = 1, i
            c(m, n) = c(m, n) + a(m,l)*b(l, n)
         end do
      end do
   end do
end subroutine matrix_mult
```

3.

```fortran
subroutine shuffle(cards)
   integer, dimension(52), intent(in) :: cards
   integer                            :: left, choice, i, temp
   real r
   cards = (/ (i, i=1,52) /)      ! Initialize deck.
   do left = 52,1,-1              ! Loop over number of cards left.
      call random_number(r)       ! Draw a card
```

```
        choice = r*left + 1        !    from remaining possibilities
        temp = cards(left)         !    and swap with last
        cards(left) = cards(choice)!    one left.
        cards(choice) = temp
    end do
end subroutine shuffle
```

4.

```
character function earliest(string)
    character(len=*), intent(in) :: string
    integer j, length
    length = len(string)
    if (length <= 0) then
        earliest = ''
    else
        earliest = string(1:1)
        do j = 2, length
            if (string(j:j) < earliest) earliest = string(j:j)
        end do
    end if
end function earliest
```

5.

```
subroutine sample
    real :: r, l, v, pi
    pi = acos(-1.)
    :
    r = 3.
    l = 4.
    v = volume(r, l)
    :
contains
    function volume(radius, length)
        real, intent(in) :: radius, length
        real             :: volume
        volume = pi*radius**2*length
    end function volume
end subroutine sample
```

7.

```
module string_type
    type string
        integer :: length
        character(len=80)   :: string_data
    end type string
    interface assignment(=)
        module procedure c_to_s_assign, s_to_c_assign
    end interface (=)
```

```
interface len
   module procedure string_len
end interface
interface operator(//)
   module procedure string_concat
end interface (//)
contains
subroutine c_to_s_assign(s, c)
   type (string), intent(out)   :: s
   character(len=*), intent(in) :: c
   s%string_data = c
   s%length = len(c)
   if (s%length > 80) s%length = 80
end subroutine c_to_s_assign
subroutine s_to_c_assign(c, s)
   type (string), intent(in)    :: s
   character(len=*), intent(out) :: c
   c = s%string_data(1:s%length)
end subroutine s_to_c_assign
function string_len(s)
   integer      :: string_len
   type(string) :: s
   string_len = s%length
end function string_len
function string_concat(s1, s2)
   type (string), intent(in) :: s1, s2
   type (string)             :: string_concat
   string_concat%string_data =                  &
                 s1%string_data(1:s1%length) // &
                 s2%string_data(1:s2%length)
   string_concat%length = s1%length + s2%length
   if (string_concat%length > 80)               &
                 string_concat%length = 80
end function string_concat
end module string_type
```

Note: The intrinsic `len` function, used in `subroutine c_to_s_assign`, is first described in Section 8.6.

Chapter 6

1.

  i) a(1, :)

  ii) a(:, 20)

  iii) a(2:50:2, 2:20:2)

  iv) a(50:2:-2, 20:2:-2)

  v) a(1:0, 1)

2.

```
where (z.gt.0) z = 2*z
```

3.

```
integer, dimension(16) :: j
```

4.

```
w       explicit-shaped
a, b    assumed-shape
d       pointer
```

5.

```
real, pointer :: x(:, :, :)
x => tar(2:10:2, 2:20:2, 2:30:2)%du(3)
```

6.

```
ll = ll + ll
ll = mm + nn + n(j:k+1, j:k+1)
```

7.

```
program backwards
    integer                :: i, j
    integer, dimension(100) :: reverse
    reverse = (/ (i, i=1, 100) /)
    read *, i, j
    reverse(i:j) = reverse(j:i:-1)
end program backwards
```

Chapter 7

1.

```
i) integer, dimension(100) ::  bin
ii) real(selected_real_kind(6, 4)), dimension(0:20, 0:20) ::  &
    iron_temperature
iii) logical, dimension(20) ::  switches
iv) character(len=70), dimension(44) ::  page
```

2.
Value of i is 3.1, but may be changed;
value of i is 3.1, but may not be changed.

3.

```
i) integer, dimension(100) ::  i=(/ (0, k=1, 100) /)
ii) integer, dimension(100) ::  i=(/ (0, 1, k=1, 50) /)
iii) real, dimension(10, 10) ::  x=reshape((/ (1.0, k=1, 100) /), &
     (/10, 10/) )
```

iv) `character(len=10) ::  string = '0123456789'`

Note: the reshape function will be met in Section 8.13.3. **4.**

	mod	outer	inner	fun
a-b	character(10,2)	-	-	-
c,d,e	real	-	-	-
f	real	-	-	real
g,h	real	-	-	-
i-n	integer	-	-	-
o-w	real	-	-	-
x	real	-	-	real
y	real	-	-	-
z	real	-	complex	-

5.

i) `type(person) boss = person('Smith', 48.7, 22)`

ii) (a) This is impossible because a pointer component cannot be a constant.
(b)
```
type(entry) current
data current%value, current%index /1.0, 1/
```

6.

The following are not:
iv) because of the real exponent, and
viii) because of the pointer component.

Chapter 8

1.

```
    program qroots        ! Solution of quadratic equation.
!
    real :: a, b, c, d, x1, x2
!
    read(*, *) a, b, c
    write( *, *) ' a = ', a, 'b = ', b, 'c = ', c
    if (a == 0.) then
       if (b /= 0.) then
          write(*, *) ' Linear: x = ', -c/b
       else
          write(*, *) ' No roots!'
       endif
    else
       d = b**2 - 4.*a*c
       if (d < 0.) then
          write (*, *) ' Complex', -b/(2.*a), '+-',      &
                       sqrt(-d)/(2.*a)
       else
          x1 = -(b + sign(sqrt(d), b))/(2.*a)
```

```
        x2 = c/(x1*a)
        write(*, *) ' Real roots', x1, x2
      endif
    endif
  end program qroots
```

Historical note: A similar problem was set in one of the first books on Fortran programming — *A FORTRAN Primer* by E. Organick (Addison-Wesley, 1963). It is interesting to compare Organick's solution, written in FORTRAN II, on p. 122 of that book, with the one above. (It is reproduced in the *Encyclopedia of Physical Science & Technology* (Academic Press, 1987), vol. 5, p. 538.)

2.

```
    subroutine calculate(x, mean, variance, ok)
      real, intent(in)  :: x(:)
      real, intent(out) :: mean, variance
      logical ok
      ok = size(x) > 1
      if (ok) then
        mean = sum(x)/size(x)
        variance = sum((x-mean)**2)/(size(x)-1)
      end if
    end subroutine calculate
```

3.

```
  F     p1 and p2 are associated with the same array elements,
        but in reverse order
  T     p1 and p2(4:1:-1) are associated with exactly the
        same array elements, a(3), a(5), a(7), a(9)
```

4.

```
  5   1     a has bounds 5:10 and a(:) has bounds 1:6
  5   1     p1 has bounds 5:10 and p2 has bounds 1:6
  1   1     x and y both have bounds 1:6
```

Chapter 9

1.

```
a) print '(a/ (t1, 10f6.1))', ' grid', grid
b) print '(a, " ", 25i5)', ' list', (list(i), i = 1, 49, 2)
or                        list(1:49:2)
c) print '(a/ (" ", 2a12))', ' titles', titles
d) print '(a/ (t1, 5en15.6))', ' power', power
e) print '(a, 10i2)', ' flags', flags
f) print '(a, 5(" (", 2f6.1, ")"))', ' plane', plane
```

2.

```
    character, dimension(3,3) :: tic_tac_toe
    integer                   :: unit
    :
    write(unit, '(t1, 3a2)' ) tic_tac_toe
```

4.

```
(a) read(*, *) grid
1.0 2.0 3.0 4.0 5.0 6.0 7.0 8.0 9.0 10.0
```

```
(b) read(*, *) list(1:49:2)
25*1
```

```
(c) read(*, *) titles
data transfer
```

```
(d) read(*, *) power
1.0 1.e-03
```

```
(e) read(*, *) flags
t f t f t f f t f t
```

```
(f) read(*, *) plane
(0.0, 1.0),(2.3, 4)
```

5.

```
    character function get_char(unit)
        integer :: unit
10      read(unit, '(a1)', advance='no', eor=10) get_char
        return
    end function get_char
```

Index